DIMENSION VARIABLE DEFAULT SETTINGS

This list is displayed on screen in AutoCAD by selecting Status from the Dimesion Menu.

COMMAND	DEFAULT	DEFINITION
DIMALT	Off	Alternate units selected
DIMALTD	2	Alternate unit decimal places
DIMALTF	25.4000	Alternate unit scale factor
DIMAPOST		Suffix for alternate text
DIMASO	On	Create associative dimensions
DIMASZ	0.1800	Arrow size
DIMBLK		Arrow block name
DIMBLK1		First arrow block name
DIMBLK2		Second arrow block name
DIMCEN	0.0900	Center mark size
DIMCLRD	BYBLOCK	Dimension line color
DIMCLRE	BYBLOCK	Extension line & leader color
DIMCLRT	BYBLOCK	Dimension text color
DIMDLE	0.0000	Dimension line extension
DIMDLI	0.3800	Dimension line increment for continuation
DIMEXE	0.1800	Extension above dimension line
DIMEXO	0.0625	Extension line origin offset
DIMGAP	0.0900	Gap from dimension line to text
DIMLFAC	1.0000	Linear unit scale factor
DIMLIM	Off	Generate dimension limits
DIMPOST		Default suffix for dimension text
DIMRND	0.0000	Rounding value
DIMSAH	Off	Separate arrow blocks
DIMSCALE	1.0000	Overall scale factor
DIMSE1	Off	Suppress the first extension line
DIMSE2	Off	Suppress the second extension line
DIMSHO	On	Update dimensions while dragging
DIMSOXD	Off	Suppress outside extension dimension
DIMSTYLE	*UNNAMED	Current dimension style (read-only)
DIMTAD	Off	Place text above the dimension line
DIMTFAC	1.0000	Tolerance text height scaling factor
DIMTIH	On	Text inside extensions is horizontal
DIMTIX	Off	Place text inside extensions
DIMTM	0.0000	Minus tolerance
DIMTOFL	Off	Force line inside extension lines
DIMTOH	On	Text outside extensions is horizontal
DIMTOL	Off	Generate dimension tolerances
DIMTP	0.0000	Plus tolerance
DIMTSZ	0.0000	Tick size
DIMTVP	0.0000	Text vertical position
DIMTXT	0.1800	Text height
DIMZIN	0	Zero suppression

COMMANDS
KEY WORD/CONCEPT
DEFINITION/INFO

STANDARD TEXT FONTS

Courtesy of Autodesk, Inc.

Fast fonts

txt   The quick brown fox jumped over the lazy dog.   ABC123

monotxt   The quick brown fox jumped over the lazy dog.   ABC123

Simplex fonts

romans   The quick brown fox jumped over the lazy dog.   ABC123

scripts   *The quick brown fox jumped over the lazy dog.*   ABC123

greeks   Τηε ϑυιχκ βροων φοξ ϑυμπεδ ο∈ερ τηε λαζψ δογ.   ΑΒΧ123

Duplex font

romand   The quick brown fox jumped over the lazy dog.   ABC123

Triplex fonts

romant   **The quick brown fox jumped over the lazy dog.**   **ABC123**

italict   *The quick brown fox jumped over the lazy dog.*   *ABC123*

Complex fonts

romanc   The quick brown fox jumped over the lazy dog.   ABC123

italicc   *The quick brown fox jumped over the lazy dog.*   *ABC123*

scriptc   *The quick brown fox jumped over the lazy dog.*   ABC123

greekc   Τηε ϑυιχκ βροων φοξ ϑυμπεδ ο∈ερ τηε λαζψ δογ.   ΑΒΧ123

cyrillic   Узд рфивк бсоцн еоч йфмпдг охдс узд лащш гож.   АБВ123

cyriltlc   Тхе цуичк брошн фож щумпед овер тхе лазй дог.   АБЧ123

Gothic fonts

gothice   The quick brown fox jumped over the lazy dog.   ABC123

gothicg   The quick brown fox jumped over the lazy dog.   ABC123

gothici   The quick brown fox jumped over the lazy dog.   ABC123

Symbol fonts

syastro   Ω∈∪ `†→'← ˙˘∧∃∇ ⊃∧£ ↑†∂'∪⊂ ∧‡∪˘ §∈∪ ↓✳©® ⊂∧∩.   ☉♀♀123

symap   ℝ⊙ ‖◊☾◑ ‡⊥◻◇ ◖◗ ♤ ◐◖◯◗♡ ◻♡◻ ⊥ ∴' ◯†♣♣ ◡♧.   ◻◻△123

symath   ⊂∞√ [[§∂‡ ↓](√ Σ ∫(∫ †)∏)√∇ (}√] {∞√ ∃←≅≈ ∇(∮. ℵ'|123

symeteo   ⌐⌐′ ∖∾∖ \∿∿) ⊢⊬ ⌐⌐∿ ⌐∿∿ ⌐∿ ⌐⊢ ⌐∾.   ◾123

symusic   ⌐♩♩♪ ☉♩♭♩♪⌐ ⌐♩♪♪:♭♩♪♫ •♩♪:♪̆ ⌐♂♂♫‖♩♩ ♩♪:♫♩♩♪ ⊕♭♩♪ ♩·ℬΨ ♩♪:♯.   ·⌐·123

	A	B	C	D	E	F	G	H	I	J	K	L	M	N	O	P	Q	R	S	T	U	V	W	X	Y	Z	[	\	]	^	_	‘
cyrillic	А	Б	В	Г	Д	Е	Ж	З	И	Й	К	Л	М	Н	О	П	Р	С	Т	У	Ф	Х	Ц	Ч	Ш	Щ	Ъ	Ы	Ь	Э	Ю	Я
cyriltlc	А	Б	Ч	Д	Е	Ф	Г	Х	И	Щ	К	Л	М	Н	О	П	Ц	Р	С	Т	У	В	Ш	Ж	Й	З	Ь	Ы	Ъ	Ю	Э	Я
greekc	Α	Β	Χ	Δ	Ε	Φ	Γ	Η	Ι	ϑ	Κ	Λ	Μ	Ν	Ο	Π	Θ	Ρ	Σ	Τ	ϒ	∇	Ω	Ξ	Ψ	Ζ	[	\	]	^	_	‘
greeks	Α	Β	Χ	Δ	Ε	Φ	Γ	Η	Ι	ϑ	Κ	Λ	Μ	Ν	Ο	Π	Θ	Ρ	Σ	Τ	ϒ	∇	Ω	Ξ	Ψ	Ζ	[	\	]	^	_	‘
syastro	⊙	☿	♀	⊕	♂	♃	♄	♅	♆	♇	☾	☄	✱	☊	☋	♈	♉	♊	♋	♌	♍	♎	♏	♐	♑	♒	[	\	]	^	_	‘
symap	○	□	△	◇	☆	+	×	✱	●	■	▲	◀	▼	▶	★	⚑	⚓	✝	⚒	⛪	✝	⛵	✥	©	✿	🔔	[	\	]	^	_	‘
symath	ℵ	′	|	‖	±	∓	×	·	÷	=	≠	≡	<	>	≦	≧	∝	∼	√	⊂	∪	⊃	∩	∈	→	↑	[	\	]	^	_	‘
symeteo	,	•	∗	▲	▬	◣	^	⌒	⌒	◡	◡	›	›	‹	S	∾	∞	⟦	б	—	⁄	|	\	—	⁄	⁄	[	\	]	^	_	‘
symusic	·	⌐	⌐	○	○	●	♯	♮	♭	▬	-	𝄽	𝄾	𝄞	𝄢	𝄡	·	›	---	⌐	^	≑	▽				[	\	]	^	_	‘

	a	b	c	d	e	f	g	h	i	j	k	l	m	n	o	p	q	r	s	t	u	v	w	x	y	z	{	|	}	~	<	>
cyrillic	а	б	в	г	д	е	ж	з	и	й	к	л	м	н	о	п	р	с	т	у	ф	х	ц	ч	ш	щ	ъ	ы	ь	э	ю	я
cyriltlc	а	б	ч	д	е	ф	г	х	и	щ	к	л	м	н	о	п	ц	р	с	т	у	в	ш	ж	й	з	ь	ы	ъ	э	ю	я
greekc	α	β	χ	δ	ε	φ	γ	η	ι	∂	κ	λ	μ	ν	ο	π	ϑ	ρ	σ	τ	υ	∈	ω	ξ	ψ	ζ	{	|	}	~	<	>
greeks	α	β	χ	δ	ε	φ	γ	η	ι	∂	κ	λ	μ	ν	ο	π	ϑ	ρ	σ	τ	υ	∈	ω	ξ	ψ	ζ	{	|	}	~	<	>
syastro	✱	‘	’	⊂	∪	⊃	∩	∈	→	↑	←	↓	∂	∇	ˆ	´	`	˘	ℵ	§	†	‡	∃	£	®	©	{	|	}	~	<	>
symap	✝	♣	♧	♀	⁂	·	•	∘	○	○	◯	◯	◯	◯	⛉	⛉	‖	⊥	∠	∴	♤	♡	◇	♧	✤	♠	{	|	}	~	<	>
symath	←	↓	∂	∇	√	∫	∮	∞	§	†	‡	∃	∏	∑	(	)	[	]	{	}	∫	∫	√	∫	≈	≅	{	|	}	~	<	>
symeteo	|	\	∖	−	⁄	ı	∖	⌒	◡	◡	⌒	◡	(	)	⌒	≀	∧	∾	∾	ℓ	∝	ϑ	℘	℘	℘	•	{	|	}	~	<	>
symusic	·	⌐	⌐	○	○	●	♯	♮	♭	▬	-	𝄽	𝄾	𝄞	𝄢	𝄡	⊙	☿	♀	⊕	♂	♃	♄	♅	♆	♇	{	|	}	~	<	>

cibt	The quick brown fox jumped over the lazy dog.	ABC123
cobt	*The quick brown fox jumped over the lazy dog.*	*ABC123*
rom	**The quick brown fox jumped over the lazy dog.**	**ABC123**
romb	**The quick brown fox jumped over the lazy dog.**	**ABC123**
sas	**The quick brown fox jumped over the lazy dog.**	**ABC123**
sasb	**The quick brown fox jumped over the lazy dog.**	**ABC123**
saso	***The quick brown fox jumped over the lazy dog.***	***ABC123***
sasbo	***The quick brown fox jumped over the lazy dog.***	***ABC123***
te	**THE QUICK BROWN FOX JUMPED OVER THE LAZY DOG.**	**ABC123**
tel	THE QUICK BROWN FOX JUMPED OVER THE LAZY DOG.	ABC123
teb	**THE QUICK BROWN FOX JUMPED OVER THE LAZY DOG.**	**ABC123**
eur	The quick brown fox jumped over the lazy dog. à á â ã ä å æ ç è é ê ë ì í î ï ð ñ ò ó Û Ý ß Ø µ ¶ © ™ ® ¢ £ ¤ ¥ ¦ § ± ¼ ½ ¾ ¿ ¡	ABC123
euro	*The quick brown fox jumped over the lazy dog.* *à á â ã ä å æ ç è é ê ë ì í î ï ð ñ ò ó Ü Ý Þ ß Ø µ ¶* *© ™ ® ¢ £ ¤ ¥ ¦ § ± ¼ ½ ¾ ¿ ¡*	*ABC123*
pan	The quick brown fox jumped over the lazy dog. ə √ Æ æ Ŋ ŋ ¿ ʰ ᵊ đ θ ß Đ Ð § ¶ á à â ǎ ā ą ã ‘a a’ Â Ǎ Ā Ä	ABC123
suf	The quick brown fox jumped over the lazy dog. £ đ ø ± ß « » ¶ { } ∈ Ł + ħ ʃ ¿ ª á à â ã ‘a a’ ą Â Ã	ABC123

STANDARD LINETYPES
Courtesy of Autodesk, Inc.

Border	— — — — —
Border2	— - — - — - —
BorderX2	—— —— ——
Center	— - — - —
Center2	— - — - — - —
CenterX2	—— — ——
Dashdot	— - — - — - —
Dashdot2	- - - - - - -
DashdotX2	—— —— ——
Dashed	— — — — —
Dashed2	- - - - - - -
DashedX2	—— —— —— ——
Divide	— - - — - - — - —
Divide2	- - — - - — - — - -
DivideX2	— - - —— - - ——
Dot	. . . .
Dot2	....
DotX2	. . . . .
Hidden	- - - - - - - - - - -
Hidden2	- - - - - - - - - - - - -
HiddenX2	—— —— —— ——
Phantom	— - - —— - - —
Phantom2	- - — - - — - - — - -
PhantomX2	—— — — ——

AutoCAD for Engineering Graphics

SECOND EDITION

Gary R. Bertoline
Technical Graphics Department
Purdue University

MACMILLAN PUBLISHING COMPANY
NEW YORK
Maxwell Macmillan Canada
TORONTO
Maxwell Macmillan International
NEW YORK   OXFORD   SINGAPORE   SYDNEY

Dedicated to Michael Giese

"Those of us who did make it have an obligation to build again, to teach to others what we know, and to try with what's left in ours to find a goodness and meaning to this life."

Platoon
Hemdale Film Corporation, 1986

Copyright © 1994 by Macmillan Publishing Company, a division of Macmillan, Inc.

Printed in the United States of America

All rights reserved. No part of this book may be reproduced or transmitted in any form or by any means, electronic or mechanical, including photocopying, recording, or any information storage and retrieval system, without permission in writing from the publisher.

Earlier edition copyright © 1990 by Macmillan Publishing Company

Macmillan Publishing Company
866 Third Avenue, New York, New York 10022

Macmillan Publishing Company is part
of the Maxwell Communication Group of Companies.

Maxwell Macmillan Canada, Inc.
1200 Eglinton Avenue East
Suite 200
Don Mills, Ontario M3C 3N1

Library of Congress Cataloging - in - Publication Data

Bertoline, Gary R.
   AutoCAD for engineering graphics/Gary R. Bertoline. — 2nd ed.
     p. cm.

   Includes index.
   ISBN 0-02-309042-1
   1. Computer graphics. 2. AutoCAD (Computer file) I. Title
   T385.B468 1994   93 - 10765
   620' .0042' 02855369 — dc20   CIP

Printing: 1 2 3 4 5 6 7 8   Year: 4 5 6 7 8 9 0 1 2 3

PREFACE

INTRODUCTION

Throughout the history of engineering graphics, one important component has been the tools used to create the graphics. Before the introduction of Computer-aided design/drafting (CADD) , the tools had not changed significantly from those developed hundreds of years ago. Such changes as the drafting machine, improved drawing media, and the mechanical drafting pencil improved the efficiency of the designer yet were not revolutionary.

The use of the computer as a tool for engineering graphics can be considered revolutionary. Although slow in development, the use of CADD for engineering graphics is a major change. When developing engineering graphics concepts with traditional tools, very little time was spent teaching how to use the tools. In fact, students mastered some tools such as the pencil, eraser, and scale before they entered the engineering graphics classroom. In an engineering graphics course how much time is spent teaching the student how to erase a line with traditional tools? After a few minutes of instruction and a few hours of drawing, students quickly master the use of traditional engineering graphics tools that soon become transparent devices to the user. The same cannot be said of a CADD system.

For all the power and flexibility of microcomputer-based CADD software, the user interface required to use the tool is more difficult to learn than the use of traditional tools. Even after the user interface is mastered, the sequence of commands or steps that must be followed for every task must be reviewed. Mastering the drawing of lines on a CADD system may not provide the prerequisite knowledge necessary to crosshatch a section view. It is from this premise that this textbook has been written. The other major consideration is whether the techniques and methods for learning engineering graphics developed for use with traditional tools are valid for CADD.

PREREQUISITES

The prerequisite for using this text is an understanding of orthographic projection, sketching, and the ANSI standard graphic language for engineering graphics, such as dimensioning, sectioning, and working drawings. This understanding is necessary so that AutoCAD software can be applied to engineering graphics principles. The text can be used to teach engineering graphics with a traditional text used as a supplement or vice versa. It is also an excellent method of learning the basics of AutoCAD software for more general purposes. Although the problems and examples are related to engineering graphics, they also provide an excellent means of learning and reinforcing the use of AutoCAD software.

CONTENT AND ORGANIZATION

The second edition of *AutoCAD for Engineering Graphics* contains many improvements compared to the first edition. Parts Two and Three contain tutorial exercises that students can use to try each AutoCAD command on an as-need-basis to create engineering drawings. Many of these exercises use lab problems that are included on a disk. A new chapter that covers the fundamentals of solid modeling using AME has been added to the text.

The text is divided into three major sections. Part One, Chapters 1 and 2 is an Introduction to Engineering Graphics and CADD; it describes the graphic language and the use of CADD to create graphics. A generic introduction to the common components of a CADD system is included to introduce to the reader the multitude of hardware and software available for CADD. This discussion is followed by an introduction to AutoCAD software and the user interface.

Part Two, Chapters 3 through 9, is CADD Applied to Engineering Graphics, including chapters on using AutoCAD for lettering and sketching, geometric construction, multiview drawings, sectional drawings, auxiliary views, dimensions, and working drawings. Each chapter describes, through examples, how AutoCAD is used for engineering graphics. These concepts are reinforced through drawing assignments at the end of each chapter and supplemental problems provided for the instructor on disk.

Part Three, Chapters 11 and 12, is CADD Applied to Engineering Design. The chapters describe how AutoCAD is used to create 3D wire-frame models, isometrics, and other pictorial views of parts. The final chapters also includes an introduction to the use of CADD for designing and manufacturing. CADD applied to the various engineering disciplines is described and illustrated. Part Three also contains drawing assignments and problems on disk for reinforcement.

KEY FEATURES

The primary goal of this book is to apply engineering graphics concepts using AutoCAD, going beyond the use of a specific software. Each chapter is written with a specific set of objectives. Learning is reinforced through drawing assignments that can be used to measure student understanding and use of engineering graphic concepts using AutoCAD. Every command is explained, and examples are shown using a tutorial format. The tutorials are highlighted by placement between ruled lines.

Many topics found in traditional texts also will be found in this text. For example, the steps necessary to create a three-view drawing are found in Chapter 6. Bisecting a line and an angle is found in Chapter 5. Many traditional engineering graphics concepts are explained using AutoCAD as the tool. Many nontraditional topics such as methods of creating 3D wireframe models and ruled surfaces are included.

Available from the publisher is an "Electronic Workbook" that contains drawing problems on disk. Many of these drawing assignments are the examples used in the textbook to describe specific operations of AutoCAD. The student will be able to learn from many of the example problems described in the text.

ACKNOWLEDGMENTS

I am grateful to everyone at Macmillan Publishing especially John Griffin. I deeply appreciate the reviews especially from Michael Pleck of the University of Illinois; and the work of Robert Bertoline, Brad Dixon, Ralph Schweers, Greg Ernest, Kathryn and Angela Reath, Anna Anderson, and my wife Ada. Writing a textbook is long and difficult but the people you work with can make it an enjoyable endeavor. I am very grateful to these people for their input and work on this text.

G. R. B.
West Lafayette, IN

CONTENTS

4   DRAWING WITH AutoCAD   95

5   GEOMETRIC CONSTRUCTION AND EDITING   153

9 AUXILIARY VIEWS AND DESCRIPTIVE GEOMETRY 307

12   SOLID MODELING   347

APPENDIX A AUTOLISP PROGRAMS   50

APPENDIX B AutoCAD'S SYSTEMS VARIABLE SETTINGS   517

APPENDIX C STANDARD HATCH PATTERNS   523

APPENDIX D USEFUL INFORMATION   529

AutoCAD 2D TUTORIAL   533

AutoCAD 3D TUTORIAL   555

CAD LITERACY   571

INDEX   575

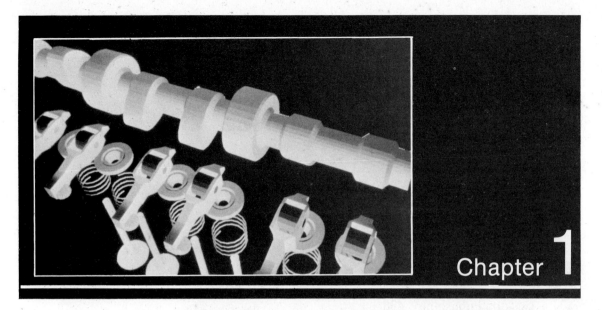

Chapter 1

THE GRAPHIC LANGUAGE

INTRODUCTION

In most engineering and technology programs, learning to communicate graphically is a basic component of the curriculum. Representing the world graphically is a fundamental communications skill used by designers, engineers, and drafters to change their conceptual designs into sketches or engineering drawings. In industry and education traditional methods of creating graphics have been with drawing instruments such as the t-square, compass, triangle, and pencil (Figure 1.1). Recently the computer has been found to be a more efficient tool to graphically represent designs. This use has led to the introduction of CADD (Computer-Aided Design/Drafting)

Figure 1.1 Traditional design/drafting tools (Hearlihy & Co.).

Figure 1.2 CADD workstation used in industry (Hewlett-Packard).

into engineering and technical drawing and other fields that require graphics for communications (Figure 1.2). **CADD** is an automated method of generating graphics for designing and drafting through computers and other peripheral devices. It can be used to supplement or replace traditional drafting and designing tools. In industry CADD is rapidly supplementing or replacing the traditional tools used to create engineering drawings.

Until very recently engineering design graphics was taught with the same basic tools that have been in existence since the time of ancient Greece. The pencil, compass, and straight-edge have been the primary tools used by the designer, and in turn, by those learning engineering graphics. In the past decade much of this has changed because the computer, interfaced with CADD software, now can be used as a tool for learning engineering graphics. By the year 2000, the overwhelming majority of drafter/designers will be using CADD rather than the pencil, straight-edge, and compass.

This chapter is an introduction to the use of CADD for engineering graphics. The design process using CADD will be explained and compared to the use of traditional tools. Finally the advantages, disadvantages, and applications of CADD will be discussed.

AUTOCAD TIP

Normally, the break command will take a piece out of an entity. The following procedure describes how to take an entity and break it into two parts.

1. Enter **BREAK** at the command prompt.
2. Pick the entity to break, then enter **F** for the first option.
3. Use the Osnap Intersection option to pick the point where the entity is to be broken.
4. When prompted to enter the second point enter **@**. This will break the entity into two parts at the point of intersection without removing part of the entity.

OBJECTIVES

After completing Chapter 1, you will be able to:
1. Describe how CADD is used to create engineering drawings,
2. Compare the design process using traditional tools or CADD,
3. List several applications of CADD,
4. List some of the advantages and disadvantages of using CADD.

A HISTORICAL OVERVIEW OF ENGINEERING GRAPHICS

Drawing is one of the oldest forms of communication. It is a universal language that dates before the formal use of verbal language and is so primitive that its history is comparable to that of humans. Through time the techniques needed for graphical communication evolved into a very complex system. By creating pictures people communicated thoughts to one another using graphic language. A **drawing** is a graphic representation of a real thing, an idea, or a proposed design. Drawings may take many forms, but the graphic method of communication is universal and timeless (Figure 1.3).

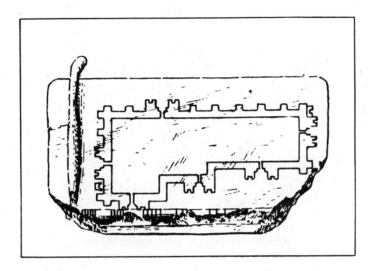

Figure 1.3 Graphic communications have been used since ancient times (From Transactions ASCE, May 1891).

AUTOCAD TIP

Before a linetype can be used on an AutoCAD drawing it must be loaded using the **LINEYTPE** command. To load all the linetypes at one time enter the Linetype command, select the Load option, then enter an * to load all the lines in the ACAD.LIN library.

Drawing has developed along two lines, artistic and technical. **Artistic drawings** have been used to express aesthetic, philosophic, or other abstract ideas. Graphic representation closely parallels human technological progress.

Technical drawings have been used from the beginning of recorded history to assist in the construction of buildings and devices. The theory of projections of objects upon imaginary planes was not developed until the early part of the fifteenth century in Italy. Leonardo DaVinci's treatise on painting is regarded as the first book written on the theory of perspective drawing. In the mid-1700s Gaspard Monge developed the principles of projection that continue to be used today as the basis of engineering drawing. **Engineering graphics** is considered to be the total field of graphical problem-solving and includes two major fields of specialization, descriptive geometry and working drawings.

During the first half of the twentieth century, the modern technology of drafting was established firmly, and the applications of graphic technology were found in engineering, design, manufacturing, production, and architecture. Engineering graphics became a concise, accurate, universal language with its own grammar and style through which engineers, drafters, and designers can communicate with one another and the public.

CADD: The Latest Tool Used for Engineering Graphics

In the last 25 years, major growth has occurred in computer technology and the use of computers to create graphics. The growth of computer graphics has followed closely the evolution of the computer. As computer hardware and software technology became more advanced and less expensive, the use of computers to generate graphics became more common in industry, leading to the development of software that could be used for engineering graphics.

This software and computer hardware came to be known as Computer-Aided Design (CAD) or Computer-Aided Design/Drafting (CADD). The development of software, improvements in hardware technology, and lower costs have led to widespread adoption of CADD systems in industry. Figure 1.4 shows a typical CADD system, which consists of a processor or computer; a monitor used to display drawings; a keyboard for alpha-numeric input; an input device such as a mouse or stylus and tablet used to control the location of drawing entities; and a plotter or hard copy device used to produce drawings on paper.

Figure 1.4 CADD workstation with peripheral devices (Courtesy of International Business Machines).

The CADD operator interacts with the system through a series of menu commands that appear on the computer screen to create, modify, and edit a drawing. By using an input device to locate points on the monitor, the operator can create a drawing. The CADD system and skilled operator can draw straight lines, perfect circles and arcs, different line types and thicknesses, various crosshatching patterns, and irregular curves. A CADD system can position and draw standard components in much the same way a template saves time drawing repetitious features on a handmade drawing. The operator can change scale quickly or one can easily zoom in on an object to perform detail work.

After the drawing is completed, dimensions are automatically calculated by the computer and placed anywhere on the drawing by the operator. Notes and labels of numerous styles and sizes can be typed and placed at any position on the drawing. A multicolored plot of any scale then can be made of the completed drawing.

With a trained user a typical CADD system can perform virtually any drawing function that can be done with traditional tools. However, all these operations are initiated by the human operator who interacts with the computer and ultimately controls the input and resulting output. CADD is not a substitute for design experience or ability. CADD is only a tool that can be used to supplement traditional tools. The underlying concepts used in engineering graphics remain the same regardless of the tool chosen to create the graphics. Orthographic projection, descriptive geometry, and other engineering graphics concepts are just as important as they always have been to the person who must communicate graphically. However, with the development of computer modeling traditional methods of communicating graphically will become less dominant in the future.

THE DESIGN PROCESS

The **design process** is used to organize the creative and analytical procedures necessary to satisfy a need or solve a problem. Although many methods have been used to describe the design process, the model depicted in Figure 1.5 has the major components traditionally associated with design. Engineering graphics and descriptive geometry are the tools used in the design process. Just as the written word is the technique used to create written documents, engineering graphics is used to create design documentation (drawings). The tools used for written documents are the typewriter and word processor. The tools used to create engineering drawings are the pencil and traditional tools and now CADD.

AUTOCAD TIP

Sometimes you will be drawing a broken line, such as hidden, phantom, or center, and it appears on screen without breaks. This may be corrected by adjusting the **LTSCALE** setting. Enter Ltscale at the command prompt then enter a number greater than one.

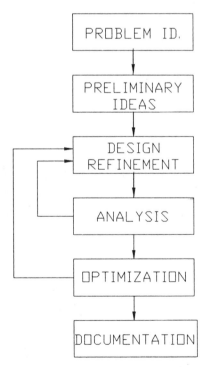

Figure 1.5 A model of the design process.

The Design Process Using Traditional Tools

The traditional tools used in the design process are those normally associated with drafting and model-making. After the problem is identified in stage one, concepts and ideas are collected for stage two, which is usually accomplished by rough sketches using paper, pencil, and eraser. These rough sketches are made quickly so that possible design solutions can be recorded before they are forgotten. From the collection of rough sketches, it is possible to select a compromise solution or solutions for stage three. Rough schematic drawings may be produced to test the design. A design layout made with instruments is produced, from which models can be created or further analysis can be performed.

Stages three, four, and five are highly interactive and iterative steps. A design solution may be analyzed and found to be needing change. This would cause the designer to return to stage three to modify the design. This process of design, analysis, and optimization may occur a number of times before the final design is chosen.

After the design has been analyzed, it will be evaluated in stage five by building models or prototypes. To accomplish this, dimensioned sketches or rough working drawings must be created for the model shop craftsperson. The model or prototype is tested, and any design modifications are noted on the drawings.

After the final design is approved, it is documented with working drawings for the manufacture of the product. The working drawings produced in stage six usually consist of detail drawings of the part(s), a parts list, and an assembly drawing. Traditionally, the design process was accomplished on drawing boards. However, much of the design process now can be performed with CADD.

The Design Process Using CADD

The use of computers for the design and documentation of a product can be grouped into four main areas:
1. Geometric Modeling
2. Engineering Analysis (CAE)
3. Design Evaluation
4. Documentation

These four areas can be interfaced with the last four stages in the design process as shown in Figure 1.6. Powerful CAD/CAM (Computer-Aided Design/Computer-Aided Manufacturing) systems are capable of replacing traditional tools used for the last four stages in the design process.

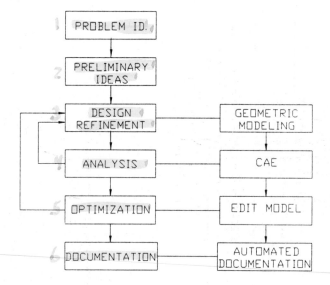

Figure 1.6 The design process integrated with CADD.

Microcomputer-based CADD, such as AutoCAD, traditionally has been used for the last stage in the design process for documentation. **Documentation** can be defined as the creation of the engineering drawings necessary to manufacture the product. This use for documentation is changing rapidly as improved hardware and software are being created. It is now possible to create with AutoCAD a 3D, wire-frame model of a part and surface shade the design using the Render Menu or to create solid models with AME (Advanced Modeling Extension). Many third-party products that have been developed for AutoCAD can be used for the design and analysis of a model. AutoCAD drawing files also can be used on powerful CAD/CAM systems through graphic translators. These procedures will be covered in detail in Chapter 11.

Geometric Modeling

Geometric modeling can be used to supplement or replace traditional tools used in stage three of the design process. A geometric model is a mathematical representation of a design created with a CADD system. Three primary methods of creating a geometric model of a part with CADD are:

1. Wire-frame
2. Surface
3. Solid

AutoCAD can create wire-frame models as shown in Figure 1.7. It is possible also to create surface models (Figure 1.8) or solid models . These mathematical computer models can be analyzed just as a prototype or model can be studied.

AUTOCAD TIP

The space bar or return key is used to repeat the previous AutoCAD command. If you press the space bar or return key twice to repeat the Line or Arc commands the new line or arc will continue from the last endpoint drawn.

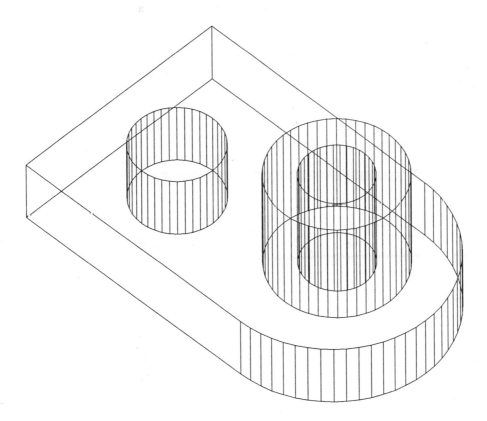

Figure 1.7 3D wireframe model.

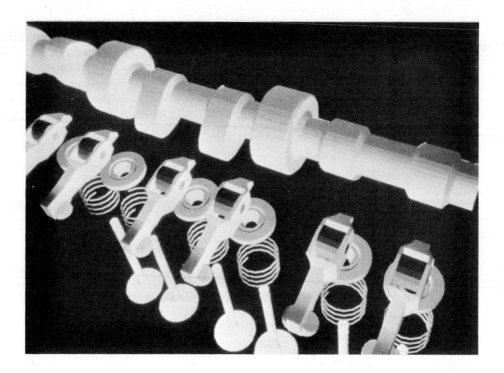

Figure 1.8 Surface model created with a CADD system.

Engineering Analysis

After the geometric model is produced, the computer can be used to analyze the part, as shown in stage four CAE (Computer-Aided Engineering), through various computer engineering analysis programs, such as stress, strain, kinematics, and heat transfer. Many of these programs can be used with AutoCAD drawings through third-party products.

Design Evaluation and Editing

With a CADD system, parts are checked for accuracy through automatic dimensioning. Details are checked by zooming in and magnifying small parts and details. Layering can be used to match parts for fit and accuracy. Three-D models also are checked for interference between mating or for parts that pass close to each other.

Documentation

CADD is used to supplement or replace traditional tools in stage six of the design process. This is what AutoCAD was primarily created to do. AutoCAD is a powerful software package for automated drafting. The basic package also can be modified with the use of its programming language, AutoLISP. Automated drafting procedures include:

1. Dimensioning
2. Cross-hatching for section drawings
3. Scaling
4. Copies
5. Mirror
6. Enlarged details
7. Rotation
8. Isometric and axonometric views
9. Symbols
10. Editing

CAD/CAM

It is now possible with CADD to supplement or replace the traditional tools used in the last four stages of the design process. In addition, once the graphic data base for the part has been created, it is possible to develop the manufacturing data base that can be used for CAM (Computer-Aided Manufacturing).

Traditionally, design and manufacturing were a two-stage process. The engineering drawings were produced by the design drafters and then used by the manufacturing engineers to produce the product, but an integrated CAD/CAM system can provide a direct link between these two processes by automating the design and manufacture of a product and their link. AutoCAD can create the graphic data base necessary for manufacturing. With the use of third-party software and graphic translators, AutoCAD drawings can be utilized for CAM are explained in Chapter 11.

APPLICATIONS OF CADD

CADD can be used to create engineering and technical drawings for a number of different uses. Probably the most common use of microcomputer-based CADD is for documentation or automated drafting. Architectural drawings can be created with CADD using special software such as AutoCAD AEC (architecture, engineering, and construction) Architectural. Pipe layout, HVAC (heating, ventilation, and air conditioning), and other building systems can also be produced with special CADD software such as AutoCAD AEC Mechanical. Electrical and electronic drawing and design also can be created with CADD. Mapping, structural, and technical illustration are other common applications of CADD. Figure 1.9 through Figure 1.13 illustrate some common application drawings produced with AutoCAD.

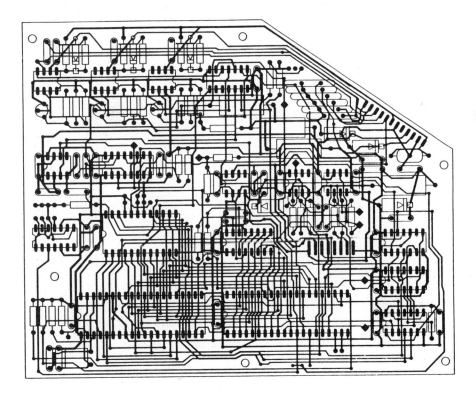

Figure 1.9 AutoCAD-produced electrical drawing (Courtesy of CAD Northwest Inc.).

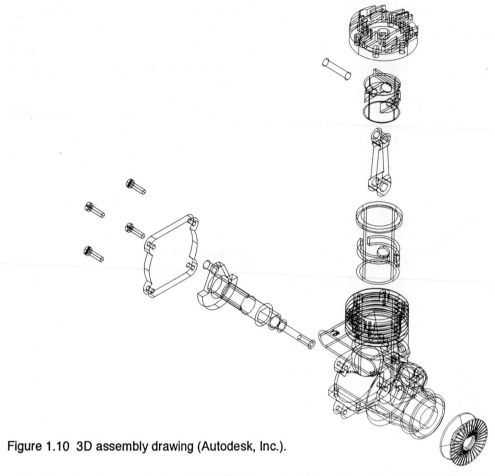

Figure 1.10 3D assembly drawing (Autodesk, Inc.).

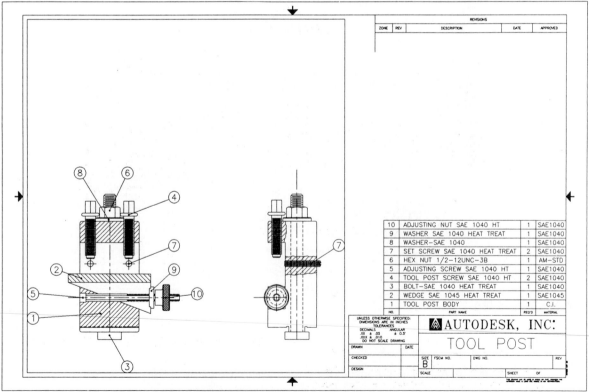

10	ADJUSTING NUT SAE 1040 HT	1	SAE1040
9	WASHER SAE 1040 HEAT TREAT	1	SAE1040
8	WASHER-SAE 1040	1	SAE1040
7	SET SCREW SAE 1040 HEAT TREAT	2	SAE1040
6	HEX NUT 1/2-12UNC-3B	1	AM-STD
5	ADJUSTING SCREW SAE 1040 HT	1	SAE1040
4	TOOL POST SCREW SAE 1040 HT	2	SAE1040
3	BOLT-SAE 1040 HEAT TREAT	1	SAE1040
2	WEDGE SAE 1045 HEAT TREAT	1	SAE1045
1	TOOL POST BODY	1	C.I.
NO.	PART NAME	REQ'D	MATERIAL

AUTODESK, INC.

TOOL POST

Figure 1.11 Mechanical assembly drawing (Autodesk, Inc.).

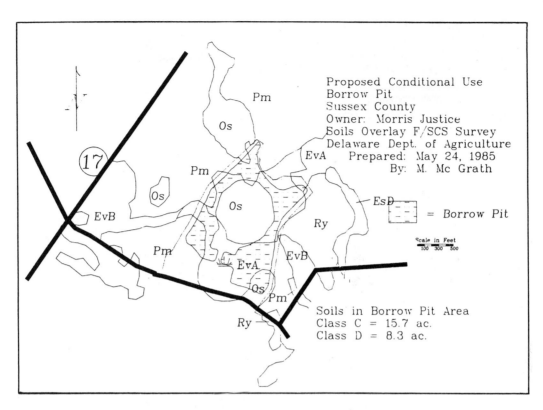

Figure 1.12 Civil engineering drawing (Autodesk, Inc.).

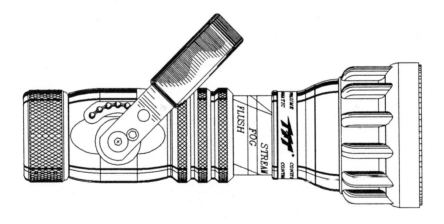

Figure 1.13 Technical illustration (Autodesk, Inc.).

Advantages of Using CADD

There are many advantages to using CADD over traditional tools. Although some advantages are quite apparent, others are more difficult to recognize, such as improved work quality, better control, and greater communication. Advantages of CADD include:

1. Faster production of some types of graphics,
2. Customer modifications that are easier to make,
3. Shorter lead time for the design of similar or family of parts,

4. Improved accuracy of the design,
5. More accurate estimates of costs,
6. Improved communications through better line weight and consistency,
7. More legible and faster placed text on drawings,
8. Automatic scaling of drawings,
9. Ability to create symbol libraries,
10. Creation of isometric and axonometric views of a 3D model.

QUESTIONS FOR REVIEW

1. Define CADD.
2. List several applications of CADD.
3. List several advantages of using CADD over traditional tools.
4. Define the design process.
5. List the four areas of design and documentation for which the computer can effectively be used.
6. Identify the stage of the design process where microcomputer-based CADD has been used until recently.

ADDITIONAL READING

From Giesecke, et al., *Technical Graphics*, 9th ed. (New York: Macmillan Co., 1991).
Chapter 1, The Graphic Language and Design.
Chapter 16, Design and Working Drawings.

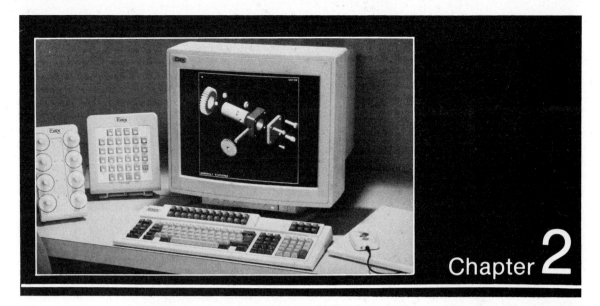

Chapter 2

THE COMPONENTS OF A CADD SYSTEM

This chapter is an introduction to the computer tools for engineering graphics. Most of the traditional engineering graphics tools such as the compass, triangles, scales, dividers, and so forth have been replaced by CADD software drawing commands. CADD (Computer-Aided Design/Drafting) is an automated method of generating graphics for designing and drafting through the use of a computer and other peripheral devices. However, additional computer components are necessary to create engineering drawings. For example, the pencil has been replaced by the computer input device, which controls the movement of the "computer pencil" or cursor. Many different types of input devices that can be used with CADD.

Hundreds of different CADD hardware and software components are available. Even when AutoCAD is the software being used for CADD, the hardware and peripheral devices that can be used can vary widely. AutoCAD runs on most microcomputers supporting PC-DOS or MS-DOS operating systems, Macintosh, and Sun workstations under UNIX. AutoCAD also supports more than 140 different peripheral devices for input and output and more hardware and peripheral devices are being added to the list.

This chapter is an introduction to the five basic devices that make a CADD system: display, input and output devices, mass memory, and the computer. Operating systems and configuring CADD software for use on specific hardware are explained also.

OBJECTIVES

After completing Chapter 2, you will be able to:
1. List the five basic components of a CADD system,
2. List common types of input devices,
3. List common types of output devices,
4. List common types of display devices,
5. Describe the three types of CADD systems,
6. Describe different types of storage devices used with CADD,
7. Define the terms, peripheral device and pixel,
8. Describe configuration of a CADD system,
9. Load AutoCAD files,
10. Configure AutoCAD.

TYPES OF CADD SYSTEMS

CADD has evolved slowly through the years, starting with early developments during the 1960s. CADD systems at that time were very large and slow, compared to the capabilities of today. CADD developed on large mainframe computers that were very expensive. As computer technology expanded, the minicomputer became popular, and some CADD packages were developed to run on this hardware. Finally in the late 1970s the microcomputer was developed, and CADD software was created that could use this type of hardware. Today CADD software is available that can run on mainframe, mini, or microcomputers. These are sometimes referred to as the CPU (Central Processing Unit), which is one of the five major components of a CADD system.

The five components are: 1) the CPU, 2) input device, 3) output device, 4) display device, and 5) mass storage.

Mainframe CADD Systems

A **mainframe computer,** such as the IBM 3033 and the Burroughs B7700, is a large computer produced by several different manufacturers. These computers cost between $200,000 and $1,000,000 and are primarily used in businesses, universities, and banks. However, it is possible to run a CADD software program on some mainframe computers. This type of system would be capable of controlling a large number of workstations. Mainframe computers must be housed in an environmentally controlled room.

The use of mainframe computers for engineering may increase in the future as the "factory of the future" develops. **Computer-integrated manufacturing (CIM)** will combine the whole design, manufacturing, assembly, sales, and other components of a factory into one integrated process. Every stage of a manufacturing operation will be controlled by the computer and will need a mainframe computer for control of large applications.

Typically, mainframe computers are used for complex engineering and scientific problems. Calculations used for computer-aided design include fluid dynamic analysis, heat transfer analysis, and structural design analysis.

The IBM 5080 graphics system typifies a CADD workstation that can be connected to a mainframe computer. This hardware can run a number of different software application programs such as CADAM, CATIA, and CAEDS. These three software programs support mechanical design, from conceptual 3D design through the analysis, documentation, and generation of numerical control (NC) machine tool data for manufacturing. This graphic system can support from 16 to 32 workstations. By using graphic translator programs, it is possible to share drawing files between mainframe computers and AutoCAD.

Only a few companies market this type of software. Because mainframe systems are very expensive, CADD software has been developed for mini- and microcomputers for some applications.

Minicomputer CADD Systems

Minicomputers, smaller versions of mainframe computers, cost from $20,000 to $200,000. Typical manufacturers include: IBM, Harris, Hewlett-Packard, Digital Equipment, Prime, Sun, Apollo, and Control Data. Minicomputers were designed originally in the early 1970s for specialized applications, like engineering, factory automation, and word processing (Figure 2.1).

Many different CADD software programs will run on minicomputers. Figure 2.2. The design can be analyzed for stress and strain, kinematics, and dynamic analysis, and the part then can be detailed and documented. Production of the part is developed through NC programming, robot programming, and automated inspection.

Minicomputer CADD systems typically cost from $30,000 to $300,000. Popular minicomputer CADD software programs are Computervision, Intergraph, Calma, Auto-Trol, Control Data Corporation, Anvil, Gerber, and Applicon. AutoCAD also can run on Sun, Apollo, and Digital Equipment minicomputer workstations. In addition, translators used to share drawings produced on different CADD systems have been developed for many of the popular minicomputer CADD software programs.

Figure 2.1 Minicomputer (Courtesy of International Business Machines).

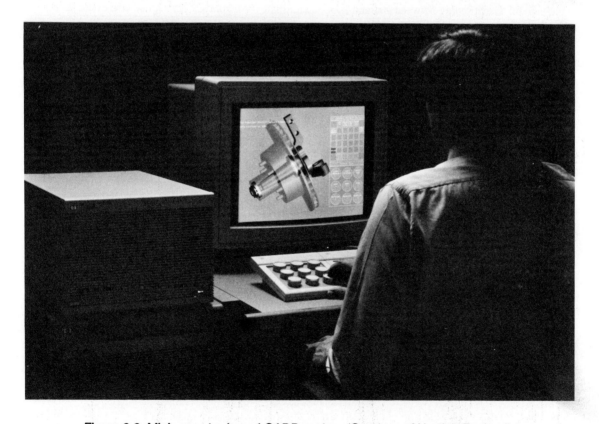

Figure 2.2 Minicomputer-based CADD system (Courtesy of Hewlett-Packard).

Microcomputer CADD Systems

In recent years the trend in CADD has been toward microcomputer workstations. In 1982 AutoCAD was one of the first CADD software programs created specifically for the microcomputer. Since then more than 100 microcomputer-based CADD software programs have been developed. Many of the popular minicomputer-based CADD companies also have developed their software to run on microcomputers, but by far the most popular microcomputer CADD software program is AutoCAD.

Microcomputers evolved in the late 1970s and now are becoming so fast and powerful that they are beginning to rival the minicomputer in performance and cost. Very powerful microcomputers have been produced by IBM, Digital Equipment, and Compaq. Cost for a typical microcomputer workstation for CADD ranges from $2,000 to $12,000. Popular microcomputers are IBM, Compaq, Tandy, Texas Instruments, Zenith, AST, Hewlett-Packard, Digital, NEC, CompuAdd, and Dell.

AutoCAD is typical of many microcomputer CADD systems. It is primarily for design documentation (detail drawings), but third-party programs have been developed for applications such as architecture, electrical, mechanical engineering, and mapping. A programming language called AutoLISP can create special applications and utilities to ease some types of work. AutoCAD will run on many types of microcomputers and peripheral devices for input and output. Drawings also can be exchanged with workstation CADD programs.

Other popular microcomputer CADD software includes VersaCAD, CADKEY, SilverScreen, Anvil 1000, IBM Fastdraft, MICRO CADAM, Generic CAD, Intergraph's Micro-station, and Computervision's Personal Designer (Figure 2.3).

AUTOCAD TIP

Sometimes AutoCAD will display circles and arcs as segmented lines to decrease redraw time. The **VIEWRES** command is used to control the display of circles and arcs. The Viewres can be set between 1 and 20000 with 100 being the default. Use a setting between 200 and 2000 to eliminate the display of segmented circles and arcs.

Figure 2.3 Microcomputer-based CADD system (Courtesy of International Business Machines).

DISPLAY DEVICES

A second major component of a CADD system is the display device or computer monitor. The display device is considered a *peripheral*, which is a device that is connected to the computer. Some of the most rapid technological development occurring in computer peripheral devices is with graphic monitors. Great advances have been made through improvements in screen resolution and the use of colors. Graphics display devices used to view the images produced with CADD software, come in different sizes and are monochrome or color (Figure 2.4).

Figure 2.4 Different devices used to display graphics (Courtesy of International Business Machines).

Usually a CADD system has one display terminal to view graphics and text; however, some systems, such as AutoCAD, support the use of two terminals, one for graphics and one for text. Having text on a separate screen allows more room for the display of graphics. Some CADD systems support two terminals for graphics and are referred to as dual displays (Figure 2.5).

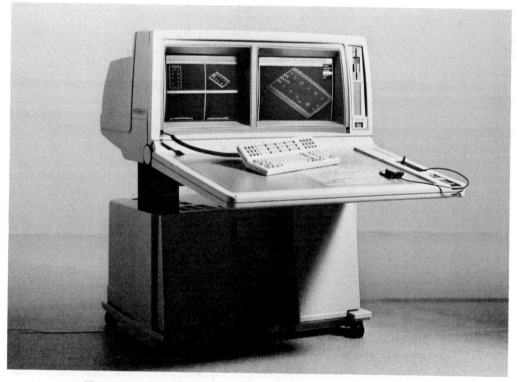

Figure 2.5 Dual display CADD system (Courtesy of Intergraph).

Display devices are grouped by resolution, screen size, graphics or text display, and monochrome or color. The resolution of a screen is determined by the number of picture elements or pixels. A **pixel** is a single dot or picture element on the display device. Each pixel can be turned on and off and can be assigned a color on color displays. Common screen sizes range from 12 to 19 inches. The use of color for CADD is becoming the standard as this technology improves. Most CADD systems support a number of different display devices, as shown in Figure 2.6. AutoCAD supports many different devices. Resolution can range from 640 by 200, to 1280 by 1024 pixels. Some monitors can display 256 colors simultaneously from a palette of more than sixteen million.

```
         A U T O C A D (R)
Copyright (c) 1982-92  Autodesk, Inc.   All Rights Reserved.
Release 12 (6/21/92) 386 DOS Extender
Serial Number:  117-10058454
EVALUATION VERSION -- NOT FOR RESALE
Licensed to:    Gary R. Bertoline, Purdue University
Obtained from:  Autodesk - neele Johnston

Available video displays:

    1.   Null display
    2.   8514/A ADI 4.2 Display and Rendering - By Panacea for Autodesk
    3.   ADI display v4.0
    4.   ADI display v4.1
    5.   Compaq Portable III Plasma Display <obsolete>
    6.   Hercules Graphics Card <obsolete>
    7.   IBM Enhanced Graphics Adapter <obsolete>
    8.   IBM Video Graphics Array ADI 4.2 - by Autodesk
    9.   SVADI Super VGA ADI 4.2 - by Autodesk
   10.   Targa+ ADI v4.2 Display and Rendering - by Autodesk
   11.   VESA Super VGA ADI v4.2 Display and Rendering - by Autodesk
   12.   XGA ADI 4.2 Display and Rendering - By Panacea for Autodesk

Select device number or ? to repeat list <8>:
```

Figure 2.6 Display devices supported by AutoCAD.

Graphic Cards

A *graphic card* is an electronic circuit board that determines the type of display monitor, resolution, and number of colors that can be used with a computer. The IBM is the defacto standard computer hardware used for microcomputer CADD software. When matched with the appropriate display device, graphic cards determine the resolution of the screen, the number of colors that can be displayed, and the palette of available colors. Five standard graphic cards have been developed for IBM and compatible hardware:

1. Monochrome Display Adapter (MDA): 720 by 348 pixels of resolution, no color,

2. Color Graphics Adapter (CGA): 640 by 200 pixels of resolution, no color. In the color mode four colors can be displayed at a lower resolution of 320 by 200,

3. Enhanced Graphics Adapter (EGA): 640 by 480 pixels of resolution, 16 colors,

4. Video Graphics Array (VGA): 640 by 480 pixels of resolution,

5. Professional Graphics Adapter (PGA): 1024 by 768 pixels of resolution, 256 displayed colors from a palette of up to 16 million.

The resolution of each graphic card can vary to some degree depending on the manufacturer. The five graphic boards listed are graphic standards not resolution standards.

AUTOCAD TIP

The name of a layer can be changed by using the **RENAME** command. Enter Rename at the command prompt then select the layer option. Enter the old name then the new name to change the layer.

INPUT DEVICES

A third major component of a CADD system is the input device. An *input device* is used to enter text and numerical data, to control movement of a screen cursor, and to make selections from the CADD program. All CADD systems have at least one input device. Many different input devices can be used with CADD software. AutoCAD supports 35 different input devices. Input and output devices connect to ports located in the rear of the computer.

Keyboard

A computer keyboard is similar to a typewriter keyboard usually with added special function keys. An IBM or compatible computer keyboard usually will have a set of keys for numeric input and arrow keys for cursor control. Two columns or a row of 10 function keys also can be used for special functions (Figure 2.7).

AutoCAD uses the keyboard primarily to input text and numerical information but also can be used to input program commands. Six of the 10 function keys normally are assigned program commands with AutoCAD:

F1 - Screen Toggle
F6 - Coordinate Toggle
F7 - Grid Toggle
F8 - Ortho Toggle
F9 - Snap Toggle
F10 - Tablet Toggle

A *toggle* is similar to an on/off light switch. Selecting the key will turn the function on or off.

Figure 2.7 Typical XT-type computer keyboard.

AUTOCAD TIP

To delete a layer use the **PURGE** command. Before a layer can be deleted all the entities must be placed on another layer using the **CHANGE** command. The drawing is saved and then loaded again. Immediately after loading enter the Purge command. Select the layer option then enter the name of the layer to delete.

The Mouse

One common and inexpensive input device is the mouse. A *mouse* is an input device used to control cursor movement and select or cancel program commands. Two common types of mice are optical and mechanical. The *optical mouse* controls cursor movement by reading the position of a light that bounces off a special reflective plate (Figure 2.8). The *mechanical mouse* has a small ball that turns when the mouse is moved across a flat surface, such as a tabletop (Figure 2.9).

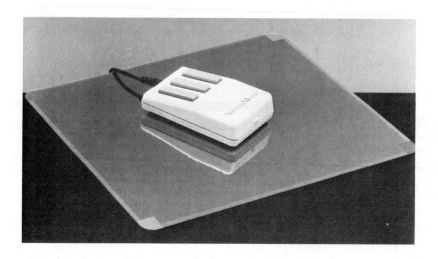

Figure 2.8 Optical mouse and reflective plate (Courtesy of Summagraphics).

Figure 2.9 Mechanical mouse.

Movement of a mouse to the left causes the screen cursor to move to the left. Movement to the right, up, or down will cause a similar movement of the screen cursor. Located on its surface, a mouse usually will have from two to 20 buttons, which can be assigned different CADD software commands. For example, the center button on a three-button mouse might be used to cancel a command. With AutoCAD, a three-button mouse may have the following functions:

1. Left button: the "pick button", used to designate the location of points in the drawing area of the screen and to select the highlighted screen and Pull-down Menu items.

2. Center button: used to select the first item on the screen menu or as a RETURN or ENTER key.
3. Right button: used to select the second item on the screen menu.

The *AutoCAD Installation and Performance Guide* can be used to determine button functions for each type of mouse that can be used with AutoCAD.

A mouse can be used to select software commands from the screen by moving the mouse into the menu area to the right of the screen, or the Pull-down Menus located at the top of the screen, pointing to the desired menu item, and pressing the pick button of the mouse. The mouse is a common pointing device used to control cursor movement and to select menu items from the screen.

Programmed Function Board

A *programmed function board* is commonly found on minicomputer-based CADD systems. Typically, this device has rows of buttons on a separate box that can be changed by programming to select CADD software commands. Often the buttons are illuminated to identify menu items that are active (Figure 2.10).

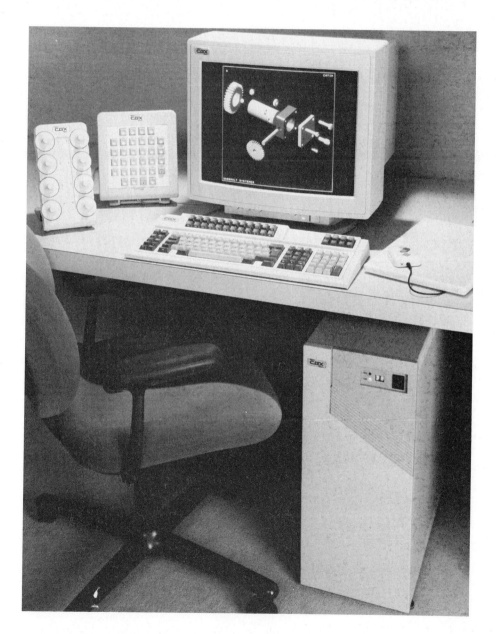

Figure 2.10 Programmed function board (Courtesy of CGX, Adage Inc).

Digitizer

A *digitizer* is an input device used to enter existing drawings or sketches into the system (Figure 2.11). The drawing is taped to the surface of the digitizer, and the puck (input device) is used to identify end points of lines, centers of circles, and other entities that are part of the drawing.

Automatic scanners have been developed to eliminate the need for a human operator to move a puck across a drawing to be digitized. An *automatic scanner* can scan a drawing and input the digitized information into the CADD system.

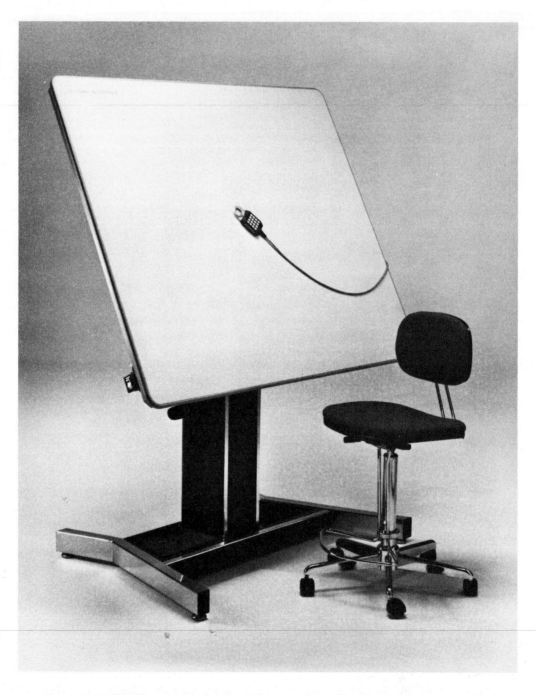

Figure 2.11 Digitizer used to input existing drawings (Courtesy of Summagraphics).

Tablet and Menu

A *menu* is a listing of software commands used to create graphics with a CADD system. A menu can be displayed on a screen (Figure 2.12), located on a tablet, or both. Most CADD systems use a tree-structure approach for their screen menus. For example, to draw a line with AutoCAD, menu item DRAW would be selected from the first menu displayed in the drawing editor. AutoCAD calls this the Root Menu. A new branch menu would appear with LINE as one of the menu commands. The LINE command would be selected to start drawing a line. To add dimensions to the drawing would involve a return to the Root Menu, where the DIM (dimension) command would be selected.

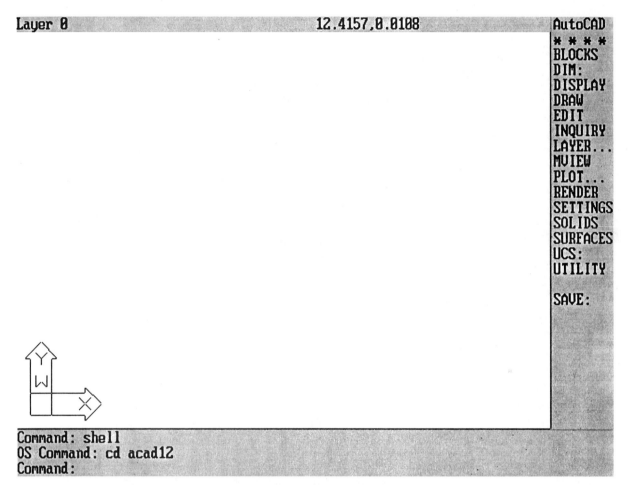

Figure 2.12 AutoCAD's screen menu.

One method of avoiding the tree structure screen menu is to type in commands from the keyboard, but a more effective procedure would be to use a tablet menu like that shown in Figure 2.13. Tablet menus are placed on a digitizing tablet, list most of the screen menu items, and include a small blank area that is used for cursor control. The LINE command can be accessed directly using AutoCAD's tablet menu by selecting the area labeled **LINE** from the tablet menu. Using the tablet menu will avoid the tree-structure approach found with the screen menu.

A *tablet* is a smaller version of the digitizer used to input drawings (Figure 2.14). Some tablets can be used as a digitizer to input existing drawings. Others only can be used for data entry and control of cursor movement. Tablets can be programmed to suit the specific needs of the user. For example, Figure 2.15 shows an architectural menu used with AEC Architectural software.

Tablets are connected to some type of pointing device. A *stylus* is one common pointing device used with tablets and is similar to a pen, as shown in the upper right of Figure 2.16. The stylus is moved across the blank surface area of the tablet to control cursor movement. It also can be used to select menu items from the tablet menu by positioning it over the menu item and pressing down on its tip. For example, to draw a line, the tip of the stylus would be positioned, then pressed, over the LINE command located on the surface of the tablet. Some styli have a button on the shaft that must be pressed to make menu selections.

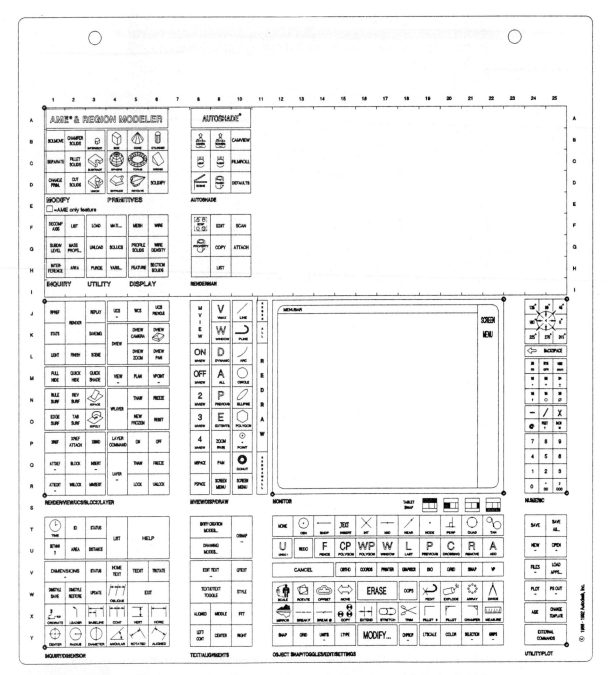

Figure 2.13 AutoCAD's tablet menu (Courtesy of Autodesk, Inc).

A *puck* sometimes is used with tablets (Figure 2.16). It usually has a number of buttons on its surface and a crosshair used for positioning. To control cursor movement, the puck is moved across the blank surface area of the tablet. To select menu items from the tablet, the crosshairs of the cursor are positioned over the menu item, and the appropriate button is pressed.

Other Input Devices

Very popular when CADD was first developing, the light pen is an input device that can be pointed at the screen to control cursor movement and make menu selections. It has lost most of its popularity and is not used often with CADD. Other input devices that are not used as often as in the past are the joy-stick, trackball, thumbwheels, and dials (Figure 2.17). These devices have been used primarily to control movement of the cursor on the screen and are sometimes referred to as pointing devices.

Figure 2.14 Tablet and input devices used for CADD (Courtesy of Houston Instruments).

Figure 2.15 AutoCAD's architectural tablet menu (Courtesy of Autodesk, Inc).

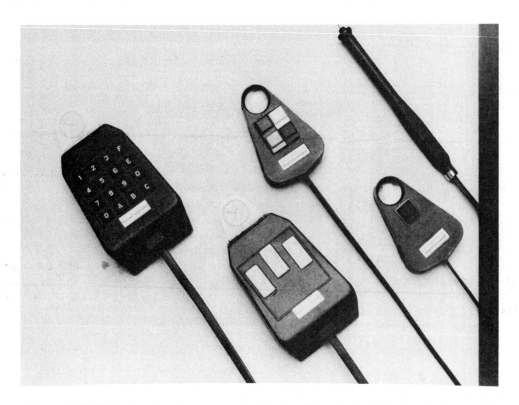

Figure 2.16 Stylus input and cursor control device (Courtesy of Houston Instruments).

Figure 2.17 Dials used for input (Courtesy of Hewlett-Packard).

OUTPUT DEVICES

An *output device* is used to present in a form common to engineers and designers the graphics created on a CADD system. Traditionally this has been in the form of drawings on paper or other types of media. Output devices are grouped by the method used to create the drawing and are the fourth major component of a computer. The two major groups of output devices are printers and pen plotters, of which AutoCAD supports many different kinds.

Pen Plotters

Pen plotters have been used with CADD for many years. *Pen plotters* are output devices that hold pens and can plot print media from A (8-1/2 by 11 inches) through E (34 by 44 inches) size. There are plotters with as few as one or as many as 14 pens. Pen plotters are the slowest type of high resolution plotters. They are rated by accuracy or repeatability, plotting speeds, and pen up/down time. Accuracy is a measure of the plotter's ability to retrace entities such as lines and circles. Pen plotters have repeatability measures from .005 to .001 of an inch. Plotting speeds can range from five inches per second (IPS) to 40 IPS.

Pen plotters can be subdivided into two groups; drum and flatbed. The *drum plotter* holds the paper by a pinch-grip, which rotates the paper across the surface of the plotter (Figure 2.18). Pens are stored in a carousel and are removed by a gripper that moves across the paper on an arm. Movement of the pen across the arm and movement of the paper 90 degrees from the arm are used to create the drawing.

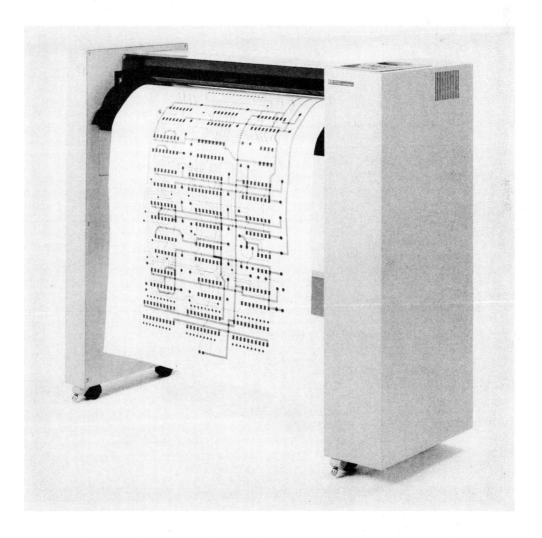

Figure 2.18 A D-size drum plotter with 8 pens (Courtesy of Hewlett-Packard).

A *flatbed plotter* holds the paper by an electrostatic charge or by a vacuum. Pens are removed from their storage along one of the edges of the plotter. The arm is free to move in the X or Y direction, and the paper is held stationary (Figure 2.19). Figure 2.20 shows a plot made with a pen plotter.

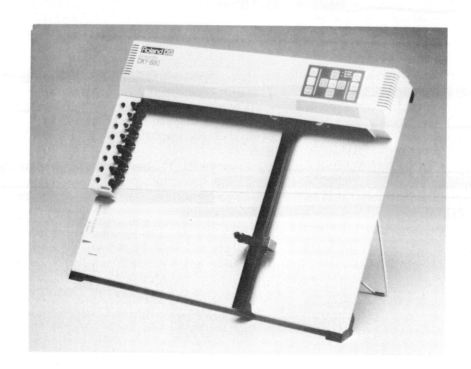

Figure 2.19 Flatbed pen plotter (Courtesy of Roland).

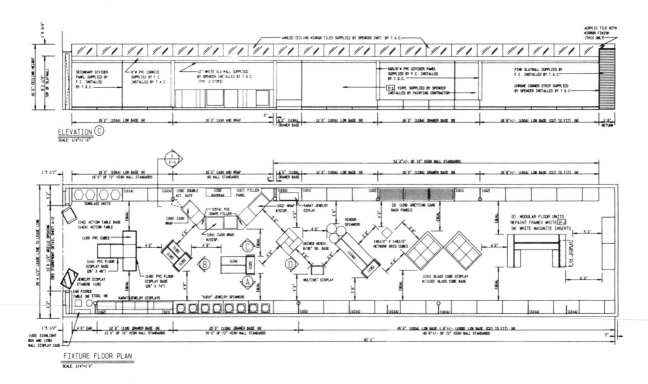

Figure 2.20 Sample pen plot (Courtesy of Hewlett-Packard).

Electrostatic Plotter

   Electrostatic plotters (Figure 2.21) use the dot or pixel as the main graphic element to create hardcopy output. An electrostatic charge is placed on the paper, and thousands of tiny writing nibs place dots on the charged surface. The resolution of electrostatic plotters range from 100 to 508 dots per inch. These plotters are the fastest of all plotters but the most expensive. They also are now capable of creating color plots. Figure 2.22 is a drawing produced with an electrostatic plotter. Notice the jagged circles and angled lines compared to the pen plot in Figure 2.20.

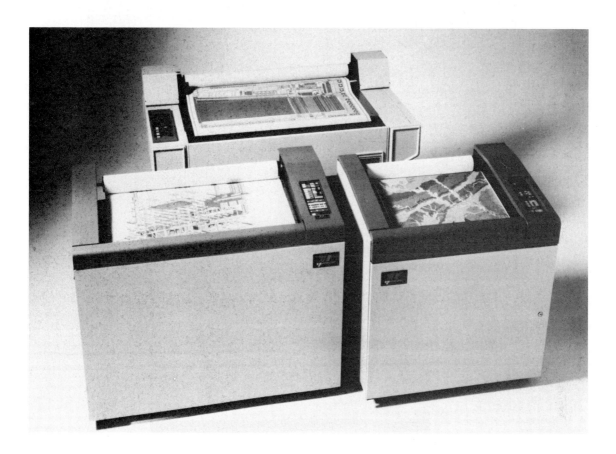

Figure 2.21 Electrostatic plotter (Courtesy of Versatec).

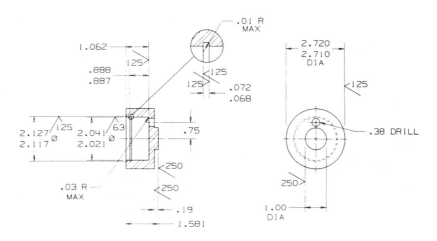

Figure 2.22 Electrostatic plot.

Ink Jet Plotters

Ink jet plotters (Figure 2.23) force tiny droplets of ink onto the surface of the media to create hardcopy output of CADD drawings. These plotters are especially useful for solid modeling applications and for shading and 3D effects by mechanical and electrical designers. A- and B-size plotters are available with resolutions in the 300 DPI range.

Figure 2.23 Ink jet plotter (Courtesy of Hewlett-Packard).

Photo Plotters

Photo plotters are used for printed circuit board artwork. This plotter uses a tiny beam of light to expose light-sensitive paper, the thickness of the beam of light being controlled. The developed print then can be used as a mask for PC boards.

Laser Printers

Laser printers (Figure 2.24) are dry types of electro-photography that use a dry toner. An 8 1/2" by 11" sheet can be printed in about eight seconds. The resolution of the print can be as high as 300 dots per inch. Figure 2.25 is an example of a plot produced by a laser printer at 300 DPI.

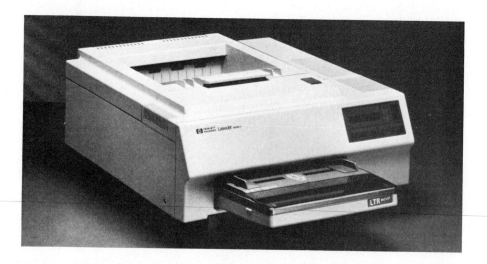

Figure 2.24 Laser printer (Courtesy of Hewlett-Packard).

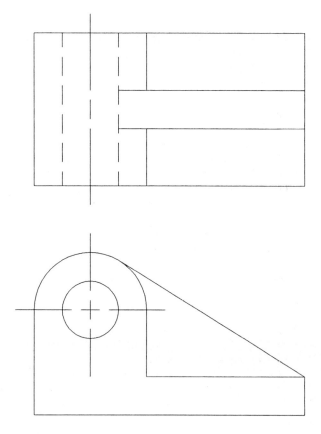

Figure 2.25 Plot produced by a laser printer.

Printers

Printers (Figure 2.26) can be used for quick check-prints of CADD drawings. Most CADD systems will print drawings on many different dot matrix graphics printers. Usually the printer output is not good enough for final copy (Figure 2.27) but is very useful for making check-prints.

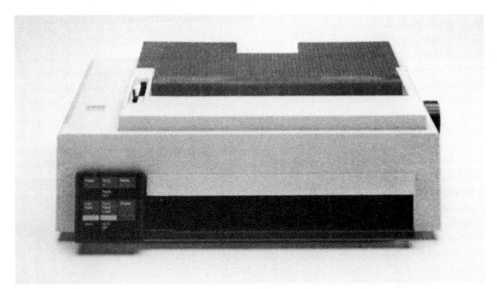

Figure 2.26 Common graphics printer that can be used for printer plots (Courtesy of International Business Machines).

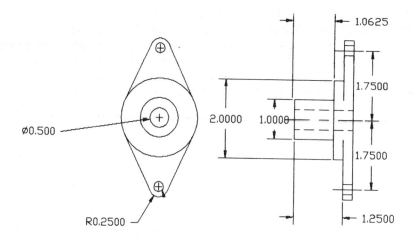

Figure 2.27 Printer plot of a drawing.

Mass Storage Devices

Storage devices are considered to be input/output (I/O) devices. Data can be input to the computer from the device, or data from the computer can be output for storage. On microcomputers five types of storage devices are:

1. 5 1/4-inch mini-floppy disk
2. 3 1/2-inch micro-disk
3. Hard disk drive
4. Bernoulli box
5. Streaming tape drive (cartridge)

The 5 1/4-inch floppy disk is a very common method of storing drawings created with CADD. Capacities range from 360KB (kilobytes) to 1.2MB (megabytes) of storage. The 3 1/2-inch micro-disk (Figure 2.28) has storage capacities of about 760KB or 1.4MB (megabytes) and can be used to store drawings. Hard disk drives can store and retrieve data much faster than floppy or micro-disks. Storage capacities range from 10MB to 200 MB and beyond. Hard drives are used to store the CADD software as well as drawings; however, any drawings stored on hard disk drives should be backed up on floppy or micro-disks for protection. Bernoulli boxes commonly can store 44 or 90 MB. They provide fast access and large storage capacities similar to a hard disk drive, but they are removable. Cartridge tape drives are used primarily for archiving of drawing files. The cartridge is similar to a cassette tape and is sometimes referred to as a streaming tape. *Archiving* is used to backup drawings files to prevent accidental loss.

Figure 2.28 A 3 1/2 inch micro disk.

THE FUTURE OF MICROCOMPUTER-BASED CADD

As microcomputer technology continues to evolve and improve, CADD software will become more powerful. The ability of a computer to process more than one task, called *multi-tasking,* will become more common. Improved bus circuitry will allow data to move faster within the computer and between the computer and peripheral devices improving processing time. Optical disk data storage will allow huge amounts of data to be stored for development of complex solid models and engineering analysis data. Screen display resolution will approach 35mm photographic quality. Workstation technology will continue to improve and drop in price so that PC-based software will increasingly be used. AutoCAD already runs on many workstation platforms under the UNIX operating system.

Software improvements will allow the growth of expert systems, which automatically will alert the designer to possible design flaws or assist her/him in making design decisions. Improved user interface will make the software both easier to learn and tomodify.

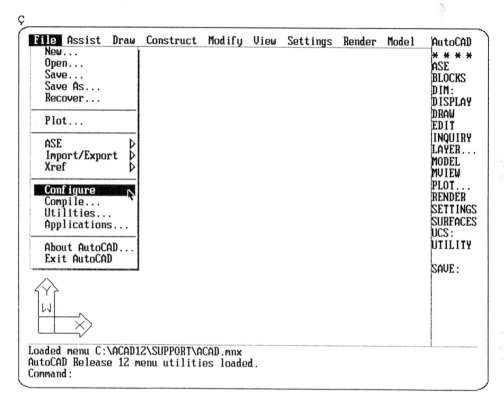

Figure 2.29 Select Configure from the File Menu for configuration.

```
          A U T O C A D (R)
Copyright (c) 1982-92  Autodesk, Inc.  All Rights Reserved.
Release Q.0.33 (5/4/92) 386 DOS Extender
Serial Number:  118-10007016
ALPHA VERSION -- NOT FOR RESALE
Licensed to:    Gary R. Bertoline, Purdue University
Obtained from:  Autodesk - Neele Johnston

Configuration menu

    0.  Exit to drawing editor
    1.  Show current configuration
    2.  Allow detailed configuration

    3.  Configure video display
    4.  Configure digitizer
    5.  Configure plotter
    6.  Configure system console
    7.  Configure operating parameters

Enter selection <0>:
```

Figure 2.30 The AutoCAD Configuration Menu.

Loading AutoCAD

Turn the computer on and at the C prompt type **ACADR12** and press RETURN. (The exact command might be different for your system) After a few moments the AutoCAD logo appears on screen then the drawing editor, as shown in Figure 2.31.

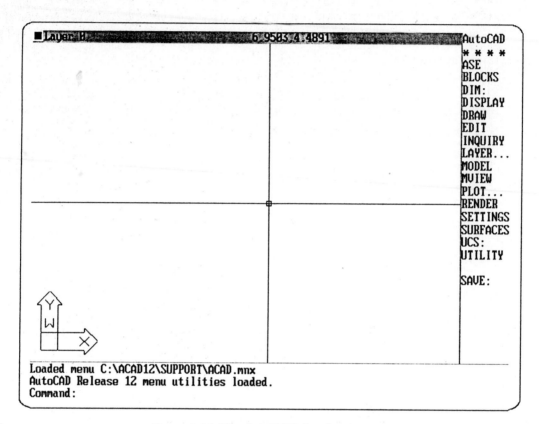

Figure 2.31 The AutoCAD drawing screen.

QUESTIONS FOR REVIEW

1. Name the five different components of a CADD system.
2. List four common types of input devices.
3. List four common types of output devices.
4. Name the three types of CADD systems.
5. Name four types of mass storage devices commonly used with CADD.
6. Define the term peripheral device and give an example.
7. Define the term pixel.
8. Describe what the term configuration is.
9. Describe some future trends in microcomputer-based CADD systems.
10. Define the word driver.
11. Name the two types of mice.
12. Describe how to configure AutoCAD.

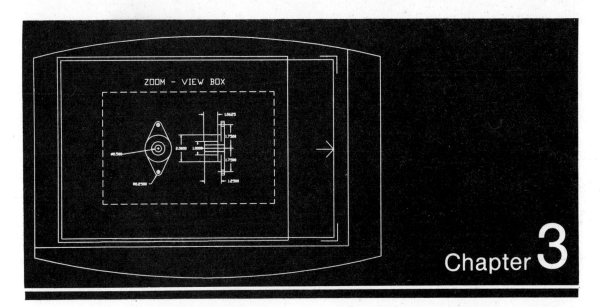

ZOOM - VIEW BOX

Chapter 3

LETTERING, SKETCHING, AND DISPLAY CHANGES

This chapter is an introduction to the use of AutoCAD to add text to drawings and sketching and to control the way a drawing is displayed. Adding text using traditional tools can take up to 20 percent of the time to create a drawing. This time-consuming process is improved considerably through the use of AutoCAD.

Text is added to a drawing through the keyboard. Different type styles or fonts are available that are different sizes and rotated. Sketches are created with a continuous line function. If a mouse or stylus is used, the sketch function is similar to using a pencil, but some AutoCAD commands make sketching easier to create and edit. AutoCAD provides many different display options to control the size of the image displayed on screen.

OBJECTIVES

After completing Chapter 3, you will be able to:
1. Add and erase single and multiple lines of text to a drawing,
2. Change the text font,
3. Change the text height, slant, rotation angle, and justification.
4. Create text at an oblique angle and in vertical orientation,
5. Change existing text style parameters,
6. Create special characters in a string of text,
7. Create a sketch using the Sketch command,
8. Use the Sketch command with Snap and Ortho Modes,
9. Use the Zoom command to enlarge or shrink the window display.
10. Pan across a drawing display,
11. Create and control the display of layers,
12. Control the display of colors, and
13. Change line types.

LETTERING ENGINEERING DRAWINGS

An engineering drawing graphically represents a design through the use of lines, arcs, and circles. However, some information about a drawing cannot be communicated clearly with only graphics. **Text** is added to a drawing to complete the description of the part and usually consists of general notes, labels for parts, title blocks, and parts lists.

Traditionally, text has been added to a drawing by freehand lettering aided by instrument-drawn guide lines. Freehand lettering is a skill that is difficult to master for some beginners. Lettering on an engineering drawing should be created quickly and in a style that is legible and consistent. To assist the designer in creating legible text, lettering templates, typing, and mechanical lettering devices have been developed.

The use of a keyboard on computers and CADD systems has created an effective method of adding text to a drawing, and the ability to freehand letter is no longer a limiting factor. An experienced CADD user can produce perfectly legible and consistent text on engineering drawings. AutoCAD provides two different commands, **DTEXT** and **TEXT**, and numerous options to add text to an engineering drawing.

The Text Command

The **TEXT** command is used to add alphanumeric text to a drawing. In a CADD system, the string of text is located by moving the cursor to the desired position then picking the point. That location may be the start point of the text, the end point, the middle, or the center. How it is located depends on the current aligned or justification mode.

Aligning Text

The default start point is usually the lower left corner of the string of text, as shown in Figure 3.1 AutoCAD features five different alignment modes, which are displayed when the **TEXT** command is selected from the second page of the Draw Menu (Figure 3.2), in the prompt:

CENTER will center a line of text about a digitized point.
FIT asks for a text height and adjusts the width of the letters to fit between two points. This command is similar to **ALIGN**, except the height is constant when using **FIT**.
MIDDLE centers the text both horizontally and vertically about the chosen point.
RIGHT justifies to the right of the text baseline.
Justify/Style<Start Point>:
Entering **J** and **RETURN** selects the Justify command with 14 options. **ALIGN** uses a start and end point for the string of text and automatically fits the text between the two digitized points. AutoCAD computes a text height to fit between the two points. Figure 3.3.

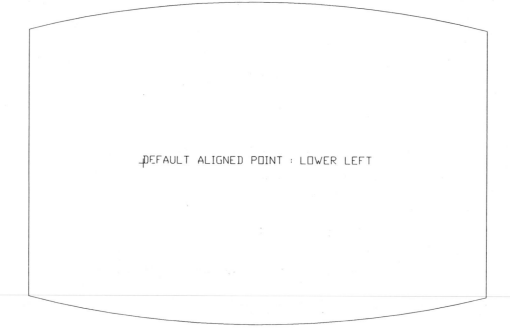

DEFAULT ALIGNED POINT : LOWER LEFT

Figure 3.1 The plus (+) indicates the digitized position for the default aligned mode.

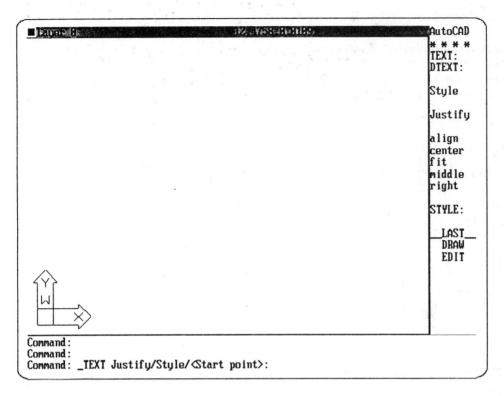

Figure 3.2 The DRAW-TEXT menu.

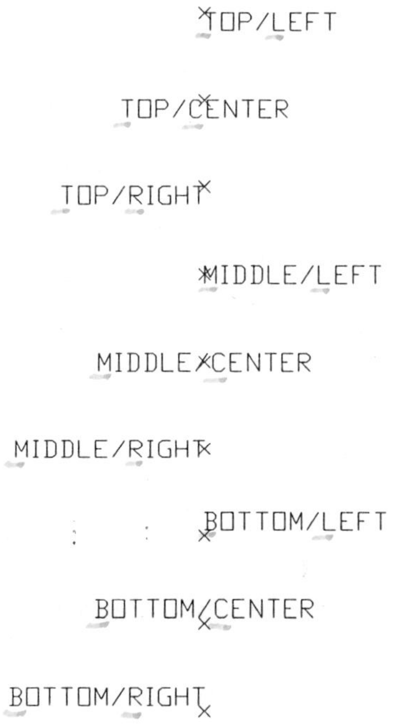

TOP/LEFT

TOP/CENTER

TOP/RIGHT

MIDDLE/LEFT

MIDDLE/CENTER

MIDDLE/RIGHT

BOTTOM/LEFT

BOTTOM/CENTER

BOTTOM/RIGHT

Figure 3.3 Examples of aligned, fit, center, middle, and right options.

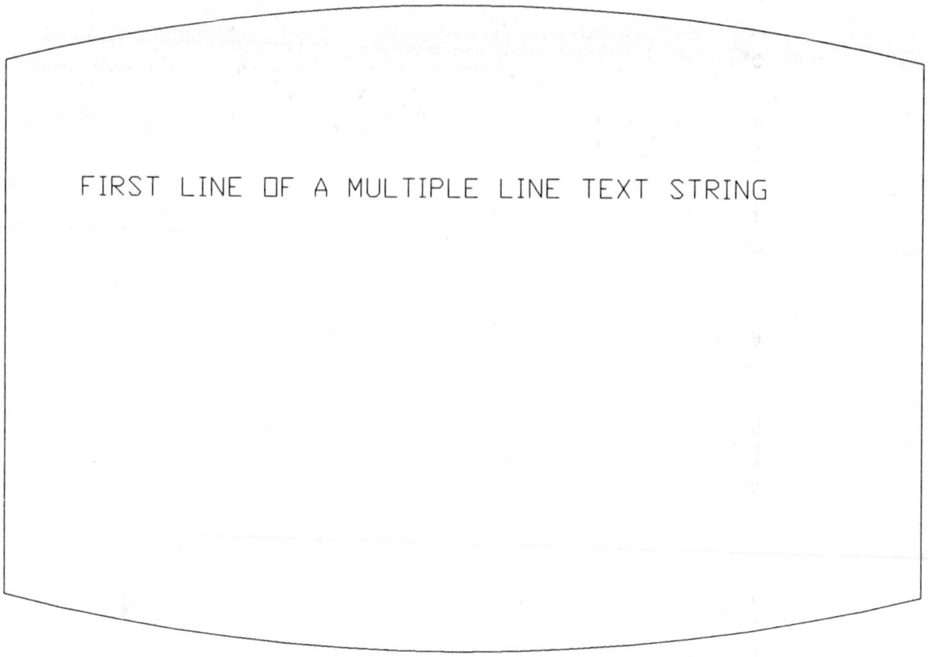

FIRST LINE OF A MULTIPLE LINE TEXT STRING

Figure 3.4 The first line of text in a multiple line text string.

TL user selects the top/left point to begin a string of text. Figure 3.4.
TC user selects the top/center point to begin a string of text.
TR user selects the top/right point to begin a string of text.
ML user selects the middle/left point to begin a string of text.
MC user selects the middle/center point to begin a string of text.
MR user selects the middle/right point to begin a string of text.
BL user selects the bottom/left point to begin a string of text.
BC user selects the bottom/center point to begin a string of text.
BR user selects the bottom/right point to begin a string of text.

Text Styles

The STYLE command determines the appearance of the text characters. The STANDARD text style is the default setting at startup with the following properties:

Style name:	Standard
Font file:	txt
Height:	0 (not fixed)
Width factor:	1
Obliquing angle:	0
Backwards:	No
Upside-down:	No
Orientation:	Horizontal

The default text style can be changed in the prototype drawing so start-up settings are different. Changes in the Standard style can be made with the **STYLE** command. Figure 3.3 uses the standard TXT font. The text font is changed by selecting the **STYLE** command from the Text Menu.

Placing Text On A Drawing: Exercise 3.1

To place a line of text using default values follow these steps.

1. Load AutoCAD and start with a blank screen or select New from the File Pull-down Menu if AutoCAD is already loaded. Select OK from the Create New Drawing Dialogue Box without naming the drawing. Select TEXT from the second page of the Draw Menu or enter TEXT at the Command Prompt.

2. A prompt reads:
Justify/Style<Start Point>:
The default text style is TXT, and the alignment point is bottom left. To accept these values, locate the start point.

3. The start point of the text is located by moving the cursor to the desired position and picking that point or by entering X,Y coordinates. For this example, the numbers 2,4 are entered.

4. The rubberband cursor stretches from the small blip indicating the start point of the text. A second prompt reads:

Height <0.2000>:.

The default value is .20 and is changed by entering a new number. To use the default value, press RETURN.

5. Rotation angle <0>:

The default setting is zero or horizontal. Enter a positive value to rotate counter-clockwise from horizontal or a negative value to rotate clockwise. Press RETURN to accept the default setting.

6. Text:

Enter the text (your name) to be added to the drawing by typing on the keyboard and pressing RETURN when finished. After RETURN is entered, the text is displayed on the screen and you are returned to the command prompt.

Erasing Text

Text is deleted by using the **ERASE** command located on the Edit Menu, typing **E** or **ERASE** at the command prompt, or selecting Erase/Single from the Modify Pull-down Menu. The cursor is positioned at any point on the text then picked. After the text is selected, press **RETURN** to delete it from the screen. A quicker method of erasing the last text string entered would be to enter **U** at the command prompt. U will undo the last command, which results in the text being erased. Another alternative would be to select Erase/Last from the Modify Pull-down Menu. Finally, picking a line of text while at the command prompt will invoke the entity grips. Entering the letter **E** will erase the selected text.

Placing Multiple Lines Of Text

Many times it is necessary to place more than one line of text on an engineering drawing. One way is to place each line separately, but AutoCAD provides a better method. After the first line of text is entered, the command prompt is displayed. Enter **RETURN** to repeat the last command entered, which is the **TEXT** command. A prompt is displayed:

Justify/Style<Start Point>:

Enter **RETURN** to add another line below the first line at the same angle, style, height, color, layer, and justification. The following steps and Figure 3.5 illustrate placing multiple lines of text:

```
FIRST LINE OF A MULTIPLE LINE TEXT STRING
SECOND LINE OF A MULTIPLE LINE TEXT STRING
```

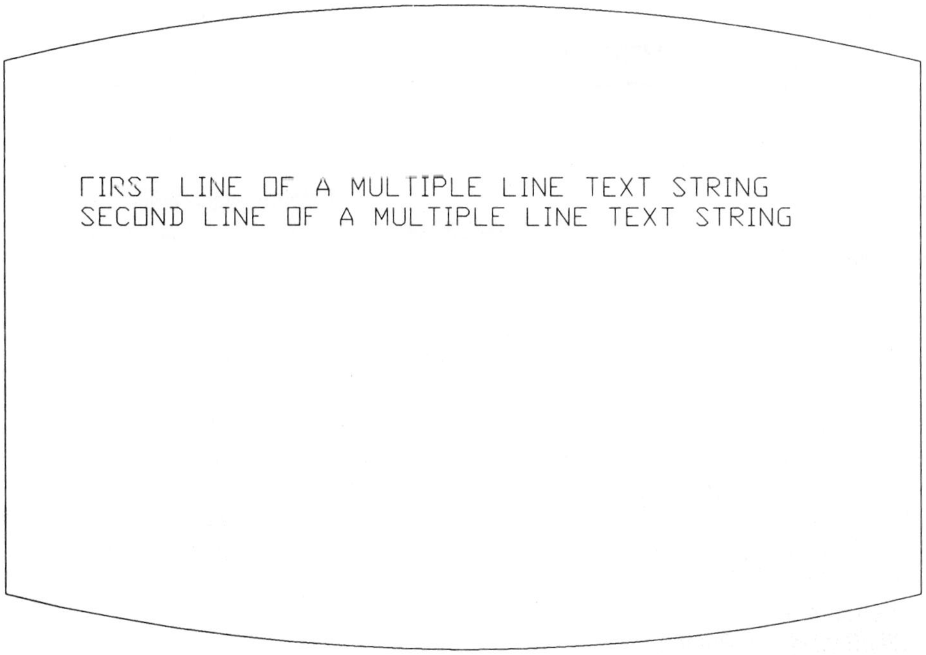

Figure 3.5 The second line of a multiple line text screen.

Multiple Lines Of Text: Exercise 3.2

1. Load AutoCAD and start with a blank screen or select New from the File Pull-down Menu. Enter **TEXT** at the command prompt and press **Return**, or select it from the Draw Menu.

2. **Justify/Style<Start Point>:**
The default text style is TXT, and the alignment point is bottom left. To accept these values, locate the start point.

3. The start point of the text is located by moving the cursor to the desired location and picking that point. The position also is determined by entering X,Y coordinates. For this example, the numbers **2,3** are entered.

4. The rubberband cursor stretches from the small blip indicating the start point of the text. A second prompt reads:
Height <0.2000>:
The default value is .20 and is changed by entering a new number. To use the default value, press **RETURN**.

5. Another prompt asks for the angle of rotation for the text:
Rotation angle <0>:
The default setting is zero or horizontal. Enter a positive value to rotate counterclockwise from horizontal or a negative value to rotate clockwise. Press **RETURN** to accept the default setting.

6. The last prompt asks that the text be entered from the keyboard:
Text:
Enter the text to be added to the drawing by typing it on the keyboard and pressing **RETURN** when finished. After RETURN is entered, the text is displayed on screen.

7. To add another line of text, enter **RETURN** at the command prompt, which repeats the last command, which is **TEXT**, and displays the following prompt:
Justify/Style<Start Point>:
Enter **RETURN**. By entering return, the height and rotation angle prompts are skipped.

8. The prompt reads:
Text:

Enter the second line of text from the keyboard.

9. The second line of text is displayed directly below the first line on the screen after **RETURN** is entered. Figure 3.5.

The Dtext Command

The **Dynamic** Text command does everything explained about the **TEXT** command. However, the main difference between the two commands is that **DTEXT** displays the text on the drawing as it is being typed from the keyboard. **DTEXT** also can be accessed from the Draw Pull-down Menu. The sequence of prompts used to enter text is identical to those used with the **TEXT** command except for the final step. The Text prompt is displayed repeatedly after entering the text string. The cursor also is positioned at the start of the second line of text. This command may be better to use when entering multiple lines of text. To terminate the **DTEXT** command, press RETURN at the Text prompt. Entering Ctrl-C to cancel the **DTEXT** command will erase all text from the screen entered during the command.

Using The Dtext Command: Exercise 3.3

1. Load AutoCAD and start with a blank screen or select New from the File Pull-down Menu. Enter **DTEXT** at the command prompt and press **Return**, or select it from the Draw Menu, or select Text/Dynamic from the Draw Pull-down Menu.

2. **Justify/Style<Start Point>:**
The default text style is TXT, and the alignment point is bottom left. To accept these values, locate the start point.

3. The start point of the text is located by moving the cursor to the desired location and picking that point. The position also is determined by entering X,Y coordinates. For this example, pick a point near the center of the screen.

4. The rubberband cursor stretches from the small blip indicating the start point of the text. A second prompt reads:

Height <0.2000>:

The default value is .20 and is changed by entering a new number. To use the default value, press **RETURN**.

5. Another prompt asks for the angle of rotation for the text:

Rotation angle <0>:

The default setting is zero or horizontal. Enter a positive value to rotate counter-clockwise from horizontal or a negative value to rotate clockwise. Press **RETURN** to accept the default setting.

6. The next prompt asks that the text be entered from the keyboard:

Text:

Enter the text to be added to the drawing by typing it on the keyboard. Notice that the text is being added directly to the screen and is being typed on the prompt line. Press **RETURN** when finished typing the first line of text.

7. A prompt reads:

Text:

A square box is displayed below the first letter in the first text string on screen. Another line of text is added by entering it from the keyboard. Pressing **RETURN** twice to finish the **DTEXT** command and return to the Command Prompt.

The Text Style

The lettering style used on engineering drawings made with traditional tools usually was the vertical, single stroke, Gothic letter style. How it appeared depended on the ability, patience, and amount of time spent on the task. With CADD, individual differences in a lettering style can be eliminated because each letter is drawn perfectly by the computer and printer or plotter. However, some individual differences can be accomplished by using different lettering styles or a different text font.

Changing Text Style

Each font can have a variety of styles because AutoCAD provides a number of variables that can be controlled

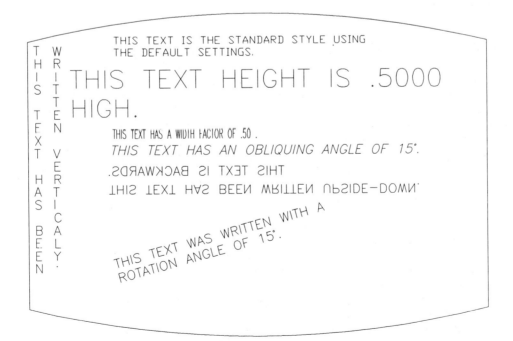

Figure 3.6 Different text style variables.

(Figure 3.6), including:
1. The height of the text.
2. The width of the text letters, called width factor.
3. The slant of the letters, called the obliquing angle.
4. Horizontal or vertical lines of text, called the orientation.
5. The text also can be drawn backwards, upside-down, or angled.
A new text style is created using the **STYLE** command that appears on the **TEXT** or **DTEXT** menu. The **STYLE** option that is listed in the **TEXT** prompt:

Justify/Style<Start Point>:

can be used to change to an existing style. The following steps describe how to create a new text style:

Creating A New Text Style: Exercise 3.4

1. Enter **STYLE** at the command prompt to display the following prompt: **Text style name (or ?) <STANDARD>:**
Entering a question mark lists the text styles created during the current drawing session. Only one is listed in the prompt line, which is the default, and appears in the prompt as **<STANDARD>**.

2. To change styles, enter the name of the new style, such as **Practice**. A new prompt reads:
New Style and the Select Font File Dialogue Box is displayed. Figure 3.7. Scroll through the files to select the font to be used with the new style. TXT is the default font file as shown in the File edit box.

3. Any one of the more than 20 AutoCAD fonts (identified by the .SHX file extension) or PostScript fonts (identified by the .PFB file extension) is selected for the new style. For this example scroll up using the scroll bar located to the right of the file list box until ROMANC is found, then double click on it. Another prompt will read:
New style. Height <0.0000>:
Setting the text height to zero allows the user to set it at the time the text is placed on the screen. Entering a value makes the style a fixed height so you are not prompted for the height every time a text string is placed.

4. Enter the default height desired, such as .125, and press RETURN.
Width factor <1.0000>:

5. Enter the default width factor to be used or press **RETURN** to select 1.0000. Numbers less than one will make letters narrow and high. Values greater than one will make letters wide and short. For this example enter **1**.
Obliquing angle <0>:

6. Enter the angle or press RETURN for zero. The obliquing angle is used to control the slant angle of the text. For this example enter **0**. The next prompt reads:
Backwards? <N>

7. To display the text backwards, enter Y or press RETURN for no. Select no for this example. The next prompt reads:
Upside-down? <N>
This prompt is for displaying upside-down text.

8. Enter Y for yes or N for no. Do not select upside-down, so enter **N**.
Vertical? <N>
This prompt is for displaying vertical or book spine text.

9. Enter Y for yes or RETURN for no. Enter **N** for horizontal text. The final prompt reads:
Practice is now the current text style
You are returned to the command prompt. Any text added to the drawing is displayed in the RomanC font using the default values assigned.

10. Practice by adding more text to the current drawing.

Changing Text Fonts

AutoCAD provides a method of changing the different text fonts through a number of different variables. A **text font** is a character pattern used to draw text. Figure 3.8 shows some of the text fonts supplied with AutoCAD.

Additional fonts can be constructed with AutoCAD's software or by reading most Adobe Type 1 (PostScript) fonts when using the STYLE command. The default text font used by AutoCAD is TXT.

AutoCAD
* * * *
STYLE:
?
Fonts
Yes
No
DTEXT:
TEXT:
LAST
DRAW
EDIT
Select Font File
Pattern: *.shx;pfb
Directory: C:\ACAD12\FONTS
Directories:
Files:
\
..
<A:>
<B:>
<C:>
<D:>
SUF_____.PFB
SYASTRO.SHX
SYMAP.SHX
SYMATH.SHX
SYMETEO.SHX
SYMUSIC.SHX
TEB_____.PFB
TEL_____.PFB
TE______.PFB
TXT.SHX
Type it
Default
File: TXT.SHX
OK
Cancel
Help...
Y
W
X
Command: style
Text style name (or ?) <STANDARD>: practice
New style.

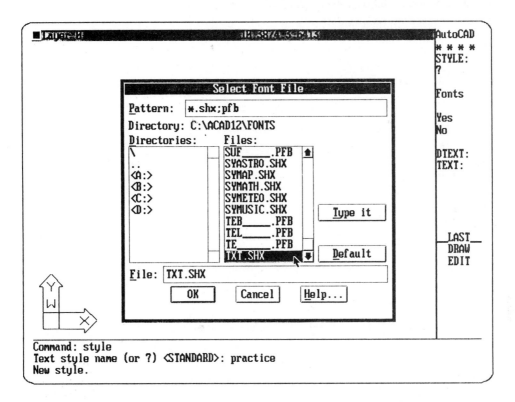

Figure 3.7 The font pop-up menu.

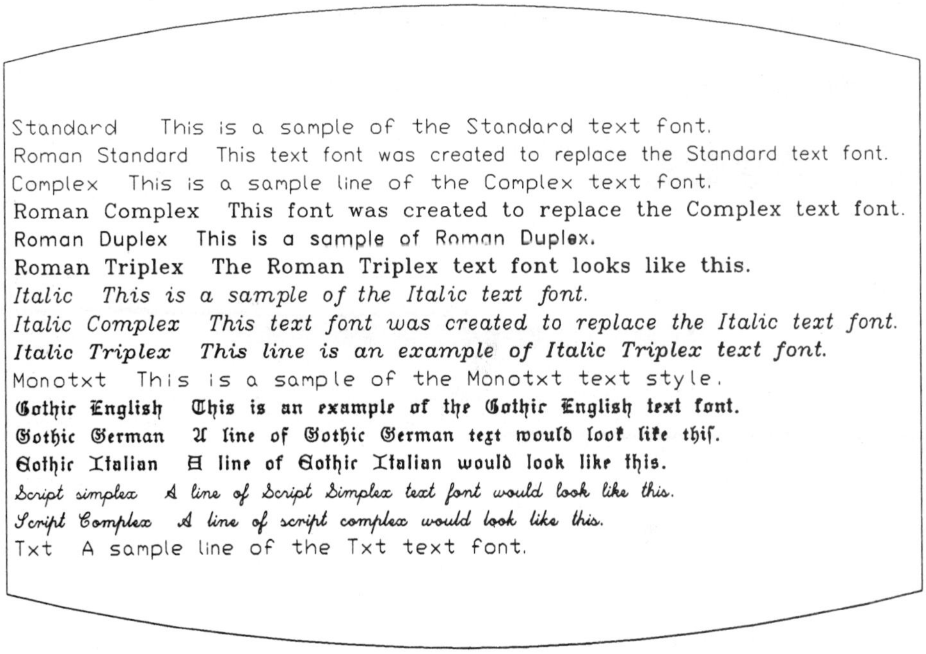

Standard This is a sample of the Standard text font.
Roman Standard This text font was created to replace the Standard text font.
Complex This is a sample line of the Complex text font.
Roman Complex This font was created to replace the Complex text font.
Roman Duplex This is a sample of Roman Duplex.
Roman Triplex The Roman Triplex text font looks like this.
Italic This is a sample of the Italic text font.
Italic Complex This text font was created to replace the Italic text font.
Italic Triplex This line is an example of Italic Triplex text font.
Monotxt This is a sample of the Monotxt text style.
Gothic English This is an example of the Gothic English text font.
Gothic German A line of Gothic German text would look like this.
Gothic Italian A line of Gothic Italian would look like this.
Script simplex A line of Script Simplex text font would look like this.
Script Complex A line of script complex would look like this.
Txt A sample line of the Txt text font.

Figure 3.8 Some of the standard text fonts.

Changing Text Fonts: Exercise 3.5

1. Select Text/Set Style... from the Draw Pull-down Menu. After choosing Set Style... from the menu, the Select Text Font Dialogue Box is displayed, as shown in Figure 3.9. Select the **Script Simplex** font by double clicking on it in the list box or in the image tile box. A prompt will read:

Height <0.0000>:

2. Enter the default height desired, such as **.125**, and press **RETURN**.

Width factor <1.0000>:

3. Enter the default width factor to be used, or press **RETURN** for 1.00.

Obliquing angle <0>:

4. Enter the angle or press **RETURN** for zero.

Backwards? <N>

5. To display the text backwards, enter Y or press **RETURN** for no.

Upside-down? <N>

This prompt is for displaying upside-down text.

6. Enter Y for yes or N for no.

Vertical? <N>

7. Enter Y for yes or **RETURN** for no. The final prompt reads:

Scripts is now the current text style.

Any text added to the drawing is displayed in the Simplex font using the default values assigned.

8. Practice by adding text to the current drawing.

Special Characters

Adding text to an engineering drawing may involve special characters that do not appear on a standard computer keyboard. For example, the degree symbol used after the numerical value for an angle is not on a standard keyboard. AutoCAD provides a method of adding these special characters to a string of text. The control characters used to display special characters are two percent signs (%%). The following control characters typed at the text prompt are used to display these special characters. Figure 3.10.

%%d is used to display the degree symbol.

%%p is used to display the plus/minus symbol commonly used for tolerancing.

%%c is used to draw the ANSI standard diameter symbol used for dimensioning circles, also known as the Greek letter *phi*.

%%% or **%** is used to display a percent symbol in a string of text.

Words also can be underscored or overscored as illustrated in Figure 3.10 by entering:

%%o before the text string to overscore and

%%u before the text string to underscore.

THE QTEXT COMMAND

Occasionally a drawing has a great deal of text. This amount of text may cause redraw time to become very long. The **QTEXT** command is used to change the text temporarily to rectangles. Figure 3.11 shows text displayed on screen when the **QTEXT** command is off, and Figure 3.12 shows the same drawing with the **QTEXT** command on after a **REGEN**. Notice that the text strings are displayed as rectangles equal in length and height to the text. The initial setting is determined by the prototype drawing. The following steps demonstrate the use of **QTEXT**:

Using Q-Text: Exercise 3.6

1. To use this command, enter **QTEXT** at the command prompt or by selecting **SETTINGS** from the Main Menu.

2. **QTEXT** is on the first page of the **SETTINGS** submenu and is selected.

3. **QTEXT ON/OFF <OFF>:**

The current setting is displayed in the prompt. Enter **ON** and press **RETURN**. Entering **REGEN** at the command prompt will change the text to rectangles. When **QTEXT** is on,

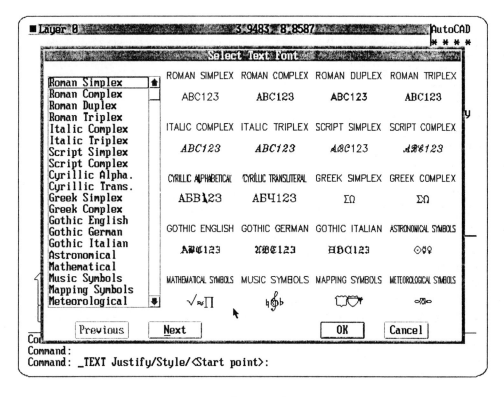

Figure 3.9 The font dialogue box.

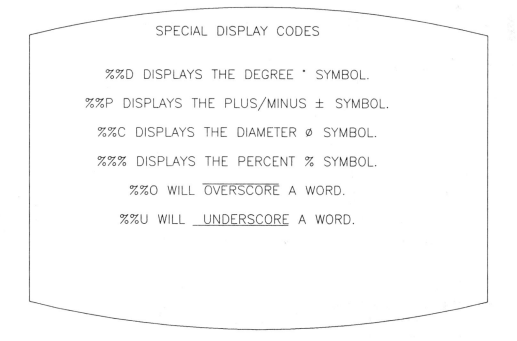

Figure 3.10 Special display codes used with text.

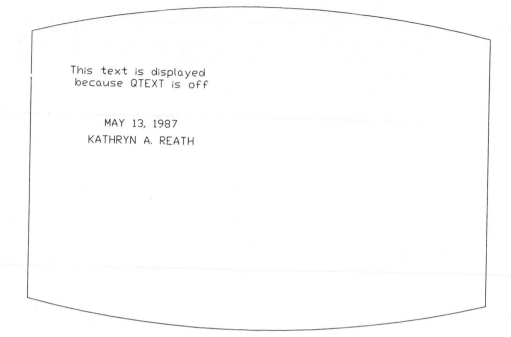

This text is displayed
because QTEXT is off

MAY 13, 1987
KATHRYN A. REATH

Figure 3.11 Text as it normally is displayed.

any new text that is added to the drawing will be displayed as text until the drawing is regenerated using the **REGEN** command. The **QTEXT** must be turned off to plot the text.

Text Scaling Factors

For most engineering drawings, the standard text height is .125. However, for the text to be drawn at .125 on the final plot, its size must be adjusted. For example, if you want .125 text on a drawing that is plotted 1/4 size, the text height must be set at .5 units. This is determined by multiplying the intended text size by the reciprocal of the drawing scale. The following list is useful in providing scaling factors for text at various plot sizes:

SCALE	TEXT HEIGHT
1/8"=1'	12
1/4"=1'	6
1/2"=1'	3
1/4 size	.5
1/2 size	.25
full size	.125
2/1	.0625
3/1	.0416
4/1	.0312
5/1	.0250
10/1	.0125

EDITING TEXT

The **DDEDIT** command is used to change text and attribute information through a dialogue box. At the command prompt, enter **DDEDIT** to display the prompt:

<Select a TEXT or ATTDEF object>/Undo:

Text is selected by picking it or using the Last option. The dialogue box is displayed on screen with the selected text string that can be changed. Pick the OK button to accept the changes.

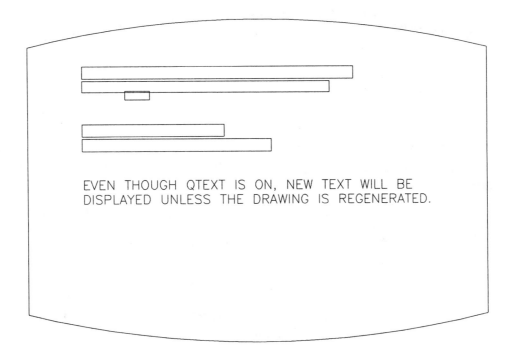

EVEN THOUGH QTEXT IS ON, NEW TEXT WILL BE
DISPLAYED UNLESS THE DRAWING IS REGENERATED.

Figure 3.12 Text as it appears when QTEXT is on.

SKETCHING

Sketching is an important communications tool for engineers and technologists. Sketching is used to record design ideas rapidly and assists the designer to think through possible solutions to problems. It is usually one of the first steps in the design process but is also used in every other stage. Sketches are used to communicate design ideas to others, to pre-plan the layout of a drawing, or to substitute for an instrument drawing.

Sketching with traditional tools is done usually with a pencil, eraser, and grid or plane paper. A technique associated with sketching includes how to hold the pencil, pencil grades and sharpness, drawing rectangles, squares, circles, lines, and ellipses. Sketches of an object can be orthographic or pictorial.

Sketching With AutoCAD

AutoCAD provides a method of creating rough, freehand sketches of an object by using the SKETCH command. The SKETCH command automatically enters entities by movement of the cursor. This mode can be used for some mapping applications and other irregular features. This is a procedure that should be used with caution if fine drawing accuracy is selected, because it is a memory intensive activity. This drawing mode interprets a sketch as a series of lines. After the sketch is completed, it can be edited as can other drawing entities.

The SKETCH command is used only with a pointing device such as a mouse. The arrow keys do not function when in this mode. The SKETCH command is a submenu item of DRAW. Turn the Snap and Ortho modes off before using this command for freehand sketches.

Creating A Sketch With AutoCAD: Exercise 3.7

1. Select SKETCH from Draw Menu or Pull-down Menu (Figure 3.13) or enter it at the command prompt. When SKETCH is chosen, the first prompt asks for a record increment

Record increment <0.1000>:

The record increment is the minimum amount of cursor movement necessary before a line segment is generated. It is used to control the length of the shortest line segment. For example, to sketch your name, a small record increment is necessary. To sketch the front view of a rectangular prism, a large record increment could be used. Use of the .1000 increment on a screen with a drawing limit of 10" makes it possible to create 100 line segments if a horizontal line is drawn from left to right across the screen. Attempt to keep this increment as large as possible to avoid using sizable amounts of memory.

2. The next prompt displays some of the **SKETCH** mode controls used with this command:

Sketch. Pen eXit Quit Record Erase Connect

Pen is a toggle used to indicate when movement of the cursor causes lines to be generated.

3. When first starting the **SKETCH** command, the pen is up, meaning that movement of the cursor will not produce lines on the screen. Before entering the letter P, position the cursor at the starting point for the sketch.

4. Enter the letter **P** or press the cursor control device's pick button to put the pen down. **<Pen down>** is added to the prompt.

5. Move the cursor now to create lines.

6. Entering the letter **P** or pressing the pick button ends the sketched line, and **<Pen up>** is displayed in the prompt line.

7. Sketched lines are not added immediately to the drawing. The **RECORD** or **EXIT** option must be used to add the sketched lines. On a color terminal, the temporary sketched lines are displayed in green. If the current color setting is green, the temporary lines are displayed in red. After the lines are added to the drawing, they are redrawn in the color associated with the current layer.

8. The **eXit** or **X** option ends the Sketch sequence, stores the line segments that have been added, and returns to the command prompt. The number of line segments added to the drawing is displayed in the prompt line. The Space Bar and RETURN have the same effect as Exit.

Quit or **Q** terminates the Sketch command without storing the temporary line segments created. **Ctrl-C** has the same effect as **Quit**.

Record or **R** saves the created segments in the drawing file without leaving the Sketch mode. These saved segments cannot be deleted using the Erase mode within Sketch. Record does not change the up/down state of the pen. The number of lines added to the drawing is displayed in the prompt line with this command.

Erase or **E** deletes those segments that have not been saved, similar to the **Undo** command described earlier. A prompt reads:

Erase: Select end of delete

The pen returns to the up position if it was down. The cursor is moved to the point at which the temporary lines are to be erased. These entities will be blanked off the screen and are erased by pressing the letter **P** or the pick button on the cursor control device. The user is returned automatically to the **SKETCH** prompt.

CONNECT or **C** is similar to the Continue function used with Line entities. It is used to connect the start point of a new Sketch segment with the endpoint of the last active sketch line. A prompt reads:

Connect: Move to endpoint of line

The crosshair cursor returns to the screen. Move the cursor to the endpoint of the last sketched line. When the cursor is within one record increment, the pen is lowered and sketching can continue.

MAKING DISPLAY CHANGES

When using traditional tools, the user focuses attention on different details and occasionally may move his/her position relative to the paper, more frequently on large drawing sheets with many details. The way CADD handles the movement or center of attention from one position on a drawing sheet to another is through the use of Display commands.

A CADD drawing is displayed on the computer monitor. These monitors come in a variety of sizes, as explained in Chapter 2. Common drawing sheets range from 8 1/2" x 11" to 34" x 44". The largest monitor size commonly used with micro-CADD is a 19 inch diagonal screen. To create large drawings on a relatively small screen, use the Display commands.

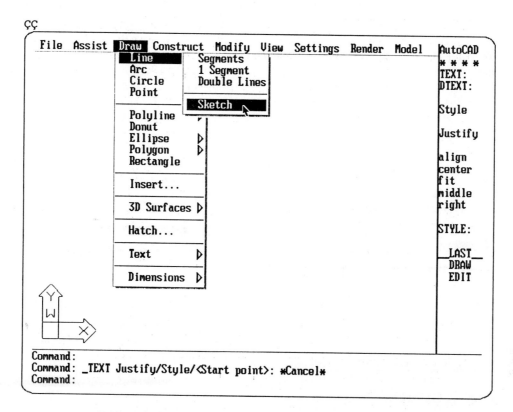

Figure 3.13 Using the SKETCH option to create a drawing.

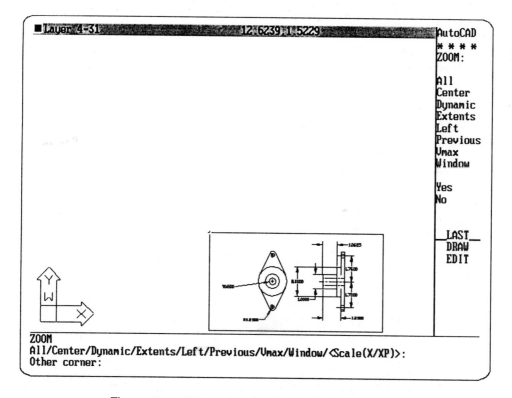

Figure 3.14 A large drawing that includes small details.

Virtually any size drawing can be created full scale with AutoCAD. Scaling does not have to be considered until the drawing is plotted; all units should be entered full size. Of course, a problem might occur when creating engineering drawings for large parts that have small details. The drawing shown in Figure 3.14 is very difficult to create on a CADD system without means of enlarging complicated areas. The Display command **ZOOM** changes the viewing window so that small details appear very large on the computer monitor, as shown in Figure 3.15. Entities are added or edited as they are when the full drawing is displayed. Any changes become part of the drawing when the full drawing again is displayed. The Display commands are some of the most helpful and commonly used commands available to shrink, enlarge, move, or redraw the screen image.

Zoom

ZOOM is a technique used in photography and cinema to enlarge or shrink a scene. A zoom lens on a camera is similar in function to the **ZOOM** command in CADD. The **ZOOM** command enlarges or shrinks the size of the displayed drawing. This command actually does not change the graphic data base; the drawing units remain the same. What does change is how large or small the drawing is displayed on the monitor. The screen display sometimes is referred to as a "window". Think of the computer display as the window on the CADD drawing. Changing the size of the window changes the size and amount of drawing displayed within the window.

The **ZOOM** command is entered at the command prompt, selected from the Display Menu, View Pull-down Menu, or used as a Transparent command by entering **Z** at the command prompt. After the **ZOOM** command is selected, a prompt reads:

All/Cente r/Dynamic/Extents/Left /Pr evious/ V max/Wi ndow/< Scale(X/XP)>:

This prompt lists the different **ZOOM** options available. The window option is the default setting so picking two points on the screen will zoom automatically into the area selected. The other options are selected by entering the name or capitalized letter of the name. Some of these options can be accessed directly through the View Pull-down Menu. Zoom is a transparent command so entering **'ZOOM or 'Z** will invoke the command while another command is in progress.

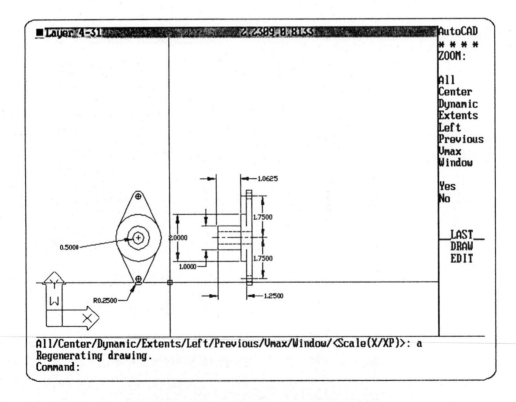

Figure 3.15 The ZOOM-WINDOW option used to enlarge the viewing area.

Zoom All

The **ZOOM ALL** option fits the entire drawing on the screen. In plan view it will zoom to the drawing's limits or the current extents, whichever is greater. In a non-plan 3D view Zoom All is the same as Zoom Extents.

Zoom All: Exercise 3.8

1. Open Exercise drawing file ZOOM by entering **OPEN** at the command prompt or by selecting Open from the File Pull-down Menu. Change to the directory where the Exercise drawing is located, then double click on the file name ZOOM. Figure 3.14 shows a drawing displayed on the screen. The rectangle surrounding the drawing represents the extents of the drawing. The drawing extents are the smallest rectangle that surrounds all the objects in a drawing.
2. Enter the letter **Z** at the command prompt, or select Zoom from the View Pull down Menu or from the Display Menu.
3. A prompt reads:
All/Center/Dynamic/Extents/Left/Previous/Vmax/Window/<Scale(X/XP)>:
Enter the letter **A** at the Zoom prompt or pick **ALL** from the screen or tablet menus. The display changes as shown in Figure 3.15.

Zoom-center

The **ZOOM-CENTER** option specifies a new center point for the drawing display. The magnification of the drawing also can be changed by entering the desired height of the window. The current height is displayed in the prompt. Entering a larger number reduces the size or magnification of the drawing. Entering a smaller number than the one displayed in the prompt increases the size or magnification of the drawing.

Zoom-Center: Exercise 3.9

1. Enter the letter **Z** at the command prompt or select Zoom from the View Pull-down Menu or from the Display Menu. Pressing **RETURN** will repeat the previous command,

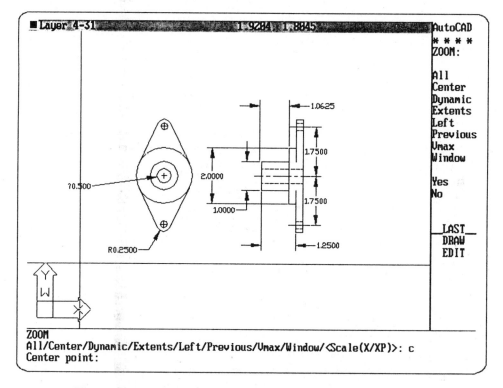

Figure 3.16 Locating a new center for the ZOOM-CENTER option.

which was Zoom from Exercise 3.8.

2. A prompt reads:

All/Ce nt er/Dyna mic/ Extents/ Left /Prev ious/Vmax /Window/<Sc ale(X/X P)>:

3. The **ZOOM-CENTER** option is selected from the Zoom Menu or **C** is entered at the Zoom prompt.

4. A prompt reads:

Center point:

Enter the center point for the display by moving the cursor with the input device and picking that location or by entering X, Y coordinate values. Figure 3.16.

5. A second prompt reads:

Magnification or Height <12.7129>:

The number displayed is the current height of the display. To change the magnification, enter a new number and press RETURN. To leave the magnification the same, press RETURN for this example. If a larger number is entered, the magnification is reduced. If a smaller number is entered, the magnification is increased. For example, entering 4.5 would increase the magnification by a factor of 2 and entering 18 would reduce the magnification by a factor of 2. Experiment with different values by entering a number then repeating steps 1-5.

Figure 3.17 shows how the display will change from Figure 3.16 after the **CENTER** option is selected, the lower left corner of the display is picked, and the height is not changed.

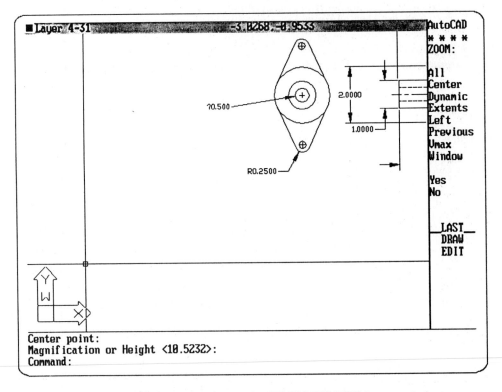

Figure 3.17 Screen display after the ZOOM-CENTER is executed.

Zoom-dynamic

The Dynamic option is used to visualize the relative sizes of the entire drawing, the generated area, and the current view screen. All three of these areas are shown on screen. This option can be entered from the View Pull-down Menu Zoom/Dynamic. When this option is selected, the graphics from the screen are replaced by rectangles representing the three areas described above. If an EGA or VGA color display is used, a solid white or black rectangle represents the drawing extents. A dotted line, shown in green or magenta on color displays, represents the current view. Four corners, drawn in red on color displays, represent the generated area that may be viewed at high speed. If the corners are not displayed, then the generated image is the same as the drawing extents. Figure 3.18 shows an example of Figure 3.17 after Dynamic is entered.

A *Panning View Box* has a large X in the center and starts out as the same size as the current view box and is part of the dynamic screen display. The box is moved by the cursor control device. This type of movement is called "panning."

A new zoom screen is created in the dynamic mode by selecting the pick button on the cursor control device. This changes the large X in the center of the view box to a large arrow located on the right side of the box (Figure 3.19). The size of the *Zoom View Box* is changed by moving the arrow cursor to the left or the right. Only horizontal movement is possible in this mode. The vertical dimension is calculated automatically. The left midpoint of the view box is stationary in this mode. By panning the view box to a different location and pressing **RETURN**, a new window is created and the drawing is displayed on screen as shown in Figure 3.20.

If a new lower left corner is needed for the new zoom window, toggle between zoom and pan modes by pressing the pick button on the cursor control device. To increase magnification, move the arrow cursor to the left, which creates a smaller view box. To decrease magnification, move the arrow cursor to the right to create a larger view box. Remember that moving the view box outside of the generated area displays an hour glass, which indicates that a longer time is required for regeneration of the new view. After the zoom box is in the desired position, press the RETURN key or the RETURN button on the cursor control device.

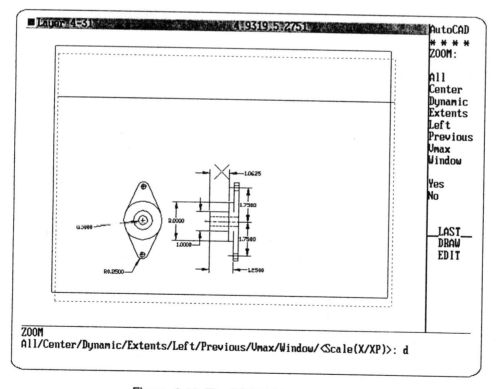

Figure 3.18 The ZOOM-DYNAMIC screen.

Extents

The Extents option displays as large as possible all of the drawing entities on the display. Figure 3.21 shows a drawing displayed before the **ZOOM EXTENTS** option is selected. The rectangle surrounding the drawing represents the limits of the drawing. If a **ZOOM EXTENTS** is executed, the display looks like Figure 3.22. Enter **ZOOM** at the command prompt or select it from the View Pull-down Menu. Enter **E** at the zoom prompt to automatically display the view shown in Figure 3.22.

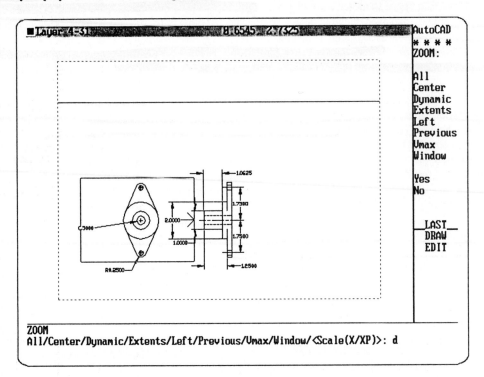

Figure 3.19 The X changes to an arrow when selecting the new display.

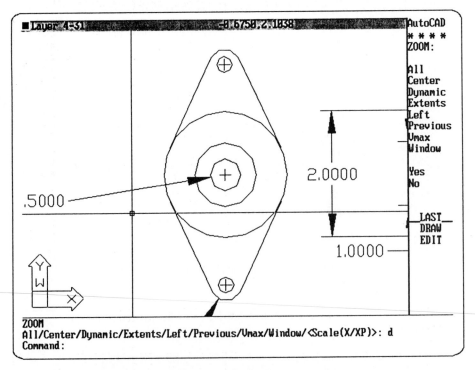

Figure 3.20 New display after using the ZOOM-DYNAMIC option.

Left

The **LEFT** option defines a new lower left corner of a display. The magnification also is changed by entering a new number in a way similar to the **CENTER** option.

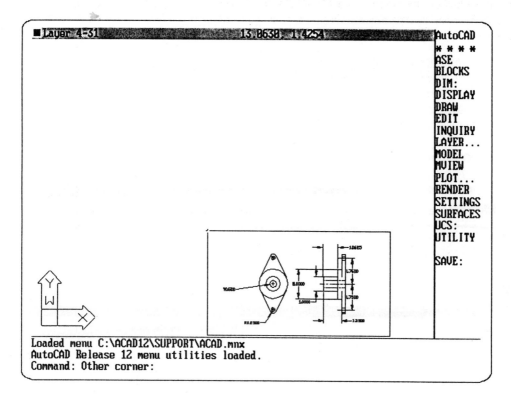

Figure 3.21 Drawing with rectangle representing the extents.

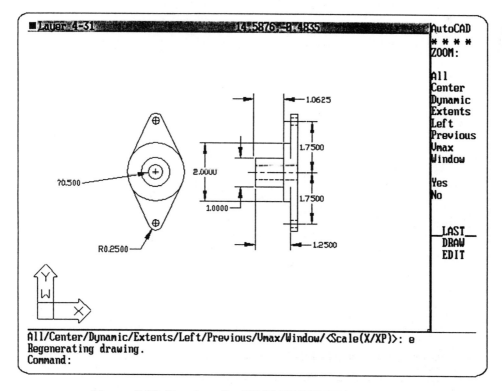

Figure 3.22 Drawing after ZOOM-EXTENTS is used.

Zoom-Left: Exercise 3.10

1. Enter **Z** at the command prompt, then **E** for extents. Repeat the Zoom command by pressing Return or the Space Bar. Choosing **LEFT** from the Zoom Menu or entering **L** at the Zoom prompt displays the following:

Lower left corner point:

2. The cursor control device can pick a point, or X, Y coordinate values can be input at the prompt. Pick the point shown in Figure 3.23. A second prompt reads:

Magnification or Height <9.3700>:

3. The number in the prompt represents the current height of the display. Entering a different number changes the magnification, as described for the **CENTER** option. Entering the same number or **RETURN** uses the same magnification and creates a new display as shown in Figure 3.24.

Zoom-previous

AutoCAD remembers the last 10 zoomed or panned windows for each viewport that has been created. The **PREVIOUS** option is used to view these other windows. Successive use of the **PREVIOUS** option is used to view the last 10 views. If only two views have been created, this command can toggle between the two views, which is extremely useful if a need to change between the full view and a magnified area for detail work is needed. As an example, if Figure 3.24 currently were displayed, Figure 3.23 could be displayed again by selecting **PREVIOUS** from the Zoom Menu or **P** from the Zoom prompt, or from the Display Pull-down Menu.

Window

The **WINDOW** option dynamically creates a new viewing window by selecting two opposing corners of a rectangle. The center of the rectangle becomes the approximate center of the new display, and the area inside is enlarged to fill the screen using left and bottom justified with closest fit to screen.

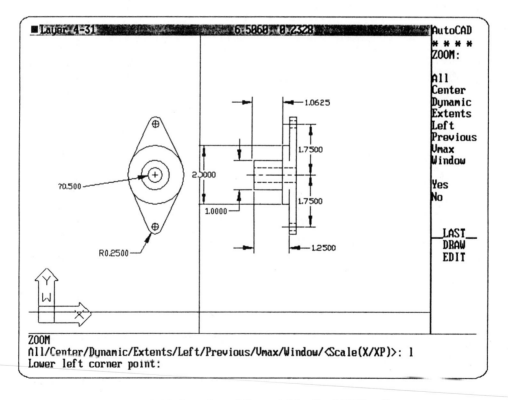

Figure 3.23 Location of the point for the LEFT option.

Zoom-Window: Exercise 3.11

1. Enter **Z** at the command prompt, then **E** for extents. Repeat the Zoom command by pressing Return or the Space Bar. Selecting the **WINDOW** option from the Zoom Menu, the Zoom prompt, or the View/Zoom/Window Pull-down Menu displays the prompt:

First corner:

2. Select the first point by entering the X, Y coordinates or by picking a point with the cursor control device, as shown in Figure 3.25. A second prompt is displayed:

Other corner:

Moving the cursor will cause a rectangle to be displayed that grows in size as the cursor is moved further from the first point picked. Enter the other corner, as shown in Figure 3.25. After the second point is picked, the new window is displayed as shown in Figure 3.26.

3. Notice that the arc and circle are drawn as a series of straight lines. AutoCAD automatically does this to make the redrawing of the screen faster. If you want to make the circle and arcs smoother on screen, then enter **VIEWRES** at the command prompt.

4. A prompt reads:

Do you want fast zooms? <Y>

Enter Y for yes to maintain fast zooms. Entering no would cause a regeneration to occur for all zooms, pans, and view restores, which will greatly increase redraw time.

5. Another prompt reads:

Enter circle zoom percent (1-20000) <100>:

100 is the default setting used by AutoCAD. Setting a higher number will result in smoother displayed circles and arcs. A lower number will result in circles and arcs with fewer line segments. Regardless of how low the number is set, AutoCAD will never represent a circle with less than eight sides.

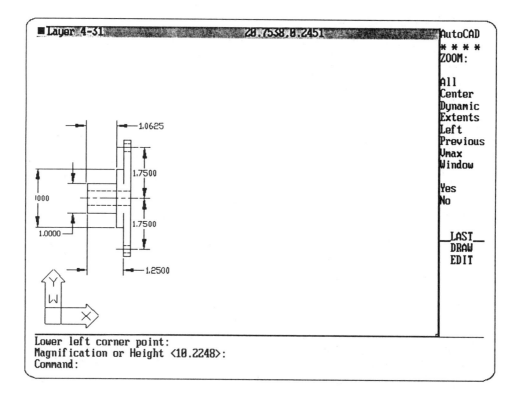

Figure 3.24 New screen display after using the LEFT option.

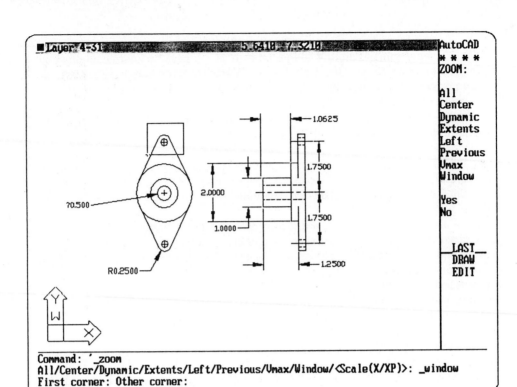

Figure 3.25 The small rectangle represents the ZOOM-WINDOW.

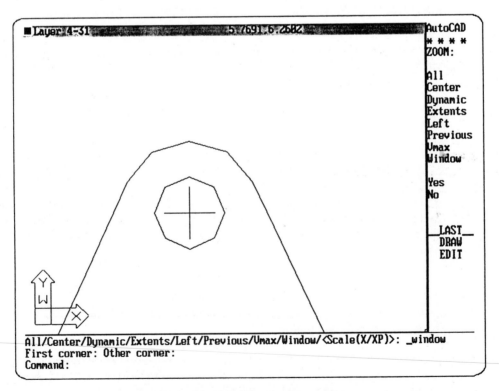

Figure 3.26 The new displayed window.

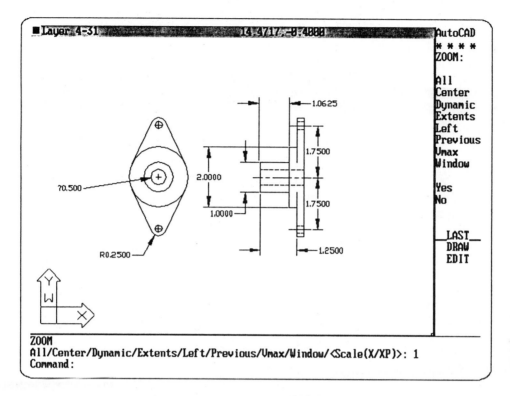

Figure 3.27 The display for a scale factor of 1.

Vmax

Zoom Vmax will zoom out as far as possible on the virtual screen without causing a regeneration of the screen. AutoCAD maintains a very large virtual screen with more than four billion pixels in each axis. Using Vmax usually will greatly reduce the displayed size of the drawing.

Scale

The **SCALE** option, the last option listed in the zoom prompt, creates a new window by entering a scale factor. To create a Scale Zoom, enter a value at the prompt and press RETURN. A scale factor of one displays the whole drawing if the drawing is within the drawing limits. Figure 3.27. Entering any other number computes a new scale relative to this full view. Entering larger numbers, such as two, doubles the size of the drawing on screen, as shown in Figure 3.28. Entering a number followed by **X** will cause a new view to be created that is relative to the current view. For example, entering **2X** will cause a new view to be created that is twice as large as the current view.

Scale: Exercise 3.12

1. Enter **Z** at the command prompt, then **E** for extents. Repeat the Zoom command by pressing Return or the Space Bar.
2. Entering a smaller number, such as .5, shrinks the drawing to one-half size, as shown in Figure 3.29. Notice that this zoom option does not change the center position of the drawing. This causes entities near the edge of the screen to be forced off the screen if a larger magnification is used.

Pan

Pan is another word that has been adopted from photography and cinematography. A camera can pan across a scene horizontally, vertically, and at an angle. The AutoCAD command **PAN** is used similar to a panning camera to produce a new view of a drawing. It does not change the size of the displayed drawing, only the relative position of the viewing window. The distance the viewing window changes is called the displacement. The displacement is entered as X, Y coordinates or by indicating the displacement distance by picking two points with the cursor control device. Pan is a transparent command so entering **'PAN** will invoke the command while another command is in progress.

Pan: Exercise 3.13

1. Enter **Z** at the command prompt, then **.5** for scale. Selecting **PAN** from the Display Menu, View Pull-down Menu, or tablet menu shows the prompt:

Displacement:

2. Enter the base point by picking a point as shown on screen by the small + in Figure 3.30.

3. A second prompt reads:

Second point:

Enter RETURN to indicate relative displacement if the coordinate values were input or pick the second point, as shown in Figure 3.30. After the second point is entered, the new window is displayed, and the drawing will be panned into its new position, as shown in Figure 3.31.

Redraw, Regen, and Regenauto

REDRAW and **REGEN** are similar commands to refresh an image on screen. The **REDRAW** command more commonly is used to clean up a drawing display that may have markers, blips, and other construction points. The display is refreshed immediately after **REDRAW** is selected from the Display, or Tablet, View Pull-down Menu, or by typing it at the command prompt. It is also a Transparent command.

For complicated drawings, the **REGEN** command redraws the display, but it usually takes longer than using the **REDRAW** command. **REGEN** takes longer because it recalculates the screen coordinates of endpoints of lines and arcs, centers of circles and arcs, and so forth. A few AutoCAD functions sometimes cause an automatic regeneration of the drawing. They include Zoom, Pan, View, Block, Insert, Layer, Style, and Line Type Scale (**LTSCALE**).

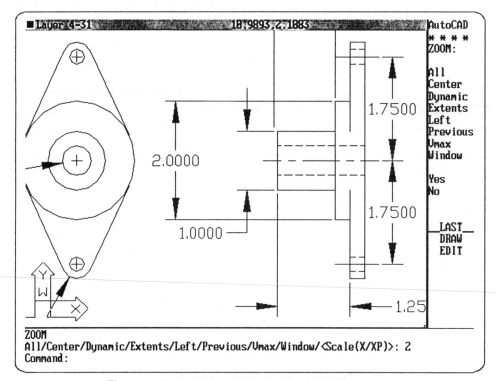

Figure 3.28 The display after a scale factor of 2.

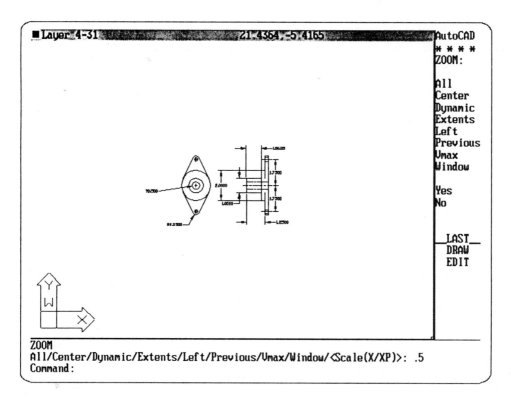

Figure 3.29 The display after a scale factor of .5.

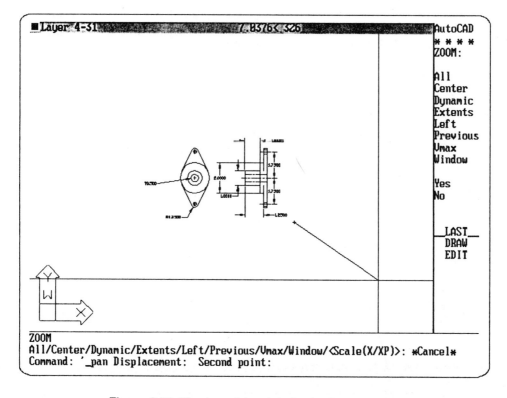

Figure 3.30 The two pick points for the PAN command.

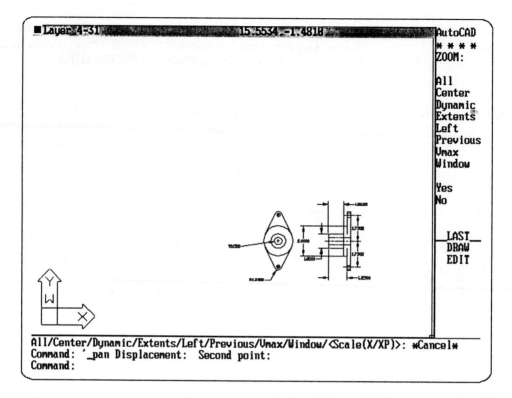

Figure 3.31 Display after using the PAN command.

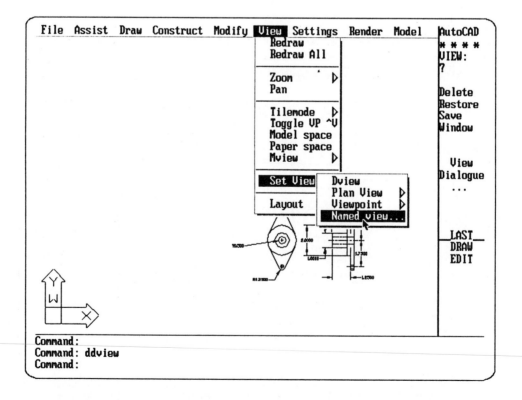

Figure 3.32 Selecting the VIEW command from the View Pull-down Menu.

The **REGENAUTO** command controls the automatic regeneration of some commands. This command is a toggle between On, Off, and Normal. If the toggle is set to off, an automatic regeneration does not occur for Block, Insert, Layer, Style, and **LTSCALE**. Zoom, Pan, and View are not affected by **REGENAUTO**.

View

VIEW is a Transparent command that identifies a unique window with a name so that it is displayed again by entering the assigned name. One possible application of the **VIEW** command is to create a view for each part or view of a working drawing. All views become part of the current drawing file. As a transparent command, entering **'VIEW** will invoke the View Command while another command is in progress.

View: Exercise 3.14

1. This command has a number of submenu options that are listed on the screen or Tablet Menu and in the prompt after **VIEW** is selected. Select the view command by entering **VIEW** at the command prompt, selecting **VIEW** from Display on the menu, or by selecting Named view... from the View Pull-down Menu. Entering **VIEW** at the command prompt displays the following prompt:

?/Delete/Restore/Save/Window:

2. The **SAVE** option is used to create a view. Selecting this option by entering **S** at the prompt displays a second prompt:

View name to save:

Entering a name saves the current display screen. View names are remembered only in the current drawing file.

Selecting Named view... from the View/Set View... Pull-down Menu, as shown in Figure 3.32, displays the Dialogue Box shown in Figure 3.33. Selecting the New Button displays the Define New View Dialogue Box, as shown in Figure 3.34. Entering a name by typing it then selecting the Save View button adds the name to the list. Select the OK button to exit the command.

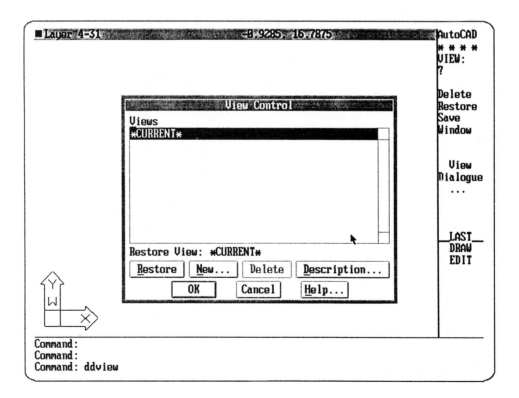

Figure 3.33 The View Control Dialogue Box.

The **RESTORE** option replaces the current display with the view name entered. The **DELETE** option removes a saved view from the drawing file. The **?** option produces a list of the views that have been created with the current drawing. This list shows the names, center points, and magnifications of each view created.

The **WINDOW** option creates a new window at the same time that the view is being created and requires that two points be identified for the new window.

LAYERS, COLORS, AND LINETYPES

For some applications in engineering drawing, different details are placed on several different sheets of paper. For example, details of houses and other buildings and printed circuit boards are drawn usually on different sheets of velum or other media. AutoCAD easily separates entities through the use of the **LAYER** command. Each layer also can be assigned a color, which is very useful when making multicolored plots or to separate or highlight certain entities on the screen.

Layers have the following properties:

Name up to 31 characters long.

Visibility either on (visible) or off (invisible). Only visible layers will be displayed on screen and plotted.

Color the default setting is color number 7.

Linetype the default setting is continuous. Several layers can use the same linetype.

Freeze/Thaw thawed layers are regenerated and frozen layers are not.

Locked/Unlocked entities on locked layers are visible but cannot be edited except for changing some properties and using object snap.

Unlike many other CADD programs, AutoCAD can assign an unlimited number of layers to a drawing. Each layer can have a name of up to 31 characters (with no spaces), can be turned on or off, and can be assigned a single

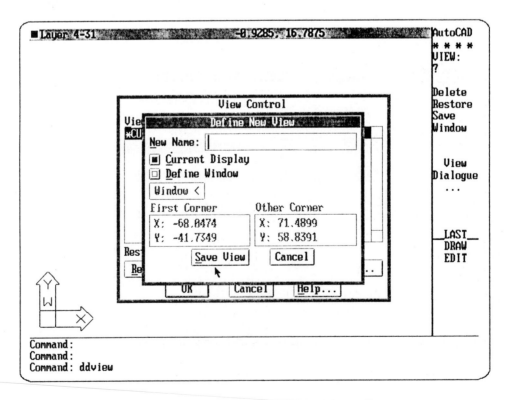

Figure 3.34 The Define New View Dialogue Box.

color or line type. The default layer found on the Prototype drawing is zero. The current layer always is displayed in the upper left corner of the screen. The default state for a layer is on, color is 7 (white), and line type is continuous (visible).

The **LAYER** command is activated by typing **LAYER** at the command prompt or by selecting **LAYER** from the Tablet, Main Menu, or **SETTINGS** Pull-down Menu. The prompt line shows:

?/Make/Set/New/ON/OFF/Color/Ltype/Freeze/Thaw/Lock/Unlock: unless the Pull-down Menu is used. These items also are listed on the screen menu. This prompt lists the layer properties that can be changed. The Layer Command will affect all viewports. For example, if layer name HATCH is turned off, entities on the hatch layer will become invisible in all the viewports. To control layer variables for a specific viewport, enter **VPLAYER** at the command prompt.

Listing Layer Information

The question mark (**?**) is used to list the layer information for the current drawing. Entering **?** at the prompt or selecting it from the screen menu toggles to the text state and lists the relevant layer information, as shown in Figure 3.35. The default layer settings are listed on the first line, **Layer Name 0**. For this example, other layers have been created. Some layers have a series of numbers for names, and one is called **DEFPOINTS**. (DEFPOINTS is created automatically when using associative dimensioning.) All of the layers are on except DEFPOINTS. Various colors and line types are assigned to different layers. The current layer is listed at the bottom. To return to the drawing screen, press the **F1** key or enter **GRAPHSCR** at the command prompt.

```
   Layer name      State      Color      Linetype
--------------------  ---------  -------------  ------------
0                     Off        7 (white)     CONTINUOUS
4-31                  On         7 (white)     CONTINUOUS
4-32                  Off        7 (white)     CONTINUOUS
4-33                  Off        7 (white)     CONTINUOUS
4-34                  Off        7 (white)     CONTINUOUS

4-35                  Off        7 (white)     CONTINUOUS
4-36                  Off        7 (white)     CONTINUOUS
4-37                  Off        7 (white)     CONTINUOUS
4-38                  Off        7 (white)     CONTINUOUS
4-39                  Off        7 (white)     CONTINUOUS

CENTERING             Off        7 (white)     CONTINUOUS
DEFPOINTS             On         7 (white)     CONTINUOUS
DIMPTS                Off        7 (white)     CONTINUOUS
LALALA                Off        7 (white)     CONTINUOUS
SCR                   Off        7 (white)     CONTINUOUS

Current layer: 4-31

?/Make/Set/New/ON/OFF/Color/Ltype/Freeze/Thaw/LOck/Unlock:
```

Figure 3.35 Layer information displayed on the text screen.

Making a Layer

The **MAKE** subcommand creates a new layer and automatically sets it as current.

Making A Layer: Exercise 3.15

1. Start a new drawing by selecting New from the File Pull-down Menu. Select the OK button from the Create New Drawing Pop-up Window. Enter **LAYER** at the command prompt. Enter **M to** select the Make option. The following prompt is displayed:

New current layer <0>:

The current layer is displayed in the prompt line within the brackets. To make a new layer type the name, such as **DIMENSIONS** then press **RETURN** twice to create a new layer, which is ON and is assigned the CONTINUOUS linetype and color 7. Figure 3.37. Notice that the new layer name is displayed in the upper left corner of the screen as DIMENSIO. The last letter is dropped because 8 letters are the maximum number that can be displayed. To view the list of layers enter **?** at the layer prompt or select Layer Control from the Settings Pull-down Menu.

Setting a New Current Layer

The **SET** subcommand changes to a new current layer very similar to the **MAKE** command, except **SET** cannot make a new layer. The **SET** command only changes to a new layer if that layer already has been created. Selecting this command from the layer prompt displays:

New current layer <0>:

The current layer is shown in the brackets. The new current layer must be entered at the prompt, followed by RETURN.

New Layers

The **NEW** subcommand creates a new layer without affecting the current layer. This command is used in the same manner as **MAKE**, except **NEW** does not make the new layer current. Selecting **NEW** displays the prompt:

New layer name(s):

The new layer name is entered at the prompt. More than one new layer is created with this command by entering each layer name separated by a comma, such as **dimension,text,border**. Entering RETURN then creates the new layers with a line type of CONTINUOUS and color 7.

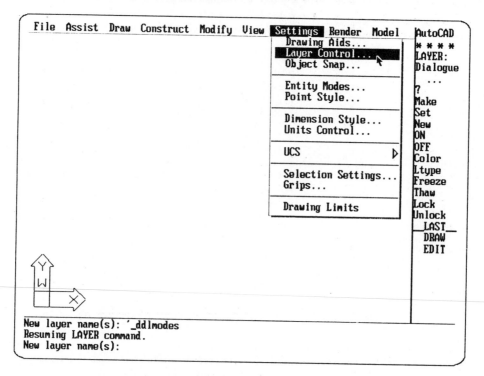

Figure 3.36 The Settings Pull-down Menu.

Creating A New Layer Using The Pull-Down Menu: Exercise 3.16

1. Select Layer Control... from the Settings Pull-down Menu. Figure 3.36.
2. The Layer Control Dialogue Box is displayed, as shown in Figure 3.37. Enter **text,border** at the flashing vertical line near the center-bottom of the dialogue box. Figure 3.37.
3. After typing the names of the new layers separated by commas, pick the New button. This will automatically display the new layer names in the list. Figure 3.38

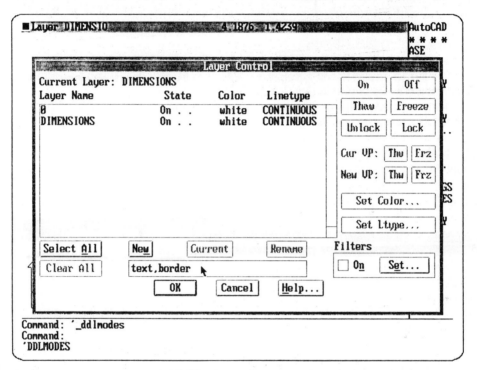

Figure 3.37 The Layer Control Dialogue Box.

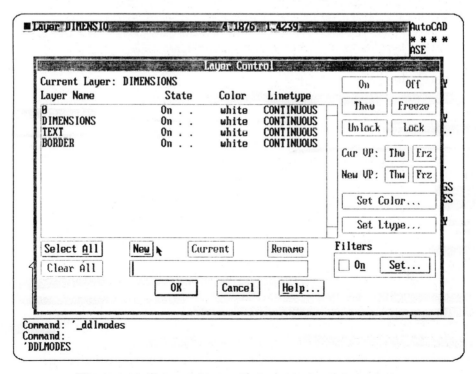

Figure 3.38 The new layers displayed in the dialogue box.

Turning Layers On

Layers that are off (not displayed) are turned on using the **ON** subcommand. Entities contained within on layers are displayed on the screen. When **ON** is selected from the screen or tablet menu or entered at the layer prompt, the following is displayed:

Layer name(s) to turn On:

A single layer is turned on by entering the name of the layer at the prompt. More than one layer is turned on by entering the layer names separated by commas. Figure 3.39 shows a drawing that has one of its layers turned off. The layer name is **Dimension** and contains the dimensions for this drawing. Entering the layer name **Dimension** at the ON prompt turns on the layer after RETURN is pressed twice.

Turning Layers On: Exercise 3.17

1. Open the file named **Layer** by selecting Open from the File Pull-down Menu. This will display the drawing shown in Figure 3.39.
2. Pull down the Settings Menu and select Layer Control...
3. The Dimensions layer is turned on by pointing at the word DIMENSIONS and picking it. This highlights the line, as shown in Figure 3.40.
4. Pick the On Button located near the upper-right of the dialogue box, then pick the OK button to display the dimensions shown in Figure 3.41.

Turning Layers Off

Occasionally, turning a layer off may be necessary to decrease redraw time, make the drawing less cluttered to facilitate adding more entities or to separate entities for plotting. The **OFF** subcommand temporarily turns off layers, which results in the entities on those layers being turned off. Layers that are off will not plot. The entities are still in the drawing data base, but they cannot be seen. Think of the **ON** and **OFF** commands like the on-off switch for a light. Choosing the **OFF** subcommand displays the prompt:

Layer name(s) to turn Off:

A single layer is turned off by entering the name of the layer at the prompt. More than one layer is turned off by entering the layer names separated by commas.

Turning Layers Off: Exercise 3.18

1. Pull down the Settings Menu and select Layer Control...
2. The Dimensions layer is turned off by pointing at the word DIMENSIONS and picking it. This highlights the line, as shown in Figure 3.40.
3. Pick the Off Button located near the upper-right of the dialogue box, then pick the OK button to turn the dimensions layer off, as shown in Figure 3.39.

Controlling Colors

Different colors are assigned to layers by using the **COLOR** subcommand. The number of colors that can be used depends on the computer hardware. AutoCAD can assign colors from 1 to 256. Each entity and each layer will have a color assigned to it. The default color is number 7 (white). The current color is shown in a small square located at the upper left corner of the screen. Different layers and entities can have the same assigned color. AutoCAD has designated the following colors to the first 7 numbers:

1- RED
2- YELLOW
3- GREEN
4- CYAN
5- BLUE
6- MAGENTA
7- WHITE

Controlling the color of entities is very useful when creating complicated drawings. However, even on a monochrome display, separating entities by color is useful for plotting. Each color can be assigned a different pen that allows the creation of multicolored plots and various line widths. Single pen plotters also create multicolor plots. AutoCAD will stop plotting and prompt the user to change pens before another color is plotted. The color number assigned to a specific layer can be changed with the **COLOR** subcommand.

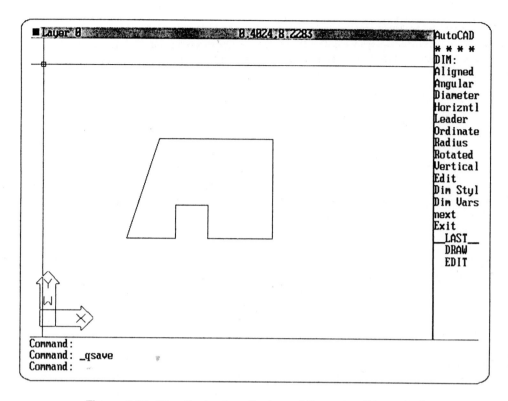

Figure 3.39 The display has the layer "dimensions" turned off.

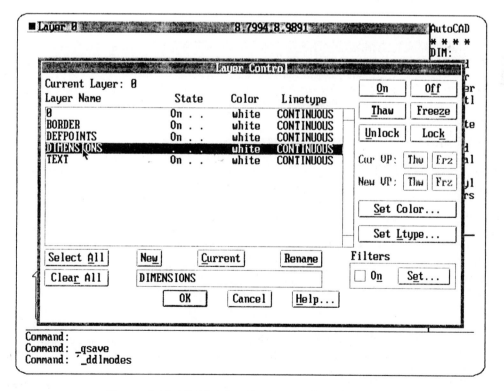

Figure 3.40 Highlighting the layer to be turned off.

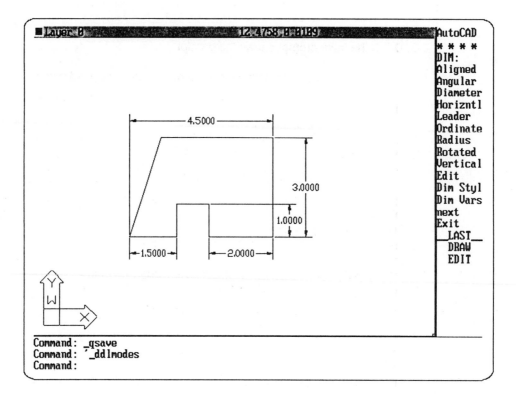

Figure 3.41 The dimension layer turned on.

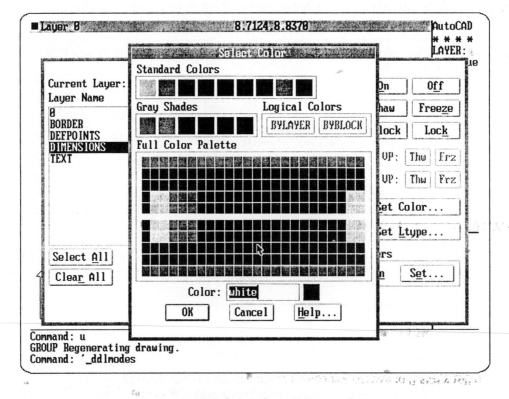

Figure 3.42 The Select Color Dialogue Box.

Assigning Colors To A Layer: Exercise 13.19

1. Entering **COLOR** at the layer prompt shows the prompt:

Color:

2. Respond to the prompt by entering the color number or one of the 7 assigned names, such as **RED**.

3. A second prompt reads:

Layer name(s) for color 1 (red) <0>:

Respond to the prompt by entering the layer name(s) to assign the color red or RETURN to assign it to the current layer 0. Assigning the layer name turns on the layer. Entering a negative sign before the color name/number assigns the color to the layer but turns it off. After entering the new layer press RETURN again. This will cause all entities on layer 0 and the small square at the upper-left corner of the screen to change colors to red.

Dialogue Box Method

1. Select Layer Control... from the Settings Pull-down Menu.

2. Pick the layer that is to be changed. For this example, highlight DIMENSIONS then pick the On Button.

3. Pick the Set Color... button located at the right side of the dialogue box.

4. The Select Color Dialogue Box is displayed as shown in Figure 3.42. The current color is displayed in the bottom of the dialogue box. The available standard colors, gray shades, and full color palette are displayed. Point at the desired color and pick it. The new color choice is displayed near the bottom of the dialogue box along with its number.

5. Pick the OK Button, which displays the Layer Control Dialogue Box with the new color number assigned to the layer.

6. Pick the OK Button to display the drawing with the dimensions shown in the new color.

Freezing and Thawing Layers

FREEZE and **THAW** are commands that are very similar to **ON** and **OFF**. **FREEZE** turns off entities on specified layers just as **OFF** is used. However, **FREEZE** also causes AutoCAD to ignore frozen entities when using **ZOOM, PAN, VPOINT, REGEN,** and entity selection. **FREEZE** decreases regen time when using these commands. **FREEZE** is a **LAYER** subcommand that displays the prompt:

Layer name(s) to Freeze:

Enter the name(s) to freeze and press RETURN. Entities on those layers selected turn off and are frozen.

THAW turns frozen entities on. A **REGEN** must be executed to display entities that have been thawed. After selecting **THAW**, a prompt is displayed:

Layer name(s) to Thaw:

Enter the name(s) of the frozen layers to be thawed and press RETURN. To display the entities again, **REGEN** must be executed. **FREEZE** can also be executed from the Layer Control... Dialog Box by picking the Freeze Button.

CHANGING LINETYPES

One of the first graphical standards introduced in engineering graphics is the alphabet of lines. A typical drawing contains a number of different linetypes. AutoCAD provides the user with many standard linetypes. Some are shown in Figure 3.43, but other linetypes can be added to the library of AutoCAD lines. To display the standard AutoCAD linetypes, enter **LINETYPE** at the command prompt, then enter **?** to display the Select Linetype File Dialogue Box. Figure 3.44. Pick the OK Button to select the default file **ACAD** to display the linetype on screen. Each entity and layer has an associated linetype and name. A linetype can be assigned to more than one layer. The default linetype is Continuous. Only lines, arcs, circles, polygons, ellipses, and polylines are affected by the linetype.

Changing Linetypes: Exercise 3.20

1. Enter **LINETYPE** at the command prompt or pick it from the Settings Menu. A prompt reads:

?/Create/Load/ Set:

To get a listing of available linetypes enter **?** at the Linetype Prompt, pick the file ACAD from the Select Linetype File Dialogue Box, then pick the OK Button. (Figure 3.45). Press the **F1** key to return to the drawing screen.

```
Linetypes defined in file C:\ACAD12\SUPPORT\ACAD.lin:

        Name            Description
------------------    -------------------
BORDER                __ __ . __ __ . __ __ . __ __ . __ __ . __ __ . __ __ .
BORDER2               _._._._._._._._._._._._._._._._._._._._._._.
BORDERX2              ___.___.    .    .    .    .    .    ___.    .    ___
CENTER                ____ ____ ____ ____ ____ ____ ____ ____ __ __ ____
CENTER2               ___ _ ___ _ ___ _ ___ _ ___ _ ___ _ ___ _ ___

CENTERX2              _____ __ _____ __ _____ __ _____ __ _____
DASHDOT               _._ _._ _._ _._ _._ _._ _._ _._ _._ _._
DASHDOT2              _._._._._._._._._._._._._._._._._._._._._._._._
DASHDOTX2             ___.    .    ___    .    ___    .    ___    .
DASHED                __ __ __ __ __ __ __ __ __ __ __ __ __ __ __ __

DASHED2               _ _ _ _ _ _ _ _ _ _ _ _ _ _ _ _ _ _ _ _ _ _
DASHEDX2              ___ ___ ___ ___ ___ ___ ___ ___ ___ ___
DIVIDE               __ . . __ . . __ . . __ . . __ . . __ . .
DIVIDE2              _.._.._.._.._.._.._.._.._.._.._.._.._.._.._.
DIVIDEX2             _____ . . _____ . . _____ . . _____
-- Press RETURN for more --


DOT                  . . . . . . . . . . . . . . . . . . . . . . .
DOT2                 .........................................
DOTX2               .   .   .   .   .   .   .   .   .   .   .   .
HIDDEN               __ __ __ __ __ __ __ __ __ __ __ __ __ __ __ __
HIDDEN2              _ _ _ _ _ _ _ _ _ _ _ _ _ _ _ _ _ _ _ _ _ _

HIDDENX2             ___ ___ ___ ___ ___ ___ ___ ___ ___ ___
PHANTOM              _____ __ __ _____ __ __ _____ __ __ _____
PHANTOM2             ___ _ _ ___ _ _ ___ _ _ ___ _ _ ___ _ _ ___ _ _
PHANTOMX2            _____ ____ ____ _____ ____ ____

?/Create/Load/Set:
```

Figure 3.43 Listing of linetypes available on AutoCAD.

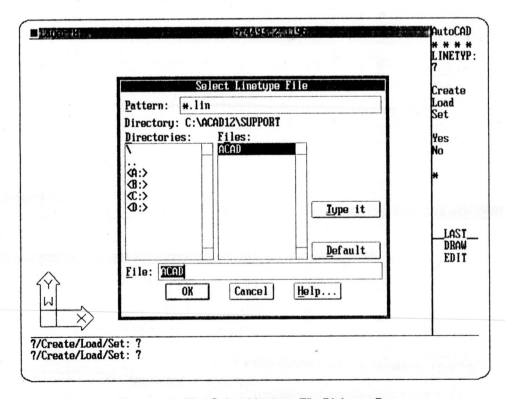

Figure 3.44 The Select Linetype File Dialogue Box.

```
Linetypes defined in file C:\ACAD12\SUPPORT\ACAD.lin:

    Name            Description
----------------    --------------------
BORDER              __ __ .  __ __ .  __ __ .  __ __ .  __ __ .
BORDER2             _._._._._._._._._._._._._._._._._._
BORDERX2            ____  ____  .  ____  ____  .  ____  ____  .  __
CENTER              ____ _ ____ _ ____ _ ____ _ ____ _ __
CENTER2             __ _ __ _ __ _ __ _ __ _ __ _ __

CENTERX2            _____  __ _____  __ _____  __ __
DASHDOT             __ . __ . __ . __ . __ . __ . __ .
DASHDOT2            _._._._._._._._._._._._._._._._._
DASHDOTX2           ____  .  ____  .  ____  .  ____  .  ____ _._
DASHED              __ __ __ __ __ __ __ __ __ __ __

DASHED2             _ _ _ _ _ _ _ _ _ _ _ _ _ _ _ _ _ _
DASHEDX2            ____  ____  ____  ____  ____  ____  __
DIVIDE              ____ . . ____ . . ____ . . ____ . . __
DIVIDE2             _._.._._.._._.._._.._._.._._.._._.
DIVIDEX2            _____ . . _____ . . _____ . .
-- Press RETURN for more --
```

Figure 3.45 AutoCAD linetypes displayed on screen.

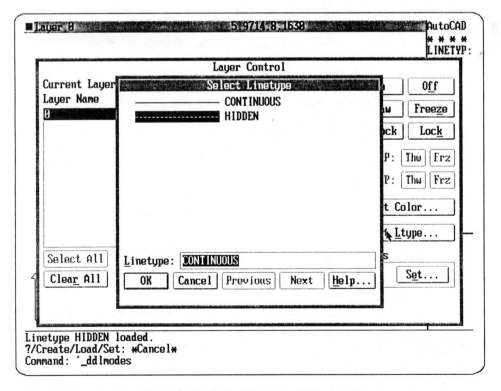

Figure 3.46 Select Linetype Dialogue Box.

2. Enter **S** to load a linetype set. Another prompt reads:
New entity linetype (or ?) <BYLAYER>:
3. Enter **HIDDEN** to set the current linetype to hidden. Press **RETURN** to get back to the command prompt. Entities added to the drawing will be shown as hidden lines until the linetype is changed again using the Set option.
4. Enter **L** at the Command Prompt, then start drawing lines. Notice that the lines are now drawn as hidden lines on screen.

To change the linetype assigned to a layer, the steps are different than used to set a current linetype.
1. Enter **LINETYPE** at the command prompt. A prompt reads:
?/Crea te/Load/ Set:
2. Enter **L** to select the Load option. A prompt is displayed:
Linetype(s) to load:
3. Enter **HIDDEN** at the prompt to load the hidden linetype or enter * to load all of the linet ypes.
4. Select Layer Control... from the Settings Pull-down Menu. Highlight the layer to assign a new linetype by picking it from the list shown on the Layer Control Dialogue Box.
5. Pick the Set Linetype... Button to display the Select Linetype Box shown in Figure 3.46.
6. Pick the hidden linetype from the displayed list or type it in, then select the OK Button. The Layer Control Box will be displayed with the hidden linestyle listed for the selected layer.
7. Enter **L** at the command prompt and draw a few lines to see that hidden lines are now assigned to the current layer.

Changing the Linetype Scale

The linetype scale is set according to the plot scale so that the plotted lines are close to ANSI standards. Use the **SETTINGS** command or enter **LTSCALE** at the command prompt to change the linetype scale. The linetype scale is set to 1/2 the reciprocal of the plot scale for ANSI standard lines. For example, if the plot scale is set at 1/8 size, then the **LTSCALE** is set to four.

AutoCAD draws lines so that they appear good at a scale of one. **LTSCALE** shrinks or stretches the line patterns used to create different linetypes. To create a new line scale, choose **LTSCALE** from the second page of the **SETTINGS** menu located on the Root Screen Menu. A prompt reads:

New scale factor <1.0000>:

To change the scale factor, simply enter a number other than one. Larger numbers stretch the lines, and smaller numbers shrink the lines, as shown in Figure 3.47.

Figure 3.47 Linetype scales of .5, 2, and 1 were used to create these line scales.

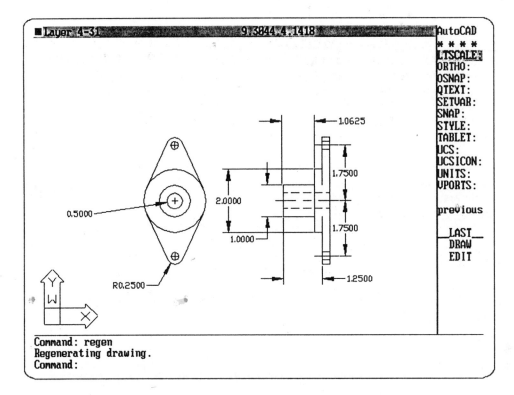

Figure 3.48 Linetype scale after using the LTSCALE command.

Changing Linetype Scale: Exercise 3.21

1. Open Exercise drawing file ZOOM by entering **OPEN** at the command prompt or by selecting Open from the File Pull-down Menu. Change to the directory where the Exercise drawing is located, then double click on the file name ZOOM.

2. Enter **Z** at the command prompt, then **E** for extents.

3. Enter **LTSCALE** at the command prompt or select it from the second page of the Settings Menu.

4. A prompt reads:

New scale factor <0.500>:

Enter a new value of 1. A prompt reads:

Regen queued:

Then you are returned to the command prompt.

5. Enter **REGEN** to display the new linetype scale. Figure 3.48. Notice the change in the lengths of the hidden lines segments.

AUTOMATIC CENTER LINES

Center lines are created with AutoCAD by using the LINETYPE-SET command as explained earlier. AutoCAD provides two center lines as shown in Figure 3.49. Center lines are added to a circle using the **CENTER** command. **CENTER** is a dimension utility explained in detail in Chapter 8. The **CENTER** command draws a center mark or center lines for circles and arcs. The **DIMCEN** dimensioning variable determines whether a center mark or center line is drawn (Figure 3.41). The default setting is .09, which will result in center marks. To create center lines for circles, enter **DIMCEN** at the command prompt, then change the setting to a negative value by entering **-.09** and **RETURN.** Select Center Mark from the Draw Pull-down Menu, as shown in Figure 3.50. A prompts reads:

Select arc or circle

Pick the arc or circle to automatically add center lines or marks to the drawing.

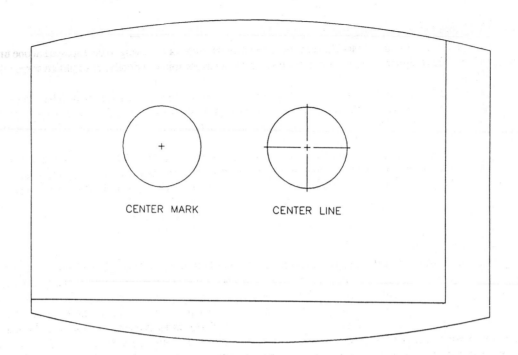

Figure 3.49 Center lines and marks.

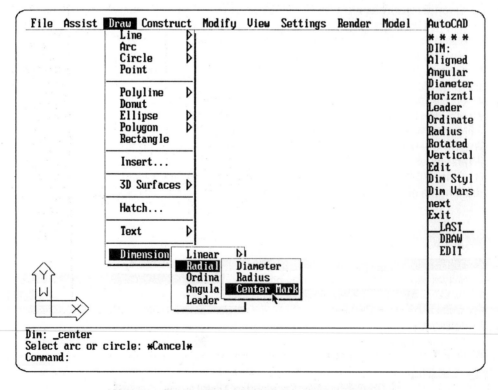

Figure 3.50 Selecting the Center Mark option.

VIEWPORTS

Viewports were added to AutoCAD to allow more than one view of a drawing to be displayed at one time. This feature allows the designer to view the object close up, far away, or misometrically, or to utilize some other user-specified view.

The rectangular portion of the drawing area on the AutoCAD screen is called a viewport. The viewing area can be divided into multiple viewports by selecting the View Option shown in Figure 3.51, which displays the Tiled Viewport Layout Menu. Figure 3.52. Each viewport can have the same or different views of the drawing in 3D, zoom, or pan portions of the drawing.

The idea of using viewports on a CADD system for engineering design is exciting because it enhances the user interface and allows the designer to concentrate on various parts of a drawing without losing the visual continuity of the whole drawing. Multiple viewports should make for a more efficient use of the display options.

Using Viewports

Each viewport will display the drawing according to the view defined by the user. The Coordinate System Icon is displayed in each viewport, as shown in Figure 3.53. Only one viewport is active or current at any given time and is identified with a heavy border line (lower-right viewport in Figure 3.53). The cursor can be moved between each viewport, but the crosshair cursor is only visible in the current viewport. The cursor will appear as a small arrow pointing to the upper left corner of the screen (Figure 3.54). Adding entities, changing the displayed image, and editing the drawing can only take place in the active viewport. However, changes to the drawing in the active viewport will also occur in the other viewports. The active viewport is changed by moving the cursor into the desired viewport and using the pick button on the input device. The cursor will change to the cross-hairs, and the viewport border will change to a thick line.

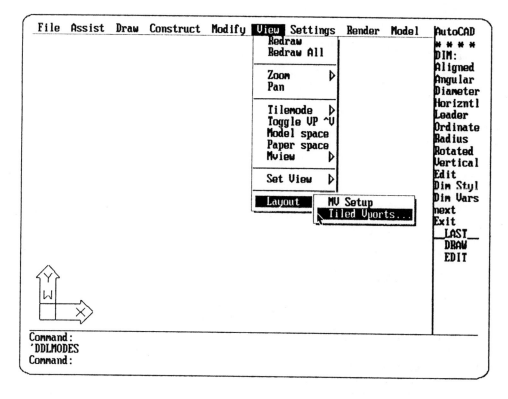

Figure 3.51 The View option Tiled Vports... selected.

Viewports are changed at mid-command by moving the cursor to the new viewport and picking it with the input device. For example, a line could be added to the drawing by picking the first point in the current viewport, then changing the current viewpoint and picking the second point in the new current viewport. Commands **SNAP, ZOOM, VPOINT, GRID, PAN, VIEWPORTS,** and **DVIEW** restrict cursor picking to the current viewport.

Viewports are changed by selecting **Layout**, then **Tiled Vports...** (Figure 3.51) from the **View** Pull-down Menu. Clicking on either one of the tiled layouts or one of the viewport options in the list will highlight the selection. Figure 3.54. Viewports are most useful when creating and editing 3D models.

Viewports: Exercise 3.22

1. Open the drawing file called **VIEWPORT.**
2. Select **Layout/Tiled Vports...** from the View Pull-down Menu.
3. Pick the four equal viewports from the icon menu and pick the OK Button.
4. Move the cursor into the upper-left viewport and set it to current by picking it. The double box will show that it is selected. This viewport will become the top view.
5. Enter **PLAN** at the command prompt or select Plan View from the Set View option on the View Pull-down Menu.
6. Use the current UCS as the method to create the plan view by picking it from the menu or entering **RETURN.** The top view of the 3D model will be displayed as shown in Figure 3.56.
7. Use the Zoom-Extents then Zoom-Scale options to center the view in the viewport by entering **Z** at the command prompt.
8. Enter **E** for extents, then **RETURN**, then RETURN again to repeat the Zoom Command then enter **1** as the scale to display the view shown in Figure 3.57.
9. Highlight the lower-left viewport by picking it with the cursor. This viewport will become the front view.
10. Select Set View..., then Viewpoint, then Presets from the View Pull-down Menu to display Figure 3.58.
11. Pick 270 degrees by moving the cursor into the area of the square with 270 degrees listed. Then pick 0 degrees by moving the cursor into the area of the semi-circle labeled 0 degrees. A new view is automatically displayed in the lower-left viewport after picking the OK Button.
12. Use the Zoom-Extents then Zoom-Scale options to center the view in the viewport by entering **Z** at the command prompt.
13. Enter **E** for extents, then **RETURN** to repeat the Zoom Command then enter **1** as the scale to display the view shown in Figure 3.59.
14. Highlight the lower-right viewport by picking it with the cursor. This viewport will become the right side view.
15. Select Set View..., then Viewpoint, then Presets from the View Pull-down Menu to display Figure 3.58.
16. Pick 0 degrees by moving the cursor into the area of the square with 0 degrees listed. Then pick 0 degrees by moving the cursor into the area of the semi-circle labeled 0 degrees. A new view is automatically displayed in the lower-right viewport after picking the OK Button.
17. Use the Zoom-Extents then Zoom-Scale options to center the view in the viewport by entering **Z** at the command prompt.
18. Enter **E** for extents then **RETURN** to repeat the Zoom Command, then enter **1** as the scale to display the view shown in Figure 3.60.

An alternate method of creating the front, top, and right side views is to use the **Vpoint** option to enter a viewing direction. Use the following X, Y, and Z coordinates for each view:

TOP: 0,0,1
FRONT: 0,-1,0
RIGHT SIDE: 1,0,0

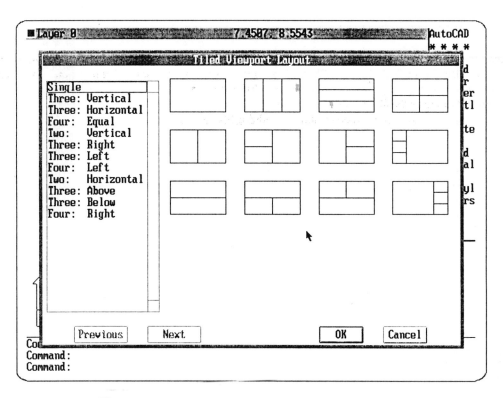

Figure 3.52 The Tiled Viewport Layout Dialogue Box.

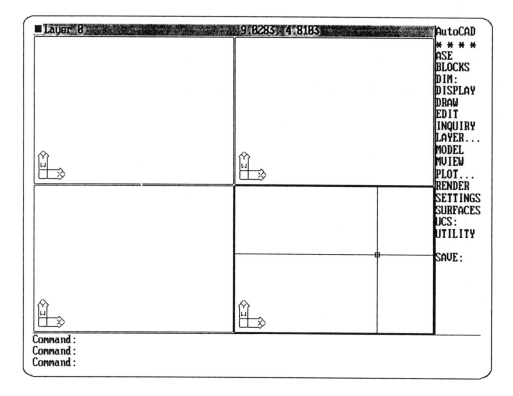

Figure 3.53 Four viewport screen.

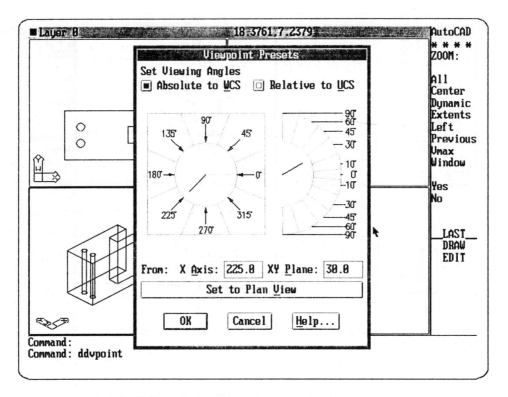

Figure 3.58 The Viewpoint Presets Dialogue Box.

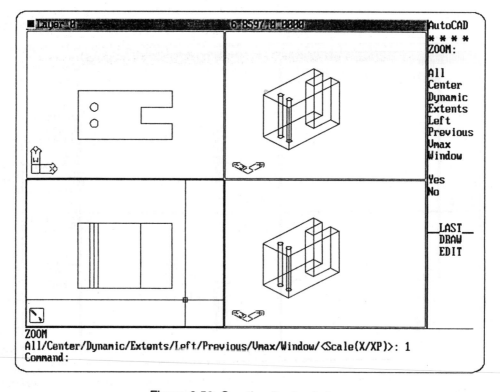

Figure 3.59 Creating the front view.

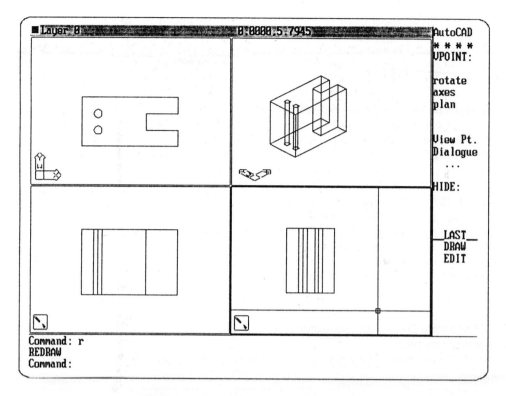

Figure 3.60 Creating the right side view.

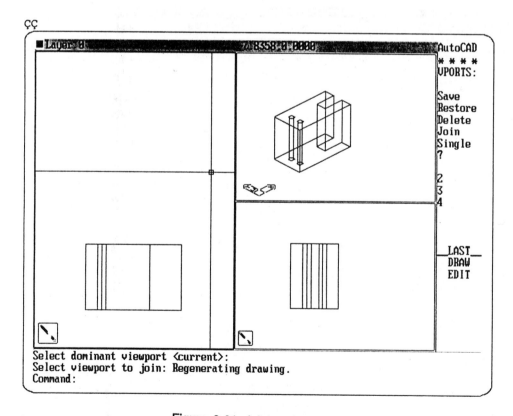

Figure 3.61 Joining viewports.

SAVING VIEWPORTS

It is possible to save viewport configurations so they can be restored later. Saved viewports can be deleted from memory and viewports can be joined. To save a viewport, enter VPORTS at the command prompt, then SAVE. A prompt reads:

?/Name For New Viewport Configuration:
Enter the name of the viewport and press RETURN.
To retrieve a previously saved viewport, select **RESTORE** from the **VPORTS** prompt. A prompt reads:
? Name of viewport configuration to restore:
Enter the name of the saved viewport and press RETURN. The saved viewport replaces the current viewports on screen.

JOINING VIEWPORTS
Viewports are joined by selecting **JOIN** from the **VPORTS** menu. A prompt reads:
Select dominant viewport:
Pick the front viewport with the cursor. Another prompt reads:
Select viewport to join:
Pick the top viewport to be joined with the cursor. Figure 3.61.

PAPER SPACE

The default AutoCAD setting is for Model Space. Most drafting and design is done in Model Space using full scale real world coordinates. However, AutoCAD provides another drawing environment called Paper Space. Paper Space is used to layout, annotate, and plot two or more views of drawings created in Model Space. Paper Space is a document composition system similar to the page composition system used in desktop publishing. Paper Space can be used to draw any entity in 2D and is especially useful for dimensioning, labeling, and drawing borders. Text does not have to be scaled for plotting as it does in Model Space. For example, to get .125" text when plotted using paper space, use .125" text.

The TILEMODE command is used to toggle between Model and Paper Space. The default tilemode setting is 1, which is model space. To change to Paper Space enter TILEMODE at the command prompt and enter 0 or pick it from the View/Tilemode Pull-dwon Menu. The UCS icon changes to a triangular shaped paper space icon. Figure 3.62. The following steps describe how to create a paper space drawing:

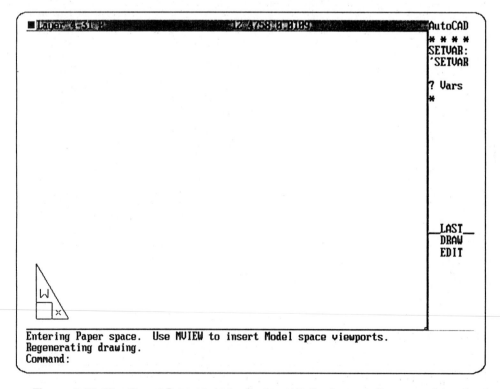

Figure 3.62 The Paper Space icon is displayed in the lower-left corner of the display.

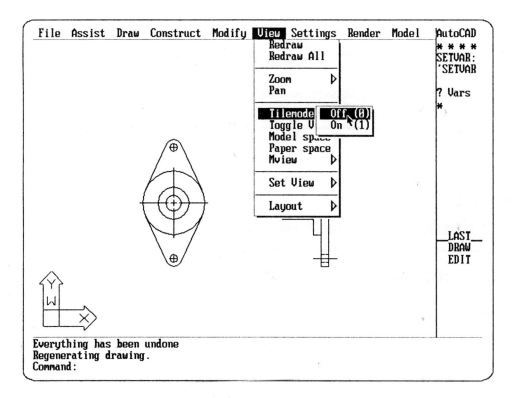

Figure 3.63 Turning the Tilemode to off.

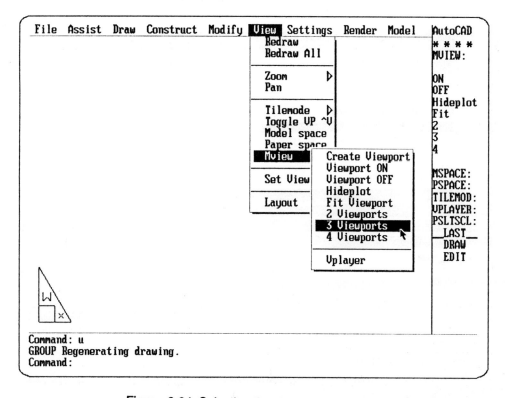

Figure 3.64 Selecting the view to be displayed.

Paper Space: Exercise 3.23

1. Open the drawing file called **VIEWPORT** from your work disk.

2. At the command prompt, enter **TILEMODE** then **0** or select Tilemode from the View Pull-down Menu then select off (0). Figure 3.63.

3. The drawing is not displayed and the UCS icon changes to the paper space icon.

4. The **MVIEW** command is used to control viewports in Paper Space. Viewports can be of varied size and number or a single viewport can be made to fit the current view. Select **MVIEW** from the View Pull-down Menu, then select 3 Viewports. Figure 3.64.

5. After selection a prompt is displayed:

Horizont al/Vertic al/Above /Bel ow/Left/<Right >:

Press RETURN to pick the Right option.

6. Another prompt is displayed:

Fit/<First Point>:

Enter Fit to automatically fit three views of the model on screen. This drawing cannot be edited but text and geometry can be added to it. A title block could be added to the drawing then plotted.

7. Enter model space by entering **MSPACE** at the command prompt.

8. Pick the lower-left viewport with the mouse to make it current. Change the viewpoint to a front view by entering **VPOINT** at the command prompt.

9. Enter **0,-1,0** to create a front view. Enter **Z** at the command prompt, then 1 to scale the front view in the viewport. Figure 3.65.

10. Pick the upper-left viewport with the mouse to make it current. Change the viewpoint to a top view by entering **VPOINT** at the command prompt.

11. Enter **0,0,1** to create a front view. Enter **Z** at the command prompt, then 1 to scale the top view in the viewport. Figure 3.66. Use the **PAN** option to center the isometric view into the right viewport.

12. To plot this layout, enter paper space by entering **PSPACE** at the command prompt.

13. Select **PLOT** from the File Pull-down Menu. Use the Display option to create a plot like that shown in Figure 3.67.

The Drag Mode

AutoCAD permits the dynamic dragging of some images, such as blocks. For example, the Edit command **MOVE** dynamically displays the entities being moved if the cursor is used to locate the new base position. The default setting for **DRAGMODE** is automatic. Drag also can be set to **ON** and **OFF**. Enter **DRAGMODE** at the command prompt to change the drag setting:

On/Off/Auto <Auto>:

Enter the new setting and RETURN.

When drag is set to **ON**, **DRAG** must be entered before picking the point to be dragged. Figure 3.68 represents an object being moved with the cursor with the **DRAGMODE** set to automatic.

ENTITY GRIPS

Entity grips are a method of editing existing AutoCAD geometry. It is possible to stretch, move, copy, rotate, scale, and mirror geometry using entity grips without entering an AutoCAD command. Grips can be used to automatically snap to geometric features, such as endpoints, midpoints, quadrants and centers. A temporary rectangular and radial snap grid is also available. Entity grips are enabled by entering **GRIPS** at the command prompt and entering 1.

Entity grips are invoked by selecting geometry at the command prompt. This will cause boxes to appear on geometric features such as the endpoints of a line and the midpoint. Figure 3.69. These boxes represent the entity grips. You will notice that as the cursor is moved on screen it will snap to the entity grips. This feature can be used in place of the OSNAP options when adding new geometry. Entering **E** will erase any entity after grip selection.

Picking one of the boxes fills it and makes it *hot*. Figure 3.70. You will also notice that a prompt appears:

STRETCH

<Stretch to point>/Base point/Copy/Undo/eXit:

You can cycle through the options by pressing the RETURN key or by entering the option from the screen menu. The default setting is stretch. Picking a new point on the drawing will cause the object to stretch from the highlighted

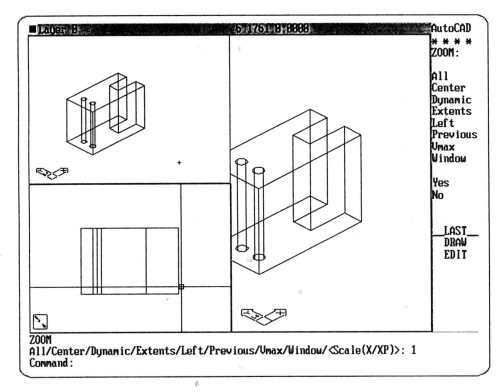

Figure 3.65 Creating a front view.

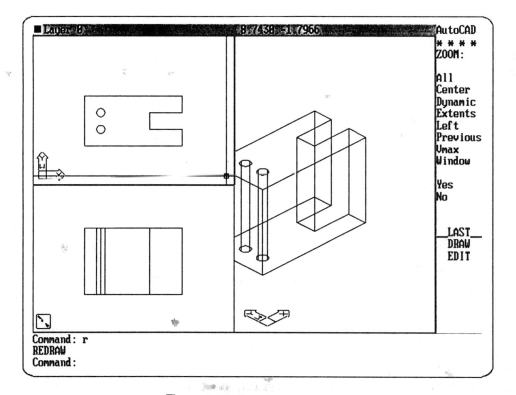

Figure 3.66 Creating a top view.

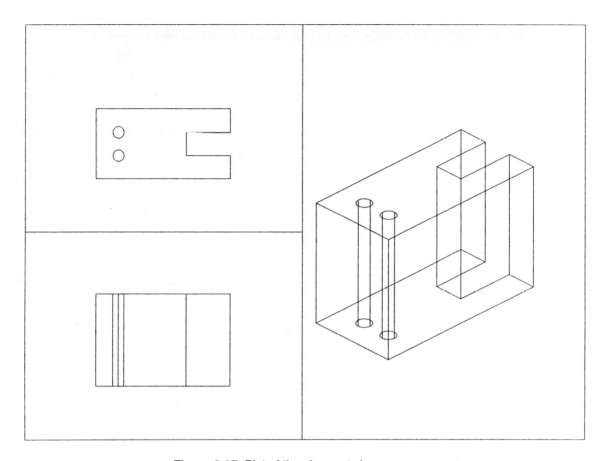

Figure 3.67 Plot of the viewports in paper space.

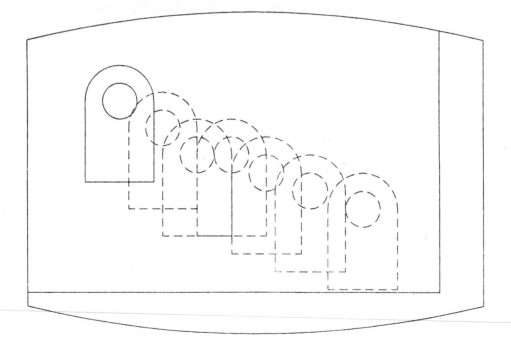

Figure 3.68 When the DRAG mode is on, the object moves with cursor movement for commands such as INSERT and COPY.

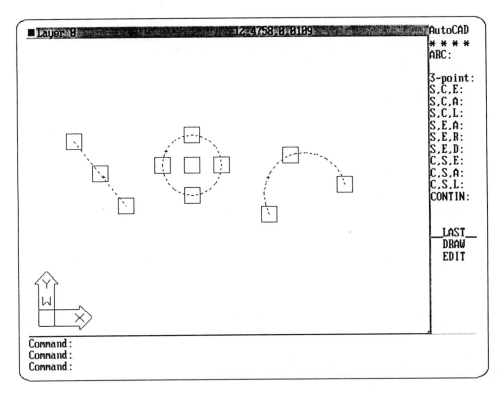

Figure 3.69 Entity grips for lines, arcs, and circles.

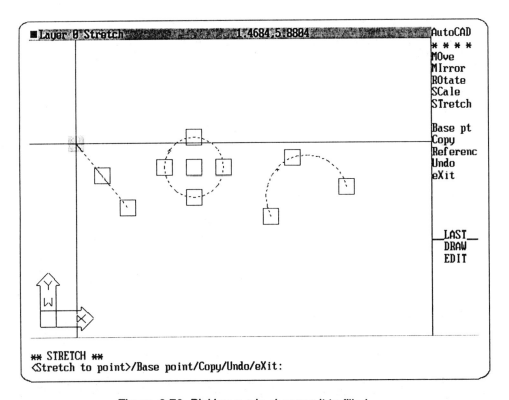

Figure 3.70 Picking a grip changes it to filled.

entity grip to the location of the picked point. Figure 3.71.

A temporary auxiliary grid is created if the copy option is used with any of the grip options after the first copy is placed. This auxiliary grid is activated by holding down the SHIFT key. The snap grid is rectangular except when using the rotate option. The multiple aligned copies of the line shown in Figure 3.72 is an example of the copy option using the shift key.

Enter X to exit the grip command. A hot entity grip is turned to warm by clicking on it again. Entering Ctrl-C twice will deselect the entities and remove the entity grips.

SELECTING ENTITIES

While at the command prompt AutoCAD is ready to select entities by simply picking a point then dragging a window around the entities then picking another point. Dragging left results in a Crossing selection and dragging to the right results in a window selection. Whenever commands such as copy, array, mirror, move, scale, stretch, erase, are used the first prompt is: **Select objects**. Objects are selected in different ways. Entering a **?** at the Select Objects prompt will display a prompt:

Expects a point or Window/Last/Crossing/BOX/ALL
/Fence/WPolygon/CPolygon/Add/Remove/Multiple
/Previous/Undo/AUto/SIngle
Select objects:

Any of these methods can be used to select objects.

Entering **FILTER** at the command prompt will display a dialogue box to create selection sets. Figure 3.73. For example, picking text and dimensions can be done with the Filter command. The selection filters are picked from a list which is activated by selecting the box below Select Filter in the dialogue box. Highlight the selection then pick the Add to List button. Pick the Apply button to invoke your selection set. The all option could be used which would only select those items in your filter selection set and would ignore all other entities.

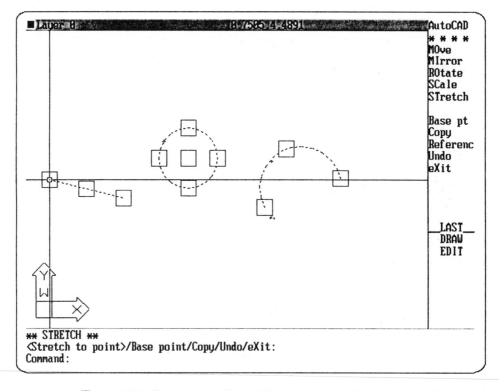

Figure 3.71 Changed position of the line after picking a point.

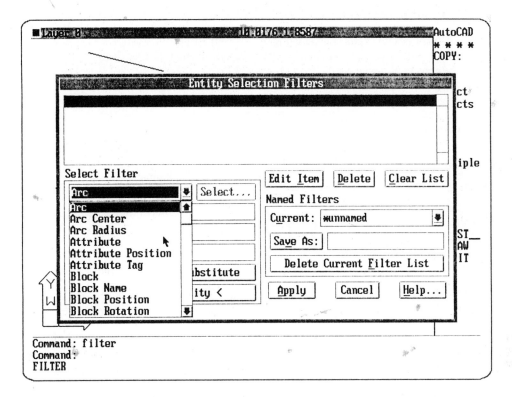

Figure 3.72 Creating a selection set using the Filter command.

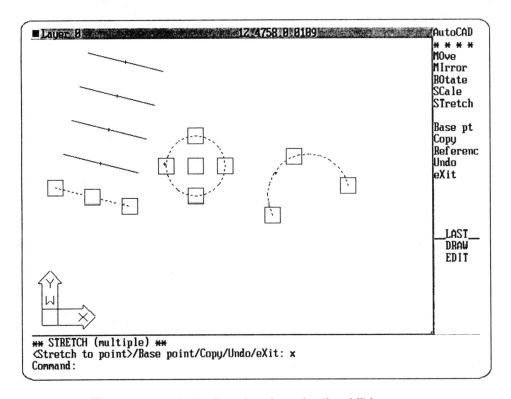

Figure 3.73 Multiple aligned copies using the shift key.

QUESTIONS FOR REVIEW

1. Name the uses of text on engineering drawings.
2. The location of text when using AutoCAD depends upon two modes, name them.
3. Specify the number of alignment modes with AutoCAD.
4. Specify the number of text styles are available with Release 12.
5. Explain how multiple lines of text can be added to a drawing.
6. Explain the difference between **TEXT** and **DTEXT**.
7. Define a text font.
8. Explain special characters, such as the degree symbol, are added to a text string.
9. Explain the use of the **QTEXT** command.
10. Identify the two command options used to add sketched lines to a drawing.
11. Define window.
12. Define pan.
13. Explain the difference between **SET** and **NEW** layer subcommands.
14. Explain the difference between **FREEZE** and **OFF**.
15. Explain how the **LTSCALE** is set to make ANSI standard linetypes.
16. Explain how the text height is controlled to create .125 lettering regardless of the plot scale.

DRAWING ASSIGNMENTS

1. Create a title block such as that shown in Figure 3.74, or one approved by your instructor. Use the display options and multiple viewports when adding text.

2. Create border lines for A, B, C, and D size engineering drawing paper.
   A size borders 8.00 x 10.50 (Figure 3.75)
   B size borders 10.00 x 16.00 (Figure 3.76)
   C size borders 16.00 x 21.00 (Figure 3.77)
   D size borders 21.00 x 33.00 (Figure 3.78)

3. Create a parts list like that shown in Figure 3.79.

4. Sketch those drawings assigned from Chapter 6.

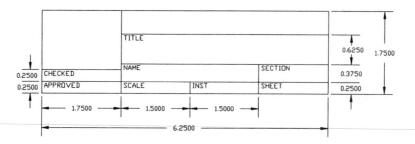

Figure 3.74 Title block.

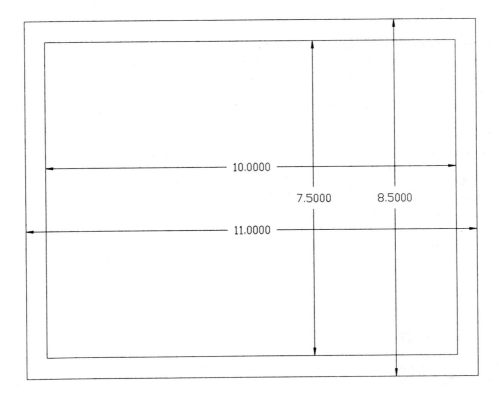

Figure 3.75 A size.

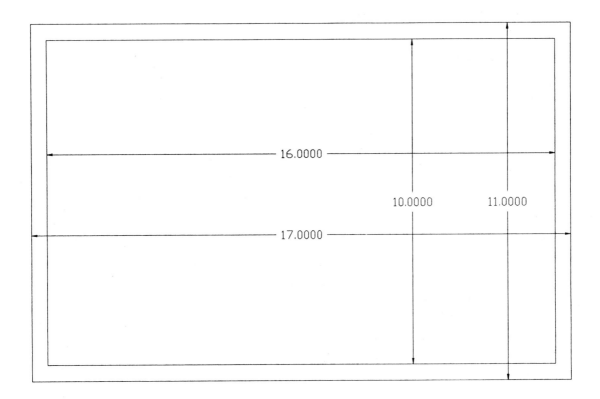

Figure 3.76 B size.

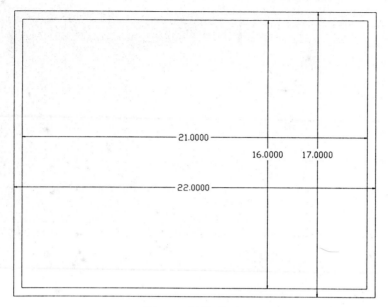

Figure 3.77 C size.

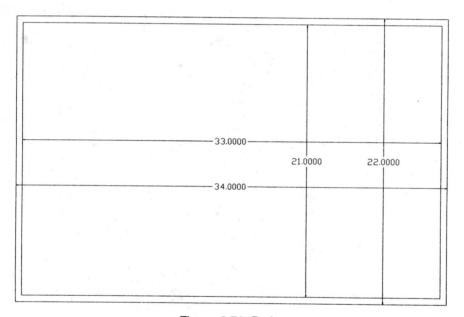

Figure 3.78 D size.

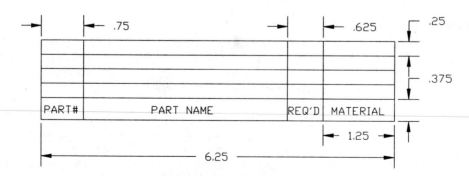

Figure 3.79 Parts list.

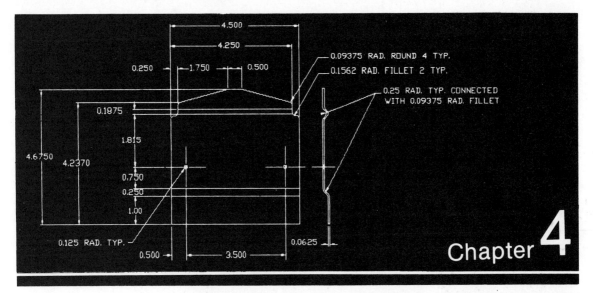

DRAWING WITH AUTOCAD

When learning to draw with traditional tools, the student spends some time exploring the use and care of drawing equipment. For example, the compass is used to draw circles and arcs, and its lead must be sharpened to a bevel for best performance. This chapter will be an introduction to drawing with the AutoCAD software program. Tools traditionally used to create drawings will be replaced by the AutoCAD software commands and the computer workstation.

OBJECTIVES

After completing Chapter 4, you will be able to:
1. Enter and exit the AutoCAD Drawing Editor,
2. Identify the four important parts of the AutoCAD screen,
3. Identify the methods to make AutoCAD command and function selections,
4. Identify the components of the status line,
5. Identify three different methods of controlling cursor movement,
6. Identify four functions of the keyboard,
7. List six methods of entering data using AutoCAD,
8. Draw lines using grid, snap, absolute, polar, and relative coordinates,
9. Draw circles and arcs,
10. Erase entities,
11. Use the **SETUP** command to create the sheet size and scale for a drawing,
12. Plot a drawing,
13. Use the **OSNAP** commands to create a drawing,
14. Use the Pull-down Menus for command selections.

STARTING AUTOCAD

Procedures to start the AutoCAD program vary between hardware devices. However, the basic procedure is the batch file ACADR12 to load the program. To load a drawing immediately type ACADR12=Directory:Filename, such as ACAD386=A:KEVIN. This will load the drawing KEVIN from the A drive. After the program is loaded, the AutoCAD screen is displayed, as shown in Figure 4.1.

The designated disk drive letter and colon must be entered before the name of the drawing file. The name must be entered from the keyboard as a string of letters or numbers up to 8 characters followed by RETURN. For example, to edit an existing drawing file called MICHAEL that is stored on a floppy disk located in disk drive A enter **A:MICHAEL** and RETURN. The text on the screen is removed, and after a few moments the drawing screen will appear. Remember to enter RETURN on the keyboard to execute any typed command or text string. On some computers the RETURN key is labeled as ENTER. This textbook will always use RETURN to enter a text string.

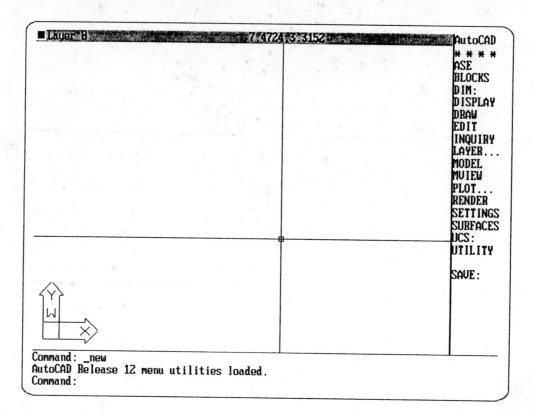

Figure 4.1 The AutoCAD screen display.

The Screen Display

AutoCAD's screen display (Figure 4.2) has a number of important parts that should be noted. How the screen appears will depend on the type of AutoCAD workstation. If two display devices are used, one for graphics and the other for prompts or text, the prompt line may not appear on the graphics screen.

The Prompt Line

The **prompt line** is located near the bottom of the screen and is used to communicate with the user through text strings. It may be located on a separate terminal on a two-terminal workstation. The prompt line will display information important to the successful use of the AutoCAD Drawing Editor.

Pressing **Ctrl-Q** turns on the print echo, which lists all of the prompts to a printer. Pressing **Ctrl-Q** again turns off the print echo. The prompt line also displays prompts that need input by the user. For example, when drawing some types of circles, a prompt requests the diameter or radius. Default values in the prompt line always appear in angled brackets as **<DEFAULT>**. Pressing RETURN selects the default value. Sometimes a prompt requests that an option for a command be chosen. When this happens the options are listed in the prompt line with one or two letters of each option being capitalized. Only the capital letters of an option need to be entered to make a selection. For example, if the option is **Freeze**, simply enter **F** and press **RETURN** to select it.

The Root Menu

The far right portion of the screen displays the **Root Menu.** The Root Menu is a very important menu because it is the window through which all of AutoCAD's Drawing Editor commands can be accessed. Various menu commands and a row of four asterisks are displayed. With the exception of the top menu command AUTOCAD and the SAVE command located at the bottom, selection of all commands and functions on the Root Menu causes a new menu to replace the Root Menu. The AutoCAD menu system is like a tree. Selection of a Root Menu item moves the user into a branch of the tree. From each menu branch are more menu items located on smaller branches of the tree.

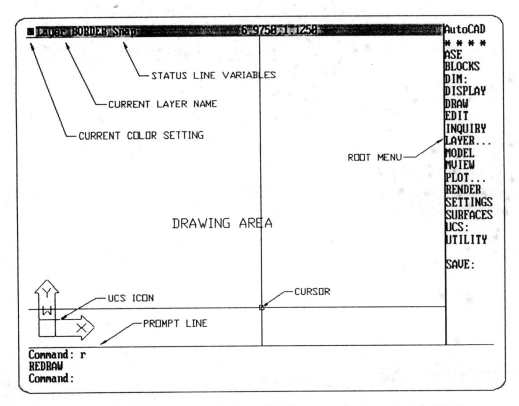

Figure 4.2 AutoCAD's screen display with labels showing important features.

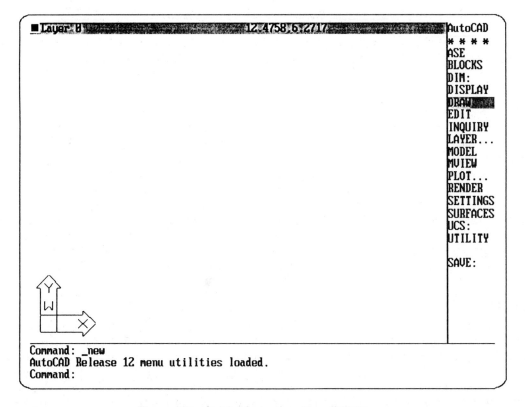

Figure 4.3 Highlighted menu item DRAW.

SELECTING AutoCAD COMMANDS

AutoCAD provides four methods to move through the branches of the menu tree:
1. Screen menu selection,
2. Keyboard typing,
3. Tablet menu selection,
4. Pull-down menu selection.

Each method has its advantages and disadvantages. Most people become proficient at using two or three methods of selecting menu items.

Screen Menu Selection

Menu items displayed along the right side of the screen are selected with a pointing device such as a mouse or puck on a graphics tablet. The pointing device is moved to a position over the desired menu item, which becomes highlighted (Figure 4.3). Pressing the left button on a mouse will activate that menu item and display a new menu on the screen. For example, if menu item DRAW is activated, the draw menu (Figure 4.4) appears replacing the Root Menu. Selecting **AUTOCAD** from the top of every screen menu will cancel a command and return the Root Menu.

The AutoCAD command that appears as the top command in the Root Menu also appears on all other menu pages. This command can be used to return to the Root Menu from any page in the AutoCAD menu structure when using the on-screen menu. Most menu commands are listed in alphabetical order from top to bottom on the screen.

Keyboard Selection

Another method to select menu items is using the keyboard to type in the name of the command. The only time that this method will work is if the prompt line, located near the bottom of the screen, displays **Command:**. If the command prompt is not shown in the prompt line, enter **CTRL-C** by holding the control key down, then pressing the letter C on the computer keyboard. Typing commands from the Command Prompt is used to jump from one branch of the program to another without returning to the Root Menu. For example, to draw a line, enter **LINE** at the **COMMAND** prompt and press RETURN.

Some commands have *aliases* which invoke a command after entering the first letter or first few letters, such as L for Line and PL for Pline. These aliases are listed by loading the Autolisp command ALIAS found in the Sample subdirectory in AutoCAD. Figure 4.5.

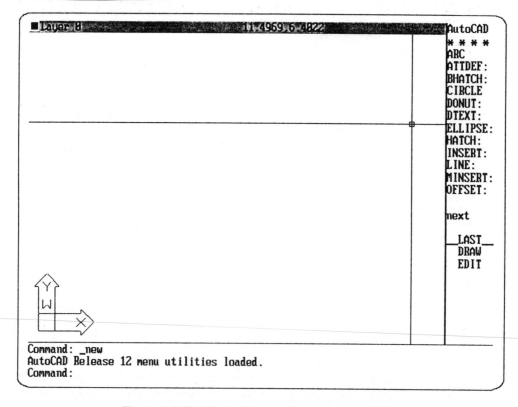

Figure 4.4 The Draw Menu replaces the Root Menu.

```
This is a list of the aliases and external commands found in
C:\ACAD12\SUPPORT\ACAD.PGP.

CATALOG       = DIR/W              DEL          = DEL
DIR           = DIR               EDIT         = EDLIN
SH            = <Null>            SHELL        = <Null>
TYPE          = TYPE              A            = ARC
C             = CIRCLE            CP           = COPY
DV            = DVIEW             E            = ERASE
L             = LINE              LA           = LAYER
M             = MOVE              MS           = MSPACE
P             = PAN               PS           = PSPACE
PL            = PLINE             R            = REDRAW
Z             = ZOOM              3DLINE       = LINE
SERIAL        = _PKSER            BOX          = SOLBOX
WED           = SOLWEDGE          WEDGE        = SOLWEDGE
CON           = SOLCONE           CONE         = SOLCONE
CYL           = SOLCYL            CYLINDER     = SOLCYL
SPH           = SOLSPHERE         SPHERE       = SOLSPHERE
TOR           = SOLTORUS          TORUS        = SOLTORUS
FIL           = SOLFILL           SOLF         = SOLFILL
CHAM          = SOLCHAM           SOLC         = SOLCHAM
EXT           = SOLEXT            EXTRUDE      = SOLEXT
REV           = SOLREV            REVOLVE      = SOLREV
SOL           = SOLIDIFY          CUT          = SOLCUT
UNI           = SOLUNION          UNION        = SOLUNION
SUB           = SOLSUB            SUBTRACT     = SOLSUB
DIF           = SOLSUB            DIFF         = SOLSUB
DIFFERENCE    = SOLSUB            SEP          = SOLSEP
SEPARATE      = SOLSEP            SCHP         = SOLCHP
CHPRIM        = SOLCHP            MAT          = SOLMAT
INTERFERENCE  = SOLINTERF         INTERF       = SOLINTERF
MATERIAL      = SOLMAT            MOV          = SOLMOVE
SL            = SOLLIST           SLIST        = SOLLIST
MP            = SOLMASSP          MASSP        = SOLMASSP
SA            = SOLAREA           SAREA        = SOLAREA
SSV           = SOLVAR            FEAT         = SOLFEAT
PROF          = SOLPROF           PROFILE      = SOLPROF
SECT          = SOLSECT           SU           = SOLUCS
SUCS          = SOLUCS            STL          = SOLSTLOUT
SW            = SOLWIRE           WIRE         = SOLWIRE
SM            = SOLMESH           MESH         = SOLMESH

Press any key to return to your drawing.
```

Figure 4.5 Listing of the alias commands.

Tablet Menu Selection

The third method of selecting menu commands is through a menu and tablet (Figure 4.6). If the AutoCAD workstation has a tablet and menu or a tablet overlay on a digitizer, commands listed on the screen menu also appear on the tablet menu. Moving the puck crosshairs or the tip of the stylus over the menu command and pressing the pick button activates the command without having to page through screen menus. The puck or stylus can be used in the blank area of the tablet that represents the screen display. Moving the puck or stylus until it highlights the desired menu item on the screen also can select commands.

Pull-down Menus

Pull-down Menus are displayed when the cursor is moved to the top of the screen (Figure 4.7). The status line and coordinate display disappear and a menu bar replaces it. The menu bar contains drawing, editing, display, and utility functions. As the cursor is moved across the menu bar each item is highlighted. Picking a highlighted menu item by pressing the button on the mouse will display the corresponding menu directly below it (Figure 4.8). Each menu item in the Pull-down Menu is highlighted as the cursor reaches it. The menu item is selected by picking it with the input device while it is highlighted. Move the cursor outside of the Pull-down Menu and press the pick button to make it disappear.

Picking an item from the pull-down menu that has a triangle drawn after it will cause another menu to appear. This is referred to as *cascading menus*. Figure 4.9. Picking menu items followed by three periods will cause a dialogue box to appear, as shown in Figure 4.10 when the Hatch... option is selected.

Using the Pull-down Menu can save time because items can be chosen without having to page through the screen menu. Many drawing and editing commands use the Auto and Single object selection modes that will repeat indefinitely until CTRL-C is used to cancel the command or another item is picked.

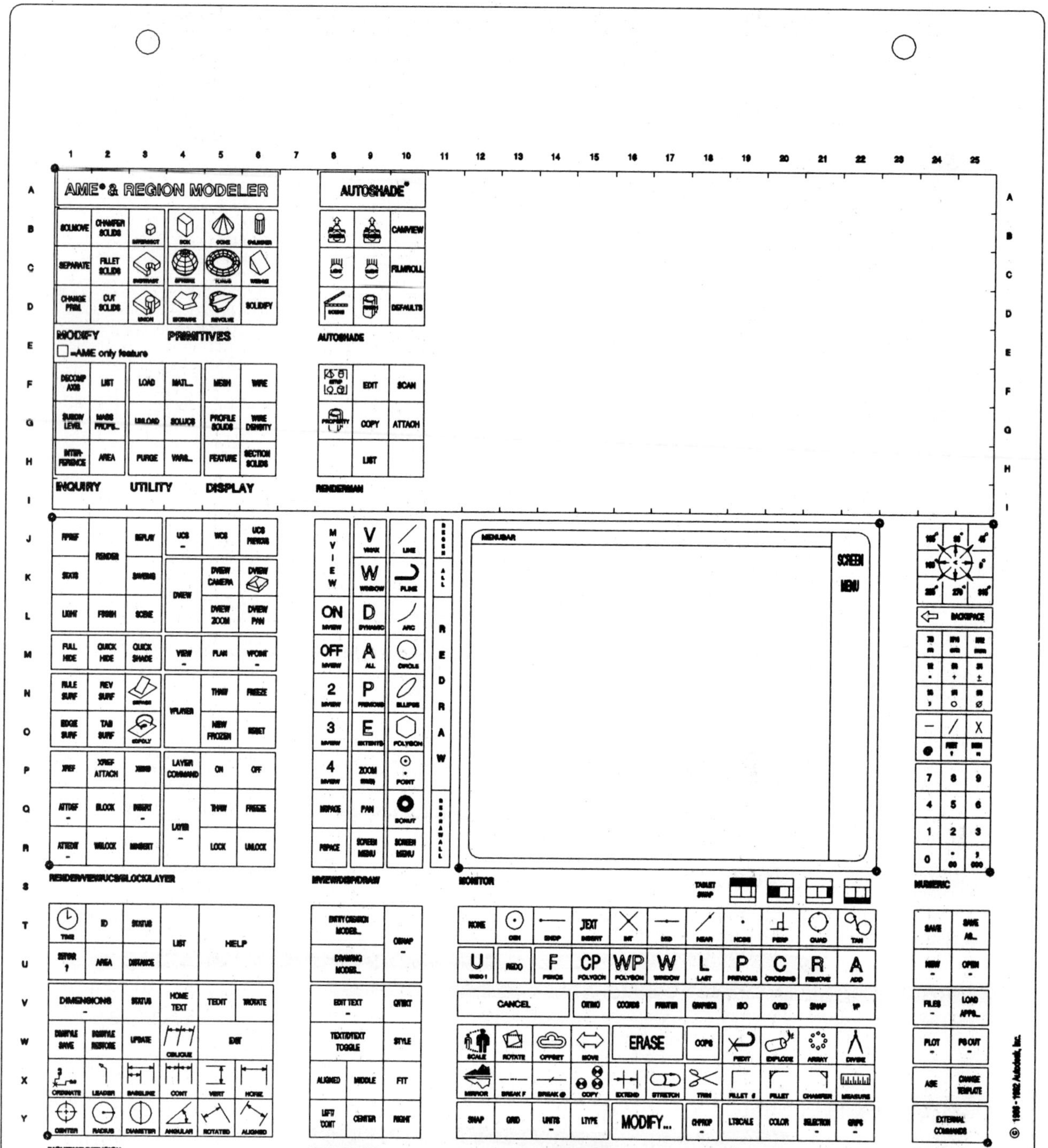

Figure 4.6 The AutoCAD tablet menu. (Autodesk, Inc.)

There are nine Pull-down Menu items:
FILE is used to open, save, recover, and plot various types of files and file formats. Figure 4.11.
ASSIST has the object snap menu, object filters and snap, inquiry, and calculator. Figure 4.12.
DRAW includes some of the drawing commands, such as line, arc, circle, polyline, 3D surfaces, insert, hatch, and text. Figure 4.8.

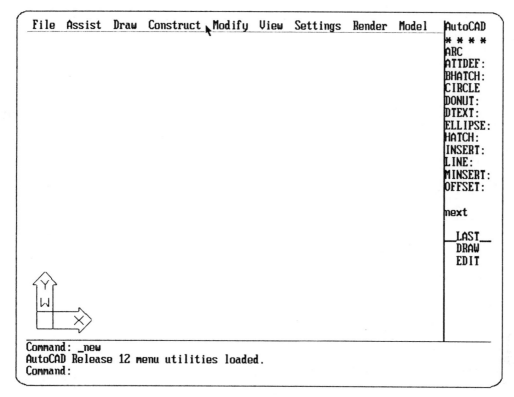

Figure 4.7 Pull-down Menu items replace the status line.

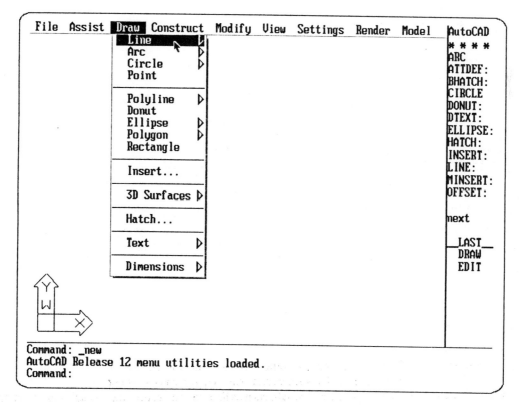

Figure 4.8 The Draw Pull-down Menu items.

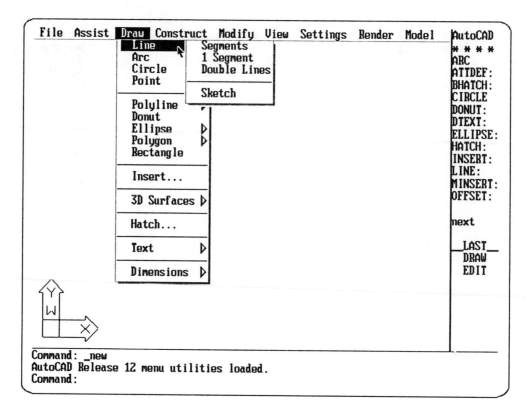

Figure 4.9 Cascading menus.

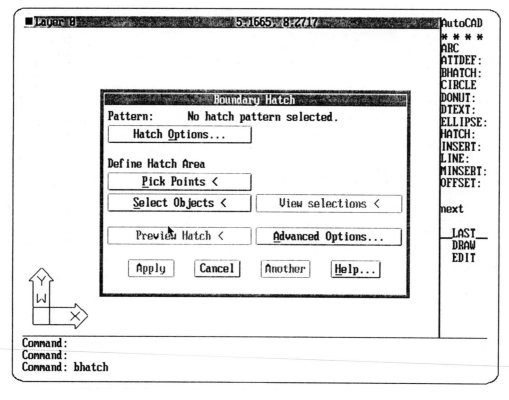

Figure 4.10 A dialogue box.

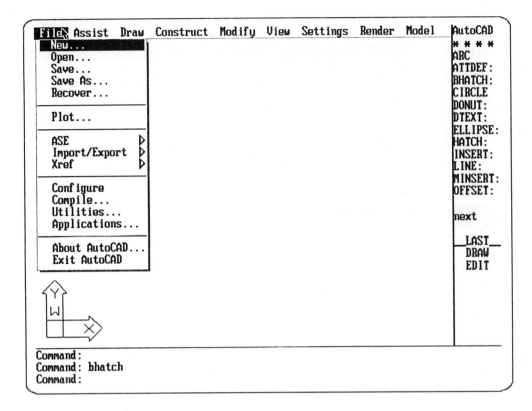

Figure 4.11 The File Pull-down Menu.

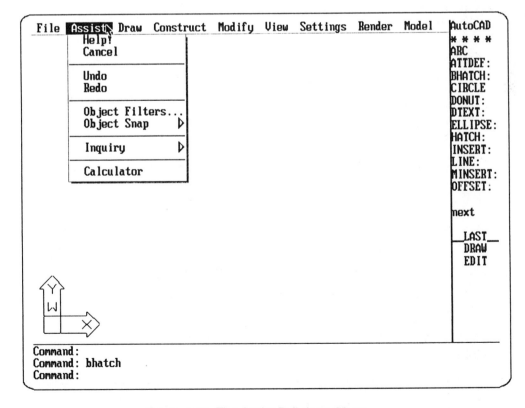

Figure 4.12 The Assist Pull-down Menu.

CONSTRUCT is used to construct arrays, copies, mirror images, chamfers, fillets, divide, measure, offset, and block commands. Figure 4.13.

MODIFY includes the editing commands of: erase, move, entity, polyedit, break, scale, mirror, trim, extend, stretch, and edit dimensions. Figure 4.14.

VIEW has display and viewport commands including: redraw, some zoom options, pan, Dview, plan views, set viewports, model, and paper space. Figure 4.15.

SETTINGS includes: UCS options, drawing aids such as grid and snap, entity modes such as color and linetype, and the layer dialogue box. Figure 4.16.

RENDER is used to render, shade, hide, and set rendering preferences. Figure 4.17.

MODEL is used for the Advanced Modeling Extension (AME). Figure 4.18.

When an item is selected from a Pull-down Menu, one of four actions can result:

1. The command is immediately activated. Rectangle and copy are examples.

2. Another menu pops up for further selection, such as when line or circle is picked. Figure 4.9.

3. An icon menu is displayed. Selecting 3D objects from the Draw Pull-down Menu displays the icon menu in Figure 4.19.

4. A dialogue box is displayed. Layer control and drawing aids are examples (Figure 4.20).

An icon menu displays choices in the form of graphic images (icons). The screen cursor turns into an arrow when the icon menu is displayed. To select an item in the icon menu, move the cursor over the icon then pick it.

A dialogue box is used to set modes or execute options by checking boxes or filling in fields. Check buttons are small rectangles used to toggle something on or off or to select items from a list.

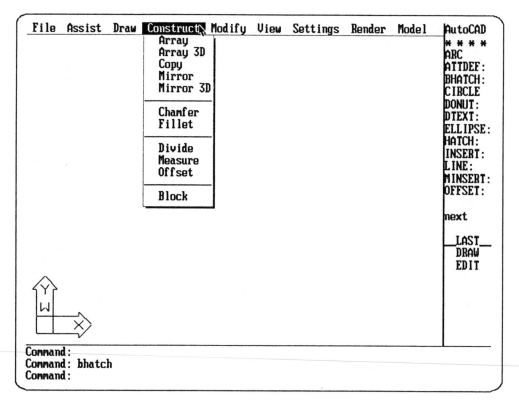

Figure 4.13 The Construct Pull-down Menu.

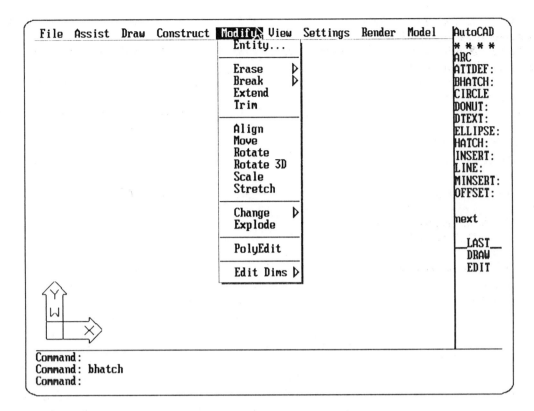

Figure 4.14 The Modify Pull-down Menu.

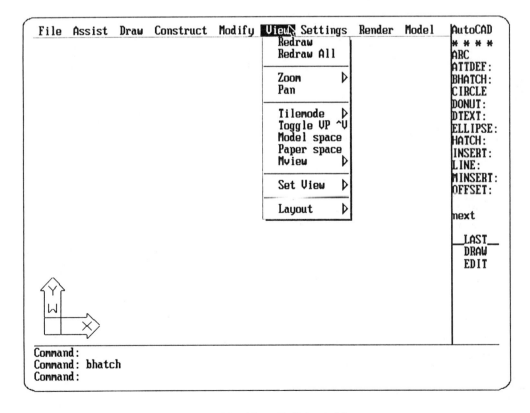

Figure 4.15 The View Pull-down Menu.

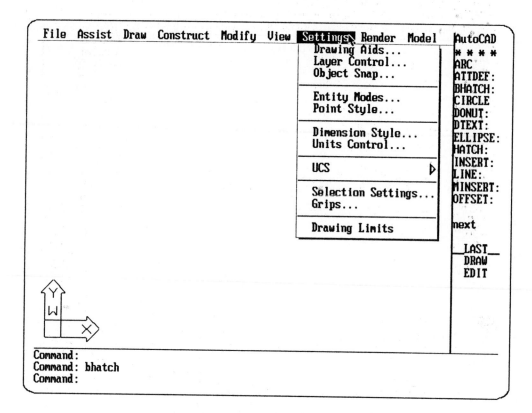

Figure 4.16 The Settings Pull-down Menu.

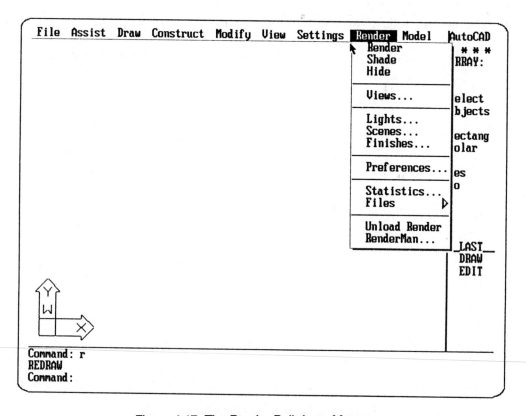

Figure 4.17 The Render Pull-down Menu.

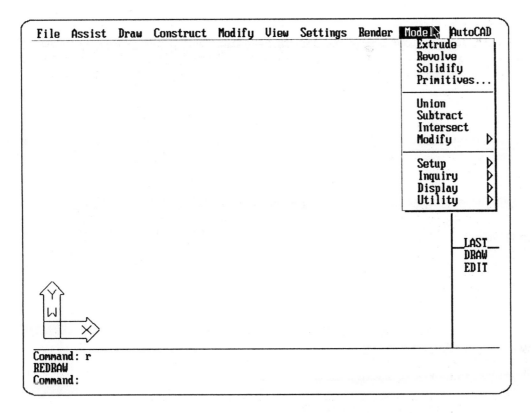

Figure 4.18 The Model Pull-down Menu.

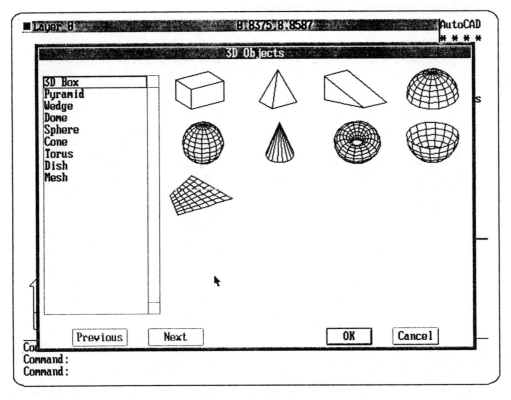

Figure 4.19 An AutoCAD icon menu.

Transparent Commands

Transparent commands can be used while another command is in operation by preceding the command with an apostrophe ('). The transparent commands are: **PAN, VIEW, REDRAW, REDRAWALL, ZOOM, SETVAR, DDEMODES, DDLMODES, DDRMODES, TEXTSCR, RESUME, GRAPHSCR,** and **HELP**. After the transparent command is complete, AutoCAD returns to the command that was being used.

THE STATUS LINE

The top of the screen, which displays some program information, is called the **status line**. At the far upper left of the screen, the current color is displayed in a small square. To the right of the color square is the current layer setting, such as **LAYER 0**. Layer 0 is the default setting. A **default** value is a setting that will be active when AutoCAD is booted up. Default values can be changed by editing the prototype drawing ACAD.DWG .

Further to the right are two strings of zeroes (**0.0000, 0.0000**). This area of the screen is used to display the X, Y coordinate position of the cursor. When SNAP is turned on, the word SNAP appears between the layer and coordinate value. When the ORTHO mode is turned on, the word ORTHO appears next to SNAP in the upper portion of the screen (Figure 4.2).

CURSOR

The **cursor** appears on the screen as a large crosshair whose movement is controlled by a pointing device or keyboard arrows. Moving the mouse, the puck, or the stylus on the graphics tablet controls the movement of the cursor on the screen. The cursor also is controlled by using the arrow keys located on the numeric keypad of an IBM PC and compatible computer keyboard.

UP ARROW moves the cursor up.
DOWN ARROW moves the cursor down.
LEFT ARROW moves the cursor to the left.
RIGHT ARROW moves the cursor to the right.
PgUp (page up) increases the speed or increment of movement when the arrow keys are used.
PgDn (page down) decreases the speed or increment of movement when the arrow keys are used.
END returns cursor control to the puck, mouse, or stylus.
HOME returns control of the cursor to the arrow keys.

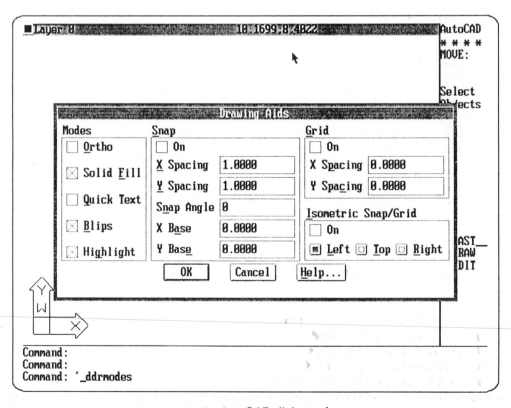

Figure 4.20 An AutoCAD dialogue box.

THE DRAWING AREA

The **drawing area** is left of the vertical line and above the horizontal line appearing on the screen. Even though the screen size may be small, the drawing area can represent virtually any size, from smaller than a postage stamp to larger than a football field. This chapter describes more about setting screen limits that control the size of the drawing area.

THE KEYBOARD

The keyboard has many special features that can be used with AutoCAD, including:

Arrow Keys
Function Keys
Return and **Space Bar**
Control Key

The arrow keys have been explained, as well as some other special function keys.

Function Keys

IBM PC and compatible computers have a row of **function keys** usually to the far left or across the top of the keyboard. Keys F1 and F6 through F10 are assigned toggle functions, which are keys that can turn a function on or off like a light switch.

F1: SCREEN TOGGLE, used to switch between the graphics screen and the text screen. The text screen lists a full 24 lines of text, commands, and prompts that have been used in the Drawing Editor. If information has scrolled off the three lines displayed in the prompt, the screen toggle or "flip screen" can be used to view them. AutoCAD will flip automatically to the text display when large amounts of text are output after a command has been invoked.

F6: COORDS TOGGLE, used to control the coordinate value output for the location of the screen cursor in X, Y values or distance and angle from a previous point. The coordinate position of the cursor can be displayed constantly in the status line at the top of the screen display by using the F6 key. If the coordinate toggle is off, the coordinate value only displays the last point input.

F7: GRID TOGGLE, used to turn the grid on and off. A grid is a series of dots that appear on the screen as a drawing aid. When the grid is turned on, the default setting of one unit is used for the spacing.

F8: ORTHO TOGGLE, used to control the orthogonal mode, which can be used when drawing lines perpendicular (orthogonal) to the coordinate system.

F9: SNAP TOGGLE, controls the snap function, which causes the cursor to snap to a set of invisible points or the grid points.

F10: TABLET TOGGLE, toggles between tablet on and off modes. When in the tablet mode, a digitizing tablet can be used as a digitizer to input existing drawings into AutoCAD. The tablet option is disabled when AutoCAD is configured for a mouse.

Return And Space Bar

The RETURN or ENTER key is used after every entry of commands or data. The SPACE BAR also can be used to terminate data or command entry with one exception. When placing text on screen, the space bar is used for spacing between words. To enter a line of text, the RETURN key must be used. The RETURN key or SPACE BAR also can repeat a command. When the command prompt appears, pressing the RETURN key or SPACE BAR activates the last command used.

Control Key Commands

The **control key,** labeled as **Ctrl** on most computer keyboards, has many special functions when used in combination with other keys. For example, the toggles that are controlled by the Function Keys also are controlled by using the **Ctrl** key.

Ctrl D is used for the coordinate toggle or **F6.**
Ctrl G is used for the grid toggle or **F7.**
Ctrl O is used for the ortho mode or **F8.**
Ctrl B is used for the snap toggle or **F9.**
Ctrl T is used to control the tablet mode or **F10.**
Ctrl Q turns the print echo on and off. The print echo is used to send all text information, such as prompts, to the printer.

Ctrl H is used like the **BACK SPACE** key to remove one character at a time from the prompt line.
Ctrl X deletes all characters input on the prompt line before **RETURN** is pressed.
Ctrl C cancels the current command or returns the program to the command prompt. Using **Ctrl C** while in a command sequence cancels the command.
Ctrl E controls the isometric cursor positions (top, left, right).

Other Important Keys

The **BACK SPACE** key deletes characters from the command line. For example, if you type "LINN" for "LINE", press the **BACK SPACE** key once to remove the second N, then type E. The **INS** or insert key turns on the menu cursor, which allows screen menu selection using the keyboard. The arrow keys position the menu cursor over the desired command; then the **RETURN** key, **SPACE BAR**, or **INSERT** key selects that menu item.

HELP!

Confused? Learning to use any CADD system to create engineering drawings is difficult at the beginning. It is not as easy as picking up a pencil and a straight-edge to draw a line. The user interface of the CADD system must be learned before beginning a drawing. The **user interface** is the method used by a software program for interaction between the computer and the operator. AutoCAD provides help for those who have difficulty remembering how different commands are used.

When the **HELP** command is entered, a description of how to use AutoCAD commands is provided. In the drawing editor, **HELP** can be used by typing **HELP** or **?** at the command prompt or by selecting **HELP!** from the Assist Pull-down Menu. The graphics screen changes to a dialogue box, which explains the operation of the Help Command. Figure 4.21.

Type in the name of the command to find help or use the index by picking the Index... Button. Picking the Index Button displays the Help Index window shown in Figure 4.22. Scroll through the commands using the scroll bar on the right then pick the one for help. For example, picking the Align command by highlighting it and then by picking the OK Button displays the information shown in Figure 4.23. Use the scroll bar to get more information, then pick the OK Button to return to the drawing screen.

If the name of the command is known, such as **LINE**, enter the command name and press **RETURN**. Information describing **LINE** and how it is used will be listed on the screen.

Help is obtained in the middle of a current command by entering **'HELP** or **'?** for any prompt that is not asking for a text string. Be sure to enter the apostrophe before HELP or ?.

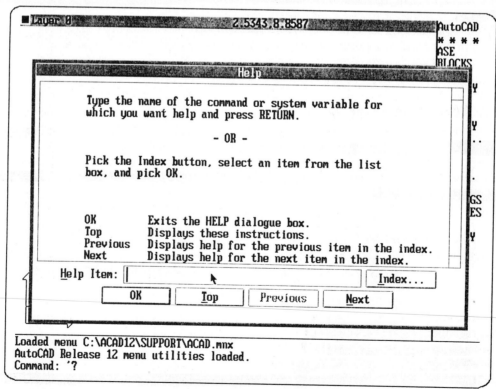

Figure 4.21 The Help dialogue box.

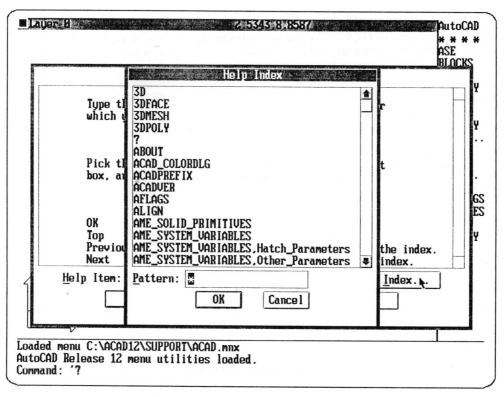

Figure 4.22 The Help Index dialogue box.

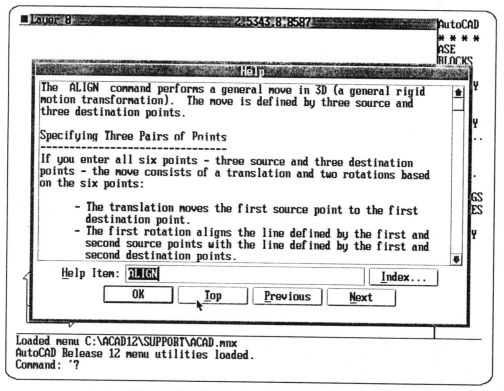

Figure 4.23 The Align help information.

THE MOUSE

AutoCAD supports the mouse input device for pointing, drawing, and selecting screen menu commands. The mouse is used for cursor control by movement over the tabletop or reflective plate. The buttons on the surface of the mouse are assigned certain functions, which *AutoCAD Installation and Performance Guide* describes. For most three-button mice, the left-most button is for "picking." **Picking** can be locating end points of lines, arcs, and circles, positioning text, erasing entities, and many other drawing functions. It is also choosing menu items from the screen by lighting the command and pressing the mouse button. The middle button on a three-button mouse is used to get the OSNAP Menu to pop-up on screen wherever the cursor is currently located. Figure 4.24. The right button on a three-button mouse serves the same function as the return key.

TABLET MENUS

A tablet menu can select menu commands more rapidly than the screen menu. Most of AutoCAD's commands are listed on a tablet menu, which allows the user to circumvent the menu hierarchy that must be followed when using the screen commands. Menu commands are chosen directly from the tablet menu through an input device such as the stylus or puck. The input device also can control the screen cursor through movement in the monitor area of the tablet menu.

STARTING A NEW DRAWING

AutoCAD is an advanced program because the user can control many different parameters or defaults of a drawing. To start a new drawing is a relatively simple task if changes to the default parameters are not wanted.

Starting A New Drawing: Exercise 4.1

1. From the Files Pull-down Menu, select **New**... Figure 4.25.

2. The Create New Drawing Dialogue Box is displayed as shown in Figure 4.26. This dialogue box is used to select the prototype drawing and new drawing name. The prototype drawing is the base information or default setting for the new drawing. ACAD.DWG is the prototype drawing provided by AutoCAD. You can make changes to this prototype drawing or create your own. For this example the default prototype drawing is used.

3. Enter the name of the drawing by typing in the word **PRACTICE**. Pick the **OK** button to start a new drawing named practice. Remember that you are limited to 8 characters with no periods for drawing file names on DOS computers. After selecting OK the AutoCAD drawing screen is displayed.

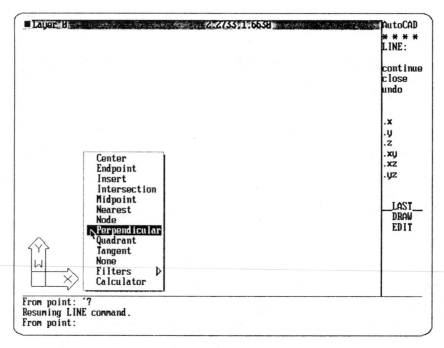

Figure 4.24 The OSNAP Menu pops-up when the middle mouse button on a three-button is selected.

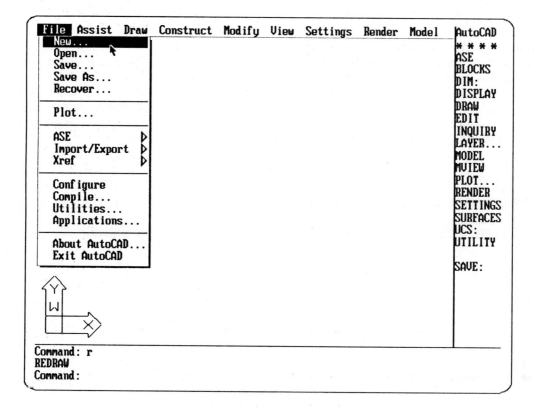

Figure 4.25 Starting a new drawing.

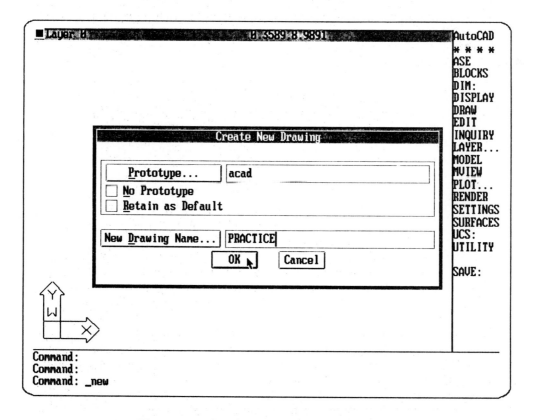

Figure 4.26 The Create New dialogue box.

AutoCAD's Prototype Drawing

The first menu that appears on the screen is the Root Menu. Before beginning on a drawing, some of the parameters or default values may have to be changed. Defaults are initial settings for different commands, such as linetype, screen color, drawing units, and so forth. Default settings appear in the prompt line in brackets such as **<DEFAULT>**. Pressing **RETURN** will accept the default value. Appendix C lists the default values for a drawing with those values set by AutoCAD using a file called ACAD.DWG. Many of the default settings are initially set in the AutoCAD prototype drawing ACAD.DWG. A listing of the current settings is displayed by entering **SETVAR** at the command prompt, followed by a question (?), mark then RETURN.

However, these default settings may not be what is needed for your drawing. For example, the **LUPREC** (linear) default setting is **Decimal, 4 decimal places.** Every time a new drawing is begun, the default units are four-place decimal. What if two-place decimal is used for most of the drawings? By changing the prototype drawing to two-place decimals, drawings would always start with the default values wanted. This can be done by changing the default values to your specifications and saving this updated version as the prototype drawing. Most default values can be changed by using the **SETTINGS** command from the Root Screen Menu then **SETVAR**.

Your new prototype drawing is used by entering the name in the Create New Dialogue Box. Actually any drawing created with AutoCAD and saved on disk can become a prototype drawing. Because prototype drawings can have custom designed title blocks and borders, preset units and scale, and many other preset parameters, a tremendous saving of time and the ability to customize any engineering drawing can result.

SETTING THE LIMITS, UNITS, SCALE, AND DRAWING BORDER

Some pre-planning is necessary before starting on a drawing with AutoCAD. Although AutoCAD can create virtually any size drawing full scale, it is best to try to determine the units used for the drawing, the size of the border, the plotting scale, and the size limits of the drawing on the screen. Most of these parameters can be determined before starting a drawing. However, even if an error is made, changes can take place at any time during the drawing.

Limits

The default setting for the drawing limits using AutoCAD's prototype drawing is 0,0 (lower left corner) and 12,9 (upper right corner), which means the effective drawing area is 12 by 9 units. For example, suppose that the object to be drawn is 18 inches long and each unit is to represent one inch. To convert all the dimensions to fit on the sheet with traditional tools, a scale of .50 would be used. AutoCAD uses an electronic sheet that can be stretched or shrunk to any size. Instead of converting all the measurements to .50 scale, the size of the drawing area can be

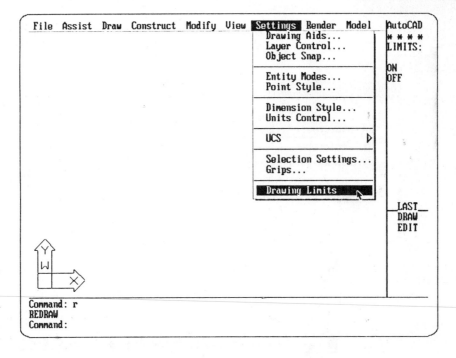

Figure 4.27 Selecting drawing limits.

expanded so that real-world coordinates can be used for all drawings. The **LIMIT** command is used to change the drawing limits of the AutoCAD screen. The following steps demonstrate setting the drawing limits:

Setting Drawing Limits: Exercise 4.2

1. From the Root Menu, choose the **SETTINGS** command. The **SETTINGS** submenu lists the **LIMITS** command. Or select Drawing Limits from the Settings Pull-down Menu. Figure 4.27.

2. Selecting **LIMITS** will show a prompt:

ON/OFF/<Lower left corner> <0.0000, 0.0000>:.

3. The default setting can be used by pressing **RETURN** but to allow some additional space for borders and plotting enter, **-1, -1** and press **RETURN**.

4. A second prompt is displayed:

Upper Right Corner: <12.0000, 9.0000>:.

Input the new upper limit so that the 18-inch part can be drawn on the screen. A new value, such as **24, 18** is input, followed by **RETURN.** Now the limits of the drawing are 25 units horizontally and 18 units vertically. To display this size drawing area, enter **ZOOM** at the command prompt then enter **All.** Turn the coordinate toggle on by selecting **F6** and check the limits by moving the input device from corner to corner of the screen.

5. Save this setting by entering **SAVE** at the command prompt, then picking the OK Button from the Save Drawing As Dialogue Box. Making each unit equal to one inch will provide enough room to draw the 18-inch part horizontally on the screen and a standard size for a C-size sheet.

LIMITS sets a fence around the working area. A grid is displayed only within the boundary of the set limits. This can be tested by turning the grid on using the **F7** key. Then enter **Z** for Zoom, then **V** for Vmax (view maximum). If the limits check is **ON,** attempting to draw outside the limits results in an **Outside limits** error message. However, parts of some entities may be drawn outside the limits even if the check is on. For example, a curve with a center within the limits may be partially outside of the set limits. The limit check is turned off by choosing **OFF,** or on by selecting **ON,** from the **LIMITS** submenu or prompt line. **LIMITS** also determines the area displayed when the **ZOOM ALL** command is used.

Units

A **unit** is any specified value, such as inches, feet, and meters. The units chosen are the required format when entering values from the keyboard. The default unit is four-place decimal. The following steps demonstrate changing the units:

Setting Units: Exercise 4.3

1. Select Units Control... from the Settings Pull-down Menu. Figure 4.28.

2. Pick the units from the Units Control Dialogue Box. Figure 4.29.

Five different units can be selected:

Scientific uses scientific notation for values, such as 1.24E+01 for 12.4 units.

Decimal uses decimal equivalent values, such as 1.5 for 1'- 6".

Engineering displays values in feet and decimal inches, such as 1'-4.8" for 12.4 units.

Architectural displays values in feet and fractional inches, such as 2'-9 3/4" for 33.75 units.

Fractional displays values with fractions, such as 33 1/2 for 33.5.

Picking the button to the left of the units will change the setting. Leave the setting at the current setting of Decimal.

2. The current precision setting is at four decimal places (0.0000). To change the precision, click on the arrow button next to the current precision setting. A pop-up box appears listing the available options. Figure 4.30. Highlight the desired value of 0.00 to change the setting.

3. The system of angle measure is displayed to the right of the units in Figure 4.29. Picking the button to the left of the units will change the setting. Decimal degrees are the default unit, which is desired, so nothing is changed.

4. The angle direction is controlled by picking the Direction... Button. A pop-up window is displayed as shown in Figure 4.31. The default AutoCAD setting for the angle convention is shown in Figure 4.32. Select the Cancel Button so no changes are made.

5. Click on the OK Button in the Unit Control Menu to accept all changes.

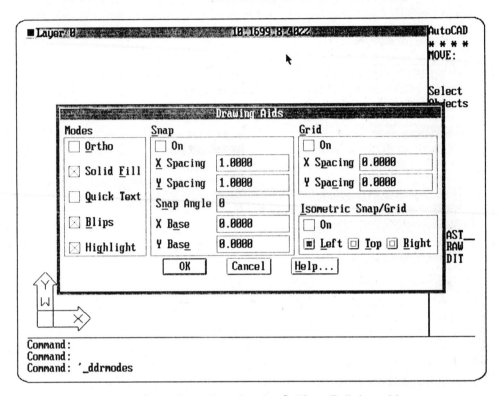

Figure 4.28 Changing units using the Settings Pull-down Menu.

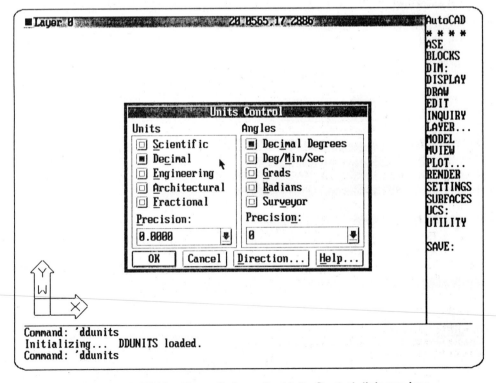

Figure 4.29 Picking the units from the Units Control dialogue box.

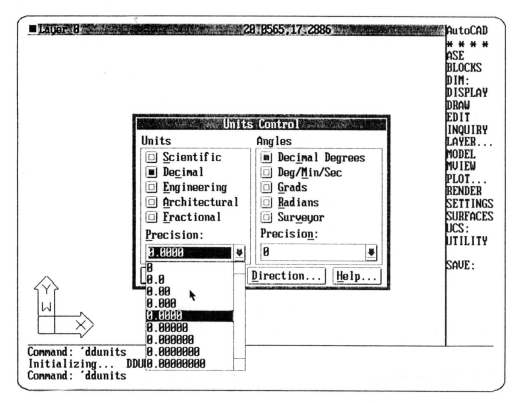

Figure 4.30 Changing the decimal precision using the pop-up box.

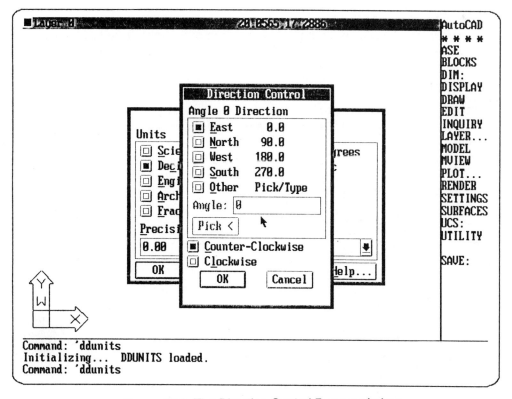

Figure 4.31 The Direction Control Pop-up window.

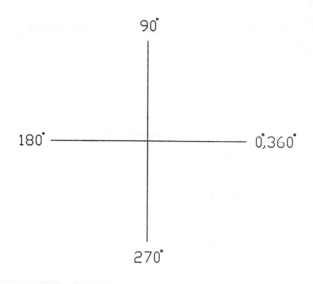

Figure 4.32 The angle convention used for polar coordinates.

Using the screen menu to make unit settings changes.

1. The units of the drawing are changed from the default value by selecting the **SETTINGS** command from the Root Menu, **NEXT** from the Settings Menu, then **UNITS.** AutoCAD changes to the text screen where Systems of Units Menu is displayed. (Figure 4.33). The default setting is shown in brackets as **<2>.**

4. Press **3** and **RETURN** to change to Engineering as the unit. The number of digits to the right of the decimal point can be set between 0 and eight. The default setting is four.

5. Change it to 2 by entering the number **2** and pressing **RETURN.**

6. The system of angle measure is then displayed. Decimal degrees are the default unit, which is desired, so **RETURN** is pressed.

7. The number of fractional places for the angle measure can be specified from 0 to 8, with 0 being the default. For this example, 2 places is selected by entering the number **2** and pressing **RETURN.**

8. The angle convention is displayed then, with 0 at three o'clock, or East on a compass. Press **RETURN** to accept this convention. Angles can be measured clockwise but press **RETURN** to measure counter-clockwise, the default setting.   The Command prompt appears. Pressing the **F1** key, the **Arrow Keys,** or the **Insert Key** returns to the graphics screen.

```
Report formats:        (Examples)

    1.   Scientific      1.55E+01
    2.   Decimal         15.50
    3.   Engineering     1'-3.50"
    4.   Architectural   1'-3 1/2"
    5.   Fractional      15 1/2

With the exception of Engineering and Architectural formats,
these formats can be used with any basic unit of measurement.
For example, Decimal mode is perfect for metric units as well
as decimal English units.

Enter choice, 1 to 5 <2>:
```

Figure 4.33 The system of units are displayed on screen.

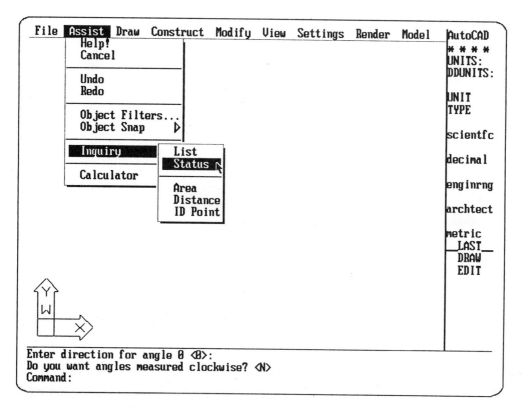

Figure 4.34 Selecting the Status option.

AUTOCAD TIP

Using the **ZOOM/EXTENTS** or **ALL** will make a drawing as large as possible on screen which can cause problems for entity selection if some are located near the edge of the screen. To avoid this repeat the Zoom command then enter **.9X**. Adding the X makes the scale relative to what is already on screen.

```
0 entities in C:\JUNK
Model space limits are X:        -1.00    Y:        -1.00    (Off)
                       X:        24.00    Y:        18.00
Model space uses       *Nothing*
Display shows          X:        -1.00    Y:        -1.00
                       X:        25.36    Y:        18.00
Insertion base is      X:         0.00    Y:         0.00    Z:        0.00
Snap resolution is     X:         1.00    Y:         1.00
Grid spacing is        X:         0.00    Y:         0.00

Current space:         Model space
Current layer:         0
Current color:         BYLAYER -- 7 (white)
Current linetype:      BYLAYER -- CONTINUOUS
Current elevation:        0.00  thickness:         0.00
Fill on  Grid off  Ortho off  Qtext off  Snap off  Tablet off
Object snap modes:     None
Free disk: 11575296 bytes
Virtual memory allocated to program: 3856 KB
Amount of program in physical memory/Total (virtual) program size: 68%
Total conventional memory: 400 KB      Total extended memory: 7360 KB
-- Press RETURN for more --
Swap file size: 388 KB
Command:
```

Figure 4.35 The current status of the drawing is displayed on screen.

Status

Many different default settings, modes, and other variables can be changed with AutoCAD. The **STATUS** command lists many of the variable settings. To enter this command, type **STATUS** at the command prompt or select **INQUIRY** from the Root Menu, then **STATUS** from the **INQUIRY** submenu or select Status from the Inquiry submenu of the Assist Pull-down Menu. Figure 4.34. The screen flips from graphics to text and displays a listing of information, as shown in Figure 4.35. To return to the graphics screen, select **F1** Flip Screen.

CREATING LINES WITH AutoCAD

An important and basic function of CADD is to create lines. Lines are created by using a pencil and straightedge with traditional tools. CADD systems use the cursor to represent the pencil point and different aids, such as grid and snap. Lines are created with CADD by locating the two end points. Picking the two end points is done by the mouse, keyboard arrow keys, or the tablet and input device. Coordinate values also can be entered through the keyboard to locate end points.

Blips

Drawing lines or other graphic entities with AutoCAD cause a small marker (+), called a blip, to appear on the screen. These **blips** are temporary markers that appear on the screen whenever a point is indicated with an input device. They are removed from the screen by using the **REDRAW** command or by selecting **F7** (grid) twice. Simply type **R** or **REDRAW** at the command prompt, and the drawing or current viewport is redrawn on the screen without the blips. Drawings are created without blips by using the **BLIPS** command, which is found on the **SETTINGS** screen menu and is turned ON or OFF from the menu. The default setting for blips is on.

Grid

To assist the user in placing lines and other entities accurately on the screen, AutoCAD places a number of dots, called a **grid,** on the screen. A grid is similar to using grid paper with traditional tools. These dots can be arranged horizontally, vertically, and isometrically. Isometric grids are explained in Chapter 11. The horizontal and vertical spacing of the dots can be different or equal. When the grid is turned on initially, the default setting using the ACAD prototype drawing is a one by one unit. Each viewport may have a different grid setting and the **GRID** command only affects the current viewport.

The grid is merely a series of construction points that will not print or plot and cannot be erased. If the grid spacing is too close for AutoCAD to display, a message appears: **Grid too dense to display**.

Turning A Grid On: Exercise 4.4

1. The grid is turned on by using the grid toggle key **F7** or **CTRL-G**. **GRID** also can be selected from the screen menu or by selecting Drawing Aids from the Settings Pull-down Menu. For this example, select Drawing Aids from the Settings Pull-down Menu. Figure 4.36.
2. The Drawing Aids Dialogue Box is displayed. Figure 4.37. Turn the grid on by picking the On button.
3. Highlight the X Spacing value of 0.00 by pointing at the value and pressing the pick button while dragging the cursor across the number. Enter a new value of .5 from the keyboard.
4. Highlight the Y Spacing value, which automatically changes the value to equal X of .5.
5. Notice that other drawing aids can be controlled from this dialogue box, such as snap and mode settings, and isometric grid values. Select the OK Button to return to the drawing screen which displays a series of horizontal and vertical rows of grid points with a spacing of .5. Figure 4.38.

Using the Screen Menu to control the grid settings.

1. From the Root Menu, select **SETTINGS** then **GRID** to display the grid options.
2. After **GRID** is selected, a prompt reads:
Grid spacing(X) or ON/OFF/Snap/Aspect <0.00>:.
Enter a value of **.5** and **RETURN** to set the grid to turn on a 1/2- unit grid. The **ON/OFF** commands also activate and/or turn off the grid. Entering an **S** will set the grid to the snap spacing. The **ASPECT** command assigns different values to the X- and Y- spacing of the grid. For example, the X spacing might be set at 1 and the Y-spacing at 2 units.

The grid is used as a guide in drawing entities. In combination with the **SNAP** function, **GRID** is very helpful. The grid is set to the snap spacing by selecting **SNAP** from the grid submenu or **S** at the grid command prompt and pressing **RETURN**. Using the grid toggle (F7) is also a quick method of redrawing the screen to remove blips.

Snap

The **SNAP function can control the position of the cursor on the screen**. After entering the Drawing Editor, the cursor is free to move to any position on the screen. The **SNAP function restricts the movement of the cursor to a spacing controlled by the user.** For example, a simple engineering drawing might have .25" as the smallest dimension unit. A .25" snap could be set, and the cursor movement would be restricted to .25" increments. **A grid that is set equal to or independent of the snap increment also could be displayed.**

The **SNAP is turned on by using the toggle F9** or **CTRL-B.** The status line displays SNAP on the screen when it is on. Figure 4.40. If the coordinate toggle is turned on, moving the cursor changes from smooth to jumping from snap point to snap point, and the coordinate readout jumps in the increments used in the snap setting. **Each viewport can have a different snap setting but the SNAP command only affects the current viewport.**

Through the Root Menu item **SETTINGS, NEXT** is selected to display the second page of the menu, where **SNAP** is found. A prompt will also read, **Snap spacing or ON/OFF/Aspect/Rotate/Style <1.00>:**. The default or current setting is displayed between the brackets and is determined by the prototype drawing. The **ON/OFF** commands are the toggle switches. **Inputting a value at the prompt sets the snap to that value and turns on the snap.** The **ASPECT** command **sets the X- and Y-spacing of the snap**. The **ROTATE command changes the coordinate direction from standard or orthogonal to any angle specified. STYLE** selects isometric or standard. **Isometric displays a grid used to create isometric drawings as isometric grid paper is used with traditional tools.**

The ORTHO Toggle

Another type of snap function is the ortho toggle, which assists in the drawing of horizontal and vertical lines. **Ortho can be used to draw lines parallel and perpendicular to rotated coordinates**. The Ortho Toggle, **F8** or **CTRL-O** turns this function on and off. When ortho is on, **ORTHO** is displayed in the status line at the top of the screen. Ortho also is turned on by typing **ORTHO** at the command prompt or from the screen menu.

Drawing A 2D Line By Screen Pointing

Creating a 2D line with AutoCAD is a simple task. From the Root Menu the **DRAW** command creates lines, as well as other graphic entities. The **LINE** command also can be chosen from the tablet menu, the Draw Pull-down Menu (Figure 4.39), or by typing **LINE** or **L** at the command prompt. The following steps demonstrate drawing a line with AutoCAD:

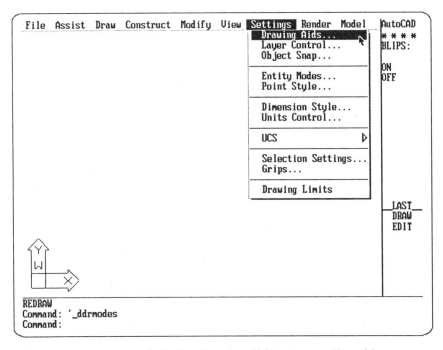

Figure 4.36 Selecting Drawing Aids to turn on the grid.

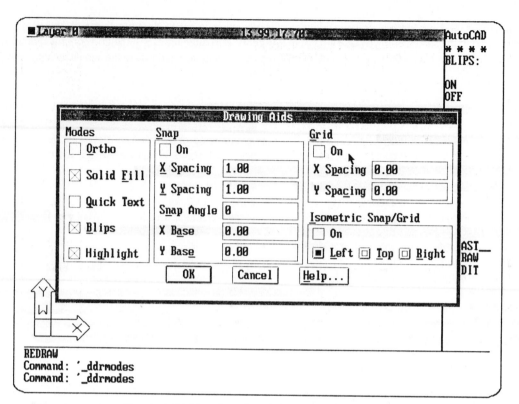

Figure 4.37 The Drawing Aids dialogue box.

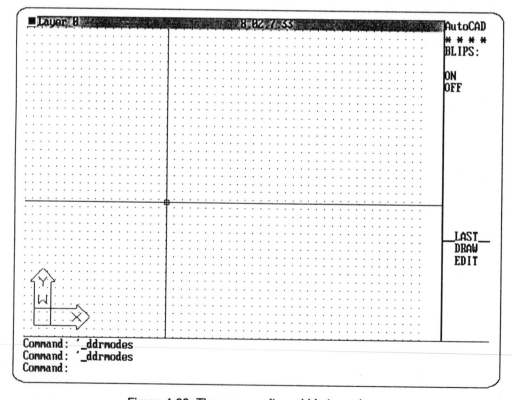

Figure 4.38 The screen after grid is turned on.

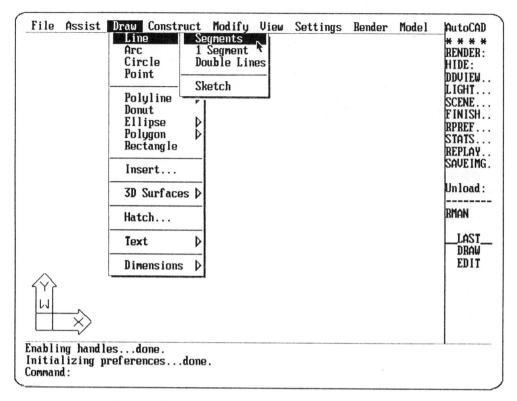

Figure 4.39 Selecting Line from the Draw Pull-down Menu.

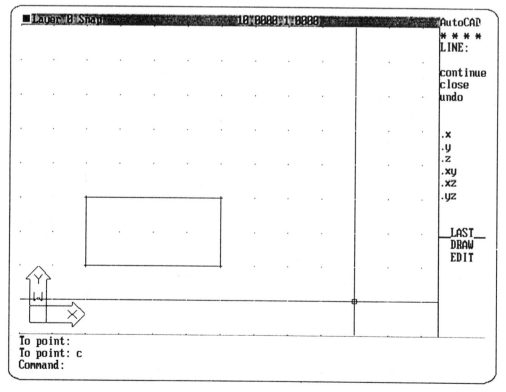

Figure 4.40 Drawing lines using grid and snap.

Drawing Lines: Exercise 4.5

1. After selecting **LINE,** then **Segments** from the Draw Pull-down Menu, a prompt displays:

From point:.

The beginning point of the line must be input. Move the cursor to a position on the screen and pick a point. A small marker (+) or blip is displayed, if blips are set ON, indicating the start point of the line. Figure 4.40.

2. A new prompt reads:

To point:.

Moving the cursor causes a "rubberband" line to stretch from the marker on the first point to the present position of the cursor (Figure 4.40). The mouse-pick button locates the endpoint of the line at the present position of the cursor.

3. Further movement of the cursor causes the rubberband line to stretch from the end point of the first line to the new cursor position (Figure 4.41). The prompt reads:

To point:.

If a single line is all that is needed, selecting **RETURN, SPACE BAR,** or the cancel command **CTRL-C** ends the line command and returns to the command prompt.

After a point is picked, the coordinate value displayed in the upper part of the screen lists the location. The Coords Toggle (**F6** or **Ctrl-D**) receives a continuous readout of the coordinate location of the cursor.

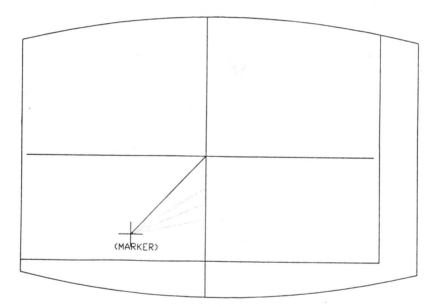

Figure 4.41   The start point of a line is marked by a blip (+) or marker. Movement of the cursor to place the end point of a line causes a rubberband line to stretch from the blip.

Drawing a 2D Line Using Snap And Grid

Accurately placed lines are created using a snap and grid for reference. When the **SNAP** mode is on, the cursor jumps to the snap points. If the grid is set equal to the snap, the cursor snaps to the grid points. A 2x4 rectangle can be created with the **LINE** command by using the grid and snap features of AutoCAD. Figure 4.40 and the following steps can be used as an example:

Drawing Lines Using Grid & Snap: Exercise 4.6

1. Turn the **SNAP** command on by pressing **F9** or **CTRL-B.** The default setting of 1.00 will be used. Snap is displayed in the status line at the top of the screen. Figure 4.40.

2. Turn the **GRID** command on by pressing **F7** or **CTRL-G.** The default setting of 1.00 is used so that the snap and grid are equal. The screen immediately displays a one-unit grid.

3. Turn the Coords Toggle on by pressing **F6** or **CTRL-D**.
4. Select **LINE** and **Segments** from the **DRAW** Pull-down Menu.
5. Move the cursor to coordinate location 2.00, 2.00 and pick that point. Notice that the cursor jumps to every grid point located on the screen when moved.
6. Move the cursor to coordinate location 6.00, 2.00 and pick the point.
7. Move the cursor to coordinate location 6.00, 4.00 and pick that point.
8. Move the cursor to coordinate location 2.00, 4.00 and pick the point.
9. Move the cursor to coordinate location 2.00, 2.00 and pick the point and press **RETURN** or choose **CLOSE** from the menu or type **C**. **CLOSE** automatically draws the last line in a closed polygon.

Drawing 2D Lines Using Ortho

The Ortho Mode can create horizontal and vertical lines. The rectangle created in the previous example could have been drawn using **ORTHO**. Use of the Ortho command would have made the movement of the cursor much faster between points. The following steps describe how to use the Ortho command to draw lines:

Drawing Lines Using Ortho: Exercise 4.7
1. Turn the Ortho mode on by pressing **F8** or **CTRL-O**. Ortho is displayed in the status line located at the top of the screen.
2. Select **LINE** and **Segments** from the **DRAW** Pull-down Menu.
3. Move the cursor to coordinate position 2.00, 2.00 and pick the point.
4. Move the cursor to coordinate position 6.00, 2.00. Notice how the cursor reacts to movement. The rubberband line only moves parallel or perpendicular to the first point input. The cursor does not have to be located exactly on the grid point 6.00, 2.00. For example, move the cursor to coordinate location 6.00, 3.00 and select the pick button or **RETURN**. The line still is drawn horizontally to coordinate location 6.00, 2.00.
5. Complete the rectangle by moving and picking coordinate points 6.00, 4.00, 2.00, 4.00, and 2.00, 2.00 or **CLOSE** or **C**. Figure 4.40.

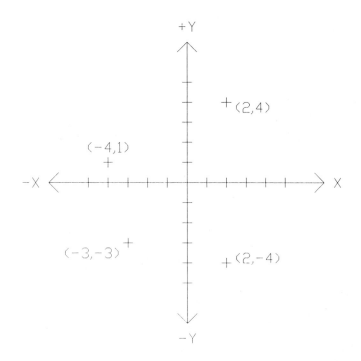

Figure 4.42 Cartesian coordinates.

Creating a 2D Line Using Absolute Coordinate Input

AutoCAD creates drawing entities by defining the coordinate locations of points. The Cartesian coordinate system (Figure 4.42) is used to define points with 2 perpendicular axes, X and Y. The intersection of the axes is called the origin and is assigned the values 0,0. The X-axis is represented by the horizontal line; positive values are assigned to points to the right and negative values to the left of the origin. The Y-axis is represented by the vertical line; positive values are assigned to points above the origin and negative values below the origin. The Z-axis is perpendicular to the screen through the intersection of the X- and Y-axes in the plan view, which is the default setting.

The location of the origin on the AutoCAD screen usually is near the lower left corner of the drawing area on the screen. The actual location of the origin is controlled by using the LIMITS command explained earlier in this chapter. AutoCAD's default prototype drawing assigns the lower left limit as the origin, 0,0, and the upper right as 12,9.

In the LINE command at the prompt: **From point:**, coordinate values can be entered from the keyboard. The start point of the line is specified using X,Y coordinate values for 2D drawings. A Z dimension could be added for 3D drawings. The numerical value for X must be input followed by a comma and the numerical value for Y and **RETURN**.

Creating Lines Using Absolute Coordinates: Exercise 4.8
A 4" horizontal line is created like this:
1. Select **LINE** and **Segments** from the **DRAW** Pull-down Menu.
2. A prompt reads:
From point:
Enter the values from the keyboard: **2, 2** then **RETURN**.
3. A prompt reads:
To point:
Enter the values from the keyboard: **6, 2** then **RETURN**.

To create a rectangle, input the following values at the line prompts:
From point: 2, 2 RETURN
To point: 6, 4 RETURN
To point: 2, 4 RETURN
To point: 2, 2 or CLOSE or C

This method of creating lines uses absolute coordinate values and draws the rectangle shown in Figure 4.40. All points are referenced from the origin of the AutoCAD display when using **absolute coordinates**.

Creating 2D Lines Using Relative Coordinate Values

For some individuals or certain situations, relative coordinate values may be easier to use when drawing lines. Relative coordinates specify the location of a point by entering coordinate values that are relative to the last point input and not the origin. The @ symbol must precede the coordinate values for AutoCAD to identify values as being relative: @X,Y RETURN. For 3D lines, the Z coordinate value is entered after Y.

Shown below are the relative coordinate values to create the rectangle drawn with relative coordinates in the previous example.

Creating Lines Using Relative Coordinates: Exercise 4.9
1. Select **LINE** and **Segments** from the **DRAW** Pull-down Menu.
2. A prompt reads:
From point:
Enter the values from the keyboard: **2, 2** then **RETURN**.
3. A prompt reads:
To point:
Enter the values from the keyboard: **@4, 0** then **RETURN**.
4. A prompt reads:
To point:
Enter the values from the keyboard: **@0, 2** then **RETURN**.

5. A prompt reads:
To point:
Enter the values from the keyboard: **@-4, 0** then **RETURN.**
6. A prompt reads:
To point:
Enter the values from the keyboard: **@0, -2** or **CLOSE** then **RETURN.** Figure 4.40.

Drawing Lines Using Polar Coordinate Values

For some situations, the use of relative polar coordinate values may be more useful. **Polar coordinates use both a distance and an angle to locate the end points of lines.** Figure 4.31 illustrates the angle convention used with AutoCAD, which can be changed by using the **UNITS** command explained earlier in this chapter.

To use relative polar coordinates, the distance preceded by the **@** symbol and the angle preceded by the less-than sign **(<)** must be input: **@DISTANCE<ANGLE**. Drawing the rectangle used in the previous examples with polar coordinate values is shown below.

Creating Lines Using Polar Coordinates: Exercise 4.10
1. Select **LINE** and **Segments** from the **DRAW** Pull-down Menu.
2. A prompt reads:
From point:
Enter the values from the keyboard: **2, 2** then **RETURN.**
3. A prompt reads:
To point:
Enter the values from the keyboard: **@4, <0** then **RETURN.**
4. A prompt reads:
To point:
Enter the values from the keyboard: **@0, <90** then **RETURN.**
5. A prompt reads:
To point:
Enter the values from the keyboard: **@-4, <180** then **RETURN.**
6. A prompt reads:
To point:
Enter the values from the keyboard: **@2, <270** or **CLOSE** then **RETURN.** Figure 4.40.

The following summarizes the various methods used to enter coordinates with AutoCAD.

COORDINATE		EXAMPLE
Cartesian Absolute	X,Y,Z	3,9,0
Cartesian Relative	@X,Y,Z	@2,5,1
Polar Absolute	Distance <Angle	5.25<45
Polar Relative	@Distance<Angle	@4<30
Cylindrical Absolute	Distance<Angle in XY Plane,Z Distance	4<45,4.5
Cylindrical Relative	@Distance<Angle in XY Plane,Z Distance	@6.5<30,4.5
Spherical Absolute	Distance<Angle in XY Plane<Angle	10<35<63
Spherical Relative	@Distance<Angle in XY Plane<Angle	@10<35<63
Last Point	@Specifies a zero offset from the last point	@
World	*Specifies world coordinate s	*4,2,7.5

The Close Subcommand

The **CLOSE** command connects the last point input with the first point input (the **From point:**) in a string of lines. It closes the last side of a polygon and terminates the string. The rectangle examples illustrated before used the **CLOSE** command as an alternative method of locating the last line of the rectangle. At the prompt: **To point:**, simply select **CLOSE** from the screen or tablet menu, or type **C** or **CLOSE**, and press **RETURN** to have the last line of a polygon drawn.

The Continue Subcommand

CONTINUE starts another string of lines from the end point of the last line or arc created. For example, after the rectangle is drawn and the string has been terminated, at the prompt **From point:**, select **CONTINUE** from the menu or tablet.

If the command prompt is displayed after drawing a string of lines, pressing **RETURN** twice is the same as using the **CONTINUE** command. Remember that **RETURN** repeats a command, which is **LINE** for this example. The second **RETURN** starts the new line from the endpoint of the last line.

ERASING ENTITIES

AutoCAD provides a number of different methods to erase entities after they have been placed on screen. This chapter explains the simplest of erase commands. More powerful features, such as erasing all entities in a window, are explained in Chapter 5. **UNDO, OOPS,** and **ERASE** are explained below.

The Undo and Redo Commands

UNDO erases connected entities in a string one at a time in reverse of the sequence in which they were drawn. **UNDO** must be used while the **LINE** or other drawing command is still active for the string. If the string is not active, **UNDO** cannot be used, and the **ERASE** command must be used. All lines of the rectangle can be erased by selecting **UNDO** four times. Entering a number after the **UNDO** command will undo that number of commands. For example, entering the number 4 causes the last four commands to undo. Using a very large number, such as 100, will undo all of your work. The **REDO** command reverses the effect of the **UNDO** command. **UNDO** also negates settings and system variables as well as drawn entities.

Undoing Lines: Exercise 4.11

1. Select **LINE** and **Segments** from the DRAW Pull-down Menu. Turn on the snap, grid, or coords if not already on.
2. Move the cursor to coordinate location 2.00, 2.00 and pick that point. Notice that the cursor jumps to every grid point located on the screen when moved.
3. Move the cursor to coordinate location 6.00, 2.00 and pick the point.
4. Move the cursor to coordinate location 6.00, 4.00 and pick that point.
5. Enter **U** then **RETURN**. Notice that the rubberband line stretches from the end of the first line 6,2 instead of 6,4. Undo can be used to erase the last point input. Entering **U** again would return the cursor to the start point.
6. Repeat steps 3 and 4.
5. Move the cursor to coordinate location 2.00, 4.00 and pick the point.
6. Move the cursor to coordinate location 2.00, 2.00 and pick the point and press **RETURN** or choose **CLOSE** from the menu or type **C**. **CLOSE** automatically draws the last line in the polygon.
7. Enter **U** for Undo to erase rectangle just drawn.
8. Enter **REDO** to return the rectangle to the screen.

It is possible also to mark a spot in the drawing session by using the **UNDO** option called **MARK**. All commands entered after the mark can be undone by using the **UNDO** command. A **MARK** should be placed before any type of action that might have a significant effect on the drawing, such as mirroring, copying, or other editing functions.

Erase

Using **UNDO** to erase lines works for some but not all errors or changes made on a drawing. AutoCAD provides an excellent and flexible method of erasing entities. **ERASE** is a submenu item of **EDIT**. **ERASE** also can be selected from the Pull-down Modify Menu. Notice that the Line Menu has Edit listed near the bottom so returning to the Root Menu to reach **ERASE** is not necessary. From the Root Menu, choose **EDIT**. The first page of the **EDIT** submenu displays the **ERASE** command. Selecting **ERASE** displays the **ERASE** menu shown in Figure 4.43. A prompt also is displayed; **Select objects.** The cursor changes from a plus (+) to a small square as shown in Figure 4.43. This square is referred to as the "PICKBOX." The size of the square is controlled by the **SETVAR** command. To erase, an entity must be within the square cursor before the pick button is selected.

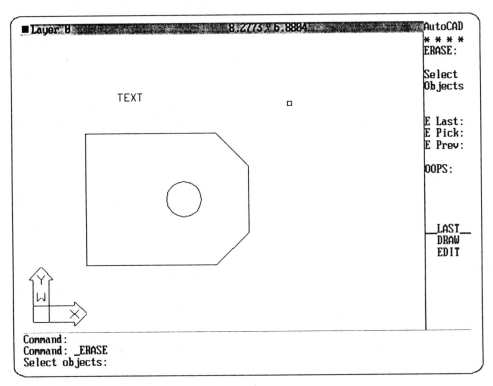

Figure 4.43 The Erase menu.

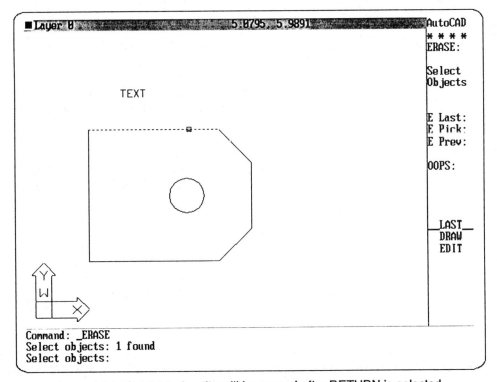

Figure 4.44 Highlighted entity will be erased after RETURN is selected.

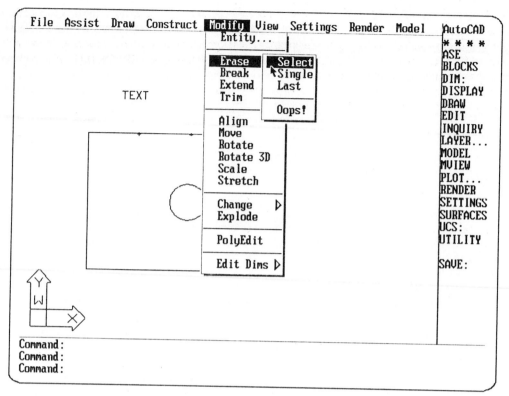

Figure 4.45 The Modify pull-down menu for erasing.

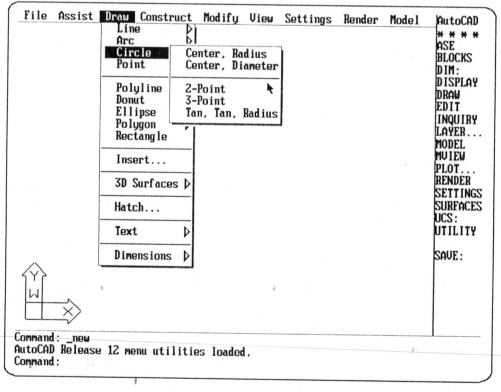

Figure 4.46 The Circle options.

The entity may be displayed as a series of dots after it is picked. For example, a solid line will change to a dotted line. Some hardware configurations will not show changes to the line. AutoCAD refers to this change as *highlighting.* Figure 4.44. The default mode for highlighting is on, but it can be turned off through the **SETTINGS** command **SETVAR.** The single entity is deleted by pressing **RETURN** or the **SPACE BAR** after picking with the cursor. If more than one entity must be deleted, move the target box over the other entities and select the pick button. After selecting all the entities, press **RETURN**. The Modify Pull-down Menu for **ERASE** deletes the entity immediately after picking without highlighting if the Single option is selected. Figure 4.45.

The following steps demonstrate the **ERASE** command:

Erasing Entities: Exercise 4.12
1. Open the file **ERASE** from the workdisk.
2. Pick **Select** from the Modify/Erase Pull-down Menu.
3. A prompt reads:
Select objects:.
Move the square cursor over the entity to be erased and pick it.
4. The solid line changes to a dotted line as shown in the figure, and a prompt will read:
1 found. To de-select an entity, enter **U** (undo) at the prompt.
A new prompt reads:
Select objects:.
5. Select the text string by moving the square cursor over the word TEXT and picking it.
6. Pick a point that does not contain any entities. A prompt reads:
Other corner:
If you move the cursor you will see a the cursor change into a expanding rectangle. Moving to the right causes a solid line rectangle to form. By totally encompassing an entity with the box then using the pick button, an entity can be erased. Partial enclosure of an entity will not erase unless the cursor is moved to the left. Moving to the left causes a dashed line rectangle to form. This is the crossing window function, which will delete any entities wholly or partially within the dashed line box.
5. Press **RETURN** or the **SPACE BAR** to erase the entities that have been selected.
6. Pick **Oops** from the Modify/Erase Pull-down Menu. All the erased entities will be returned to the screen.
6. Experiment with the other erase options found on the Pull-down Menu and the Undo option by entering **U**.

Oops

The **OOPS** command recovers entities erased. This command only recovers the most recently erased entities. When entities are erased, they are saved by AutoCAD. Executing **OOPS** restores them to the drawing. Once another **ERASE** is executed, the entities saved change, and **OOPS** restores only those from the most recent **ERASE.** The OOPS command is located on the Erase submenu, Pull-down Menu, or can be typed at the command prompt.

DRAWING CIRCLES

A circle is a basic geometric entity that is created with traditional tools by a compass or circle template. Circles are created with AutoCAD by using the **CIRCLE** command located on the **DRAW** submenu or by entering **CIRCLE** at the command prompt. The **CIRCLE** menu is displayed in Figure 4.46. AutoCAD provides five methods to create circles. The two most common methods, center-radius and center-diameter, are explained in this chapter.

The **Center, Radius** options create a circle by locating the center of the circle and a point on the circumference, or entering the size of the radius through keyboard input or by picking a point. The **Center, Diameter** command creates circles by locating the center point and inputting the diameter of the circle. The following steps demonstrate how to create circles with AutoCAD:

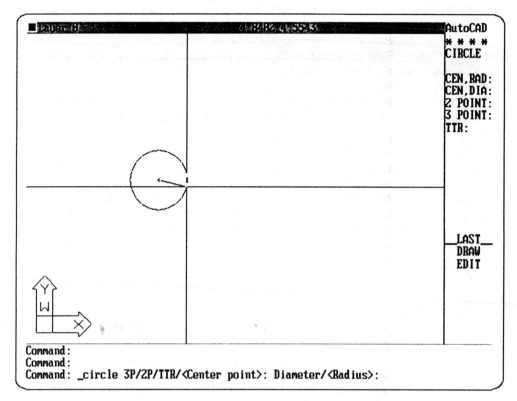

Figure 4.47 Drawing a circle using center point radius option.

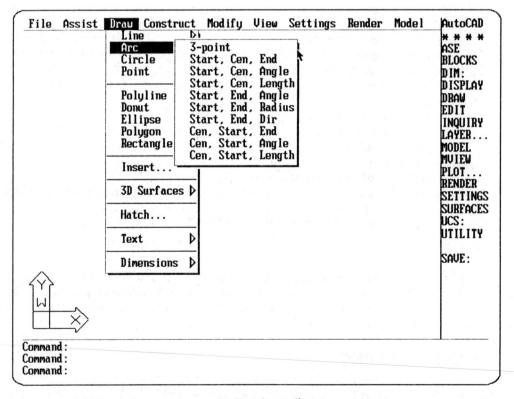

Figure 4.48 The Arc option.

Drawing Circles: Exercise 4.13

1. Load a new drawing to start with a blank screen.
2. Select **Center, Radius** from the Draw/Circle Pull-down Menu.
3. This command displays a prompt:

3P/2P/TTR/<Center point>:.

Center point is the default setting with the other circle drawing options listed in the prompt. The center point is located by inputting coordinate values or by picking a point on the

screen with the pointing device. Figure 4.47. A blip is displayed at the center point, if blips are on, and a prompt reads:

4. **Diameter/<Radius>:**

Enter the size of the radius from the keyboard and press **RETURN**. A point on the circumference of the circle could also be located by moving the cursor to the desired radius and picking the point. To specify a diameter instead of a radius, which is the default setting, type **D** at the prompt, press **RETURN** then enter the diameter.

5. Entering U will erase the circle. Experiment with the other circle drawing functions by repeating the command.

DRAWING ARCS

Arcs are created with AutoCAD through the **ARC** command located on the **DRAW** submenu or from the Draw Pull-down Menu. Figure 4.48. Ten different methods of creating arcs are provided by AutoCAD. Many of these methods are for special cases. For most uses the **S,C,E** (Start, Center, End) option is sufficient to locate the starting point of the arc (S), the center point of the arc (C), and the end point (E). Figure 4.49 and the following steps demonstrate one method to create an arc:

Drawing Arcs: Exercise 4.14

1. Open the drawing file **ARC** from the workdisk. Figure 4.49.
2. Select **Start, Center, End** from the Draw/Arc Pull-down Menu.
3. A prompt reads

Center/<Start point>:.

Locate the start point of the arc by moving the cursor to the desired position and pick it. A blip marks the point selected. Because the default method of creating arcs and circles is in a counter-clockwise direction, the first point selected for this example is important. Selecting the end point of the upper line in Figure 4.49 would result in the arc being drawn incorrectly.

4. **Center/End/<Second point>: c Center:**

The second point entered is the location of the center of the arc. Pick the location of the center point by locating the cursor and pressing the button. A blip will mark the center point on the screen.

5. **Angle/Length of chord/<End point>:**

The final point to be entered is the endpoint of the arc. For this example, the end of the upper line must be picked.

6. Enter U to erase the arc and experiment with other arc drawing options.

Moving the cursor after the second point is input results in a rubberband line and arc, as shown in Figure 4.49. The default setting is the automatic drag mode for some functions, such as the placement of arcs. The drag mode is turned on and off or set to automatic by typing **DRAGMODE** at the command prompt. It can also be changed by selecting **SETTINGS** from Root Menu.

SAVING A DRAWING

After work progresses on a drawing for a period of time, it should be saved. Saving avoids loss caused by a hardware or software failure or the loss of power to the computer. Although drawings are infrequently lost, saving the work every 15 to 20 minutes is a good habit to form. The **SAVE** command updates drawing files and returns

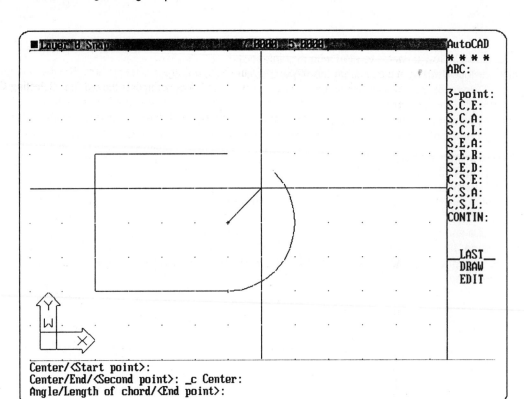

Figure 4.49 Drawing an arc.

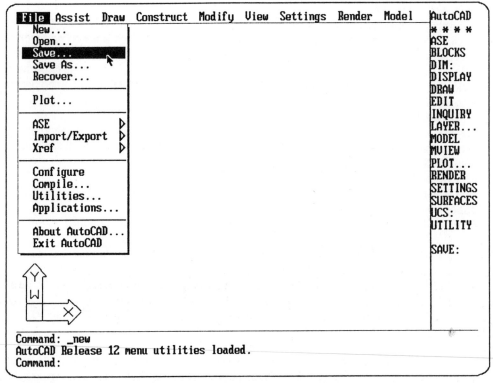

Figure 4.50 Selecting the Save command.

the user to the Drawing Editor to continue work on the drawing. This command provides the option to save the drawing under the same file name used to enter the Drawing Editor or to create another file.

Selecting **SAVE AS** from the File Pull-down Menu (Figure 4.50) displays a dialogue box, as shown in Figure 4.51. Typing a new file name and selecting **OK** creates a new file and does not update the old file. Selecting **OK** from the Pop-up Menu will save the drawing in the directory shown at the top using the file name displayed in the File box located near the bottom. To change the directory or file name, point at the area on screen to highlight it and type in a new name or directory. Selecting **Type it** from the Pop-up Menu closes the menu and allows the entry of a file name in the prompt line. The long rectangular box in the center of the Pop-up Menu displays the drawing files in the current directory. Point and click in the scroll bar with the input device to display more files.

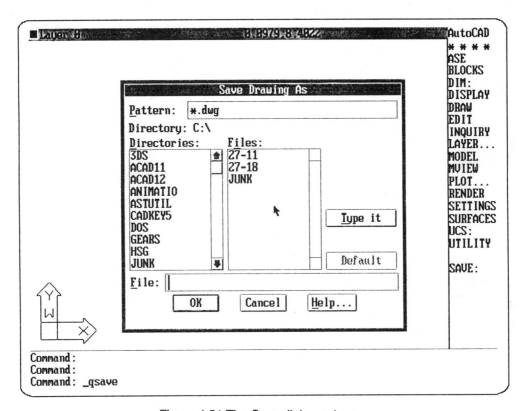

Figure 4.51 The Save dialogue box.

ENDING A DRAWING SESSION

To conclude a drawing session and save a drawing before exiting AutoCAD, use the **END** command, which is located on the Utility submenu. **END** saves the current drawing under the current drawing name and makes a backup file of the previous file. For example, a drawing called BRYAN created a few days ago is retrieved and edited today. The **END** command saves the edited drawing under the same name, BRYAN.DWG, and makes the original file a backup under the name BRYAN.BAK if the drawing was not saved during the editing session.

Selecting Exit AutoCAD from the File Pull-down Menu will end the drawing session. However, before ending the drawing session, a dialogue box will ask if you want to save the changes to the drawing since the last save, discard changes, or cancel the command. Figure 4.52. Pick the Save Changes... Button to end the session and save the drawing with changes.

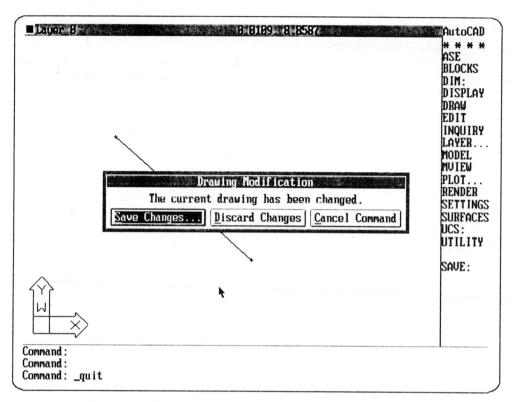

Figure 4.52 Saving changes to a drawing before exiting AutoCAD.

QUITTING A DRAWING SESSION

QUIT is a fast method to exit the Drawing Editor, but it does not save any work created during the drawing session. QUIT is located on the Utility submenu as is **End**. QUIT does not erase a previously saved drawing file; it simply does not update it. If a saved drawing is retrieved and changes are made to it, these changes can be discarded, and the original drawing is not altered after the **QUIT** command is used. **QUIT** will prompt, **Really want to discard all changes to drawing?** Type **Y** for yes and enter **RETURN** to discard all changes to a previous drawing or any work created on a new drawing. The Main Menu then is displayed.

THE FILE UTILITIES

AutoCAD provides a means of editing drawing files saved on a disk. Some of these procedures are similar to the DOS commands: Delete, Dir, and Copy. The advantage of using AutoCAD is that these operations can be performed within the AutoCAD program. Figure 4.53 shows the File Utility Dialogue Box, which is displayed after selecting Utilities... from the Files Pull-down Menu or by selecting Files: from the Utilities Screen Menu.

Selecting List Files... from the dialogue box displays the drawing files contained on a specified drive or directory. The drive letter followed by a colon (:) displays all the drawing files on the specified disk. Drawing files have **.DWG** as an extension. The directories can be changed by scrolling through them then picking one.

To erase files from a disk, use Delete files... Files can also be renamed by using Rename files... Files are copied by using Copy file... option.

Locking and Unlocking Files

AutoCAD can be used in a networked environment where two or more computers are electronically linked to share files. This means that it is possible for one user to try to load a drawing that is currently being worked on by another. To prevent this from happening, AutoCAD automatically locks a file that is currently being used and denies access to it except by the person who originally opened it. A locked file is unlocked using the File Utility Menu item, Unlock file.

Other Types of Files Created with AutoCAD

AutoCAD provides a method to create other types of files, which are useful to exchange files between different CADD systems and to create slides of drawings. Occasionally, a user might find the need to use an AutoCAD drawing with some other CADD software or to use a drawing file created on another system on AutoCAD. For example, an AutoCAD file can be saved in a form that can be used by a CAD/CAM system, such as Computervision or Intergraph, using the IGES (Initial Graphics Exchange Standard) format. IGES, DXF, Postscript, and Slide files are created by selecting them from the Utility submenu or by selecting Import/Export from the File Pull-down Menu, as shown in Figure 4.54.

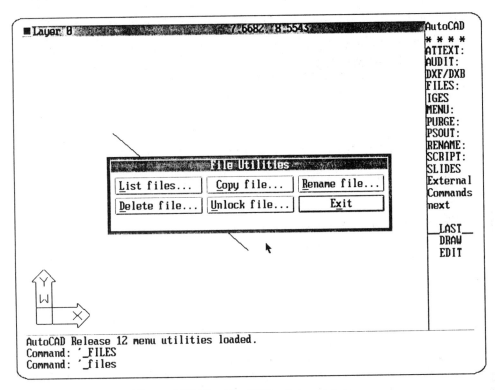

Figure 4.53 The File Utility dialogue box.

Reading and Creating IGES Files

From the Import/Export submenu two commands are available, **IGES in...** and **IGES out..**. Both options use a dialogue box to load or create the IGES file. IGES IN is used to read an IGES file into AutoCAD. IGES OUT is used to create an IGES file from an AutoCAD drawing. When the IGES file is created, the extender **.igs** is added to the file name.

Reading and Creating DXF and DXB Files

Another drawing interchange file created by AutoCAD is called a **DXF** file. A DXF file is used to exchange files between other microcomputer-based CADD programs, such as CADKEY and VersaCAD, and for desktop publishing programs, such as Ventura. A **DXB** file created from a program such as CAD/camera also can be read into AutoCAD. UTILITY submenu item **DXF** and **DXB** is used for this type of interchange files. To create a DXF file, the **DXF out** command is used. To read a DXF file created with another software program, the **DXF in** command is used. These files will have **.dxf** as the file name extender.

Creating Slide Files

Slide files are created with AutoCAD using **UTILITY** submenu command **SLIDES**. A slide file is similar to a picture of a drawing. These pictures or slides are combined with a written script to produce slide shows of drawings or text created with AutoCAD. The **SLIDE** command is used to make a slide using menu item **MSLIDE**. **SLIDES** are viewed by selecting menu item **VSLIDE**. The **MSLIDE** command creates a slide file with the extender **.sld**. Only those entities currently displayed on the screen will become part of the slide.

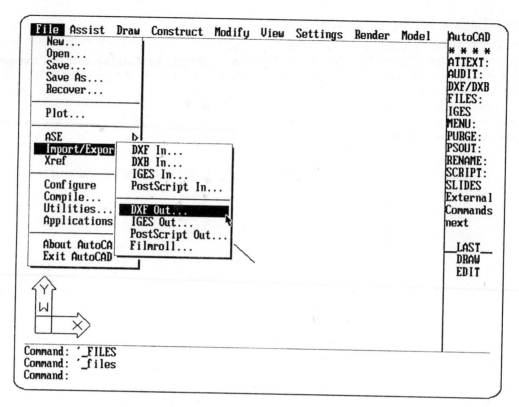

Figure 4.54 Saving a drawing to other file formats.

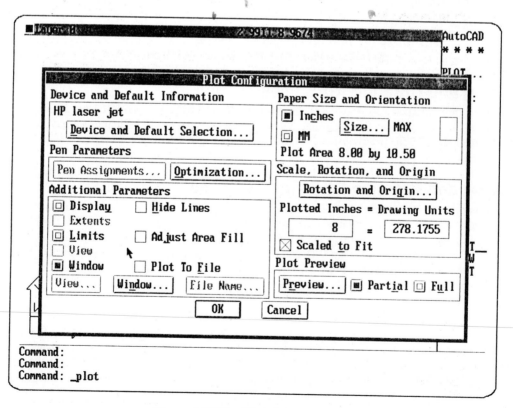

Figure 4.55 The Plot dialogue box.

PLOTTING AUTOCAD DRAWINGS

All CAD drawings can be created full scale. If the drawing is too big or small for the screen, use **ZOOM** to change the viewing window. The drawing is scaled when it is plotted. AutoCAD automatically changes the drawing units to plot units. Drawings are scaled by fitting the drawing to a specified drawing sheet. The preferred method is to specify plotted units = drawing units. For example, to scale a drawing to 1/4 size, enter **1 = 4** at the plot scale prompt. To scale a drawing 10/1, enter **10 = 1**.

AutoCAD provides many different options for creating plots and printer plots of drawings. Before plotting a drawing, AutoCAD must be configured for the plotter or printer plotter on the workstation. AutoCAD is configured for both a plotter and printer plotter using the File Pull-down Menu Command Plot or from the Root Menu Plot. A pop-up dialogue box is displayed, as shown in Figure 4.55.

There are four major steps when making a plot:

1. Selection of drawing area to plot under Additional Parameters in the Plot Dialogue Box.
2. Selection of paper size and orientation.
3. Selection of plot scale, rotation, and origin.
4. Selection of plotting device and default information.

There are 5 options to define the drawing area that is plotted are explained below using the drawing in Figure 4.56.

Plotting Using Display: Exercise 4.15

1. Open the drawing file PLOT.
2. Select PLOT from the File Pull-down Menu or from the Root Menu.
3. A pop-up dialogue box is displayed, as shown in Figure 4.55.
4. Pick the Display button under the Additional Parameters Heading.
5. Select the Plot Preview button to view the effective plotting area. The Preview pop-up dialogue box is displayed to show the paper size, and plotting area and if there are any warnings. Figure 4.57.
6. Pick the OK button on the Preview and plot configuration dialogue boxes to begin the plotting sequence. A prompt reads:

Effective plotting area: 7.57 wide by 10.50 high
Position paper in plotter.
Press RETURN to continue or S to Stop for hardware setup

7. Press RETURN to plot the drawing as shown in Figure 4.58.

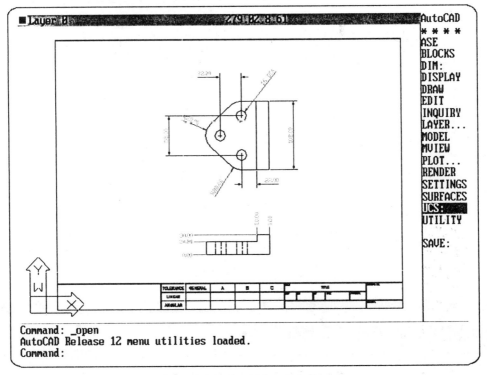

Figure 4.56 Drawing to be plotted.

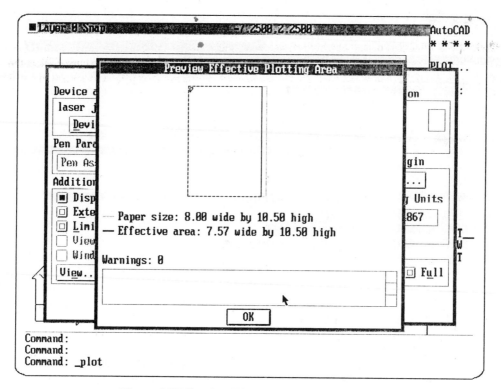

Figure 4.57 Preview Plot pop-up dialogue box.

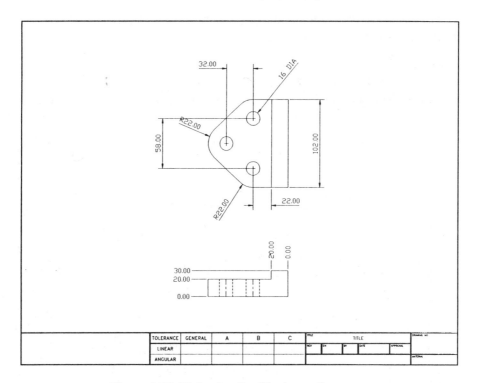

Figure 4.58 Plot using the Display option.

Extents plots those entities currently displayed. Before plotting an edited drawing using the **Extents** option, the **Zoom All** or **Zoom Extents** should be executed to get all the drawing to plot.

Limits plots all the entities in the defined limit area. Entities drawn outside of the limits of the drawing are not drawn. Figure 4.59 is an example of the same drawing plotted in Figure 4.56, except the **Limits** command was used.

View only plots a view as defined using the **View** Command from Root Menu Command Display. When using **View** to make a plot, the name of the view must be entered.

Window plots that part of the drawing defined by a window. With this selection a pop-up dialogue box is used to enter coordinate values for the window or a pick button can be selected to cursor select the window. Figure 4.60. A window is created by specifying a lower left and upper right corner point that will

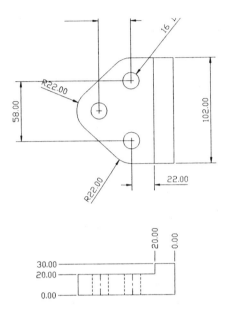

Figure 4.59 Plot using the Limits option.

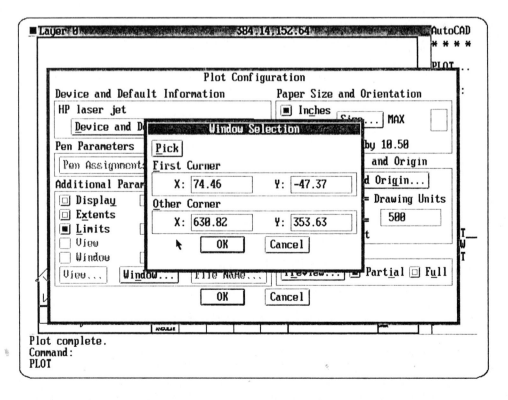

Figure 4.60 The window selection pop-up dialogue box.

create a rectangle. Figure 4.61. Any entity that appears within the window is plotted. This option is useful to make enlarged plots of small complicated parts. When using this command, AutoCAD requests that the first point be specified **First point:** A point is specified by entering X, Y coordinate values or, if in the Drawing Editor, by moving the cursor to the desired location. After the first point is specified, a second prompt reads:

Second point: Figure 4.62 shows a printer plot using the **Window** option.

A plot file can be created on a floppy disk instead of being sent directly to the plotter or printer. The floppy disk could then be taken to a workstation with a printer or plotter and the hardcopy made without AutoCAD software. A plot file is made by selecting Plot to File from the Additional Parameters section of the Plot Configuration Dialogue Box.

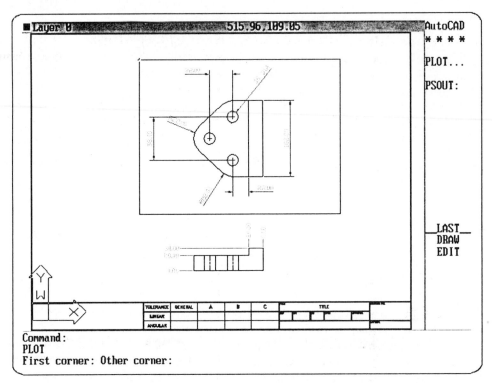

Figure 4.61 Picking the window to plot.

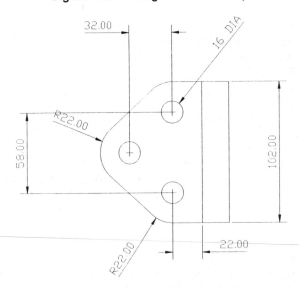

Figure 4.62 Plot using window.

Changing Plot Parameters

After the type of plot is selected, AutoCAD provides different plot variables that can be controlled. The plot parameters determine the paper size, plot units and origin, pen colors, pen widths, rotation angle, and so on. These variables are changed in the Plot Dialogue Box.

The plot scale is specified, such as 1/2"=1". The scale is determined automatically by AutoCAD to fit on the sheet when the Scaled to Fit button is selected from the Plot Dialogue Box. Layers are frozen to control the amount of information before plotting. Entities that are on layers that are frozen will not plot. Freezing layers is especially useful to make plots of architectural drawings because it can separate floor plans as well as, electrical, mechanical, and other plans. Layers are frozen using the Layer command before the Plot command is selected.

Controlling the Line Weight of Engineering Drawings

Engineering drawings use different line weights to promote clarity. Different line weights are assigned to AutoCAD drawings through a pen plotter. By assigning entities to each layer of a drawing, line weight is controlled. Layers are assigned colors, which are given different pen numbers in the **PLOT** command. The following standards are suggested for engineering drawings:

1. Color- white, pen number- 1, layer number 1, .7mm pen, visible, cutting plane, and short break lines.
2. Color- red, pen number- 2, layer number 2, .35mm pen, all other line types. (Hidden line types may be assigned a .5mm pen.)

The **PLOT** command is used to assign different pen numbers to the entity colors by selecting Pen Assignments from the Plot Dialogue Box.

The OSNAP Options

With traditional tools, geometry is added to a drawing by connecting endpoints of lines, drawing lines tangent to circles, and many other methods. This task is usually accomplished by positioning the straight-edge or compass between the entities and adding the line, arc, or circle. AutoCAD provides a method to connect new entities to the endpoints or tangents through the **OSNAP** (object snap) options. **OSNAP** provides a method of snapping to or attaching to existing entities. For example, sometimes it is important to start a new line from the endpoint of an existing line. Moving the cursor to the endpoint of the line and "eyeballing" it might produce a line that appears to attach to the endpoint of the existing line. However, to take advantage of AutoCAD's extreme accuracy, the **OSNAP** option should be used.

A user of AutoCAD must be able to use and understand the necessity of using **OSNAP** to create accurate drawings. Using the correct **OSNAP** option will result in accurate placement of entities relative to endpoints, intersection, midpoints, centers, perpendiculars, and tangents (Figure 4.63). **OSNAP** is selected from the second page of the Root Menu item **SETTINGS** or from the **ASSIST** Pull-down Menu (Figure 4.64) or by selecting the * * * * option from any menu in AutoCAD. The middle button on a three button mouse when pressed will result in the OSNAP Menu being displayed on screen.

When an **OSNAP** option is selected, the cursor turns into a target. The existing entity must fall within the target area to be selected. The size of the target or aperture can be controlled with the **SETTINGS** option called **APERTURE**. The target size can be set between 1 and 50 pixels in size. The default setting is 10 pixels. A pixel is the smallest dot that can be displayed on screen. Setting a large target makes the selection of an entity easy if there are not many entities on screen; however, it takes longer to find the point. A small target area will make it possible to find points more quickly and is more accurate on drawings with many entities, but more difficult to get the cursor to align with the desired entity.

OSNAP can be used with the LINE command to set a snap option without interrupting the drawing of the line by selecting * * * * from the menu, the **ASSIST** Pull-down Menu or by picking the center button on a three-button mouse. This method of selecting an **OSNAP** option will apply only to the next cursor pick. If there are many cursor picks using the same object snap option, select **OSNAP** from the **ASSIST** Pull-down Menu, then pick the option, such as intersections. The OSNAP option will remain in effect until turned off by selecting **NONE** from the OSNAP Menu. The following steps demonstrate how the **OSNAP** option is used:

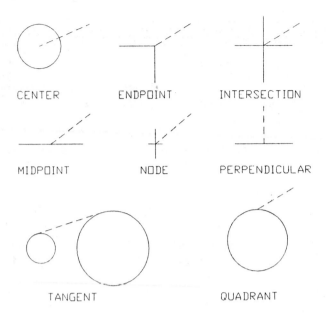

Figure 4.63 Examples of the **OSNAP** option.

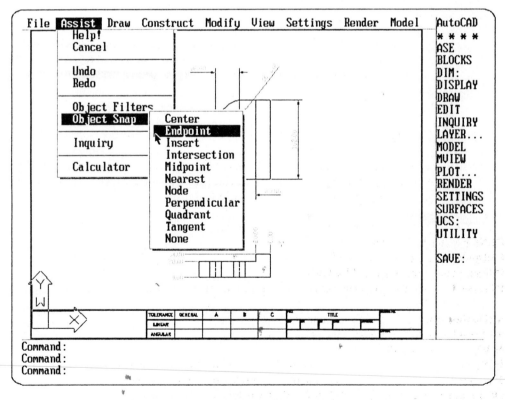

Figure 4.64 The OSNAP Pull-down Menu.

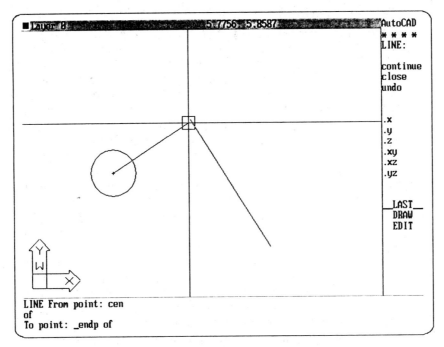

Figure 4.65 Using the **OSNAP** option endpoint.

Drawing A Line Using Osnap: Exercise 4.16

1. To draw a line from the center of a circle to the endpoint of the line shown in Figure 4.65, select **LINE** from the **DRAW** Menu.

2. A prompt reads:

From point:

Enter **CEN**, which is short for center, to set the object snap to seek the center of a circle.

3. The cursor displays the aperture target area. Move the target so that any part of the circle is inside the square area, then pick it. The start point of the line will snap to the center of the circle.

4. A prompt reads:

To point:

Enter **END**, which is short for endpoint, to set the object snap to seek the endpoint of a line.

5. The cursor displays the aperture target area. Move the target so that any part of the line is inside the square area, then pick it. Make sure that the target is closest to the endpoint of the line to which you want the line to snap.

The object snap options are listed and defined as follows:

CENter snaps to the center of arcs or circles.

ENDpoint snaps to the nearest end of an arc or a line.

INSert snaps to the origin of **BLOCKS** or text.

INTersec snaps to the intersection of two entities, such as two lines, an arc and a line, two circles, an arc and a circle, a line and a circle.

MIDpoint snaps to the middle of a line or an arc.

NEArest snaps to the nearest point on an entity.

NODe snaps to a **POINT** entity.

PERpend snaps to a point on a line that would create a line perpendicular to the existing entity.

TANgent snaps to an arc or a circle that is tangent from the last point picked.

QUAdrant snaps to the 0, 90, 180, or 270 degree point on a circle or an arc.

QUIck snaps to the first target point.

Setting a Running Object Snap

When planning to use a single or multiple object snap modes frequently, a running Osnap setting should be set. For example, suppose you are going to dimension a part and most of the dimensions are located using the endpoints of lines. A running Osnap set to Endpoint would be the best method to place the dimensions. Once a running object snap mode is set, it remains active until it is chagnged using the Osnap command. To set a single running Osnap mode, enter **OSNAP** at the command prompt, then enter the desired object snap, such as **End**. To set multiple running object snaps, enter **OSNAP** at the command prompt, then enter the first three letters of each object snap separated by commas, such as **Int,End** to set the mode to intersection and endpoint.

CREATING A PROTOTYPE DRAWING FOR ENGINEERING GRAPHICS

AutoCAD has a default prototype drawing called ACAD.DWG. This drawing has all the default settings as listed in Appendix C. AutoCAD's default setting may not be the one you need to create an engineering drawing. Instead of changing the parameters necessary to create an engineering drawing every time a new drawing is started, a prototype drawing file can be created. This prototype drawing then can be loaded with each new engineering drawing, which will have the settings you need. The following steps describe how to create a prototype drawing with default settings useful for engineering drawings:

Creating a Prototype Drawing: Exercise 4.17

1. Begin a new drawing file by selecting New from the File Pull-down Menu.
2. Enter the drawing file name **ENG-B**.
3. Select **Units Control** from the Settings Pull-down Menu.
4. Pick the Engineering button from the Units Control Dialogue Box to set the units to engineering.
5. Pick the number of digits for the engineering units from the Precision box by selecting the three decimal place option.
6. Set the system of angle measure to decimal degrees by selecting it from the dialogue box.
7. Pick the OK button to complete the unit selections.

Select a paper size to be used for this prototype drawing. For this example, a B-size sheet is selected. Different prototype drawings can be created for each size sheet if needed.

1. Select Drawing Limits from the Settings Pull-down Menu.
2. Use the default setting of 0,0 for the lower left corner by entering **RETURN** at the first prompt.
3. Enter **17,11** to set the upper right limit for a B-size sheet at the prompt line.
4. Enter **ZOOM** at the command prompt, then **ALL** to display the new drawing limits.

The next step is to create new layers, colors, and linetypes for an engineering drawing. The following is a list of layer names and properties recommended for an engineering drawing.

Layer Name	Color	Linetype
0	White 7	Continuous
Hidden	Green 3	Hidden
Center	Magenta 6	Center
Object	White 7	Continuous
Text	White 7	Continuous
Dimension	Yellow 2	Continuous
Border	Blue 5	Continuous
Section	Red 1	Continuous

1. Enter **LAYER** at the command prompt.
2. Enter the new layer names separated by commas.
HIDDEN,CENTER,OBJE CT,TEXT,DIMENSI ON,BORD ER,SECTIO N
3. Set the new colors for each layer by entering **COLOR.**
4. Enter **3** (green).
5. Enter the layer name **HIDDEN.**
6. Enter **COLOR.**
7. Enter **6** (magenta).
8. Enter the layer name **CENTER.**
9. Enter **COLOR.**
10. Enter **2** (Yellow).
11. Enter the layer name **DIMENSION.**
12. Enter **COLOR.**
13. Enter **5** (Blue).
14. Enter the layer name **BORDER.**
15. Enter **COLOR.**
16. Enter **1** (Red).
17. Enter the layer name **SECTION.**

The linetypes for each layer must be set.
1. Enter **LTYPE** at the Layer Prompt.
2. Enter **HIDDEN** for the linetype.
3. Enter **HIDDEN** for the layer to assign the hidden linetype.
4. Enter **LTYPE** to repeat the command.
5. Enter **CENTER** for the linetype.
6. Enter **CENTER** for the layer to assign the center linetype.
7. Check the layers you have just created by entering **?** at the Layer Prompt, then **RETURN.** The text screen will display the layer listings.
Other settings can be changed if desired.
1. Enter **SNAP** at the command prompt.
2. Enter **.25** to change the snap setting.
3. Select **F6** to turn the coordinate display on.
4. Enter **LTSCALE** to set the linetype scale.
5. Enter **.5** to set the linetype scale.
6. Enter **END** at the command prompt to save the prototype drawing.

To use the engineering prototype drawing just created, a new drawing file must be started. Select New from the File Pull-down Menu. Enter the name of the new drawing, followed by an equal sign and the name of the prototype drawing. For example, to create a new drawing named TOOLREST using the newly created prototype drawing enter **TOOLREST=ENG-B**. This new drawing will have all the default settings created in the prototype drawing ENG-B.

QUESTIONS FOR REVIEW

1. Name the four important parts of the AutoCAD screen.
2. List the four methods used to make AutoCAD command selections.
3. Identify the information displayed in the status line.
4. List three methods to control cursor movement.
5. List four functions of the keyboard.
6. Describe how the print echo is turned on and off.
7. Define the function of the Root Menu.
8. Explain transparent commands.
9. Explain a cursor.
10. Explain defaults.

11. Describe a prototype drawing.
12. Describe blips and how are they removed from the screen.
13. Identify the command used to list AutoCAD default settings.
14. Explain why a grid is used.
15. Name the ortho toggle.
16. Explain how relative coordinates are different from absolute coordinates.
17. Define polar coordinates.
18. Explain the difference between **SAVE**, **END**, and **QUIT**.
19. List the four major steps to make a print or plot of a drawing.
20. Explain how line weight of engineering drawings are controlled with AutoCAD.
21. List the AutoCAD transparent commands.
22. List the Control key commands.
23. Describe the use for **OOPS**.

DRAWING ASSIGNMENTS

1. Do those drawings assigned by your instructor using the dimensions shown. Do not dimension, save the drawings on disk, and plot.
2. From Giesecke et al. *Technical Graphics 9th ed.* Instrument drawing problems from Chapter 2.
3. Create a prototype drawing for an A-, B-, C-, and D-size engineering drawing.

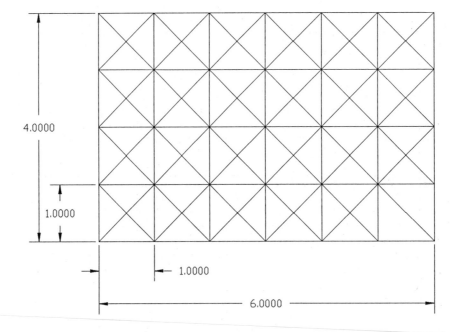

Figure 4.66 Lines.

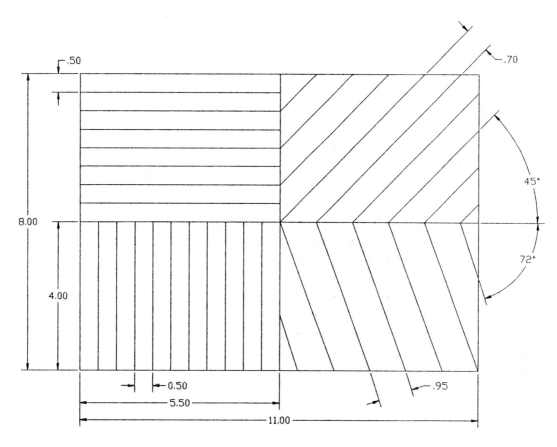

Figure 4.67 More lines.

Figure 4.68 Circles and arcs.

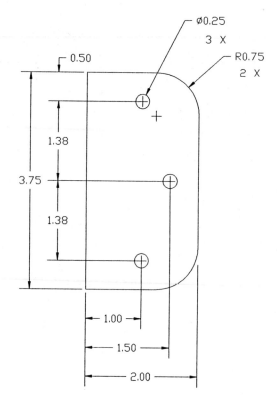

Figure 4.69 Hinge Plate.

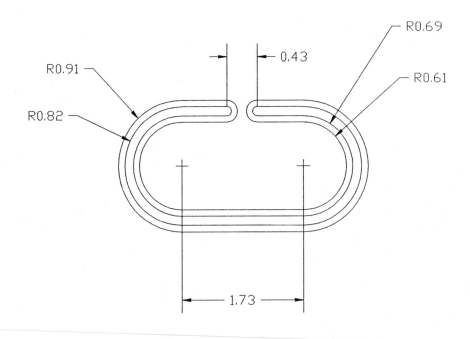

Figure 4.70 Link.

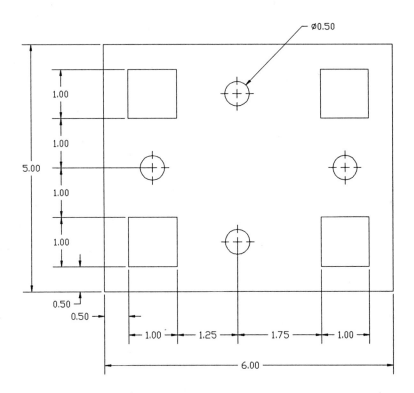

Figure 4.71 Centering Plate.

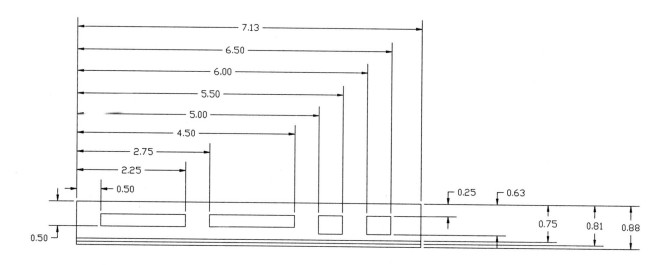

Figure 4.72 Front Panel.

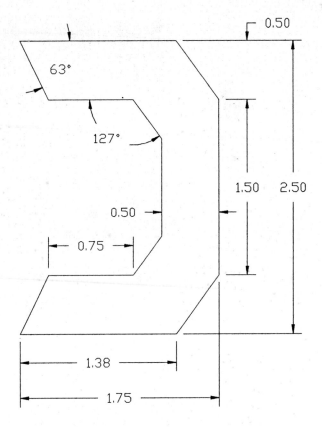

Figure 4.73 Locator.

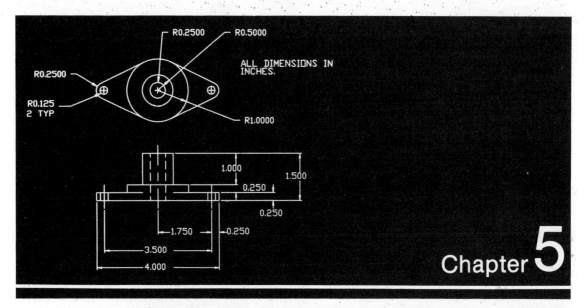

GEOMETRIC CONSTRUCTION AND EDITING

Creating two-dimensional engineering drawings requires some knowledge of geometric construction, which is based on plane geometry. Common figures include points, lines, arcs, circles, and polygons. The knowledge of geometric construction can be used to solve of many drawing and design problems.

The solution of some geometric construction problems can take considerable time by traditional methods. Creating a pentagon is accomplished by dividing the circle into five equal parts. Drawing circles or arcs tangent to circles, arcs, and lines also can be quite time-consuming using traditional tools. Most CADD software has automated many of the geometric construction tasks. AutoCAD provides flexible and powerful means of constructing geometry for engineering drawings.

This chapter is an introduction to using AutoCAD for creating complex geometry, performing complex geometric construction, and editing geometry. Many complex geometric construction tasks are solved very easily with AutoCAD. Figure 5.1 is an example of a complex geometric figure that can be created with AutoCAD. Included in this chapter are the useful copy and mirror commands. The techniques and applications explained are used throughout the remainder of the text. The concepts are extremely important for the successful use of CADD in creating engineering drawings.

OBJECTIVES

After completing Chapter 5, you will be able to:
1. Place points on a drawing,
2. Create filled or unfilled lines of a specified width (Traces),
3. Create a connected sequence of lines and arc segments called Polylines,
4. Create arcs and circles,
5. Create polygons and ellipses,
6. Create filled rings and circles,
7. Create solid or hollow quadrilaterals or triangles,
8. Snap to any existing entity or point on the entity,
9. Edit existing entities, including erasing, trimming, copying, mirroring, stretching, exploding, inserting, **dividing, measuring, extending, and changing** some of the characteristics of entities,
10. Draw parallel and perpendicular lines,
11. Bisect and divide lines into equal parts,
12. Draw lines and circles tangent to existing entities,
13. Draw irregular curves and splines.

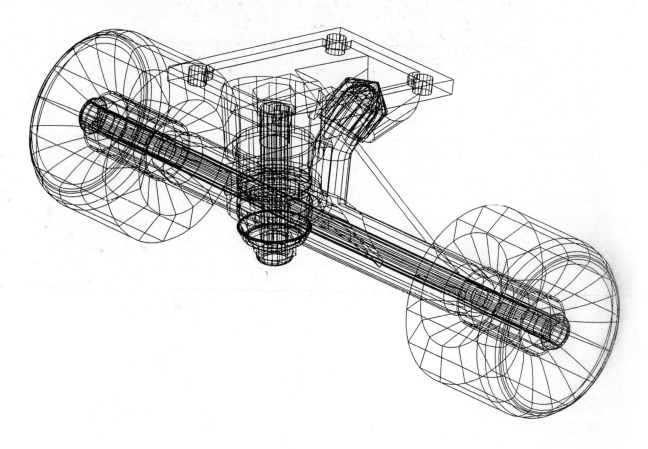

Figure 5.1 Complex geometric shapes can be created with AutoCAD. (Courtesy of Autodesk, Inc.)

PLACING POINTS ON A DRAWING

A point has no length or width but is represented on a drawing by a small dot. Points are used to construct more complex geometric shapes. AutoCAD provides different graphic representations of points by selecting **COMPLEX POINTS** example from the Point Menu, as shown in Figure 5.2. These points also can be drawn at different sizes. The **POINT** command is located on the second page of the Draw Menu. Points can act as **NODES** for entity construction using **OSNAP**.

Representing Points: Exercise 5.1

1. Open file **LAB5-1**. Zoom into the upper-left part of the drawing sheet using the **ZOOM** command. To create a point, enter **POINT** at the command prompt, or select it from the Draw Menu. A prompt reads:
Point:
2. Select the point by entering X, Y coordinate values separated by a comma, such as **4, 5**, or by moving the cursor to the desired position and pressing the pick button on the input device.
3. A blip (+) will appear on the screen at the selected position. A **REDRAW** removes the blip and leaves a very small dot on the screen. This small dot is the default point display setting.

The following steps demonstrate how to change the type of point displayed:

Changing the Displayed Point: Exercise 5.2

1. Zoom out then zoom into 5.2 on the drwaing sheet. Select Point from the Draw Pull-down Menu. Pick **Pdmode** from the on-screen menu located on the right. A prompt is displayed:

New value for PDMODE <0>:

The current default setting is displayed in the brackets.

2. Selecting **Type and Size...** from the Point submenu displays all the points in a dialogue box, as shown in Figure 5.2.

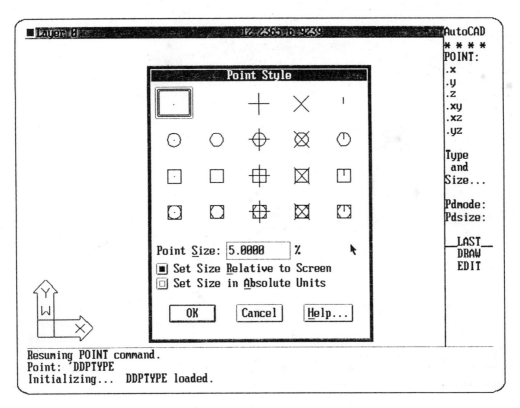

Figure 5.2 AutoCAD point options.

3. Click on the desired point to be displayed by pointing at it with the mouse then picking the OK button.

4. Enter **POINT** at the command and place a few points on screen by picking a position with the cursor.

The size of the points displayed is controlled using the Point submenu command **PDSIZE.**

Changing the Point Size: Exercise 5.3

1. The size can be set relative to the screen or in absolute units by picking the respective buttons from the Points dialogue box. Selecting **Points** from the Draw Pull-down Menu then **Type and Size...** displays the Point Dialogue box.

2. Enter the new value in the Point Size box then pick the OK button. When set to size relative to screen the number entered is a percent of the screen size. When set to size in absolute units the number entered is the current units. Figure 5.3 shows points drawn using different sizes relative to screen size.

3. At the command prompt enter **POINT** and add a few points using the new size.

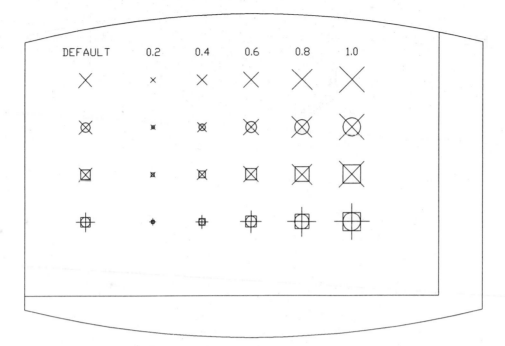

Figure 5.3 Different point sizes created with **PDSIZE**.

CREATING PARALLEL LINES

To create parallel lines separated by a specified distance, use the **LINE** command to draw separate lines. However, AutoCAD provides a command called **TRACE** that can be used to draw lines of a specified width. In addition, the space between the lines can be filled. Traces are created like lines, except the **TRACE** command is used, and the distance between the lines must be entered. Another method of creating parallel lines is to use the Double Line option or the Entity Grip option Copy. The alternative and preferred method to create parallel lines is to use **OFFSET**. All four methods are explained starting with **TRACE**.

Drawing Parallel Lines Using TRACE: Exercise 5.4

1. To create parallel lines enter **TRACE** at the command prompt, or select it from the Draw submenu located on the screen or the tablet.

Trace width <.0500>:
The default setting or the current setting is displayed in the brackets.

2. To define a new width, enter a number, such as **.25** and press RETURN. The new width could also be defined by selecting two points with the cursor.

3. **From Point:** Enter the coordinate values, such as **1,2,** or move the cursor to the desired starting point. A small blip is displayed on screen at the chosen point.

4. **To point:** Enter the second point using the cursor position or coordinate values, such as **3,4**. Another blip is displayed, but the lines will not be drawn until a third point is selected or RETURN is entered. The points specified are located at the center between the end points.

The trace is solid unless the Fill mode is turned off. Figure 5.4 shows filled and unfilled parallel lines created using **TRACE**. The initial setting for trace lines is with **FILL** on. The Fill mode is turned off by selecting **FILL OFF** from the Trace submenu or by typing **FILL** at the command prompt. Using **TRACE** for parallel lines should only be used for construction purposes because of its limitations.

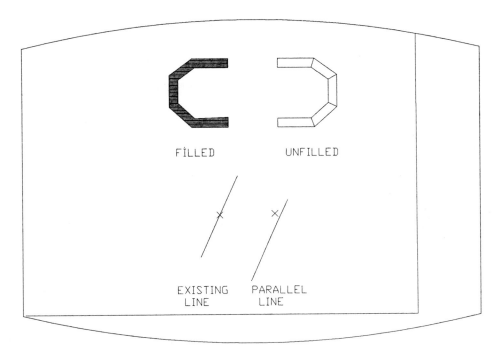

Figure 5.4 Filled and unfilled parallel lines using **TRACE** and **OFFSET** commands to create a line parallel to an existing line.

PARALLEL LINES USING OFFSET

The preferred method of creating parallel lines is through the use of the **OFFSET** command. The **OFFSET** command creates a line entity parallel to an existing entity by entering a distance or specifying a point, as shown at the bottom of Figure 5.4.

Drawing Parallel Lines Using OFFSET: Exercise 5.5

1. The **OFFSET** command is an Edit Menu item and is selected from the menu, picking it from the Construct Pull-down Menu, or by entering it at the command prompt.

2. **Offset distance or Through <Through>**
The bracket displays the last distance entered or **Through** if there is none. A distance can be entered at the prompt, such as 2, or **T** for specifying a distance with the pick device.

3. **Select object to offset:**
Pick the line as shown in Figure 5.4.

4. **Side to offset:** is displayed if a distance was entered or **Through point** if the **Through** option was selected.
This prompt is requesting at which side of the existing line to place the new parallel line. Move the cursor to one side or the other, such as the right, and pick that point. A parallel line is drawn. Figure 5.4.

Drawing Parallel Lines Using DOUBLE LINE: Exercise 5.6

1. The Double Lines option will draw two lines similar to the trace command except there is no fill option and there are many different ways to create the line. Select the Draw Pull-down Menu then Line then Double Lines or enter **DLINE** at the command prompt.

2. A prompt reads:
Break/Caps/Dragline/offset/Snap/Undo/Width/<start point>:
Enter **W** to set the width of the double line. This would be the distance between the parallel lines. For this example enter **1**.

3. The default setting is to draw two lines which are centered about the picked points. To change it so that the picked points are one of the parallel lines enter **D** for the Dragline option then **R** for the right option.

4. Turn the Caps option off by entering **C** then None.
5. Pick the start point of the lines then the end point then RETURN. Two parallel lines are drawn on screen, as shown in Figure 5.5.

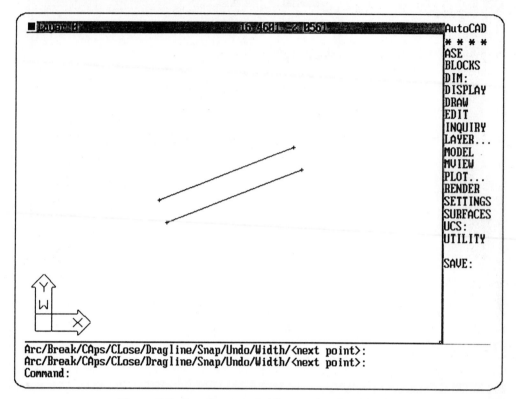

Figure 5.5 Creating parallel lines using Double Lines.

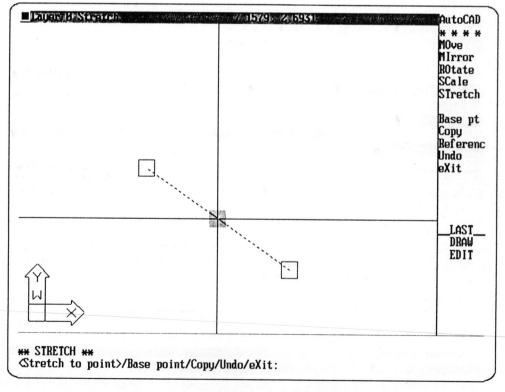

Figure 5.6 Line after picking a grip point.

Drawing Parallel Lines Using Entity Grips: Exercise 5.7

1. Open file **LAB5-2.** At the command prompt pick the line that is to be drawn parallel with the pick device. The grips will appear as small squares located at the ends and the center of the line. Pick the middle grip point with the input dvice. The entity grips are displayed as squares. Figure 5.6.

2. A prompt reads:

<Stretch to point>/Base point/Copy/Undo/eXit:

Enter **C** to make a copy of the picked line.

3. Pick a point on either side of the given line to create new line that is parallel to it.

4. Enter **X** to exit the copy sequence. Figure 5.7.

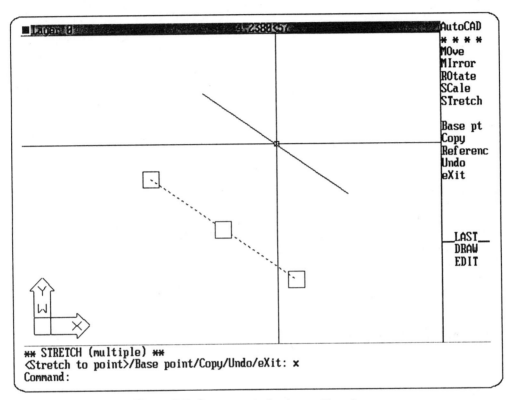

Figure 5.7 Copy created using entity grips.

SNAPPING TO EXISTING ENTITIES

A line drawn from an existing point or some other entity is accomplished using traditional tools by simply positioning the straight-edge through the given entity before adding the line. AutoCAD provides a method of drawing entities from existing entities through the Object Snap functions. These commands can snap to existing entities in much the same way as the **SNAP** command is used to lock onto a grid or other coordinate points. The Object Snap functions snap to end points, centers, midpoints, intersections, and other positions of existing entities on a drawing, as described in Chapter 3. These functions are used to produce complex geometric construction.

The **OSNAP** command activates the object snap. **OSNAP** can be used whenever AutoCAD requests a point. For example, in creating a line, AutoCAD requests a start point and subsequent points for the string of lines. Object Snap is used for any or all of the point choice requests.

Object Snap is activated in a number of ways:

1. One method is to enter an **OSNAP** function, such as **CENTER,** when AutoCAD requests the entry of a point.

2. Another way is to use the **SETTINGS** command from the Root Menu to preset an Object Snap function by selecting **OSNAP** from the **SETTINGS** submenu. The **OSNAP** Menu displays the eleven Object Snap functions. Selecting an Object Snap function through the **SETTINGS** Menu makes that setting active whenever AutoCAD requests that a point be entered.

3. A third method of selecting an Object Snap function is to select * * * * from the screen menu when AutoCAD requests a point to be entered. The fourth method is to pick the center button on a three-button mouse. The **OSNAP**

Menu is displayed, which can be used to select the snap option necessary to locate a point. Setting the object snap in this manner activates that Object Snap function for only one point. Subsequent points entered are not affected.

When an **OSNAP** option is activated, the cursor displays a target area in the form of a square to act as a guide in picking points (Figure 5.8). For example, to draw a line from the end point of an existing line using the

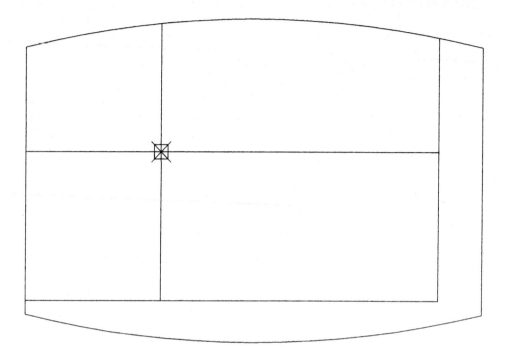

Figure 5.8 Object snap target area represented by a small square.

ENDPOINT option, the end point of the line or any point of the line between the midpoint and desired end point must be located inside of the target, as shown in Figure 5.9. The size of the target is controlled by the APERTURE command.

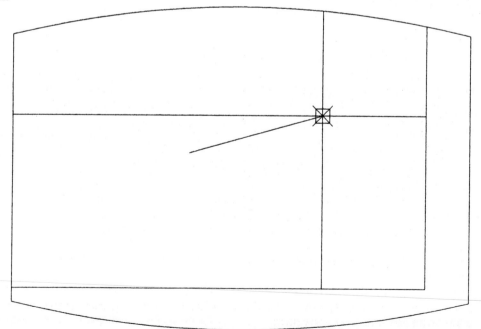

Figure 5.9 Locating the end point of a line in the target area.

The **APERTURE** command is activated by typing it in at the command prompt.

A prompt is displayed.

Object snap target height (1-50 pixels) <10>:

The number in brackets is the default or current setting. Enter the number desired and press **RETURN**. The larger the number entered, the larger the target area. Smaller settings are necessary to increase AutoCAD's search time and to make the Object Snap command more discriminating on complicated drawings with many entities. To compare the relative sizes of aperture settings, Figure 5.10 displays two different settings.

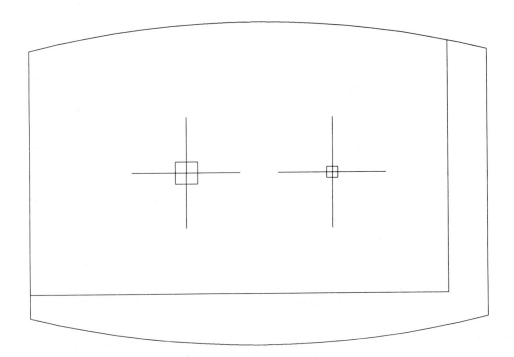

Figure 5.10 Aperture settings of ten and five.

BISECTING A LINE

The Object Snap mode includes different options that can assist in the placing of entities on a drawing. Through the Object Snap mode, many geometric construction problems can be solved, such as bisecting a line. AutoCAD automates many of the more difficult or time-consuming geometric construction tasks. The **OSNAP** command **MIDPOINT** and the **LINE** or **POINT** command is used to bisect a given line.

Bisecting a Line: Exercise 5.8

Figure 5.11 and the following steps describe how to bisect line A-B using AutoCAD.

1. Enter **LINE** at the command prompt or pick it from one of the menus.

2. **From point:**

Move the cursor to the start point of the line C and enter the position.

3. **To point:**

Select * * * * from the screen menu, or use any of the methods previously described to display the **OSNAP** Menu.

4. Select **MIDpoint** from the screen menu or type **MID** and RETURN.

5. The target cursor is displayed. Move the target cursor so that it contains some portion of the given line and select that point.

6. A new line is drawn from the first point C to the midpoint of the given line A-B. Figure 5.12.

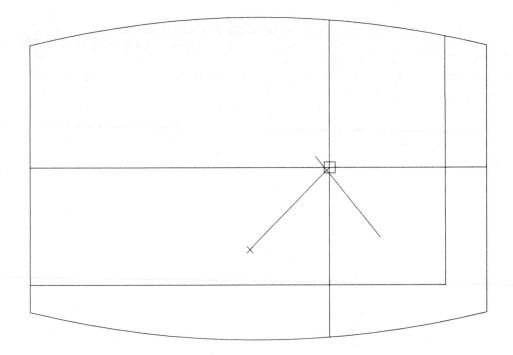

Figure 5.11 Bisecting a line using the **MIDPOINT** command.

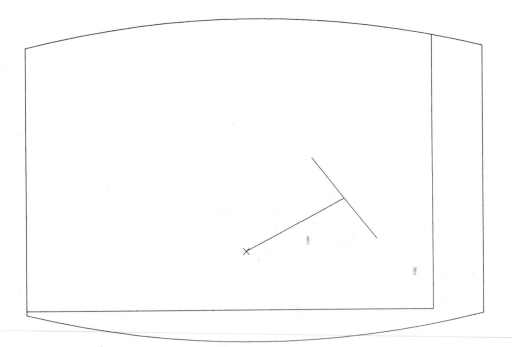

Figure 5.12 A line drawn to the midpoint of the given line.

Bisecting a Line or Arc Using Midpoint: Exercise 5.9

1. The bisector of a line or arc can be found by simply placing a point using the OSNAP option MIDpoint. Enter **PDMODE** from the command prompt.
2. Enter a new value of 3 for the type of point to be displayed.
3. Select Point from the Draw Pull-down Menu.
4. Enter **MID** at the **Point:** prompt to activate the midpoint OSNAP option.
5. Pick the line then the arc. A small X is placed at the midpoint of the line and arc. Figure 5.13.

    An alternate method would be to use entity grips to first select the line and arc at the command prompt, then use the point command to place a point at the midpoint entity grip.

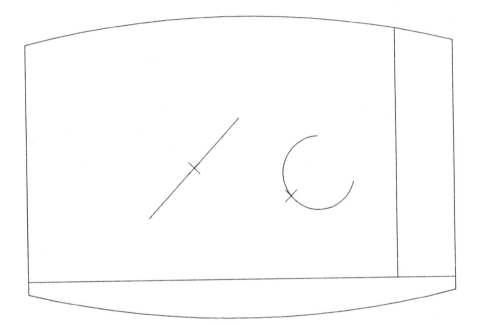

Figure 5.13 Finding the midpoint of a line.

BISECTING AN ANGLE

One method of bisecting an angle is to draw a circle tangent to the two sides of the angle, then draw a line from the vertex of the angle through the center of the circle. Figure 5.14, and the following steps can be used to bisect an angle.

Bisecting an Angle Using a Circle: Exercise 5.10

1. Given angle ABC, shown in Figure 5.14, draw a circle of any diameter tangent to the lines. Before drawing the circle, it is recommended to change linetype from solid to dot and the layer. Select **CIRCLE** from the Draw Menu or type it at the command prompt.
2. **CIRCLE 3P/2P/TTR/<Center point>:**
Select **TTR** from the menu or enter it from the keyboard.
3. **Enter Tangent spec:**
Pick one of the lines of the angle.
4. **Enter second Tangent spec:**
Pick the other line of the angle.
5. **Radius:**
Input the radius of the circle. Any radius can be used; however, a small radius such as the one shown in the figure as a dotted circle is preferred.

6. After the circle has been created, the angle is bisected by selecting the **LINE** command from the Draw Menu.

7. **From point:**

Enter **INT** or select the * * * * **OSNAP** Menu and select **INTERSEC**.

8. The aperture or target is shown at the intersection of the cursor on screen. Move the target over the vertex of the angle and select that point. A small blip or marker is displayed at the vertex.

9. **To point:**

Enter **CEN,** or select the * * * * **OSNAP** Menu and select **CENTER**.

10. Move the cursor to any point on the circumference of the circle and select that point. A line is drawn from the vertex of the angle to the center of the circle, which is the bisector (Figure 5.14).

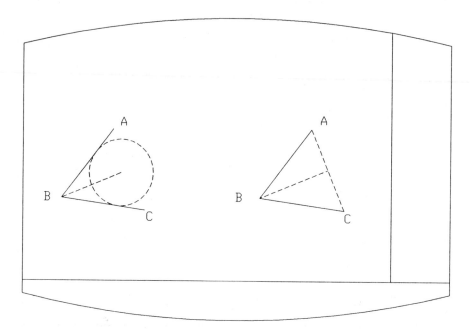

Figure 5.14 Bisecting an angle.

Bisecting an Angle Using a Line: Exercise 5.11

1. Draw a line from point A to C by entering **L** at the command prompt.
2. Enter **END** (endpoint) at the line prompt and pick point A.
3. Enter **END** at the line prompt and pick point B.
4. Repeat the Line command then enter **MID** and pick line A-C for one endpoint of the bisector.
5. Enter **END** and pick point B to draw the bisector of the angle. Figure 5.14.

DIVIDE A LINE INTO EQUAL PARTS

AutoCAD has automated the task of dividing a line or other entity into equal parts using the **DIVIDE** command, which is on the Edit Menu. Lines, arcs, circles, or polylines can be divided into any number of equal parts from 2 through 32,767. Points are placed along the entity after it is divided. The points will not be visible because the line hides the dots used as the default point setting. To get an **X** to display, the **PDMODE** is set to 3 by selecting **SETVAR** from the Settings Menu. A prompt reads **SETVAR Variable name or ?:** Enter **PDMODE** at the prompt. Another prompt reads **New value for PDMODE <0>:**. Enter the number **3** to display points. The following steps and Figure 5.15 describe how to divide line A-B into 5 equal parts.

Dividing a Line or Circle into Equal Parts: Exercise 5.12

1. Make sure the PDMODE is set to three before starting this exercise. From the Edit Menu select **DIVIDE** or select Divide from the Construct Pull-down Menu. A prompt reads: **Select object to divide:** Move the cursor over line A-B or the circle and select it.

2. **<Number of segments>/Block:**
Enter a number, such as **5**, and press RETURN. Four X's are displayed over the line, as shown in Figure 5.15, dividing the line into 5 equal parts.

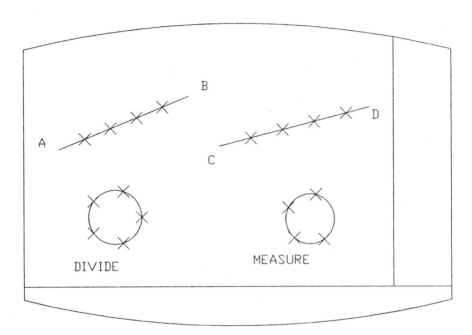

Figure 5.15 Dividing a line and circle into parts.

To divide other entities such as circles and arcs into equal parts use the **DIVIDE** command as described. After the entity is divided, the points can be used as Object Snap nodes for further construction. Instead of displaying an X for each point, a **BLOCK** could be used. The **BLOCK** must be defined within the current drawing to be used with **DIVIDE**. Blocks are explained in detail in Chapter 6.

Another command similar to **DIVIDE** is called **MEASURE**. The **MEASURE** command is located on the Edit Menu and is used to segment a line, arc, circle, or polyline into user-specified distances. Instead of the entity being divided automatically into the specified equal parts, as done with **DIVIDE**, the entity is measured into segments of the user-specified length starting at the endpoint nearest the digitized selection point. This may result in the last line segment being shorter than the specified length. **MEASURE** is described using the line C-D in Figure 5.15 and the following steps:

Segmenting a Line or Circle into Parts: Exercise 5.13

1. Open file **LAB5-3**. Select **MEASURE** from the Edit Menu or select Divide from the Construct Pull-down Menu or by entering it at the command prompt.
2. **Select object to measure:**
Pick line C-D or the circle with the cursor.
3. **<Segment length>/Block:** Enter the numerical distance to be used to segment the line, such as **1** and press RETURN.
4. Points drawn on the line are spaced every one inch as shown in the Figure 5.15. The last segment may not be equal to one inch.

DRAWING A LINE THROUGH A POINT AND PERPENDICULAR TO A LINE

Drawing a line through a point and perpendicular to an existing line is a common construction practice when creating engineering drawings. AutoCAD automates this task by using the **OSNAP** commands along with the **LINE** command. Figure 5.14 and the following steps can be used as a guide:

Drawing a Perpendicular Line: Exercise 5.14

1. Given point C and line A-B shown in Figure 5.16, select **LINE** from the Draw Menu or at the command prompt.
2. **From point:**
Enter **NEAREST** or **NODE**. **NEAREST** to or **NODE OF** is displayed in the prompt.
3. Move the cursor target over the point and pick it. Another prompt reads:
To point:
Enter **PERPEND** or select it from the Osnap Menu.
4. Pick any point on the line. A new line is drawn from the point perpendicular to the line, as shown in Figure 5.16.

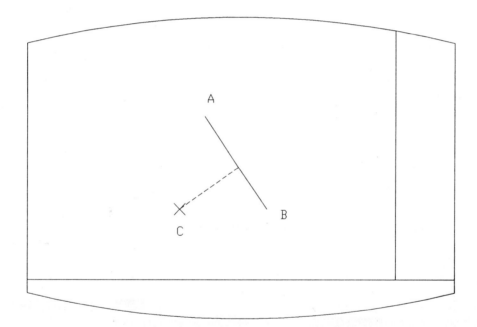

Figure 5.16 Drawing a line from a point perpendicular to a line.

DRAWING EQUILATERAL TRIANGLES, SQUARES, AND OTHER REGULAR POLYGONS

Triangles, rectangles, and other irregular polygons are created using lines, as described in Chapters 3 and 4. To create equilateral triangles, squares, and other regular polygons with AutoCAD, the **POLYGON** command is used. This command is part of the Draw Menu and creates regular polygons in a number of ways. Polygons can be created as circumscribed or inscribed about an imaginary circle, as shown in Figure 5.17. They also can be created by the edge method, as shown in Figure 5.18. Regular polygons can be created with 3 to 1024 sides. Polygons are created as polylines so that PLINE edit will work with these entities. The polygon is erased by using the **ERASE** command and selecting one side. To dynamically view the polygon as it is being placed on screen, turn the Drag Mode on by entering **DRAGMODE** at the command prompt. Figure 5.19 and the following steps show how to create an equilateral triangle:

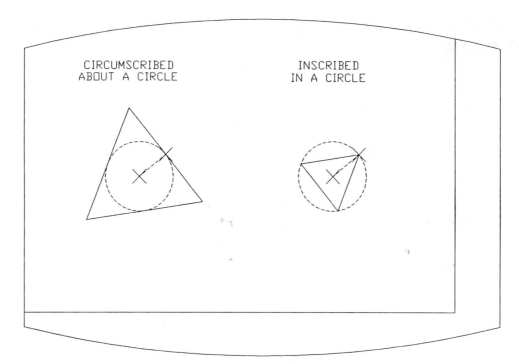

Figure 5.17 Polygon created by selecting the center point and a point on one side if it is circumscribed, or a point on a corner if it is inscribed.

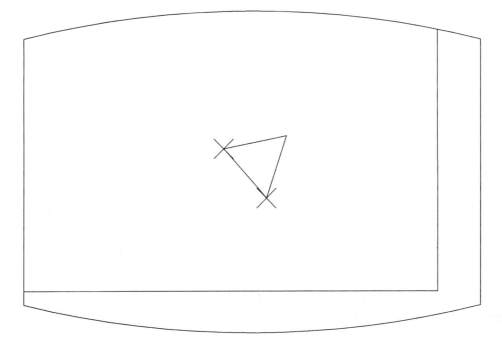

Figure 5.18 The edge method can be used to create polygons by picking the start and end point of

Creating an Equilateral Triangle: Exercise 5.15

1. From the Draw Pull-down Menu select **Polygon** then **Inscribed** or enter it at the command prompt.

2. **Number of sides:**

Enter the number **3** for a triangle.

one edge.

3. Edge/<Center of polygon>:
The default setting is the center of the polygon. Move the cursor to the desired center point and pick the location. Figure 5.19 show this point as a small plus (+). All sides of the polygon are equidistant from the picked point.

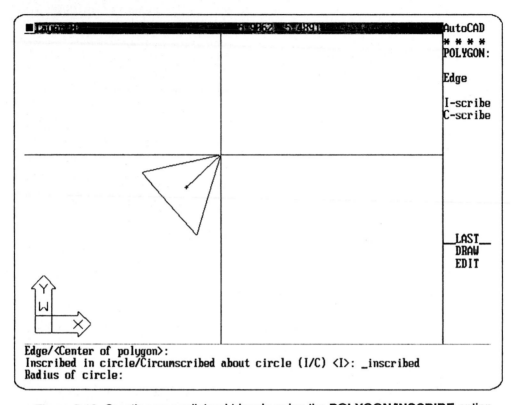

```
■ [░░░░░░ ░░]                       ░░░ ░░░░  ░░░░░░                    AutoCAD
                                                                       * * * *
                                                                       POLYGON:

                                                                       Edge

                                                                       I-scribe
                                                                       C-scribe






                                                                       LAST__
                                                                       DRAW
                                                                       EDIT



Edge/<Center of polygon>:
Inscribed in circle/Circumscribed about circle (I/C) <I>: _inscribed
Radius of circle:
```

Figure 5.19 Creating an equilateral triangle using the **POLYGON/INSCRIBE** option.

4. Inscribed in circle/Circumscribed about circle (I/C) <C>:
Enter an **I** to select the inscribed option or a **C** to select the circumscribed option. Figure 5.19 was created by entering **I** at the prompt.
5. The radius of the polygon can be entered at the **Radius of circle:** prompt by entering X, Y coordinate values or by moving the cursor and picking a point. The radius of the circle will contain all the vertices of the polygon. If the cursor is moved before picking a point and the Drag Mode is on, the polygon expands or shrinks and rotates on the screen. The final cursor position determines the radius of the polygon and the angle it is positioned on screen, as shown in Figure 5.19.

The circumscribed option is used in the same way, except the radius polygon contains the midpoint of each side of the polygon. Enter the letter **E** at the **Edge/<Center of polygon>:** prompt to define the ends of one of the polygon's edges. Figure 5.18 shows a triangle created using the **Edge** command by picking two points that define one side of the triangle.

GEOMETRIC CONSTRUCTION: CIRCLES, ARCS, AND LINES

AutoCAD provides a number of different commands that can be used for geometric construction. The software automatically performs some construction, such as finding the center of a circle. Other geometric construction must be created using AutoCAD commands.

Drawing a Circle Through Three Points

Occasionally it is necessary to draw a circle through three given points. AutoCAD has automated this task with the **3 Point** Circle submenu command. After **CIRCLE** is selected, enter **3P** at the prompt or select Circle then 3 Point from the Draw Pull-down Menu. AutoCAD then prompts for the location of the first, second, and third points. These points can be entered as X, Y coordinate values or as points picked with the input device. Figure 5.20A shows the three picked points on the circumference of the circle as small markers (+). The circle then is drawn through the three points. The Object Snap Menu also can draw circles tangent to existing entities, as shown in Figures 5.20B and 5.20C, by entering **TANGENT** at the prompt for each point.

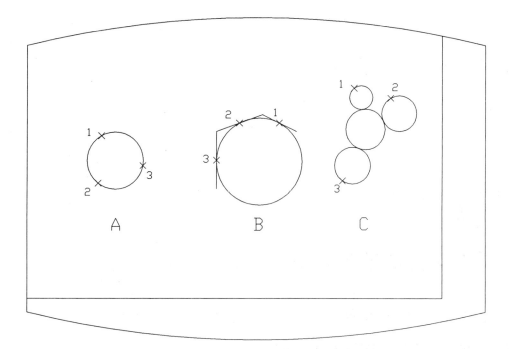

Figure 5.20 A circle drawn through three points.

Locating the Center of a Circle

Locating the center of a circle or an arc with AutoCAD is accomplished by using the Osnap option called **CENTER**. This option is used with a **DRAW** sub-command, such as line, arc, circle, or pline. Figure 5.21 shows an example of locating the center of a circle to create concentric circles. The small circle was drawn by locating the center point of the large circle and picking a point on the circumference, or entering the radius or diameter. Refer to Figure 5.21 and the following steps to locate the center of a circle:

1. Select the circle radius (CEN,RAD) or circle diameter (CEN,DIA) command from the CIRCLE submenu.
2. Enter CENTER or select it from the Osnap Menu.
3. Move the cursor to a point on the circumference of the large circle and pick the point. A small plus (+) is displayed.
4. A prompt asks for the radius or diameter. Enter a radius or diameter or move the cursor to a location on the circumference of the new circle and pick that point. A circle is drawn that is concentric to the large circle, as shown in Figure 5.21.

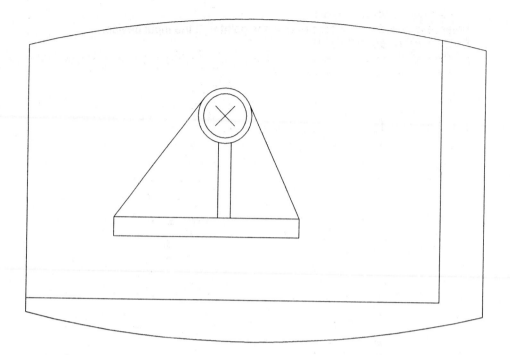

Figure 5.21 Creating a concentric circle by locating the circle's center point.

Drawing a Circle Through Two Points

The **2P** option draws a circle through two points, which define the diameter of the circle.

Drawing a Circle Through Two Points: Exercise 5.17

1. Select **2 Point** from the Circle Submenu or enter it at the circle prompt.

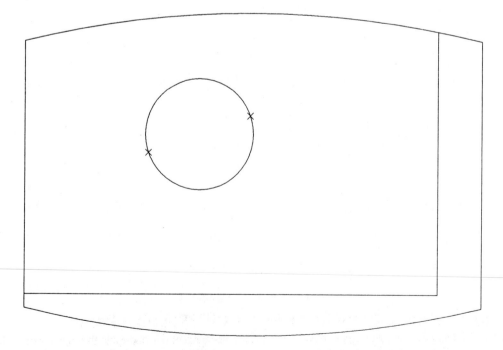

Figure 5.22 Creating a circle using the **2 Point** option.

2. **First point on diameter:**
Enter X, Y coordinate values or pick the point with the input device.
Second point on diameter:
Input the X, Y coordinate values or pick the point with the input device. Figure 5.22 shows
a circle created with the **2P** command.

Drawing a Circle Tangent to a Line at a Given Point

Many geometric forms have lines tangent to circles that can be created with AutoCAD's Osnap command called
TANGENT. The **3 Point** option draws a circle tangent to a line at a given point. Figure 5.23 shows a circle drawn
tangent to the midpoint of the line.

Drawing a Tangent Circle: Exercise 5.18

1. Select the **CIRCLE** command.
2. **3P/2P/TTR/<Center point>:**
Enter **3P** and RETURN.
3. **First point:**
Enter **TANGENT** or select it from the Osnap Menu.
4. Pick any point on the line, and a marker is displayed on the line.
5. **Second point:**
Enter **MIDPOINT** or select it from the Osnap Menu.
6. Pick any point on the line, and a marker will be displayed at the midpoint of the line.
7. **Third point:**
Pick any point with the cursor to draw the circle tangent to the midpoint of the line, as
shown in Figure 5.23.

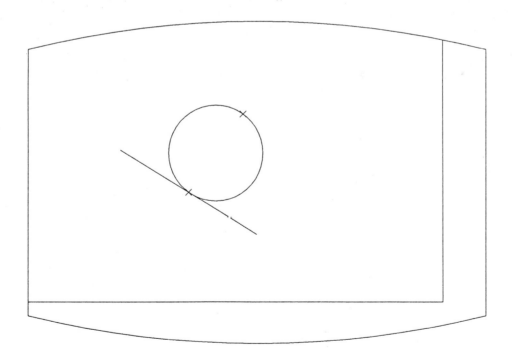

Figure 5.23 Drawing a circle tangent to a line and through a point.

Drawing a Line Tangent to a Circle and Through a Point

Figure 5.24 and the following steps show how to draw a line tangent to a circle and through a point. The line
is tangent to the large circle and through the upper right corner of the rectangular base.

Drawing Tangent Lines: Exercise 5.19

1. Open file **LAB5-4.** Select **LINE** from the Draw Menu or enter it at the command prompt.

2. **From point:**

Either the circle or the corner of the base can be the first point. For this example the base is used as the first point. Select **ENDPOINT** from the Osnap Menu, then pick the point on the base. A small blip or marker is displayed on the corner and the rubberband line stretches from it.

3. **To point:**

Select **TANGENT** from the Osnap Menu and digitize a point on the circumference of the circle that is to the right of the center point. A line is drawn from the point tangent to the circle, as shown in Figure 5.24.

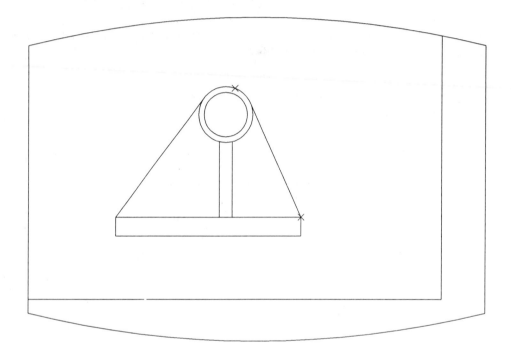

Figure 5.24 Drawing a line tangent to a circle and through a point.

Drawing Lines Tangent to Two Circles

Lines are drawn tangent to circles using the **TANGENT** Osnap command. Figure 5.24 shows a set of three circles with lines of tangency running between them. The following steps demonstrate how to draw lines tangent to circles:

Drawing Lines Tangent to Two Circles: Exercise 5.20

1. Select **LINE** from the Draw Menu or enter it at the command prompt.

2. **Start point:**

Enter Osnap command **TANGENT** or select it from the Osnap Menu.

3. Pick a point on the circumference of the top circle, labeled as point 1. A small marker and a rubberband line will stretch from the circle.

4. **To point:**

Enter the **TANGENT** command at the prompt.

5. Digitize the lower left circle, labeled as point 2. A tangent line is drawn between the circles. To draw lines 3-4 and 5-6, repeat steps one through five.

Drawing Circles Tangent to Lines or Circles

The **TTR** (tangent, tangent, radius) command draws a circle of a specified radius tangent to lines, arcs, and circles. Figure 5.26 shows three examples of a circle drawn tangent to lines and/or circles. The following steps describe how to use the **TTR** command:

Drawing Tangent Circles: Exercise 5.21

1. Select the **CIRCLE** command from the Draw Menu or enter it at the command prompt.
2. **3P/2P/TTR/<Center point>:**
Enter **TTR** at the prompt.
3. **Enter Tangent spec:**
Pick the first line or circle as indicated by the number 1 in Figure 5.26.
4. **Enter second Tangent spec:**
Pick the second line or circle as indicated by the number 2 in Figure 5.26.
5. **Radius:**
Enter a numerical value such as .5. A one-inch diameter circle is drawn tangent to the two entities picked, as shown in Figure 5.26.

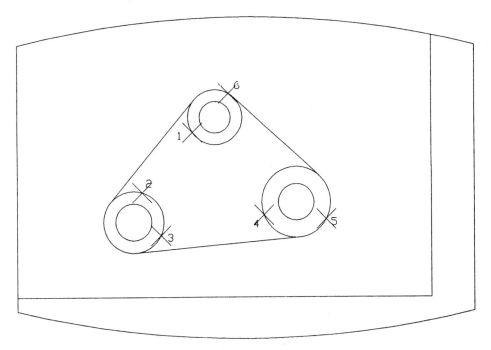

Figuro 5.25 Drawing lines tangent to two circles.

Drawing an Arc Tangent to Two Lines

Drawing an arc tangent to two lines at any angle is accomplished most effectively by using the AutoCAD **FILLET** command found on the Edit Menu. The **FILLET** command draws an arc of a specified radius between two intersecting or non-intersecting lines, arcs, circles, or polylines. If a fillet is added to the intersection of two lines, the fillet is added and the lines are trimmed automatically from the corner to the point of tangency, as shown in Figure 5.27. The following steps demonstrate the use of **FILLET** to create arcs tangent to two lines:

Drawing an Arc Tangent to Two Lines: EXERCISE 5.22

1. Open file **LAB5-5.** From the Edit Menu select **FILLET** or enter it at the command prompt
2. **Polyline/Radius/<Select first object>:**
Enter the letter **R** to set the desired fillet radius.

3. **Enter fillet radius <0.0000>:**

The number in brackets is the current setting. For this example, enter **.25** at the prompt and press **RETURN**. This returns you to the command prompt.

4. At the command prompt enter **RETURN** to repeat the fillet command.

5. **Polyline/Radius/<Select first object>:**

Pick each line that is to be filleted. After the second line is selected, the arc is drawn tangent to the lines, and the lines are trimmed, as shown in Figure 5.27.

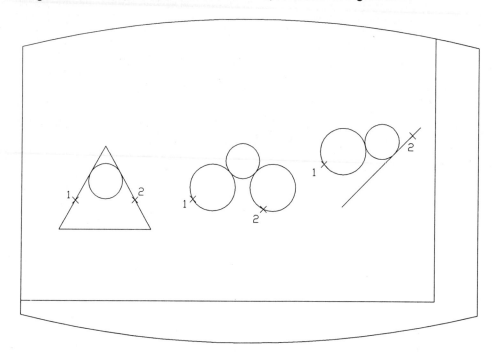

Figure 5.26 Drawing circles tangent to lines and circles.

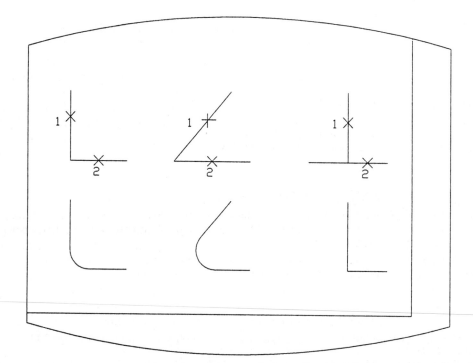

Figure 5.27 Use the **FILLET** command to drawn an arc tangent to two lines.

If the fillet radius is set at zero, it can trim the corners of intersecting lines, as shown in Figure 5.27. It also can extend lines that are too short for the input radius. The polyline option automatically fillets all the corners of a polyline (Figure 5.28). At the Fillet Prompt, **Polyline/Radius/<Select first objects>:**, enter the letter **P**. A prompt reads: **Select 2D polyline:**. Pick any single entity of the polyline. AutoCAD automatically places fillets of the specified radius at the vertices of the intersecting PLINES segments.

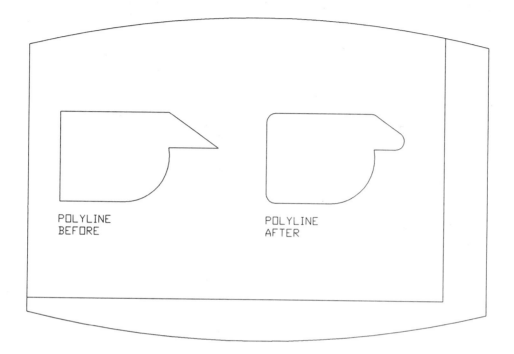

POLYLINE
BEFORE

POLYLINE
AFTER

Figure 5.28 Using **FILLET** on a polyline.

Drawing an Arc of a Given Radius Tangent to Two Circles

The Fillet command also draws an arc tangent to two circles, as shown in Figure 5.29. The Fillet command will not trim the circles as it does for lines. To create the large arc and circle tangent to the two circles shown in Figure 5.29, a large radius, such as ten, must be set and the circle, TTR option used. After the Fillet or Circle command is selected, pick the circles approximately where indicated, and the arc or circle is added as shown.

The Fillet command cannot create the large arc shown on the right of Figure 5.29. This arc only is created by using the Circle command **TTR** with a large radius such as ten. After the circle is added to the drawing, the **TRIM** command must be used to trim the unwanted portion of the circle. **TRIM** is an Edit command that can clip or erase part of an entity. It can be compared to an erasing shield that is used with traditional tools.

Drawing an Arc Tangent to Two Circles: Exercise 5.23
1. From the Construct Pull-down Menu pick **Fillet**. Enter **R** then enter a radius of 2.0.
2. Press RETURN to repeat the Fillet command. Pick point one on the circle then point
2. An arc is added between the circles.
3. Pick Circle then Tan, Tan, Radius from the Draw Pull-down Menu.
4. Pick point three then point four for the tangent points.
5. Enter a radius of 2. A circle is drawn tangent to the given circles as shown in Figure 5.29.
6. Pick **TRIM** from the Modify Pull-down Menu. A new prompt reads:
Select cutting edge(s). . .
Select objects:
For this example, the cutting edges are the two circles.

2. Pick both circles, as indicated by the numbers 5 and 6 in Figure 5.30. A RETURN must be entered after the cutting edges have been specified.

3. **Select object to trim/undo:**

The object to be trimmed is the large circle drawn tangent to the two smaller ones. It is very important the large circle be picked at the correct position so that the portion of the circle between the small circles is left. If the large circle is picked between the small circles, that portion running between the circles to the point of tangency is deleted. If the large circle is picked as indicated in Figure 5.30 labeled as number 7, the large portion of the circle is trimmed, as shown in Figure 5.31.

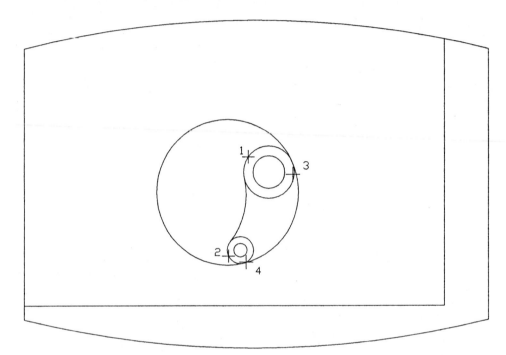

Figure 5.29 Drawing arcs tangent to two circles.

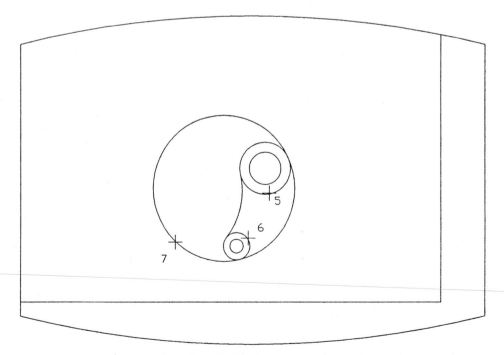

Figure 5.30 Trimming the circle.

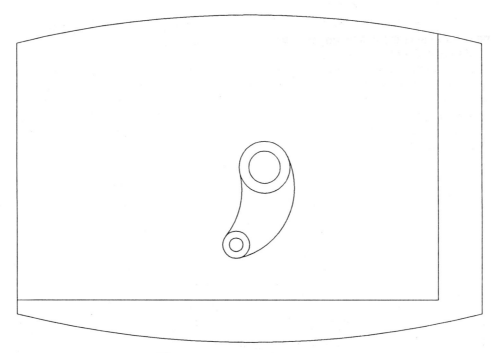

Figure 5.31 After trim is executed.

Drawing an Arc Tangent to an Arc and a Straight Line

The **FILLET** command is the most effective method of creating an arc tangent to a given arc or circle and a line. An alternate method would be the **CIRCLE/TTR** option and **TRIM.** Figure 5.32 shows an application of this construction technique. The one flaw with using **FILLET** is the line to which the arc is drawn tangent automatically is trimmed. If the line should be left on the drawing, it will have to be added after the fillet is created. The arc drawn between the line and the circle in Figure 5.32 was created using a 2-inch radius fillet.

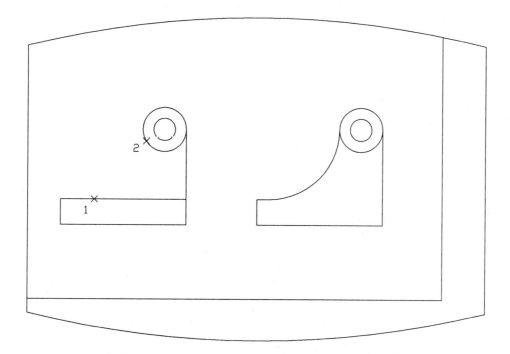

Figure 5.32 Drawing an arc tangent to a circle and a line.

Drawing an Arc Tangent to a Circle and a Line: Exercise 5.24

1. After the **FILLET** command is entered, a prompt reads:
   Polyline/Radius/<Select first objects>:
2. Enter the letter **R** to set the radius.
3. **Enter fillet radius <0.0000>:**
The current value is the last value input. Enter the new value of **2** and press RETURN.
3. The command prompt is displayed. Press RETURN to repeat the **FILLET** command.
4. **Polyline/Radius/<Select first objects>:**
Pick the line and the circle in the figure, and the arc is drawn, as shown in Figure 5.32.
Use the Line command to add the line that was erased when the fillet was added.

DRAWING AN OGEE CURVE

An ogee curve is created using the **S,E,R** Arc command. Picking the start and end points and entering the radius of the arc creates an ogee curve, as shown in Figure 5.33.

Drawing an Ogee Curve: Exercise 5.25

1. Select **S,E,R** (Start, End, Radius) from the Arc Menu.
2. **Center/<Start point>:**
Pick the start of the arc labeled as point 1 in the figure.
3. **Center/End/<Second point>:** Pick the end point of the arc labeled as point 2 in the figure.
4. **Angle/Direction/Radius/<Center point>:**
Pick the location of the center of the arc labeled as point 3 in the figure. Make sure the Drag Mode is on to visually check the accuracy of tangent arc to the line.
5. Repeat the preceding steps to create the second arc and complete the ogee curve shown in Figure 5.33.

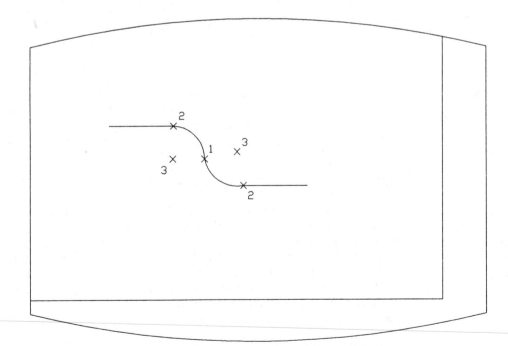

Figure 5.33 Drawing an ogee curve.

DRAWING IRREGULAR CURVES

Drawing a series of tangent arcs through given points or through the end points of lines using traditional tools is accomplished with a French or irregular curve. The AutoCAD command used to create irregular curves is **PEDIT** (polyline edit), which only can be used if the line is drawn as a polyline.

Figure 5.34 shows a polyline created with the **PLINE** command. Polylines are a connected sequence of lines and arc segments that are treated as a single entity.

Drawing an Irregular Curve: Exercise 5.26

1. Open file **LAB5-6**. To draw a polyline, enter the **PLINE** command.
2. **From point:**
Pick the starting point of the polyline.
3. **Arc/Close/Half width/Length/Undo/Width/<Endpoint of line>:**
The default setting is to draw lines. To draw a line, move the cursor to a new position and pick the point with the input device. Continue to move the cursor and pick points until the polyline is complete, then enter RETURN.

After a polyline is created, it can be edited to create a series of tangent arcs through the end points of the line segments. The **PEDIT** command from the Edit command list changes the straight line segments into tangent arcs.

1. After **PEDIT** is selected from the Edit Menu, a prompt reads:
Select objects:
2. Pick any line segment of the polyline and Return.
Close/Join/Width/Editvertex/Fitcurve/Splinecurve/Decurve/Undo/eXit <X>:
3. Enter the letter **F** and press RETURN. The **FIT CURVE** option immediately changes the straight line segments to a series of tangent arcs by running through all the vertices of the polyline Figure 5.34. The curve is edited using the **EDIT VERTEX** option by assigning tangent directions or adding more vertices.

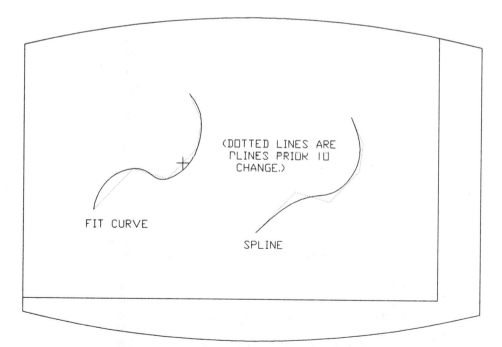

Figure 5.34 Creating tangent arcs through a series of points.

DRAWING A CUBIC B-SPLINE

A cubic B-spline is a smooth curve that passes through start point and points and is pulled toward all points between. Figure 5.34. Unlike an irregular curve, the cubic B-spline does not pass through all the points. The closer the points, the closer the spline comes to passing through them. AutoCAD creates a cubic B-spline of a polyline using the **SPLINE** command located on the **PEDIT** submenu.

Creating a Cubic-B-spline: Exercise 5.27

1. Enter **PEDIT** at the command prompt or from the Edit Menu.
2. After **PEDIT** is selected a prompt reads:
Select polyline
2. Pick the polyline to be made into a cubic B-spline.
3. The prompt reads:
Close/Join/Width/Editvertex/Fitcurve/Splinecurve/Decurve/Undo/eXit <X>:
Enter **S** or select **SPLINE** from the menu.
4. The polyline is replaced by a cubic B-spline, as shown in Figure 5.34. Notice the difference between the two curves produced by the **Fit Curve** and **Spline** commands.

DRAWING ELLIPSES

An ellipse is formed by a plane intersecting a right circular cone or cylinder or when viewing a circle or hole at an angle between 0 and 90 degrees. Ellipses are used in engineering graphics to create isometric views of circles and holes. The long axis of an ellipse is called the major diameter and the short axis the minor diameter. AutoCAD provides the **ELLIPSE** command to draw a variety of ellipses using a number of techniques. This is accomplished by answering the ellipse prompts in different ways. When in the isometric snap mode, the **ELLIPSE** command automatically projects the ellipse into the current isometric drawing plane. Ellipses are constructed by defining the axis and eccentricity, or by the center and two axes. The isometric ellipse is explained in Chapter 11. Set the **DRAG MODE** on to dynamically display the ellipse as it is being placed with the cursor.

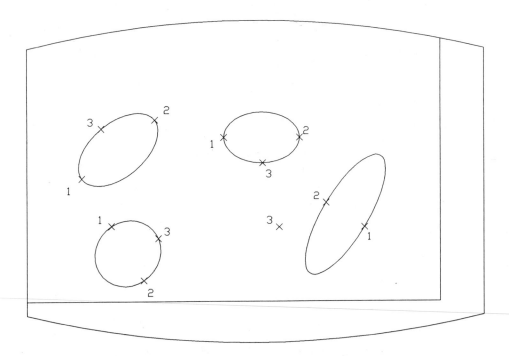

Figure 5.35 Drawing ellipses by defining three points.

Drawing Ellipses (Axes Option): Exercise 5.28

1. The **ELLIPSE** command is activated by choosing it from the Draw Menu or by entering **ELLIPSE** at the command prompt.

2. **<Axis endpoint 1>/Center:**
Pick a point to identify the first end point of one of the axes.

3. **Axis endpoint 2:**
Pick the other end point of the axis. The angle between the two end points will determine the angle at which the ellipse is drawn.

4. The next prompt determines which axis has been defined. The prompt reads:
<Other axis distance>/Rotation: A rubberband line stretches from the cursor to the midpoint of the first axis. Pick the third point on the circumference of the ellipse to create the ellipse.

Figure 5.35 shows some examples of ellipses produced using the axis and eccentricity option. The **ROTATION** option specifies the angle into which circle is rotated, the third dimension creating an elliptical view of the circle. Values between 0 and 89.4 are accepted. A value of zero will produce a circle. Examples of different rotation angles are shown in Figure 5.36. The following steps show how the **CENTER** option is used.

Drawing Ellipses (Center Option): Exercise 5.29

1. The ellipse by center and two axes is activated by choosing the **CENTER** option at the first prompt.

2. **<Axis endpoint1>/Center:**
Enter the letter **C** to identify the first digitized point at the center of the ellipse.

3. **Axis endpoint:**
Pick the end point of either axis. The angle between the center point and the axis end point determines the orientation of the ellipse.

4. **<Other axis distance>/Rotation**
Pick the third point to draw the ellipse. The rotation angle also can be specified as described.

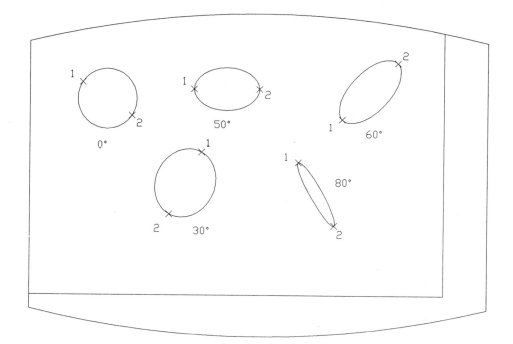

Figure 5.36 Drawing ellipses by entering the rotation angle.

Figure 5.37 shows a few examples of the center and two axes method of constructing ellipses.

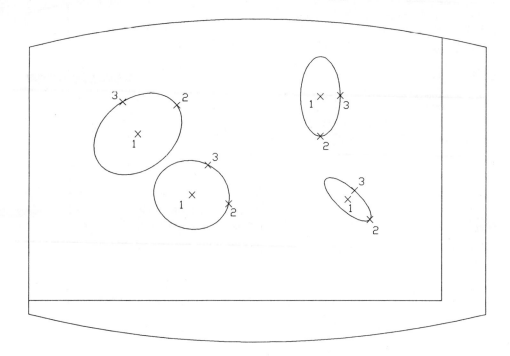

Figure 5.37 Drawing ellipses by locating the center and location of the major and minor diameter.

OTHER METHODS OF CREATING GEOMETRIC ENTITIES WITH AutoCAD

Most CADD programs provide a number of methods of creating geometric entities. Traditional tools draw an arc with basically two methods, using a compass or a circle template. AutoCAD provides eleven different "tools" to create arcs. AutoCAD also creates some uncommon geometric entities, such as **DONUTS** and **SOLIDS**. This section briefly describes other methods of creating geometric entities.

Drawing Arcs

When the **ARC** command is selected from the menu, a new menu lists the eleven methods of creating arcs. Each menu item is abbreviated, except the first, which is **3-POINT**. Menu items are not abbreviated if the pull-down menu is used. The 3-Point option is used just as the 3-Point Circle option is used. The first point is the beginning of the arc, and the second and third are points that define the arc curvature, as shown in Figure 5.38.

This list describes the meaning of each letter that appears in the Arc Menu.

S: START POINT
C: CENTER POINT
E: END POINT
A: INCLUDED ANGLE
L: LENGTH OF A CHORD
R: RADIUS
D: TANGENT DIRECTION
CONTIN: CONTINUES AN ARC FROM THE LAST ENTITY ENDPOINT ENTERED

Figure 5.38 shows how each command creates arcs. Each number represents the order in which a point is picked on the screen. If the **DRAG** function is activated, the arc is displayed on the screen as the cursor is moved to locate the third point. Coordinate values can be entered for any of the points instead of using the cursor.

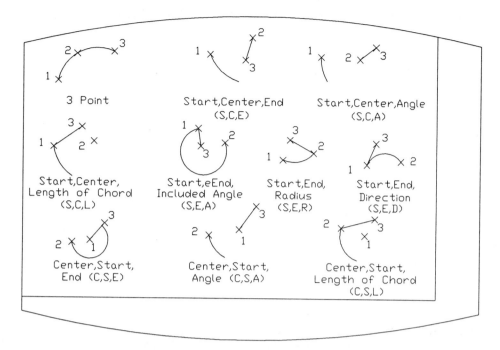

Figure 5.38 Different methods of creating arcs with AutoCAD.

Drawing Filled Circles

The **DONUT** or **DOUGHNUT** command is used to create filled circles or rings like that shown in Figure 5.39.

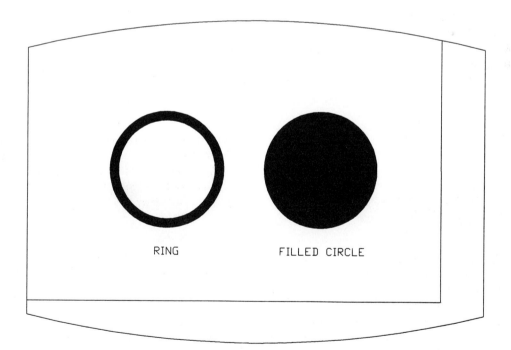

RING   FILLED CIRCLE

Figure 5.39 Using the **DONUT** Command to draw filled rings or circles.

Drawing Filled Circles: Exercise 5.30

1. **DONUT** is activated from the Draw Menu or by entering **DONUT** or **DOUGHNUT** at the command prompt.

2. **Inside diameter <0.5000>**

The most recent setting is displayed in the brackets. Enter the desired inside diameter, such as **2.75**.

3. **Outside diameter <1.0000>**

Enter the outside diameter, such as **3.25**.

4. **Center or doughnut:**

If **DRAGMODE** is set to AUTO, the donut is displayed with the center at the center of the cursor. Pick a point to place the donut on the drawing and press RETURN to cancel the command.

A ring is drawn as shown in Figure 5.39 if the **FILLMODE** is set to ON by entering a numerical value of 1. If zero is entered at the first prompt, a filled circle is drawn as shown in the figure. Instead of entering numeric values, points can be picked with the cursor.

Drawing Filled Squares, Rectangles, and Triangles

The **SOLID** command is used to create filled areas bounded by lines. The filled areas can be squares, rectangles, quadrilaterals, or triangles. Solids are created by specifying the end points of lines or points in space through keyboard input or by cursor picking.

Drawing Filled Areas: Exercise 5.31

1. The **SOLID** command is activated by selecting it from the second page of the Draw Menu or entering it at the command prompt. To draw a solid rectangle, define two opposite sides of the rectangle by specifying the end points of each line, then enter RETURN.

2. **First point:**

Pick the first endpoint of a line.

3. **Second point:** Pick the opposite end of the line.

3. **Third point:** Pick the first endpoint for the second line.

4. **Fourth point:** Pick the opposite end fo the line. Figure 5.40A is the type of drawing created if the endpoints of the two lines are selected in the order shown. Figure 5.40B is a rectangle created using the endpoint selection shown.

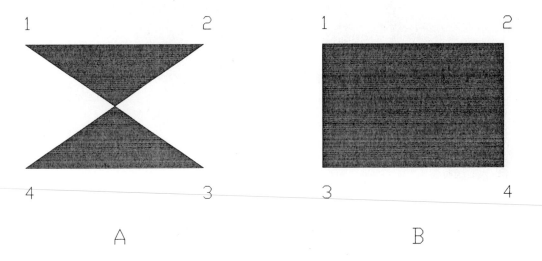

Figure 5.40 Creating a filled rectangle using the **SOLID** Command.

Creating a Rectangular Array: Exercise 5.34

1. Open file **LAB5-8**. A rectangular array (Figure 5.42) is created by entering **ARRAY** at the command prompt, picking it from the Construct Pull-down Menu, or from the Edit Menu.

2. **Select objects:**
Pick each line of the square or stretch a window to select the square.

3. **Rectangular or Polar array (R/P):**
Enter the letter **R** for rectangular.

4. **Number of rows (—) <1>:**
For this example, five rows are needed, so the number **5** is entered.

5. **Number of columns (| | |) <1>:**
The number of columns to be entered is **3**.

6. **Unit cell or distance between rows (—):**
Enter the distance between the cell rows as **.5** for this example.

7. **Distance between columns (| | |):**
For this example, enter a distance of **1**. The rectangular array is created as shown in Figure 5.43.

Entering negative numbers for the row distance causes the rows to be created below the original entity. Likewise, entering negative numbers for the column distance creates columns to the left.

Creating a Circular Array: Exercise 5.35

1. A polar array is created by entering **ARRAY** at the command prompt, picking it from the Construct Pull-down Menu, or from the Edit Menu.

2. **Select objects:**
Pick the smallest circle in the figure.

3. **Rectangular or Polar array (R/P):**
Enter the letter **P** for a polar array.

4. **Center point of array:**
To create the bolt circle shown in Figure 5.43, **pick the largest circle** using the Center Osnap option.

5. **Number of items:**

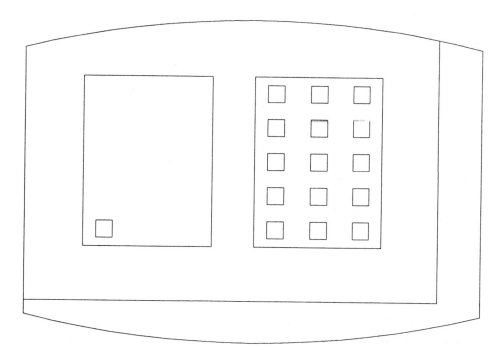

Figure 5.43 Creating a rectangular array.

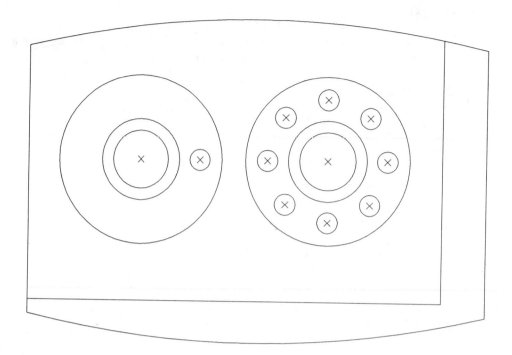

Figure 5.44 Creating a circular (polar) array.

Enter the number of items to be copied, including the original. For this example, the number **8** is entered.

6. **Angle to fill (+=CCW, -=CW) <360>:**
To create a partial circular array, an angle less than 360 is entered. The sign entered with the angle determines if the array is created clockwise or counter-clockwise from the original. For this example, enter RETURN for a full 360-degree array.

7. **Rotate objects as they are copied?(Y):**
Enter YES at the prompt. The circular array is completed and drawn as shown in the figu re.

Moving Geometry

The **MOVE** command moves selected entities, such as geometry and text, to a new location. This option is very useful when an engineering drawing is created on a CADD system, giving the user the flexibility to draw entities and move them to a location that best communicates the desired information.

The **MOVE** command is activated by selecting it from the Edit Menu or Modify Pull-down Menu, or by entering it at the command prompt. Figure 5.45 is an example.

Moving Geometry: Exercise 5.36

1. For this example, the move command is used to align the right side view with the front view in a three-view drawing.

2. After **MOVE** is selected, a prompt reads:
Select objects:
Entities are selected one at a time, by window or some other means. For this example, a window is used to identify the figure to be moved. Select the first corner, the second corner of the window, then return as shown in Figure 5.45.

3. **Base point or displacement:**
The base point or handle for moving the figure must be defined. Pick the lower left corner of the figure, labeled as point 3 in Figure 5.45.

4. **Second point of displacement:**

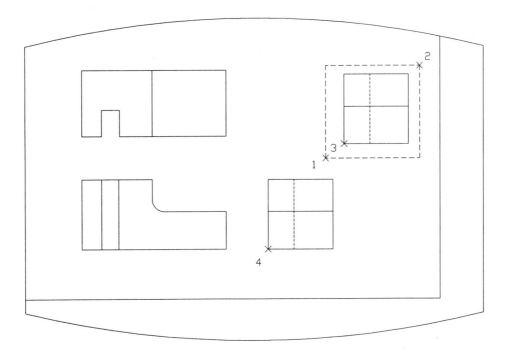

Figure 5.45 Moving entities on a screen.

Move the cursor to a position that aligns the figure with the front view. A grid with snap is used to move the view, as shown in Figure 5.45. If **DRAGMODE** is on, the objects will move with the cursor.

A quick way to make a copy is to select the entities by stretching a window while at the command prompt. This is the entity grip selection. Enter the letter M at the command prompt after selection to start the move command. Pick the base point then the displacement point to move the entities.

Rotating Figures

Entities, such as text and geometry, are rotated on screen by using the **ROTATE** command. They are rotated by defining the base point of rotation and entering the rotation angle. Positive angles cause a counter-clockwise rotation, and negative angles cause a clockwise rotation. Entities to be rotated are selected by cursor or by window. The **ROTATE** command can solve descriptive geometry problems as described in Chapter 9. Figure 5.46 shows how entities are rotated.

Rotating Geometry: Exercise 5.37

1. The **ROTATE** command is selected from the Edit Menu, input at the command prompt or picked from the Modify Pull-down Menu.
2. **Select objects:**
Select the objects to be rotated. For this example, use the Window Option by picking the first corner to create a window.
3. **Base point:**
Indicate the point of rotation as the bottom right corner of the object, as shown in the Figure 5.46.

4. **<Rotation angle>/Reference:**
Input the rotation angle of **45** degrees for this example. The object is rotated as shown in Figure 5.47.

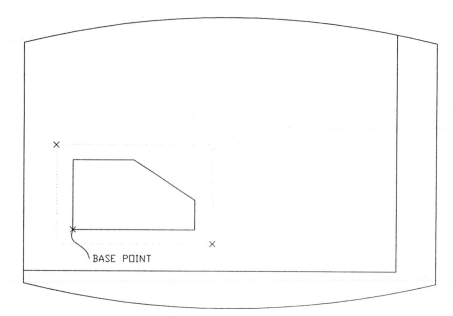

Figure 5.46 Using the **WINDOW** option to define objects to be rotated.

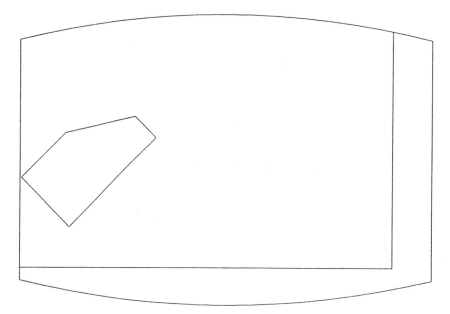

Figure 5.47 Object rotated 45 degrees.

Mirroring Entities

AutoCAD has a command called **MIRROR** that can be used to make a mirror image of existing entities. The existing entities can be retained or deleted during the mirroring operation. After the items to be mirrored are selected, the mirror axis is defined by any two points and at any angle. The **MIRROR** command is especially useful in drawing complicated parts that are symmetrical. Figure 5.48 is an example of a part that is completed using the **MIRROR** command.

Mirroring Entities: Exercise 5.38

1. Open file **LAB5-9**. Select **MIRROR** from the Edit Menu, enter it at the command prompt or pick it from the Construct Pull-down Menu.
2. **Select objects:**
Objects can be selected in a number of different ways, but using the Window Option for this example is the most effective.

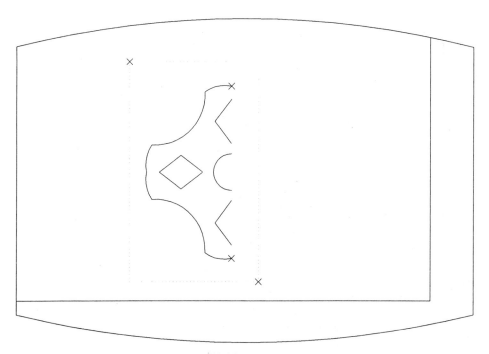

Figure 5.48 Drawing to be mirrored.

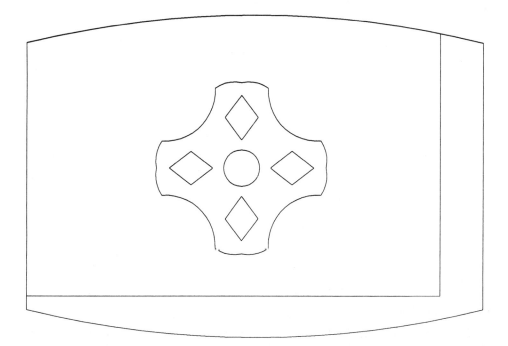

Figure 5.49 Drawing after it has been copied and mirrored.

3. After the objects are selected another prompt reads:
First point of mirror line:
For this example a point along the vertical center line must be picked. Use the Osnap option **ENDPOINT** to snap to the end point.
4. **Second point:**
Pick another point on the vertical center line as shown in the figure.
5. **Delete old objects? <N>:**
Enter RETURN or N if the old object is to remain. The object is copied and mirrored, completing the part shown in Figure 5.49.

ENLARGING OR REDUCING THE DRAWING SCALE

Enlarging or reducing the size of a drawing using traditional tools can be very time-consuming. Using CADD for the same purpose is extremely fast and accurate. One way of changing the size of a drawing is to control the scale at which it is plotted. This method only changes the plotted size of the drawing and not the actual size stored in the geometric data base. To change the size of a drawing in the data base, the Edit command **SCALE** or Modify pull-down menu item Scale must be used.

Figure 5.50 is a dimensioned drawing that will be scaled to different sizes to demonstrate how AutoCAD changes the size of a drawing.

Scaling a Drawing: Exercise 5.39

1. Select the **SCALE** command Modify Pull-down Menu.
2. After the **SCALE** command is selected a prompt reads:
Select objects:
Objects can be selected in different ways, but using the Window Option is the most effective to select the entire drawing, shown in Figure 5.50.
3. After the window is created and the objects are selected another prompt reads:
Base point:
The base point is located at any position on the drawing by moving the cursor to a position and picking that point. However, good practice suggests using a base point such as a corner of the object or center of a hole.
4. **<Scale factor>/Reference:**
To enlarge an object enter a number larger than one. To reduce the size of an object enter a number between zero and one. Entering a two doubles the size of the drawing. Entering .25 makes the drawing one-quarter size. For this example, enter **.5** to make the drawing half size as shown in Figure 5.51. Notice the dimensions change to 1/2 size. This is called associative dimensioning and is explained later.

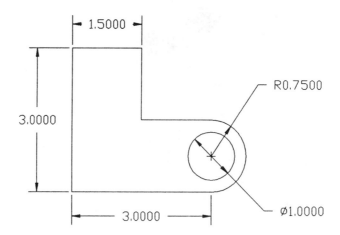

Figure 5.50 Object to be scaled.

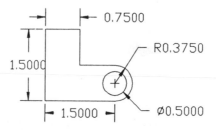

Figure 5.51 Object after a new scale of .50 is entered.

STRETCH A DRAWING

AutoCAD provides a method for moving or stretching part of an object. The **STRETCH** command stretches or shrinks a drawing. A crossing window most effectively identifies the part of the object to be stretched. A base point and a new point then are identified to stretch the object.

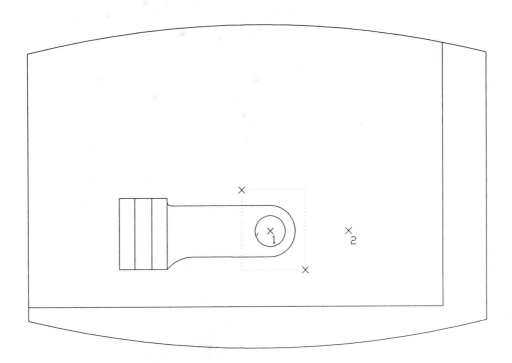

Figure 5.52 **WINDOW** used to stretch a part.

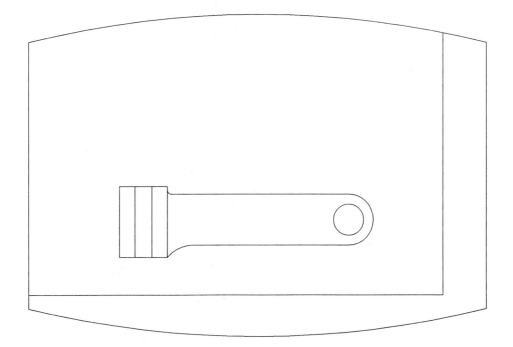

Figure 5.53 Object after **STRETCH** is executed.

Stretching Geometry: Exercise 5.40

1. The **STRETCH** command is an Edit Menu item or Modify Pull-down Menu item that will display the prompt:

Select objects to stretch by window. . .
Select objects:

The window is created by picking two points as shown in Figure 5.52. Entities located entirely within the window, such as the circle in Figure 5.52, are moved. Entities that cross the window will have the end point that is within the window stretched.

2. After the window is selected and Return entered, another prompt reads:

Base point or displacement:

The base point is the handle used to stretch the object. For this example, the center of the hole makes a good base point.

3. **Second point of displacement:**

Pick the new location of the handle or base point. The object is stretched as shown in Figure 5.53.

OTHER COMMANDS USED TO CREATE OR EDIT GEOMETRY

The flexibility of AutoCAD provides many other methods to create and edit geometry than those covered in this chapter. Experience with any CADD system reveals some of the more subtle methods of effectively using the software. An effort has been made to show the basic methods that can be employed to create an engineering drawing. However, there are other powerful commands that should be described that do not fit within the normal boundaries of geometric construction using traditional tools. For example, using traditional tools, a chamfer is created easily after the user learns to draw horizontal, vertical, and inclined lines. Most CADD systems have a special command just to create chamfers that is automatic and much more effective than creating a chamfer using basic geometric construction techniques. This part of the chapter describes some of the special AutoCAD commands that do not fall within the traditional framework of geometric construction.

Breaking Entities

The **BREAK** command edits existing entities by breaking or erasing part of the entity. The **BREAK** command is similar to an erasing shield when using traditional tools. Figure 5.54 is an example of how the **BREAK** command edits a drawing. For this example, the part of the circle located between the two lines must be erased.

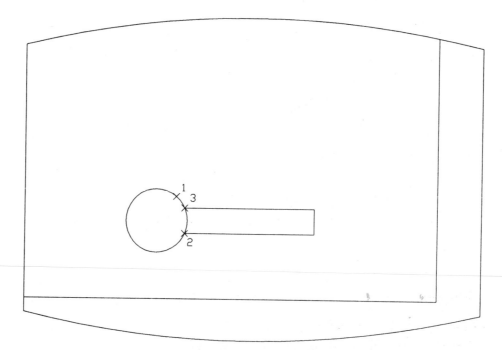

Figure 5.54 Selecting points to break the circle.

Breaking Geometry: Exercise 5.41

1. After the **BREAK** command is selected from the Edit Menu or Modify pull-down menu, a prompt reads:
Select object:
The object to be broken (the circle) is selected by moving the cursor and picking it.
2. **Enter second point (or F for first point):**
Enter F at the prompt.
3. A prompt reads:
Enter first point:
The intersection between the circle and the line is selected by using Osnap option **INTERSE C**.
4. **Enter second point:**
Use the intersection identified as point 3 in Figure 5.54 with Osnap option **INTERSEC**. Part of the circle is deleted as shown in Figure 5.55. When breaking circles, always work in a counter-clockwise direction. Figure 5.55 shows the different results between counter-clockwise and clockwise selection.

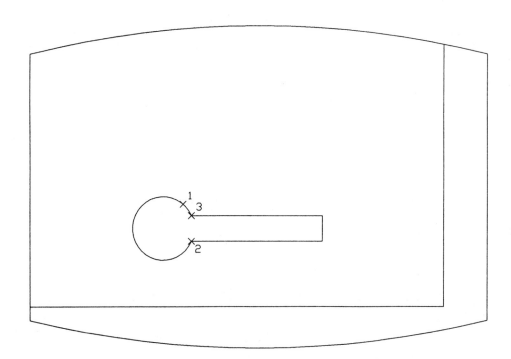

Figure 5.55 The drawing after break is executed.

Changing Properties Of Existing Entities

The **CHANGE** command modifies the color, linetype, layer of entities, and an object's three-dimensional thickness.

Changing Properties: Exercise 5.42

1. **CHANGE** is an Edit Menu item that will display the following prompt after selection:
Select objects:
Pick the object(s) to change with the cursor.
2. **Properties/<change point>:**
To change entity properties, enter the letter **P** and press RETURN.

3. Change what property (Color/Elev/LAyer/Ltype/Thickness) ?
Enter the word or the letter of the property to be changed.
If color is selected, a prompt requests **New color <current>:** Enter RED.
Elevation displays **New elevation <current>**
Layer displays **New layer <current>:** Enter CONSTRUCTION.
Linetype displays **New linetype <current>:** Enter HIDDEN.
And thickness requests **New thickness<current>:**
Respond to the prompt by entering the new property desired then two RETURNS to change the entity property.

Other characteristics of entities are modified if a point is entered at the second change prompt, **Properties/ <Change point>:.** The point entered becomes a new end point of the line selected; the new radius of the circle selected; or the new location, style, height, and so forth of the text string selected. Figure 5.56 shows a change in radius of a circle from three to two using the **CHANGE** option **CHANGE POINT**.

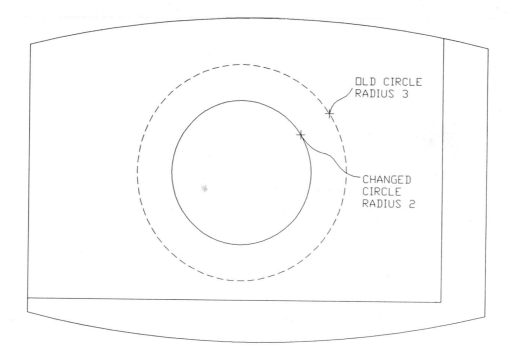

Figure 5.56 Using the **CHANGE** Command to edit a circle radius.

Extending Entities

The **EXTEND** command is similar to the **STRETCH** command for stretching entities. However, **EXTEND** lengthens objects only to a specific edge or boundary. This command is very useful to create auxiliary views, solve descriptive geometry problems, and aid basic geometric construction. The **EXTEND** command lengthens lines, arcs, and polylines. The two long horizontal lines shown in Figure 5.57 are used to demonstrate the use of the **EXTEND** command.

Extending Geometry: Exercise 5.43

1. After **EXTEND** has been selected from the Edit Menu, picked from the Modify Pull-down Menu or entered at the command prompt, a prompt is displayed:
Select boundary edge(s). . .
Select objects:
Pick the entity that is used as a boundary for the extension and Return when all the entities are selected. The selected entity becomes highlighted and remains that way until the command is terminated.

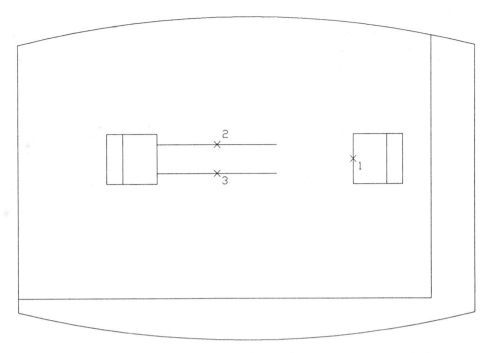

Figure 5.57 Pick points for boundary and two lines to be extended.

2. **Select objects to extend/undo:**
The lines that need to be extended have to be picked. After the entities are identified, the lines are extended as shown in Figure 5.58.

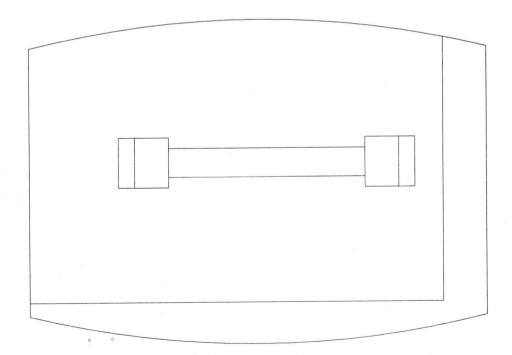

Figure 5.58 Object after **EXTEND** is executed.

QUESTIONS FOR REVIEW

1. Name the command to create filled or unfilled lines of a specified width.
2. Name the most effective command to create parallel lines.
3. Name the command to connect a sequence of lines and arcs segments.
4. List the **OSNAP** command options and their functions.
5. Identify the difference between **BREAK** and **ERASE**.
6. Name which submenu the **CHANGE** command is located.
7. Specify the difference between the **MOVE** and **COPY** command.
8. List the types of objects best suited for the **MIRROR** command.
9. Explain the difference between the two types of arrays.
10. Identify the difference between **BREAK** and **TRIM**.
11. Name the command used to bisect a line.
12. What is the difference between **DIVIDE** and **MEASURE**?
13. Name the command used to create irregular curves.
14. Define a cubic B-spline.
15. List the types of areas that can be filled using the **SOLID** command.
16. Name the command used to change the size of a drawing in the data base.

DRAWING ASSIGNMENTS

1. Do those drawings assigned by your instructor from Figures 5.59 through 5.66.
2. From Giesecke et al.., *Engineering Drawing* , 5th ed., or *Technical Drawing*, 9th ed. Drawing assignments from Chapter 4.

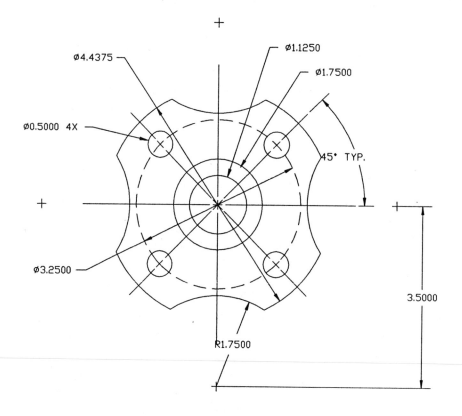

Figure 5.59 Spacer.

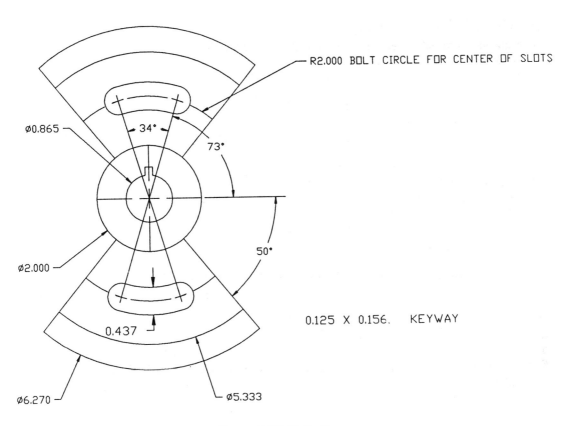

R2.000 BOLT CIRCLE FOR CENTER OF SLOTS

Ø0.865

34°

73°

Ø2.000

50°

0.437

0.125 X 0.156.   KEYWAY

Ø6.270

Ø5.333

Figure 5.60 Butterfly.

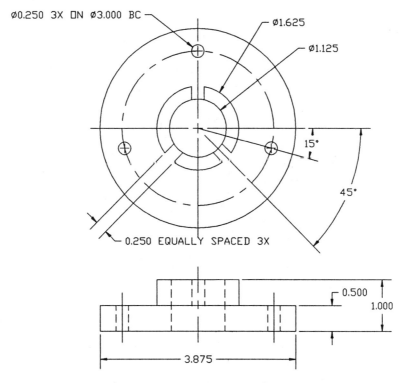

Ø0.250 3X ON Ø3.000 BC

Ø1.625

Ø1.125

15°

45°

0.250 EQUALLY SPACED 3X

0.500

1.000

3.875

Figure 5.61 Slot Support.

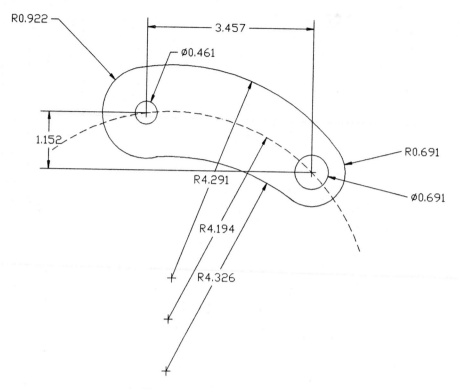

Figure 5.62 Cam Arm.

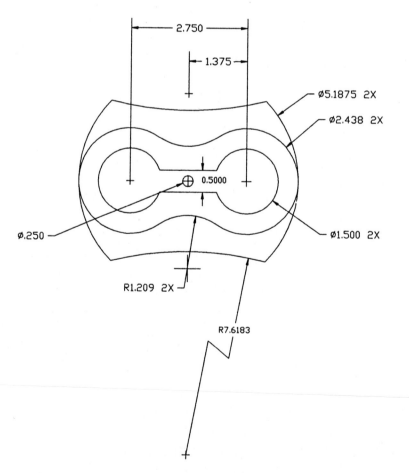

Figure 5.63 Eye Stop.

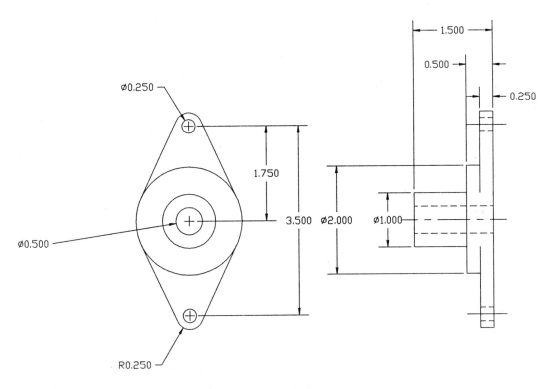

Figure 5.64 Spindle Support.

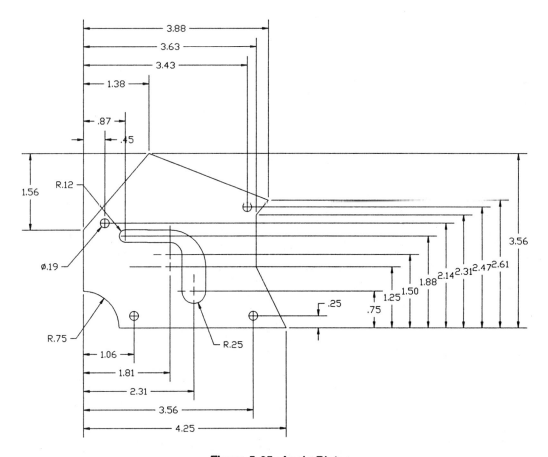

Figure 5.65 Angle Plate.

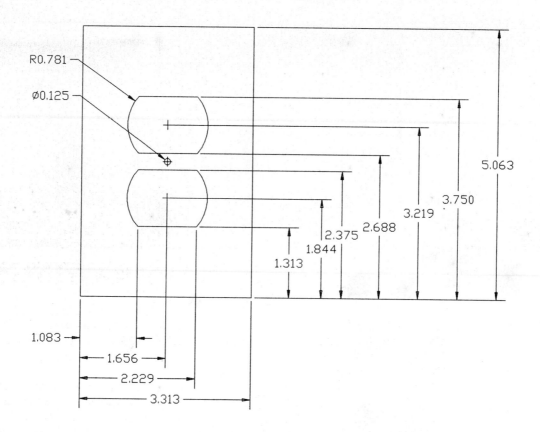

Figure 5.66 Outlet Plate.

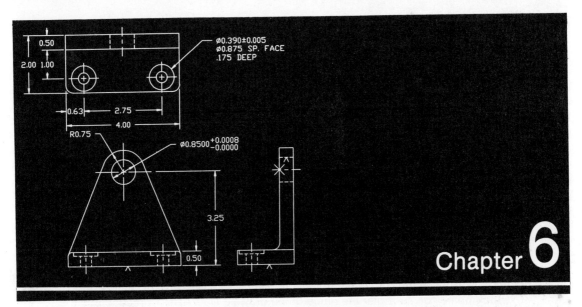

Chapter 6

MULTIVIEW DRAWINGS

Designers normally conceptualize a design in their minds then refine their ideas by sketching on paper. After the design has been refined further, the instrument or CADD drawings are created. These final design drawings, created to manufacture the part, are usually in the form of multiview drawings. This chapter describes how to most effectively create multiview drawings with CADD.

One of the most efficient methods of creating multiview drawings is through the use of templates. With traditional tools, templates are used to create circles, fasteners, doors, windows, or other common features of a drawing that are frequently used. Templates are thin plastic instruments with cutouts of shapes commonly used in engineering drawings. CADD provides a method to create templates similar to those used with traditional tools. Common names used for these electronic templates are macros, symbols, blocks, and patterns. Any object to be used more than once on a CADD-produced drawing is a candidate for creation of an electronic template.

AutoCAD calls the electronic symbols **BLOCKS** or **WBLOCKS**. To speed drawing, users of a CADD system usually create their own set of symbols or blocks for commonly used objects. For example, an industry that frequently uses fastening devices produces them as blocks. After several related blocks are created, they usually are referred to as a library of symbols. A **library** can be defined as a collection of related blocks. This chapter also describes how to create, store, retrieve, manipulate, and edit blocks.

OBJECTIVES

After completing Chapter 6, you will be able to:
1. Create a multiview drawing of a design,
2. Create a Drawing Plan before starting the multiview drawing,
3. Create a block,
4. Store a block,
5. Retrieve and position a block on a drawing,
6. Edit a block,
7. Draw fillets, rounds, chamfers, and runouts,
8. Create a break line for a partial view.

CREATING TEMPLATES

Creating symbols with CADD is something that should be understood and used frequently because it can save the designer many hours of time when creating an engineering drawing. Before a designer starts any engineering drawing, some thought is given to the most effective method to create a drawing with the CADD system to maximize its efficient use. This initial preparation, called a Drawing Plan, is described in detail later in this chapter.

One area that should be considered carefully is the use of blocks. **BLOCK** is the AutoCAD command to create a template of any single entity or group of entities even whole drawings. Given names up to 31 characters, blocks can be inserted into a drawing at any scale and rotation angle. Blocks created from entities of different colors, linetypes, and layers retain those properties unless they were created on layer zero. Blocks created on layer zero take on the properties assigned to the layer where they are inserted. Use the **CHANGE** command to move blocks to another layer. Blocks not only save time but help create a customized set of drawing parts. Changes in drawings are accomplished more easily if parts of the drawing are blocks. Blocks also save disk storage space, which is important for large drawings.

BLOCKS can only be used in the drawing file in which they were created unless they are copied into a new drawing file. The steps below show how to use **BLOCKS** created on another drawing:

Copying Blocks into a New File: Exercise 6.1

1. Open a new drawing.
2. Enter **INSERT** at the command prompt or select it from the **BLOCK** menu.
3. **Block name (or ?):** Enter the name of the drawing file **LAB6-1** preceded by the directory location of the file.
4. **Insertion point:** Enter **CTRL-C.** This cancels the command but invisibly places the drawing file into the current drawing so any blocks can be used. This can be verified by using **BLOCK** and the **?** option to list the block names.

CREATING WBLOCKS

A **WBLOCK** is one of the **BLOCK** options than can be used on any drawing because it is an individual drawing file (DWG extension). Therefore any drawing file (DWG extension) already is a **WBLOCK** ready for insertion into another drawing. **WBLOCKS** are entire drawings so they take more file space than **BLOCKS.** To create a **WBLOCK** from a **BLOCK,** use the following steps:

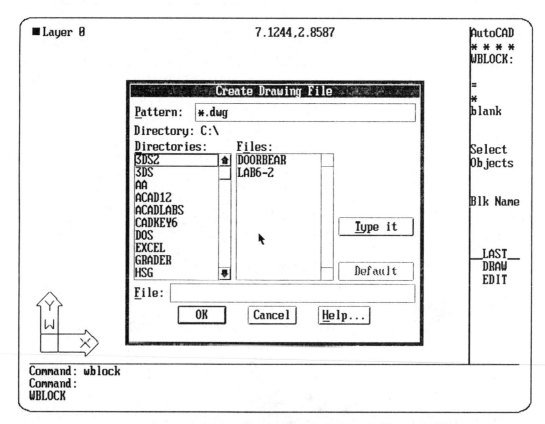

Figure 6.1 The WBLOCK Pop-up Menu used to create a WBLOCK of the hexagon.

Creating a Wblock: Exercise 6.2

l. Enter **WBLOCK** at the command prompt or select it from the **BLOCK** menu.

2. The drawing file dialogue box is displayed on screen as shown in Figure 6.1. Enter the name to be used for the **WBLOCK** by pointing at the file line in the dialogue box and entering the name. You are limited to 8 characters for a **WBLOCK** file name.

3. After the name of the drawing file is entered, a prompt reads

Block Name:

Enter the name of the **BLOCK** to be made into a **WBLOCK** or enter the = (equal) symbol to assign the same name.

To make a **WBLOCK** from a drawing which is not a **BLOCK** use the same steps discribed above except at step 3:

3. **Block name:**   Select **RETURN.**

4. **Insertion base point.** Pick a point on the drawing with the cursor or enter **W** and use a window. All the entities selected will become a new **WBLOCK** that can be inserted into any drawing.

CREATING A BLOCK

The **BLOCK** command creates new blocks from the currently displayed drawing. Blocks also are created in an editing session solely to create a library of symbols for a drawing. This session is where the pre-planning of a drawing may indicate that parts of a drawing may be created most effectively using blocks. These blocks are created before the drawing is started and are placed in a library. For example, suppose that an assembly drawing must be created of the roller support like that shown in Figure 6.2. Standard ANSI features such as nuts, bolts, and washers may be available from third-party software companies, as shown in Figure 6.3, or they can be created with AutoCAD. Other parts of the assembly can be created by making part of the working engineering drawing a block. For example, Figure 6.4 shows the three-view engineering drawing of the angle created earlier. A block is made of the right-side view and used for the assembly drawing. Figure 6.4 and the following steps describe the creation of the right-side view as a block.

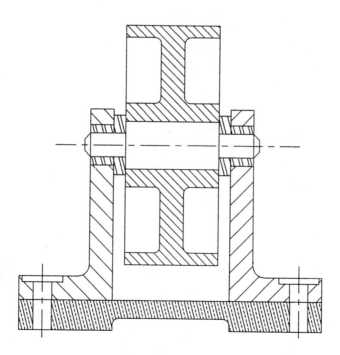

Figure 6.2 An assembly drawing that can be created entirely from blocks.

Creating a Block: Exercise 6.3

1. Open file **LAB6-2**. Enter the **BLOCK** command from the tablet menu, at the command prompt, or from the Root Menu.

2. **Block name (or?):**

Enter **?** to list the names of the blocks in the drawing on the screen. Enter the name of the block by typing up to 31 characters and press RETURN. The characters can be letters, numbers, or special characters. For this example, enter **ANGLE** and press RETURN.

3. If the name **ANGLE** has already been used, a prompt reads:

Block ANGLE already exists. Redefine it? <N>:

Entering **NO** exits the **BLOCK** command. Entering **YES** redefines the block. Enter yes for this example.

4. **Insertion base point:**

The base point is similar to the one used for copying entities as explained in Chapter 5. It is the "handle" used to position the block onto the drawing and uses any of the entity selection methods described in Chapter 5. Some pre-planning should be done before the point is selected. When creating an assembly drawing, the center lines of drilled holes are usually good locations for base points. Enter **INTERSECT** and select the intersection of the center line and object line, as shown with **X** in Figure 6.4.

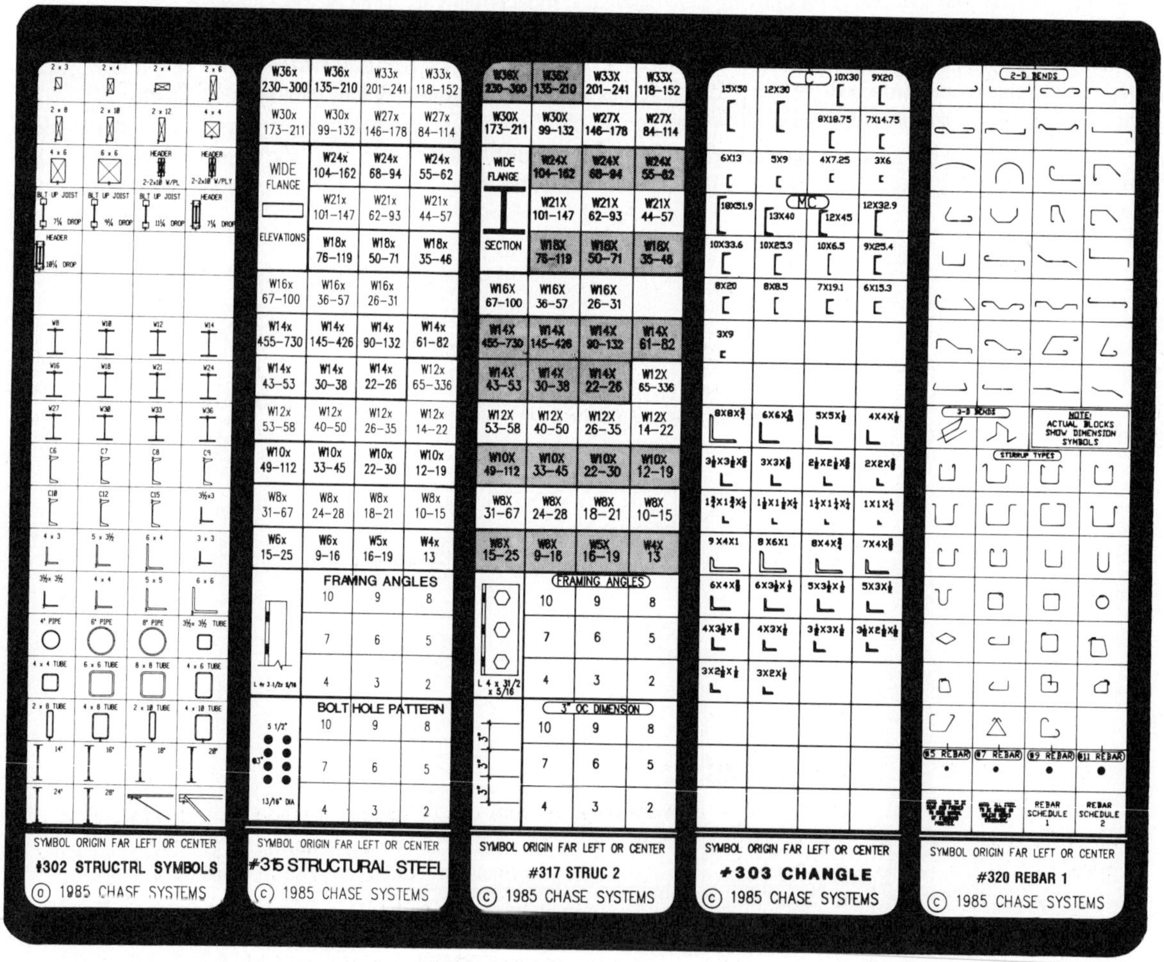

Figure 6.3 Third-party software companies provide ANSI standard and other common parts (Courtesy of Chase Systems).

5. **Select objects:**
The quickest method of selecting all the entities in the side view is with the **WINDOW** option. Select two opposite corners of a rectangle that surrounds the side view. Enter RETURN after the objects are highlighted on the screen. The entities are selected and erased from the screen. Enter **OOPS** to restore the entities to the screen. The block has been created and the definition is stored in the drawing data base. To save the block on disk, the **WBLOCK** command must be used.

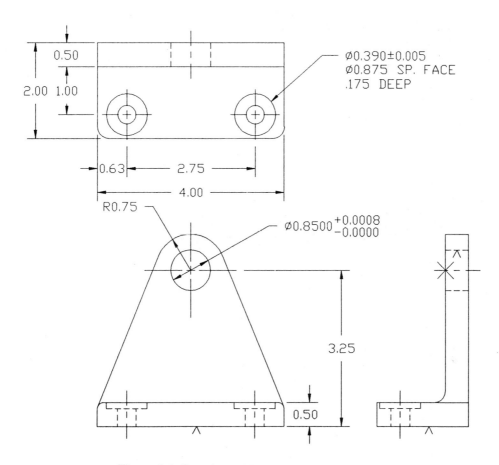

Figure 6.4 Creating a block of the right side view.

Placing Blocks On a Drawing

The **INSERT** command places a block on a drawing. A block can be scaled with independent values used for the X and Y axes. The block also can be rotated, using the **INSERT** option. By entering negative scale values, mirrored images can be created. When a block is created, it is considered one entity, no matter how many entities make up the block. To break the block into separate entities, an asterisk * can be entered before the block name when placing it on a drawing.

If a block is to be inserted into another drawing, such as the Angle block onto the assembly drawing, it first must be accessible to any drawing with the **WBLOCK** command. The following steps describe the **WBLOCK** command:

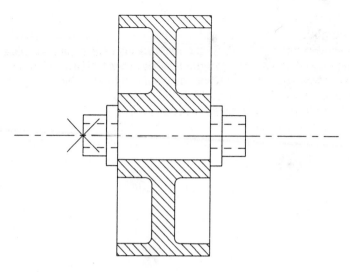

Figure 6.5 Location of insertion points.

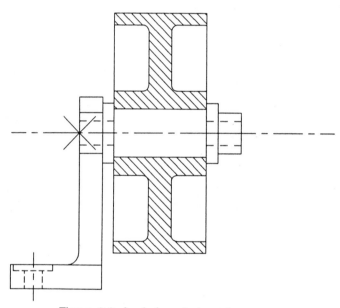

Figure 6.6 Angle inserted as shown.

Creating a Wblock of the Angle: Exercise 6.4

1. Enter **WBLOCK** at the command prompt.
2. **File name:**
Enter the name of the file to be created from the block on the disk limited to 8 characters. For this example, use the name **ANGLEBLK** preceded by the directory and press RETURN.
3. **Block name:**
Enter the name of the block, which for this example is **ANGLE**. AutoCAD creates a new file called **ANGLEBLK.DWG**. Now that it is in the DWG format, it can be inserted into any drawing file.

Figure 6.6 and the following steps describe the **INSERT** command.

1. Load file **LAB6-3**. Select **INSERT** from the Block submenu.
2. **Block name (or ?):**

For this example, enter **ANGLEBK** preceded by the directory and press RETURN.

3. **Insertion point:**

Enter the osnap command **INTERSECT** and pick the center line and outside edge of the bushing, as indicated by **X** on Figure 6.5. If the **DRAGMODE** is on, the Angle drags across the screen as the cursor is moved.

4. **X scale factor <1> / Corner/ XYZ:**

The default scale setting is 1 and is indicated in the brackets. **CORNER** defines the corners of a box, similar to a window, with the X, Y dimensions of the box becoming the X, Y scale of the block. **XYZ** is used for 3D applications that are described in Chapter 11. For this example, the assembly drawing has a full scale so press RETURN.

5. **Y scale factor (default=X):**

For this example, press RETURN to use the same scale factor used for X.

6. **Rotation angle <0>:**

No rotation is necessary, so enter RETURN. The Angle is added to the drawing, as shown in Figure 6.6.

To place the Angle on the other side of the assembly, it must be mirrored. The following steps describe how to mirror a block:

Mirroring a Block: Exercise 6.5

1. Select **INSERT** from the Block submenu.
2. **Block name (or?):**

Enter a **?** to list the block names. For this example, enter **ANGLEBLK** preceded by the directory and press RETURN.

3. **Insertion point:**

Enter the command **INTERSECT** and pick the center line and outside edge of the bushing, as indicated by **X** on Figure 6.7.

4. **X scale factor <1> / Corner/ XYZ:**

To mirror the block enter **-1** and press RETURN.

5. **Y scale factor (default=X):**

Enter the number **1** and press RETURN.

6. **Rotation angle <0>:** No rotation is necessary, so enter RETURN. The Angle is added to the drawing, as shown in Figure 6.8.

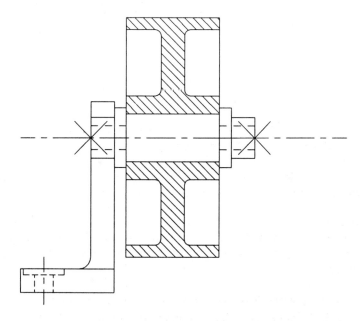

Figure 6.7 Location of insertion point for a mirrored block.

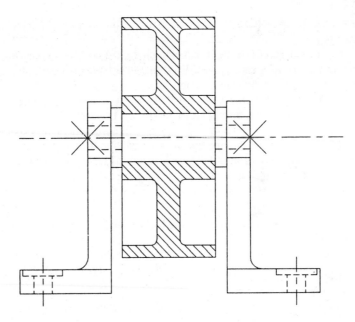

Figure 6.8 Angle mirrored and drawn on the assembly.

Placing Multiple Copies of a Block

Blocks can be copied in a series of rows and columns similar to an Array, as described in Chapter 5. The **BLOCK** submenu command **MINSERT** creates the pattern of holes on the Drying Plate shown in Figure 6.9. The block to be copied is shown in the upper left corner of the screen in Figure 6.9. It already has been defined as a block called "HOMEPLATE." The point (X) to start the block array is located near the upper left corner of the plate. Four rows and six columns with 1.5 spacing are needed for the block array. The following steps demonstrate how the **MINSERT** command creates multiple copies of blocks:

Placing Multiple Copies of a Block: Exercise 6.6

1. Load file **LAB6-4.** Select **MINSERT** from the Block submenu.
2. **Block name (or?):**
For this example, enter **HOMEPLATE** and press RETURN.
3. **Insertion point:**
Enter the command **NODE** , if a POINT is used, and pick the point, as indicated by **X** on Figure 6.9.
4. **X scale factor <1> / Corner/ XYZ:**
The full scale is used by entering RETURN.
5. **Y scale factor (default=X):**
Enter RETURN.
6. **Rotation angle <0>:**
No rotation is necessary so enter RETURN.
7. **Number of rows (—)<1>:**
The number of rows needed for this example is four. Enter the number **4** and press RETURN.
8. **Number of columns (III)<1>:**
Enter **6** for the number of columns.
9. If a number other than one is entered, another prompt reads:
Unit cell or distance between rows (—):
Enter the distance between rows as **-1.5** and press RETURN. The negative value is used to draw the rows below the insertion point. Positive values are used to draw rows above the insertion point.

10. Unit cell or distance between columns (III):
Enter the distance between the columns as **1.5** and press RETURN. Positive values are used to draw to the right and above of the insertion point; negative values draw to the left and below. The Drying Plate is completed as shown in Figure 6.10.

Figure 6.9 The **MINSERT** command is used to create multiple copies of a block.

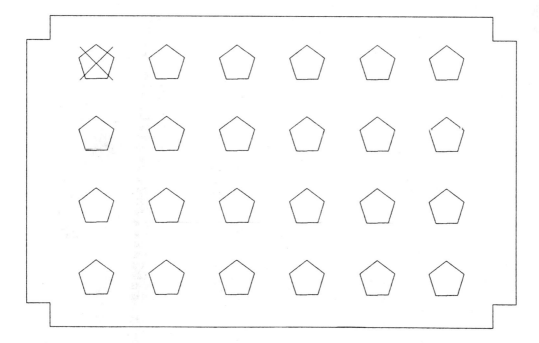

Figure 6.10 Four rows and six columns with 1.5 spacing created using **MINSERT**.

Editing and other Special Block Functions

A block is considered as one whole entity though it may contain many entities. As described earlier, a block is separated into multiple entities by entering an asterisk * before the name of the block for the Insert command. Another method is to use the Edit subcommand **EXPLODE**. Entering the **EXPLODE** command and picking any entity on an inserted block forces a redraw of the block. The object is no longer a block if the X, Y, and Z scale factors are the same.

The names of blocks also can be changed, using the Utility submenu command **RENAME**. The **RENAME** command displays a prompt **Block/LAyer/LType/Style/View:**. Select the Block option from the list, then enter the name of the block to change at the **Old block name:** prompt. Then enter the new name of the block at the **New block name:** prompt.

CREATING A DRAWING PLAN

A Drawing Plan is a critical part of creating any drawing with CADD. It plans the most effective method of using the software to create the drawing. The time and reflection spent with the Drawing Plan are recovered quickly as the drawing is produced. A Drawing Plan organizes the drawing so that the most effective features of CADD are

DRAWING PLAN

Drawing Name:_____ **Part #:**_____

Drawing Assembly:_____

File Name:_____ Sub-Directory:_____

Drawn By: _____ Date:_____

Revised By:_____ Date:_____

Units:_____ Drawing Limits:_____

Drawing Border:_____ Width of Drawing:_____

Height of Drawing:_____ Depth of Drawing:_____

Distance between views:_____ Centering Dimensions:_____

Edit commands (Mirror, Copy, etc.) _____
_____

Plotting Scale:_____

Special Linetypes:_____

Hatch Patterns:_____

Note Text Style:_____ Dimension Text Style:_____

Height:_____ Width/Aspect:_____

LAYER	DESCRIPTION	COLOR	PEN

Blocks:_____

Notes:_____
_____
_____
_____
_____
_____
_____

Figure 6.11 A drawing plan sheet.

used at the proper times. For example, symmetrical objects sometimes are created more quickly using the **MIRROR** option. Separating entities by layers, color, and pen numbers before the drawing is started results in a much more organized drawing file. This type of file better lends itself to editing by the user (Figure 6.11).

Before the Drawing Plan is created, visualize the design by sketching the necessary views. Appropriate views must be selected that describe the part completely with the fewest hidden lines. After those decisions are made, the Drawing Plan can be completed.

MULTIVIEW DRAWINGS

Engineering graphics is the method used to describe accurately the geometry of 3D shapes by means of drawings on flat 2D sheets of paper (Figure 6.12). This problem of representing 3D shapes on 2D paper has been overcome through the development of orthographic projection. The use of pictorial views also was developed to give technical drawings a sense of depth. However, pictorial views are not very useful for describing with enough detail to be manufactured a complicated shape.

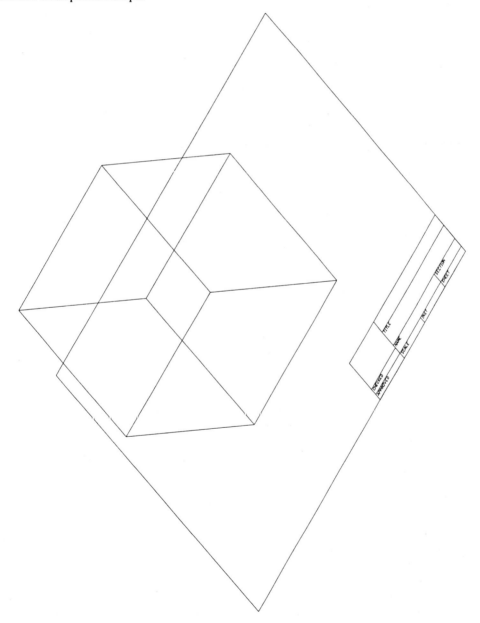

Figure 6.12 Graphically communicating a 3D shape onto a 2D paper is solved through orthographic projection.

To effectively communicate 3D shapes on 2D paper, the part is commonly viewed from the front, top, and right side. These views are created by rotating the object so that a line of sight is perpendicular to its major faces. Another method is to imagine that the part is stationary then move yourself into a position so that your line of sight is perpendicular to the major surfaces of the shape (Figure 6.13). Theoretically, you are positioned at infinity, resulting in the rays of light leading from the object to your eyes being parallel for each principal view. These views then are drawn on paper to represent the 3D shape (Figure 6.14). The top, front, left, and right side views, and the seldom used bottom and rear views comprise the six principal views.

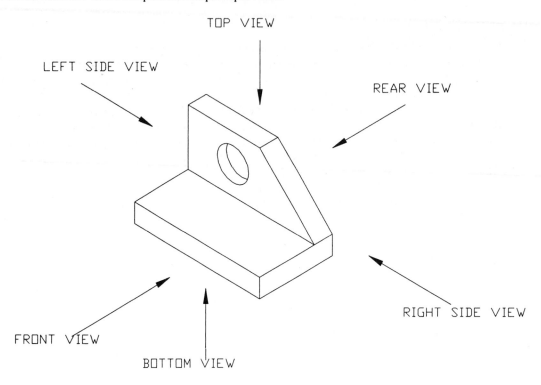

Figure 6.13 Positions of lines of sight to create the six principal views.

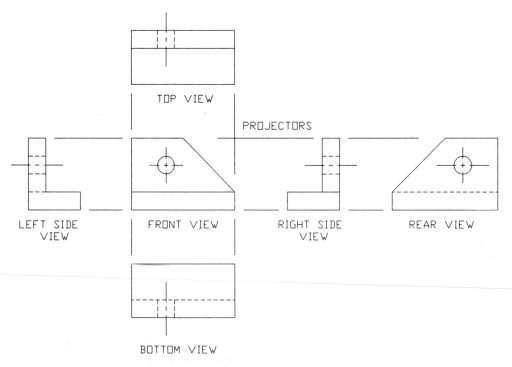

Figure 6.14 The six principal views.

Two dimensions can be viewed in any one principal view. For example, the front view shows the height and width of the object. However, the depth of the object is lost because of the 2D nature of the paper. That is why the front view appears to be flat when in fact it is not.

Multiview drawings are arranged according to the convention shown in Figure 6.14. Projectors can be drawn between adjacent views so that each feature of an object in one view is aligned with those same features in the adjacent view. That is why the side views are of the same height as the front and rear views and are aligned horizontally on the drawing. The top and bottom views are the same width as the front view and aligned vertically on the drawing.

ONE-VIEW DRAWINGS

Occasionally, a part can be described completely with one view. Very thin parts like gaskets, developments for thin metal or paper containers, and printed circuit boards may be effectively described with one view. The thickness of the material is specified in a note.

Before a one-view drawing is created with AutoCAD, the Drawing Plan should be completed. For this example, the "Gasket" shown in Figure 6.15 is used. Determine the overall width and height dimensions of the part to select the appropriate limits and drawing border for the drawing. If AutoCAD's Prototype drawing is being used, the limits will not have to be changed from 0,0 and 12,9 for the Gasket. If the limits must be changed, use the **LIMITS** command from the Settings submenu. If a customized drawing sheet has been created earlier with the **WBLOCK** command, it can be added to this drawing with the **INSERT** command.

The customized drawing border and title block shown in Figure 6.16 are inserted into the drawing using the following steps:

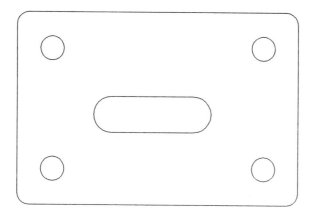

Figure 6.15 One-view drawing of a gasket.

Inserting a Title Block and Border: Exercise 6.7

1. Open a new drawing then select the **BLOCK** command.
2. Select the **INSERT** command.
3. **File name:**
Enter **A-SHEET** preceded by the directory location and press RETURN.
4. **Insertion point:**
Enter **1,1** and press RETURN.
5. **Scale factor <1>/Corner/XYZ:**
Enter RETURN.
6. **Rotation angle <0>:**
Enter RETURN. The drawing sheet is displayed as shown in Figure 6.16.

The one-view drawing should be centered onto the drawing sheet. This is accomplished by subtracting the height of the Gasket (4) from the working height of the drawing sheet (7) and dividing the difference by two. For this example, 4 is subtracted from 7 then divided by 2 to give an answer of 1.5.

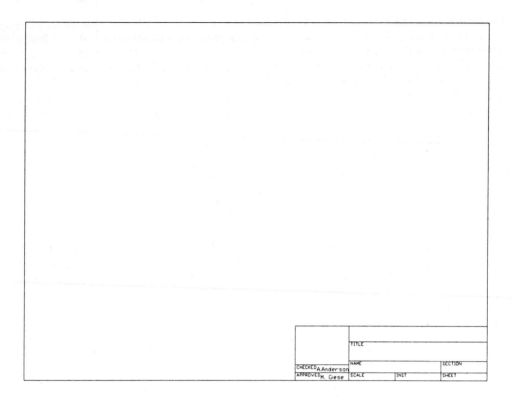

Figure 6.16 Customized A-size drawing sheet.

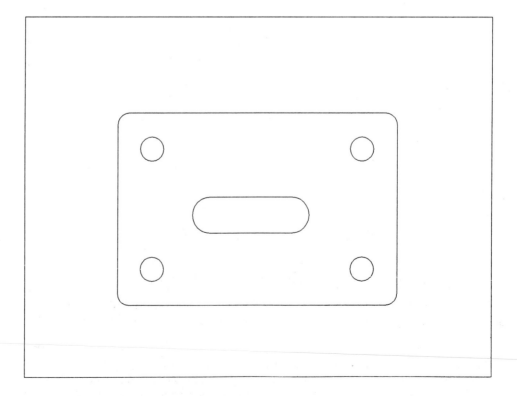

Figure 6.17 The centered gasket.

The drawing is centered from left to right by subtracting the width of the Gasket from the working length of the drawing sheet and dividing the difference by two. For this example, 6 is subtracted from 10, then divided by 2 to give an answer of 2. The drawing is started by creating a rectangle using the **LINE** command and a grid or coordinate point entry. The lower left corner of the rectangle is located at coordinate points 3,2.5. The upper right corner of the rectangle is located at coordinate points 9, 6.5. Remember that the drawing sheet was located at coordinate points 1,1 so the 1 had to be added to the distances to properly center the drawing, as shown in Figure 6.17. The rectangle can be edited and other details added to create the Gasket. A note would also be added to the drawing to indicate that it is .125 thick.

Centering the drawing also can be done by using the **MOVE** command. Each view is moved independently of the others using the **WINDOW** option from the **MOVE** command. The views could then be properly spaced after each is completed.

Using Construction Lines to Create a Drawing

Construction lines are used to make drawings when using traditional tools. Construction lines also are used with AutoCAD to lay out a drawing. The **DOT** linetype is used to represent construction lines on a drawing. Visible, hidden, and center lines are drawn over the top of the dot linetype by snapping to the intersection of the construction lines using **OSNAP** option **INTERSEC**. Construction lines are assigned a separate layer, then frozen after the drawing is completed so they are not displayed or plotted. Figure 6.18 shows the layout of a drawing using **DOT** linetype for construction. Use the Settings subcommand **LINETYPE** to set the linetype to DOT.

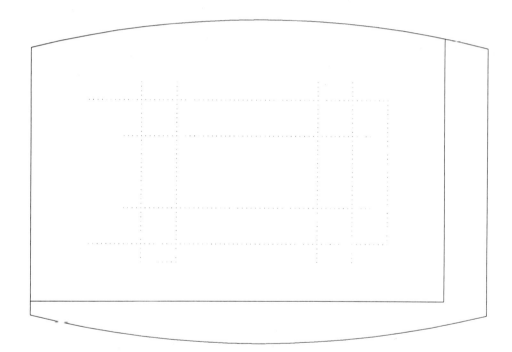

Figure 6.18 Dot lines used for construction.

CREATING TWO-VIEW ENGINEERING DRAWINGS

Occasionally, a part can be described completely with two views. Symmetrical objects, such as wheels, cylinders, and cones, can be described with two views. The Wheel shown in Figure 6.2 of the Roller Assembly can be described completely with two views, as can the Base and Shaft.

Before a two-view drawing is created with AutoCAD, the Drawing Plan should be completed. For this example, the Wheel from the Roller Assembly is used. Determine the overall width, height, depth, and distance between the views of the part to select the appropriate limits and drawing border for the drawing. For the Wheel, the diameter is 5, the depth is 1, and distance between the views is 2 to allow for dimensions. A B-size sheet must be used to accommodate the two-view Wheel drawing.

If AutoCAD's Prototype drawing is used, the limits are changed from 0,0 and 12,9 for the Wheel and B-size sheet using the **LIMITS** command from the Settings submenu. The following steps are used as an example.

Starting a Two-view Drawing: Exercise: 6.8

1. Open a new drawing then select **LIMITS** to display the following prompt:
ON/OFF<Lower left corner> <0, 0>:
The default setting is 0,0 and can be changed by entering new coordinate values. Allowing some additional space for drawing and plotting the border is insured by entering **-1, -1** and pressing RETURN.
2. **Upper right corner: <12,9>:**
To accommodate a B-size drawing sheet and some space for plotting, the coordinate values **18,12** are entered.

If a customized drawing B-size drawing sheet has been created earlier with the **WBLOCK** command, it can be added to this drawing with the **INSERT** command.

The customized sheet shown in Figure 6-19 is inserted into the drawing using the following steps:

Inserting a B-size Title Block and Border: Exercise 6.9

1. Select the **BLOCK** command.
2. Select the **INSERT** command.
3. **File name:**
Enter **B-SHEET** and press RETURN.
4. **Insertion point:**
Enter **0,0** and press RETURN.

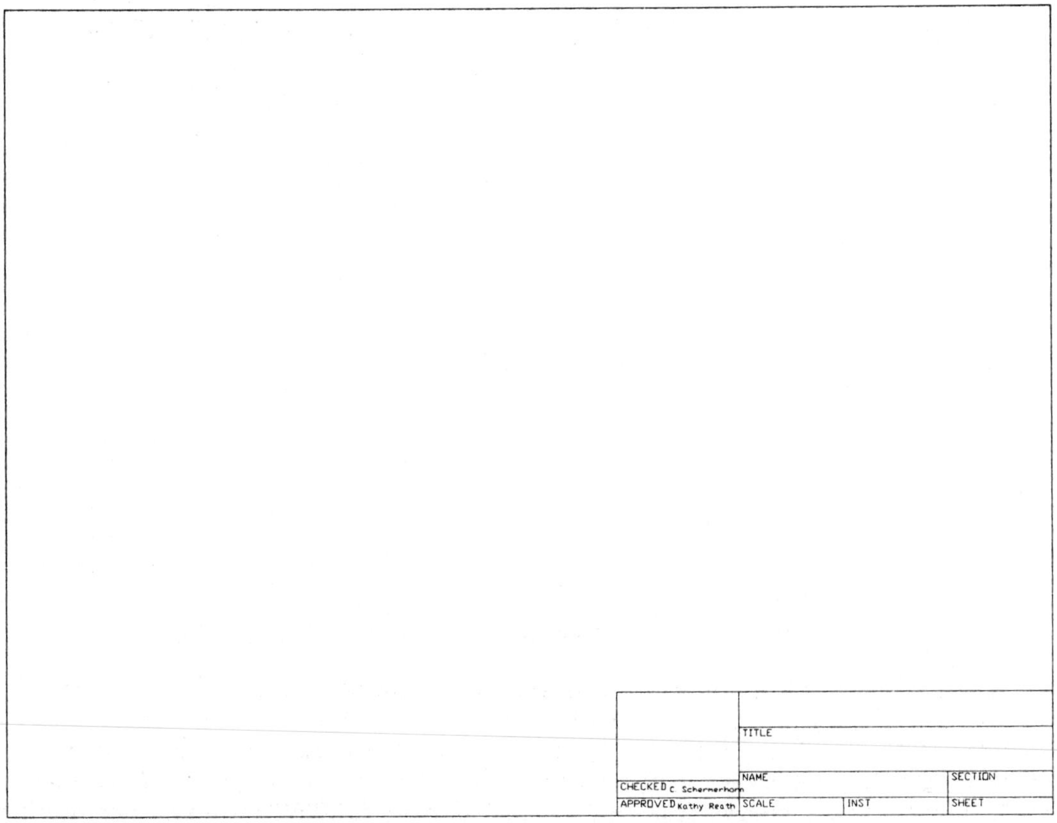

Figure 6.19 Customized B-size drawing sheet.

5. Scale factor <1>/Corner/XYZ:
Enter RETURN.
6. Rotation angle <0>:
Enter RETURN. The drawing sheet is displayed as in Figure 6.19.

The two-view drawing is vertically centered on the drawing sheet by subtracting the diameter of the Wheel from the working height of the drawing sheet and dividing the difference by 2. For this example, 5 is subtracted from 10, then divided by 2 to give an answer of 2.5 to center the drawing vertically.

The drawing is centered from left to right by subtracting the diameter and depth of the Wheel and the space between the views from the working length of the drawing sheet and dividing the difference by two. For this example, 5 (Wheel diameter) is added to 2 (depth of Wheel) and 2 (space between the views) for a sum of 9. Nine is subtracted from 15 then divided by 2 to give an answer of 3. The Wheel is located 3 from the left and right border lines and 2.5 from the top and bottom borders.

To start this drawing, the center lines of the Wheel first should be located on the drawing sheet using DOT linetype. The radius of the Wheel is 2.5 and the distance from the lower border line to the edge of the views is determined to be 2.5. The horizontal center construction line is located on the drawing sheet 5 from the bottom border line. Turn the **Coords** toggle **ON** and the **Ortho** toggle **ON**, then enter the **LINE** command. Draw a horizontal line with a Y coordinate value of 5 as shown in Figure 6.20. Five can be used because the bottom and left sides of the border were located at coordinate points 0,0 when the B-size border was positioned on the drawing.

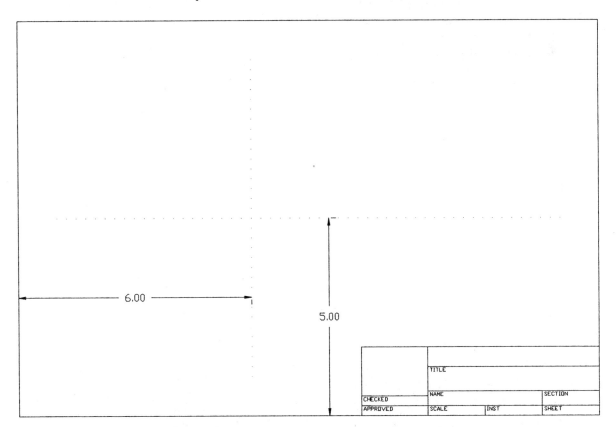

Figure 6.20 Locations of center lines to start the drawing.

The vertical center line for the front view of the Wheel is located by determining the distance from the left border line at which the view is to be located (3), then adding the radius of the Wheel (2.5). The sum of these two values locates the vertical center line. With the **Coords** and **Ortho** toggles **ON**, use the **Line** command to draw a vertical center line with a X coordinate value of 6.0, as shown in Figure 6.20. The wheel is created as shown in Figure 6.21.

Centering the drawing could be done after it is created by using the **MOVE** command. Each view is moved independently of the other using the **WINDOW** Option from the **MOVE** command. The views then are spaced properly after the drawing is completed.

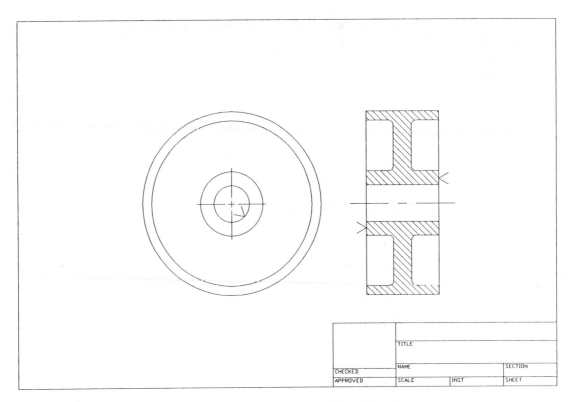

Figure 6.21 The completed Wheel drawing.

THREE-VIEW DRAWINGS

Frequently, a part must be described with three views. A three-view drawing is necessary to describe more complicated parts, such as the Angles found on the Roller Assembly. Although the Angles are not extremely complicated, three views eliminate hidden lines and accommodate dimensions. A section view possibly could be used to eliminate one view of the Angle but that will be discussed later in Chapter 7.

Before a three-view drawing is created with AutoCAD, the Drawing Plan should be completed. For this example, the Angle from the Roller Assembly is used. Determine the overall width, height, and depth of the part, and the distance to be used between the views to select the appropriate limits and drawing border. For the Angle, the width is 4, the depth is 2, the height is 3.5, and the distance between the views is 2 to allow for dimensions. A B-size sheet accommodates the three-view Angle drawing.

If AutoCAD's Prototype drawing is being used, the limits have to be changed from 0,0 and 12,9 for the Angle and B-size sheet. The limits are changed using the **LIMITS** command from the Settings submenu. The following steps are used as an example.

Starting a Three-view Drawing: Exercise: 6.10

1. Open a new drawing then select **LIMITS** to display the following prompt:
ON/OFF<Lower left corner> <0, 0>:
The default setting is 0,0 and is changed by entering new coordinate values. Allow some additional space for plotting the border by entering **1, -1** and pressing RETURN.
2. **Upper right corner: <12,9>:**
To accommodate a B-size drawing sheet and some space for plotting, the coordinate values **18, 12** are entered.

A B-size drawing sheet is used for this drawing by selecting **SETUP** from the Root Menu. If a customized drawing sheet has been created earlier with the **WBLOCK** command, it can be added to this drawing with the **INSERT** command.

The customized sheet is inserted into the drawing using the following steps:

Inserting a B-size Title Block and Border: Exercise 6.11

1. Select the **BLOCK** command.
2. Select the **INSERT** command.
3. **File name:**
Enter **B-SHEET** and press RETURN.
4. **Insertion point:**
Enter **1,1** and press RETURN.
5. **Scale factor <1>/Corner/XYZ:**
Enter RETURN.
6. **Rotation angle <0>:**
Enter RETURN. The drawing sheet is displayed on screen.

The three-view drawing is centered vertically on the drawing sheet. This is accomplished by subtracting the height (3.5) and depth (2) of the Angle and the distance between the views (2) from the working height (10) of the drawing sheet and dividing the difference by 2, leaving 1.25 to center the drawing vertically.

The drawing is centered from left to right by subtracting the width (4) and the depth (2) of the Angle and the space between the views (2) from the working length of the drawing sheet (15) and dividing the difference by 2, leaving 3.5 as the centering distance. The Angle will be located 3.5 from the left and right border lines and 1.25 from the top and bottom borders.

The drawing then is started by creating a rectangle using the **LINE** command. The lower left corner of the rectangle is located at coordinate points 3.5, 1.25. The upper right corner of the rectangle is located at coordinate points 11.5, 8.75, as shown in Figure 6.22. The rectangle can be edited and other details added to create the Angle.

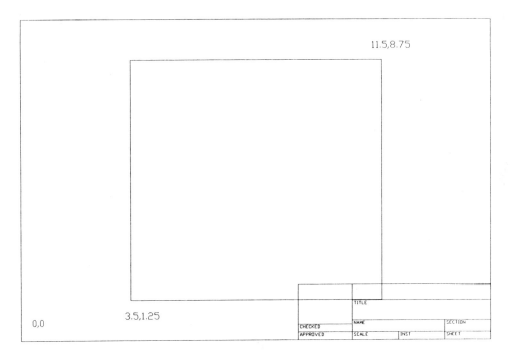

Figure 6.22 Locating a rectangle to create the three-view drawing.

Part of the rectangle falls within the title block located in the lower right corner of the drawing. A number of options can be used to solve this problem. The drawing could be located slightly off center. The views also could be arranged as shown in Figure 6.23. A different type of title block can be used or the title block can be moved to another location. The flexibility of a CADD system allows the user to solve problems in a number of ways. Centering the drawing could be done after it is created by using the **MOVE** and **ROTATE** commands. Each view could be moved independently of the other using the **WINDOW** Option from the **MOVE** command. The views then could be properly spaced after the drawing is completed. It may be easier to move the border rather than the drawing especially if the border is on its own layer.

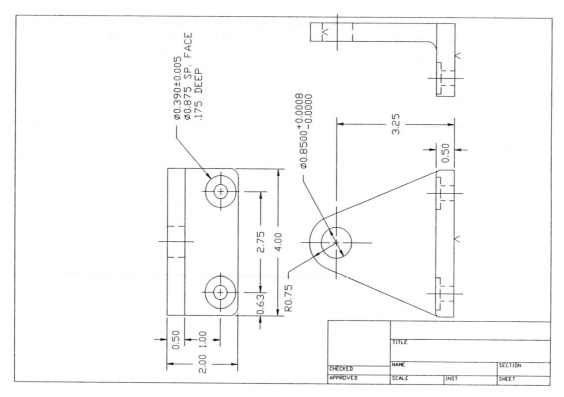

Figure 6.23 An alternative method of arranging views.

OTHER DRAWING CONVENTIONS

Through the years, drawing conventions have developed to standardize engineering drawing practices. For example, partial views commonly are used for symmetrical parts or complicated views like that shown in Figure 6.24. Using AutoCAD to create some of the more common drawing conventions, such as partial views, break lines, chamfers, runouts, fillets, rounds, and hidden line conventions, is explained.

Partial Views and Break Lines

Occasionally a drawing is so complicated that creating partial views of the part is acceptable practice. Figure 6.24 shows an L-shaped part that is better represented as a partial view. Partial views are created as normal orthographic views, except a part of the drawing is incomplete. A break line limits the extent of the part, as shown in Figure 6.24. The break line is drawn with traditional tools as a freehand object line.

A break line is created with AutoCAD using the **SKETCH** command. As explained in Chapter 5, the **SKETCH** command creates lines of any specified length, making it the perfect command for creating a break line. The following steps describe the use of the **SKETCH** command to draw a break line:

Creating Break Lines: Exercise 6.12

1. Open file **LAB6-5**. Select the **SKETCH** command.
2. **Record increment <0.1000>:**
The default value is listed in the brackets and is used for this example. To accept the value, enter RETURN.
3. **Sketch. Pen eXit Quit Record Erase Connect .**
Position the cursor at the start location of the break line and press the button on the input device.

4. **<Pen down>** is added to the prompt. Any movement of the cursor results in the creating of a sketched line. To create a break line like that shown in Figure 6.24, slowly move the cursor in an erratic manner from one end point of a line to the other.
5. Press the button once again on the input device to end the sketched line. **<Pen up>** is added to the prompt.
6. Enter the letter **R** or **RECORD** to accept the break line. A message displays the number of sketched lines needed to be created for the break line, such as **9 lines recorded**. Save the drawing as **LAB6-8.**

An alternate method of making a break line is to use the **LINE** option and create short line segments. **OSNAP** options then can be used to accurately start and end the break line at the ends of current lines.

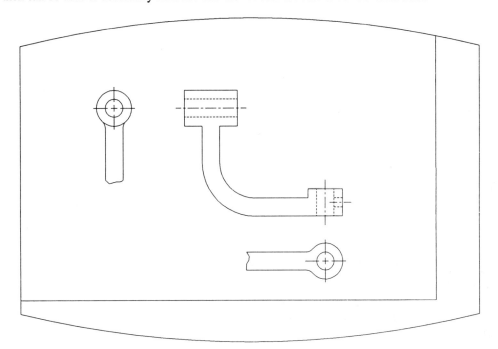

Figure 6.24 Partial views of a part.

Fillets and Rounds

Parts that are designed as castings or forgings are drawn with rounded interior and exterior corners unless one or both of the surfaces are machined finished. Fillets and rounds are easily produced on a drawing with AutoCAD using the **FILLET** command. The **FILLET** command automatically trims lines and arcs before the radius is drawn on the object. The **FILLET** command was explained in Chapter 5 as it relates to the drawing of an arc tangent to two lines. The following steps describe how to create a fillet or round tangent to two lines. Figure 6.25 demonstrates the uses of the **FILLET** command;

Applications of the Fillet Command: Exercise 6.13

1. Load file **LAB6-6.** To create a round tangent to two lines as shown in 6.25A, select the Edit command **FILLET.**
2. **Polyline/Radius/<Select first object>:**
The radius of the round is entered first. This is done by entering the letter **R** or **Radius.**
3. **Enter fillet radius <0.0000>:**
The default value is shown in the brackets. Leaving the value at zero trims corner lines that extend too far, Figure 6.25B, or extend two lines until they intersect and form a corner. For this example, enter **.25** for the radius of the round.

4. Press RETURN again to repeat the **FILLET** command.
5. **Polyline/Radius/<Select first object>:**
Use the pointing device to select the first intersecting line.
6. **Polyline/Radius/<Select second object>:** Pick the second intersectiong line to create the round shown in Figure 6.25A.

The **FILLET** command trims lines and adds the arc shown in Figure 6.25C. Fillets also are drawn between two circles as shown in Figure 6.25D. When using the **FILLET** command circles are never are trimmed. Circles are trimmed later, if required, using the **TRIM** command.

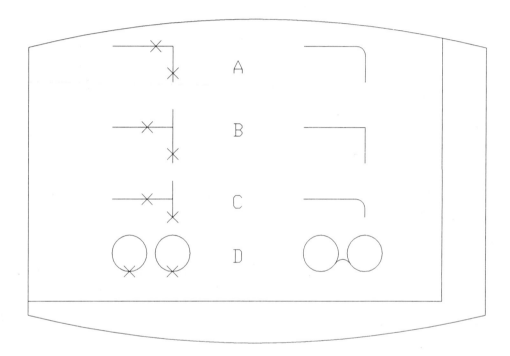

Figure 6.25 Different applications of the **FILLET** command.

Chamfers

A chamfer is a beveled or sloping edge commonly used to break sharp corners that have been machine finished like the end of the bottom shaft in Figure 6.26. AutoCAD provides an automated method of adding chamfers to the corners of drawings. **CHAMFER** is an **EDIT** subcommand that is used to trim corners automatically and add chamfers to lines or extend and add a chamfer to non-intersecting lines. Its operation is very similar to the **FILLET** command used in Figure 6.25B. Two different distances are used to create chamfers that are not at 45 degrees. Setting the chamfer distance equal to zero also trims corners or extends lines to create corners similar to the **FILLET** command.
The following steps and Figure 6.26 demonstrate the use of the **CHAMFER** command;

Drawing Chamfers: Exercise 6.14

1. Load file **LAB6-7** then select the **CHAMFER** command.
2. **Polyline/Distances/<Select first line>:**
The default chamfer distance is set at zero. The distance is set by entering **D** or **Distance** at the prompt.

3.
4.
The
loc
be
5.
If t
ma
loo
prc
rur
6.

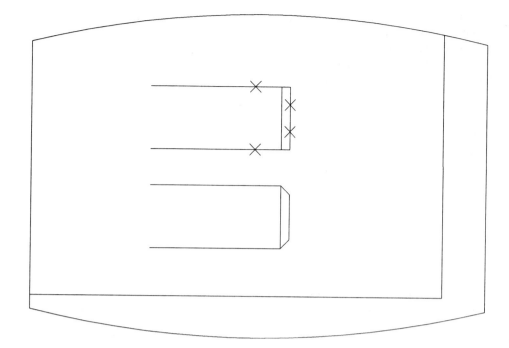

Figure 6.26 Using the **CHAMFER** command to add chamfers to the corners of a part.

3. **Enter first chamfer distance <0.0000>:**
For this example, enter the value **.25** and press RETURN.
4. **Enter second chamfer distance <0.2500>:**
The second distance automatically takes on the value entered at the previous prompt.

QUES

1.
2.
3.
4.
5.
6.
7.
8.
9.
10.
11.
12.
13.
can be u
14.

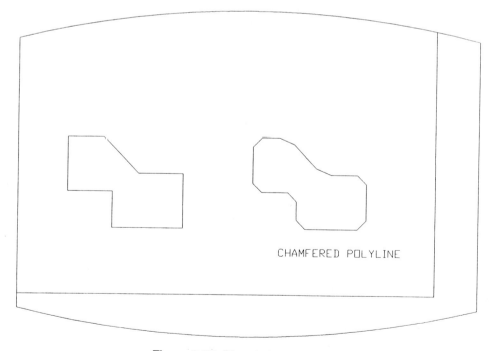

CHAMFERED POLYLINE

Figure 6.27 Chamfering a Polyline.

DRAWING ASSIGNMENTS

1. From Figures 6.30 through 6.50, complete those drawings assigned by your instructor.
2. From Giesecke et al., *Engineering Graphics, 5th ed.* Multiview drawing problems from Chapter 6.
3. Create WBLOCKS of the A-, B-, C-, and D-size drawing sheets created at the end of Chapter 3.

Rur

R
6.28.
of a ci
comm
view
snap
runou

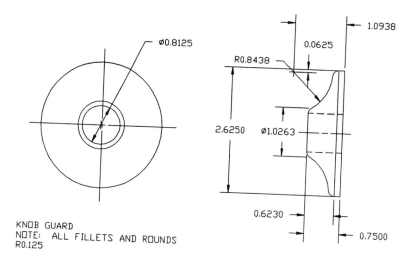

KNOB GUARD
NOTE: ALL FILLETS AND ROUNDS
R0.125

Figure 6.30 Knob Guard.

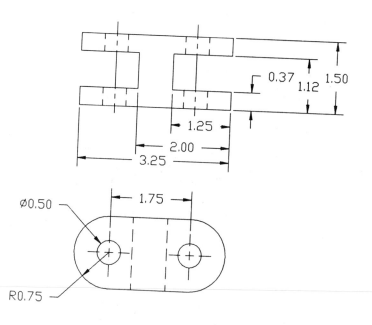

Figure 6.31 Link Pin.

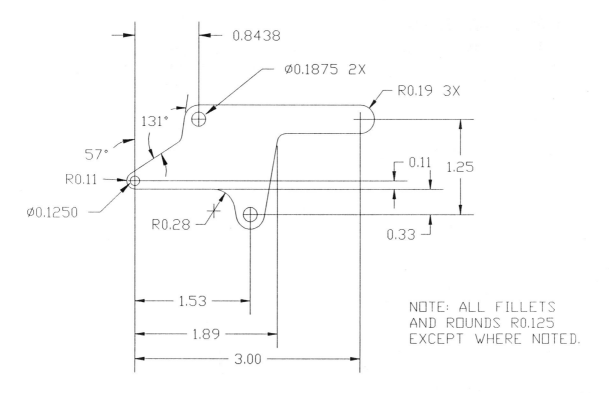

Figure 6.32 Tie Down.

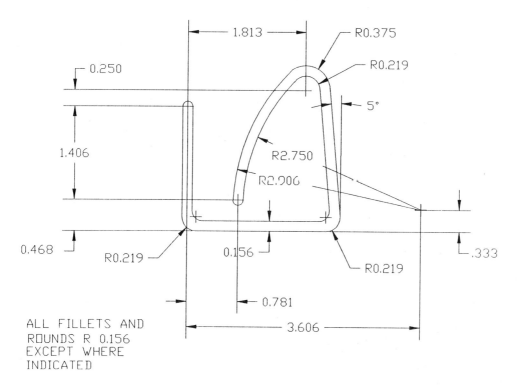

Figure 6.33 Spring Clip.

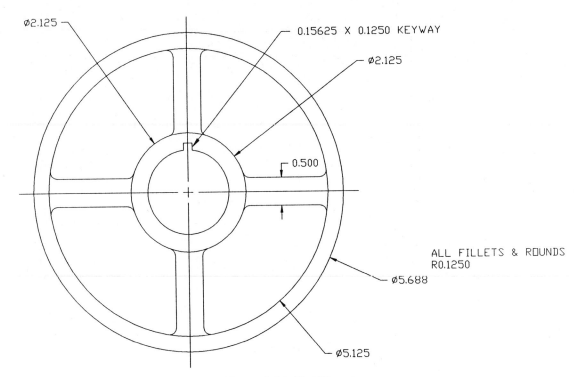

Ø2.125

0.15625 X 0.1250 KEYWAY

Ø2.125

0.500

ALL FILLETS & ROUNDS
R0.1250

Ø5.688

Ø5.125

Figure 6.34 Flat Wheel.

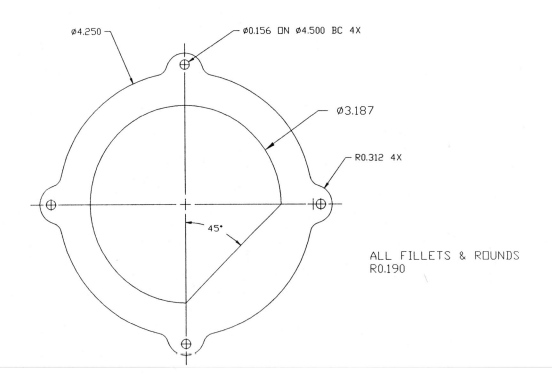

Ø4.250

Ø0.156 ON Ø4.500 BC 4X

Ø3.187

R0.312 4X

45°

ALL FILLETS & ROUNDS
R0.190

Figure 6.35 Gasket.

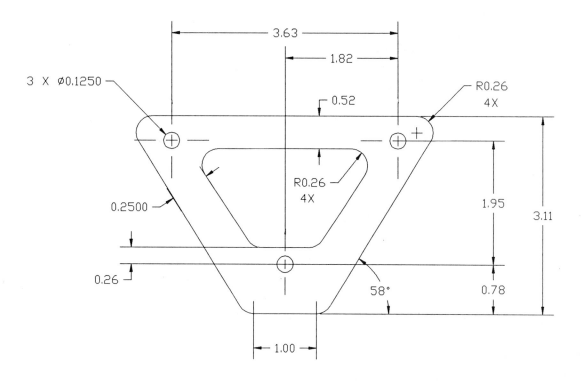

Figure 6.36 Elbow Support.

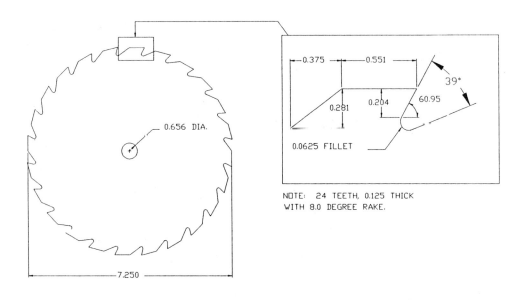

Figure 6.37 Rip Saw.

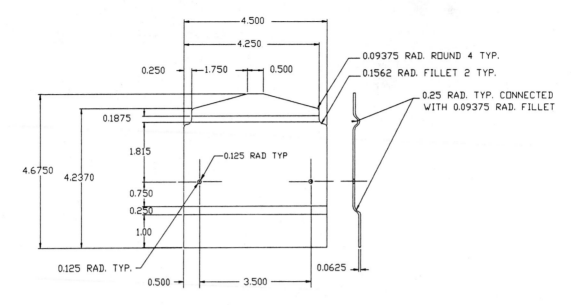

Figure 6.38 Saw Guard. All fillets and rounds .125 Radius.

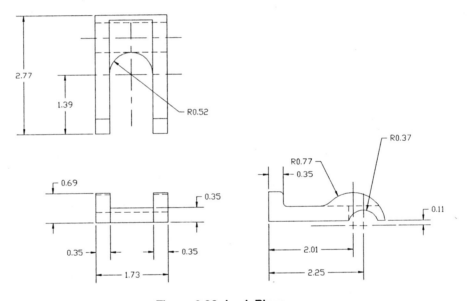

Figure 6.39 Lock Piece.

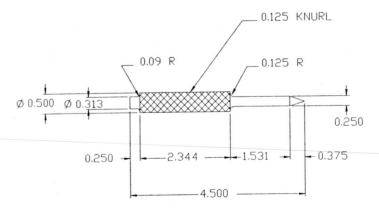

Figure 6.40 Center Punch.

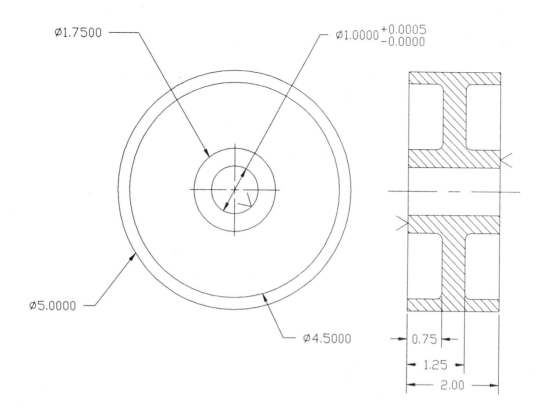

Figure 6.41 Pulley Wheel. Do not section.

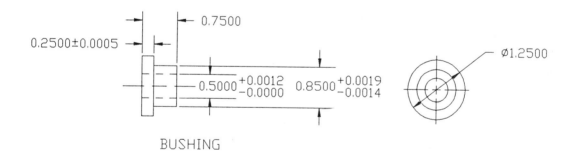

BUSHING

Figure 6.42 Bushing.

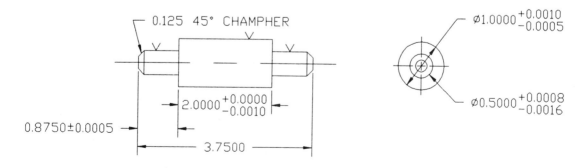

Figure 6.43 Shaft.

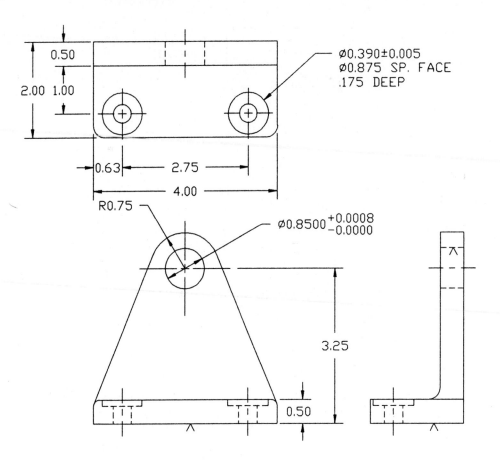

Figure 6.44 Arm.

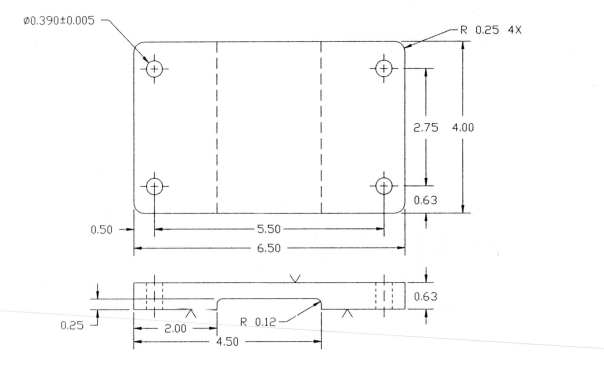

Figure 6.45 Base Plate.

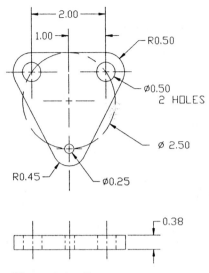

Figure 6.46 Centering Support.

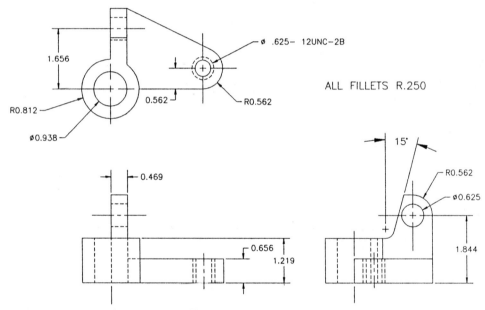

Figure 6.47 Cable Clip.

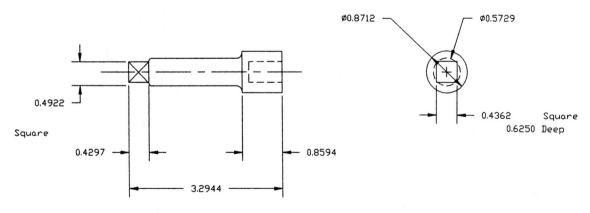

Figure 6.48 Extension.

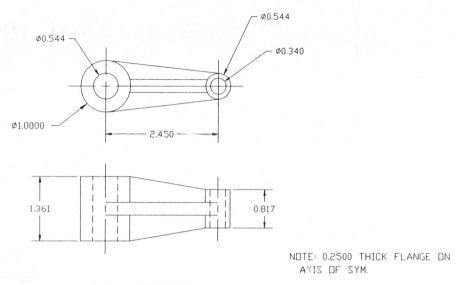

Figure 6.49 Shaft Support.

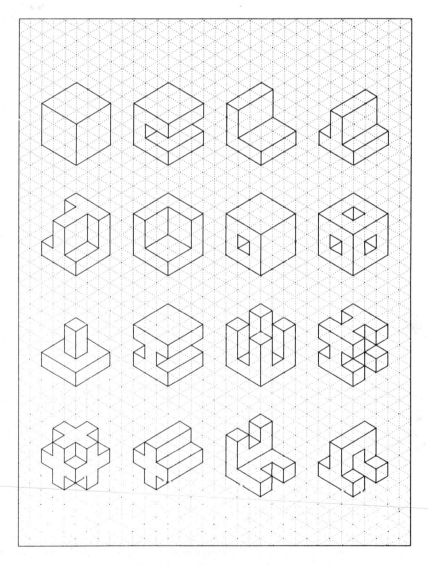

Figure 6.50 Create multiview drawings.

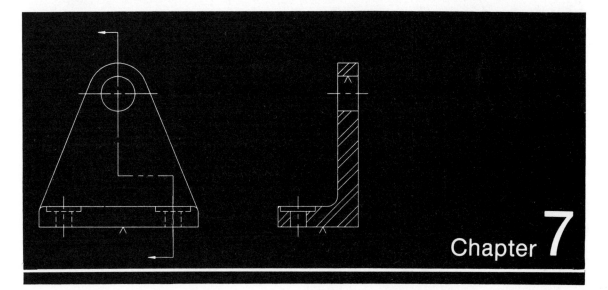

Chapter 7

SECTIONAL VIEWS

Frequently an engineering drawing is so complicated the orthographic views of the design can be very confusing. Drawings that contain many hidden features can result in drawings that are difficult to visualize and dimension. Conventional treatment of this type of drawing is to use a technique of cutting away part of the object to reveal interior details. This type of drawing is called a sectional view.

Sectional views have cross-hatching patterns added to the details of the part. This cross-hatching pattern is added to a drawing with traditional tools by creating successive parallel lines drawn at an angle. This procedure can be very time consuming for large cross-hatched areas. CADD systems have automated this procedure through a command or series of commands. AutoCAD automatically fills an area with any one of 41 predefined cross-hatching patterns, using the HATCH command. This chapter describes how the HATCH command creates different types of sectional views.

OBJECTIVES

After completing Chapter 7, you will be able to:
1. Create and draw a cutting plane line,
2. Fill any enclosed polygon with a hatch pattern,
3. Erase a hatch pattern from a drawing,
4. Define your own type of hatch pattern,
5. Create a full, half, offset, removed, revolved, or broken-out section view,
6. Create orthographic assembly sections, and
7. Create thin parts for sections using conventional practices.

SECTION VIEWS

Section views simplify dimensioning a part, eliminate hidden lines, and more clearly reveal interior features. A sectional view is produced by passing an imaginary cutting plane through an object. Figure 7.1. The cutting plane functions similar to a saw blade that cuts through the object. The cut portion is removed (Figure 7.2) to reveal interior features of the object. The arrows represent the line of sight necessary to view orthographically the sectioned part. Surfaces physically touched by the cutting plane have hatch lines added to them, as shown in Figures 7.2 and 7.3. With AutoCAD, cross-hatching lines are added to a drawing using the **HATCH** command. Hidden lines usually are not drawn in the sectioned view. This is demonstrated in the front sectional view of Figure 7.3 where the slot in the back of the part intersects the sectioned area. Hatch patterns can also be used as artistic patterns and for shading.

The orthographic view of the part shows the front view as the sectioned view. Notice that all visible edges and contours behind the cutting plane are drawn. This is demonstrated in the front view of Figure 7.3 at the holes and the slot in the bottom. The imaginary cutting plane line is shown in the top view where it appears as an edge. Cutting plane lines are terminated by short perpendicular lines with arrows. The arrows point in the direction of the line of sight necessary to see the sectioned view. Letters are sometimes drawn near each end of the cutting plane lines for identification purposes, as shown in Figure 7.4.

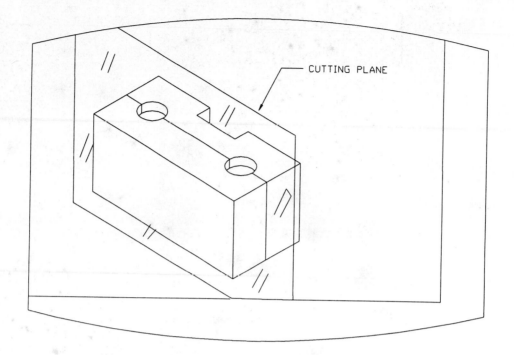

Figure 7.1 Imaginary cutting plane used to create sectional drawings.

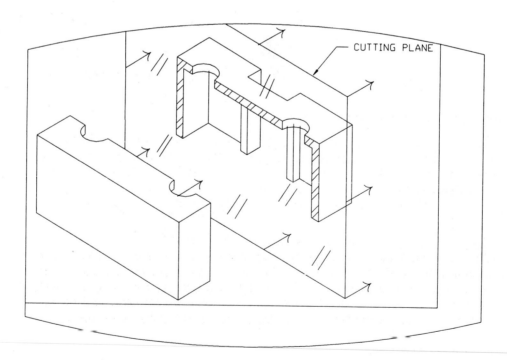

Figure 7.2 Removing part of the object for the sectional view.

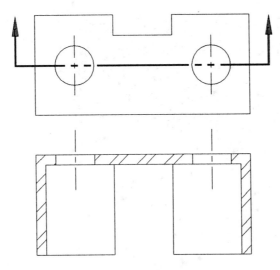

Figure 7.3 Orthographic views of the sectioned part.

Figure 7.4 The two acceptable methods of representing the edge view of the cutting plane on an orthographic drawing.

CUTTING PLANE LINES

Three acceptable methods of representing cutting plane lines on a drawing are shown in the figure. One method uses a series of 1/4-inch dashes, which are drawn with AutoCAD using the Hidden line style. The second cutting plane line can be drawn with AutoCAD using separate line segments, the phantom linetype or by creating your own line style and adding it to the linetype file using the **CREATE** option of the **LINETYPE** command. Each type of cutting plane line is terminated by an arrow drawn perpendicular to the line.

Adding Cutting Plane Lines: Exercise 7.1

1. For this problem the base plate shown in Figure 7.5 is used to create a full section of the front view. Load **LAB7-1** from the data disk. The first step in creating a section is to choose the position of the cutting plane line and add it to the top view. For this example, the cutting plane passes horizontally through the two counterbored holes. Before the line is drawn on screen, it is changed to a cutting plane line. Select the **LINETYPE** command from the Settings Menu.

2. **?/Create/Load/Set:**

Enter the letter **L** or **LOAD** to change the linetype to the cutting plane line. If the linetype is already loaded, enter **S** or **SET**.

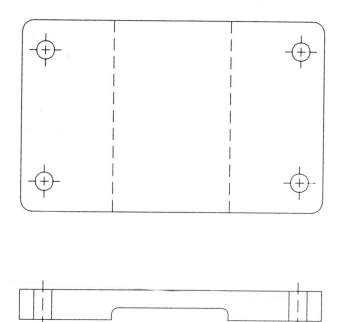

Figure 7.5 The Base Plate ready for sectioning.

3. Linetype(s) to load:
Enter the cutting plane line name **PHANTOM** and press RETURN.
4. A dialogue box is displayed to select the file to search for the linetype. Use the ACAD file to load the phantom line. Enter RETURN if the linetype is located in the default file shown in the dialogue box.
5. The cutting plane is drawn on the top view by entering the **PLINE** command. Pick the start point and the end point of the cutting plane line using snap or coordinate input, as shown in Figure 7.6.
6. A cutting plane line is drawn thicker than object lines. Change the thickness of the Pline representing the cutting plane by entering **PEDIT**.
7. Pick the cutting plane line then press Return.
8. At the Pedit prompt enter **W** to change the line width.
9. Enter **.025** as the new thickness then enter Return to exit Pedit. The line thickness is immediately updated on the drawing. Figure 7.6.
10. Change the linetype back to the CONTINUOUS style using the **LINETYPE** command as described in Steps 1 through 4.
11. Arrows are added to the Pline using the Leader command. The size of the arrow is changed by entering **DIMASZ** at the command prompt. Diamsz is the dimension variable setting for the arow size with a default setting of .18. Enter **.30** as the new dimension arrow size.
12. Arrows drawn perpendicular to the cutting plane line are added to the drawing by using the **LEADER** command found on the Dimension Menu or by selecting it from the Draw/Dimension Pull-down Menu.. A prompt reads:
Leader start:
Pick the left end point of the Pline.
12. **To point:**
Pick the corner of the Pline to terminate the leader line.
13 **To point:**
Enter RETURN to end the leader line.
14. **Dimension text < >:.**
No text is required, so simply enter Ctrl-C. The leader line is drawn as shown in Figure 7.7 with an arrow. Repeat Steps 11 through 14 to add the other leader line to the cutting plane.
15. Save the drawing as **Lab7-4**.

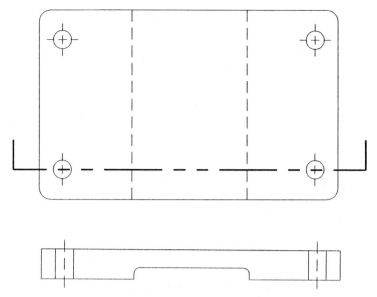

Figure 7.6 Adding the cutting plane line.

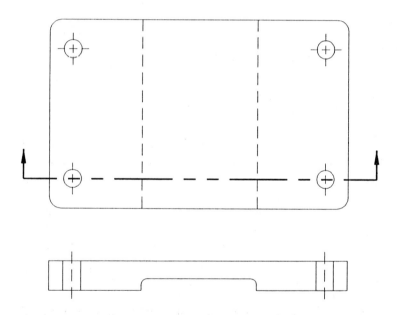

Figure 7.7 Adding arrows to the cutting plane line by using the Leader command.

SECTION LINES

Section lines are added to a part to represent those surfaces that are created by the cutting plane. Different section line patterns have been developed to represent different materials. However, so many different materials can be produced, the cast iron is used as the general purpose symbol for many section drawings. Different section line symbols are used commonly for an assembly in section.

AutoCAD Section Lines

Drawing section lines with traditional tools can be a tedious job. AutoCAD has automated the placement of section lines on a drawing through the use of the **HATCH** command. The **HATCH** command is a **DRAW** submenu option that has 53 different section lining symbols available. AutoCAD refers to section lines as hatch patterns. A listing of the hatch pattern names can be displayed by entering **HATCH** then **?** at the command prompt in Figure 7.8. Select **F1** (flip screen) when finished.

Each hatch pattern is changed from the original form by varying the scale of the pattern and angle at which the pattern is drawn. For example, Figure 7.9 shows two squares filled with the cast iron or general purpose hatch pattern ANSI31. The pattern at the left is at full scale and the default angle. The pattern at the right is drawn at .5 scale and an angle of 60 degrees. You should use a larger scale factor when hatching big areas to save time plotting and regeneration.

The hatch pattern scale is set both relative to the plot scale used and at the reciprocal of the plot scale. For example, if the plot scale is 1/2, then the hatch pattern scale is set to 2.

New hatch patterns can be added to the 53 supplied with the AutoCAD software. New hatch patterns can be created using the **HATCH** command by inputting the spacing and angle between the lines. Hatch patterns added to a drawing are in the form of blocks. This method of drawing hatch patterns is especially convenient if the pattern must be erased. Because the pattern is in the form of a block, each line used for the hatch pattern does not have to be individually selected for erasure. Hatch patterns are erased by picking any single entity in the pattern.

```
ANGLE             -  Angle steel
ANSI31            -  ANSI Iron, Brick, Stone masonry
ANSI32            -  ANSI Steel
ANSI33            -  ANSI Bronze, Brass, Copper
ANSI34            -  ANSI Plastic, Rubber
ANSI35            -  ANSI Fire brick, Refractory material
ANSI36            -  ANSI Marble, Slate, Glass
ANSI37            -  ANSI Lead, Zinc, Magnesium, Sound/Heat/Elec Insulation
ANSI38            -  ANSI Aluminum
AR-B816           -  8x16 Block elevation stretcher bond
AR-B816C          -  8x16 Block elevation stretcher bond with mortar joints
AR-B88            -  8x8 Block elevation stretcher bond
AR-BRELM          -  Standard brick elevation english bond with mortar joints
AR-BRSTD          -  Standard brick elevation stretcher bond
AR-CONC           -  Random dot and stone pattern
AR-HBONE          -  Standard brick herringbone pattern @ 45 degrees
AR-PARQ1          -  2x12 Parquet flooring: pattern of 12x12
AR-RROOF          -  Roof shingle texture
AR-RSHKE          -  Roof wood shake texture
-- Press RETURN for more --
AR-SAND           -  Random dot pattern
BOX               -  Box steel
BRASS             -  Brass material
BRICK             -  Brick or masonry-type surface
BRSTONE           -  Brick and stone
CLAY              -  Clay material
CORK              -  Cork material
CROSS             -  A series of crosses
DASH              -  Dashed lines
DOLMIT            -  Geological rock layering
DOTS              -  A series of dots
EARTH             -  Earth or ground (subterranean)
ESCHER            -  Escher pattern
FLEX              -  Flexible material
GRASS             -  Grass area
GRATE             -  Grated area
HEX               -  Hexagons
HONEY             -  Honeycomb pattern
HOUND             -  Houndstooth check
INSUL             -  Insulation material
-- Press RETURN for more --
LINE              -  Parallel horizontal lines
MUDST             -  Mud and sand
NET               -  Horizontal / vertical grid
NET3              -  Network pattern 0-60-120
PLAST             -  Plastic material
PLASTI            -  Plastic material
SACNCR            -  Concrete
SQUARE            -  Small aligned squares
STARS             -  Star of David
STEEL             -  Steel material
SWAMP             -  Swampy area
TRANS             -  Heat transfer material
TRIANG            -  Equilateral triangles
ZIGZAG            -  Staircase effect

Command:
```

Figure 7.8 Listing of AutoCAD's standard hatch patterns.

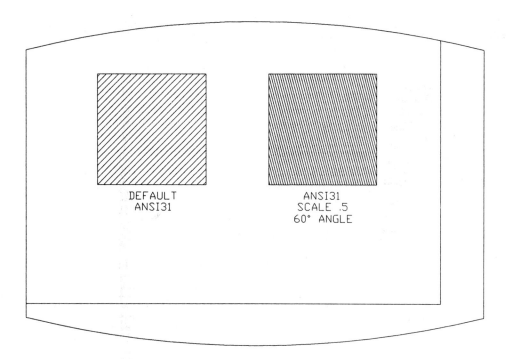

Figure 7.9 The same hatch pattern drawn at different scales and angles.

THE HATCH BOUNDARY

Hatch patterns are added to drawings that are enclosed by a boundary made of lines, polylines, arcs, and circles. Hatch boundaries are defined using any of the object selection methods. The **BHATCH** command automatically defines a boundary. Using the **HATCH** command, the boundary must be selected manually.

Boundary Hatching

BHATCH is the automatic boundary hatching command that hatches a region by simply picking a point inside the region. The boundary of the region is defined automatically, and a polyline is created from the entities that make the boundary. By default the polyline is deleted after the hatching is drawn but it can be retained as an option. Unhatched islands within the hatched region can be defined by picking them. Before the hatching is added to the defined region, it can be previewed for accuracy.

Selecting **BHATCH** from the Draw Pull-down Menu displays the Boundary Hatch dialogue box shown in Figure 7.10. To define the hatch pattern pick the Hatch Options... button which displays the dialogue box shown in Figure 7.11. Pick the Pattern... button to view the standard hatch patterns available from AutoCAD. Figure 7.12. Each pattern is represented graphically with the name of the pattern listed below. ANSI standard patterns are listed as ANSI followed by a number. More patterns can be viewed by picking the Next button. To select a hatch pattern point at the icon and pick it. The icon menu is replaced by the Hatch Options dialogue box with the selected hatch pattern added next to the Pattern... button.

Each hatch pattern is defined with an initial scale and rotation angle of 0 degrees. Use a larger scale to expand the hatch pattern and a smaller scale to contract the pattern. If the user defined option button is selected, then the angle, spacing, and double hatching options must be specified. The hatching style is controlled by the Normal, Outer, and Ignore buttons. The results of the different hatching styles are shown in Figure 7.13.

N- normal, hatch every other feature.

I- interior, hatches entire object ignoring all closed interior areas.

O- outer, hatches outermost area only.

The Exploded Hatch button is turned on if you want the hatch pattern to be made of individual lines. Normally, a hatch pattern is formed as a block containing all its hatch lines. When erasing a hatch pattern only one line in the pattern must be selected to delete all the lines if the exploded button is not selected. The **EXPLODE** command will break hatch blocks into individual lines.

After setting your hatch options select the OK button. The Boundary Hatch dialogue box is displayed. To automatically construct a boundary, select the Pick Point options. A prompt is displayed:

Select internal point

Prompts scroll through the prompt line:

Selecting everything...
Selecting everything visible...
Analyzing the selected data...
Select internal point

Enter RETURN to end the selection. The Boundary Hatch Dialogue box is displayed again. Pick the Preview Hatch button in the dialogue box. The hatching is displayed on the drawing for you to verify its accuracy. The prompt reads: **Press RETURN to continue.** Entering Return displays the hatch dialogue box. To place the hatch pattern onto the drawing select the Apply button. The following steps describe how to hatch the object shown in Figure 7.14:

Using Boundary Hatch: Exercise 7.2

1. Load **LAB7-2** from your data disk.
2. From the Draw Pull-down Menu select **Hatch...**
3. From the hatch dialogue box select Hatch Options...
4. From the Hatch Options Dialogue Box select the **Pattern...** button.
5. An icon menu is displayed showing the various standard hatch patterns. Pick the desired pattern with the mouse by pointing at the pattern and using the pick button on the mouse. For this example pick **ANSI31.**
6. ANSI31 is displayed next to the Pattern... button in the Hatch Options Dialogue Box. Pick the **OK** button to return to the hatch dialogue box.
7. Select the **Pick Points** button to define the area to be hatched.
8. The dialogue box is removed and you can move the cursor to any position inside the area bounded by the lines and arcs that make the drawing. Once the cursor is inside the boundary of the object use the pick button on the input device. The boundary for the hatch area is automatically defined and highlighted.

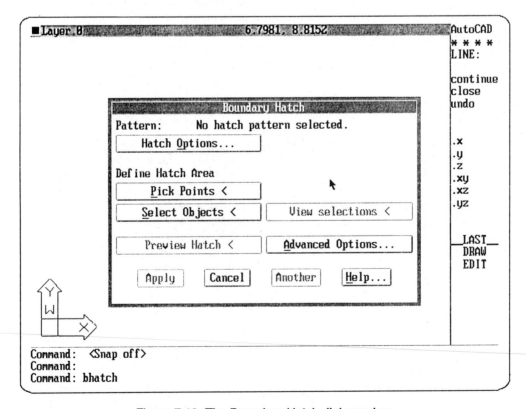

Figure 7.10 The Boundary Hatch dialogue box.

9. At the next **Select internal point** prompt enter Return to end the selection mode.
10. The hatch dialogue box is again displayed. Pick the **Preview Hatch** button to show the hatch pattern on the drawing. Press Return after examining the hatch pattern.
11. If the hatch pattern type and location are acceptable, pick the **Apply** button. The hatch pattern is added to the object as shown in Figure 7.15.

To erase a hatch pattern enter **E** at the command prompt and select any hatch line with the cursor, then enter Return. The hatch pattern will be removed from the drawing. Different steps must be followed to hatch an area with a hole. The following steps describe how to create hatch patterns around holes:

Hatching Around Holes: Exercise 7.3

1. Load **LAB7-3** from your data disk.
2. From the Draw Pull-down Menu select **Hatch...**
3. A different hatch style will be used for this problem. From the hatch dialogue box select **Hatch Options...**
4. From the Hatch Options Dialogue Box select the **Pattern...** button.
5. An icon menu is displayed showing the various standard hatch patterns. Pick the desired pattern with the mouse by pointing at the pattern and using the pick button on the mouse. For this example pick **ANSI32**.
6. ANSI32 is displayed next to the Pattern... button in the Hatch Options Dialogue Box. Pick the **OK** button to return to the hatch dialogue box.
7. Select the **Pick Points** button to define the area to be hatched.
8. The dialogue box is removed and the drawing is displayed. Pick any point inside the boundary of the object except inside the circle. The border is highlighted after selection. Notice that the circle is not highlighted meaning it is not part of the selected border. If the object were to be hatched now the circle would crosshatched. To avoid crosshatching the circle pick a point inside the circle.
9. At the next **Select internal point** prompt enter Return to end the selection mode.

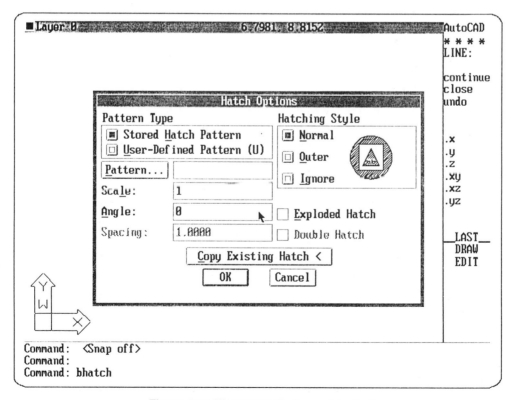

Figure 7.11 The Hatch Options dialogue box.

10. The hatch dialogue box is again displayed. Pick the **Preview Hatch** button to show the hatch pattern on the drawing. Press Return after examining the hatch pattern.
11. If the hatch pattern type and location are acceptable, pick the **Apply** button. The hatch pattern is added to the object as shown in Figure 7.16.

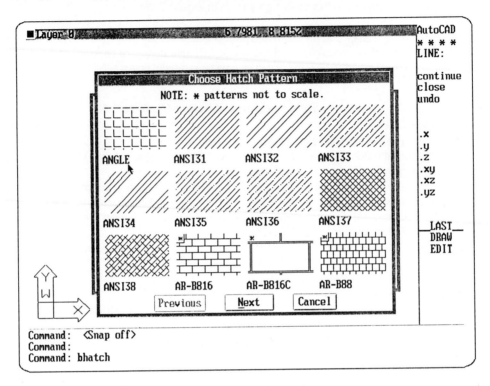

Figure 7.12 The hatch pattern icon menu.

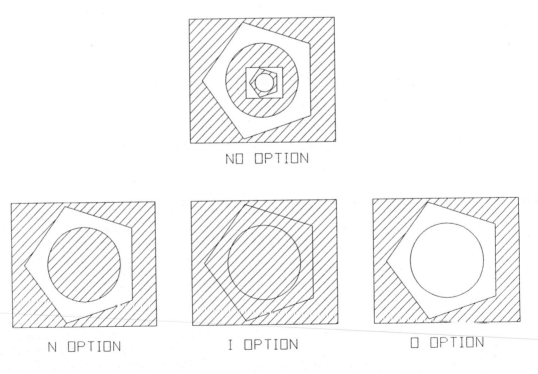

Figure 7.13 The hatching styles.

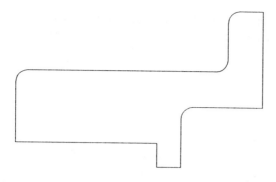

Figure 7.14 Area to be hatched.

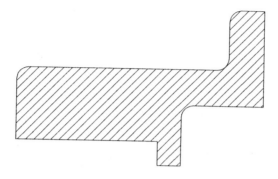

Figure 7.15 Area after hatching.

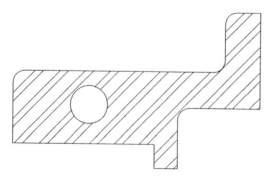

Figure 7.16 Area after hatching.

Using AutoCAD to Manually Place Section Lines on a Drawing

AutoCAD can place a hatch pattern inside of any enclosed polygon made of lines, arcs, circles, and polylines. Each entity of the enclosed polygon must be identified for manual hatching to occur. The manual method of creating a hatch pattern is to use a window or to pick each entity for the hatch boundary. Manual hatching usually demands a considerable amount of pre-planning because of the way AutoCAD needs to have entities drawn for hatch patterns. A hatch pattern only works successfully on enclosed polygons that are bounded by separate entities. In order to create a sectional drawing like that shown in Figure 7.17, each entity of the enclosed polygon must be separate and not overhanging. Lines must not form a "T" as they do in the counterbored hole in Figure 7.17. The exploded view shown to the right in Figure 7.17 better illustrates how each line is drawn separately before the hatch pattern is added.

There are three alternatives to drawing separate entities for the hatch boundaries. One is to use the **BREAK** command to break each entity at the intersecting corners. This may be the most undesirable of the choices because it slows plotting. By selecting the same two points for the **BREAK** command, the entity is broken into two parts.

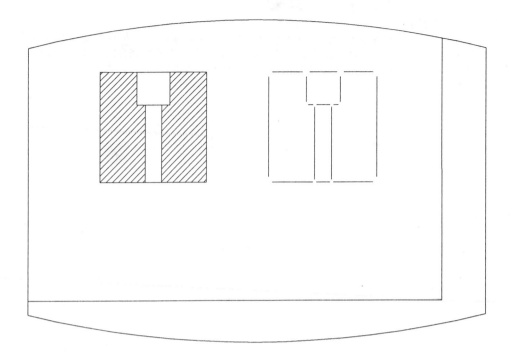

Figure 7.17 Each entity bounding the hatch area must be a separate entity.

The second method of creating the boundaries for a hatch pattern is to trace each entity on a different layer. The third is to trace only the entities that will not be captured in a selection window and put them on a new layer. In the second and third methods the new layer should be turned off after the section lines are created.

CREATING A FULL SECTION VIEW USING MANUAL HATCHING

Many types of sectional views can be used for part description in engineering graphics. Each type of sectional view is used for a specific purpose and depends upon the complexity and general shape of the part being described. A **full section** is a view created by passing a cutting plane completely through a part. The Base Plate of the Wheel Assembly demonstrates the creation of a full sectional view drawing using AutoCAD.

For dimensioning purposes and clarity of the drawing, a full section view of the Base Plate is appropriate. If preplanning is carefully followed, the front view of the Base Plate is created with separate entities as described earlier and without hidden lines in preparation for a full section view. Figure 7.7 shows the Base Plate before hatch lines are added. The following steps are a guide to create full section drawings.

Creating a Full Section View: Exercise 7.4

1. Load **LAB7-4** which was created earlier in Exercise 7.1.
2. For this example, the hatching is added using one of AutoCAD's standard patterns. Enter **HATCH** at the command prompt or select it from the tablet or screen menu.
12. **Pattern (? or name/U,style)**
If a pattern already was used in this drawing session, it will be listed in brackets at the prompt. A listing of the standard patterns is seen on screen by entering **?** at the prompt and pressing RETURN. If the name is known it can be entered at the prompt. For this example enter **ANSI31** and press RETURN. ANSI31 is the standard iron symbol used for most engineering drawings.
13. **Scale for pattern <1.0000>:**
Use the default scale by entering RETURN.
14. **Angle for crosshatch lines <0>:**
The default value is shown in brackets. Actually the default setting draws the pattern at the recommended angle of 45 degrees. Press RETURN to use the default setting.

15. Select objects:

Entities are selected using the standard methods. Each entity is picked, as shown in Figure 7.18. After the last entity is selected enter RETURN at the **Select objects:** prompt. The areas are section-lined as shown in Figure 7.19.

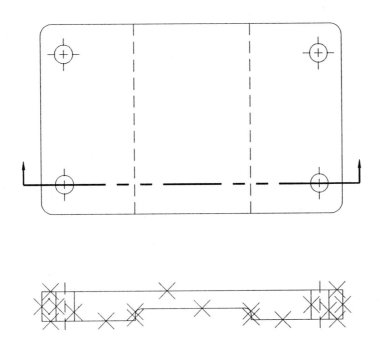

Figure 7.18 Selecting each entity for the crosshatching.

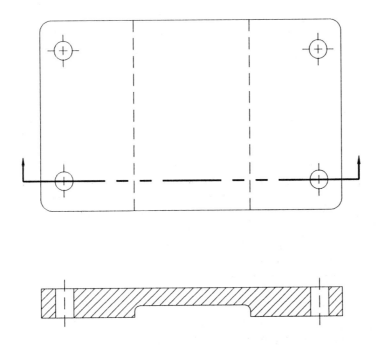

Figure 7.19 Area after hatching.

Another method that can be used to section line the front view is with the **WINDOW** Option.

1. At the first **select objects:** prompt enter **W** or **WINDOW**.
2. **First corner:**
Pick the first corner of a box.
3. **Other corner:**
Picking another corner displays the number of entities found, and the area will be crosshatched. Three windows (Figure 7.20) would have to be used to complete the front view, as shown in Figure 7.19.

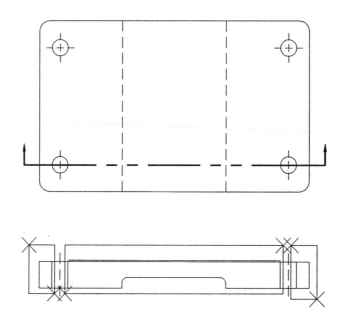

Figure 7.20 Using windows to crosshatch.

HALF SECTION VIEWS FROM A USER-DEFINED HATCH PATTERN

A half-section drawing is used mainly for symmetrical objects and is created by passing a cutting plane halfway through an object, as shown in Figure 7.21. Hidden lines are omitted in both halves of the drawings. A center line is drawn between the sectioned and unsectioned half of the section view. The following steps show how to create a half-section view of the Wheel from the Wheel Assembly using a user-defined hatch pattern:

Crosshatching a Half Section View: Exercise 7.5

1. Load **LAB7-5** from the data disk. Enter **BHATCH** at the command prompt or select it from the tablet or screen menu.
2. From the hatch dialogue box select **Hatch Options...**
4. From the Hatch Options Dialogue Box select the **User-Defined Pattern** button.
5. Enter **135** for the angle and **.25** as the spacing of the user defined hatch pattern.
6. Pick the **OK** button to return to the hatch dialogue box.
7. Select the **Pick Points** button to define the area to be hatched.
8. The dialogue box is removed and you can move the cursor to any position inside the area bounded by the lines and arcs that make up the area to be crosshatched. Once the cursor is inside the boundary of the object use the pick button on the input device. The boundary for the hatch area is automatically defined and highlighted.
9. At the next **Select internal point** prompt enter Return to end the selection mode.
10. The hatch dialogue box is again displayed. Pick the **Preview Hatch** button to show the hatch pattern on the drawing. Press Return after examining the hatch pattern.
11. If the hatch pattern type and location is acceptable, pick the **Apply** button. The hatch pattern is added to the object as shown in Figure 7.22.

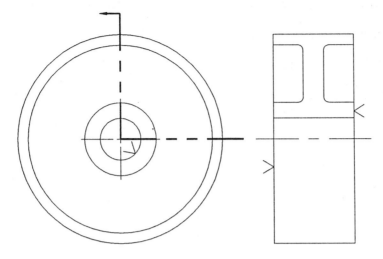

Figure 7.21 Creating a half-section view.

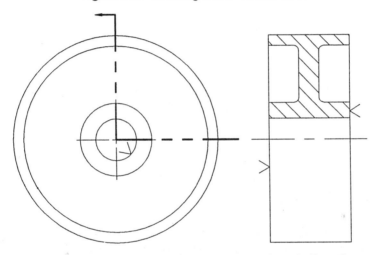

Figure 7.22 User-defined hatch pattern for a half section.

To erase a hatch pattern enter **E** at the command prompt and select any hatch line with the cursor, then enter Return. The hatch pattern will be removed from the drawing.

CREATING OFFSET SECTION DRAWINGS

Some complicated parts are shown better in section using an offset cutting plane. This type of section uses a cutting plane that bends or "offsets" so that all the important details of a drawing are represented in a section view. It is very similar to a full section except that the cutting plane is bent. Figure 7.23 is an example of an offset section view. Notice that all the offsets in the cutting plane line are at 90 degrees and that these bends are never shown in the sectioned view. For this example, the right-side view of the Angle from the Wheel Assembly will be used.

Offset Section View: Exercise 7.6

1. Load **LAB7-6** from the data disk. The cutting plane line is drawn on the front view as shown in Figure 7.23.
2. For this example, the hatching is added using one of AutoCAD's standard patterns. Enter **BHATCH** at the command prompt or select it from the tablet or screen menu.
3. From the hatch dialogue box select **Hatch Options...**
4. From the Hatch Options Dialogue Box select the **Pattern...** button.
5. An icon menu is displayed showing the various standard hatch patterns. Pick the desired pattern with the mouse by pointing at the pattern and using the pick button on the mouse. For this example pick **ANSI32**.

6. ANSI32 is now displayed next to the Pattern... button in the Hatch Options Dialogue Box. Pick the **OK** button to return to the hatch dialogue box.

7. Select the Pick Points button to define the 3 areas to be hatched.

8. The dialogue box is removed and the drawing is displayed. Pick any point inside the boundary of the object except inside the holes. The border is highlighted after selection. Pick the other two areas to be crosshatched.

9. At the next **Select internal point** prompt enter Return to end the selection mode.

10. The hatch dialogue box is again displayed. Pick the **Preview Hatch** button to show the hatch pattern on the drawing. Press Return after examining the hatch pattern.

11. If the hatch pattern type and location are acceptable, pick the **Apply** button. The hatch pattern is added to the object as shown in Figure 7.24.

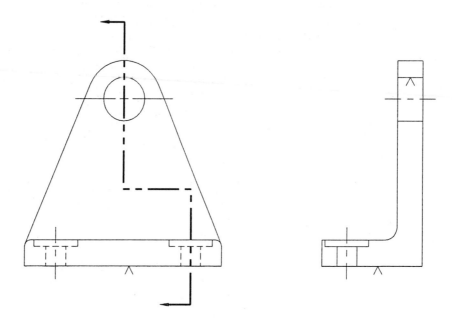

Figure 7.23 Creating an offset section drawing.

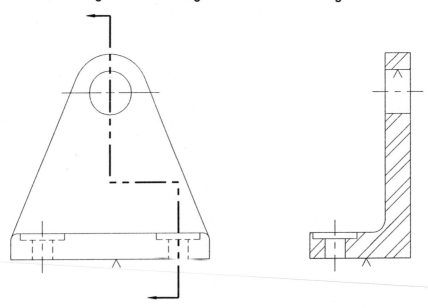

Figure 7.24 An offset section using the steel pattern ANSI 32.

BROKEN-OUT SECTIONS

Occasionally there is a need to show only part of an object in section to reveal interior details Figure 7.25. This type of view is called a broken-out section. The sectioned and unsectioned halves of the view are separated by a break line. The cutting plane is extended only as far as needed and is not shown on the drawing. Figure 7.25 and the following steps demonstrate the creation of a broken-out section view:

Creating a Broken-out Section View: Exercise 7.7

1. Load **LAB 7-7** from the data disk. The break line can be drawn with AutoCAD using the **SKETCH** command, as explained iearlier in the text.
2. For this example, the hatching is added using one of AutoCAD's standard patterns. Enter **BHATCH** at the command prompt or select it from the tablet or screen menu.
3. From the hatch dialogue box select **Hatch Options...**
4. From the Hatch Options Dialogue Box select the **Pattern...** button.
5. An icon menu is displayed showing the various standard hatch patterns. Pick the desired pattern with the mouse by pointing at the pattern and using the pick button on the mouse. For this example pick **ANSI33**.
6. ANSI33 is now displayed next to the Pattern... button in the Hatch Options Dialogue Box. Pick the **OK** button to return to the hatch dialogue box.
7. Select the Pick Points button to define the 3 areas to be hatched.
8. The dialogue box is removed and the drawing is displayed. Pick any point inside the boundary of the object where crosshatching is to be placed. The border is highlighted after selection. Pick the other two areas to have crosshatching.
9. At the next **Select internal point** prompt enter Return to end the selection mode.
10. The hatch dialogue box is again displayed. Pick the **Preview Hatch** button to show the hatch pattern on the drawing. Press Return after examining the hatch pattern.
11. If the hatch pattern type and location is acceptable, pick the **Apply** button. The hatch pattern is added to the object as shown in Figure 7.26.

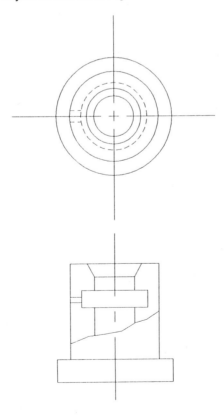

Figure 7.25 Creating a broken-out section view.

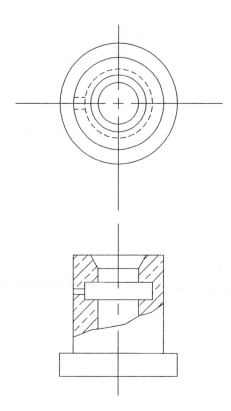

Figure 7.26 A broken-out section using AutoCAD's ANSI 33.

REVOLVED SECTIONS

The shape of elongated parts is shown with revolved section views. Objects with more than one type of cross section or with complicated shapes are shown best with a revolved section. These views are created by passing a cutting plane perpendicular to the axis or center line of the object. The cross section of the part at the point where the cutting plane was passed then is revolved 90 degrees about the center line. This cross-section view is drawn on top of the object as shown in Figure 7.27.

Creating a Revolved Section View: Exercise 7.8

1. Load **LAB7-8** from the data disk.
2. For this example, the hatching is added using one of AutoCAD's standard patterns. Enter **BHATCH** at the command prompt or select it from the tablet or screen menu.
3. From the hatch dialogue box select **Hatch Options...**
4. From the Hatch Options Dialogue Box select the **Pattern...** button.
5. An icon menu is displayed showing the various standard hatch patterns. Pick the desired pattern with the mouse by pointing at the pattern and using the pick button on the mouse. For this example pick **ANSI32**.
6. ANSI32 is now displayed next to the Pattern... button in the Hatch Options Dialogue Box. Pick the **OK** button to return to the hatch dialogue box.
7. Select the Pick Points button to define the 3 areas to be hatched.
8. The dialogue box is removed and the drawing is displayed. Pick any point inside the boundary of the larger of the two concentric circles. The border is highlighted after selection. Pick the smaller of the two concentric circles.
9. At the next **Select internal point** prompt enter Return to end the selection mode.
10. The hatch dialogue box is again displayed. Pick the **Preview Hatch** button to show the hatch pattern on the drawing. Press Return after examining the hatch pattern.
11. If the hatch pattern type and location are acceptable, pick the **Apply** button. The hatch pattern is added to the object as shown in Figure 7.28.

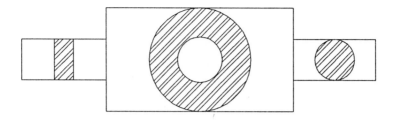

Figure 7.27 Creating a revolved section view.

Figure 7.28 A revolved section view of a tubular cross section.

REMOVED SECTION VIEWS

A removed section is created in the same way as a revolved section. The difference between the two sectioning methods is that the cross section is not drawn on the object but removed from the object and drawn to the outside of the part, as shown in Figure 7.29. Removed sections are labeled to match the labels assigned to the cutting plane line. Occasionally the removed section is drawn to a larger scale to show small details and to facilitate dimensioning. Use **BHATCH** to section line the removed view.

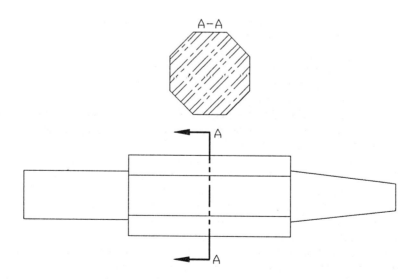

Figure 7.29 A removed section view.

SECTION ASSEMBLY DRAWINGS

Sectioned assembly views are used to describe the relationship of parts in an assembly. When these drawings are created, it is important that adjacent parts be section lined differently by varying the angles of the section lines and/or using different section-line material symbols. Figure 7.30 is an example of a section assembly drawing. It was created by using AutoCAD section-line symbols ANSI31 and ANSI33, drawn at two different angles. The ANSI31 symbol was drawn at its default value. The ANSI33 was drawn at a 120-degree angle.

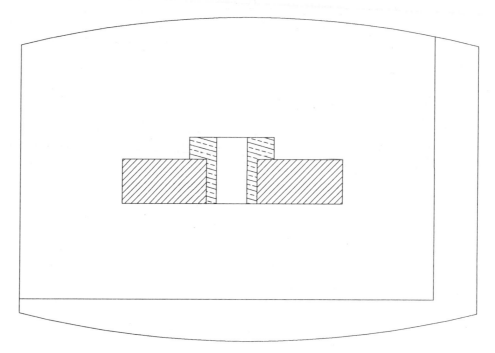

Figure 7.30 An assembly section.

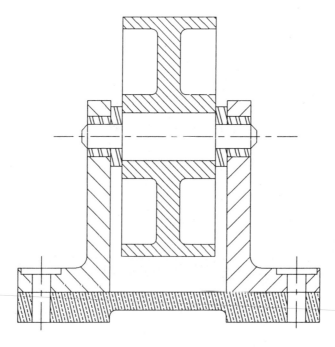

Figure 7.31 Section assembly drawing created with blocks from the detail drawings.

Section assembly drawings also are created from detail drawings that are copied or brought into a drawing as a block. This basic procedure was explained in Chapter 6 using the **WBLOCK** command. Each detail can be edited to create a section view, and each view can be assembled to create a section assembly drawing, as shown in Figure 7.31.

Thin Parts in Section

Thin parts, such as washers and gaskets, in section are represented usually as solid-filled areas. The washers on each side of the Wheel in the Wheel Assembly drawing in Figure 7.32 are examples of thin parts in section. With AutoCAD thin parts in section can be created using the Draw subcommands **TRACE, SOLID,** or **PLINE. LINE** or **PLINE** could be used with **OFFSET** to create thin parts in section. The **POLYLINE** command creates thin parts in section by changing the width of the polyline using the **WIDTH** subcommand. The **TRACE** command is used by entering the trace width so that it is equal to thickness of the thin part. For example, to create a .125 thick washer in section using the **TRACE** command, enter **.125** at the first prompt, **Trace width <>:**. The line then is drawn **From point: To point:** using one of the standard methods.

The **SOLID** command is probably the quickest method to make a thin part in section by creating solid-filled quadrilaterals or triangles. The **FILL** Mode must be on for this command to work for thin parts in section. The following steps describe how to create thin parts in section:

1. The Settings subcommand **SETVAR** toggles the Fill Mode on and off.

2. After the **SOLID** command is selected, a prompt will request:

First point:.

Pick the location of the first point to describe the quadrilateral for the washer.

3. **Second point:**

Continue to pick the corners of the rectangle to describe the shape of the washer, then enter RETURN to complete the Solid. If the Fill Mode is on, the washer is drawn on screen and filled as shown in Figure 7.32. Make sure the sequence of points is picked correctly or the filled area will look like a bowtie instead of a rectangle.

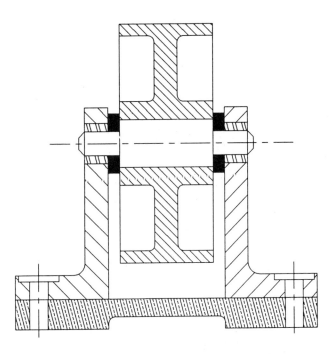

Figure 7.32 Section assembly drawing showing two washers as thin parts in section.

A USER-DEFINED HATCH PATTERN

The following steps demonstrate how to create a section view of the part shown in Figure 7.33.

1. Enter **HATCH** at the command prompt or select it from the tablet or screen menu.

2. **Pattern (? or name/U,style)**

If a pattern was used already in this drawing session, it will be listed in brackets at the prompt. Enter the letter **U** to define a simple hatch pattern.

3. **Angle for crosshatch lines <0>:**

The default value is shown in brackets. For this example enter the value of **60** and press RETURN.

4. Another prompt will read:

Spacing between lines <1.0000>:

Enter the value of .125 and press RETURN.

5. **Double hatch area? <N>:**

Figure 7.33 shows the difference between the single and double hatch patterns. For this example enter RETURN for a single hatch pattern.

6. **Select objects:**

Pick the object by stretching a window around the object. Enter RETURN at the **Select objects:** prompt. The areas are section lined, as shown in Figure 7.33.

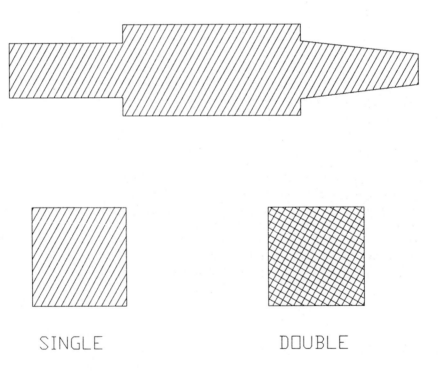

Figure 7.33 Single and double hatch patterns.

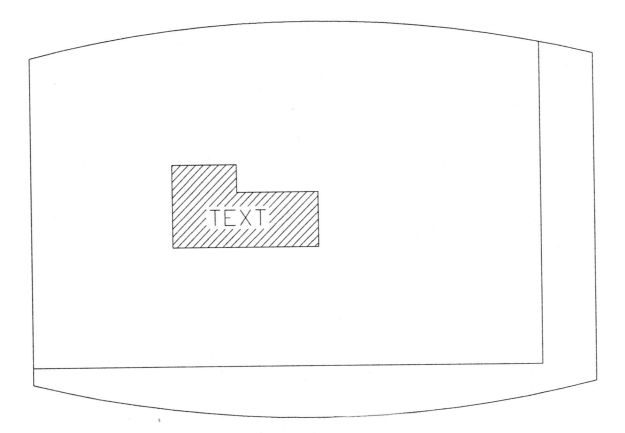

Figure 7.34 Text inside hatching.

QUESTIONS FOR REVIEW

1. Name the AutoCAD command used to create section lines.
2. Name the command used to create a line.
3. Name the type of line supplied with AutoCAD software that is used for a cutting plane line.
4. Name the two variables that can be changed on a hatch pattern.
5. Explain why hatch patterns are added to a drawing in the form of blocks.
6. Name the two methods used to draw separate entities for hatch boundaries.
7. Name the command used to draw perpendicular arrows for cutting plane lines.
8. Name the hatch pattern used for the standard iron symbol.
9. Name the AutoCAD command used to create the break line in a broken-out section drawing.
10. List two methods of drawing a thin part in section.
11. Explain how the scale of the hatch pattern is determined.

DRAWING ASSIGNMENTS

1. Do those drawings assigned by your instructor from Figures 7.35 through 7.49.
2. Create a section assembly drawing of the Wheel Assembly using dimensions from Chapter 6.
3. From Giesecke et al., *Engineering Graphics*, 4th ed. Section view problems from Chapter 7 Sectional Views.

20.10

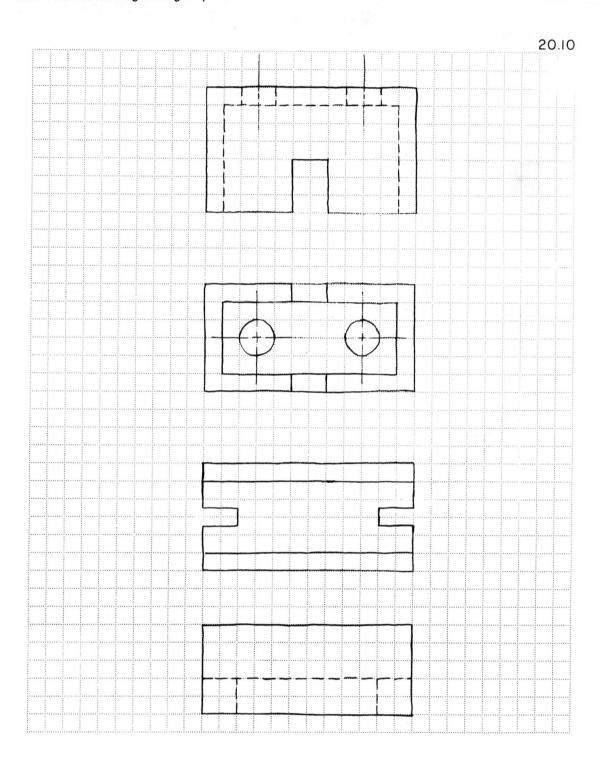

Figures 7.35 through 7.36 Complete the front views as full-sections. Each grid square = .25 inches or 6 mm.

20.10

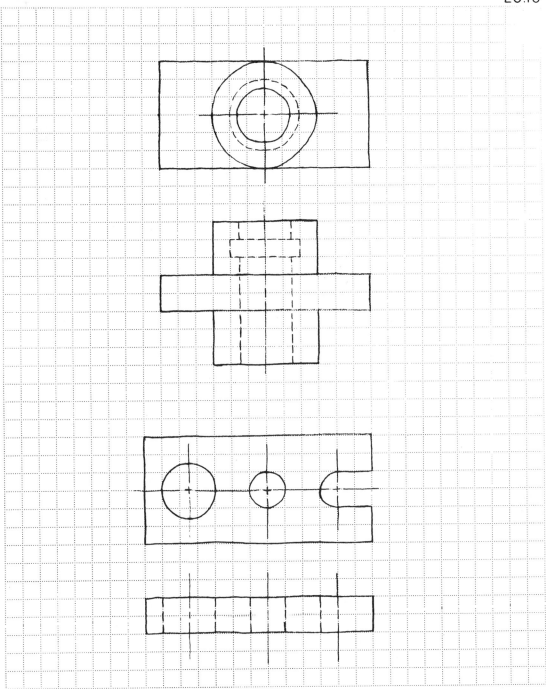

Figures 7.37 through 7.38 Complete the front views as full-sections. Each grid square = .25 inches or 6 mm.

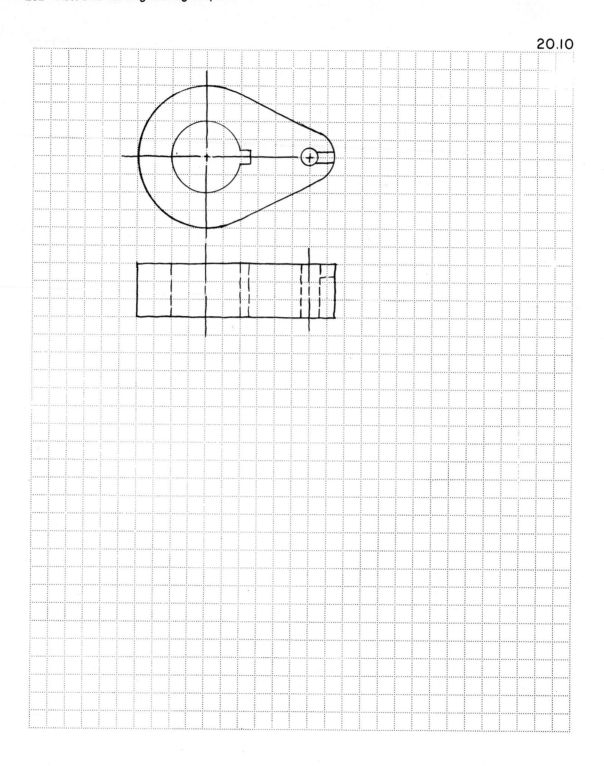

20.10

Figure 7.39 Complete the front views as full-sections. Each grid square = .25 inches or 6 mm.

20.10

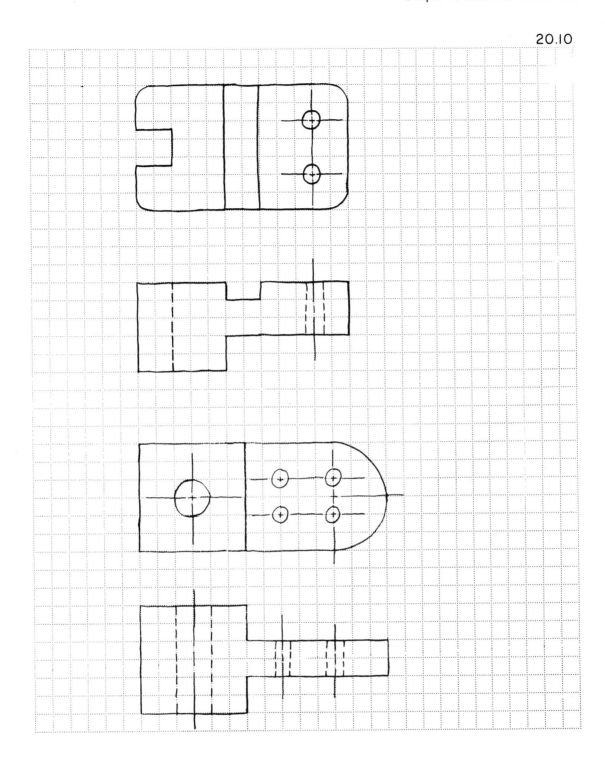

Figures 7.40 through 7.41 Complete the front views as offset-sections. Each grid square = .25 inches or 6 mm.

20.10

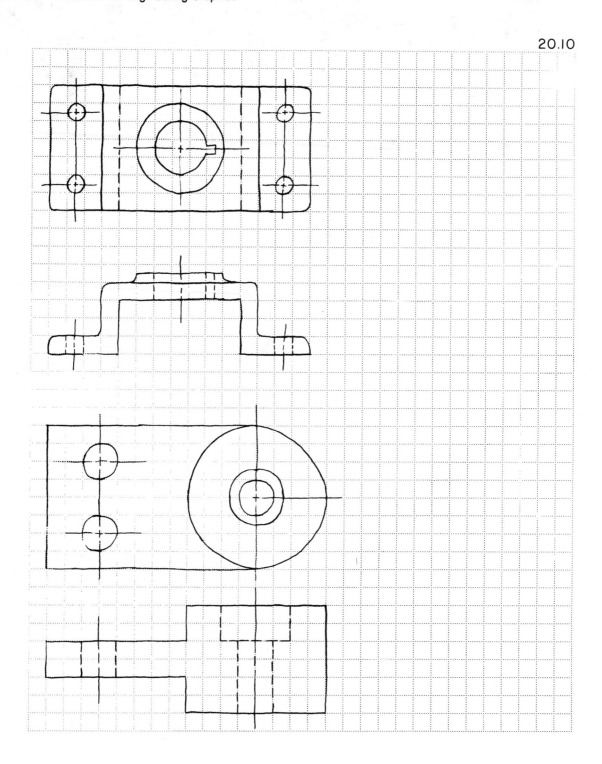

Figures 7.42 through 7.43 Complete the front views as offset-sections. Each grid square = .25 inches or 6 mm.

20.10

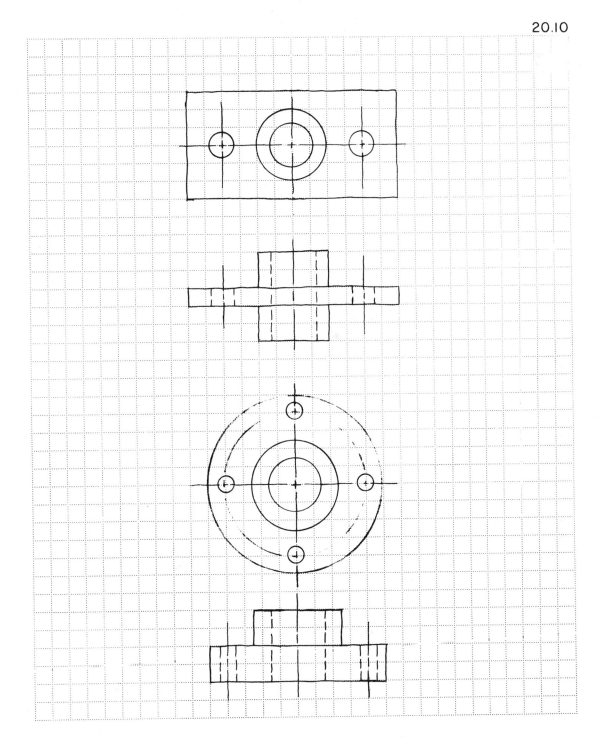

Figures 7.44 through 7.45 Complete the front views as half-sections. Each grid square = .25 inches or 6mm.

20.10

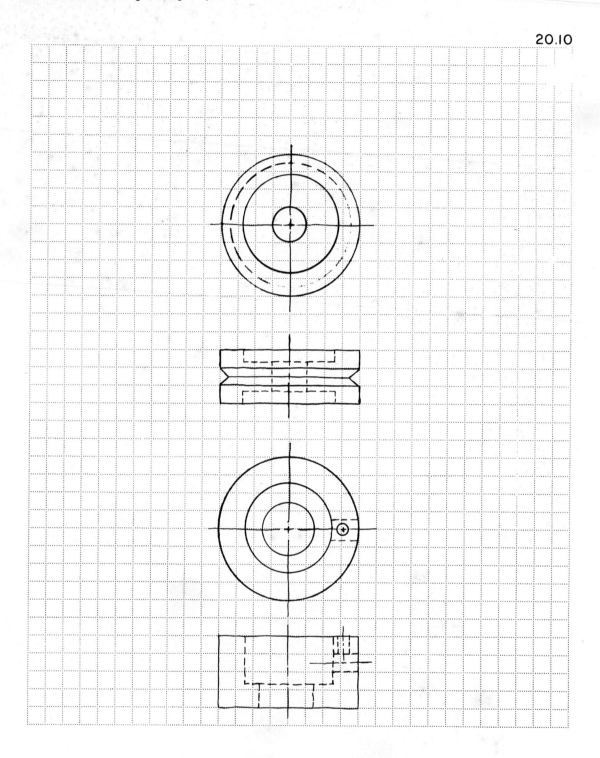

Figures 7.46 through 7.47 Complete the front views as half-sections. Each grid square = .25 inches or 6mm.

20.10

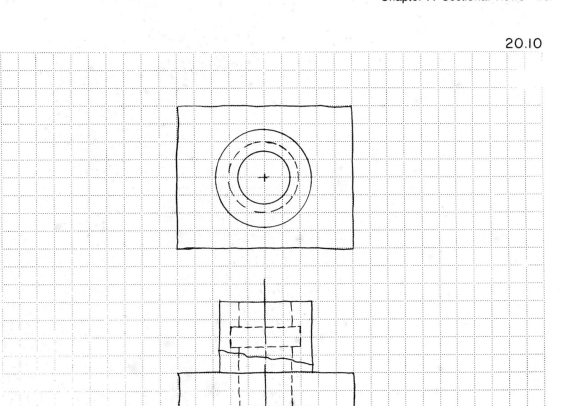

Figures 7.48 and 7.49 Complete the front views as broken-out sections. Each grid square = .25 inches or 6mm.

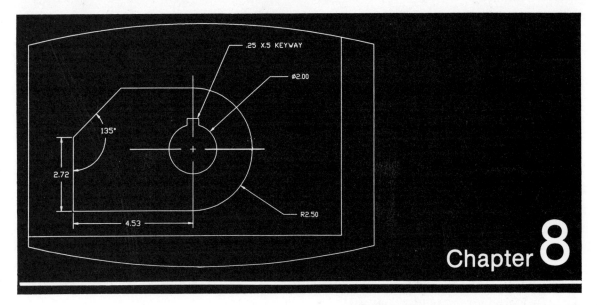

.25 X.5 KEYWAY

Ø2.00

135°

2.72

4.53

R2.50

Chapter 8

DIMENSIONING

An engineering drawing is produced to describe completely a part so that it can be manufactured. The drawing involves three major components, shape, location, and size description. Describing the shape of a part is accomplished with orthographic projection, sections, and detail drawings. Location dimensions describe the location of details, such as centers of holes. Size description is accomplished by completely dimensioning the part.

Modern manufacturing techniques and the need for interchangeability of parts have resulted in the development of a system of tolerancing size descriptions. This chapter describes the size description and tolerancing of parts using AutoCAD.

OBJECTIVES

After completing Chapter 8, you will be able to:
1. Completely describe a part using AutoCAD,
2. Place horizontal, vertical, aligned, rotated, baseline, and continued dimensions,
3. Place angular, radial, and diametral dimensions,
4. Control the dimension variables of AutoCAD, such as dimension type, size of characters, and arrow type,
5. Place tolerancing values on dimensions,
6. Place geometric tolerancing symbols on a drawing,
7. Dimension parts for size and locations,
8. Place leaders and notes on a dimensioned drawing,
9. Dimension prisms, pyramids, cones, cylinders, tapers, chamfers, keyways, knurls, necks and undercuts, and threads,
10. Place finish marks and other symbols on a drawing,
11. Place limit values on dimensions, and
12. Place center lines on holes.

DIMENSIONING PRACTICES

Dimensioning is the practice of completely describing a part's size, form, and location of geometric entities (Figure 8.1). The two basic components of part description are size and location dimensions. Size dimensions describe the size of each geometric component of a part (Figure 8.2). For example, the width, height, and depth, size of drilled holes and slots, and other details are size dimensions. Location dimensions are used to locate geometric details on a part, (Figure 8.2) such as the center points of holes, slots, and other geometric components.

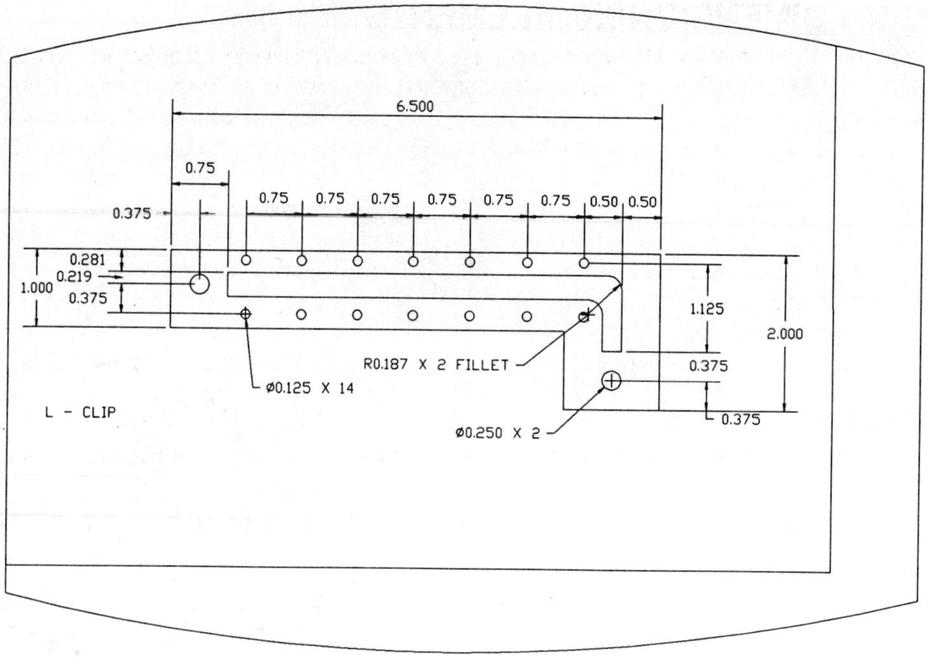

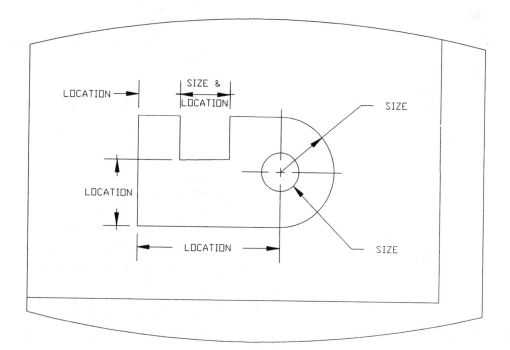

Figure 8.1 Drawing dimensioned by using AutoCAD.

Figure 8.2 Size and location dimensions.

If all the size and location dimensions are included on a part, the part is most probably completely dimensioned. Size and location dimensions are placed on an AutoCAD drawing using the Dimension subcommands **LINEAR, ANGULAR, DIAMETER,** and **RADIUS.**

CHANGING DIMENSIONING ELEMENTS

The dimensioning technique used for a particular engineering drawing can vary according to the standards being followed or the engineering discipline. Architectural and civil engineering drawings commonly use unbroken dimension lines. Drawings created for manufacturing purposes use broken dimension lines and decimal inches or metric units. AutoCAD provides a way to change the different dimensioning techniques to facilitate the creation of engineering drawings of many types.

The AutoCAD Prototype drawing has a number of default dimension settings. The default dimension settings are listed with the Dimension subcommand **STATUS**. **STATUS** shows a listing of the current dimensioning variables and settings, as shown in Figure 8.3. These default settings are changed by using the Dimension subcommand **DIM VARS**.

A most important dimensioning variable for plotting is the **DIMSCALE** option, which is used to control the overall scale factor of most dimensioning variables that specify sizes, distances, or offsets. **DIMSCALE** is determined by calculating the reciprocal of the plot scale. For example, a plot scale of 1/4 would mean a **DIMSCALE** of four.

Dimensions are placed on a different layer so they can be separated from other elements of a drawing. Finished drawings can be plotted with or without dimensions using the **FREEZE** option.

```
DIMALT    Off                   Alternate units selected
DIMALTD   2                     Alternate unit decimal places
DIMALTF   25.4000               Alternate unit scale factor
DIMAPOST                        Suffix for alternate text
DIMASO    On                    Create associative dimensions
DIMASZ    0.1800                Arrow size
DIMBLK                          Arrow block name
DIMBLK1                         First arrow block name
DIMBLK2                         Second arrow block name
DIMCEN    0.0900                Center mark size
DIMCLRD   BYBLOCK               Dimension line color
DIMCLRE   BYBLOCK               Extension line & leader color
DIMCLRT   BYBLOCK               Dimension text color
DIMDLE    0.0000                Dimension line extension
DIMDLI    0.3800                Dimension line increment for continuation
DIMEXE    0.1800                Extension above dimension line
DIMEXO    0.0625                Extension line origin offset
DIMGAP    0.0900                Gap from dimension line to text
DIMLFAC   1.0000                Linear unit scale factor
-- Press RETURN for more --
DIMLIM    Off                   Generate dimension limits
DIMPOST                         Default suffix for dimension text
DIMRND    0.0000                Rounding value
DIMSAH    Off                   Separate arrow blocks
DIMSCALE  1.0000                Overall scale factor
DIMSE1    Off                   Suppress the first extension line
DIMSE2    Off                   Suppress the second extension line
DIMSHO    On                    Update dimensions while dragging
DIMSOXD   Off                   Suppress outside extension dimension
DIMSTYLE  *UNNAMED              Current dimension style (read-only)
DIMTAD    Off                   Place text above the dimension line
DIMTFAC   1.0000                Tolerance text height scaling factor
DIMTIH    On                    Text inside extensions is horizontal
DIMTIX    Off                   Place text inside extensions
DIMTM     0.0000                Minus tolerance
DIMTOFL   Off                   Force line inside extension lines
DIMTOH    On                    Text outside extensions is horizontal
DIMTOL    Off                   Generate dimension tolerances
DIMTP     0.0000                Plus tolerance
DIMTSZ    0.0000                Tick size
-- Press RETURN for more --
DIMTVP    0.0000                Text vertical position
DIMTXT    0.1800                Text height
DIMZIN    0                     Zero suppression

Dim:
```

Figure 8.3 Listing of current dimension variables and settings using the STATUS command.

DIMENSIONING ELEMENTS

A dimension is made from a number of different components (Figure 8.4). The extension line describes the termination points of a dimension. AutoCAD's **LINEAR** dimensioning commands automatically draw extension lines; however, AutoCAD allows for the suppression of one or both extension lines. The **DIM VARS** (dimension variable) subcommand **DIMSE1** suppresses the first extension line. **DIMSE2** command is used to suppress the second extension line. The default values are off for both of these variables.

Normally, an extension line starts with a visible gap from the outline of the part as shown in Figure 8.4. The default setting of AutoCAD is 0.0625. This distance is changed with the **DIM VAR** command **DIMEXO**. Extension lines also extend past the related dimension line. The AutoCAD default setting is 0.18 and can be changed using the **DIM VAR** command **DIMEXE**.

The dimension line is terminated with arrows at each end and indicates the direction and extents of a dimension. Dimension lines are either broken to facilitate the placement of the dimension text or unbroken, in which case the text is located above the dimension line. An example of each type is shown in Figure 8.4, although types should not be mixed on engineering drawings. The default setting breaks the dimension line. To change the dimension line from broken to unbroken, use the **DIM VAR** command **DIMTAD**.

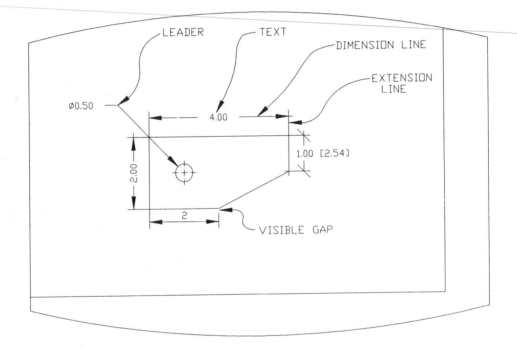

Figure 8.4 Different parts of a dimension that can be changed using the DIM VAR command.

The size of the arrows or the symbol used at the end of the dimension line also can be controlled. The default size of the arrow is 0.1800, which may be too small if the drawing is scaled less than full size when plotted. To change the size of the arrow, use the **DIM VAR** command **DIMASZ**. For example, if the plotted scale of the drawing is .50, double the arrow size to 0.3600. The symbol used at the end of the dimension line can be changed from an arrow to a tick, as shown on the 1.00 vertical dimension in Figure 8.4, or to a symbol of your choice. The **DIM VAR** command **DIMTSZ** turns on the tick symbol to a specified size. When the tick value is set to zero, the arrow symbol is used. The **DIM VAR** command **DIMBLK** specifies the name of a block to be used for the dimension line symbol. The arrow symbol can be any block defined by the user.

Two accepted methods of placing dimension text on a drawing are unidirectional and bidirectional, or aligned. The unidirectional method draws all dimension text horizontally and is the default setting for AutoCAD. Bidirectional dimensioning draws all dimensions parallel to the dimension line, as shown at the 2.00 vertical dimension in Figure 8.4. The **DIMTIH** and the **DIMTOH** commands change AutoCAD to bidirectional dimensions.

The dimension text height is controlled using the **DIM VAR** command **DIMTXT**. The default setting for text is 0.18 units. To scale the plotted drawing, change the dimension text size so that it is not too large or small. For example, if the drawing is to be plotted at double size (2:1), the dimension text size should be halved to 0.09. The dimension distance is measured automatically and placed on a drawing with the Dimension command. However, it is possible to activate a rounding value by using the **DIM VAR** command **DIMRND**. It is also possible to show decimal inches and metric units in one dimension, as shown in the 1.00 [2.54] vertical dimension in Figure 8.4. The **DIMALT** command toggles on and off the alternate units capability. The default setting is off. The alternate units scale factor and decimal precision also are controlled using the **DIMALTF** and **DIMALTD** commands.

DIMENSION STYLES DIALOG BOX

Many of the dimension variables described above can be changed with a dialogue box instead of the **DIMVARS** commands. Selecting Dimension Style... from the Settings Pull-down Menu displays the Dimension Style Dialogue box. Figure 8.5. More than one dimensioning style can be created and listed in the dialogue box. For example, to dimension engineering drawings you may want to create a special dimensioning style called ANSIY14-5M use of the Dimension Style box. This will replace Unamed as the dimension style. The style is defined by selecting the various variables buttons located to the right of the named styles. Pick Dimension Line to display the Dimension Line Dialogue Box shown in Figure 8.6. Settings are changed in the dialogue box instead of using the **DIMVAR** commands.

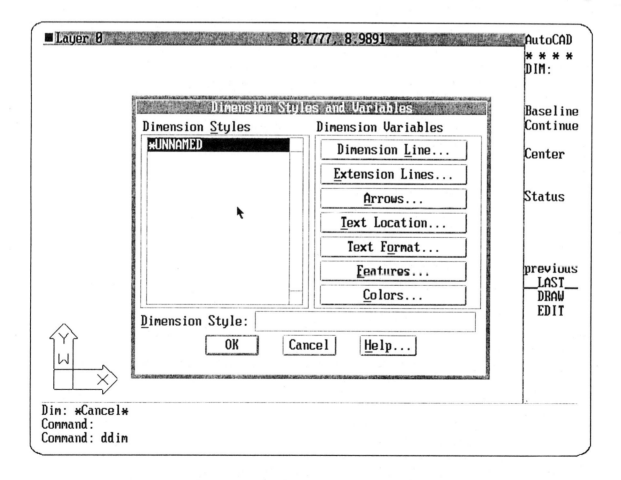

Figure 8.5 Dimension styles dialogue box.

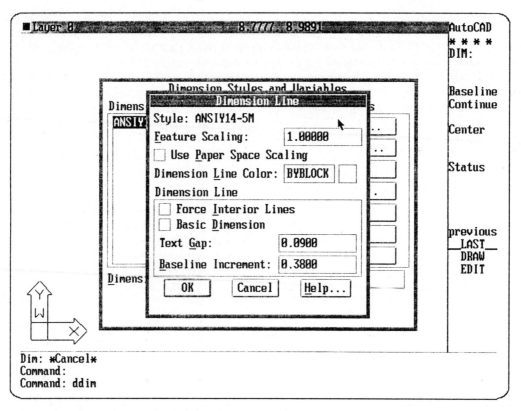

Figure 8.6 Dimension line dialogue box.

DIMENSIONING STANDARDS

Several different dimensioning practices have developed over the years to standardize the part description of engineering drawings using ANSI Y14.5M standards. More common dimensioning rules for engineering drawings include:

1. Dimensions should be placed in the most descriptive view.

2. Dimensions should be located outside the boundaries of the object. Using AutoCAD, pick the dimension text location point outside the boundaries of the view.

3. Each size and location dimension should be specified only once.

4. Crossed dimension lines should be avoided.

5. The space between the first dimension line and the object should be at least .375" or 10mm. Use a grid to assist in the accurate placement of dimension lines; X, Y coordinate display; or drawing of construction lines using AutoCAD's dot line and **OFFSET** feature.

6. The space between dimension lines should be at least .25 or 6mm.

These dimensioning practices are illustrated in the following examples using AutoCAD.

Size and Location Dimensions

Placing size and location dimensions on a drawing uses most of the AutoCAD dimensioning commands. Figure 8.7 will be used to demonstrate the use of AutoCAD to dimension an engineering drawing.

Linear Dimensions

The location and size of features on an engineering drawing are created with AutoCAD using the **HORIZONTAL, VERTICAL, ALIGNED,** and **ROTATED** Dimension commands. After selecting **DIM** from the Root Menu or Tablet Menu, the **DIM:** prompt is displayed. If only one dimension is to be created, use the **DIM1:** command, which returns to the command prompt after the dimension is placed. Entering RETURN at the **DIM:** prompt repeats the last dimension command.

HORIZONTAL DIMENSIONS

The **LINEAR** subcommand **HORIZONTAL** places horizontal dimensions on a drawing. To place a horizontal dimension on Figure 8.7 follow the steps below. Before starting to dimension a drawing with AutoCAD, it is helpful to place a .25 grid on the screen and set the Snap function at .25 to allow the accurate placement of dimension lines at the specified distances from the object. The first dimension line is located .5 from the object line. Each succeeding dimension line can be located .25 from the inside dimension line. If using metric, set the grid and snap to 2mm.

If the drawing is to be plotted at a scale other than 1:1, the grid distance should be changed so that the scaled plot still has the .5 and .25 distances. For example, if plotting at half scale, the distance to the first dimension line should be drawn one inch from the object, instead of .50, to meet the standard after plotting.

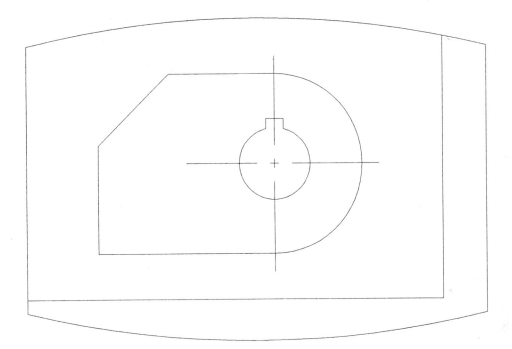

Figure 8.7 A simple engineering drawing that requires a variety of dimension commands.

Placing Horizontal Dimensions: Exercioc 8.1

1. Open **LAB8-1** from the data disk. From the Draw Pull-down Menu select Dimension/Linear/Horizontal or pick **HORIZNTAL** from the Dimension Menu. A prompt reads:
First extension line origin or RETURN to select:
AutoCAD provides two different methods to select the entity to be dimensioned. Extension lines are located automatically at the end points of lines and arcs by entering RETURN at the prompt. Extension lines are located manually by picking the first point with the cursor. This second method is described later. For this example enter RETURN.
2. **Select line, arc, or circle:**
Pick with the cursor the horizontal line to be dimensioned. It may be necessary to turn off the Snap toggle to accurately pick the line for dimensioning.
3. **Dimension line location (Text/Angle):**
Make sure the Snap toggle is on. Move the cursor a minimum of two grid points from the outside of the object. Position the cursor at the desired location for the text and pick that point.

4. **Dimension text (5.00):**
AutoCAD automatically measures the line and inserts that distance in the brackets. If that is the desired text simply press RETURN. The text, extension lines, dimension line, and arrows are located on the drawing as shown in Figure 8.8. Figure 8.8 also shows the points picked as a small X for locating the horizontal dimension.

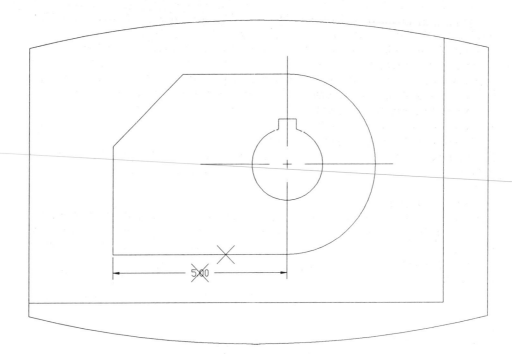

Figure 8.8 A horizontal size dimension placed on a drawing.

DIMENSION TEXT

There are two options for the **Dimension text:** prompt shown in step 4 above. One option is to enter a text string from the keyboard and replace the one shown in brackets. The other option is to eliminate entirely the text string from the dimension by entering a single SPACE and RETURN.

The dimension text style also can be changed to any of the available text fonts.

1. To change the current text format select **Text/Set Style...** from the Draw Pull-down Menu.
2. Select the text font from the dialogue box then pick the **OK** button.
3. **Height <.2000>:**
Enter the desired text height then press **RETURN**.
4. **Width factor (1.00):** Enter a new width factor or **RETURN** to accept the default. A factor of 1 will result in square text characters.
5. **Obliquing angle (0):** Set the angle of the dimension text or enter **RETURN** for no angles.
6. **Backwards ? (N):** Enter **RETURN** to reject backwards text.
7. **Upside down ? (N):** Enter **RETURN** to reject upside down text.
8. **Vertical? (N):** Enter **RETURN** to reject vertical text. After entering Return a prompt indicates that the new text style is current.

New text styles cannot be created with the Dimension Mode. The text height can also be changed using the **DIM VAR** subcommand **DIMTXT**.

MANUALLY PLACING DIMENSIONS

The same dimension can be placed on the drawing by manually selecting the position of the extension lines. This procedure is explained below:

Manually Placing Dimensions: Exercise 8.2

1. Use **LAB8-1** from the data disk. From the Draw Pull-down Menu select Dimension/ Linear/Horizontal or pick **HORIZNTAL** from the Dimension Menu. A prompt reads:
First extension line origin or RETURN to select:
To manually select the extension line locations, move the cursor to one of the end points of the line and pick that point. You will want to have the snap on or use Osnap Endpoint to make the selection. AutoCAD will automatically place a gap between the object and the start of the dimension if a value is entered for the **DIMEXO** variable.
2. **Second extension line origin:**
Pick the other end point of the line.
3. **Dimension line location (Text/Angle):**
Make sure the Snap toggle is on. Move the cursor a minimum of two grid points from the outside of the object. Position the cursor at the desired location for the text and pick that point.
4. **Dimension text (5.00):**
AutoCAD automatically measures the horizontal distance between pick points and inserts that distance in the brackets. If that is the desired text simply press RETURN. The text, extension lines, dimension line, and arrows are located on the drawing as shown in Figure 8.9. Figure 8.9 also shows the points picked for manually locating the horizontal dimension.

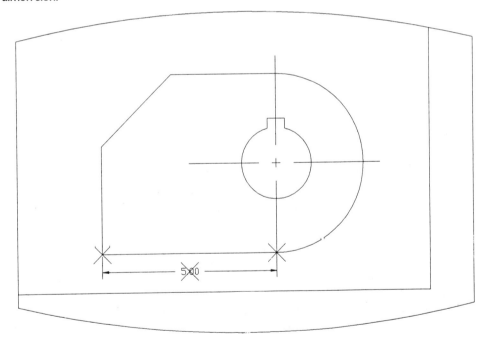

Figure 8.9 Location of picked points to manually place a dimension on a drawing.

ERASING DIMENSIONS

The most recent dimension is erased quickly using the **UNDO** command. The **ERASE** command also can be used to erase dimensions. Picking any point on the dimension line, extension line, or text erases the entire dimension if the dimension was created with **DIMASO** on, which is the default. To erase multiple dimensions use **Window** or **Crossing.** To erase parts of dimensions, such as the text, use the **EXPLODE** option to separate the entities and edit the dimensions.

DIMENSION ENTITY GRIPS

Another method of erasing dimensions is to use entity grips. At the command prompt pick a dimension. Handle points are displayed on screen as shown in Figure 8.10. After selection enter the letter **E** and RETURN to erase the selected dimension. Entity grips can also be used to edit dimensions. Pick either of the grips over the arrow heads to lengthen or shorten the distance between the dimension line and the extension line origins. The dimension text grip is used to reposition the text. Selecting one of the extension line grips is used to change its position which changes the length of the extension line and the dimension itself. Arc and circle dimension grips are used to rotate the dimension around the circle or arc for repositioning.

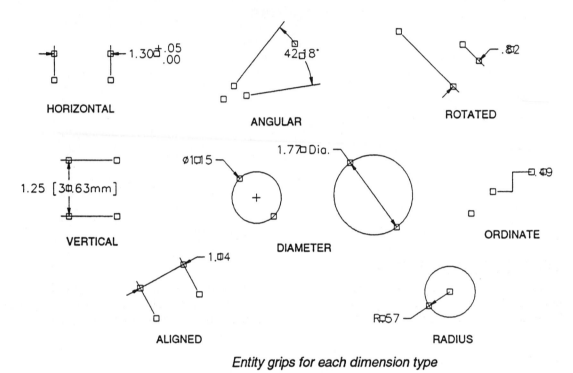

Entity grips for each dimension type

Figure 8.10 Entity grips for each type of dimension. (Courtesy of Autodesk, Inc.)

VERTICAL DIMENSIONS

Vertical dimensions are placed on an AutoCAD drawing with the **VERTICAL** command, which is used in a way nearly identical to the **HORIZONTAL** command. Vertical dimensions can be placed automatically or manually. The following example demonstrates the placement of a vertical dimension using the automatic mode:

Placing Vertical Dimensions: Exercise 8.3

1. After selecting **VERTICAL** from the Dimension Menu a prompt reads:
First extension line origin or RETURN to select:
For this example, enter RETURN.
2. **Select line, arc, or circle:**
Pick with the cursor the vertical line to be dimensioned. It may be necessary to turn the Snap toggle off to accurately pick the line for dimensioning.
3. **Dimension line location:**
Make sure the Snap toggle is on. Move the cursor a minimum of two grid points from the outside of the object. Position the cursor at the desired location for the text and pick that point.
4. **Dimension text (3.00):**
AutoCAD automatically measures the line and inserts that distance in the brackets. If that is the desired text simply press RETURN. The text, extension lines, dimension line, and arrows are located on the drawing as shown in Figure 8.11. Figure 8.11 also shows the points picked for locating the vertical dimension.

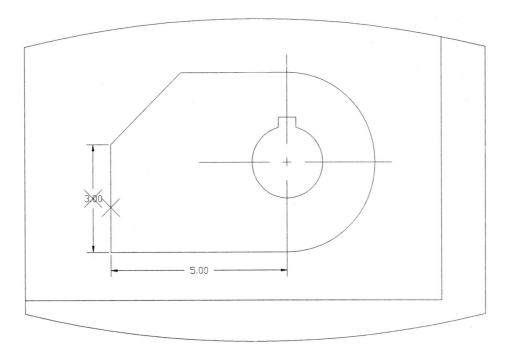

Figure 8.11 Placing a vertical location dimension.

ALIGNED DIMENSIONS

Occasionally, to place a dimension parallel to a line or other entity that is neither horizontal nor vertical is necessary. AutoCAD refers to this type of dimension as aligned. The **LINEAR** subcommand **ALIGNED** places dimensions parallel to the entity. An aligned dimension is placed on Figure 8.7 using the following steps.

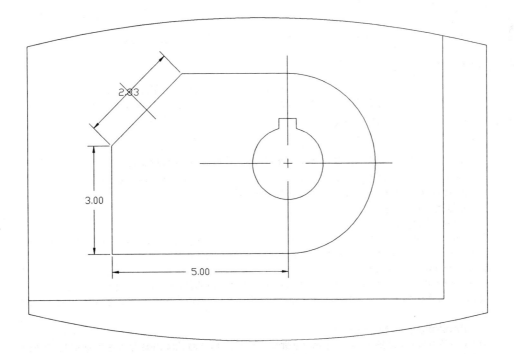

Figure 8.12 Placing an aligned dimension.

Placing Aligned Dimensions: Exercise 8.4

1. After selecting **ALIGNED** a prompt reads:
First extension line origin or RETURN to select:
For this example, enter RETURN.
2. **Select line, arc, or circle:**
Pick with the cursor the angled line in the upper left corner of the part. The snap toggle may need to be turned off to accurately pick the line.
3. **Dimension line location:**
Make sure the Snap toggle is on. Move the cursor a minimum of two grid points from the outside of the object. Position the cursor at the desired location for the text and pick that point.
4. **Dimension text (2.83):**
AutoCAD automatically measures the line and inserts that distance in the brackets. If that is the desired text simply press RETURN. The text, extension lines, dimension line, and arrows are located on the drawing as shown in Figure 8.12. Figure 8.12 also shows the points picked for locating the aligned dimension. Save the drawing on your data disk.

The dimension text is drawn horizontally for the aligned dimension just created. However, the text can be drawn parallel to the dimension line by changing the **DIM VAR** subcommand **DIMTIH** from the default value On to Off.

DIMENSIONING CIRCLES

Drilled holes normally are dimensioned in the view that shows the hole as a circle. The AutoCAD command used for dimensioning circles is **DIAMETER** which automatically measures the size of the hole, places the dimension line outside the hole with arrowheads, and places the text and phi symbol commonly used for ANSI standard dimensions (Figure 8.13).

To force the dimension text inside the circle set **DIMTIX** to 1. Figure 8.14 shows a circle dimensioned with the text forced inside,

With ANSI standard dimensioning practices, concentric circles are specified in the longitudinal views when practical, as shown in Figure 8.15. These dimensions can be added to an AutoCAD drawing with the **VERTICAL** command. The phi symbol preceding the dimension text can be added after the dimension is placed on the screen in the form of a note. The character string necessary to create the phi symbol in a string of text is **%%C**. It also can be added at the **Dimension text:** prompt line. The following steps describe how to dimension circles in the longitudinal view:

Dimensioning Circles in the Longitudinal View: Excercise 8.5

1. Open **LAB8-2** from the data disk. Select Dimension/Linear/Vertical from the Draw Pull-down Menu.
2. **First extension line origin or RETURN to select:**
For this example, enter RETURN.
2. **Select line, arc, or circle:**
Pick with the cursor the vertical line representing the smallest circle. It may be necessary to turn off the Snap toggle to accurately pick the line for dimensioning.
3. **Dimension line location:**
Make sure the Snap toggle is on. Move the cursor a minimum of two grid points from the outside of the object. Position the cursor at the desired location for the text and pick that point.
4. **Dimension text (0.5000):**
Enter %%C.500 at the prompt to display the dimension with a phi symbol.
5. Repeat steps 1-4 for the remaining vertical dimensions. Figure 8.15.

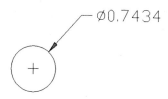

Figure 8.13 Dimensioning a circle with AutoCAD.

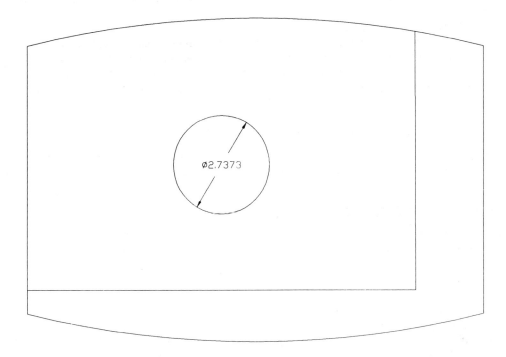

Figure 8.14 Forcing dimension text inside the circle by setting DIMTIX to 1.

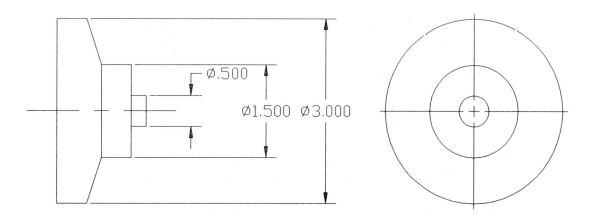

Figure 8.15 Dimensioning concentric circles.

Dimensioning circles or holes where they appear as circles on a drawing will automatically place the phi symbol to precede the numerical dimension. The following steps describe how to dimension a circle:

Dimensioning a Circle: Exercise 8.6

1. Open **LAB 8-1** saved in Exercise 8.4. Select Dimension/Radial/Diameter from the Draw Pull-down Menu.
2. **Select arc or circle**: Pick any point on the circumference of the circle to begin dimensioning.
3. **Dimension text (2.00)**: Select **Return** to accept the displayed dimension value.
4. **Enter leader length for text**: Moving the cursor displays the dimension if the Drag Mode is on. Move the cursor to the desired location for the text and pick the point. The dimension is placed as shown in Figure 8.16.

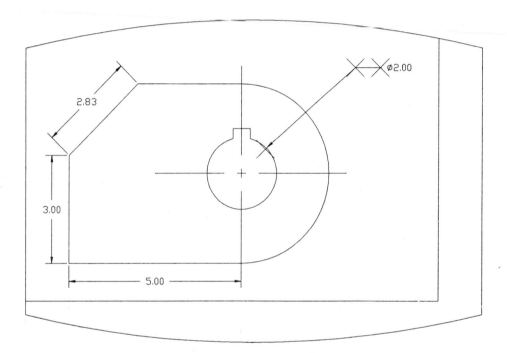

Figure 8.16 Dimensioning a circle.

CENTER MARKS OR CENTER LINES

With **DIAMETER** or **ARC** dimension functions, a center mark is added to the center of the circle or arc. The Dimension Variable **DIMCEN** controls the dimension mark or dimension line placed on a circle or arc. If the value of **DIMCEN** is set to zero, no mark is added to the drawing when dimensioned. The default value is set at 0.090. For engineering drawings a value of .125 is more appropriate. If **DIMCEN** is a negative value, center lines are drawn instead of center marks which is standard practice for engineering drawing. The absolute value determines the size of the center mark. Figure 8.17.

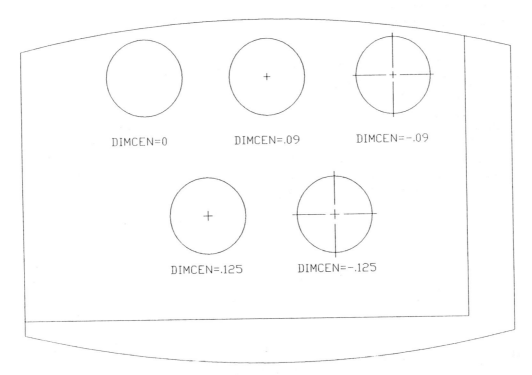

Figure 8.17 Center marks.

DRAWING LEADER LINES

Leader lines commonly are used in dimensioning to specify special conditions on engineering drawings. For example, the keyway shown in Figure 8.7 is specified by adding a leader line and the appropriate text. Leaders also are used to dimension circles by interrupting the **DIAMETER** command.

To specify the keyway shown in Figure 8.18, the following steps are used:

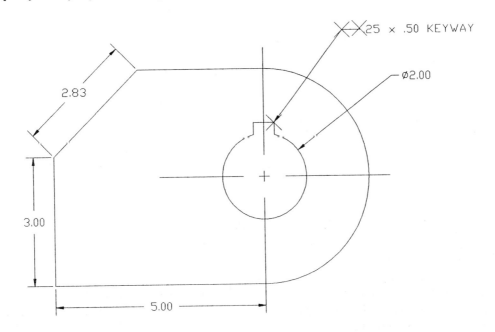

Figure 8.18 Dimensioning a keyway using the LEADER command.

Adding Leader Lines: Exercise 8.7

1. Enter **LEADER** at the **Dim:** prompt.

2. **Leader start:**

Pick a point on the keyway.

3. **To point:**

Pick the end point of the leader.

4. **To point:**

Pick another point horizontal to the last point input to create the short leg of the leader. Use **ORTHO** toggle by entering F-8 or CTRL-O.

5. **To point:**

Enter RETURN to display the following prompt:

Dimension text (2.00):

The default measurement is the most recent dimension and cannot be used for the keyway.

6. For this example, the keyway is dimensioned by keyboard entry as: **.25 X .50 KEYWAY**, followed by RETURN. The keyway is dimensioned as shown in Figure 8.18.

A circle also can be dimensioned with a leader line by interrupting the **DIAMETER** command when prompted by the dimension text. Entering a single space and pressing RETURN breaks the DIAMETER command. Enter **LEADER** at the **DIM** prompt and pick the points necessary to create a leader for the hole to be dimensioned. When the points have been chosen, enter RETURN at the **To point:** prompt. The **Dimension text (2.00]:** prompt with the dimension value of the circle is displayed. Enter RETURN to add the dimension text to the leader, as shown in Figure 8.19. This procedure will also work with the **ARC** command.

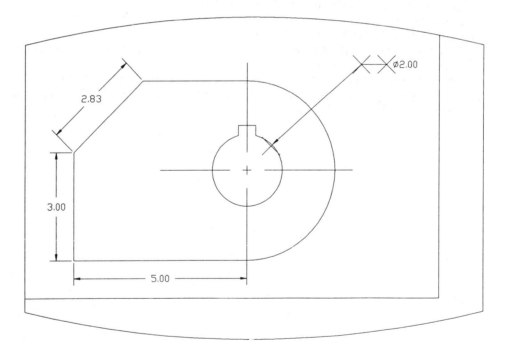

Figure 8.19 Dimensioning a circle using LEADER.

DIMENSIONING ARCS

Arcs are dimensioned with the **RADIUS** command which specifies their radii with a leader and arrow from the center to a point on the arc Figure 8.20. The dimension text is preceded by the letter **R** to denote that it is a radius dimension. Figure 8.20 shows the effect of the Dim Vars **DIMTIX** on a radial dimension. When dimensioning small arcs use **DIMTIX** off, which is the default. When dimensioning larger arcs use **DIMTIX** on.

The following steps show how to use the **RADIUS** command to dimension the arc in Figure 8.7:

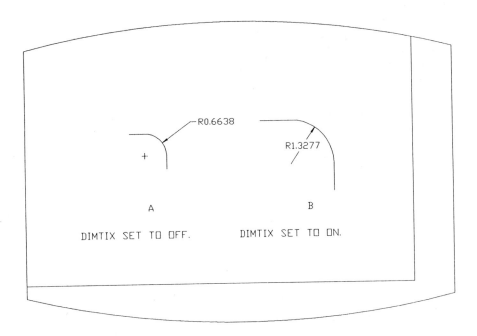

Figure 8.20 Accepted methods of dimensioning arcs.

Dimensioning Arcs: Exercise 8.8

1. At the **Dim:** prompt enter the **RADIUS** command.
2. **Select arc or circle:**
Pick a point on the circumference of the arc.
3. **Dimension text (2.50):** is displayed in the prompt line. Press Return to accept the value automatically given by AutoCAD.
4. **Enter leader length for text** is displayed in the prompt line and you can dynamically drag the dimension into position. Move the cursor to the location for the text and pick the point then press RETURN. Figure 8.21.

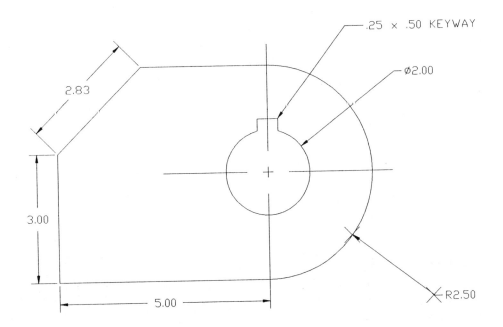

Figure 8.21 Dimensioning an arc with AutoCAD.

DIMENSIONING ANGLES

Linear dimensions for lines which are neither horizontal nor vertical are created by locating the two end points of the angled line using the **ALIGNED** dimensioning command. Angles are dimensioned automatically by locating one end point and specifying the angle by creating an arc with the center point at the vertex of the angle. The AutoCAD command **ANGULAR** specifies the angle of a feature. As soon as the angle vertex and extension endpoints are known, an angular dimension is dragged along as the cursor is moved. So the same angle can be dimensioned in several different ways as shown in Figure 8.22. While dragging the location for the dimension, the text and the rotation angle can be changed. Figure 8.23. Figure 8.24 and the following steps illustrate the use of the **ANGULAR** command:

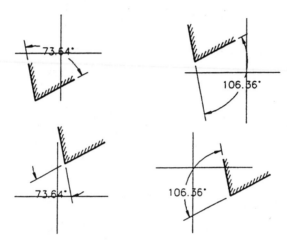

Angular dimension being dragged to new locations

Figure 8.22 Angular dimensions being dragged to new locations. (Autodesk, Inc).

Angular Dimensioning: Exercise 8.9

1. Select **Angular** from the Dim Menu or pick Draw/Dimension/Angular from the pull-down menus.
2. **Select arc, circle, line or RETURN:** is the first prompt displayed.
Pick a point on the line to be dimensioned.
3. **Second line:**
Pick a point on the second line.
4. **Dimension arc line location (Text/Angle):** is displayed in the prompt line. To change the numerical value displayed on screen enter **T** to enter the new number. To rotate the position of the text enter **A** and then the new angle. Moving the cursor will display the 4 different angular dimensions possible. Pick the position shown in Figure 8.24.
5. **Dimension text (135):** is displayed in the prompt line.
The measured angle is displayed in the brackets. To accept the value press RETURN.
6. **Enter text location (or RETURN):** is displayed in the prompt line. Entering Return automatically places the text along the arc and puts a space in it. An alternative to automatic placement would be to move the cursor to any position on screen. Notice that the text follows the location of the cursor and picking a point will place the text at that position.
If manually placing an angular dimension, enter **%%D** preceeding the numerical value to display the degree symbol.

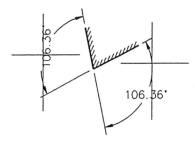

Angular dimension being dragged, while text is rotated

Figure 8.23 Angular dimension being dragged while text is rotated. (Autodesk, Inc).

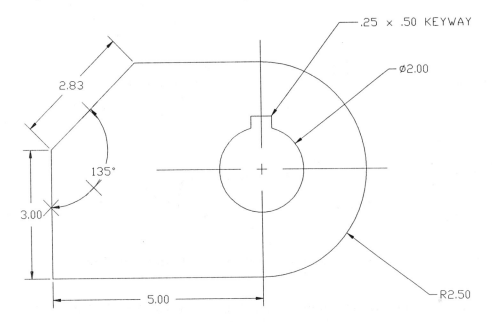

Figure 8.24 Dimensioning an angle.

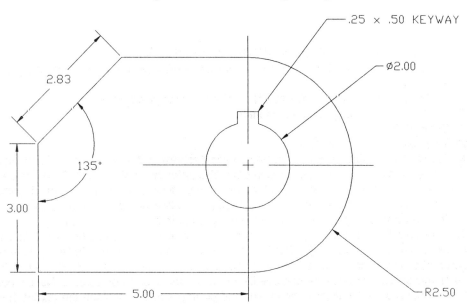

Figure 8.25 A completely dimensioned engineering drawing.

EDITING A DIMENSIONED DRAWING

AutoCAD provides associative dimensions capabilities. Associative dimensions are automatically changed when the part geometry is changed with Edit commands, such as **SCALE, TRIM, EXTEND, STRETCH, ROTATE,** and **MIRROR.** Associative dimensions are created when the dimension variable **DIMASO** is on. The default setting is on and is changed with the **SETVAR** command.

The completed dimensioned drawing of Figure 8.7 is shown in Figure 8.25. Changes are made by erasing dimensions and placing them in different locations. The dimension variables can be changed after the dimensions are placed on a drawing by using the **DIM VAR** command. The **UPDATE** command updates the dimension variables on a finished, dimensioned drawing to the new current variable setting. The following steps demonstrate how to change the size of dimension text and arrows on Figure 8.25:

Updating Dimensions: Exercise 8.10

1. Select **DIM VARS** from the Dimension Menu or pick **Dimension Style...** from the Settings Pull-down Menu. This displays the Dimension Style and Variables Dialogue Box as shown in Figure 8.5.

2. Select **DIMASZ** to change the size of the arrows from the Dim Vars Menu or pick the **Features...** button from the dialogue box which displays the dialogue box shown in Figure 8.26.

3. Change the arrow size from .1800 to .2500. Then change the text height from .1800 to .2500 in the dialogue box. Pick the **OK** button on the Features dialogue box, then **OK** on the Dimension Style dialogue box.

4. Pick **Dim:** from the Main Menu. At the DIM prompt enter **UPDATE** to change the dimension variables to the current settings.

5. **Select objects:**

Use any of the standard object selection methods available. For this example **WINDOW** is used. Pick the first corner of the window to surround the entire drawing.

6. **Other corner:**

Pick the other corner of the window. A message displays the number of objects found such as, **32 found,** and the arrows and text are changed, as shown in Figure 8.27.

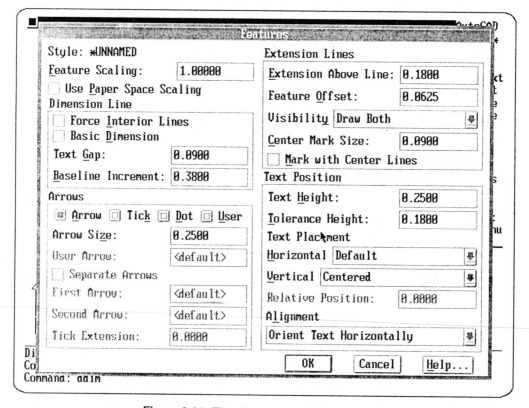

Figure 8.26 The dimension style dialogue box.

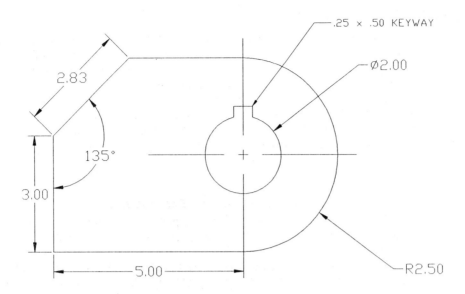

Figure 8.27 Using the UPDATE command to change dimension variables.

Notice that the leader arrows and text did not change. These dimensions cannot be updated and must be redrawn using the new variable settings.

BASELINE DIMENSIONING

Baseline or datum dimensioning commonly is used on parts that are to be toleranced. Baseline dimensioning avoids the accumulation of tolerances from feature to feature on a part. AutoCAD's **BASELINE** command creates datum dimensions on a drawing. This command automatically starts a linear dimension from the baseline or datum surface of the first dimension. To use Baseline the first dimension must be placed on the drawing using the Horizontal or Vertical dimensioning options. To use the **BASELINE** option, a value must be specified for the DIM variable **DIMDLI** which has a default setting of .3800. This numerical value controls the space between each dimension line in baseline dimensioning. Figure 8.28 and the following steps demonstrate baseline dimensioning:

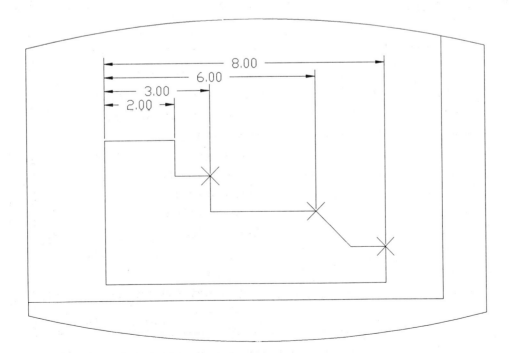

Figure 8.28 Baseline dimensioning.

Creating Baseline Dimensions: Exercise 8.11

1. Open **LAB 8-3** from your data disk. Select Horizontal from the Dim Menu or pick Draw/ Dimension/Horizontal from the pull-down menus.

2. **First extension line origin or RETURN to select:** is displayed in the prompt line. For this example, the vertical surface on the left of the part is used as the datum. Pick the left endpoint of the 2.00 horizontal line using the Osnap Endpoint option.

3. **Second extension line origin:** Pick the right endpoint of the 2.00 horizontal line using the Osnap Endpoint option.

4. **Dimension line location:** is displayed in the prompt line. Pick a point .500 from the object.

5. **Dimension text <2.00>:** is displayed in the prompt line. Enter Return to accept the value and place the first dimension on the drawing.

6. Select **BASELINE** from the pull-down menu or enter it at the Dim prompt.

7. **Second extension line origin or RETURN to select:** Pick the corner of the part to be dimensioned using the Osnap Endpoint option.

8. **Dimension text (3.00):**
Entering RETURN automatically places the dimension on the drawing without having to specify the location of the text.

9. Enter RETURN to repeat the **BASELINE** command to complete the dimensions, as shown in Figure 8.28.

POINT-TO-POINT DIMENSIONING

Point-to-point dimensioning is used for simple parts without tolerances. This type of dimensioning is commonly used for dimensioning parts for locations. The AutoCAD command **CONTINUOUS** is used to more effectively place point-to-point dimensions on a drawing. Figure 8.29 and the following steps are used as an example:

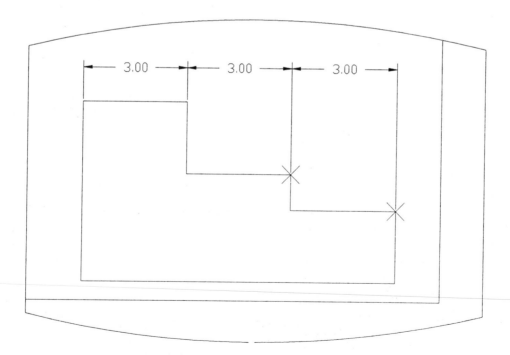

Figure 8.29 Continuous dimensioning.

Continuous Dimensions: Exercise 8.12

1. Open **LAB 8-4** from your data disk. Select **Dim:** from the menu or select Dimension from the Draw Pull-down Menu.
2. At the **DIM:** prompt select **HORIZONTAL** from the menu and place the first dimension on the drawing.
3. Select **CONTINUE** from the Dim menu or enter it at the Dim prompt.
4. **Second extension line origin or RETURN to select:**
Pick the next location to be dimensioned as shown by the X in figure 8.29.
5. **Dimension text (3.00):**
Entering RETURN automatically places the dimension on the drawing without having to specify the location of the text.
6. Enter RETURN to repeat the **CONTINUOUS** command and complete the dimensions, as shown in Figure 8.29.

THE TROTATE OPTION

The **TROTATE** option is used to change the angle of dimension text. This command can be used to change unidirectional dimensions to bi-directional. The following steps describe how to use the **TROTATE** option:

Rotating Dimension Text: Exercise 8.13

1. Use the dimensions placed in Exercise 8.12. Select **DIM**: from the Main Menu.
2. Select **TROTATE** from the DIM EDIT Menu.
3. **Enter text angle:** Enter a value of **90** to rotate the dimension text in Figure 8.30 from horizontal to vertical.
4. **Select objects:** Pick the dimension to change and press **Return.** The dimension text is rotated from horizontal to vertical as shown in Figure 8.30.

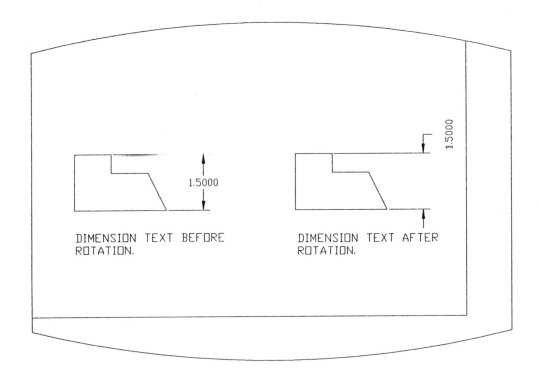

Figure 8.30 Effects of the TROTATE option.

ORDINAL DIMENSIONING

Ordinal dimensions are used to display the X and Y coordinates of a feature. Ordinal dimensions have no arrows or dimension lines only extension lines and text. Ordinal dimensions are commonly used for NC (Numerical Control) drawings. Figure 8.31 and the following steps describe how to create ordinal dimensions with AutoCAD:

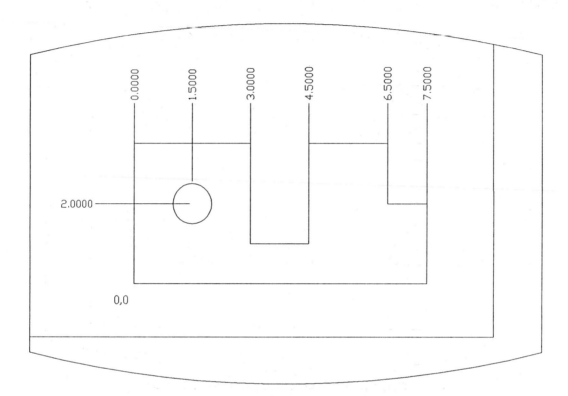

Figure 8.31 Ordinal dimensioning.

Placing Ordinal Dimensions: Exercise 8.14

1. Open **LAB 8-5** from your data disk. Select **DIM** from the Main Menu. Turn **Ortho** on by pressing the **F8** key.
2. Select **ORDINATE:** from the DIM Menu.
3. **Select Feature:** Pick the feature to be dimensioned.
4. **Leader Endpoint (X datum/Y datum):** Enter **X** to place the X coordinate value of the feature.
5. **Leader Endpoint:** Pick the location for the start of the dimension text.
6. **Dimension text (0.0000):** The dimension text is displayed in the prompt line. To accept the value enter **Return** or enter your own value. After RETURN is selected the dimension is placed on the drawing.
7. Enter **Return** to repeat the ORDINATE option to finish the dimensioning.
Figure 8.31 shows the X coordinate values of the features across the top of the drawing. The Y coordinate value of the hole located to the left of the drawing was drawn by picking the center of the circle and entering Y at the **Leader endpoint (X datum/Y datum)** prompt

DIMENSIONS FOR VARIOUS SHAPES

Many parts designed and documented with engineering drawings are made from simple geometric shapes such as prisms, cylinders, and cones. These simple shapes are dimensioned differently. Prisms, for example, must have the height, width, and depth specified. Figures 8.32 and 8.33 show how to dimension some basic geometric shapes.

The pyramid in Figure 8.32 is dimensioned with AutoCAD using the **HORIZONTAL** and **VERTICAL** commands. Cones are dimensioned by specifying the altitude and diameter of the base. With AutoCAD use the **HORIZONTAL** and **VERTICAL** commands. Regular prisms, as shown in Figure 8.33, are dimensioned using **HORIZONTAL** and **VERTICAL** dimension commands. Dimensioning cylinders requires the diameter and length to be specified. With AutoCAD use the **HORIZONTAL, VERTICAL,** and **LEADER** , or **DIAMETER** commands.

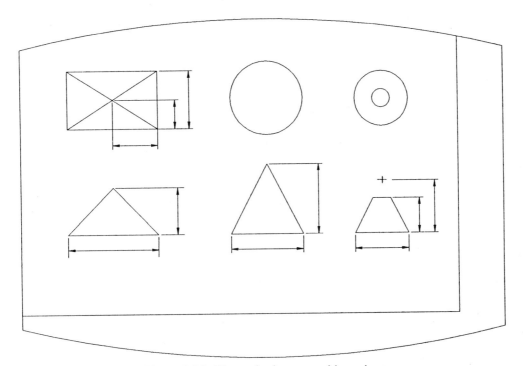

Figure 8.32 Dimensioning pyramids and cones.

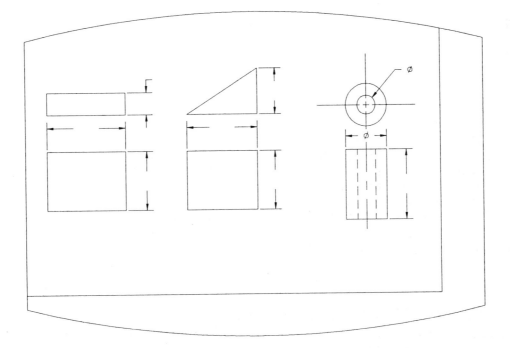

Figure 8.33 Dimensioning prisms and cylinders.

USING LEADERS AND NOTES TO DIMENSION OTHER COMMON FEATURES

Many features of an engineering drawing must be specified other than size, location, and basic geometric shape. Many of the features that must be specified with a note and/or leader are details that are created with special machining operations. The keyway that was dimensioned earlier in this chapter is a good example. Other special features that must be specified are fillets and rounds, chamfers, threads, and holes.

Fillets and rounds usually are specified as a note away from the detail drawing using the **TEXT** command, as explained in Chapter 3. Varying the text style and height can add to the clarity of notes added to an engineering drawing.

Figure 8.34 shows special types of holes that must be specified with a leader and note using AutoCAD commands **LEADER** and **TEXT**. The following steps dimension a counterbored hole as shown in Figure 8.34:

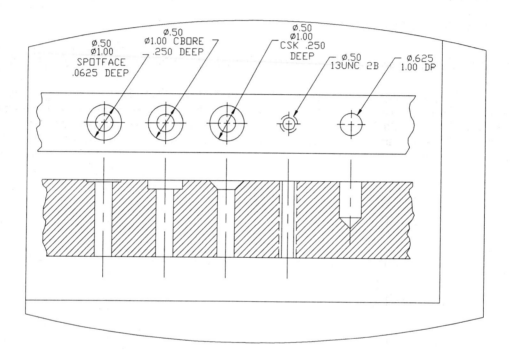

Figure 8.34 Dimensioning holes.

Dimensioning a Counterbored Hole: Exercise 8.15

1. Open **LAB 8-6** from your data disk. At the **DIM:** prompt select **LEADER** or pick it from the Draw/Dimension pull-down menu.
2. **Leader start:**
Pick a point on the circumference of the large hole.
3. **To point:**
Pick a point that is radial with the two holes and approximately one inch from the large hole.
4. **To point:**
Pick a point located approximately 1/4 of an inch horizontally to the right. Use the Ortho Snap (F8) to assist in placing the point.
5. Enter RETURN at the next **To point:** prompt.
6. **Dimension text ():**
Enter the first line of text for the counterbored hole. **%%C .50** displays the phi symbol and the size of the small hole.
7. Select the **TEXT** command from the **DRAW** submenu.

8. **Justify/Style (start point):**
Pick a point below the first line of text at the end of the leader.
9. **Height (0.2000):**
Enter the current value set in the dimensioning variables, such as the default value of **0.18**
and RETURN.
10. **Rotation angle (0):**
Enter RETURN.
11. **Text:**
Enter **%%C 1.00 CBORE** to specify the diameter of the counterbore.
12. **Command:**
To start another line of text directly below the last line enter RETURN.
13. **Justify/Style (start point):**
Enter RETURN.
14. **Text:**
Enter **.250 DEEP** and RETURN.

This procedure can be used for most holes and other features, such as chamfers, knurls, necks and undercuts, threads, and tapers.

When specifying some details it is acceptable to use symbols instead of text. Figure 8.35 shows a number of symbols that can be used instead of text for features such as counterbored and countersunk holes. These symbols can be added to drawings with the **INSERT** command and added to a dimension note if desired. Finish marks identify those surfaces of a part that are to be machined finished and are placed in every view where the finished surface appears as an edge.

Figure 8.35 Symbols used for dimensioning can be made into **BLOCKS** and inserted into a dimension note.

TOLERANCING ENGINEERING DRAWINGS

A tolerance is the total amount a specified dimension can vary. It carefully controls the size of parts so they can be assembled even if they are manufactured at different locations. Tolerances are applied to the basic size of parts, following industry standards. They are specified in an engineering drawing through a general note or in the title block, or are applied directly to the dimension. If applied to the dimension, tolerances can be expressed as limits and plus/minus. If manually placing tolerancing values with text, enter %%P to draw the plus/minus symbol.

The plus/minus method is used two different ways. When the plus/minus dimension allows variation in only one direction from the basic size, the tolerancing is called unilateral. When the dimension can vary in both directions from the basic size, it is called bilateral. AutoCAD is used for plus/minus tolerancing of linear and diametral dimensions by turning on the **DIMTOL** variable. The upper and lower limits of a dimension are set using the dimension variable commands **DIMTP**, for plus tolerances, and **DIMTM** for minus tolerances. Figure 8.36 and the following steps are a guide for placing bilateral tolerances on a drawing:

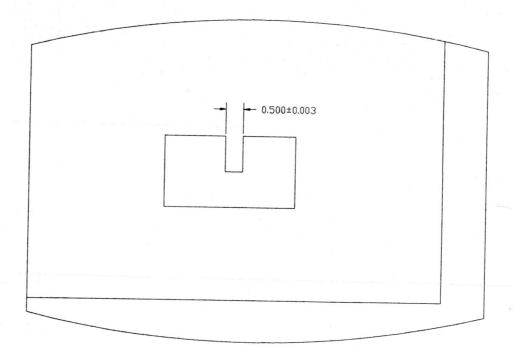

Figure 8.36 Bilateral plus/minus dimensions.

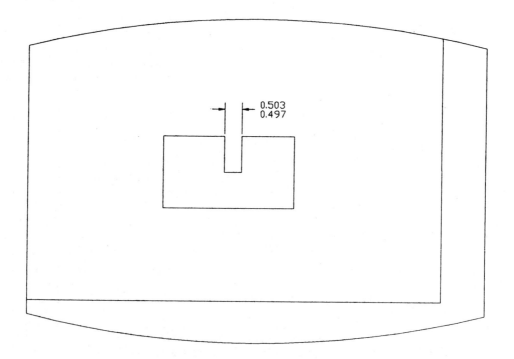

Figure 8.37 A limit form of dimension.

Placing Bilateral Tolerances: Exercise 8.16

1. Open **LAB 8-7** from your data disk. Before tolerancing a drawing, change the decimal precision of the dimensions if necessary. The decimal precision is changed by using the **SETTINGS** option **UNITS**, as described in Chapter 2. For this example select **Decimal** as the units and **3** as the number of digits to the right of the decimal point.

2. To set the upper and lower limits of the dimension, enter **DIM VARS** at the **DIM:** prompt

3. Select **DIMTP** from the third Dim Vars Menu to set the upper limit or plus tolerance.
4. **DIMTP Current value (0.0000) New value:**
Enter the new value as **0.003** and press RETURN.
5. **Dim:**
Select **DIMTM** to set the lower limit or minus tolerance.
6. **DIMTM Current value (0.0000) New value:**
Enter the new value as **0.003** and press RETURN. All zeroes could be entered at this step to create a unilateral tolerance.
7. **Dim:**
Select **DIMTOL** to turn on the tolerancing.
8. **Current value (Off) New value:**
Enter **ON** to create plus/minus tolerances.
9. **Dim:**
Go to the Dimension Menu and select **Horizontal** to create the bilateral plus/minus toleranced dimension shown in Figure 8.36.

The limits method shows the largest and smallest sizes permitted for a feature (Figure 8.37). The AutoCAD dimension variable command **DIMLIM** is turned on to create linear and diametral limit dimensions. The same steps described for the plus/minus method of tolerancing can be used for limits, except Step 7 would need **DIMLIM** to turn on the limits dimensioning. **DIMTOL** and **DIMLIM** cannot be on at the same time. AutoCAD automatically turns off one if both are turned on simultaneously.

BASIC DIMENSIONS

A basic dimension is a theoretical dimension value applied to the size or location of a feature on a part. General tolerances specified in notes or a title block do not apply to a basic dimension. One method of identifying a basic dimension is to draw a rectangle around the dimension value. AutoCAD automatically draws a rectangle around any dimension value if the **DIMGAP** is set to a negative value. When DIMGAP is positive no gap is produced. The absolute value of the DIMGAP setting determines the space between the dimension text and the sides of the box. Figure 8.38 show basic diemesions with a setting of -.09 on the left and -.30 on the right. The following steps describe how to create a basic dimension.

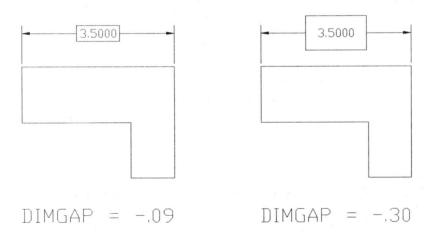

Figure 8.38 Using a negative DIMGAP setting to create a basic dimension.

Basic Dimensions: Exercise 8.17

1. Open **LAB8-8** from your data disk.
2. Enter **DIMGAP** at the command prompt.
3. **New value for DIMGAP <0.0900>:** is displayed in the prompt line. Enter a new value of **-.09**.
4. From the Draw Pull-down Menu select Dimension/Linear/Horizontal or pick **HORIZNTAL** from the Dimension Menu. A prompt reads:
First extension line origin or RETURN to select:
Pick one endpoint of the line to be dimensioned.

2. **Second extension line origin:**
Pick the other endpoint of the line.
3. **Dimension line location (Text/Angle):**
Make sure the Snap toggle is on. Move the cursor a minimum of .5 units from the outside of the object. Position the cursor at the desired location for the text and pick that point.
4. **Dimension text (3.5000):** Enter Return to add the basic dimension to the drawing.

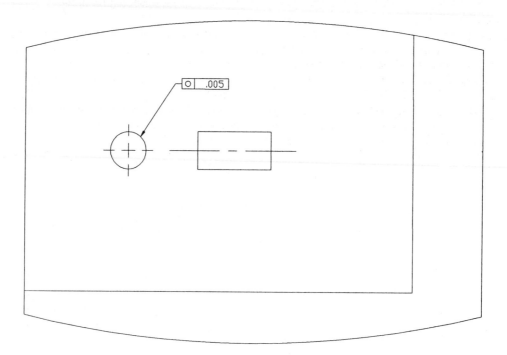

Figure 8.39 A simple geometric tolerance.

	CHARACTERISTIC	SYMBOL
FORM TOLERANCES	STRAIGHTNESS	—
	FLATNESS	⟋▱
	ROUNDNESS	◯
	CYLINDRICITY	⌀
	PROFILE OF A LINE	⌒
	PROFILE OF A SURFACE	⌓
	ANGULARITY	∠
	PERPENDICULARITY	⊥
	PARALLELISM	//
LOCATION TOLERANCES	POSITION	⊕
	CONCENTRICITY	◎
	SYMMETRY	≡
RUNOUT TOLERANCES	CIRCULAR	⟋
	TOTAL	⟋

Figure 8.40 Table of position and form symbols.

GEOMETRIC TOLERANCING

Geometric tolerancing specifies tolerances of position and form of mating parts. It specifies the amount of variation allowable from perfect forms such as prisms, cylinders, and cones. It is impossible to manufacture perfect forms, so geometric tolerances are used to limit the possible variation of a part. Geometric tolerances are used along with the coordinate dimensioning system and are specified through a combination of symbols and numerical values in a feature control symbol. Figure 8.39 is a typical feature control symbol specifying the amount of roundness variation allowed on the cylindrical piece. Figure 8.40 shows a table of position and form symbols used for geometric tolera ncing.

To effectively use AutoCAD for geometric tolerancing, the symbols must be created and saved on a symbols disk or in a symbols library. The **INSERT** command then is used to place the symbols onto the drawing. The AutoCAD command **LEADER** could be used to create the leader line. The line drawing command and grid can create the rectangles that contain the symbols and text for a geometric tolerance. However, it may be easier to create the symbols with rectangles so they do not have to be drawn every time a geometric tolerance is used on an engineering drawing. The geometric tolerance shown in Figure 8.41 is produced with AutoCAD by suppressing the text of a **VERTICAL** dimension and by entering a single blank space with the space bar, followed by RETURN. The geometric tolerance symbols are added to the drawing as **WBLOCKS.**

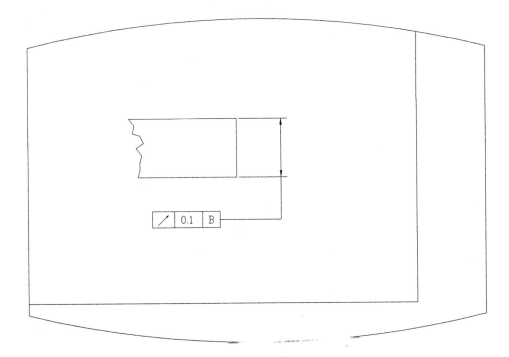

Figure 8.41 Suppressing text on a vertical dimension to produce a feature geometric tolerance.

DUAL DIMENSIONING

Occasionally it is necessary to display both English and Metric dimensions on a drawing. This is referred to as dual dimensioning. To draw dual dimensions with AutoCAD three Dim Vars must be set:

DIMALT - Alternate units
DIMALTF - Alternate units scale factor
DIMALTD - Alternate units decimal places.

Use the following steps to create metric millimeters (mm) dual dimensions:

Dual Dimensioning: Exercise 8.18

1. Load **LAB 8-9** from your data disk. Select **DIM:** from the Main Menu.

2. Select **DIMVARS** from the menu.

3. Select **DIMALT** from the menu.

4. **New value for DIMALT <0>:** is displayed in the prompt line. Enter the number 1 to set the alternate units.

5. Select **DIMALTD** from the DimVars menu.

6. **New value for DIMALTD <2>:** is displayed in the prompt line. **DIMALTD** is used to set the number of decimal places for the alternate dimensions. For millimeter dimensions set the value to zero.

7. Select **DIMALTF** to set the alternate dimension scale factor.

8. **New value for DIMALTF <25.4000>:** To convert decimal inches to mm use a scale of 25.40 which is the default setting.

9. Dimension the rectangle with the Horizontal and Vertical dimension commands. Figure 8.42 shows a dual dimensioned drawing.

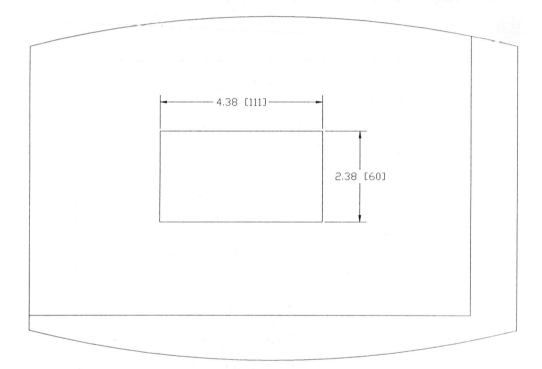

Figure 8.42 Dual dimensioning.

ASSOCIATIVE DIMENSIONS

An associative dimension will change its value when the geometry of the drawing is changed. For example, when using the **Edit** commands **Stretch, Trim,** or **Extend** to change geometry on a drawing the dimension will also be changed if associative dimensioning is on. With AutoCAD the Dim Vars command **DIMASO** must be set to **ON** for associative dimensioning. Figure 8.43 shows the effect of stretching a part's length with **DIMASO** on and the automatic change in dimension from 3.75 to the new length of 5.88. If **DIMSHO** is set to on the new dimension length is displayed as the part is being stretched.

EDITING DIMENSIONS

Selected dimensions can be edited by using the **UPDATE, HOMETEXT, NEW TEXT, TROTATE, TEDIT,** or **OBLIQUE** commands found on the Edit Menu of the DIM Menu. The **UPDATE** command will change selected dimension to all the current DimVar settings, units or text style. To change a dimension to the current setting enter **UPDATE** at the DIM: prompt then select the dimension to be changed.

The **NEWTEXT** command is used to edit the current dimension text. At the **DIM:** prompt enter **NEWTEXT**. At the **Enter new dimension text:** prompt enter the new text. Select the dimension to change the text.

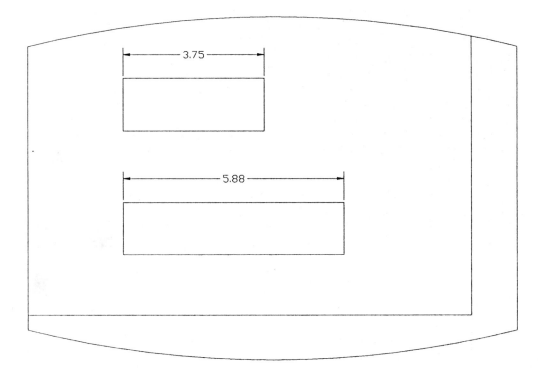

Figure 8.43 Associative dimensioning.

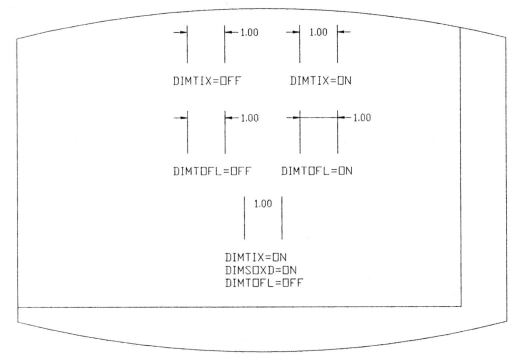

Figure 8.44 Dimensioning in small spaces.

Dimensioning in small spaces.

Some time the space available to place a dimension is too small for the text and arrows. On full-scale drawings dimensions of 1/2 inch or less will need to have a dimension variable changed before adding the dimension to the drawing. The **DIMTIX** option controls the placement of the dimension text. When **DIMTIX** is set to off, the dimension text is placed outside the extension lines as shown in Figure 8.44. The **DIMTOFL** option can be used to force the dimension line inside the extension lines. Figure 8.44. The **DIMSOXD** option supresses the outside extension line as shown in Figure 8.44.

QUESTIONS FOR REVIEW

1. Specify how a listing of dimension settings can be displayed.
2. Define the function of **DIMASO**.
3. Name the AutoCAD commands used to place linear dimensions.
4. Explain how to accurately place dimensions at a specified distance from the object.
5. Explain the difference between manual and automatic dimensioning.
6. Explain how the most recent dimension is erased quickly.
7. Explain how center lines and center marks are added to dimensioned circles.
8. Specify how the **DIMSCALE** value is set?
9. Explain how dimension variables are changed on dimensions already placed on a drawing.
10. List how datum dimensions are created with AutoCAD.
11. Name the command used to place plus/minus tolerances on dimensions.
12. Identify is the difference between **DIM** and **DIM1**.
13. Specify the function of the **CONTINUOUS** option found on the dimension menu.
14. Explain why dimensions should be placed on a separate layer.

Figure 8.45 Dimensioning problem set one.

DRAWING ASSIGNMENTS

1. Dimension those drawings assigned by your instructor from previous chapters by loading the files into the Drawing Editor and adding dimensions following ANSI standards.

2. Create orthographic views and add dimensions to those drawings assigned from Figures 8.45 through 8.49. Each grid mark is equal to .25" or 5mm.

3. Draw and dimension Figure 8.50 using bilateral tolerances. Set the decimal precision to three places and place upper and lower limits of .003".

4. Draw and dimension Figure 8.51 and 8.52. Set the decimal precision to four places and use the limit method by turning the dimension variable **DIMLIN** on.

5. From Giesecke et al., *Engineering Graphics* and *Technical Graphics* drawings from Chapter 11.

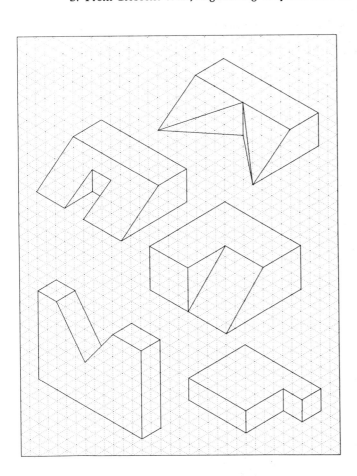

Figure 8.46 Dimensioning problem set two.

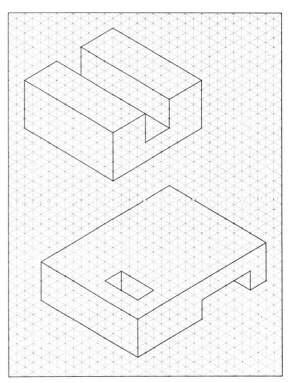

Figure 8.47 Dimensioning problem set three.

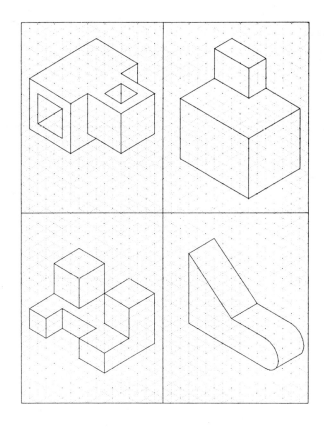

Figure 8.48 Dimensioning problem set four.

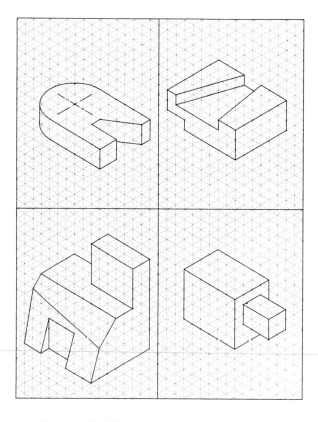

Figure 8.49 Dimensioning problem set five.

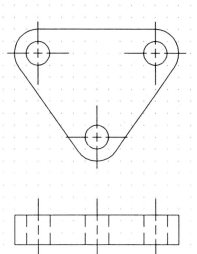

Figure 8.50 Tolerancing problem one.

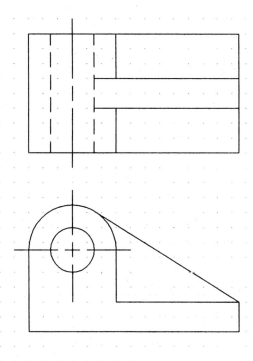

Figure 8.51 Tolerancing problem two.

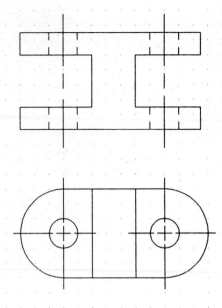

Figure 8.52 Tolerancing problem three.

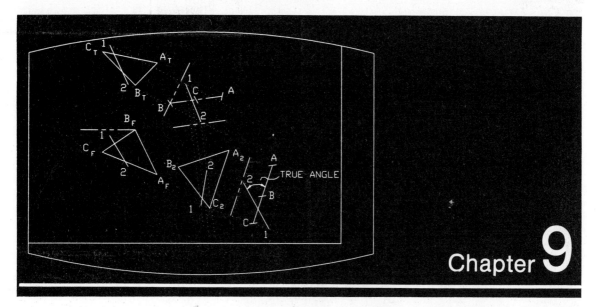

Chapter 9

AUXILIARY VIEWS AND DESCRIPTIVE GEOMETRY

Human beings exist in a three-dimensional world. The task of a designer is to determine the most acceptable solution to a problem. Initially, the solution of a problem may occur in the mind of the designer. The design solution must be communicated to other people in a manner that can be understood easily. Sketches and engineering drawings commonly are used to describe design ideas. Generally, engineering drawings are two or three principal views of a part. However, in special cases one of the six principal views may not adequately describe the design, as shown in Figure 9.1. The surface containing the elliptical view of the hole in the front view is described better using an auxiliary view. This chapter describes the use of AutoCAD to create primary auxiliary views.

As a design solution is being created and evaluated, it may be necessary to determine the spatial relationship between parts of the same object or between one part and another. Figure 9.2 shows a tower and supporting guy wires. The normal orthographic views of the design do not reveal the true lengths of the guy wires. Descriptive geometry has been developed to assist in determining the spatial relationship between parts. Descriptive geometry is based on the fundamentals of orthographic projection. This chapter describes the use of AutoCAD to solve descriptive geometry problems using auxiliary views and rotation. The four fundamental views necessary to solve all descriptive geometry problems are explained and constructed using AutoCAD. These views are: (1) the true length of a line, (2) point view of a line, (3) edge view of a plane, and (4) the normal or true size of a plane.

OBJECTIVES

After completing Chapter 9, you will be able to:
1. Create an auxiliary view of a part,
2. Determine the true length of a line,
3. Find the point view of a line,
4. Find the edge view of a plane,
5. Determine the true size of a plane,
6. Find the piercing points between lines and planes,
7. Draw the line of intersection between planes,
8. Determine the angle between lines and planes and between two planes,
9. Develop patterns for simple geometric shapes,
10. Use the rotation method to solve simple descriptive geometry problems,
11. Construct the four fundamental views necessary to solve descriptive geometry problems with AutoCAD.

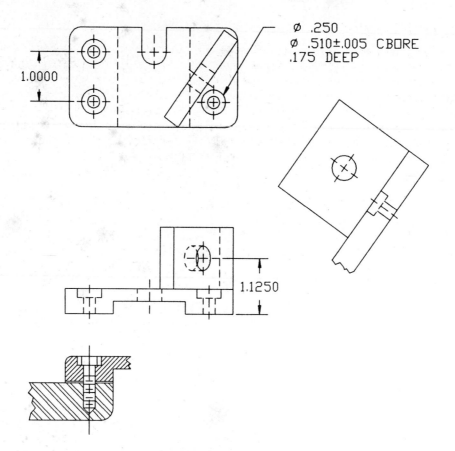

Ø .250
Ø .510±.005 CBORE
.175 DEEP

1.0000

1.1250

Figure 9.1 An auxiliary view.

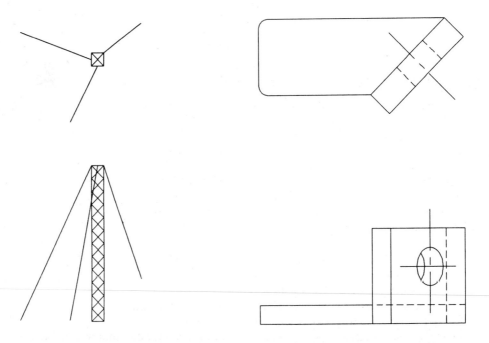

Figure 9.2 An application of descriptive geometry.

Figure 9.3 Drawing of a part that can use an auxiliary view.

AUXILIARY VIEWS

Many objects are designed so that some of the details are not parallel to one of the six principal planes. For example, neither of the two principal views in Figure 9.3 shows the drilled hole or the surface containing the hole true size. To determine the true size and shape of the hole and surface a new view must be created so that the line of sight is perpendicular to the surface, as shown in Figure 9.4. This new view is called an auxiliary view.

An auxiliary view is created by drawing parallel projectors that are perpendicular to the edge view of the surface to be found true size. Measurements are taken from the front view and transferred to the parallel projectors to create the auxiliary view. Although the same procedures used to create an auxiliary view with traditional tools can be used with a CADD system, it is more effective to determine the strengths and weaknesses of the software and use a technique most appropriate for the problem.

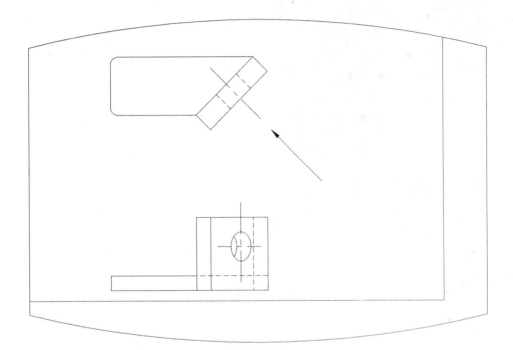

Figure 9.4 Line of sight for the auxiliary view.

DRAWING AN AUXILIARY VIEW WITH AutoCAD

The following steps create an auxiliary view of Figure 9.4. The versatility of AutoCAD makes these steps only one of several methods that can create a simple auxiliary view. AutoCAD can create parallel and perpendicular lines in such a way that projectors or reference planes are unnecessary. The **VERTICAL** dimension option determines measurements in the front view for the auxiliary view. However, the **VERTICAL** option is canceled after the distance is displayed in the prompt line and before the dimension is placed on the drawing. The **LIST** option can also be used to determine distances. The **OFFSET** option creates parallel lines at a specified distance in the auxiliary view. The following steps and related figures explain in detail the construction of an auxiliary view using AutoCAD.

To create the auxiliary view for Figure 9.4, three important dimensions must be taken from the front view: (1) the total height of the surface, (2) the diameter or radius of the hole, and (3) the vertical position of the hole.

Drawing an Auxiliary View: Exercise 9.1

1. Open **LAB9-1** from your data disk. Set the **OBJECT SNAP** Mode to **ENDPOINT** by entering **OSNAP** at the command prompt then **END** followed by Return.
2. Select the **VERTICAL** dimension option from the **DIM** Menu.
3. **First extension line origin or RETURN to select:**
To find the total height of the surface in the front view pick the endpoint of the line.
4. **Second extension line origin:**
Pick the second line.

5. Dimension line location:
Pick a point near the front view. The exact location is not important because the command is canceled before the dimension is placed on the drawing.

6. Dimension text <.5000:>
The height of the surface is shown in brackets in the prompt line. Record the distance before canceling the command.

7. The same procedures described in steps 2 through 6 are used to find the vertical position of the hole. For this example, the distance from the top of the front view to the center of the hole is 1.0000.

8. The top view must be used to determine the size of the hole because the **DIAMETER** or **RADIUS** dimension option will not work with ellipses. The **ALIGNED** dimension option is used to measure the diameter of the circle in the top view. It is determined that the diameter of the circle is 1.0000.

To start the auxiliary view, use the **OFFSET** option to create new lines parallel and at a specified distance from the edge view of the inclined surface in the top view.

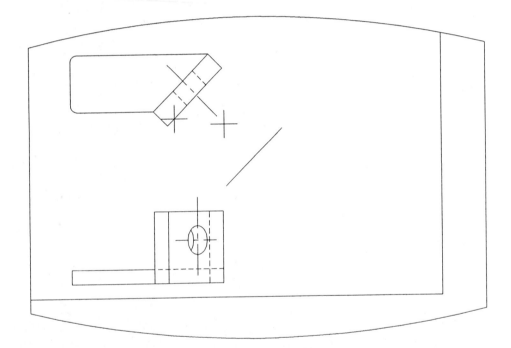

Figure 9.5 Offsetting a line for the auxiliary view.

1. Select the Edit command **OFFSET**.

2. Offset distance or Through <Through>:
The first line to be drawn in the auxiliary view must be placed so it will not interfere with the given views. For this example, the auxiliary view is located **3.000** from the top view so that distance is entered.

3. Select object to offset:
Pick the edge view of the inclined surface in the top view, as shown in Figure 9.5. The line is highlighted on screen.

4. Side to offset?
Pick a point to the right of the edge view in the top view. A line equal in length, parallel to, and projected perpendicular to the line picked in Step 3 is added to the drawing as shown in Figure 9.5.

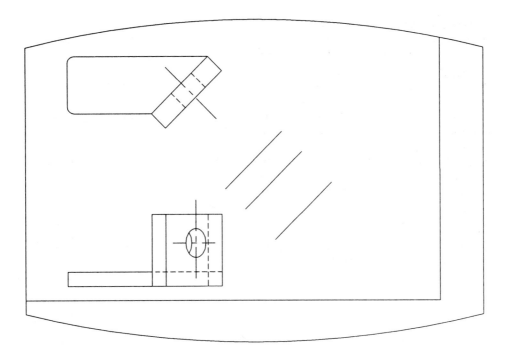

Figure 9.6 Offsetting lines for the center line and total height of the view.

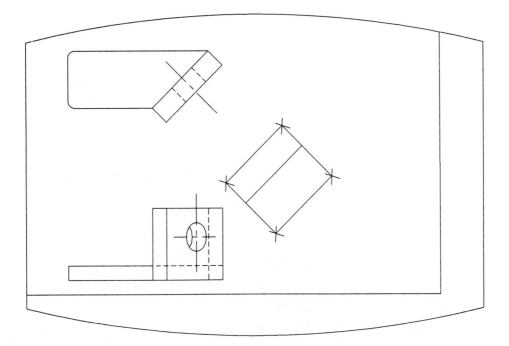

Figure 9.7 Adding lines to the view.

5. Repeat Steps 1 through 4 using an offset distance of **4.0000** and **5.5000** to locate the center of the hole and the total height of the surface, as shown in Figure 9.6.
6. Two lines are added to the auxiliary view by using the **LINE** function and snapping to the **ENDPOINT** of the lines created in Steps 1 through 5, as shown in Figure 9.7.
7. The Edit option **EXTEND** is used to extend the center line of the hole in the top view into the auxiliary view.

8. **Select boundary edge(s). . .**
Select objects:
The center line is extended from the top view to the most distant line in the auxiliary view. The most distant line is picked, as shown in Figure 9.8. After RETURN is entered, the line is highlighted.
9. **Select object to extend:**
Pick the center line in the top view as shown in Figure 9.8. The center line immediately extends as shown in the figure.
10. The hole is added to the auxiliary view by using the two crossing lines as a center

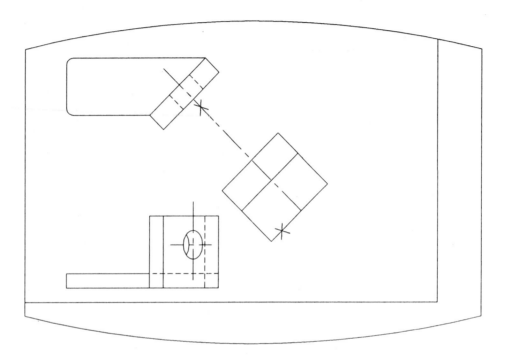

Figure 9.8 Using the **EXTEND** option to draw the center line.

point for the **CIRCLE** option. Change the **OSNAP** option to **INTERSECTION** and select the **CIRCLE** option.
11. **3P/2P/TTR/<Center point>:**
Pick the intersecting lines in the auxiliary view.
12. **Diameter/<Radius>:**
Enter the radius of the circle, **.5** and RETURN. The circle is added to the view.
13. The auxiliary view has to be edited to complete the view to engineering graphics standards. The extended center line is edited using **BREAK** and **TRIM** or **ERASE**.
14. The other center line has to be changed from a solid line to the center line by using the **CHANGE** option **LINETYPE**. The completed auxiliary view is shown in Figure 9.9.

This example is only one of several ways to create an auxiliary view wioth AutoCAD. It may be possible to create this auxiliary view in less time by rotating the **SNAP**, which rotates the grid. The snap and grid axes then are parallel and perpendicular to the edge view of the surface in the top view. The angle of the edge view of the plane in the top view is determined using the INQUIRY/LIST option. That is the angle used to rotate the snap shown in Figure 9.10. The **SNAP** is rotated with the **SETTINGS** option **SNAP** and **ROTATE**. The rotation angle would be 45 degrees, and the rotation origin would be the intersection of the center line of the hole and the edge view of the plane in the top view. The auxiliary view then is created using **LINE** with the **SNAP** and **ORTHO** Modes ON.

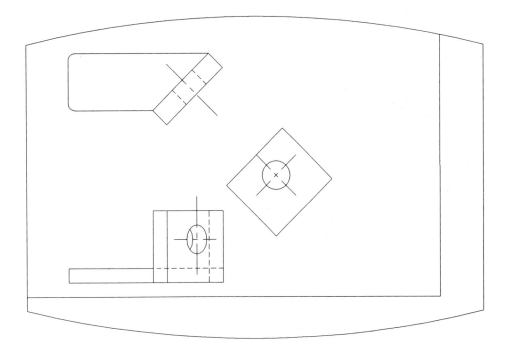

Figure 9.9 The completed auxiliary view of the oblique surface.

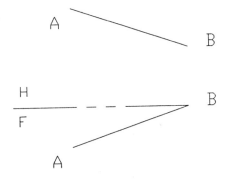

Figure 9.10 Front and top view of oblique line AB.

ALTERNATE METHOD AUXILIARY VIEWS

The alternate method uses techniques that are not very similar to traditional contruction methods but take advantage of AutoCAD commands. The technique uses the same principles used for traditional solutions, such as projecting perpendicular to the edge view of the inclined plane to create the auxiliary view. The followoing steps describe how to create an auxiliary view using AutoCAD. *(The following technique was developed by Professor Michael H. Pleck at the University of Illinois, Champaign/Urbana).*

Auxiliary View Alternate Method: Exercise 9.2

1. Open **LAB9-1** from your data disk. Measure the angle of the line in the top view which represents the edge view of the inclined plane by picking Assist/Inquiry/List from the Pull down Menus.

2. **Select objects:** is displayed in the prompt line. Pick the line in the top view, then enter Return. Information about the line is displayed on the text screen. Look for the *Angle in the XY Plane.* For this example the angle is 225 degrees. Zero degrees is at 3:00 o-clock making this a 45-degree line from the horizontal. Record the length of the line which is 2.2973.

3. Repeat the List command by entering Return, then pick one of the horizontal lines of the face to be drawn in the auxiliary view. Record the length of the line which is 1.6245 for this example. Notice that the line length is foreshortened because its true length is shown in the top view as 2.2973. These lengths will be used later when creating the auxiliary view.

4. Make a block of the face that is to be drawn in auxiliary. Pick Construct/Block from the Pull-down Menus.

5. **Block name (or?):** is displayed in the prompt line. Enter the name **VIEW** at the prompt.

6. **Insertion base point:** is displayed in the prompt line. Pick one of the corners using Osnap Endpoint.

7. **Select objects:** is displayed in the prompt line. Pick each entity that consists of the face to be drawn in the auxiliary view including the center lines. When finished picking, enter Return.

8. Enter **OOPS** after making the block to display it again on screen.

9. Rotate the snap so that one axis is parallel to the edge view of the plane by entering **SNAP** at the command prompt.

10. **Snap spacing or ON/OFF/Aspect/Rotate/Style <1.0000>:** Enter R to set the rotation angle to 45 degrees as measured in Step 2.

11. **Base point <0.0000, 0.0000>:** Enter Osnap Endpoint and pick one corner of the edge view of the plane in the top view.

12. **Rotation angle <0>:** Enter 45 degrees then F8 to turn on the grid. The other endpoint of the line could have been selected instead of entering the degrees. The grid is displayed on screen with the cursor turned parallel to the grid marks.

13. Everything is set to create the auxiliary view. To place the block, begin by entering **INSERT** at the command prompt or by picking it from the contruct menu.

14. **Block name (or?):** Enter the name used in Step 5 called View.

15. **Insertion point:** Pick a point along the grid aligned with the top view.

16. **X scale factor <1> / Corner / XYZ:** Divide the true length of the face 2.2973 by the foreshortened distance 1.6245 obtained in Steps 2 and 3. The resulting value of 1.4142 is the X-scale value entered.

17. **Y scale factor (default=X):** Enter 1 for full scale.

18. **Rotation angle:** The rotation angle is 45 degrees. The auxiliary view is displayed on screen as shown in Figure 9.9.

DESCRIPTIVE GEOMETRY

Before designs can be manufactured, a complete description must be produced. Orthographic projection and descriptive geometry are the graphic tools used to describe objects. The fundamental elements of descriptive geometry are based upon orthographic projection. However, orthographic projection is primarily used to produce drawings that communicate an exact description of a part for its manufacture. Descriptive geometry is used primarily to solve spatial problems encountered in the design of a product.

Descriptive geometry is concerned with determining the true length of entities, areas of surfaces, intersections of entities, and other relationships between two or more parts. This is accomplished by creating a series of successive auxiliary views. AutoCAD, like most other microcomputer-based CADD programs, was developed primarily for the documentation of parts using multiview drawings. Therefore, the command structure and the availability of commands that facilitate the creation of successive auxiliary views for the solution of descriptive geometry problems are not available readily.

AutoCAD is a very diverse and powerful CADD software program that can solve descriptive geometry problems. However, the techniques used differ from the traditional methods. For example, a divider is used to transfer measurements with traditional tools. What is the most effective method of transferring a measurement with AutoCAD?

In this text, the techniques described to solve descriptive geometry problems with AutoCAD are not the only methods that work. The power and flexibility of the program allow different techniques to be used to solve problems. Experience in writing programs can help create special commands, such as parallel and transfer, to solve descriptive geometry problems with AutoCAD's AutoLISP programming language.

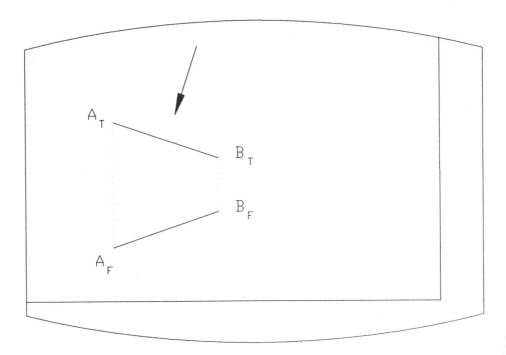

Figure 9.11 The line of sight necessary to find its true length.

TRUE LENGTH OF A LINE

The true length of a line is found by creating an auxiliary view perpendicular to a given foreshortened view of the line. It is one of the four fundamental views necessary to solve descriptive geometry problems. Figure 9.10 shows the front and top views of line segment A-B. It is determined that line A-B is a foreshortened line because the projectors between the views are not perpendicular to the line in either view. To find the true length of line A-B, an auxiliary view is created by projecting perpendicular to the top view, as represented by the arrow in Figure 9.11. Before starting, change the decimal precision to 8 with the Units commands. A reference plane is drawn perpendicular to the projectors between the two given views. Another reference plane is drawn parallel to the top view of the line. Before any descriptive geometry problem is started, the **LAYERS** command should be used to create a construction layer with the **DOT** linetype and a reference plane layer with **PHANTOM** linetype. The **OSNAP** command should be set to **ENDPOINT**. The following steps demonstrate finding a true length of a line. *(The following technique was developed by Professor Michael H. Pleck at the University of Illinois, Champaign/ Urbana).*

Finding the True Length of a Line: Exercise 9.3

1. Open **LAB 9-2** from your data disk. Set the active linetype to **PHANTOM** lines.
2. Set the **ORTHO** Mode ON and set Osnap to Endpoint. To increase your accuracy in making measurements, increase the decimal precision to the maximum value of 8 using the **UNITS** command.
3. Projectors are drawn between the views to serve as a means of measuring distances needed when creating the auxiliary view to find the true length of the line. Select **LINE** to draw a line from Point B in the top view to point B in the front view.
4. Select **LINE** to draw a line from point A in the top view to a point perpendicular to the reference plane H/F using the Perpendicular Osnap option.
5. Repeat the **LINE** command and draw a line from point A in the front view to a point perpendicular to the reference plane H/F using the Perpendicular Osnap option.
6. Select one view of the line to create the auxiliary view to find the true length of the line. Either view could be used but for this example the top view is selected. Rotate the snap so that it is aligned with the line in the top view by entering **SNAP** at the command prompt.
7. **Snap spacing or ON/OFF/Aspect/Rotate/Style <1.00000000>:** Enter R to rotate the snap.

8. **Base point <0.00000000,0.00000000>:** Pick point B in the top view.

9. **Rotation angle <0>:** Pick point A in the top view. The cursor is rotated so one axis is parallel with line A-B in the top view. Turn the grid on by entering F7. Figure 9.12.

10. Draw a reference line parallel to the top view of line A-B by using **LINE** and snapping to the grid. Label this refernce line H/1 using the **DTEXT** command.

11. Draw projectors from points A and B in the top view to reference line H/1 using the Line command. Use the Perpendicular Osnap option to draw the lines perpendicular to the reference line. Figure 9.13.

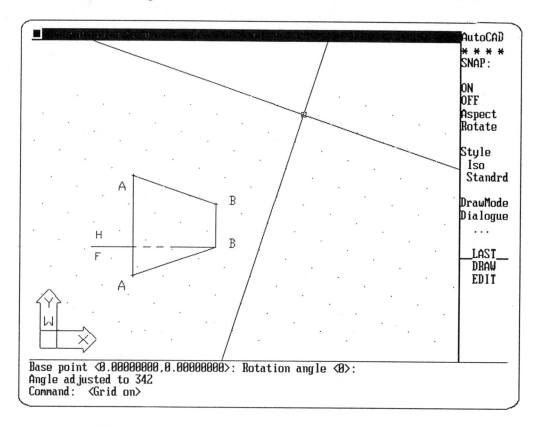

Figure 9.12 Snap rotated parallel to the top view of line A-B.

12. The perpendicular distance that point A lies from reference plane H/F must be determined. Select Assist/Inquiry/List from the Pull-down Menus and pick the line segment. The length will be listed on screen as 1.00000000. This distance must be transferred to the auxiliary view to locate point A.

13. To locate point A in the auxiliary view, the angle of reference line H/1 must be determined. Repeat the @ command and pick the reference line. The angle of the line is listed as 341.56505118.

14. To locate point A in the auxiliary view, draw a perpendicular line from the intersection of reference line H/1 and the projector of point A from the top view at a distance and angle determined in Steps 12 and 13. Enter **LINE** at the command prompt.

15. Snap to the intersection of the projector from point A with the reference line uisng Osnap Intersection. At the **To point:** prompt enter **@1<71.56505118**. The angle measured in Step 13 was subtracted from 270 to get the angle of the projector for point A.

16. Complete the true length view of line A-B by using the **LINE** command to snap to the endpoint of the projector and the intersection of the projector from point B and the reference line H/1. Use **DTEXT** to label the endpoints of the line. Figure 9.14.

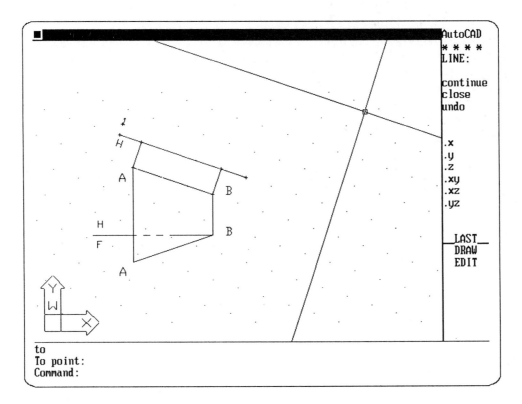

Figure 9.13 Reference plane and projectors for the new view.

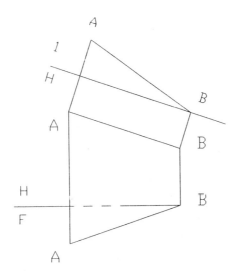

Figure 9.14 The true length view of line A-B.

POINT VIEW OF A LINE (SECONDARY AUXILIARY VIEWS)

The point view of a line is created by viewing the end of a true length line. This is the second fundamental view necessary to solve descriptive geometry problems. Another reference plane must be drawn perpendicular to the true length view of the line using the **Snap/Grid**. Layers should be created to construct and separate auxiliary views from the given views. The following steps use the true length line found in the previous example to create the point view of a line. This procedure also shows how to create a secondary auxiliary view.

Creating a Point View of a Line: Exercise 9.4

1. Continuing with the previous exercise, enter **SNAP** at the command prompt, then enter R to rotate the snap parallel to true length view of line A-B. Snap to the endpoints of line A-B to define the new snap roation angle.

2. Draw a reference line perpendicular to the true length view of line A-B by using **LINE** and snapping to the grid. Label this reference line 1/2 using the **DTEXT** command.

3. Draw a projector from point B in view 1 using Osnap Endpoint perpendicular to reference line 1/2 using Osnap Perpendicular. Figure 9.15.

4. The perpendicular distance that points A and B lie from reference plane 1/H must be determined. Select Assist/Inquiry/List from the Pull-down Menus and pick the line segment. The length will be listed on screen as 1.00000000. This distance must be

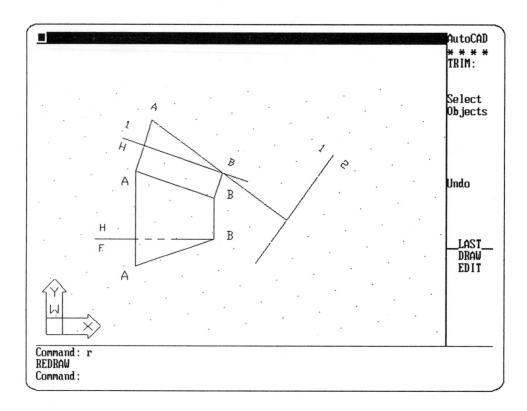

Figure 9.15 Drawing the reference line and projector for line A-B.

transferred to the auxiliary view to locate the point view of line A-B.

5. In order to locate point A in the auxiliary view the angle of reference line 1/2 must be determined. Repeat the List command and pick the reference line. The angle of the line is listed as 234.01665056.

6. To locate the point view of line A-B in the auxiliary view draw a perpendicular line from the Intersection of reference line 1/2 and the projector of line A-B from view 1 at a distance and angle determined in Steps 4 and 5. Enter **LINE** at the command prompt.

7. Snap to the intersection of the projector from point A with the reference line uisng Osnap Intersection. At the **To point:** prompt enter **@1<-36.01665056**. The angle measured in Step 5 was subtracted from 270 to get the angle of the projector for line A-B.

8. Set the Point Mode to 3, then draw a point at the end of the projector to locate the point view of line A-B. Figure 9.16.

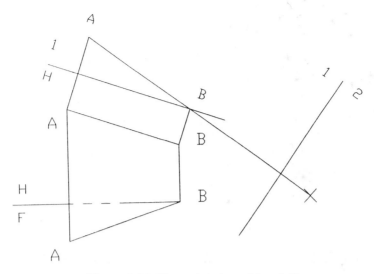

Figure 9.16 The point view of line A-B.

Finding the point view of a line has many applications in descriptive geometry. To determine the shortest distance between a point and a line, view the line as a point. To determine the shortest distance between two lines, view one of the lines as a point. The edge view of a plane can be constructed by finding the point view of a line in the plane. The angle between two planes can be determined by finding a point view of the line of intersection between the planes. Many applications exist for the point view of a line, and the basic steps that have been shown can be used with AutoCAD.

FINDING THE EDGE VIEW OF A PLANE

The edge view of a plane can be drawn by finding the point view of a line that lies in the plane. This is the third fundamental view necessary to solve descriptive geometry problems. To make the solution of these problems easier, a true length line is installed in the plane if none of the sides of the plane are true length (Figure 9.17). The following steps describe how to find the edge view of a plane using AutoCAD:

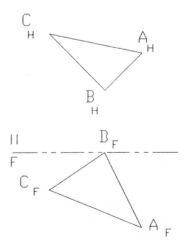

Figure 9.17 Oblique plane.

Creating an Edge View of a Plane: Exercise 9.5

1. Open **LAB9-4** from your data disk. Create a construction layer with dot linetype.
2. Install a true length line in plane ABC by drawing a line in the front view that is parallel with the given reference plane. This new line when constructed in the top view will be a true length line in the plane from which an edge view of the plane can be created. Use the **ORTHO** function and **LINE** to create a horizontal line in the front view of plane ABC, as shown in Figure 9.18, by picking point C and any point to the right of line A-B.

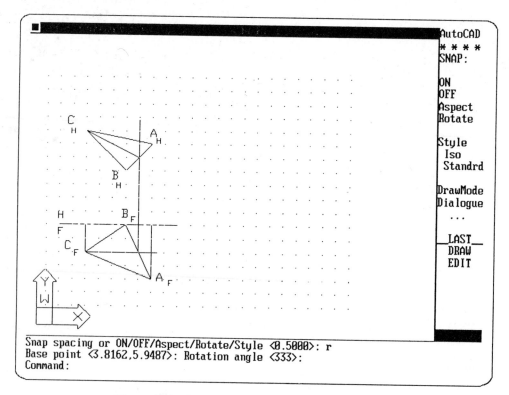

Figure 9.18 Creating a true length line in plane ABC.

3. Project the new line to the top view by picking the **INTERSECTION** of the new line and side AB of the plane in the front view. Draw this line to the reference plane H/F using the Osnap Perpendicular. Draw a line from the intersection of the projector and reference plane H/F to a point in the top view so that the projector intersects side AB of plane ABC. Pick a point like that shown in Figure 9.18 in the top view.

4. A new line is drawn from point C in the top view to the intersection of the projector from the front view.   This new line in the top view is a true length line located in plane ABC. Figure 9.18.

5. Draw projectors from points C and A in the front view perpendicular to reference plane H/F.

6. Enter **SNAP** at the command prompt then enter R to rotate the snap parallel to true length view of line in plane ABC. Snap to the endpoints of the line to define the new snap rotation angle.

7. Draw a reference line perpendicular to the true length view of line A-B by using **LINE** and snapping to the grid. Label this reference line H/1 using the **DTEXT** command.

8. Draw a projector from the true length line using Osnap Endpoint perpendicular to reference line H/1 using Osnap Perpendicular. Repeat this step to draw projectors for points A and B. Figure 9.19.

9. The perpendicular distance the new line in the front view lies from reference plane H/F must be determined. Select Assist/Inquiry/List from the Pull-down Menus and pick the line segment. The length will be listed on screen as 1.00000000. This distance must be transferred to the auxiliary view to locate the point view of line A-B.

10. Determine the distances that point A is from reference plane H/F in the front view by repeating the **LIST** command. The length of 2.00000000 is listed on screen.

11. To locate the edge view of plane ABC in the auxiliary view, the angle of reference line H/1 must be determined. Repeat the List command and pick the reference line. The angle of the line is listed as 153.43494882.

12. To locate the edge view of plane ABC in the auxiliary view draw perpendicular lines from the intersection of reference line H/1 and the projectors of points A, B, and C from the top view at a distance and angle determined in Steps 9, 10, 11. Enter **LINE** at the command prompt.

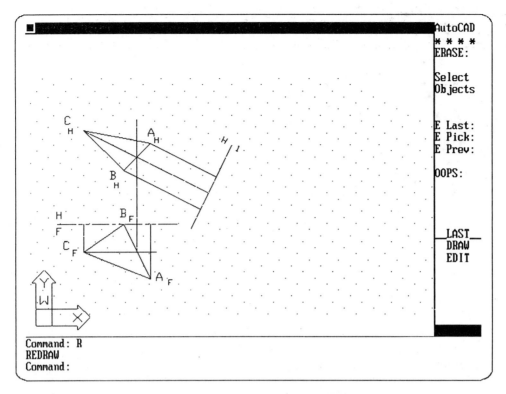

Figure 9.19 Starting the auxiliary view.

13. Snap to the intersection of the projector from point A with the reference line using Osnap Intersection. At the **To point:** prompt enter **@2<-27.43494882**. The angle measured in Step 11 was subtracted from 180 to get the angle of the projector for point A.

14.   Snap to the intersection of the projector from point C with the reference line using Osnap Intersection. At the **To point:** prompt enter **@1<-27.43494882**. This locates point C in the auxiliary view.

15.   Draw a line using the endpoints of the projectors to create the edge view of plane ABC. Figure 9.20.

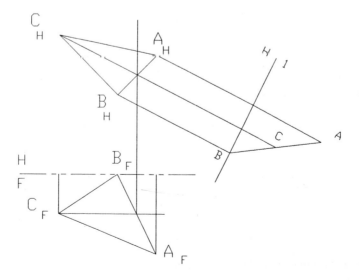

Figure 9.20 The edge view of plane ABC.

TRUE SIZE OF A PLANE

Finding the true size of a plane involves the use of a secondary auxiliary view, as described in finding the point view of a line. The true size of the plane is the fourth fundamental view necessary to solve descriptive geometry problems. Many of the steps to find the point view of a line can be used to find the true size of a plane. To find the true size of a plane, project a view perpendicular to the edge view of the plane. The following steps describe how to create the true size of a plane from the edge view created in the previous example:

Finding the True Size View of a Plane: Exercise 9.6

1. Continuing with the previous exercise enter **SNAP** at the command prompt then enter R to rotate the snap parallel to the edge view of plane ABC. Snap to endpoints A-B to define the new snap rotation angle.

2. Draw a reference line perpendicular to the edge view of plane ABC by using **LINE** and snapping to the grid. Label this refernce line 1/2 using the **DTEXT** command.

3. Draw projectors from points A, B, and C in view 1 using Osnap Endpoint perpendicular to reference line 1/2 using Osnap Perpendicular. Figure 9.21.

4. The perpendicular distance that points A, B, and C in the top view lie from reference plane 1/H must be determined. Select Assist/Inquiry/List from the Pull-down Menus and pick the line segment. The length for A is 2.77639320, for B is 3.22360680, and C is 5.23606798 These distances must be transferred to the auxiliary view to locate the points A, B, and C.

5. To locate the points in the auxiliary view, the angle of reference line 1/2 must be determined. Repeat the List command and pick the reference line. The angle of the line is listed as 6.68836446.

6. To locate the edge view of plane ABC in the auxiliary view, draw a perpendicular line from the intersection of reference line 1/2 and the projectors of points A, B, and C from view 1 at a distance and angle determined in Steps 4.7. Enter **LINE** at the command prompt

8. Snap to the intersection of the projector from point A with the reference line uisng Osnap Intersection. At the **To point:** prompt enter **@1<-84.68836446**. The angle measured in Step 5 was subtracted from 90 to get the angle of the projector for the points.

9. To view all the points on screen enter **ZOOM** at the command prompt then enter **ALL**.

10. Draw lines from the end of the projectors to locate the edge view of plane ABC. Figure 9.22.

Figure 9.21 Projecting points A, B, and C into the auxiliary view.

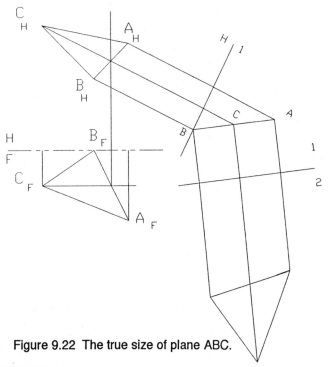

Figure 9.22 The true size of plane ABC.

PIERCING POINTS

Determining the piercing point of a line with a plane is solved by either (1) the edge view of a plane method or (2) the cutting plane or projection method. The edge view of a plane method is explained first, even though the cutting plane method can be executed more rapidly with AutoCAD.

The piercing point between a line and a plane can be found in a view that shows the plane as an edge. The piercing point is then projected to the adjacent view. Finding the edge view of a plane with AutoCAD was explained in Exercise 9.5. To find the piercing point with the edge view method with AutoCAD use the same basic steps explained above except the endpoints of the line would also be projected into the auxiliary view constructed for the edge view of the plane, as shown in Figure 9.23. The piercing point is projected from the edge view to the top and front views as explained in the following steps:

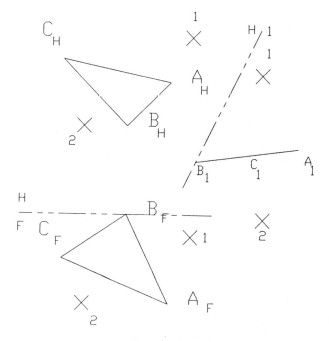

Figure 9.23 Finding the piercing point in a plane.

Finding Piercing Points: Exercise 9.7

1. Open **LAB9-5** from your data disk. Figure 9.23. The piercing point is projected from the auxiliary view to the top view using the DOT linetype and layer. The **OFFSET** or **COPY** command can be used to copy one of the existing dot line projectors through the piercing point using the **OSNAP** option **INTERSECT**, as shown in Figure 9.24.

2. The intersection of the piercing point projector and the line in the top view are the point of intersection, as shown in Figure 9.24.

3. Turn the **ORTHO** Mode ON and draw a vertical construction LINE from the piercing point in the top view to the front view, as shown in Figure 9.25. The line and piercing point are drawn as shown in the figure.

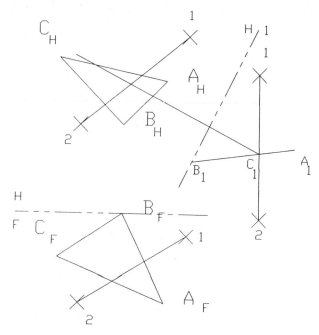

Figure 9.24 Projecting the piercing point into the top view.

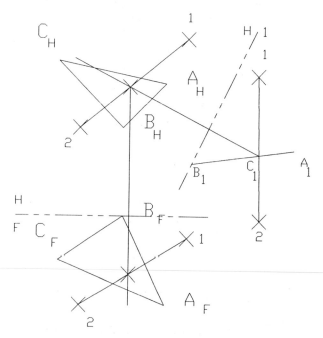

Figure 9.25 Locating the piercing points in the top and front views.

Determining Visibility

When the user is dealing with the intersection of lines and planes, and between two planes, the correct visibility between entities must be determined and represented on the engineering drawing through solid or hidden lines. Before the linetype is determined a visibility check is performed. This can be accomplished by drawing projectors between adjacent views to determine which entity would be in front of the other, as shown in Figure 9.26.

Figure 9.29 Cut

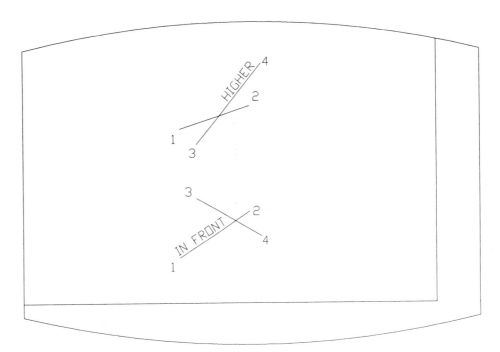

Figure 9.26 Drawing projectors between the views to determine visibility.

3. Draw a
the plane
to determi
line 1-2 ir
Figure 9.
4. Projec
check an

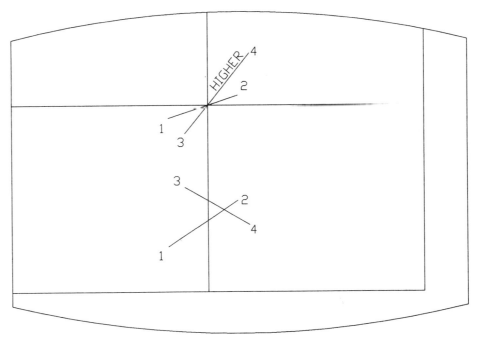

Figure 9.27 Using the cursor to check visibility.

The AutoCAD
The cursor is used i
the cursor to the po
check visibility. Us
in Figure 9.28 beca
AutoCAD.

Figur

Piercing P

Solving des
is avoided when
a plane is by pr

The projecti
and the plane in
the piercing poi
a guide to findi

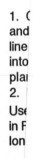

1. (
and
line
into
plar
2.

Us
in F
lon

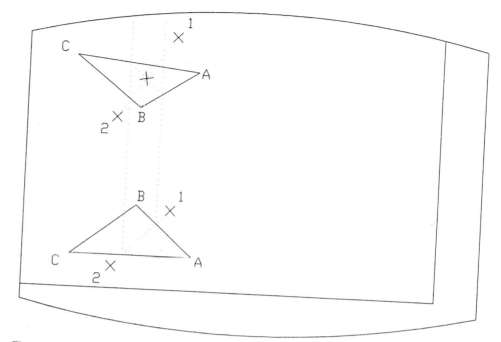

Figure 9.31 The piercing point between the line and the plane is located in the top view.

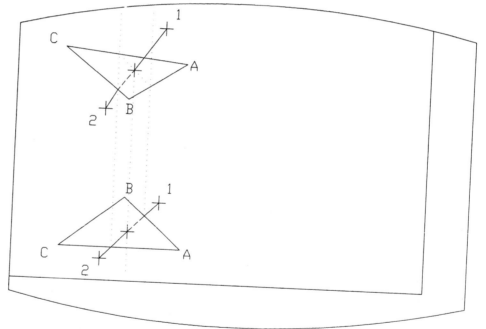

Figure 9.32 The piercing point is projected to the front view, visibility is determined, and the line is drawn.

INTERSECTION OF PLANES

The intersection of planes is located by finding the piercing points of two lines in one plane with the other plane. Solving this problem graphically is done through the same methods described for finding the piercing point between a line and a plane. Piercing points can be determined with the auxiliary view method or by projection. When using AutoCAD, it is recommended that the projection method be used. Both methods were explained previously and can be used as a guide to solve the intersection of planes problems.

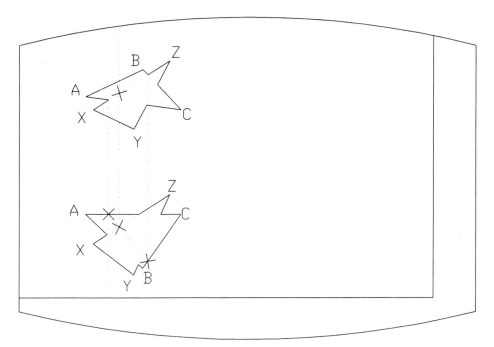

Figure 9.33 Cutting plane XZ is projected to the front view to locate the piercing point for line XZ in plane ABC.

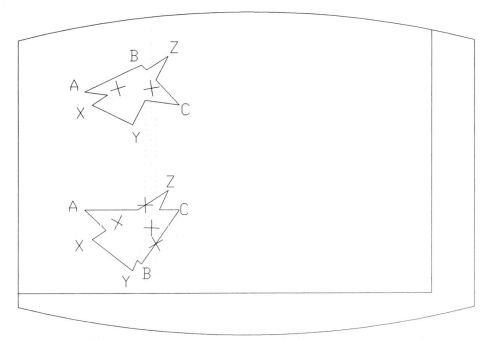

Figure 9.34 Cutting plane YZ is projected to the front view to locate the piercing point for line YZ in plane ABC.

Intersection of Planes: Exercise 9.9

1. Open **LAB9-8** from your data disk. Lines X-Z of plane XYZ in the top view has a cutting plane line passed through it, as shown in Figure 9.33, using the **LINE** command.
2. The points of intersection between the cutting plane and the edges of plane ABC are projected to the front view using **LINE** and **ORTHO**, as shown in Figure 9.33.

3. One piercing point is determined by drawing the trace in the front view. The intersection of the trace with line X-Z is the piercing point, which is marked with the **POINT** command and projected and marked in the top view, as shown in Figure 9.33.

4. A cutting plane is passed through line Y-Z of plane XYZ in the top view, and the trace is projected to the front view using **LINE** and **ORTHO**, as shown in Figure 9.34.

5. The trace is located in the front view by drawing a **LINE** from the **INTERSECTION** of the projectors with lines B-C and A-C, as shown in Figure 9.34.

6. The second piercing point is located at the intersection of the trace line and line Z-Y in the front view and is marked with a **POINT**.

7. The piercing point is projected into the top view using **LINE** and **ORTHO** and marked with a **POINT**.

8. The piercing points are connected with a solid line, and a visibility check is made with the cursor. Figure 9.35 shows the completed views of the intersecting planes.

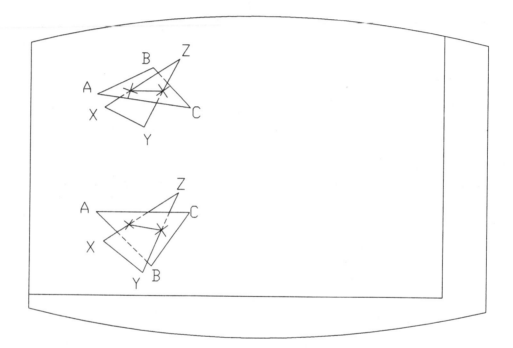

Figure 9.35 Visibility is determined and the views are completed.

SOLVING OTHER DESCRIPTIVE GEOMETRY PROBLEMS WITH AutoCAD

Virtually any descriptive geometry problem can be solved by auxiliary views or by projection. Each method has been explained in detail. The methods employed on the various problems in this chapter can solve other descriptive geometry problems.

To find the angle between a line and a plane, find either the plane true size or the line true length. Another auxiliary view then is created that shows the plane as an edge view and the line true length. From this view the angle can be measured. Figure 9.36 shows the true angle between line 1-2 and plane ABC by finding the true size of the plane and projecting perpendicular to the line to get an edge view of the plane and true length of the line. To try this problem, open **LAB9-9** from your data disk.

To find the shortest distance between two lines, find one line true length from which a point view of a line is constructed. The shortest distance then can be measured. The basic steps to solve this problem were explained earlier in this chapter under "Finding the Point View of a Line."

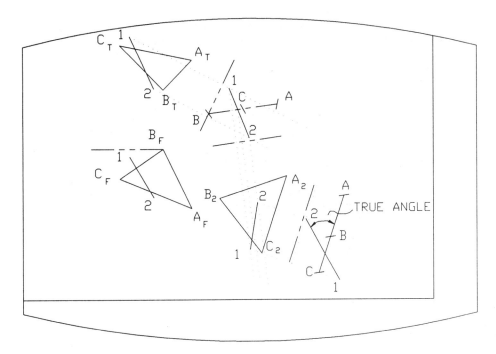

Figure 9.36. Finding the angle between a line and a plane.

LEMS

An alternative to the auxiliary view method of solving descriptive geometry problems is to use the revolution technique. This technique revolves an orthographic view into a new position to determine the true length of a line or the edge view of a plane, which may be a more effective method of finding the true length of a line. The following steps show how to use AutoCAD to create the true length of a line by revolution:

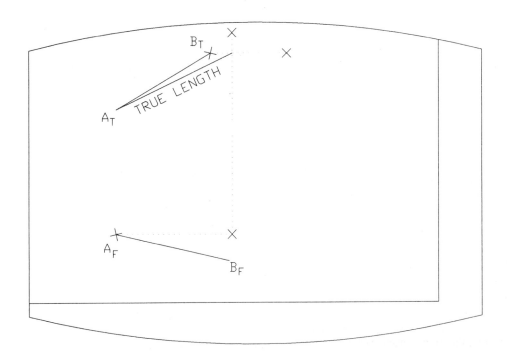

Figure 9.37 Using the revolution technique to find the true length of a line.

True Length of Line Revolution Method: Exercise 9.10

1. Open **LAB9-10** from your data disk. Set the layer and linetype to **DOT** for construction lines.

2. Use the **LIST** command to determine the length of line A-B in the front view of Figure 9.37. It is determined that the length is 3.3541.

3. Select **LINE** and **OSNAP** option **ENDPOINT**. Pick point A in the front view.

4. The second point is input using absolute coordinate values. Input **@3.3541,0** and enter RETURN. The construction line is drawn in the front view, as shown in Figure 9.37.

5. Set the **ORTHO** Mode ON and use the **LINE** command to draw a vertical projection line to the top view, as shown in Figure 9.37.

6. Draw a horizontal line from point B in the top view that intersects the vertical projector created in step five. Use **LINE** and **ORTHO** to draw the line shown in Figure 9.47.

7. Change the layer and linetype to solid before drawing the true length of line A-B. Turn **ORTHO** Mode OFF and use **LINE** and **OSNAP** options **ENDPOINT** and **INTERSECT** to draw the true length, as shown in Figure 9.37.

8. Use the **LIST** command to determine the measured true length of line A-B. For this example, the length is 4.1833.

SPATIAL GEOMETRY USING 3D MODELS

Many designs are initially created as 3D computer models. Because they are initially created as 3D models, there is no need to use traditional descriptive geometry techniques to solve spatial problems. In fact many spatial distances can be determined using AutoCAD's **LIST** or **DISTANCE** commands which will give the true length of lines from any viewpoint. However, it is still important to use traditional descriptive geometry concepts in engineering design. The difference when using 3D geometry is to use non-traditional techniques to solve these problems. The following section describes how to use non-traditional techniques to solve spatial problems using AutoCAD.

Finding the True Length View of a Line

Many techniques can be used to create a view of a line on a 3D model, which is perpendicular. One method is to position AutoCAD's UCS so that it is parallel to the line then get a plan view of the UCS. This will create a true length viewpoint of a line. The following steps describe how to create a true length view of a line on a 3D model.

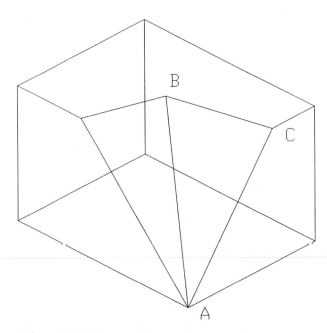

Figure 9.38 3D model for spatial geometry problems.

Creating a True Length View of a Line: Exercise 9.11

1. Open **LAB 9-11** from your data disk. Figure 9.38. Lab 9-11 is a simple solid model with two oblique planes having a common side A-B which is an oblique line. The problem is to create a viewpoint which will be perpendicular to line A-B. The UCS will have to be repositioned so that it is parallel to line A-B. To determine visibility enter **HIDE** at the command prompt to hide the hidden lines.

2. Set the Osnap mode to Endpoint and set units decimal precision to 8 places.

3. Enter **UCS** at the command prompt or pick Settings/UCS/Origin from the Pull-down Menus.

Origin/ZAxis/3 point/Entity/View/X/Y/Z/Prev/Restore/Save/Del/?/<World>: is displayed in the prompt line.

4. Enter **3** to select the 3-point option to define the new UCS.

Origin point <0,0,0>: is displayed.

5. Pick point B with the cursor.

Point on positive portion of the X-axis: is displayed.

6. Pick point A to align the X-axis of the UCS with line A-B of the plane.

Point on positive-Y portion of the UCS XY plane: is displayed.

7. Pick point C to align the UCS with plane ABC. Notice that the UCS icon changes positions on screen as it aligns itself with plane ABC.

8. To create a view perpendicular to line A-B and the current UCS setting, enter **PLAN** at the command prompt.

<Current UCS>/UCS/World: is prompted.

9. Enter **Return** to make the plane view the current UCS. This automatically creates a viewpoint perpendicular to line AB. Use a Zoom-All to create a view like that shown in Figure 9.39.

10. To verify that the current view is a true length view of line A-B pick Assist/Inquiry/Distance from the Pull-down Menus. Pick the endpoints of line AB to list the coordinate information for the line. The true length of the line is listed as distance = 3.535553391 and the angle from the XY plane is listed as 0 meaning that line AB is parallel with the screen and our line of sight is perpendicular to it. (*At this point it would be possible to verify that lines AC and BC are also true length making the current view a true size view of a plane*).

11. To determine visibility of lines enter **HIDE** at the command prompt to temporarily remove the hidden lines.

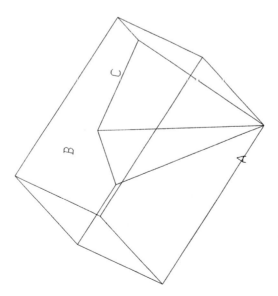

Figure 9.39 True size view of line A-B and plane ABC.

The 3D model is now in a convenient positon to create a pojnt view of line AB. This is done by again using the UCS and Plan commands. The following steps describe the techique used to find a point view of a line with AutoCAD.

Finding the Point View of a Line: Exercise 9.12

1. Continue from the preceeding exercise and enter **UCS** at the command prompt or pick Settings/UCS/Origin from the pull-down menus.
Origin/ZAxi s/3 point/Entity/V iew/X /Y/Z/P rev /R estore/S ave /Del/?/< World>: is displayed in the prompt line.
4. Enter **Y** to rotate the current UCS 90 degrees about the Y axis.
Rotation angle about Y axis <0>:
5. Enter **90** at the prompt.
6. To create a view perpendicular to line A-B and the current UCS setting enter **PLAN** at the command prompt.
<Current UCS>/UCS/World: is prompted.
7. Enter **Return** to make the plane view the current UCS. This automatically creates a viewpoint parallel to line AB. Figure 9.40. (*You will also notice that both oblique planes appear on edge because the comon line between the planes is a point. Remember, that to find the edge view of a plane find a point view of a line that lies in the plane*)
8. It is now possible to determine the angle between the oblique planes by using the angular dimension command as shown in the figure.

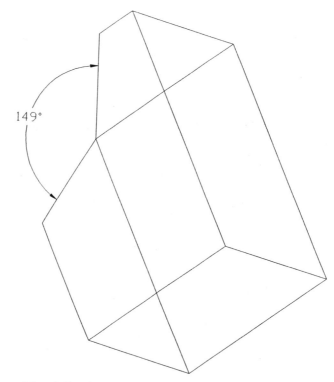

Figure 9.40 Point view of line A-B, edge view of the planes, and true size view of the angle between the planes.

Finding the True Size and Edge View of Planes

The same steps to find the true length and point view of a line are used to create true size and edge views of planes. First create a perpendicular viewpoint of any line in the plane by making the UCS parallel to two lines in the plane, then use the Plan command to create a viewpoint perpendicular to the UCS. This will create the true size view of the plane. (See Exercise 9.11). To create the edge view of a plane create a viewpoint parallel to any line in the plane. This is done by rotating the UCS 90 degrees about an axis perpendicular to a line in the plane, then using the Plan command to create the viewpoint perpendicular to the UCS and parallel to the line. (See Exercise 9.12).

Summary

AutoCAD creates the four fundamental views necessary to solve many descriptive geometry problems. The cutting plane or projection method is more effective to solve some types of problems using AutoCAD. AutoCAD can be used for many types of descriptive geometry problems that have not been explained in detail. For example, the intersection of planes and solids can be solved because AutoCAD can be used to determine piercing points and lines of intersections.

It is important to recognize that AutoCAD and virtually all other microcomputer-based CADD programs were not developed to solve descriptive geometry problems, which are primarily design functions. Most microcomputer-based CADD systems were developed primarily to document design solutions and not the actual design and analysis. Using AutoCAD and other CADD programs to solve complex descriptive geometry problems may not be the most effective tools. However, CADD can be extremely valuable if the solution must reveal accurate results. AutoCAD can provide eight-place decimal inch accuracy. AutoLISP programs can be developed to create new commands that facilitate the solution of descriptive geometry problems.

DEVELOPMENTS

The preceding descriptive geometry examples can be used to find the line of intersection between various surfaces and geometric solids. At times it is important to be able to create the flat patterns of geometric surfaces and solids. These unfolded patterns are called developments, which are created usually by determining the true length of all the lines of the geometric shape. The true length distances then can be used to create a flat development.

Patterns are placed into three major groups: (1) parallel line development used for prisms and cylinders, (2) radial line development used for pyramids and cones, and (3) triangulation development for transition pieces, such as a heating duct that changes from a round to rectangular cross-section. AutoCAD can create developments through a combination of editing and draw commands. The following examples show one way that AutoCAD creates simple pattern developments. Other combinations of commands will work, and the use of AutoLISP programs can simplify the process.

Parallel Line Development-Right Prism

The right truncated prism shown in Figure 9.41 is developed using AutoCAD. The following steps show the commands used to construct the flat pattern. The prompts and detailed use of each command have not been included because all the commands used have already been explained in detail.

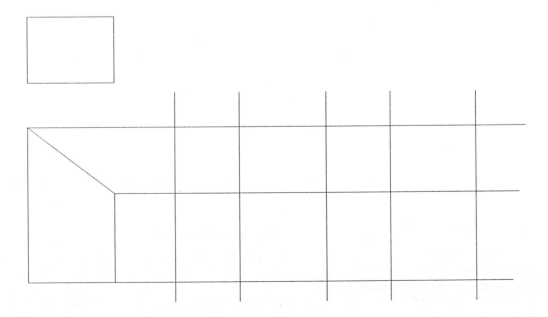

Figure 9.41 Constructing the layout of the prism.

Developing a Right Prisim: Exercise 9.13

1. Open **LAB9-12** from your data disk. The **LIST** command is used to determine the height, width, and depth dimensions of the prism shown in Figure 9.41.

2. Create a new **LAYER** with **DOT** linetype for construction lines.

3. Use **LINE** and **ORTHO** to draw the horizontal base line and projectors from the front view.

4. Use **LINE** and **ORTHO** to draw a vertical construction line for the start point of the pattern. This line should be placed about one inch to the right of the front view of the prism.

5. The **OFFSET** command draws the vertical fold lines. Pick the vertical construction line and input the first distance of 1.5 for this example. Pick another point to the right of the vertical construction line. A new line is drawn.

Repeat the **OFFSET** command and pick the new vertical line, input a distance of two and pick a point to the right. This procedure is repeated until the layout of the pattern is complete, as shown in Figure 9.41.

6. To create the pattern for the bottom of the prism, use **OFFSET** to offset the baseline 1.5 below the pattern.

7. Use **EXTEND** to draw the vertical fold lines to the newly offset line.

8. The top of the pattern is created by drawing a **LINE** from points 1 and 2.

9. The **OFFSET** command draws the other side of the top 1.5 inches from line 1-2.

10. Use **LINE** and **OSNAP** option **ENDPOINT** to complete the top of the pattern Figure 9.42.

11. Change the **LAYER** to **CONTINUOUS** to draw solid lines.

12. Use **LINE** and **ORTHO** option **INTERSEC** to draw the pattern outline.

13. Use **TRIM** and **ERASE** to edit the drawing so that the **DOT** linetype represents the fold lines shown in Figure 9.42.

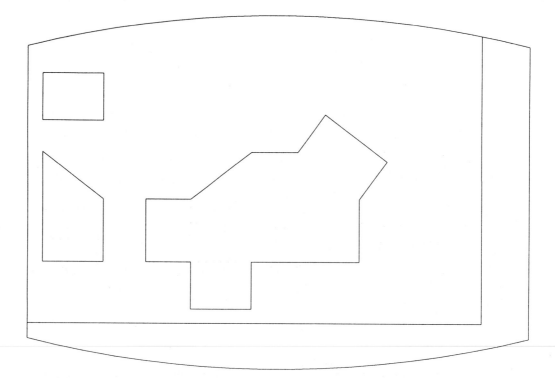

Figure 9.42 Finishing the layout of the prism.

Parallel Line Development-Right Circular Cylinders

The following steps show how to create a pattern development of the truncated cylinder shown in Figure 9.43. Only half of the pattern is drawn, then the **MIRROR** command is used to complete the development.

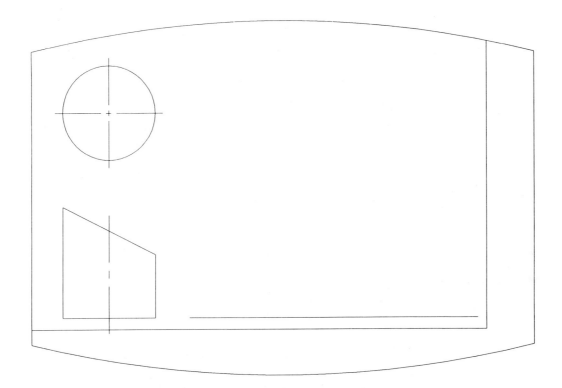

Figure 9.43 Drawing the baseline for the cylinder layout.

Developing a Right Circular Cylinder: Exercise 9.14

1. Open **LAB9-13** from your data disk. Use the **SETTINGS** command option **LIMITS** to change the drawing boundaries to 17 by 11 to accommodate the pattern development for the cylinder.
2. Determine the circumference of the cylinder by using the **LIST** command and picking the top view of the circle. For this example, the circumference is determined to be 9.4248.
3. Create a new **LAYER** with the **DOT** linetype.
4. Use **LINE**, **ENDPOINT**, and **ORTHO** to draw the baseline of the pattern by picking the bottom right corner of the front view and another point to the far right of the drawing area.
5. Use the **CONTINUOUS** linetype **LAYER** to draw a solid line over the dot linetype baseline.
6. Use **LINE** and **ORTHO** option **NEAREST** and pick a point on the dot line close to the front view. Enter absolute coordinate values **@4.7124,0** to create a solid baseline equal in length to one half the circumference of the cylinder, as shown in Figure 9.43.
7. Change the active **LAYER** to **DOT**.
8. Change the point mode to **3** with the **PDMODE** option. **DIVIDE** the top view of the cylinder into **16** equal parts.
9. **DIVIDE** the baseline into 8 equal parts.
10. Use **LINE** and **ORTHO** and **OSNAP** to **NODE** to draw vertical construction lines from the points along the circumference of the cylinder in the top view to the front view, as shown in Figure 9.44.

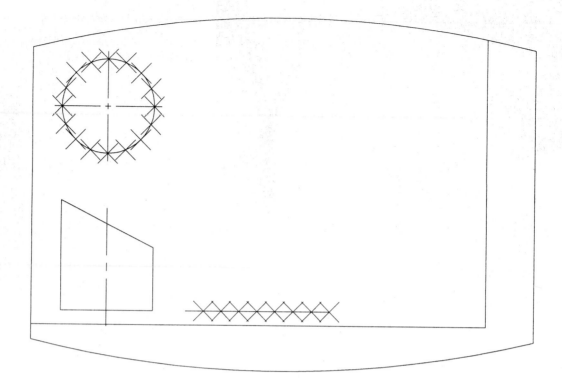

Figure 9.44 Dividing the circle and baseline into equal parts.

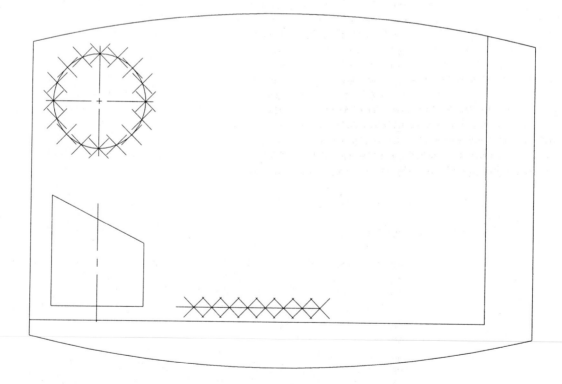

Figure 9.45 Projecting the lines for the pattern.

11. Set **OSNAP** to **INTERSEC** and use **LINE** to draw horizontal projectors to the pattern development from the intersection of the vertical projectors and the cylinder in the front view (Figure 9.45).

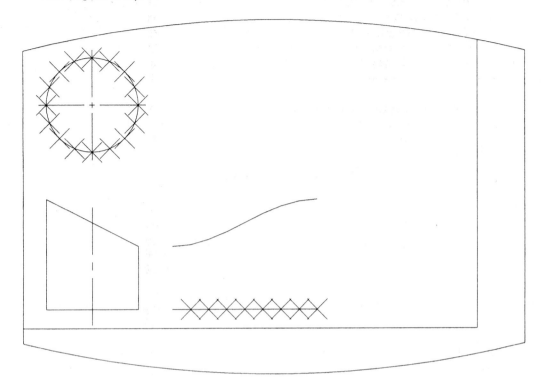

Figure 9.46 Using **PLINE** to draw the irregular curved surface.

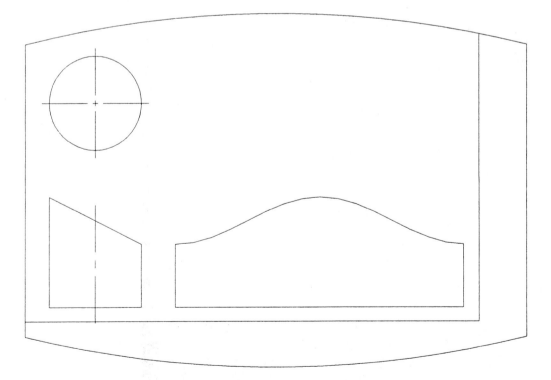

Figure 9.47 Using the **MIRROR** command to complete the pattern.

12. The distance between two of the points along the baseline must be determined. This distance is equal to 1/16 of the circumference, or 0.58905. This distance also could be determined by using the **DIMENSION** option **HORIZONTAL** to measure the distance between two points on the baseline.

13. The **RECTANGULAR ARRAY** command is used to layout half the circumference of the circle. Use 1 **ROW** and 9 **COLUMNS** and a **DISTANCE** between columns equal to .58905 to create the array.

14. The **PLINE** command is used to draw the top of the pattern. Change the **LAYER** to CONTINUOUS to draw solid lines.

15. Use **PLINE** and **OSNAP INTERSEC** to draw the smooth, curved surface by picking the intersection of the horizontal and vertical projectors (Figure 9.46).

16. Use the **MIRROR** command to complete the development of the smooth curved surface. Add **LINES** to the ends of the pattern to complete the development, as shown in Figure 9.47.

Radial Line Development-Cones

All pyramids and cones are constructed using radial line developments. The edges of pyramids and the elements of cones appear as straight lines that radiate from the vertex. The truncated cone shown in Figure 9.48 and the following steps demonstrate radial line development of cones:

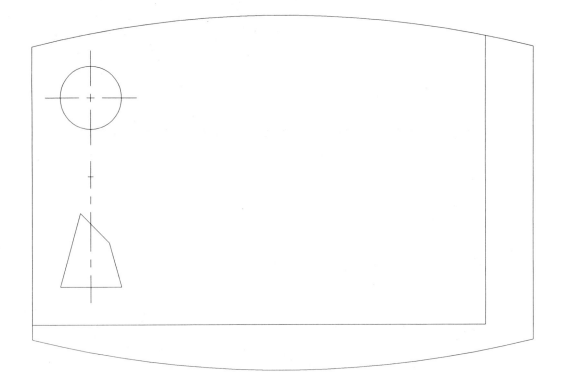

Figure 9.48 Truncated cone to be developed.

Developing a Cone: Exercise 9.15

1. Open **LAB9-14** from your data disk. Use the **DIMENSION** option **ALIGNED** to measure the true length of the cone's element. Pick the vertex, the intersection of the base, and the side of the cone in the front view. For this example, the distance is 3.6401.

2. Begin the development of the pattern by calculating the arc distance using the formula, $A=r/l \times 360$. The angle is equal to the radius of the cone divided by the length of its elements multiplied by 360 degrees. For this example, $1/3.6401 \times 360 = 98.8984$.

3. Knowing the included angle of the arc is important to use the **ARC** command **C,S,A** (center, start, angle) to begin the pattern layout. Pick a point to the right of the front view of the truncated cone for the center of the arc. Input the absolute coordinate value for the start of the arc, **@3.6401,0**. Input the angle of the arc, **98.8984.** The arc is drawn as shown in Figure 9.49.

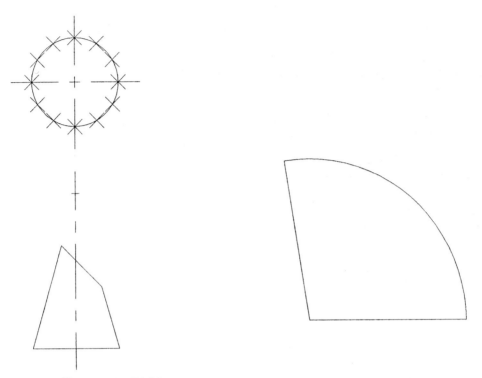

Figure 9.49 Dividing the base into equal parts and drawing the layout.

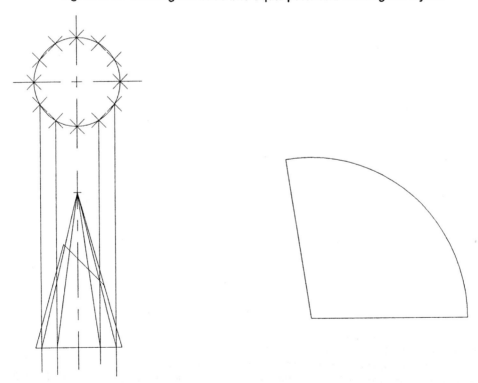

Figure 9.50 Projecting construction points to the front view.

4. Change the **LAYER** to **DOT** linetype for construction lines and use **LINE, OSNAP-CENTER** to pick the center of the arc. Pick the **ENDPOINTS** of the arc as shown in Figure 9.49.

5. Change the **PDMODE** to 3. **DIVIDE** the top view of the cone into 12 equal parts, as shown in Figure 9.49.

6. Project the points along the circumference of the top view to a point below the base of the front view using **LINE, ORTHO, OSNAP, NODE** (Figure 9.59). This step is necessary to create the elements of the cone.

7. Draw the elements by projecting the intersection of the projectors from the top view along the base of the cone in the front view to the vertex using **LINE, ORTHO-OFF, INTERSEC, NODE** (Figure 9.50).

8. Change the **DISPLAY** window using **ZOOM** to include only the front view of the cone.

9. Change the **LAYER** and linetype to **PHANTOM**.

10. Use **LINE, ORTHO, INTERSEC** to draw horizontal lines from the intersection of the projectors from the base to the vertex with the edge view of the truncated portion of the cone to the true length element (Figure 9.51).

11. Use the **DIMENSION ALIGNED** option to measure the true length distances of each element of the cone. For this example they are found to be:

1.2134
1.2506
1.3650
1.5600
1.8200
2.0729
2.1840

12. **DIVIDE** the arc to be used in the pattern development into **12** parts.

13. Use **DRAW, LINE, CENTER,** and **ENDPOINT** to draw a construction line from the center of the arc to the start point of the arc.

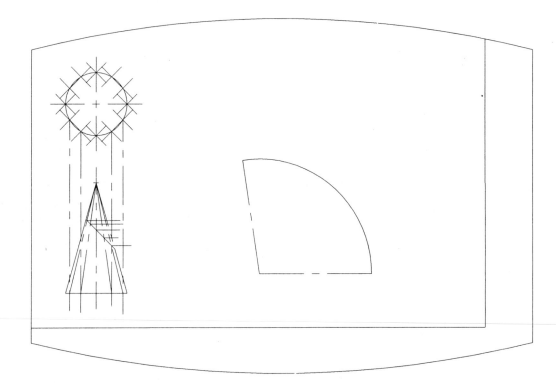

Figure 9.51 Determining true lengths in the front view.

14. Use the **POLAR ARRAY** command to copy the line drawn in Step 13. Pick the line; pick the center of the arc for the center of the array; enter **7** as the number of copies for the array; enter half of the angle of the arc; **49.4492** and **CCW** for a counter-clockwise array pattern (Figure 9.52).

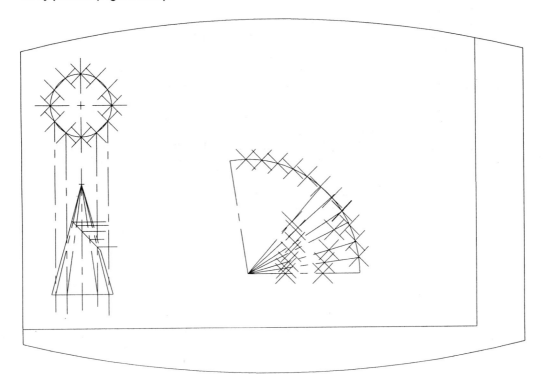

Figure 9.52 Locating the true length construction lines in the pattern.

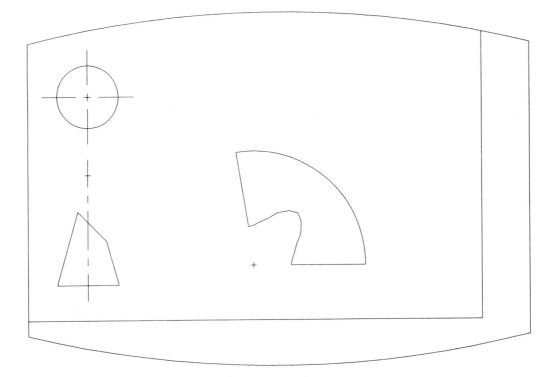

Figure 9.53 Using **PLINE** and **MIRROR** to complete the pattern.

15. Use the **MEASURE** command to transfer the true length distances of each element. Pick a point on the element closest to the vertex in the development view and input the corresponding distance. Repeat this step for each element, using the distances determined in Step 11 (Figure 9.52).

16. Change the **LAYER** and linetype to **CONTINUOUS** to draw solid lines. Use **PLINE, NODE** to draw a smooth curve through each point on the elements.

17. Use the **MIRROR** command to complete the smooth curve.

18. Draw the end lines of the pattern using **LINE, ENDPOINTS** (Figure 9.53).

Radial Line Development-Pyramid

The following steps show how to use AutoCAD to create a pattern of the truncated pyramid shown in Figure 9.54:

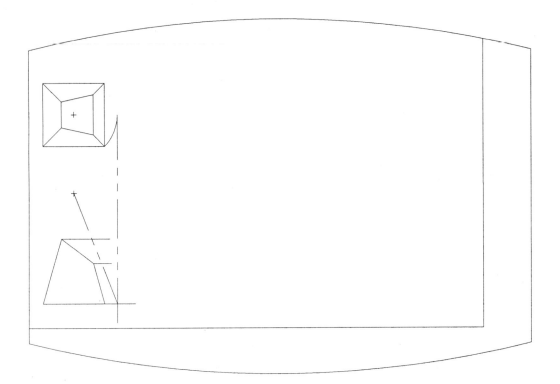

Figure 9.54 Radial line development of a pyramid.

Developing a Pyramid: Exercise 9.16

1. Open **LAB9-15** from your data disk. Use **LIST** to determine the length of the baselines of the pyramid. Pick each baseline in the top view. For this example, each baseline is equal to 2 inches.

2. Change the **LAYER** and use **DOT** linetype for construction lines. Use the rotation method to determine the true length of the edges of the pyramid in the top view. This is done by using the **ARC, C,S,E** command and picking the vertex as the center, the intersection of the edge line with the corner of the base, and a point above the horizontal center line of the pyramid in the top view. Repeat this procedure to determine the true length of each line segment of the pyramid.

3. Project the intersection of the arc and the center line to the baseline of the front view using **LINE, ORTHO, INTERSEC**.

4. Extend the baseline and the end points of the edges of the pyramid in the front view horizontally using **LINE, ORTHO, INTERSEC**.

5. Draw a line from the intersection of the baseline in the front view with the projector from the top view to the vertex using **LINE, ORTHO-OFF, INTERSEC.** This length is the true length of side of the pyramid (Figure 9.54).

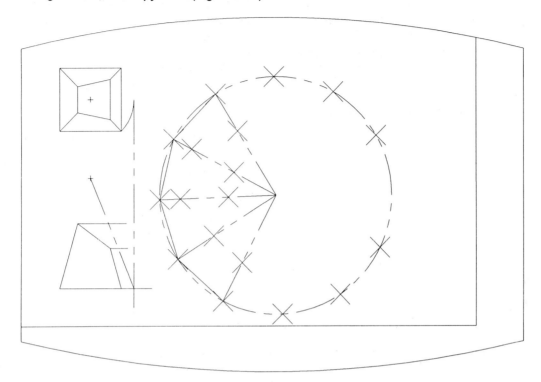

Figure 9.55 Developing the pattern.

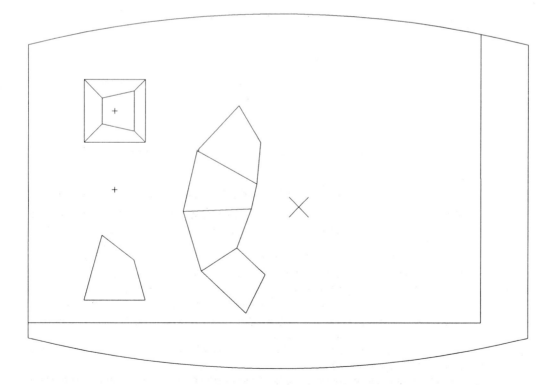

Figure 9.56 The complete pyramid pattern.

6. The intersection of the true length line and the horizontal projectors of the endpoints of the edges of the pyramid are the true length of each edge. Use the **DIMENSION, ALIGNED** option to determine the true length distances. For this example, the distances are: 3.7749, 2.4022, and 1.5544.

7. The development of the pattern begins by drawing a **CIRCLE** equal in radius to the length of the pyramid edge, **3.7749**.

8. Use **PDMODE** of **3** to **MEASURE** 2 inch increments on the circle. The 2-inch measurement is the length of the baselines of the pyramid found in step one.

9. Select four, 2-inch segments on the circle and **DRAW, LINES** from the center of the circle to the points (Figure 9.55).

10. Use the **MEASURE** command to transfer the distances of each edge of the pyramid to the pattern view. Pick a point on the construction line closest to the center of the circle in the development view. Input the distances measured in Step 6.

11. Change the **LAYER** and linetype to **CONTINUOUS** to draw solid lines. Use **LINE, NODE** to complete the pattern development shown in Figure 9.56. Fold lines can be left as construction lines if desired.

Summary

AutoCAD can be used for most types of pattern developments. The basic knowledge necessary to create patterns of solids has been demonstrated and can be applied to other types of patterns, such as the intersection of solids. Determining the line of intersection between planes was demonstrated earlier. This knowledge can be combined with the pattern developments to create very complex patterns. It is important that the full abilities of AutoCAD be used through preplanning if it is to be a more effective method of creating patterns than traditional tools.

QUESTIONS FOR REVIEW

1. Name the AutoCAD command to create new lines parallel to a given line at a specified distance.

2. List two methods that can be used to measure distances.

3. Measured distances are transferred to auxiliary views using the _____ or _____ function.

4. Name the option used to rotate the grid.

5. List two methods of checking visibility with AutoCAD.

DRAWING ASSIGNMENTS

1. Use the 1/4" or 5mm grid to create drawings from Figures 9.57 through 9.63 before solving the problems.

2. Figure 9.57 Line AB is 2" or 40mm long. Point B is located generally below point A. Draw line AB in the front view.

3. Figure 9.58 Draw the true length and point view of line AB.

4. Figure 9.59 Draw the true length and point view of line AB.

5. Figure 9.60 Find the true size of plane ABC.

6. Figure 9.61 Find the edge view of plane ABC.

7. Figure 9.62 Determine the angle between angles ABC and ACD.

8. Figure 9.63 Determine the piercing point between line 1-2 and plane ABC.

9. Develop a pattern for drawing Figures 9.64 through 9.71.

10. Figure 9.72 Draw an auxiliary view of the oblique surface.

11. From Giesecke et al., *Engineering Graphic*, 4th ed. Do the drawing assignments at the end of Chapters 19, 20, 21, and 22.

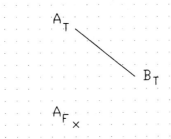

Figure 9.57 Line AB is 2inches or 40mm long. Point B is located generally below point A. Draw line
AB in the front view.

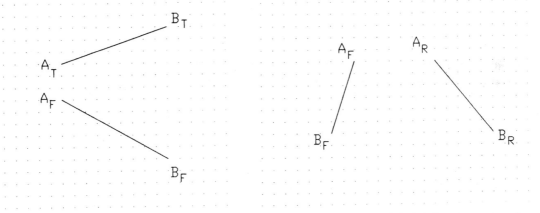

Figure 9.58 Draw the true length and point
view of line AB.

Figure 9.59 Draw the true length and point
view of line AB.

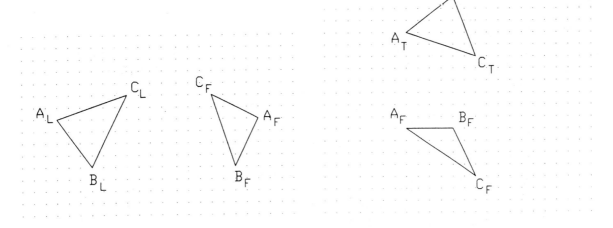

Figure 9.60 Find the true size of plane ABC.

Figure 9.61 Find the edge view of plane ABC.

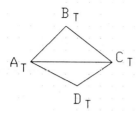

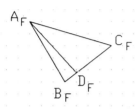

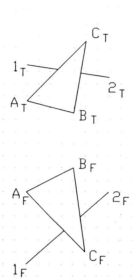

Figure 9.62 Determine the angle between angles ABC and ACD.

Figure 9.63 Determine the piercing point between line 1-2 and plane ABC.

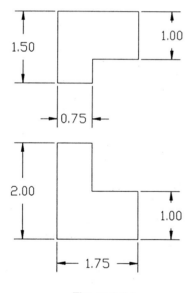

Figure 9.64

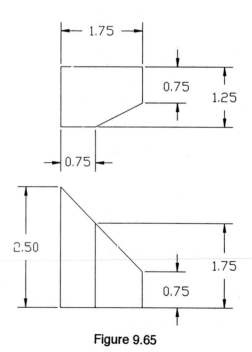

Figure 9.65

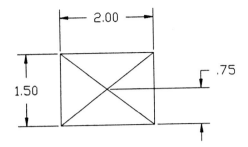

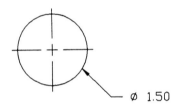

Figure 9.66

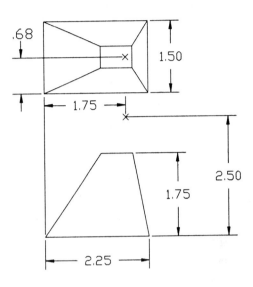

Figure 9.67

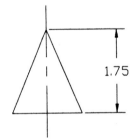

Figure 9.68

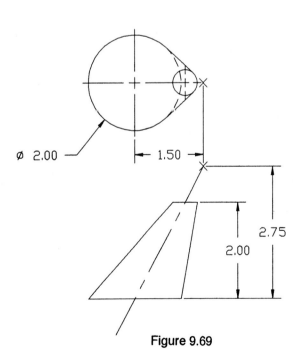

Figure 9.69

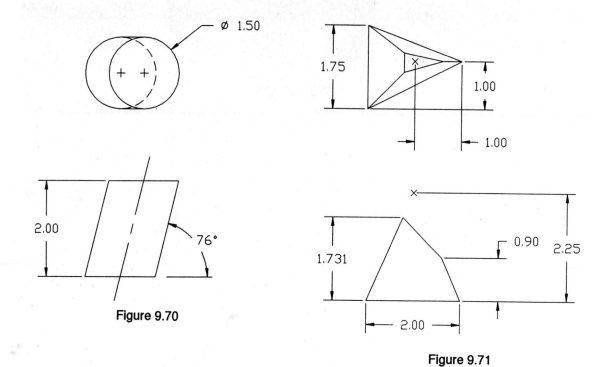

Figure 9.70

Figure 9.71

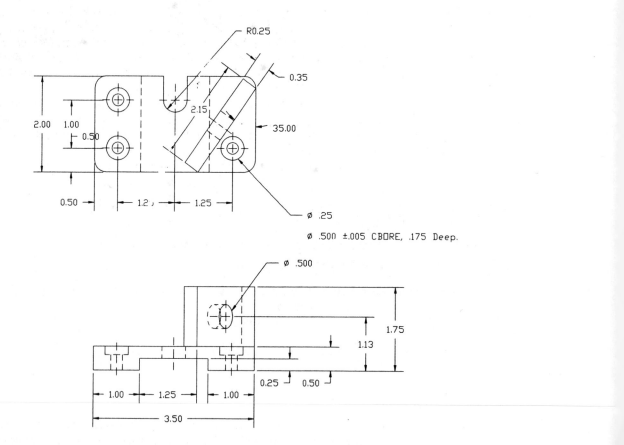

Figure 9.72

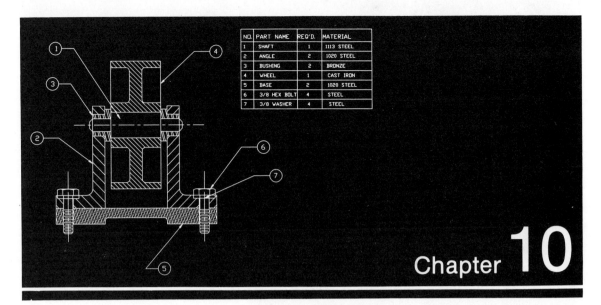

NO.	PART NAME	REQ'D.	MATERIAL
1	SHAFT	1	1113 STEEL
2	ANGLE	2	1020 STEEL
3	BUSHING	2	BRONZE
4	WHEEL	1	CAST IRON
5	BASE	2	1020 STEEL
6	3/8 HEX BOLT	4	STEEL
7	3/8 WASHER	4	STEEL

Chapter 10

WORKING DRAWINGS

Engineering graphics is dependent upon the output of the design process. The design process using CADD was explained in Chapter 2. CADD can be integrated into the design process at an early stage if the software is capable of creating 3D images that can be manipulated, edited, and analyzed. Micro-based CADD systems are used more commonly in the last stage of the design process for documentation. Documentation of a design for production purposes is usually in the form of working drawings. The working drawings necessary to manufacture a design can vary. They can consist of a complete set of dimensioned detail drawings, assembly drawings, parts lists, bill of materials, and patent drawings.

AutoCAD is a powerful tool that can create working drawings. The information provided in the previous chapters includes the prerequisite knowledge necessary to produce working drawings. Careful preplanning and an effort to exploit the power and versatility of AutoCAD make the production of working drawings an easier task. This chapter demonstrates the most effective use of AutoCAD to create working drawings.

OBJECTIVES

After completing Chapter 10, you will be able to:
1. Create detail drawings of parts to be used more effectively for assemblies and parts lists,
2. Create an assembly drawing of a design,
3. Create a bill of materials,
4. Use layers to prepare more effectively detail drawings that can be used for assembly drawings,
5. Use the **WBLOCK** command to create assembly drawings,
6. Create a parts list with or without the use of attributes,
7. Create blocks with attributes, and
8. Create a complete set of working drawings for the manufacture of a design.

WORKING DRAWINGS

Working drawings are the specifications necessary to manufacture a design and normally consist of individual detail drawings of each part of the design and an assembly drawing. Starting on the working drawings involves several initial decisions.

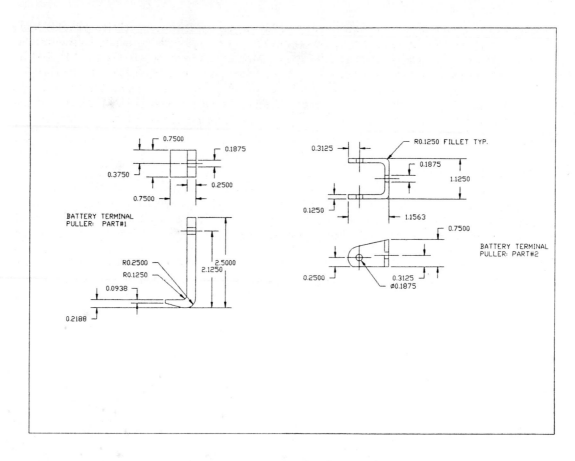

Figure 10.1 Multiple details on a sheet.

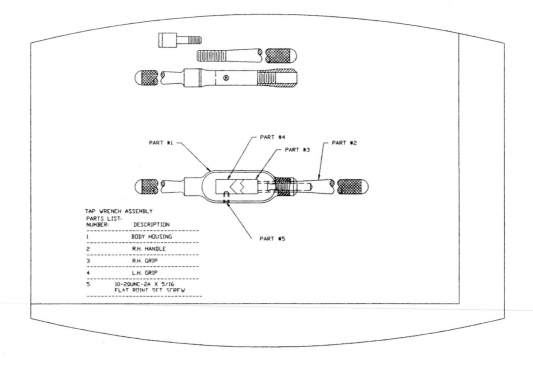

Figure 10.2 Single detail on a sheet.

The number of details per sheet must be determined. If the design is small, with relatively few parts, the details can be shown on one sheet (Figure 10.1). The maximum size of the plotter output is also important. Large assemblies may have two or three details on a sheet, and multiple sheets, to describe fully the design (Figure 10.2). To have one detail per sheet regardless of the size or complexity of the design is not uncommon. If more than one detail is to be used per sheet, make sure enough room is between the views for dimensions and notes. This is not a major concern when using a CADD system because views can be moved within a sheet or moved to another sheet, if necessary. Other considerations include size of drawing sheet, title block, bill of material requirements, and type of assembly drawing that best describes the design.

DETAIL DRAWINGS

Many of the examples explained in earlier chapters focused on the Roller Assembly. The Roller Assembly again is used to demonstrate the use of CADD for working drawings. The Roller Assembly requires detail drawings of five different parts: the wheel, shaft, angle, base, and bushings. Each part must have a detail drawing including all the dimensions necessary to manufacture the part. The nuts and bolts do not need detail drawings because they are standard parts and are specified in the parts list.

To start on the detail drawings of the parts, the type of assembly drawing and scale to be used must be determined. For this example, a simple orthographic, full-section view of the assembly is created, as shown in Figure 10.3. The assembly is made by passing a cutting plane through the center line of the shaft through the full length of the Roller Assembly. This means that one view of each detail should be drawn on a separate layer without dimensions. The view is assigned an attribute that describes the part so that a bill of materials can be extracted from the assembly drawing. Blocks are made of the view, and the assembly drawing is created from the blocks.

After the sheet size and title block are selected, each detail drawing is created by laying out construction lines or by using grid and snap. Figure 10.4 shows the layout for the detail drawing of the Wheel. Dot lines are used for construction lines and are drawn on a separate layer so they can be frozen after the drawing is complete. Frozen layers do not appear on the screen and will not plot. Center lines are used for the location of centers of holes and are located on the screen using a grid and snap, or X, Y coordinate input.

The outline of the Wheel is created with solid lines, arcs, circles, and fillets. All lines in the right-side view are drawn as object lines, as shown in Figure 10.5, to create a full-section view to facilitate dimensions. The right-side view of the Wheel is used as a block for the assembly drawing. The assembly drawing is a full section so section lines are added to the left-side view of the Wheel. Before dimensions are added to the drawing, attributes are added to the right-side view and a Wblock is made using a window to define the entities. This Wblock can be used in the assembly drawing, which is created after all the detail drawings, blocks, and attributes are created for the Roller Assembly.

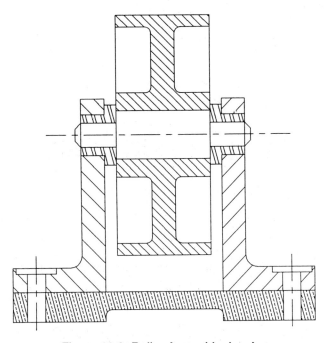

Figure 10.3 Roller Assembly drawing.

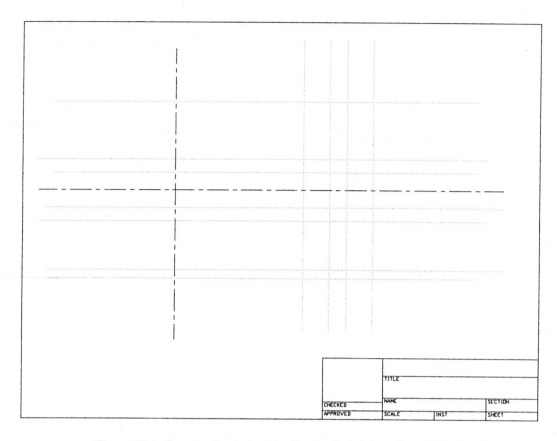

Figure 10.4 Construction layout for the detail drawing of the Wheel.

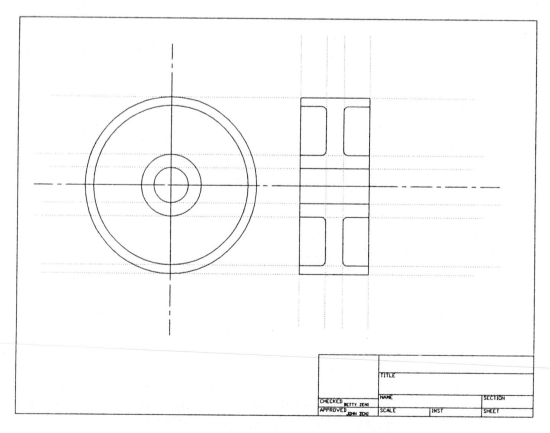

Figure 10.5 Creating the views for the Wheel.

ATTRIBUTES

Attributes are special drawing entities that contain text. It is a method to describe parts through text information that can be extracted from a drawing to create a bill of materials or used with a spread sheet program like Lotus 1-2-3 or dBase III. Attributes can be assigned to any entity if they are part of a BLOCK. Attributes can be displayed on a drawing or made invisible.

Attributes can be assigned to each part of an assembly drawing for a bill of materials program. They also are used for architectural drawings to tag windows, doors, and electrical fixtures. Another application of attributes assigns information to each electronic component, such as integrated circuit chips. The IC chips can be stored as blocks, then placed on the circuit board.

After attributes are assigned to graphic entities, they can be made into blocks and placed into drawings. For example, the detail views of the Roller Assembly for the assembly drawing can have the attributes necessary to create a bill of materials and can be made into blocks. The blocks are then brought together to create a complete assembly drawing. The attribute information is extracted from the drawing and used to create the bill of materials. The Roller Assembly drawing is an example of creating, editing, and extracting attributes.

Defining Attributes

Attributes are defined using the Draw subcommand **ATTDEF**. The information to be extracted from a drawing and the format that attributes are to take must be determined. A bill of materials usually has the part number, name, material, and number of each part necessary for the assembly. For a simple bill of materials, four attribute variables must be created for each part of the assembly.

An attribute can have four optional modes. The **INVISIBLE** Mode toggles between having the attribute text on or off when the block is placed on a drawing. The Display subcommand **ATTDISP** overrides the invisible option. The **CONSTANT** Mode gives the attribute a fixed value for all insertions of the block and cannot be changed without changing the block. The **VERIFY** Mode checks the attribute values assigned to a drawing before accepting them. The **PRESET** Mode creates attributes that are variable but not requested during block insertion.

To create an attribute with four variables for the bill of materials, the following steps are used as a guide:

Creating Attributes: Exercise 10.1

1. Draw two views of the Wheel, as shown in Figure 10.6, or open the completed drawing from your data disk using filename **LAB10-1**. Select **ATTDEF** from the Draw submenu.

2. **Attribute modes — Invisible:N Constant:N Verify:N Preset:N Enter (ICVP) to change, RETURN when done:**

The four attribute modes are listed with the default values of NO.

3. Enter a letter **I** to make the attribute invisible and press RETURN.

4. **Attribute modes — Invisible:Y Constant:N Verify:N Preset:N Enter (ICVP) to change, RETURN when done:**

Notice that the Invisible Mode now reads Y. Enter the letter **V** to turn the Verify Mode on and press RETURN.

5. **Attribute modes — Invisible:Y Constant:N Verify:Y Preset:N Enter (ICVP) to change, RETURN when done:**

No other modes are changed so RETURN is entered.

6. **Attribute tag:**

The first attribute variable is defined by giving it a name. Enter **PART-NUMBER** at the prompt and press RETURN. A tag can be any characters without blank spaces.

7. **Attribute prompt:**

This step creates a prompt to assist in making the attribute definition when the block is inserted. For this example, enter **PLEASE ENTER PART NUMBER**. A null response results in the attribute tag being the prompt. This step does not appear if the Constant Mode is used for the attribute.

8. **Default attribute value:**

This step creates a default response to the prompt made in Step 7. It is used to assist the user of the attribute to enter the correct type of response. For example, the default attribute value for a part number might be **XX**, which means that a one- or two-digit number is required for input.

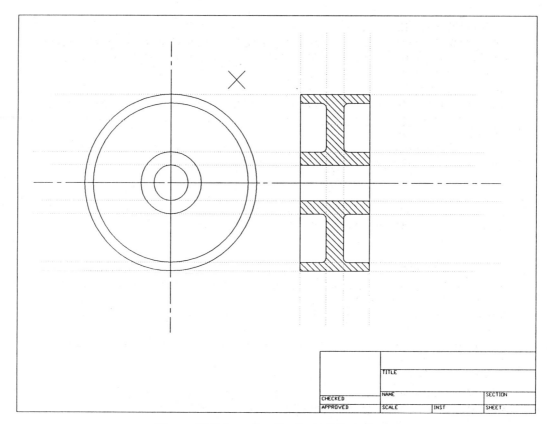

Figure 10.6 Locating the first attribute tag.

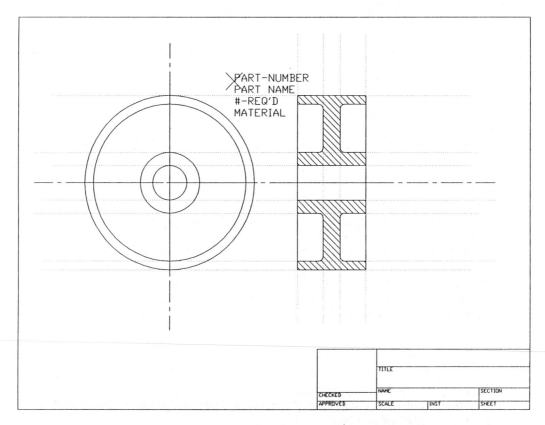

Figure 10.7 The Wheel with attribute tag.

9. Justify/Style (Start point):
The location of the attribute tag is entered. The attribute tag should be located close to the view so that it is easily included in the defined block. Figure 10.6 shows the point picked for the Wheel.
10. Height (0.080):
The size of the attribute text is requested. The default setting is 0.0800 and is changed to .2000 by entering a new value and RETURN.
11. Rotation angle (0):
The text can be rotated by entering an angle and RETURN. No rotation is requested for this example, so RETURN is entered. The tag is drawn on screen.

The first attribute tag has been created for the bill of materials. The same steps are followed to create the other three variables necessary to create a bill of materials for the assembly drawing. The following steps create the attribute tag for the part name.

1. Select **ATTDEF** from the Draw submenu.
2. **Attribute modes — Invisible:Y Constant:N Verify:Y Preset:N Enter (ICVP) to change, RETURN when done:**
The same modes are used for all other attribute tags, so RETURN is entered.
3. **Attribute tag:**
The second attribute variable is defined by first giving the variable a name. Enter **PART-NAME** at the prompt and press RETURN.
4. **Attribute prompt:**
This step creates a prompt to assist in making the attribute definition when the block is inserted. For this example, enter **PLEASE ENTER PART NAME**.
5. **Default attribute value:**
Enter **NAME** and press RETURN.
6. **Justify/Style (Start point):**
Entering RETURN locates the second tag immediately below the first.

The third text string included in the attribute is for the number of each part in the assembly. The following steps create this attribute tag:

1. Select **ATTDEF** from the Draw submenu.
2. **Attribute modes — Invisible:Y Constant:N Verify:Y Preset:N Enter (ICVP) to change, RETURN when done:**
The same modes are used for all other attribute tags, so RETURN is entered.
3. **Attribute tag:**
The third attribute variable is defined by giving the variable a name. Enter #-REQ'D and press RETURN.
4. **Attribute prompt:**
This step creates a prompt to assist in making the attribute definition when the block is inserted. For this example, enter:
PLEASE ENTER THE NUMBER OF PARTS TO BE USED IN THE ASSEMBLY.
5. **Default attribute value:**
Enter **XX** and press RETURN.
6. **Justify/Style (Start point):**
Entering RETURN locates the third tag immediately below the second.

The last tag to be defined is for the type of material used for the part, described by the following steps:

1. Select **ATTDEF** from the Draw submenu.
2. **Attribute modes — Invisible:Y Constant:N Verify:Y Preset:N Enter (ICVP) to change, RETURN when done:**
The same modes are used for all other attribute tags, so RETURN is entered.

3. **Attribute tag:**
The second attribute variable is defined by first giving the variable a name. Enter **MATERIAL** at the prompt and press RETURN.
4. **Attribute prompt:**
This step creates a prompt to assist in making the attribute definition when the block is inserted. For this example, enter:
PLEASE ENTER NAME OF MATERIAL.
5. **Default attribute value:**
Enter **MATERIAL** and press RETURN.
6. **Justify/Style (Start point):**
Entering RETURN locates the fourth tag immediately below the third.
The finished attribute tag is shown in Figure 10.7.

Attributes can be edited after creation using the Edit subcommand **ATTEDIT**. Repeat Exercise 10.1 for each part in the assembly.

Creating the Attribute WBlock for the Assembly Drawing

After the attribute tags have been defined for each view to be used for the assembly drawing, the Wblock containing the attribute information is created. The Wblock is defined as described in Chapter 6. The Wheel attribute will be made into a block for an example. Be sure to save the current drawing of the Wheel before the Wblock is created so that it can be retrieved and completed with dimensions for the detail drawing.

Creating a Block: Exercise 10.2

1. Enter **BLOCK** at the command prompt.
2. **Block name (or ?):**
Enter **WHEEL** and RETURN.
3. **Insertion base point:**
The selection of the insertion point is extremely important when creating an assembly drawing and can save a lot of time. For the Wheel, the base point is the intersection of the left side with the center line, as shown in Figure 10.8. Use **OSNAP** command **INTERSE C**.
4. **Select objects:**
Enter the letter **W** to use a window for selection.
5. **First corner:**
Pick a point like that shown in Figure 10.8.
6. **Other corner:**
Pick another point that includes the view and the attribute tags, as shown in Figure 10.8, then enter RETURN.
7. All the entities and the attribute tags disappear from the screen as the block is created.
The **OOPS** command can be used to restore the object that was just turned into a block.
8. Now make a **WBLOCK** out of the **BLOCK** so that it can be inserted into the assembly drawing. Select **BLOCKS** then **WBLOCK** from the menu.
9. A dialogue box is displayed on screen. Enter the filename WHEEL in the dialogue box then select OK.
10. **Block name:** Enter = to make the Block and Wblock names the same.

The procedure just described is repeated for all the parts of the Roller Assembly.

CREATING THE ASSEMBLY DRAWING

Attribute tags have to be created for all the views used in the assembly drawing. After the tags and blocks have been defined, the assembly drawing can be made. To create an assembly drawing from blocks, the scale is selected and the drawing sheet must be prepared by drawing the center and construction lines necessary to place the blocks on the screen (Figure 10.9).

The first block placed on the screen for the assembly is the Shaft.

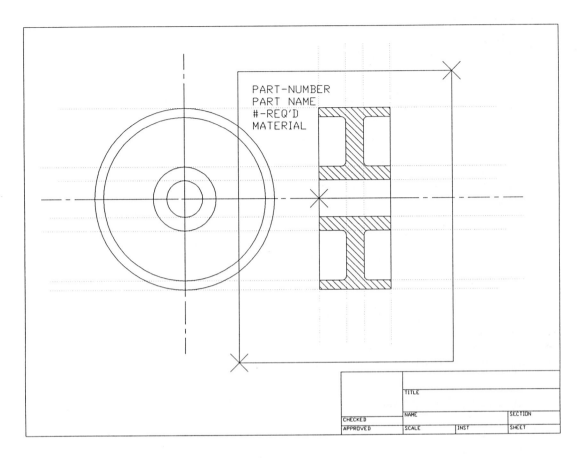

Figure 10.8 Window used to define the BLOCK containing the attribute tag.

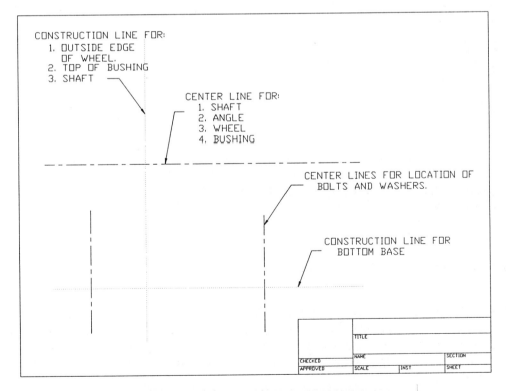

Figure 10.9 Layout for the assembly drawing.

Creating the Assembly using Blocks: Exercise 10.3

1. Open **LAB10-2** from your data disk. Select **INSERT** to place the Shaft on the drawing.
2. **Block name (or ?):**
Enter **SHAFT** and RETURN.
3. **INSERTION POINT:**
Select **OSNAP** subcommand **INTERSEC**.
4. Pick the intersection shown in Figure 10.10.
5. **X scale factor (1) / Corner / XYZ:**
Enter RETURN for full scale.
6. **Y scale factor (default=X):**
Enter RETURN.
7. **Rotation angle (0):**
Enter RETURN.
8. **Enter Attribute values PLEASE ENTER NAME OF MATERIAL (MATERIAL):**
The attribute prompts are displayed after the block is defined in reverse order. The prompts are the ones created when the attribute variables were defined using the **ATTDEF** function. Enter the material name **1113 STEEL** and RETURN.
9. **PLEASE ENTER THE NUMBER REQUIRED FOR THIS ASSEMBLY (XX):**
Enter **1** and RETURN.
10. **PLEASE ENTER PART NAME (NAME):**
Enter **SHAFT** and RETURN.
11. **PLEASE ENTER PART NUMBER (XX):**
Enter **1** and RETURN.

The Shaft appears on the screen, as shown in Figure 10.10. The attribute text is not displayed because the Visible Mode was off. To turn on the text, use the Display subcommand **ATTDISP**.

All the other parts of the assembly will be located on the drawing sheet similar to those described, using different insertion points and attribute variable information. The assembly drawing appears, as shown in Figure 10.11.

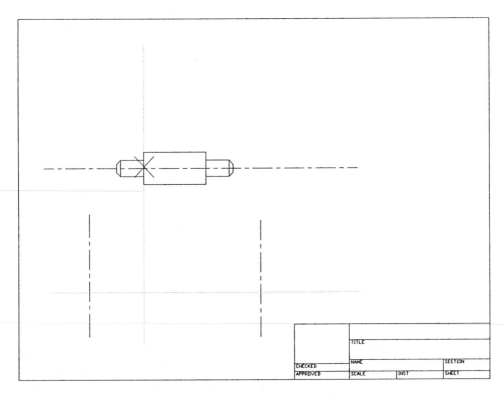

Figure 10.10 Insertion point for the Shaft.

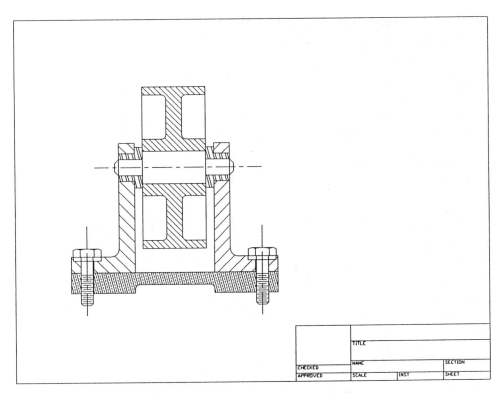

Figure 10.11 Completed assembly drawing.

EXTRACTING ATTRIBUTE INFORMATION

After the blocks with attributes are assembled on the drawing, the information must be extracted, but a Template File first must be created. Template Files are created by using a text editor such as EDLIN or WordStar or data base software such as dBASE III. Each line in the Template File specifies one of the attribute variables. To create a parts list of the Roller Assembly, four attribute variables were created. Each of these variables must have a line in the Template File that extracts the information, including the name, the width necessary to display the name, and its numerical precision if necessary.

The Template File used to create a bill of materials for the Roller Assembly is shown below. It was created as a non-document file on a word processor and saved with the file name **ASSEMBLY.TXT**.

PART-NUMBER	**N005000**
SPACE1	C002000
PART-NAME	C015000
SPACE2	C002000
#-REQ'D	N005000
SPACE3	C002000
MATERIAL	C015000

The C or N following the field name extracts (N)umerical or (C)haracter information. The next three digits define the number of character spaces for the extracted information. For example, the first three digits (015) after PART-NAME mean that 15 character spaces are provided for the name of the part. If the part name is longer than 15 characters, it automatically is truncated at the sixteenth character. The last three digits specify the decimal precision for numeric information. All of the numeric information necessary for the bill of materials are whole numbers, so three zeros are used in this Template File. The first line extracts the part number from the block. Lines labeled as SPACE1, SPACE2, and SPACE3 are used to leave two empty spaces between the extracted information.

The last line in the Template File must end with a RETURN and is saved with **.TXT** as the file name extender.

The Utility subcommand **ATTEXT** extracts attribute information from a drawing. AutoCAD provides three different formats for extracting text from a drawing file: **CDF, SDF,** and **DXF**. CDF and SDF are formats that can be used by data base programs, spread sheets, and text editors. The DXF file is used by programmers and is generally much more complicated and difficult to interpret.

To create a bill of materials, the SDF format is recommended. To create an SDF format file, follow these steps:

Creating a Parts List Using Extracted Data: Exercise 10.3

1. At the command prompt, enter **ATTEXT** and RETURN.
2. **CDF, SDF, or DXF Attribute extract (or Entities)? (C):** Enter the file type to be created, **SDF** and RETURN. SDF is a file format like that produced by dBASE III and is the standard input for microcomputer data base systems. CDF is the default format and produces a file that contains at most one record. The fields in each record are separated by a comma and enclosed by quotes. DXF is the AutoCAD drawing interchange file format. Entities are used to select the objects for attribute extraction.
3. A Pop-up dialogue box is displayed on screen. Enter the file name and select OK. Enter the template file name and disk drive specifier, **ASSEMBLY** without the .**TXT** file type.
4. **Extract file name ():**
Enter the name of the file, **BOM**, and RETURN. Do not use the same name as that of the Template File, or it will be deleted when the extract file is created.
5. **1 records in extract file.**
This prompt appears after a brief pause. AutoCAD automatically extracted the information from every block in the assembly drawing and saved it as a file called BOM on the current disk drive.

The extract file then can be loaded into a text editor, data base, or spread sheet program for manipulation and analysis. To create the bill of materials for the Roller Assembly, the extract file is loaded into a word processor headers are added. It is printed as shown here.

NO. PART NAME		REQ'D MATERIAL	
1	SHAFT	1	1113 STEEL
2	ANGLE	2	1020 STEEL
3	BUSHING	2	BRONZE
4	WHEEL	1	CAST IRON
5	BASE	1	1020 STEEL
6	3/8 HEX BOLT	4	STEEL
7	3/8 WASHER	4	STEEL

This table now can be brought back into AutoCAD and added to the Roller Assembly drawing file as the bill of materials (Figure 10.12).

PART IDENTIFICATION NUMBERS

The final element that must be added to an assembly drawing is the method of identifying each part of the design. Normally this is accomplished by placing a leader line with arrow an touching the part. At the end of the leader, a circle, called a balloon, is drawn that contains the number of the part. The part call-outs are created with AutoCAD using the **LEADER**, **CIRCLE**, and **TEXT** functions (Figure 10.13). These three functions also may be combined into a block to facilitate the adding of balloons to an assembly drawing.

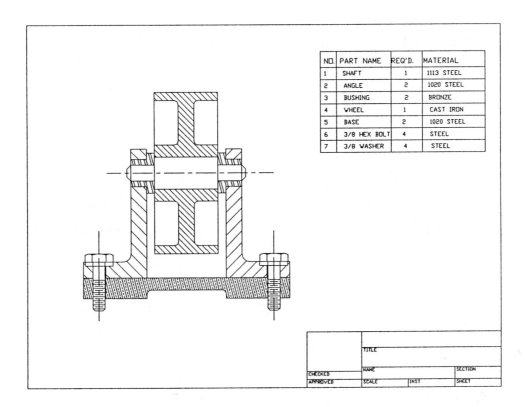

NO.	PART NAME	REQ'D.	MATERIAL
1	SHAFT	1	1113 STEEL
2	ANGLE	2	1020 STEEL
3	BUSHING	2	BRONZE
4	WHEEL	1	CAST IRON
5	BASE	2	1020 STEEL
6	3/8 HEX BOLT	4	STEEL
7	3/8 WASHER	4	STEEL

Figure 10.12 Assembly drawing and parts list.

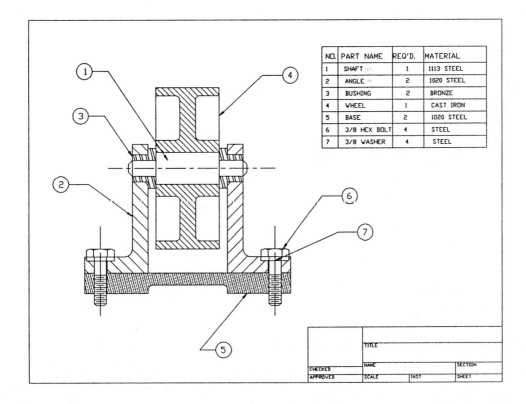

NO.	PART NAME	REQ'D.	MATERIAL
1	SHAFT	1	1113 STEEL
2	ANGLE	2	1020 STEEL
3	BUSHING	2	BRONZE
4	WHEEL	1	CAST IRON
5	BASE	2	1020 STEEL
6	3/8 HEX BOLT	4	STEEL
7	3/8 WASHER	4	STEEL

Figure 10.13 Assembly drawing, parts list, and balloons for part identification.

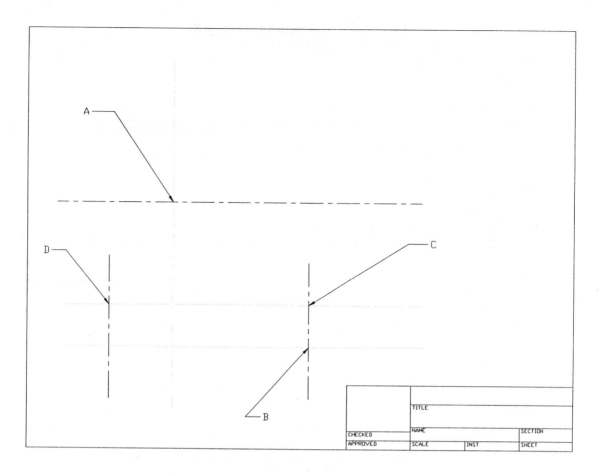

Figure 10.14 Starting points for the assembly.

CREATING AN ASSEMBLY DRAWING WITHOUT ATTRIBUTES

To create an assembly drawing using the **INSERT** command, the scale is selected and the drawing sheet must be prepared by drawing the center and construction lines necessary to place the blocks on the screen (Figure 10.14). Each part making up the assembly must be edited and saved as a drawing file. For example, the detail drawing of the wheel must be edited so only the sectioned view is shown without dimensions. This is then saved as a drawing file. This must be done for each part in the assembly. The first drawing placed on the screen for the assembly is the Shaft.

Placing the Shaft: Exercise 10.4

1. Open drawing file **LAB10-3**. Select **INSERT** to place the Shaft on the drawing.
2. **Block name (or ?):**
Enter **SHAFT** and RETURN.
3. **INSERTION POINT:**
Select **OSNAP** subcommand **INTERSEC**.
4. Pick the intersection labeled point A.
5. **X scale factor (1) / Corner / XYZ:**
Enter RETURN for full scale.
6. **Y scale factor (default=X):**
Enter RETURN.
7. **Rotation angle (0):**
Enter RETURN. The Shaft appears on the screen, as shown in Figure 10.13.

Placing the Bushings: Exercise 10.5

1. Select **INSERT** to place the Bushing on the drawing.
2. **Block name (or ?):**
Enter **BUSHING** and RETURN.
3. **INSERTION POINT:**
Select **OSNAP** subcommand **INTERSEC**.
4. Pick the intersection between the large diameter of the shaft on the right end and the center line.
5. **X scale factor (1) / Corner / XYZ:**
Enter RETURN for full scale.
6. **Y scale factor (default=X):**
Enter RETURN.
7. **Rotation angle (0):**
Enter RETURN. The bushing appears on screen.
8. Repeat the **INSERT** command to place the other Bushing by pressing the RETURN key.
9. **Block name (or ?):**
Enter **BUSHING** and RETURN.
10. **INSERTION POINT:**
Select **OSNAP** subcommand **INTERSEC**.
4. Pick the intersection labeled as point A.
5. **X scale factor (1) / Corner / XYZ:**
Enter RETURN for full scale.
6. **Y scale factor (default=X):**
Enter RETURN.
7. **Rotation angle (0):**
Enter 180 to rotate the Bushing for the other side of the assembly.

Placing the Wheel: Exercise 10.6

1. Select **INSERT** to place the Wheel on the drawing.
2. **Block name (or ?):**
Enter **WHEEL** and RETURN.
3. **INSERTION POINT:**
Select **OSNAP** subcommand **INTERSEC**.
4. Pick the intersection point labeled A.
5. **X scale factor (1) / Corner / XYZ:**
Enter RETURN for full scale.
6. **Y scale factor (default=X):**
Enter RETURN.
7. **Rotation angle (0):**
Enter RETURN. The Wheel appears on screen, as shown in Figure 10.13.

Placing the Base: Exercise 10.7

1. Select **INSERT** to place the Base on the drawing.
2. **Block name (or ?):**
Enter **BASE** and RETURN.
3. **INSERTION POINT:**
Select **OSNAP** subcommand **INTERSEC**.
4. Pick the intersection labeled B.
5. **X scale factor (1) / Corner / XYZ:**
Enter RETURN for full scale.
6. **Y scale factor (default=X):**
Enter RETURN.
7. **Rotation angle (0):**
Enter RETURN to show the base.

Placing the Angles: Exercise 10.8

1. Select **INSERT** to place the Angles on the drawing.
2. **Block name (or ?):**
Enter **ANGLE** and RETURN.
3. **INSERTION POINT:**
Select **OSNAP** subcommand **INTERSEC**.
4. Pick the intersection between the center line for the shaft and the far right end of the right bushing.
5. **X scale factor (1) / Corner / XYZ:**
Enter RETURN for full scale.
6. **Y scale factor (default=X):**
Enter RETURN.
7. **Rotation angle (0):**
Enter RETURN. The Angle appears on screen.
8. Repeat the **INSERT** command to place the other Angle by pressing the RETURN key.
9. **Block name (or ?):**

Enter **ANGLE2** and RETURN.
10. **INSERTION POINT:**
Select **OSNAP** subcommand **INTERSEC**.
4. Pick the intersection between the center line for the shaft and the far left end of the left bushing.
5. **X scale factor (1) / Corner / XYZ:**
Enter RETURN for full scale.
6. **Y scale factor (default=X):**
Enter RETURN.
7. **Rotation angle (0):**
Enter RETURN. The Angle appears on screen.

Placing the Bolts: Exercise 10.9

1. Select **INSERT** to place the Bolts on the drawing.
2. **Block name (or ?):**
Enter **HEXBOLT** and RETURN.
3. **INSERTION POINT:**
Select **OSNAP** subcommand **INTERSEC**.
4. Pick the intersection labeled C.
5. **X scale factor (1) / Corner / XYZ:**
Enter RETURN for full scale.
6. **Y scale factor (default=X):**
Enter RETURN.
7. **Rotation angle (0):**
Enter RETURN. The Bolt appears on screen.
8. Repeat the **INSERT** command to place the other Bolt by pressing the RETURN key.
9. **Block name (or ?):**
Enter **BOLT** and RETURN.
10. **INSERTION POINT:**
Select **OSNAP** subcommand **INTERSEC**.
4. Pick the intersection labeled D.
5. **X scale factor (1) / Corner / XYZ:**
Enter RETURN for full scale.
6. **Y scale factor (default=X):**
Enter RETURN.
7. **Rotation angle (0):**
Enter RETURN.

Placing the Washers: Exercise 10.10

1. Select **INSERT** to place the Washers on the drawing.
2. **Block name (or ?):**
Enter **WASHER** and RETURN.
3. **INSERTION POINT:**
Select **OSNAP** subcommand **INTERSEC**.
4. Pick the intersection labeled C.
5. **X scale factor (1) / Corner / XYZ:**
Enter RETURN for full scale.
6. **Y scale factor (default=X):**
Enter RETURN.
7. **Rotation angle (0):**
Enter RETURN. The Washer appears on screen.
8. Repeat the **INSERT** command to place the other Washer by pressing the RETURN key.
9. **Block name (or ?):**
Enter **WASHER** and RETURN.
10. **INSERTION POINT:**
Select **OSNAP** subcommand **INTERSEC**.
4. Pick the intersection labeled D.
5. **X scale factor (1) / Corner / XYZ:**
Enter RETURN for full scale.
6. **Y scale factor (default=X):**
Enter RETURN.
7. **Rotation angle (0):**
Enter RETURN. The Washer appears on screen as shown in Figure 10.13.
8. Erase the construction lines to complete the assembly.

PART IDENTIFICATION NUMBERS

The final element that must be added to an assembly drawing is the method of identifying each part of the design. Normally this is accomplished by placing a leader line with an arrow touching the part and a bill of materials. At the end of the leader, a circle, called a balloon, is drawn that contains the number of the part. The part call-outs are created with AutoCAD using the **LEADER, CIRCLE,** and **TEXT** functions (Figure 10.13). These three functions also may be combined into a block to facilitate the adding of balloons to an assembly drawing. The bill of materials is created by drawing horizontal and vertical lines to create the table, then to add text.

Placing a Part Identification Number: Exercise 10.11

1. Select **DIM** from the menu or from the Draw Pull-down Menu.
2. Select **LEADER** from the Dimension Menu.
3. A prompt reads:
Leader Start:
Pick the edge of the part to be identified.
4. A prompt reads:
To point:
Pick the point where the bend in the leader line should be located.
5. Another prompt reads:
To point:
Pick the endpoint of the leader line, then enter RETURN.
6. A prompt reads:
Dimension text <>:
Enter a space, then the part number.
7. Cancel the dimension command by entering Ctrl-C, then select the **CIRCLE** command and draw a circle around the part number. Repeat these steps for each part as shown in Figure 10.13.
8. Construct a parts list and add text to complete the assembly drawing.

QUESTIONS FOR REVIEW

1. Define an attribute.
2. Name three different uses for attributes.
3. Identify AutoCAD command used to define attributes.
4. List the four attribute modes.
5. Identify AutoCAD command used to edit attributes.
6. Name the type of file that must be created before attribute information is extracted.
7. Name the AutoCAD command used to extract attribute information from a drawing.
8. Explain **ATTDISP**.

DRAWING ASSIGNMENTS

1. Create a complete set of working drawings of the Wheel Assembly, including a sectioned assembly drawing with parts list and dimensioned detail drawings of each part.

2. From Giesecke et al., *Engineering Graphics*, 4th ed., or *Technical Graphics*, 8th ed.. Working drawing problems from Chapter 14.

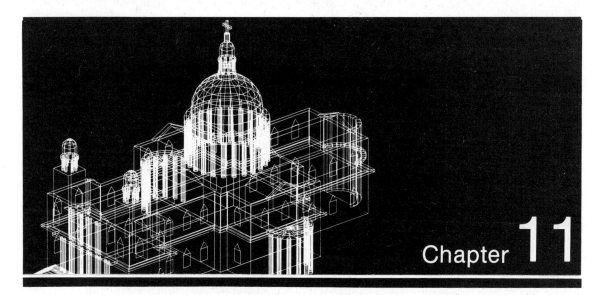

Chapter 11

THREE-DIMENSIONAL DRAWINGS
AND APPLICATIONS OF AutoCAD

AutoCAD has been used for many applications, such as architectural, chemical, civil, facility planning, mapping, piping, medical technology, theater, and many others. The user's training and background determine the application of the CADD software. AutoCAD is a general CADD software program flexible enough to be used for many applications. This chapter describes some of the more common uses for the engineering profession.

One of the most exciting developments in microcomputer-based CADD software is the ability to create three-dimensional (3D) drawings. Drawing an object in three dimensions can assist the designer in visualizing the shape and form of the design. Three-dimensional drawings assist the designer in creating the object and in communicating the design to others. AutoCAD can create 3D models that can be viewed in any direction. Hidden lines can be removed from the model to improve visualization. The 3D model can be converted to a 2D drawing for documentation. The 3D model also can be surface modeled and shaded using AutoShade. This chapter describes how AutoCAD can create 3D wireframe and surface models.

Finally, this chapter describes how AutoCAD can be integrated into the design process described in Chapter 1. The automation of the design and manufacture of a product are described. AutoCAD's role in design and manufacturing is described, along with specific examples and applications. This chapter shows how AutoCAD can be used for different applications. Knowing the application of any tool is the only true measure of its worth.

OBJECTIVES

After completing Chapter 11, you will be able to:
1. Describe the applications of AutoCAD to the engineering profession,
2. Create 3D wireframe models of designs,
3. Create surface models of designs,
4. Create 2D drawings from a 3D model,
5. Apply AutoCAD to the analysis and evaluation of a design,
6. Describe the merging of design and manufacturing, CAD/CAM,
7. Describe how AutoCAD can document a design,

2D VERSUS 3D DRAWINGS FOR DESIGN

Engineering design is a creative process based on sound scientific principles. This creative process can be enhanced through the use of various tools. The documentation of a design idea traditionally was accomplished with paper and pencil and other tools that assisted the user in drawing straight lines and consistent curves and arcs. The use of traditional tools for design can be supplemented with CADD software programs. How CADD fits into the design process has not been determined fully because the hardware and software continue to evolve and improve.

The development of microcomputer-based CADD starts with automating the documentation of a design. Documentation takes the form of 2D engineering or technical drawings necessary for the manufacture of product. A 3D CADD system should be thought of as a tool that can be used to integrate more fully the design and documentation of an idea. By integrating the design process with a 3D CADD system, it is possible to create a 3D model of the design, analyze and edit the model, and then create the 2D drawings necessary for documentation for manufacturing. The ultimate CADD system allows the designer to model, analyze, edit, and document the design without the use of prototypes. A prototype is a working model of the proposed design. To a certain extent, AutoCAD and third-party software developments can be used as described for simple mechanical components and electronic designs.

Designing in 3D has many advantages over designing in 2D. The interference or clearance of parts can be checked visually by changing the viewpoint relative to the model. The ability to visualize the design is much greater with a 3D model. A 3D model also can automate the manufacture of the part.

COMPUTER-AIDED DESIGN/DRAFTING

The design process shown in Figure 11.1 depicts the integration of CADD. After the preliminary ideas have been sketched, the geometric modeling of the part can begin on AutoCAD. As shown in Figure 11.1, CADD can be used for geometric modeling, analysis (sometimes called computer-aided engineering), editing or optimization, and automated drafting or documentation.

The process works by creating a 3D model of the design. The object is then analyzed, edited, and manipulated to complete the the design and documentation.

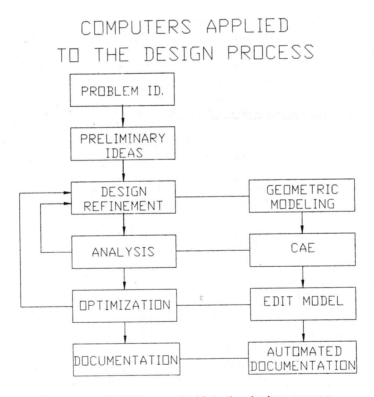

Figure 11.1 CADD integrated into the design process.

GEOMETRIC MODELING

Geometric modeling is the conversion of rough design sketches into accurate 3D models on the computer. Computer-generated 3D models can be created several ways, depending on the software being used. One method is to create a wireframe model like that shown in Figure 11.2. Geometric models can be grouped into three areas:

1. Wireframe
2. Surface
3. Solid

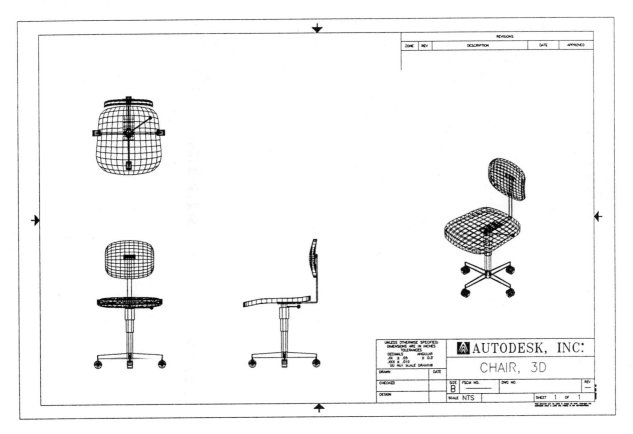

Figure 11.2 3D wireframe model. (Courtesy of Autodesk, Inc).

Creating Wireframe Models with AutoCAD

A wireframe model is a representation of a geometric form that uses lines for the outside elements, giving the appearance of a wireframe. AutoCAD provides four methods of creating a 3D wireframe model:

1. Extrusion
2. 3D lines, polylines, circles and arcs, oriented in 3D coordinate space
3. 3D faces
4. 3D objects

The extrusion method of creating 3D models uses the **ELEV** command to set the Z depth. Extruded forms are limited in that they cannot be used to draw 3D diagonal lines. **LINE** is used to create any line by assigning a Z coordinate value and is used for point-to-point model construction. **LINES** cannot be extruded, but the **COPY** command can be used to copy them to a new Z depth.

THE AutoCAD 3D HUMAN INTERFACE

When AutoCAD is loaded into the computer memory using the default prototype drawing, the 3D axis appears as shown in Figure 11.3. The X and Y axes lie in the plane of the screen. The X axis is horizontal, with positive values located to the right of the Y axis and negative values located to the left. The Y axis is vertical, with positive values located above the X axis and negative values located below. The Z axis is located perpendicular to the screen, with a Z value of zero assigned to the surface of the screen. A positive Z value moves the point out of the screen toward the viewer. A negative Z value moves the point into the screen away from the viewer.

The default setting illustrated in Figure 11.3 is the **PLAN VIEW** or top view with AutoCAD and is assigned values of 0,0,1. AutoCAD considers the entire drawing to be at 0,0,0. However, it is not possible to assign these values to a viewpoint to look inside the model. The name **PLAN VIEW** is associated with architectural drawings showing floor plans, plot plans, and other one-view drawings. AutoCAD provides a method of controlling the viewpoint from which a drawing is viewed through the **VPOINT** (viewpoint) command, View Presets, and the **DVIEW** (dynamic view) command. **VPOINT** is used to get off the Z axis to look from any of the sides and create any number of axonometric views.

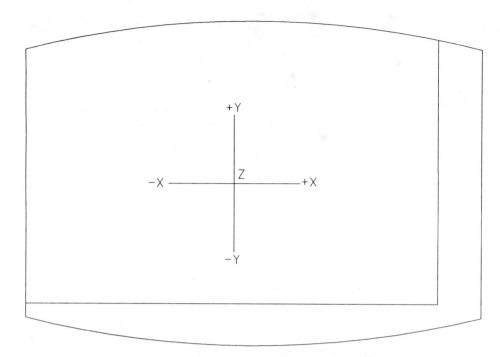

Figure 11.3 AutoCAD's default axis position.

Using View Presets

The Presets option is an easy way to create the six principal views and any pictorial view of a part. Figure 11.4 shows the Pull-down Menus to select for the Presets option. Figure 11.5 shows the Presets dialogue box. The dialogue box has two major components: (1) The angle from the X-axis icon located to the left of the dialogue box,

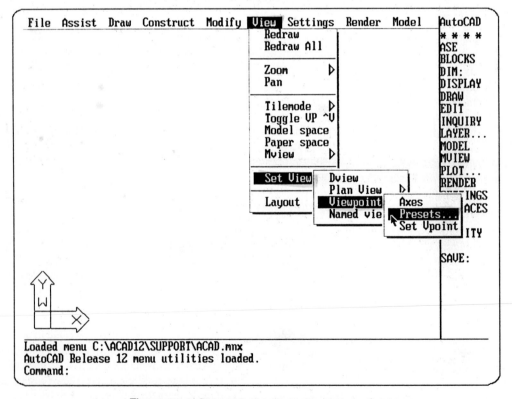

Figure 11.4 Selecting the Presets command.

and (2) the angle from the XY plane icon located to the right of the dialogue box. Remember that the default settings for AutoCAD are to be in the plan view with world coordinates, as shown in Figure 11.6. This figure shows how the X-axis angle from the Presets dialogue box relates to a plan view drawing. Notice that 0 degrees is at 3:00 at default settings. To create the view shown (top view) in Figure 11.6, the presets are set to 270 degrees from the X-axis and 90 degrees from the XY plane, as shown in Figure 11.5.

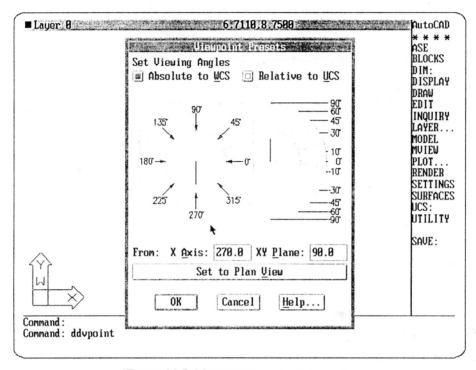

Figure 11.5 Viewport presets dialogue box.

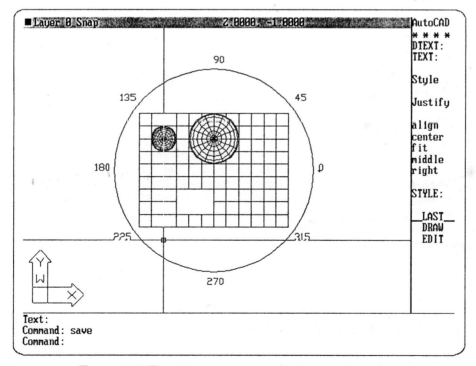

Figure 11.6 The default plan view with the presets marked.

To change the viewpoint with the Presets dialogue box pick a new angle with the cursor. For example to create a front view of parts change the XY plane setting to 0 degrees. To create any of the six principal views use the following presets:

View	Angle from X-axis	Angle from XY plane
Top (plan)	270	90
Front	270	0
Right side	0	0
Left side	180	0
Rear	90	0
Bottom	270	-90

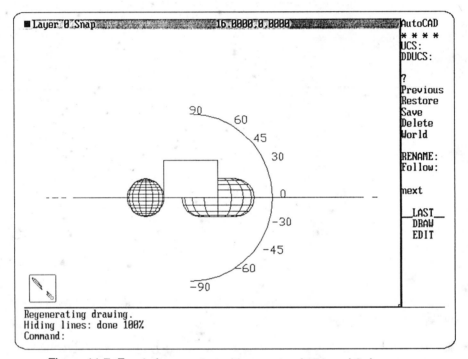

Figure 11.7 Front view created with presets of 270 and 0 degrees.

To create pictorial views of the parts use presets between 0 and 90 to get a view from above or presets between 0 and -90 to get views from below. Figure 11.8 shows a view of the parts using settings of 315 from the X-axis and 30 above the XY plane. This produces a view front above and to the right of the object. Use the following settings to create pictorials:

View	Angle from X-axis	Angle from XY plane
Front Above/Right	315	10 to 75
Front Above/Left	225	10 to 75
Rear Above/Right	135	10 to 75
Rear Above/Left	45	10 to 75
Front Below/Right	315	-10 to -75
Front Below/Left	225	-10 to -75
Rear Below/Righr	135	-10 to -75
Rear Below/Left	45	-10 to -75

Using the Presets Option to Create New Viewpoints: Exercise 11.1

1. Open **LAB11-1** from your data disk.
2. Select View/Set View/Viewpoint/Presets... from the Pull-down Menus.
3. Using the values shown above create the six principal views of the objects. Use the **HIDE** command to verify the viewpoints.
4. Using the values shown above create 8 pictorial viewpoints. Again use the **HIDE** command to verify viewpoints.

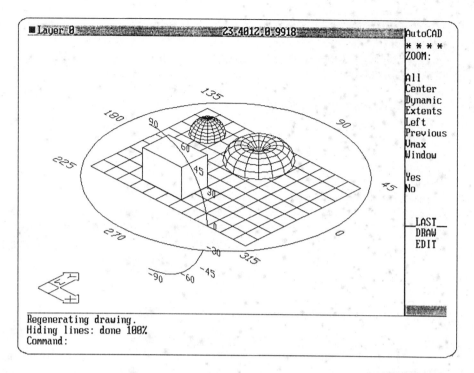

Figure 11.8 Pictorial view using presets of 315 and 30 degrees.

The Viewpoint Command

Three methods of using the **VPOINT** command are provided. One technique is to enter X, Y, Z view coordinate values that represent the viewpoint target. For example, the default target position is 0,0,0 which is the plan or top view. The second method is to use the **AXES** Option, which displays the X, Y, and Z axes on screen and a target to locate the new viewpoint. The third method is to use the Rotate option to specify the new viewpoint in terms of two angles: one from the X-axis and the other above or below the XY plane similar to the Presets option described above. The Presets option described previously is a graphic representation of the Vpoint/Rotate option.

To use the Vpoint command enter it at the command prompt or pick it from the View/Set/View/Viewpoint/Set Vpoint Pull-down Menu. A prompt is displayed: **Rotate/,View point> <0.0000, 0.0000, 0.0000>:** The default selection is to enter view coordinate values. The following coordinate values can be used to create the six principal viewpoints:

View	View Coordinates
Top (plan)	0,0,1
Front	0,-1,0
Right side	1,0,0
Left side	-1,0,0
Rear	0,1,0
Bottom	0,0,-1

Pictorial views are created using the following values:

View	View Coordinates
Front Above/Right	1,-1,1
Front Above/Left	-1,-1,1
Rear Above/Right	-1,1,1
Rear Above/Left	1,1,1
Front Below/Right	-1,1,-1
Front Below/Left	1,1,-1
Rear Below/Right	1,-1,-1
Rear Below/Left	-1,-1,-1

Using the Vpoint View Coordinates Option to Create New Viewpoints: Exercise 11.2

1. Open **LAB11-1** from your data disk.
2. Select View/Set View/Viewpoint/Set Vpoint... from the Pull-down Menus or enter **VPOINT** at the command prompt.
3. Using the values shown above create the six principal views of the objects. Use the **HIDE** command to verify the viewpoints.
4. Using the values shown above create 8 pictorial viewpoints. Again use the **HIDE** command to verify viewpoints.

It is not uncommon to become "lost in space" when changing viewpoints on a wireframe model. If this occurs, select the **VPOINT** command and enter 0,0,1 to return to the plan or top view. Values of 1,-1,1 generate a viewpoint from above and to the right of the object, similar to an isometric view.

To prevent getting lost in space, draw a small circle around a corner of the drawing in the plan view, display a base grid, Figure 11.7, or draw important elements, such as the base of the object, in a different color. This will give some visual continuity to your drawing and aid in determining the viewpoint from which the object is being seen. The circle then can be erased or placed on a different layer and frozen after the model is completed. Finally, the best method of learning the **VPOINT** command is to practice with simple objects until you are proficient at creating a limited number of new viewpoints.

The Vpoint Bull's-eye Option

At the Vpoint prompt entering Return displays the bull's eye option. The concentric circles or bull's-eye shown at the upper right of the icon menu is the second method of changing viewpoints. It is selected from the **VPOINT** Menu using the **AXES** Option from the Pull-down Menu or by entering Return after **VPOINT** is entered at the command prompt. The X, Y, and Z axes also are displayed on the screen with the bull's-eye, as shown in Figure 11.9. Moving the cursor within the bull's-eye causes the X, Y, and Z axes to move. Placing the cursor at the center of the bull's-eye is the same as the plan view or 0,0,1. The horizontal line represents the X-axis, the vertical line represents the Y-axis, and the intersection is the origin. Movement anywhere within the small circle creates a view looking down on the object. Movement anywhere between the small and large circles creates a view looking from under the object. Picking a point anywhere within the bull's eye will automatically generate a new view of the object. Figure 11.10 shows where to position the crusor in the target to get various views.

The **SNAP** and **COORDS** Toggle functions can be used with the bull's-eye. The **SNAP** function is useful in keeping the cursor along the axes of the circle and snaps to the plan view, which is the center of the two concentric circles. Having the Coords Toggle ON is useful because the X,Y coordinates of the viewpoint are displayed on screen. Movement of the cursor along the X axis of the bull's-eye causes the X and Z axes to rotate about the Y axis. Movement of the cursor along the Y axis of the bull's-eye causes the Y and Z axes to rotate about the X axis. Using the bull's-eye to create new views can be a tricky method at first. Some time should be spent with a simple object like Figure 11.6 to learn how to change viewpoints.

Using the Vpoint Axis Option to Create New Viewpoints: Exercise 11.3

1. Open **LAB11-1** from your data disk.
2. Select View/Set View/Viewpoint/Axes from the Pull-down Menus or enter **VPOINT** at the command prompt then Return.
3. Using Figure 11.10 as a guide practide using the Axes option to create new viewpoints. Use the **HIDE** command to verify the viewpoints.

The Vpoint Rotate Option

The **ROTATE** option creates a new view by entering an angle in the X-Y plane and angle from the X-Y plane to create a new sight vector through the origin.

For example, to use the **ROTATE** option to change the line of sight from the top view, enter **VPOINT** at the command prompt. Figure 11.11.

A prompt is displayed: **Rotate/<View point> (0,0,1):**
Enter **R** to select the rotate option.
A prompt is displayed: **Enter the angle in the X-Y plane from the X-axis (270):**
Enter an angle of **-30** degrees to create a view that will show a front exposure of the block.
A prompt is displayed: **Enter angle from the X-Y plane (90):**

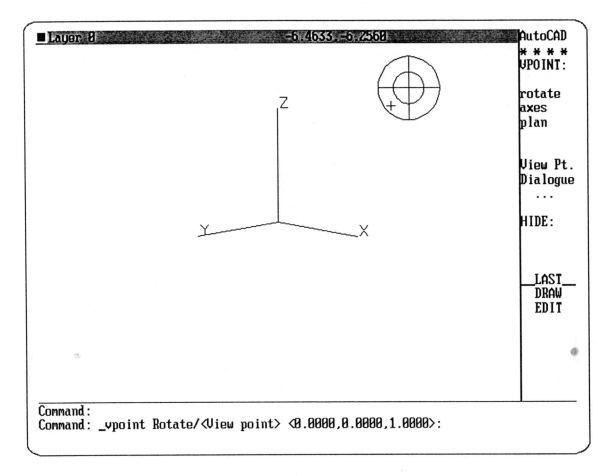

Figure 11.9 The axes and target.

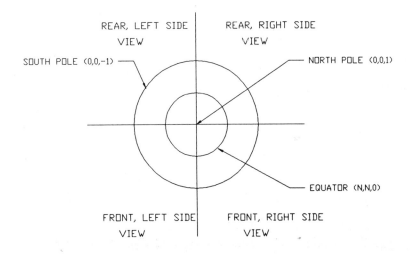

Figure 11.10 The bull's-eye showing the view created at various locations.

Enter an angle of **30** degrees to create a view from above the object. Figure 11.11.

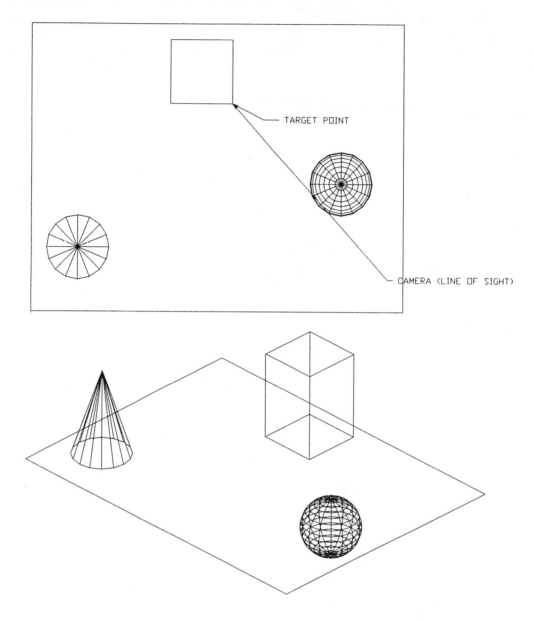

TARGET POINT

CAMERA (LINE OF SIGHT)

Figure 11.11 The relationship between the target and viewpoint and the resulting view.

Using the Vpoint Rotate Option to Create New Viewpoints: Exercise 11.4

1. Open **LAB11-1** from your data disk.
2. Select View/Set View/Viewpoint/Set Viewpoint from the pull-down menus or enter **VPOINT** at the command prompt then R.
3. Practide using the Rotate option to create new viewpoints.   Use the **HIDE** command to verify the viewpoints.

DYNAMIC VIEW (DVIEW)

VPOINT is a static method of creating a new viewing position relative to the object. **DVIEW** is another method of viewing an object by dynamically moving the object (target) or the viewpoint (camera). By controlling the camera position relative to the target, it is possible to define virtually any line of sight vector. Figure 11.11 shows the relationship between the the target and viewpoint, as defined by AutoCAD. In the figure, the target point is 4 units above the ground and the camera is 10 units above the ground and 150 units from the target. AutoCAD always uses a camera and target relationship to determine the current view. The camera represents the position of the viewer, and the target is the point at which the camera is aimed.

With **DVIEW** it is possible to develop the parallel projections necessary to create orthographic views, such as the six principal views, and any number of auxiliary views. It is also possible to create any number of axonometric views of 3D models, as it is with the **VPOINT** command. **DVIEW** allows the creation of perspective views, as shown in Figure 11.12.

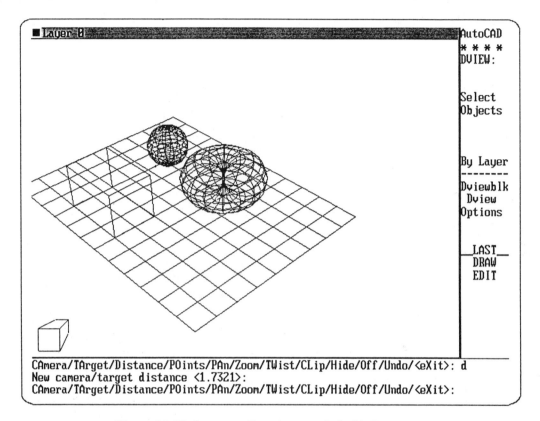

Figure 11.12 A perspective view created with Dview.

Views are created with the **DVIEW** command by moving the camera, target, or both relative to the 3D model. After the line of sight is created, the camera can be moved in or out or the camera lens can be changed to adjust the field of view. It is also possible to create cutting planes through the model by locating back or front clipping planes.

The **DVIEW** command is activated by entering **DVIEW** at the command prompt, selecting View/Set View/ Dview from the Pull-down Menus, or by selecting it from the tablet or the first page of the **DISPLAY** screen menu option listed on the Root Menu. After the command is entered, a prompt reads:

Select objects:

Objects are selected using any of the traditional methods, such as single and window. Only choose enough entities to visualize the object adequately as it is dynamically moved on the screen. Choosing too many entities will slow view redraw time. Entering RETURN at the select objects prompt will cause a block named **DVIEWBLOCK** to be displayed. The AutoCAD default block is a wireframe 3D model of a house, as shown in Figure 11.13. The block is displayed in the same orientation as your drawing and can be used to change the view dynamically. The DVIEWBLOCK house will be replaced by your drawing in the new view when **DVIEW** is exited. It is possible to create your own VIEWBLOCK using the **BLOCK** command.

After the objects are selected or the DVIEWBLOCK is displayed, a prompt is displayed.

CAmeraT Arget/Distance/POin ts/PAn/Zoom/TWist/CLip/Hi de/Off/Und o/<eXit>:

This prompt lists the **DVIEW** options available. An option is selected by entering it at the prompt.

CAMERA Dynamic View

The **CAMERA** option is used to create new views by rotating the camera around the target position. The camera is rotated by moving the cursor or entering the angle of the camera up or down relative to the XY plane. The second variable is the left to right angle of rotation of the camera relative to the X axis.

DISTANCE Dynamic View

This option is used to move the camera position in or out along the line of sight relative to the object or target. Using this option turns the perspective option on and allows absolute distances to be entered from the camera to the object (target). After the distance is entered, the perspective icon is displayed in the lower left corner of the screen (Figure 11.12). Distances are entered from the keyboard or the slider bar is used to set a new distance from zero to 16 times its current length.

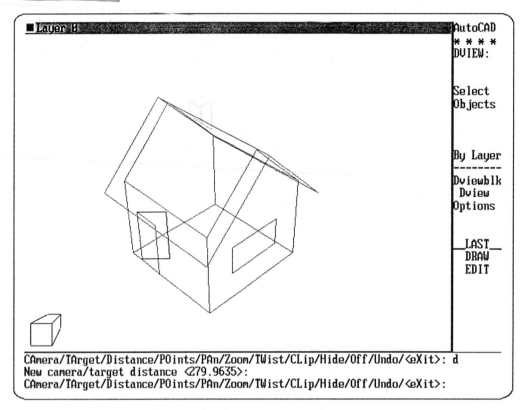

Figure 11.13 The **DVIEWBLOCK** of a house.

ZOOM Dynamic View

The **ZOOM** option can work in two different ways, depending on whether the perspective view has been turned on using the **DISTANCE** option. If the perspective view is on, **ZOOM** is used to change the field of view, similar to changing lenses on a 35 mm camera. The default lens is 50 mm. Values less than 50 mm, such as 35, create a wide field of view and values greater then 50mm, such as 75, create a narrow field of view and make the object larger.

If the perspective option is not turned on, the **ZOOM** option works nearly the same way as the **ZOOM CENTER** command. Entering values larger than 1 zooms in on the object, and entering values smaller than 1 zooms out from the object. The slider bar can be used to display the new zoom factor dynamically. The new zoom factor is displayed in the status line.

PAN Dynamic View

The **PAN** option is used to change the position of the object in the active window by picking or entering two points. Coordinate entry from the keyboard works only if the perspective is off.

POINTS Dynamic View

POINTS is used to change the position of the camera and the target point. Values for the camera and the target position can be entered from the keyboard or by selecting points with the **OSNAP** options. The target point is entered first; then a rubber-band line is stretched to the cursor location for defining a new line of sight.

TWIST Dynamic View

TWIST is used to twist or rotate the current view around the line of sight. Values are entered from the keyboard, with zero located at 3:00 on the face of a clock and angles measured counter-clockwise. The twist angle also is defined by picking a point on the screen. A rubberband line stretches from the center of the view to the current cursor position. As the cursor is moved, the view dynamically twists on the screen.

CLIP Dynamic View

The **CLIP** option is used to position invisible front and back cutting planes on a view. Entities located behind the back clipping plane are removed by AutoCAD, and entities in front of the front clipping plane are removed (Figure 11.14). One or both clipping planes can be used in a view. The planes are positioned by using the sliding bars or entering a distance from the current target position.

The current distance is displayed in the prompt, and the slide bar is shown in the viewport. Sliding the bar to the left dynamically moves the clip plane toward the camera or viewer. Moving the slide bar to the right moves the clip plane farther from the camera. A positive distance places the clip plane between the target and the camera. A negative number places the clip plane behind the target. The clip plane also is turned on by entering the current distance value displayed in the prompt.

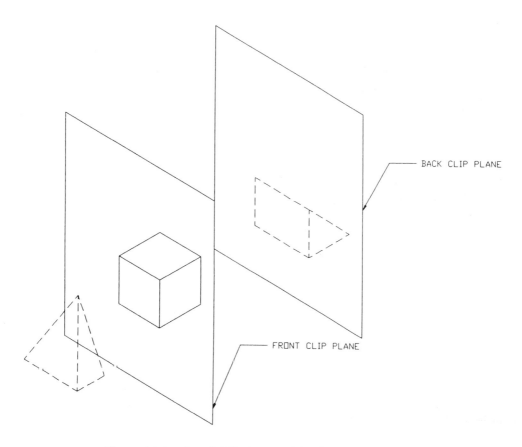

Figure 11.14 AutoCAD's front and back clipping planes.

Using the Dview Command to Create New Viewpoints: Exercise 11.5

1. Open **LAB11-1** from your data disk.
2. Select View/Set View/Dview from the pull-down menus or enter **Dview** at the command prompt.
3. Practide using the Dview options to create new viewpoints. Use the **HIDE** command to verify the viewpoints.

THE USER COORDINATE SYSTEM (UCS)

AutoCAD developed a special method of moving around in 3D space to facilitate drawing. This system is called the User Coordinate System (UCS) and is the method to orient a coordinate system anywhere in 3D space. Drawing in 3D space presents some problems for users of CADD. There are times when it is easier to define a point in 3D space by picking a point or drawing on an oblique surface rather than trying to determine its X, Y, and Z coordinates.

In 2D drawing, the X and Y axes form a plane called the plan view in AutoCAD. The plan view is called the World Coordinate System. To assist in drawing 3D models, use the UCS to define a new plan view. This temporary, user-defined plan view simplifies drawing on surfaces that are not parallel with the plan view. A UCS can be given a name up to 31 characters so that it can be easily retrieved later. So a UCS can be created and viewed from all principal views and any auxiliary or isometric view. A UCS is necessary because most drawing aids are functional in the X-Y plane of a coordinate system.

The UCS can be thought of as a method of defining the current construction plane. The UCS or construction plane is the planar surface in space that can be defined by the user. Because the user has control of the position of the UCS, creating 3D models becomes easier. The principle of the UCS is simple: if the entity is hard to draw in 3D space, create a UCS to make drawing easier. Figure 11.15 shows how the UCS is positioned to facilitate the drawing of the part. To draw the hole in the inclined face, the UCS was placed so that its origin was on the corner of the surface. The X and Y axes were placed parallel to the edges of the surface so that the center point could be located by entering the coordinate distance from the UCS origin.

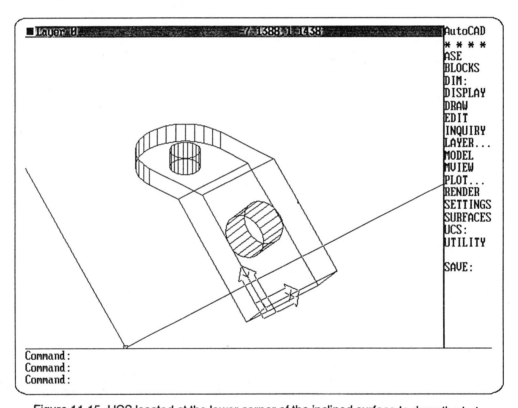

Figure 11.15 UCS located at the lower corner of the inclined surface to draw the hole.

The UCS Icon

AutoCAD provides an icon as a visual aid to determine the position of the UCS in relation to the model. The UCS icon normally is displayed in the lower left corner of the screen. It shows how the X, Y, and Z axes are oriented in 3D space and what the viewing direction is relative to the XY plane. The **UCSICON** command is used to control the display of the icon. Figure 11.16 shows how the UCS icon can be displayed, depending on its position in space.

The axes are labeled with letters. The X and Y letters represent the positive directions of the X and Y axes. If the letter W appears on the Y leg of the icon, the UCS is the same as the World Coordinate System. A plus (+) at the base means that the icon is located at the origin of the current UCS. A box is drawn at the base of the icon if one is viewing the UCS from above (positive Z axis). No box is shown at the base of the icon if one is viewing the UCS from below (negative Z axis). Figure 11.16 shows how the icon appears if one is viewing the current UCS or the X and Y axes on edge.

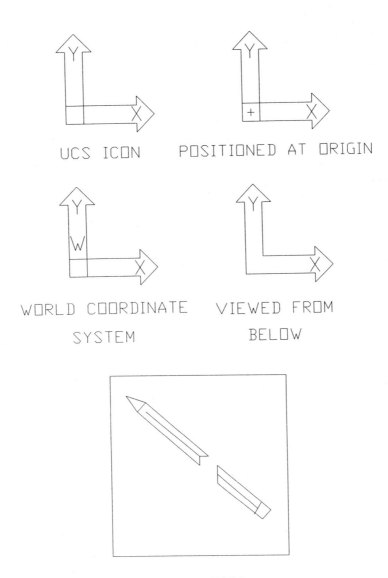

Figure 11.16 UCS icons.

The UCS icon is turned on or off by entering **UCSICON** at the command prompt. A prompt reads:

On/Off/All/Noorigin/ORigin/<ON>:

OFF turns the icon off and ON turns it on. The **ALL** option is used to make changes in all active viewports. The prompt is repeated to make changes in each viewport if desired. The **NOORIGIN** option displays the icon in the lower left corner of the viewport even if the UCS origin is located somewhere else. **NOORIGIN** is the default setting. **ORIGIN** forces the icon to be displayed at the origin of the current UCS. If the origin is not within the current display, it is shown in the lower left corner of the viewport.

The World Coordinate System

AutoCAD has defined its World Coordinate System (WCS) as X horizontal, Y vertical, and Z at right angles to X and Y (Figure 11.17). The origin is located at the intersection of the three axes. The default setting is for the X and Y axes to be parallel to the display screen which is the plan or top view. The pointing device can be used to pick X and Y points, but the Z point must be entered from the keyboard. AutoCAD will automatically assign the Z axis to the current elevation if the Z value is not entered from the keyboard. The elevation setting determines the current construction plane. The World Coordinate System is fixed, but the UCS can be changed within the WCS.

AutoCAD uses the standard right-hand rule to determine all coordinate systems and the direction of rotation. Figure 11.17. Figure 11.18 indicates the positive direction of angles for the coordinate systems used with AutoCAD.

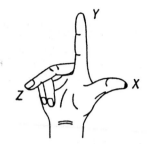

Figure 11.17 The right-hand rule for AutoCAD. (Courtesy of Autodesk, Inc.)

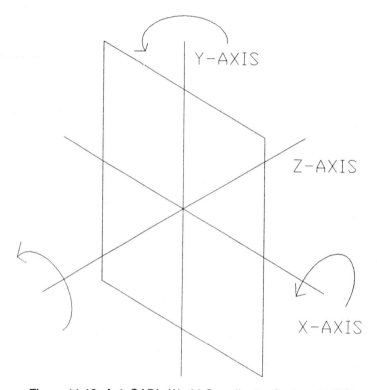

Figure 11.18 AutoCAD's World Coordinate System (WCS).

The UCS Command

Many different options are given to define a new UCS. To change the UCS setting, enter **UCS** at the command prompt, picking it from the Root Menu, or by picking the **Settings** option from the Pull-down Menu bar.

UCS Origin

The **ORIGIN** option is used to change the current UCS origin to a new position. After entering **UCS** at the command prompt, enter **O** from the prompt:

> **Origin/ZAxis/3point/Entity/View/X/Y/Z/Prev/Restore/Save/Del/?/<World>:**

After entering **O** a prompt reads:

> **Origin point <0,0,0>:**

The new origin point is specified by using any of the normal AutoCAD methods of specifying points. In Figure 11.19 the origin is moved from 0,0,0 to its new position by using Osnap Center then picking the circle.

UCS ZAxis

The **ZAxis** option is used to specify a new origin by changing the Z axis. The X and Y axes are determined automatically after the new Z axis is defined. This option is used to define a new extrusion direction. Use this command to create oblique surfaces and oblique extrusions. Enter **UCS** at the command prompt to display:

Origin /ZAxis/ 3poin t/Entity/View /X/Y /Z/Pre v/Restor e/Save/De l/?/<World >:

Enter **ZA** to change the Z axis.

Origin point <0,0,0>:

Define the new origin point or press RETURN to select the default.

Point on positive portion of the Z axis < >:

A rubberband line stretches from the origin. Pick a point or enter coordinates to define the positive Z axis.

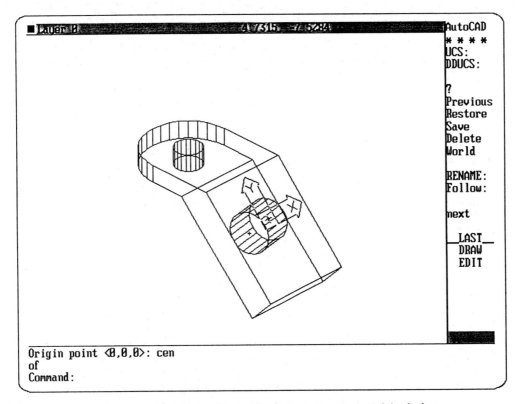

```
Origin point <0,0,0>: cen
of
Command:
```

Figure 11.19 Moving the UCS origin to the center of the hole.

UCS 3Point

The **3point** option is used to create a new UCS by picking three points. The first point selected is the location of the origin, the second point is the positive direction for the X axis , and the third point is the positive direction for the Y axis. This option is particularly useful when trying to align the UCS with a given surface. Coordinate points are used or points are picked with the cursor, using any of AutoCAD's OSNAP options.

At the command prompt enter **UCS**. A prompt reads:

Origin /ZAxis/ 3poin t/Entity/View /X/Y /Z/Pre v/Restor e/Save/De l/?/<World >:

Enter the number **3** for the **3point** option. Another prompt reads:

Origin point <0,0,0>:

Select the origin point with the cursor, enter numerical values, or enter RETURN to select the old origin. For this example enter **END** to use the OSNAP option **END OF**. Pick the corner of the object where the UCS origin is located as, shown in Figure 11.20.

Point on positive portion of X axis < >:

Enter a value or pick a point. For this example, enter **END** and pick the endpoint of the line that is to be parallel to the X axis.

Point on positive-Y portion of the UCS X-Y plane < >:

Enter a value or pick a point. For this example, enter **END** and pick the endpoint of the line that is to be parallel to the Y axis (Figure 11.20).

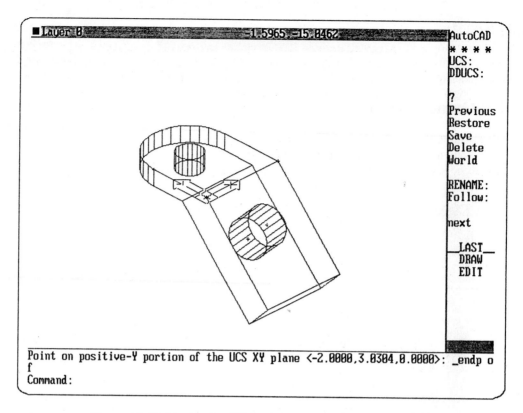

Figure 11.20 Moving the UCS origin to a corner using 3points.

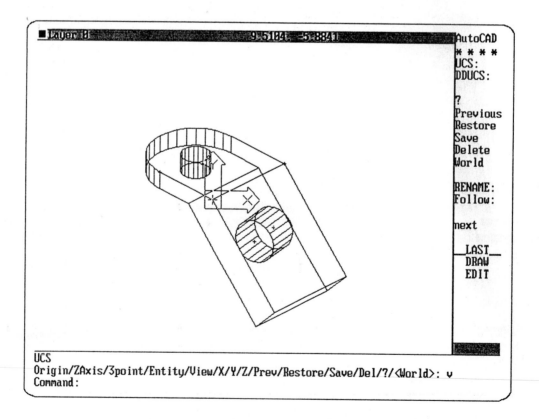

Figure 11.21 Moving the UCS origin parallel to the screen using the View option.

UCS Entity

The **ENTITY** option is used to define a new UCS by picking any entity except a polyline or polyline mesh. The extrusion direction will be the same as the selected entity. This option positions the X-Y axes of the UCS parallel to the selected entity. For arcs and circles, the center becomes the new origin and the X axis aligns itself with a point on the arc or circle closest to the pick point. For lines, the end closest to the pick point becomes the new origin and the second endpoint lies in the X-Z plane with a Y coordinate value of zero. Only object pointing is allowed with this option.

At the command prompt enter **UCS**. A prompt reads:

Origin /ZAxis/ 3poin t/Entity/View /X/Y /Z/Pre v/Restor e/Save/De l/?/<World >:

Enter **E** to select the **Entity** option.

Select object to align UCS:

UCS View

The **VIEW** option is used to move the UCS so that it is parallel to the screen in the current viewport. This option automatically places the X and Y axes parallel to the screen. This changes the current view to the plan view. One application of the **VIEW** option is to add text to pictorial drawings.

At the command prompt enter **UCS**. A prompt reads:

Origin /ZAxis/ 3poin t/Entity/View /X/Y /Z/Pre v/Restor e/Save/De l/?/<World >:

Enter **V** to select the **VIEW** option. The new UCS is located on screen at the old origin location, as shown in Figure 11.21.

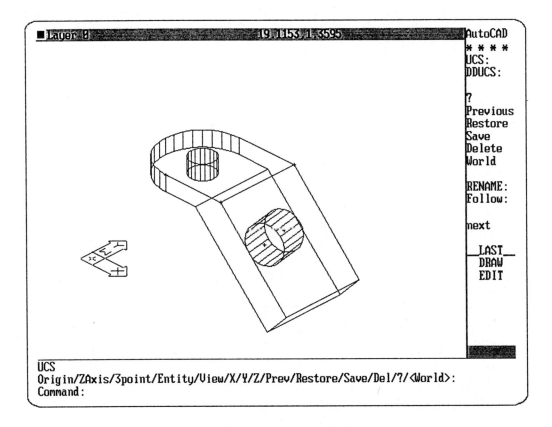

Figure 11.22 UCS at the world position.

UCS XYZ

The X, Y, or Z options are used to rotate the current UCS about one of the three axes. Either an angle is specified or a point is picked. The right-hand rule angle convention is used with this option. Figure 11.22 shows the UCS at the WORLD setting.

At the command prompt enter **UCS**. A prompt reads:

Origin /ZAxis/ 3poin t/Entity/View /X/Y/Z/Pre v/Restor e/Save/De l/?/<World >:

Enter one of the three axes, such as X.

Rotation angle about X axis <0,0>:

Pick two points to define an angle or enter a numerical value, such as **90**. The new UCS is displayed on screen, as shown in Figure 11.23.

Changing the Y and Z axes requires the same steps. Figure 11.24 shows the axes after the Y axis is rotated 90 degrees. Figure 11.25 shows the axes after the Z axis is rotated 90 degrees.

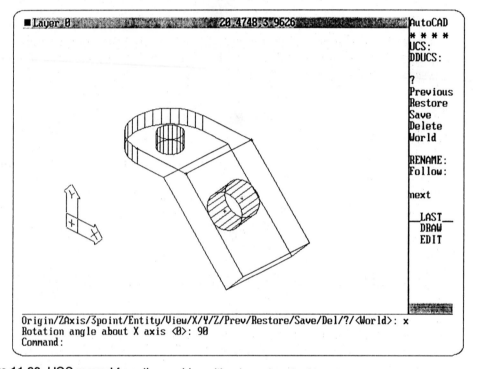

Figure 11.23 UCS moved from the world position by using the **X** option and an angle of 90 degrees.

UCS Previous, Restore, Save, and Delete

The **Previous** option is used to redisplay the previous UCS positions. It is similar in operation to the **Zoom Previous** option. Entering **P** at the UCS prompt:

Origin /ZAxis/ 3poin t/Entity/View /X/Y /Z/Pre v/Restor e/Save/De l/?/<World >:

will automatically display the previous UCS position. Up to 10 UCS positions can be recalled by repeatedly selecting the **Previous** option.

The **Save** option is used to name and save the location of the current UCS. The name used can be up to 31 characters. The **Restore** option is used to display a UCS that was saved using the **Save** option. When the **Restore** option is selected a prompt reads:

?/Name of UCS to restore:

Enter a question mark to list the names of the saved UCS's or enter the name at the prompt.

The **Delete** option is used to delete from memory a saved UCS. When this option is selected, a prompt reads:

Name of coordinate system(s) to delete:

Enter the name or use DOS wild card characters, such as ? and *.

Entering a **?** at the UCS prompt displays the name of the current UCS and the name, origin position, and XYZ axes for all saved coordinate systems. If the current coordinate system is not named, it is listed as "world" or "no name."

The **World** option is used to set the current UCS to the World Coordinate System.

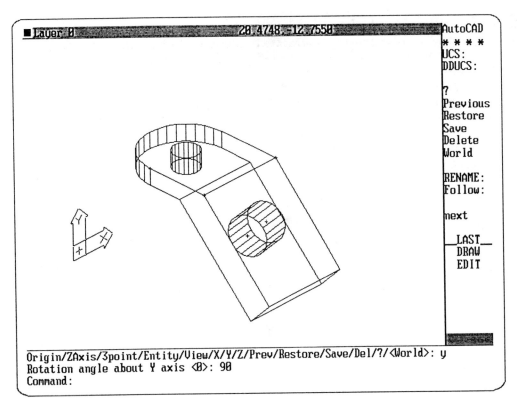

```
Origin/ZAxis/3point/Entity/View/X/Y/Z/Prev/Restore/Save/Del/?/<World>: y
Rotation angle about Y axis <0>: 90
Command:
```

Figure 11.24 Y axis rotated 90 degrees.

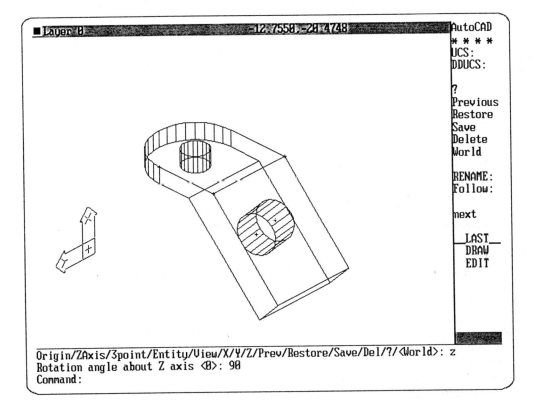

```
Origin/ZAxis/3point/Entity/View/X/Y/Z/Prev/Restore/Save/Del/?/<World>: z
Rotation angle about Z axis <0>: 90
Command:
```

Figure 11.25 Z axis rotated 90 degrees.

The UCS Pull-down Menus

The UCS Pull-down Menus are used to assist in the management of the UCS commands and contains all of its functions. Figure 11.26. The named UCS dialogue box is used to name or select a named UCS. Figure 11.27. This dialogue box lists the names of each UCS that was saved and is used to define a new current UCS. The World Coordinate System is always the first entry in the list. If the current UCS is not named, *NO NAME* is displayed.

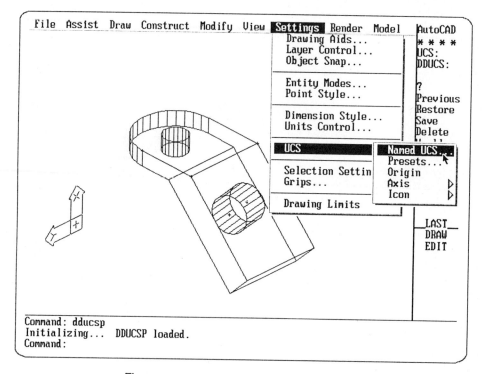

Figure 11.26 The **UCS** Pull-down Menu.

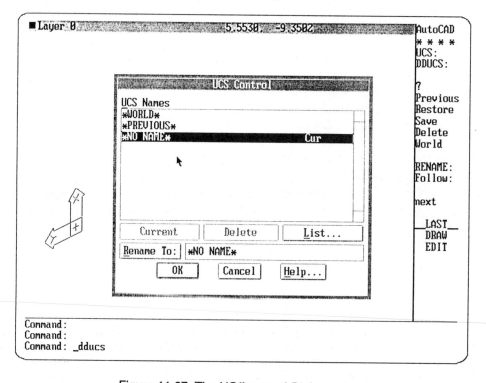

Figure 11.27 The UCS named Dialogue box.

Click on the Current field to change the current UCS. The list button displays the coordinate system's origin and the direction of its X, Y, and Z axes relative to the user coordinates. Pick the delete button to delete a UCS entry. UCS names or renames are entered in the coordinate system's field by pointing at it.

Picking UCS Presets from the Settings Pull-down Menu displays the Dialogue Box in Figure 11.28. This menu is used to change the current UCS to World, Screen, or one of the six principal orthographic views. The orthographic views are defined relative to the current UCS or absolute with the WCS.

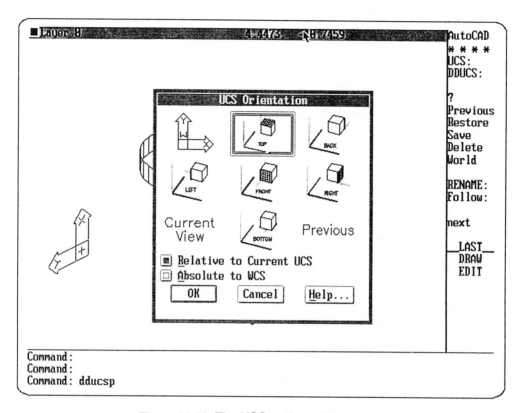

Figure 11.28 The UCS settings dialogue box.

Using the Vpoint Axis Option to Create New Viewpoints: Exercise 11.6
1. Open **LAB11-2** from your data disk.
2. Enter **UCS** at the command prompt.
3. Practice changing the UCS using each of the options. Use the **HIDE** command to verify the viewpoints.

Using Viewports to Create Standard Orthographic Views

Most engineers and designers are accustomed to viewing a model in the standard orthographic view arrangement of front view below the top view and in alignment and the right side view to the right of the front view and in alignment. Although users of AutoCAD can use any method they feel comfortable with when creating a 3D model, arranging the views in the standard way is more appropriate when following accepted engineering drawing standards. Once these views are created they can be made into **BLOCKS** and inserted into a drawing border to create standard orthographic views from a 3D model. The **BLOCKS** are exploded and dimensions added to create a detail drawing. Further editing of the views is necessary to avoid large files caused by duplication of entities, poor output to the plotter, and editing of hidden lines.

Figure 11.29 shows the plan view of a 3D model. Other views of the model are simultaneously viewed using the **VIEWPORTS** command. The four-viewport option is a good choice when creating a 3D model. Three of the viewports could be used to display the standard front, top, and profile orthographic views. The fourth view could be used to display an axonometric view. To create this type of viewing arrangement, select the four-viewport option after entering **VIEWPORTS** at the command prompt. The 3D model is displayed in the viewports as shown in Figure 11.30. All the viewports are set to the plan view and must be changed using the **DVIEW** command. The following steps describe how to create a front, top, right side, and isometric view of the model:

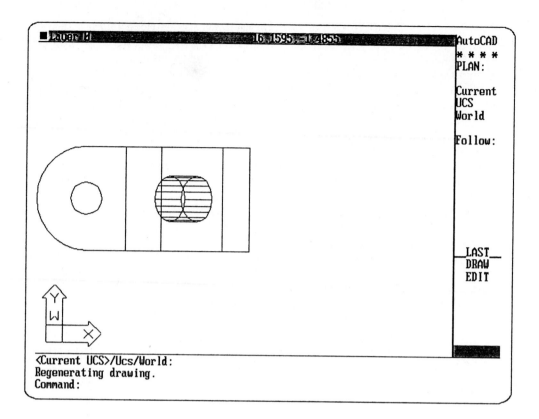

Figure 11.29 The plan view of the part.

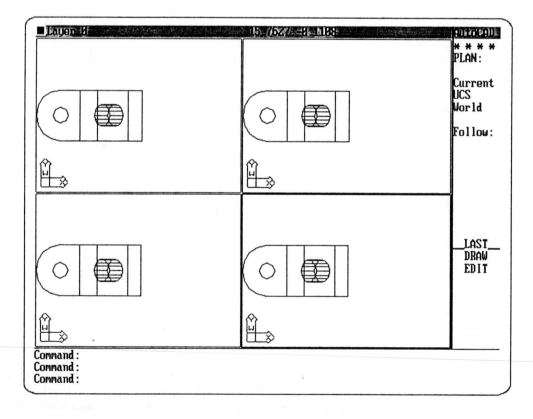

Figure 11.30 The 4 equal tiled viewports.

Creating Aligned Orthographic Views: Exercise 11.7

1. Open **LAB11-3** from your data disk. Pick View/Layout/Tiled Vports... from the Pull-down Menus.
2. Pick the 4 equal layout from the dialogue box.
3. After the four-viewport option is displayed, activate the lower right viewport by moving the cursor into it and pressing the pick button on the input device. The arrow cursor changes to a crosshairs. The lower right viewport will be the location of the right side view.
4. Enter **VPOINT** at the command prompt.
5. Enter **1,0,0** to display the right side view.
6. Move the cursor to the lower-left viewport and activate it by picking it.
7. Enter **RETURN** to repeat the **VPOINT** command.
8. Enter **0,-1,0** to display the front view.
9. Pick the upper-right viewport to activate it.
10. Enter **RETURN** to repeat the **VPOINT** command.
11. Enter **1,-1,1** to create an axonometric view.
12. Figure 11.31 shows the view in each viewport. The views should be reduced in size by using the **ZOOM** command. Enter **ZOOM** at the command prompt. Enter **1** to display a smaller view of the axonometric view.
14. Pick each viewport to activate it and repeat the **ZOOM** command to approximately align all the views as shown in Figure 11.32.

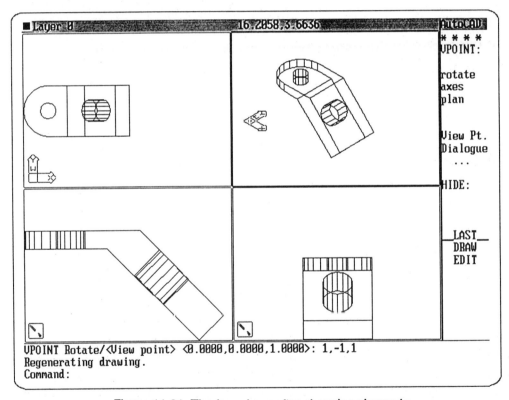

Figure 11.31 The four views after changing viewports.

CREATING 3D WIREFRAME MODELS BY EXTRUSION

The extrusion method is a quick means of creating parts with thickness. Always try to use Pline construction for your base geometry so that it can be used with the Advanced Modeling Extension (AME) described in Chapter 12. The Settings command **ELEVATION** is used to set the extrusion thickness of a part before it is drawn. Setting an extrusion thickness draws entities with a Z value. It is important that the current elevation and thickness be known when creating wireframe models to prevent errors. The **STATUS** command can display the current settings. The **LIST** command determines the elevation and thickness of displayed entities. The following steps describe how to use the extrusion method to create a simple drawing:

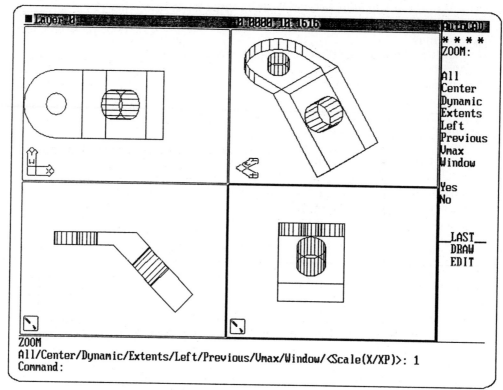

Figure 11.32 Orthographic views and pictorials.

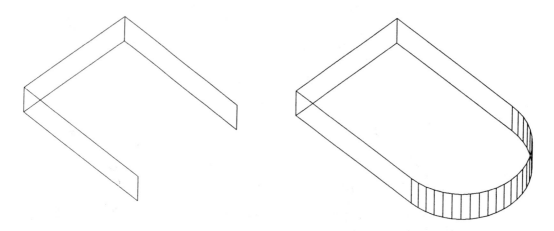

Figure 11.33 Drawing lines with a thickness.   Figure 11.34 An arc added with a thickness of .75.

Creating a Model Using Extrusion: Exercise 11.8

1. Start a new drawing with the plan view; set the snap to .5, grid ON, and coordinate display ON.
2. From the SETTINGS side menu select **ELEVATION.**
3. **New current elevation <.0000>:**
Leave the elevation at zero by entering RETURN so that the bottom of the part is resting at zero on the Z plane.
4. **New current thickness <.0000>:**
Enter the thickness of the part, **.75**, and RETURN.

5. Draw three sides of the part by picking the corners located on grid points using the **PLINE** command. As each line is created, the 3D thickness is added automatically to the drawing.

6. To view the 3 sides of the part select **VPOINT** from the DISPLAY Menu and enter the values **1,-1,1** for an isometric view. Figure 11.33 shows the three lines drawn with a thickness of .75.

7. An **ARC** is added to the open end of the part using **S,C,E** and picking the ends of the lines and the center of the arc. An arc with a number of elements is drawn on the end of the lines as shown in Figure 11.34.

8. Two cylinders are extruded from the completed base by changing the elevation and thickness with the **ELEVATION** command.

9. **New current elevation .0000:**

Set the elevation to the top surface of the base by entering **.75** and RETURN.

10. **New current thickness .7500:**

Enter the thickness or height of the cylinders, **2**, and RETURN.

11. Use the **CIRCLE** command to draw a cylinder equal in radius to the arc on the base. Pick the center point of the circle to be the same as the arc.

12. Add a negative cylinder (hole) with the **CIRCLE** command. Enter a radius value that is less than the arc and pick the same center point. Figure 11.35 shows the completed part.

13. AutoCAD provides a method of automatically removing hidden lines from a 3D model by entering **HIDE** at the Command prompt. The following prompt is displayed while the hidden lines are being removed from the drawing:

Regenerating drawing

Hidden lines: done 100%

AutoCAD will display these prompts while it determines which lines are hidden and removes them from the current view. After the calculations have been completed, the 3D model is displayed with hidden lines removed. Figure 11.36.

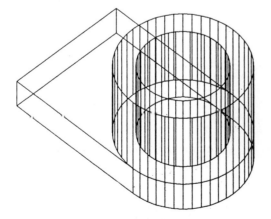

Figure 11.35 Positive and negative cylinders added to the model.

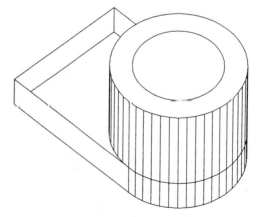

Figure 11.36 Model after HIDE is executed.

A shaded view of the model can be created by selecting **SHADE** from the Render Menu or by entering **SHADE** at the command prompt. The default **SHADE** setting will display the model as shown in Figure 11.37.

EDITING THE MODEL

As mentioned earlier most AutoCAD commands will work with 3D drawings. To erase an extruded entity, use the **ERASE** command and pick the entity. If the entity was extruded, all the entities of the extrusion are erased. For example, picking a point on the large circle erases the circle and all of its elements.

AUTOMATIC HIDDEN LINE REMOVAL OF 3D MODELS

Most CADD software programs provide a method of automatically removing hidden lines from a 3D wireframe model. The time needed to calculate hidden line removal will vary according to the complexity of the object and the computing power of the workstation.

The **HIDE** or **SHADE** option is used to automatically blank hidden entities on a drawing. Hidden lines are temporarily removed from the current viewport when **HIDE** is selected and redisplayed when the viewport is regenerated.

The **HIDE** option works successfully with objects that have been created with entities that represent solid surfaces, such as **3D FACES** or extruded **TRACES, SOLIDS,** or **POLYLINES. HIDE** considers solids as opaque surfaces and removes entities located behind these surfaces, as shown in Figure 11.36. **HIDE** will not remove hidden lines from objects made from lines.

To get a more accurate 3D model with hidden lines removed, the **3D FACE** command can be used to create the wireframe. The backs of the circles in Figure 11.36 have had all the lines removed even though some of the elements of the small negative cylinder should be seen. This can be avoided by drawing the circle as an **ARC**. Figure 11.38 shows two extruded cylinders. The one on the left was created with **CIRCLE,** and the one on the right was created with two 180 degree arcs with **ARC** command **S,C,E.** The **HIDE** command produced Figure 11.39, showing the different effect it has on circles and arcs.

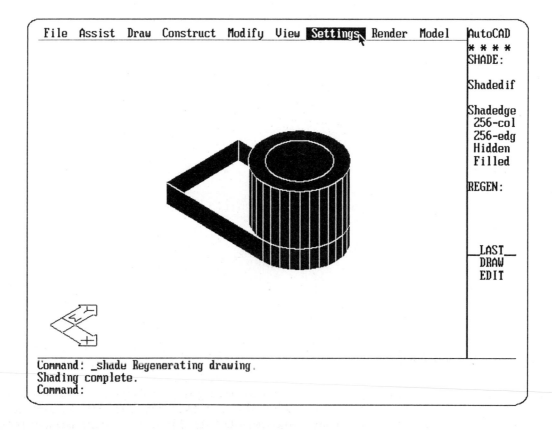

Figure 11.37 Model after shading.

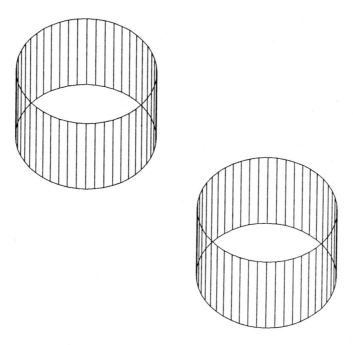

Figure 11.38 Two cylinders, one drawn on the left with **CIRCLE** and the other with **ARC**.

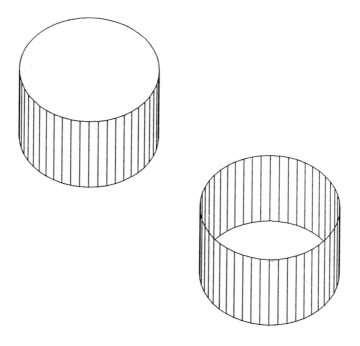

Figure 11.39 The different effect of **HIDE** on the two cylinders.

POINT-TO-POINT 3D WIREFRAME MODELS

The **LINE** command is used to create 3D wireframe models. Lines can be defined by picking points or entering X, Y, and Z coordinates. The following steps show how to create a triangular prism using the **LINE** command. This will create a model without any surface properties so the **HIDE** and **SHADE** commands will have no effect. In addition the wireframe model cannot be solidified to be used with AME. *This technique is not recommended for any purpose other than illustration or documentation.*

Creating a Wireframe Model Using Lines: Exercise: 11.9

1. Start a new drawing in the plan view and set the elevation and thickness to zero. Display the grid and enter **VPOINT** then the coordinates **1, -1, 1** to view your construction in isometric.

2. Select **LINE** to draw the base of the prism on the current elevation.

3. **From point:**
Enter **1,1** and RETURN.

4. **To point:**
Enter **4.5,1** and RETURN.

5. **To point:**
Enter **4.5,3** and RETURN.

6. **To point:**
Enter **1,3** and RETURN.

7. **To point:**
Enter **CLOSE** and RETURN. The rectangular base is created.

8. Enter RETURN to repeat the **LINE** command.

9. **From point:**
Enter **4.5,1,0** and RETURN or pick that coordinate point using **OSNAP** command **ENDPOI NT.**

10. **To point:**
Enter **4.5,3,3** and RETURN.

11. **To point:**
Enter **1,3,3** and RETURN.

12. **To point:**
Enter **1,1,0** and RETURN or pick that coordinate point.

13. Set **OSNAP** to **ENDPOINT** and select **LINE**. Figure 11.40 shows the model that has been created. Two more lines must be added to complete the prism.

14. Pick the endpoints of the oblique lines and the base points to complete the drawing, as shown in Figure 11.41.

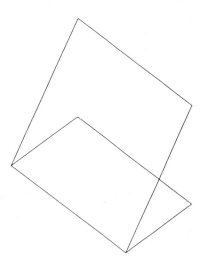
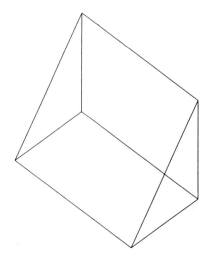

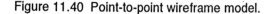

Figure 11.40 Point-to-point wireframe model.   Figure 11.41 Completed triangular prism.

Creating Flat and Approximate Curved 3D Surfaces

AutoCAD provides different methods to create flat and curved 3D surfaces. These surfaces are created with a mesh by defining the boundaries and the area inside the boundaries. Five commands are available to create meshed surf aces.

3DMESH is used to construct a general polygon mesh by defining the coordinate points of each vertex.
RULESURF creates a polygon mesh between two selected objects.
TABSURF creates a polygon mesh by moving a direction vector along a defined path.
REVSURF creates a polygon mesh by sweeping an object around a specified axis.
EDGESURF creates a Coons surface patch between four selected objects.

AutoCAD defines a flat or curved surface through a matrix of vertices called M and N. The M and N vertices are columns and rows of points defining each vertex. The system variable **SURFTAB1** controls the density of the mesh created with the **RULESURF** and **TABSURF** commands. The system variables **SURFTAB1** and **SURFTAB2** control the density of the mesh in the M and N directions.

The polygon mesh commands replace the **3DFACE** command for most situations where a surface is defined as one entity. These meshes are edited using the conventional commands used with other AutoCAD geometry. **HIDE** and **SHADE** options will work with 3D surfaces. Select Draw/3D Surfaces to pick one of the surfacing commands. Figure 11.42

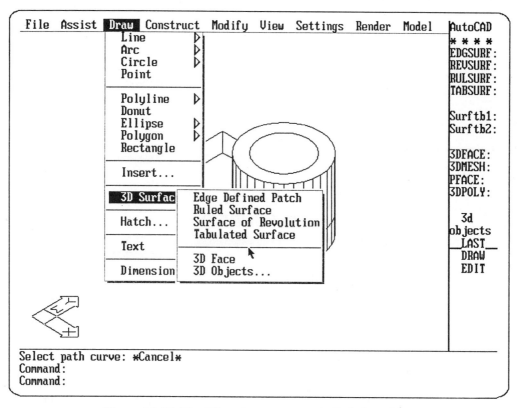

Figure 11.42 The 3D surface commands Pull-down Menus.

Creating a Surface Entering the Location of Vertices

Three-dimensional polygon surfaces or meshes are defined by using the **3DMESH** command. Each vertex in the mesh must be specified in the M and N directions. This is the manual method of creating surfaces primarily used for AutoLISP applications. The other surface commands are less tedious to use and are recommended. To use the **3DMESH** option follow these steps:

Creating a Meshed Surface: Exercise 11.10

1. Start a new drawing then enter **3DMESH** at the command prompt.
2. **Mesh M size:**
Enter the number of columns for the mesh, for this example enter **3**.
3. **Mesh N size:**
Enter the number of rows for the mesh, for this example enter **4**. The M and N values determine the number of vertices in the mesh, for this example 12 (3 x 4). AutoCAD will

prompt for each vertex. Enter the X, Y, and/or Z coordinate location for each vertex. The following values will create the mesh shown in Figure 11.43.

Vertex (0,0): Enter **1,1,0**.
Vertex (0,1): Enter **1,2,1**.
Vertex (0,2): Enter **1,3,0**.
Vertex (0,3): Enter **1,4,-1** .
Vertex (1,0): Enter **2,1,1**.
Vertex (1,1): Enter **2,2,0**.
Vertex (1,2): Enter **2,3,3**.
Vertex (1,3): Enter **2,4.5,2** .
Vertex (2,0): Enter **3,1,0**.
Vertex (2,1): Enter **3,2,1**.
Vertex (2,2): Enter **3,3,0**.
Vertex (2,3): Enter **3,4,3**.

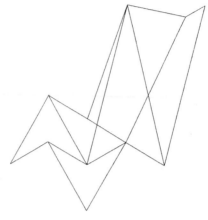

Figure 11.43 Mesh created by entering the locations of vertices.

Creating a Surface with the RULESURF Command

The **RULESURF** command is used to create a polygon mesh between two entities. Half of the vertices are equally spaced on one of the curves and the other half on the other curve. To change the number of vertices use the **SETVAR** option **SURFTAB1**. The following steps describe the **RULESURF** command:

Creating a Rulesurf Surface: Exercise 11.11

1. Open **LAB11-4** from your data disk then enter **RULESURF** at the command prompt or pick it from the Draw Pull-down Menu..
2. **Select first defining curve:**
Pick the first curve with the cursor.
3. **Select second defining curve:**
Pick the second curve with the cursor. Lines are drawn between the two curves, as shown in Figure 11.44.

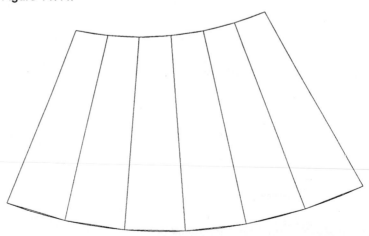

Figure 11.44 Surface created between two curves with the **RULESURF** command.

Notice that each selected entity has been divided into an equal number of parts and a line drawn to the same corresponding point on the other entity. AutoCAD starts the ruled surface from the endpoint of each curve nearest the point used to select the entity. Figure 11.45 shows what happens if the points chosen are not closest to the same endpoints.

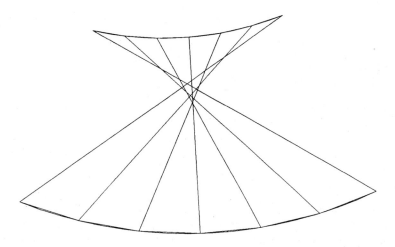

Figure 11.45 Result of picking points along the defining curves that are not closest to the same endpoints.

Changing the Number of Vertices of Polygon Meshes

The number of vertices for a polygon mesh is controlled by the **SURFTAB1** and **SURFTAB2** options. To change the number of vertices enter **SETVAR** at the command prompt. Enter one of the options, such as **SURFTAB1**. A prompt reads: **New value for SURFTAB1 <6>:**. Enter the number of vertices desired. Figure 11.46 is a mesh created with the **RULESURF** command using 12 vertices instead of the default setting of six.

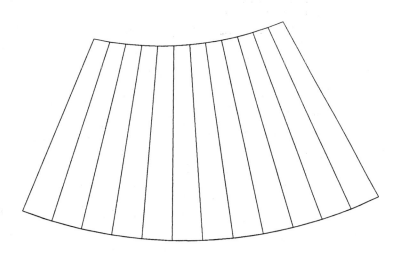

Figure 11.46 Result of changing the number of vertices with the **SURFTAB1** option.

Creating a Surface with the TABSURF Command

The **TABSURF** command creates a mesh by drawing lines from the selected entity in the direction and at the length of a specified vector. The length of the direction vector determines the length of the tabulated surface created. In plane geometry terms it is called the generatrix. The path that the mesh creates is called the path curve. In plane geometry terms it is called the directrix. The following steps describe the **TABSURF** command:

Creating a Tabsurf Surface: Exercise 11.12

1. Open **LAB11-5** from your data disk then enter **TABSURF** at the command prompt.
2. **Select path curve:**
Pick the entity of the path for the mesh.
3. **Select direction vector:**
Pick the entity that will define the length of the mesh. Figure 11.47 shows the mesh created using the selected path curve and direction vector.

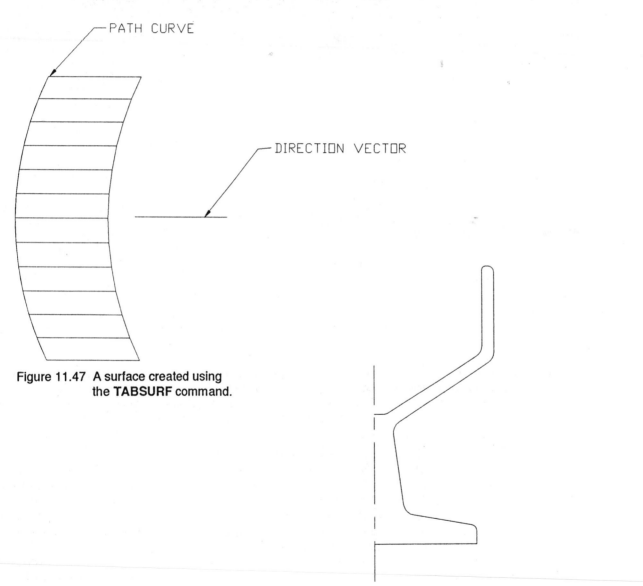

Figure 11.47 A surface created using the **TABSURF** command.

Figure 11.48 Polyline profile and axis of revolution.

Creating a Surface with the REVSURF Command

The **REVSURF** command is used to create a mesh by copying and revolving selected entities about a specified axis. The angle of the revolution is specified with an angle of 360 degrees, creating a complete revolution surface, as shown in Figure 11.49. The axis of revolution can be a line or polyline. The density of the mesh is controlled by **SURFTAB1** and **SURFTAB2**. The following steps describe how to create a revolved surface:

Creating a Revsurf Surface: Exercise 11.13

1. Open **LAB11-6** from your data disk then enter **REVSURF** at the command prompt.
2. **Select path curve:**
Pick the entity to be revolved, such as a line, arc, circle, or polyline. For this example, the polyline shown in Figure 11.48 is selected.
3. **Select axis of revolution:**
Pick the center line created for an axis.
4. **Start angle <>:**
Usually the start angle will be zero; however, the start point of the revolved surface could be offset to your specifications by entering an angle greater than zero.
5. **Included angle (+=ccw, -=cw) <Full circle>:**
Entering an angle of less than 360 degrees will create a revolved surface that does not close. Figure 11.49 is the result of using zero as a start point and full circle as the included angle.

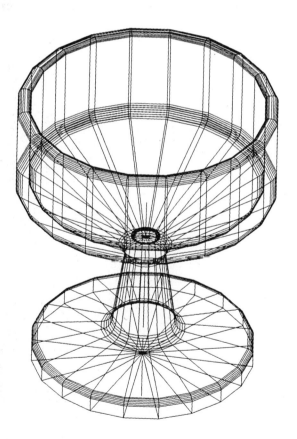

Figure 11.49 Surface created with the **REVSURF** command.

Creating a Coon's Surface

The **EDGESURF** command is used to create a Coon's surface by picking four intersecting edges. A Coon's surface or patch is a surface description technique used to define complex surfaces. The mathematical method for defining complex shapes was developed by Steve Coons and is used to prepare aircraft, automobile, and ship designs. This command is especially useful to create a smooth surface between spline curves. The first edge selected determines the M direction, and the two edges that intersect it are the N direction. **SURFTAB1** determines the number of M divisions and **SURFTAB2** determines the number of N divisions. The following steps demonstrate the use of the **EDGESURF** command to create a Coon's surface:

Creating a Coon's Surface: Exercise 11.14

1. Open **LAB11-7** from your data disk1. Enter **EDGESURF** at the command prompt.
2. **Select edge 1:**
Pick the first edge of the surface, the polyline shown in Figure 11.50. Lines, arcs, and polylines are the types of entities that can be defined for an edge surface.
3. **Select edge 2:**
Pick the second edge.
4. **Select edge 3:**
Pick the third edge.
5. **Select edge 4:**
Pick the fourth edge. After the fourth edge is selected, the Coon's surface is generated, as shown in Figure 11.51.

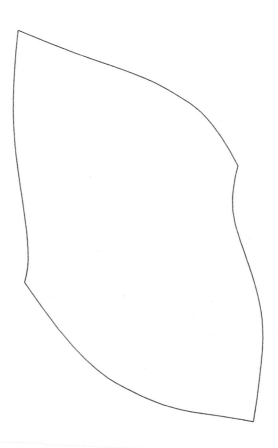

Figure 11.50 Polyline edges used to create a Coon's surface.

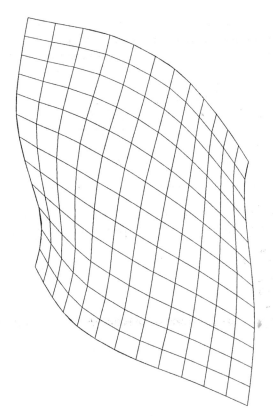

Figure 11.51 The Coon's surface created from the polylines.

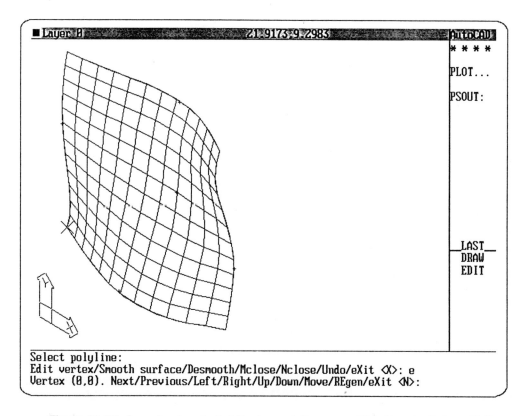

Figure 11.52 A marker located at the lower left corner of the Coon's surface (0,0).

Editing a 3D Polygon Mesh

Individual vertices of a polygon mesh can be edited by using the **PEDIT** command. The **EDIT** option is used to select the vertex to change. After the vertex is selected, a new location is defined by picking a point or entering new coordinate values. The following steps describe how to edit a mesh:

Editing a 3D Surface: Exercise 11.15

1. Enter **PEDIT** at the command prompt. Pick the 3D surface to be edited with the cursor.
2. **Editvertex/Smoothsurface/Desmooth/Mclose/Nclose/Undo/eXit <X>:**
    Enter **EDIT**. A marker is placed on vertex (0,0) (Figure 11.52). The marker can be moved to a new position by using one of the options listed in the prompt.
3. **Vertex(m,n).Next/Previous/Left/Right/Up/Down/Move/REgen/eXit <>:**
    Move the marker to the desired vertex using **Next, Previous, Left, Right, Up,** or **Down** option s.
4. After the marker is placed, enter **Move** to change the vertex.
5. **Enter new location:**
    Enter the new coordinate values or pick a new point (Figure 11.53).

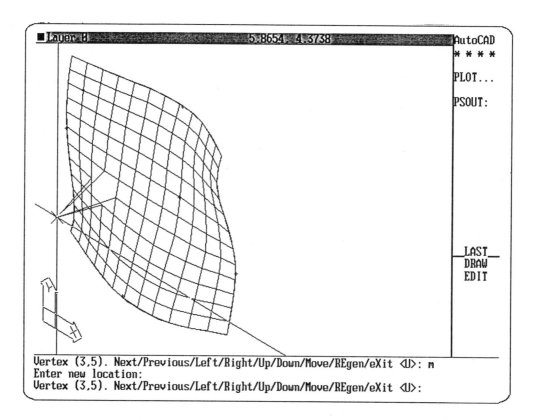

Figure 11.53 Result of using the **PEDIT** command to change the location of a vertex.

CREATING SURFACE MODELS WITH AutoCAD

A surface model of a part is different from a wireframe. The surface model defines the edges of a part, as does a wireframe, but it also defines the surface bounded by the wireframe. Surface models can be created by drawing the wireframe and then adding the surface, or by drawing the surface by defining its boundaries. Although AutoCAD cannot create surface models, **3D FACE** creates surfaces that are very similar to them. This will result in a more accurate automatic hidden line removal when using the **HIDE** or **SHADE** commands. After the surface model is created, it can be displayed with or without hidden lines.

3D FACE is similar to the 2D **SOLID** command, except that a Z dimension can be specified to form a plane in 3D space. In fact, each corner of the 3D face can have a different Z value to produce nonplanar objects. The prompt sequence is the same as for the **SOLID** command. However, points are entered in a clockwise or counterclockwise direction for a face instead of in the bow-tie order used with solid. Faces are displayed as wireframes and are never filled. They cannot be extruded but can be copied to a new depth or Z plane. Coplanar faces are considered opaque by the **HIDE** command. The following steps show how to create a simple rectangular solid prism using **3D FACE**:

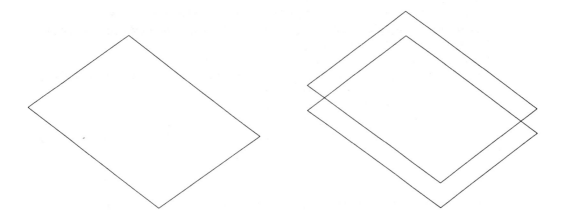

Figure 11.54 A **3D FACE** at elevation of zero.   Figure 11.55 The face copied to an elevation of .75.

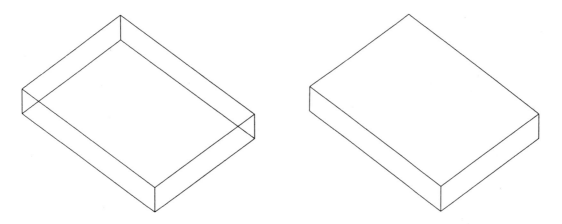

Figure 11.56 Faces added to the four perpendicular
sides of the prism.

Figure 11.57 Prism after **HIDE** is executed.

Creating a Surface Model: Exercise 11.16

1. Open a new drawing then set the elevation and thickness to zero with the **ELEVATION** command.
2. Select **3D FACE** from the second page of the Draw Menu or select Draw/3D Surfaces/ 3D Face from the pull-down menus.
3. **First point:**
Pick a point on screen or enter X, Y, Z coordinate values, such as 2,2,0.
4. **Second point:**
Pick a point or enter X, Y, Z coordinate values, such as 6,2,0.
5. **Third point:**
Pick a point or enter X, Y, Z coordinate values, such as 6,5,0.

6. **Fourth point:**
Pick the last point or enter coordinate values, such as 2,5,0. After the point is picked a line is drawn from point one to point four.

7. **Third point:**
Cancel the command by entering CTRL-C. Enter **VPOINT** at the command prompt and change the view direction to 1,-1,1, as shown in Figure 11.54.

8. Enter **COPY** at the command prompt to replicate the 3D face and place it .75 above the original face.

9. Pick one of the sides of the face. All the line entities of the face are highlighted.

10. Select one of the corners of the 3D face as the base point by using **OSNAP ENDOF.**

11. Enter **2,2,.75.** DISPLACEMENT HEIGHT

12. A new face is displayed on the screen, as shown in Figure 11.55.

13. Faces are added on the four perpendicular sides between the top and bottom faces. Set the **OSNAP** to **ENDPOINT**, use **3D FACE**, and pick the corners of the two faces. Figure 11.56 shows how the object appears after adding the perpendicular faces.

14. Use the **HIDE** command to remove hidden lines, as shown in Figure 11.57. Notice that all hidden lines have been removed without error. Using **3D FACES** results in more accurate automatic hidden line removal.

CREATING A 3D MODEL FROM A 2D DRAWING

It is possible to create a 3D model of a 2D drawing by using the **CHANGE** command. This is a variation of the extrusion method described earlier. Figure 11.58 is an example using the following steps:

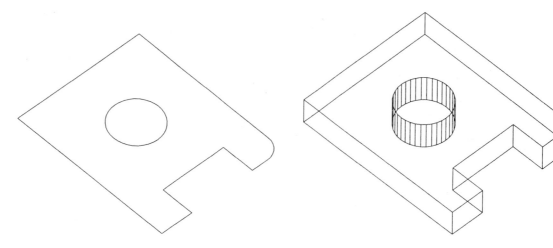

Figure 11.58 View to be used for a 3D model construction from a 2D drawing.

Figure 11.59 Using the **CHANGE** option to extrude the view into a 3D model.

Using Change to Create a 3D Model: Exercise 11.17

1. Open **LAB11-8** from your data disk.

2. Enter **CHANGE** at the command prompt.

3. The object selection prompt appears. Choose **WINDOW** and pick points that include all entities and enter RETURN.

3. At the properties prompt enter **PROPERTIES** or **P**, then **THICKNESS** or **T**.

4. **New thickness :**
Enter a thickness of **.75** and select the RETURN key twice. The object is extruded to a thickness of .75, as shown in Figure 11.59.

CREATING WIREFRAME MODELS FROM PRIMITIVES

Wireframe models can be created by defining basic geometric shapes, such as cones, cylinders, and pyramids. Primitive shapes are defined by specifying the basic dimensions of the shape. For example, to define a cylinder, the diameter of its base, height, and number of elements must be specified to create a circular cylinder. The bonus disk provided with AutoCAD software has a number of AutoLISP programs that can be used to create 3D wireframe models with primitives.

The 3D primitive shapes can be loaded through the Pull-down Menu command Draw/3D Surfaces/3D Objects.... The 3D objects dialogue box is displayed on screen as shown in Figure 11.60. These primitives cannot be used in AME.

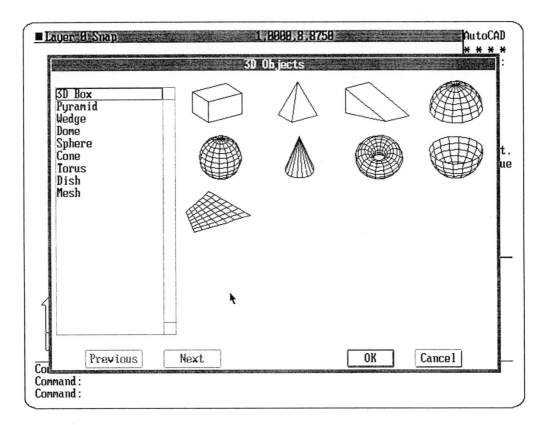

Figure 11.60 3D Objects Menu.

Creating a Cone

The following steps show how to create a wireframe model of a cone:

Creating a Cone: Exercise 11.18

1. Open a new drawing then select **CONE** from the Draw/3D Surfaces/3D Objects Menu or the Pull-down Menu.

2. **Base center point:**
Enter the center point of the base by picking a point or entering the X, Y, Z coordinates.

3. **Diameter/<radius> of base:**
Pick a point on the circumference of the base or enter the radius or diameter.

4. **Diamter/<radius> of top <0>:**
A truncated cone is created by giving a second radius or diameter that is smaller than the base diameter but greater than zero. The default setting is zero, which is entered by pressing RETURN.

5. **Height:**
Enter the height of the cone and RETURN.

6. **Number of segments <16>:**
The number of elements or segments needed to create the cone is input. The default setting of 16 is selected by entering RETURN. The cone is created and displayed on screen.

7. At the command prompt enter **VPOINT** to change to an isometric view.

8. Enter **1,-1,1.5** and RETURN to display the cone in Figure 11.61.

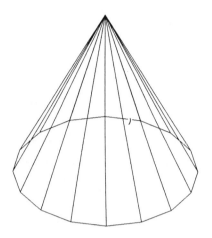

Figure 11.61 Wireframe model of a cone.

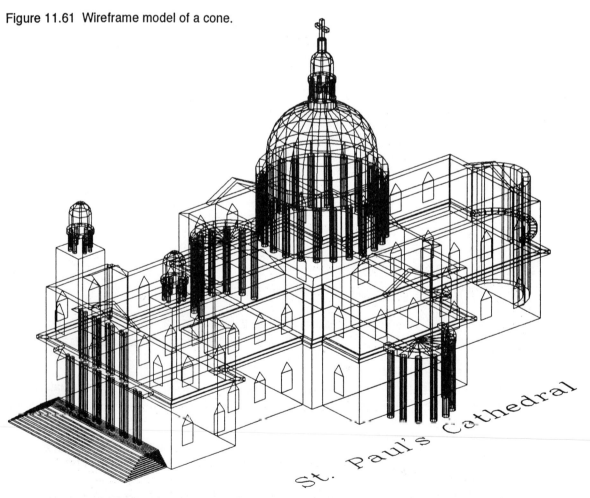

Figure 11.62 Domes used to create this drawing. (Courtesy of Autodesk, Inc).

Creating Spheres

The AutoCAD program includes a method of creating half-spheres. The bottom half of a sphere is called a **DISH**; the top half is called a **DOME**. Both can be combined to form a whole sphere or the **SPHERE** option can be used. St. Paul's Cathedral (Figure 11.62) is an example of the use for a half sphere. The following steps show how to create the bottom and top halves of a sphere:

Creating a Sphere: Exercise 11.19

1. Begin a new drawing then select **DISH** from the 3D Objects Menu.
2. **Center of dish:**
Pick the center point for the half-sphere.
3. **Diameter/<radius> of dish:**
Pick a point for the radius of the half-sphere.
4. **Number of logitudinal segments (8-24) (16):**
5. **Number of latitudinal segments (8):**
The number of segments determines the number of faces on the surface of the sphere. Sixteen is the default setting and is selected by entering RETURN. The half-sphere is displayed on screen. Use the **VPOINT** command and enter **1,-1,1.5** to display the sphere, as shown in Figure 11.63.

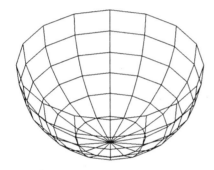

Figure 11.63 The bottom half of a sphere
is called a **DISH**.

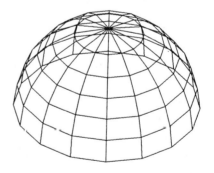

Figure 11.64 The top half of a sphere
is called a **DOME**.

A **DOME** is created with the same steps used for the **DISH** except that **DOME** is selected in step 1. Figure 11.64 shows a dome created and viewed from 1,-1,1. The AutoCAD command **SPHERE** creates a complete sphere. The prompt sequence shown here is used to create a sphere.

Center of sphere:
Diameter/(radius):
Number of longitudinal segments (16):
Number of latitudinal segments (16):

Figure 11.65 shows a sphere created and viewed from 1,-1,1.5. The **HIDE** command can be used with 3D primitive models just as it can with other 3D drawings created with AutoCAD. Figure 11.66 shows the sphere after the hidden lines are removed using the **HIDE** option.

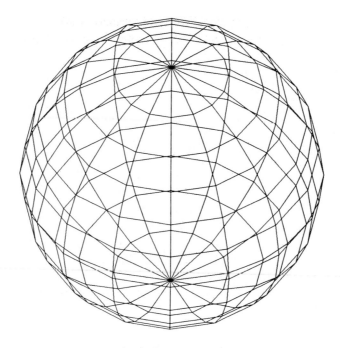

Figure 11.65 A wireframe model of a sphere.

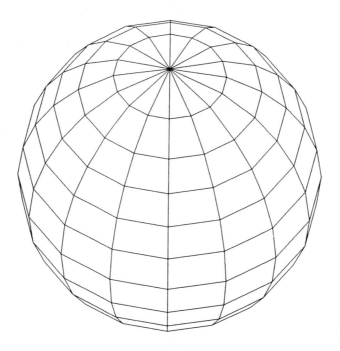

Figure 11.66 A sphere with hidden lines removed.

Creating a Torus

A torus is a solid formed by a circle or other geometric shape (hexagon) revolving around an axis that is eccentric to the circle or shape. The 3D Objects command **TORUS** creates a torus by specifying the radius or diameter of the torus, the radius or diameter of the geometric shape called a tube, the number of radial segments, and the number of tube segments. The following steps show how to create a torus:

Creating a Torus: Exercise 11.20

1. Start a new drawing then select **TORUS** from the 3D Objects Menu.
2. **Center of torus:**
Pick the location of the center point for the torus.
3. **Diameter/(radius) of torus:**
Enter the radius (3) or pick a point.
4. **Diameter/(radius) of tube:**
Enter the radius (1) or pick a point.
5. **Segments around tube circumference(16):**
Enter the number of segments (16) and RETURN.
6. **Segments around torus circumference(16):**
Enter the number of segments (16) and RETURN. Change the **VPOINT** to 1,-1,1. Figure 11.67 shows the torus produced using the values in parentheses.

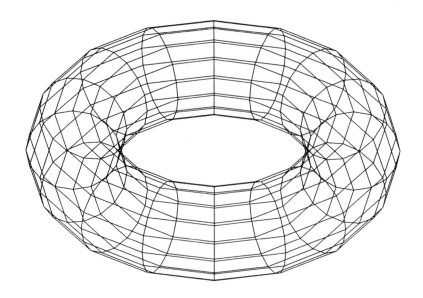

Figure 11.67 A torus.

Creating Pyramids

Right, truncated, and oblique pyramids can be produced with the **PYRAMID** command. The following steps show how to create an oblique pyramid:

Creating a Pyramid: Exercise 11.21

1. Start a new drawing then select **PYRAMID** from the 3D Objects Menu.
2. **First base point:**
Pick a point for the location of the first corner.
3. **Second base point:**
Pick a point for the location of the second corner.
4. **Third base point:**
Pick a point for the location of the third corner.
5. **Tetrahedron/<Fourth base point>:**
Pick a point for the location of the fourth corner or enter **T** to draw a tetrahedron.
6. **Ridge/Top/<Apex point>:**
Pick a point for the apex that is off-center from the base to create an oblique pyramid.
Change the **VPOINT** to 1,-1,1 Figure 11.68.

Creating Boxes

The **BOX** option is used to create rectangular prisms or cubes. Boxes are defined by entering the length, width, and height dimensions. Only the length dimension is necessary to create a cube. The following steps describe how to create a rectangular box:

Creating a Box: Exercise 11.22

1. Start a new drawing then select **BOX** from the 3D Objects Menu or from the Pull-down Menu.
2. **Corner of box:**
Pick a point to locate the corner of the box.
3. **Length:**
Enter the desired length from the keyboard or by picking a point.
4. **Cube/<width>:**
Enter **C** to create a cube or pick a point or enter coordinates to define the width of a rectangular box.
5. **Height:**
Enter the height of the rectangular box.
6. **Rotation about Z axis:**
This step allows for a rotation angle if desired. Enter zero for no rotation, and then change the **VPOINT** to 1, -1, 1 to view it as shown in Figure 11.69

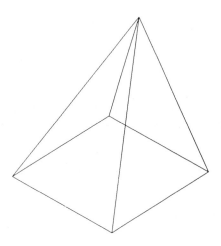

Figure 11.68 A pyramid.

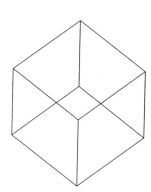

Figure 11.69 A box.

Creating a Wedge

A **WEDGE** is a primitive 3D geometric object that is defined by entering length, width, and height dimensions. A **WEDGE** is a box cut diagonally across its width. The following steps describe how to create a **WEDGE**:

Creating a Wedge: Exercise 11.23

1. Select **WEDGE** from the 3D Objects Menu or from the Pull- down Menu.
2. **Corner of wedge:**
Pick the starting point of the wedge or enter coordinate values.
3. **Length:**
Enter the length of the wedge.
4. **Width:**
Enter the width of the wedge.
5. **Height:**

Enter the height of the wedge.
6. **Rotation about Z axis:**
This step allows for a rotation angle if desired. Enter zero for no rotation, and then change
the **VPOINT** to 1, -1, 1 to view it as shown in Figure 11.70.

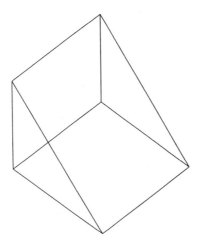

Figure 11.70 A wedge.

PLOTTING 3D MODELS

The plotting and printing options work in the same way for 3D models except for plot rotations and hidden lines.
3D models cannot be rotated when printed or plotted. Hidden lines can be removed before plotting by entering **YES**
at the hidden lines prompt. Removal of hidden lines from plots will take time, just as it does when using the **HIDE**
command in the drawing editor.

CREATING ORTHOGRAPHIC VIEWS FROM 3D WIREFRAME DRAWINGS

As computer hardware and CADD software programs become more advanced, they will be used more often
for the design of a product from the very early stages in the design process. Three dimensional models of the design
are created on the CADD system.

After the design is finalized, it must be documented through orthographic drawings. Figure 11.71 shows a three-
view drawing created from a 3D model. The front view is created by using the plan view of the 3D model and
inserting it into a blank drawing sheet. The top and front views are added, along with dimensions, to create a detail
drawing of the 3D model (Figure 11.72).

BLOCKS can be made of each view of the 3D model and inserted in the desired orientation on a drawing border.
The **BLOCKS** for the orthographic views can be created after using the Viewports to create the standard views, as
described earlier. The block is then exploded and dimensions are added to create the detail drawings. However,
this method will cause large files from duplicated entities, poor output for plotting, and editing for hidden lines.

With Release 12 is an AutoLISP program called **PROJECT.LSP**, which can be loaded using the File/
Applications Pull-down Menu. Project.Lsp is located in the ACAD Sample directory. PROJECT1 creates 2D
entities by projecting 3D entities onto the current UCS plane. The entities to be projected are selected by the user,
which avoids the duplication of entites caused when making orthographic views from a 3D model using a **BLOCK**.
The selected entities can be made into a block that can be inserted onto a drawing border. Each view is created by
orienting the UCS to the desired view because **PROJECT.LSP** always projects the view normal to the current UCS
X, Y plane. Before projecting, it is recommended that a different layer and color be created for clarity. To facilitate
selection of entites, it is recommended that the viewpoint be changed to an isometric or other axonometric view.
PROJECT2 projects entities from the current UCS onto a designated construction plane for the construction of 3D
wireframe models.

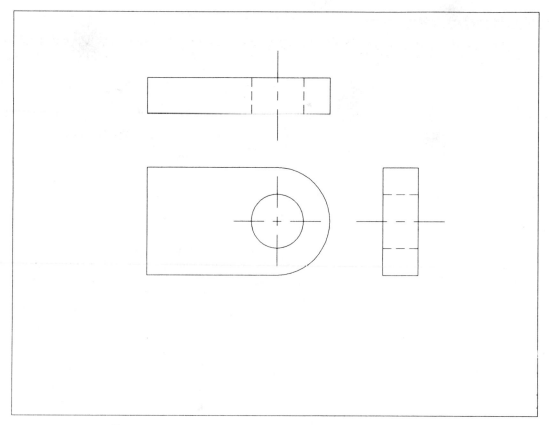

Figure 11.71 Three-view drawing created from a 3D model.

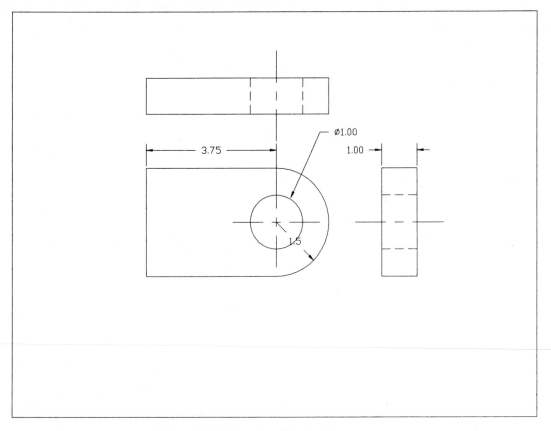

Figure 11.72 Details added to the drawing.

DESIGN ANALYSIS

Design analysis is the process of evaluating a design through mathematical modeling, calculations, graphics, and/or creating a prototype. Analysis of the model through the use of computers is called Computer-aided Engineering (CAE).

CADD software programs are capable of very sophisticated analyses of 3D models, including finite element, kinematics, and mass properties. Although AutoCAD does not provide integrated analysis capabilities, third-party software programs are available that can be integrated with AutoCAD or use AutoCAD DXF drawing files. Design analysis includes factors such as human engineering, functional analysis, economic analysis, strength, and size. These analyses can be performed using mathematics, graphics, and engineering tasks.

Finite Element Analysis

Finite element analysis (FEA) is a method of evaluating different properties of a design. FEA evaluates the strength of the material when it is subjected to different loads, such as vibrations, stress, deflections, buckling, and thermal stresses. FEA can be used for simple structural problems, solid and fluid mechanics, heat transfer, seepage flow, and electric and magnetic fields. FEA offers advantages over building prototypes. A load subjected to a prototype may only break in one place and may not reveal weaknesses in other areas unless several tests are performed. This iteration of the design process is time-consuming and expensive. FEA can ensure the strength of a part by creating a mathematical model to simulate its deformation under various loads.

FEA is a computational-intensive task that can be performed on some microcomputers. FEA programs have been developed that use the geometry created by AutoCAD as the outline of the part for creating a finite element model (FEM). The following steps demonstrate how AutoCAD and a third-party software program can analyze the simple T-bracket shown in Figure 11.73.

1. The design of the t-bracket is documented on AutoCAD by creating orthographic views and adding dimensions to a separate layer.

2. The dimension layer is turned off and frozen before the FEM is created. If the FEA program is integrated with AutoCAD's software, select it from the menu. This is usually located near the bottom of the Root Menu in the drawing editor. If the FEA program is not integrated, use the **DXF/OUT** function to create a DXF file to load into the FEA program.

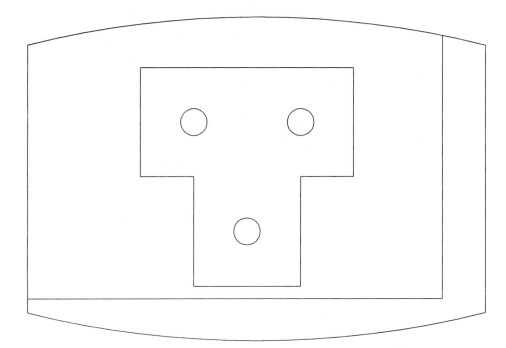

Figure 11.73 AutoCAD produced drawing of a t-bracket to be analyzed.

3. The mathematical model of a part is created by separating the outline of the structure into square and triangular pieces called finite elements. This process is called meshing because the drawing looks like a mesh when finished. Figure 11.74. The mesh can be created with AutoCAD's 3D surfaces described earlier in this chapter.

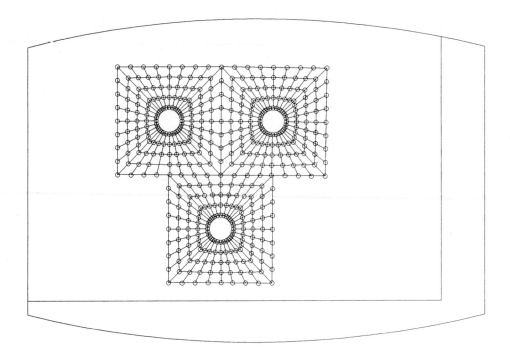

Figure 11.74 FEM model of the t-bracket showing the meshing and nodes.

Figure 11.75 The solid lines represent the exaggerated deflection of the nodes after load values have been assigned. The hidden lines represent the model before loading.

4. The points at which these elements meet are called nodes. The node points can be assigned load or temperature values, or they can be constrained to indicate a point that cannot be moved.

5. The FEA program calculates the relationship of each nodal value and produces a set of data. One set of data might show the deflection of all the nodes on the model with solid lines Figure 11.75. This deflection is graphically reproduced on screen. The deflection is exaggerated so that the designer can determine more easily the characteristics of the part under the specified load. The display may show the undeformed shape in one color and the exaggerated shape in another color.

6. A second set of data that may be produced by the FEA program is the stresses on all the elements. The stresses on the elements are displayed on screen as a multicolor plot. Each color signifies a different stress level, such as red for high levels of stress and blue for low areas of stress.

7. This information can be used to modify the design by adding reinforcement to weak areas or lightening areas with no stress. FEA models are used to optimize designs. AutoCAD can be used to edit the design which truly integrates the design and analysis process.

```
            LINE        Layer: 0
                        Space: Model space
                Thickness =    -4.0000
            from point, X=    7.0000  Y=    2.5000  Z=   -1.4142
              to point, X=    3.1109  Y=    2.5000  Z=    2.4749
Extrusion direction relative to UCS:
                   X=    0.0000  Y=   -1.0000  Z=    0.0000
     In Current UCS, Length =    3.8891,  Angle in XY Plane =      180
              3D Length  =    5.5000,  Angle from XY Plane =       45
              Delta X =  -3.8891, Delta Y =     0.0000, Delta Z =    3.8891


            CIRCLE      Layer: 0
                        Space: Model space
                Thickness =     0.7500
        center point, X=    1.5251  Y=    4.5000  Z=    2.4749
        radius     0.6250
   circumference   3.9270
           area    1.2272


Command:
```

Figure 11.76 Property information found with the List command.

PROPERTY CALCULATIONS OF A MODEL

After the geometry of a model has been created with AutoCAD, the Root Menu command **INQUIRY** can be used to extract useful information about a drawing. Engineers, architects, and other designers need to determine surface areas of rooms, sections of mechanical parts, lengths of electronic circuits, and so forth. The inquiry commands **AREA**, **DISTANCE**, **LIST**, and **ID** can be used to determine information about entities on a drawing.

The List Command

The **LIST** command can be used to determine specific information about entities. The information that is extracted from the entity depends on the type.

The command is activated by entering **LIST** at the command prompt or selecting from the menu. A prompt requests: **Select objects:** Pick the entities about which information is to be extracted, then enter RETURN. The text screen lists the information about the entities selected. If too much information is available to show on one screen, press **CTRL S** to pause the display. Figure 11.76 shows the listing for one of the faces in a 3D model. The information includes the coordinates of its endpoints, length, angle from start point to end point, and change in X and Y. Figure 11.76 also shows the listing for one of the drilled holes in the t-bracket. The center point location, radius, area, and circumference are given for circles.

The Distance Command

The **DIST** command is used to determine the length and angle between two points. **DIST** can determine the length of a line or the distance between any two points on a drawing. For example, **DIST** can be used to determine the shortest distance between two points in the design of circuit boards, clearances between parts, and so forth.

Enter **DIST** at the command prompt or from the menu. A prompt will request **First point:**. Pick the first point which displays a second prompt: **Second point:**. Pick the second point to display the distance, angle, and change in X and Y (delta values). Figure 11.77 displays the distance from the bottom left corner of the t-bracket to the center of the bottom hole.

```
<First point>/Entity/Add/Subtract: e

Select circle or polyline:
Area = 1.2272, Circumference = 3.9270

Command: dist
First point:  Second point:
Distance = 3.3941,  Angle in XY Plane = 1,  Angle from XY Plane = 0
Delta X = 3.3936,  Delta Y = 0.0580,    Delta Z = 0.0000

Command: id
Point:  X = 5.7177     Y = 3.2101     Z = 0.0000

Command: time

Current time:              29 Dec 1992 at 23:36:26.380
Times for this drawing:
  Created:                 20 Feb 1989 at 15:50:23.990
  Last updated:            20 Feb 1989 at 16:47:19.800
  Total editing time:      0 days 01:19:21.820
  Elapsed timer (on):      0 days 01:19:21.820
  Next automatic save in:  0 days 01:37:57.110

Display/ON/OFF/Reset:
```

Figure 11.77 The Area, Distance, ID, and Time displays.

The Id Command

The **ID** command is used to specify a point on a drawing and displays that point on the screen. This command is useful for designing, locating points before drawing the entity, or determining the location of a block before insertion.

Enter **ID** at the command prompt. The prompt reads: **Point:**. Pick the point to display the X, Y, and Z coordinates. At the point prompt, coordinate values can be entered. AutoCAD will display the point with a small temporary blip, if the blip mode is on. Figure 11.77 displays the X, Y, and Z coordinates.

The Area Command

The **AREA** command can specify any number of points enclosing a space on a drawing. The area and perimeter of the space are automatically calculated and displayed in the prompt line. AutoCAD keeps a running count of the area being calculated as the points are selected.

It is also possible to subtract areas from the running count. Arcs must be drawn as polyline arcs using the **PEDIT** command because AutoCAD does not calculate areas for arcs.

To determine the area of the t-bracket, select **AREA** from the menu. The prompt reads: {**First point**}/**Entity**/**Add/Subtract:**. Moving clockwise or counter-clockwise, pick the eight corners of the t-bracket and enter **RETURN**. The prompt line displays the area and perimeter.

To subtract the circles from the calculated area, enter **S** and RETURN. Enter the letter **E** to select entities, then pick each circle on the t-bracket. Enter RETURN to display the Area prompt. Enter the letter **A** to add new areas Figure 11.77.

Summary

The **INQUIRY** commands are used to determine information about a drawing. The ones described are the most useful for designing and editing parts. However, several other **INQUIRY** commands are very useful. The **DBLIST** (data base list) command gives a complete listing of every entity on a drawing. The **STATUS** command displays general information about frequently used settings. **STATUS** displays the number of entities, limits, snap resolution, grid spacing, current layer, color, linetype, elevation, and much more. Figure 11.78.

```
11 entities in C:\JUNK\3DPART
Model space limits are X:      0.0000   Y:      0.0000   (Off)
                       X:     12.0000   Y:      9.0000
Model space uses       X:     -0.4749   Y:     -1.5000   **Over
                       X:      8.4357   Y:     10.5000   **Over
Display shows          X:     -0.4749   Y:     -1.5000
                       X:     16.1740   Y:     10.5000
Insertion base is      X:      0.0000   Y:      0.0000   Z:       0.0000
Snap resolution is     X:      0.5000   Y:      0.5000
Grid spacing is        X:      0.0000   Y:      0.0000

Current space:         Model space
Current layer:         0
Current color:         BYLAYER -- 7 (white)
Current linetype:      BYLAYER -- CONTINUOUS
Current elevation:     0.0000  thickness:   -1.5000
Fill on  Grid off  Ortho off  Qtext off  Snap off  Tablet off
Object snap modes:     None
Free disk: 60366848 bytes
Virtual memory allocated to program: 4028 KB
Amount of program in physical memory/Total (virtual) program size: 75%
-- Press RETURN for more --
Total conventional memory: 384 KB      Total extended memory: 5312 KB
Swap file size: 388 KB
Command:
```

Figure 11.78 Status of a drawing.

MASS PROPERTY CALCULATIONS

More sophisticated calculations can be made of solid models. A solid model can be assigned the properties of different materials. The model then becomes a mathematical model of the design itself and can be analyzed to determine its characteristics. Typical mass property calculations that can be extracted from a solid model include volume, mass, surface area, center of gravity, and moments of inertia.

INTERFERENCE CHECKING AND SPACE GEOMETRY

Two other important analysis procedures that can be performed with CADD are interference checking and kinematics. An assembly of parts can be checked for interference with AutoCAD by creating a section assembly drawing, as described in Chapter 7. Zooming into areas that have mating parts can reveal visually whether errors exist in the design. To determine interferences more accurately, use the **DIST** command to measure the critical dimensions of an assembly to verify clearances.

If a 3D model of the assembly is created, **VPOINT** can be used to change the line of sight to determine clearances. For example, to determine the clearance between two pipes, the point view of one of the pipe's center lines must be found. Chapter 8 describes how to use descriptive geometry to find clearances on 2D drawings. The same theory is used with 3D drawings. However, the viewpoint is used to change the line of sight so that it is parallel to one of the pipe's center lines, and the **DIST** command is used to measure the distance.

Figure 11.79 shows two 3D pipes created with AutoCAD. The **VPOINT** and **DIST** commands are used to determine the clearance, as shown in Figure 11.80. As 3D capabilities and user friendly interfaces improve, traditional descriptive geometry problems are solved with the 3D model using the theory developed with 2D drawings.

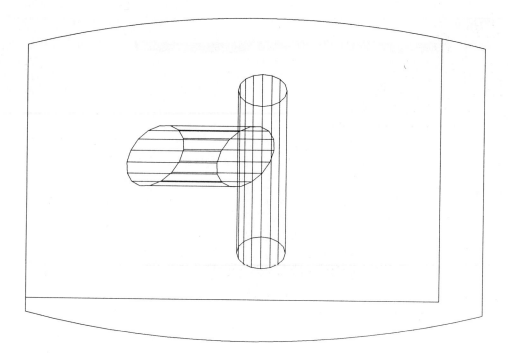

Figure 11.79 Two oblique 3D pipes.

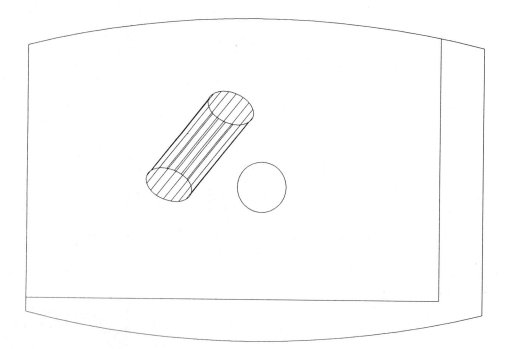

Figure 11.80 Changing the VPOINT and then using DIST to determine the shortest distance between the two pipes.

KINEMATICS

Kinematics is somewhat related to interference checking except that the model is not static. With some CADD software programs it is possible to display dynamically the movement of parts. Interferences can be determined through a whole range of motions. For example, a robot workcell used for assembly must be programmed for its

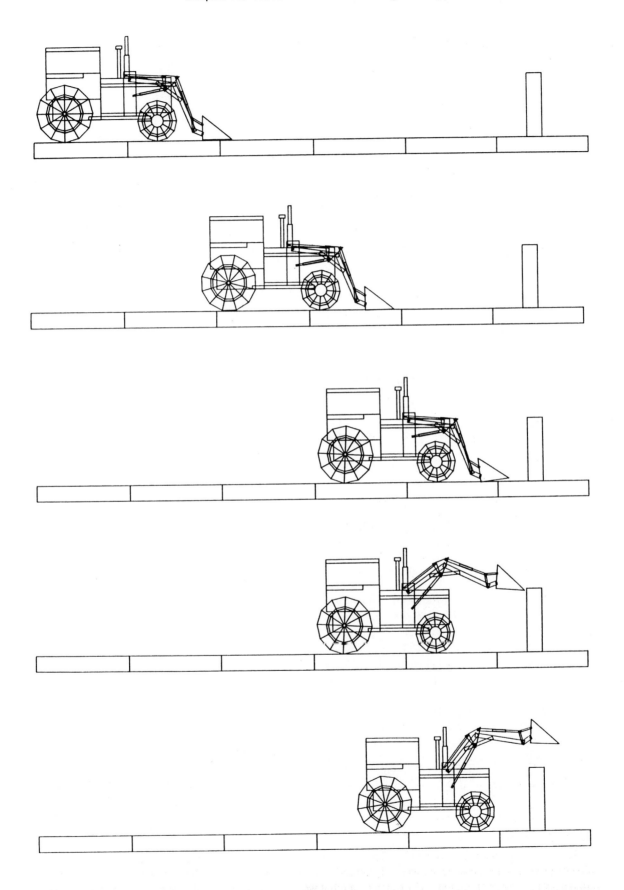

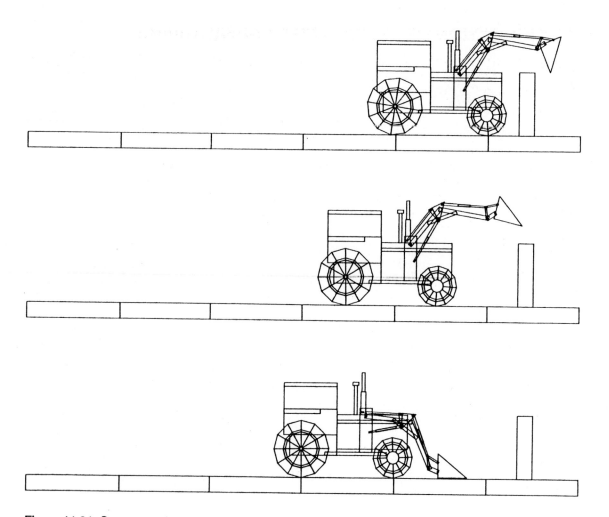

Figure 11.81 Sequence of drawings used for kinematic analysis (Computer Aided Design Software, Inc).

movements relative to everything within its workcell. These movements can be displayed on a CADD system, and the viewpoint changed to avoid possible collisions. The movement of the suspension system of an automobile can be displayed dynamically to check for interference with the exhaust system and other body parts.

AutoCAD has the capability to animate the motion of parts. The AutoLISP programming language can be used to create a program for animation. One method might be to create the moving part as a **BLOCK** and use **MOVE, ERASE, COPY, INSERT, ROTATE,** and other commands to simulate motion. Third-party software is also available that will allow animation of a drawing produced with AutoCAD and saved as a DXF file (Figure 11.81).

AUTOMATED DRAFTING

After the design of the part has been analyzed, it can be modified with AutoCAD as described in previous chapters. If the design of the part was created outside AutoCAD, the engineering drawings must be created for production and documentation. AutoCAD was originally created as an automated method of drafting. As the software became more advanced, powerful design functions could be performed. However, the strength of AutoCAD is in documenting designs.

The last stage in the design process, as shown in Figure 11.1, is documentation through automated drafting. Documentation includes detail drawings that orthographically describe each part, including dimensions. Assembly drawings frequently are used to show how the parts are assembled. Assembly drawings are drawn either orthographically or pictorially, depending on the complexity of the design. Orthographic assembly drawings were described in Chapter 7. Pictorial assembly drawings can be created from the 3D models. A bill of materials is usually included with the assembly drawing.

THE INTEGRATION OF DESIGN AND MANUFACTURING

The integration of design and manufacturing is accomplished with the geometry created from a CADD system and the computer-controlled manufacturing facility. Design and manufacturing can be linked using powerful software programs called Computer-aided Design/Computer-aided Manufacturing (CAD/CAM).

For many years machine tools have been automated. These automated machine tools are called numerical control (NC) machine tools. More recently, machine tools have been computer controlled and are called Computer Numerical Controlled (CNC). Postprocessors can use the geometry created by a CADD system, such as AutoCAD, to create the computer code necessary to control CNC machines.

CADD software is not limited to creating the geometry of parts. It is used to design robots and robot workcells, tools and fixtures, plant layouts, and other related tasks. Computer-aided manufacturing (CAM) is a process that uses computers to assist or control the manufacture of a product. CAM usually is used when many of the same parts have to be fabricated.

INTERCHANGE FILES

AutoCAD is not an integrated CAD/CAM program. However, AutoCAD does provide several methods to automate the manufacture of a part, either through third-party software programs or through file transfers to CAD/CAM systems. File transfers are done through the DXF (drawing interchange) or IGES (Initial Graphics Exchange Standard) format or through graphic translators.

DXF files are standard ASCII text files that can be used by many other CADD systems. The **DXF/OUT** command creates an ASCII file of an AutoCAD program. The filename automatically has **.DXF** as the file extender. When making this type of file, a prompt requests the decimal point accuracy of the entities.

IGES files are made of AutoCAD drawings by selecting **UTILITY** item **IGES**. The **IGESOUT** command creates an IGES file with **.igs** as the file name extender. The **IGESIN** command reads an IGES file created on another CADD program. IGES and DXF files are not 100 percent accurate for all CADD systems. Graphic translators also have been developed for particular CAD/CAM systems. Some entities and special procedures may not transfer very well between software programs.

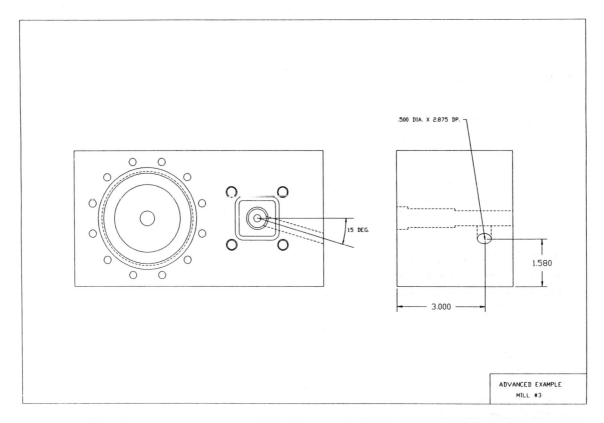

Figure 11.82 Drawing used to create an NC milling program (SmartCAM, Point Control Company).

CAD/CAM

A number of third-party programs can use AutoCAD drawing files to create CAM programs. AutoCAD drawing files are saved in the DXF or IGES format. The CAM program loads the AutoCAD file shown in Figure 11.82. A job plan must be created that provides information about cutting-tool size, speeds, feeds, and so forth.

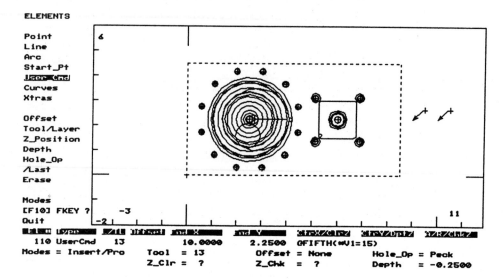

Figure 11.83 Tool path display (SmartCAM, Point Control Company).

```
FILE: MILL1                                          PAGE: 1

%
N100 G49 G40 G90 G17
N105 G00 X-0.425 Y-0.375 T1 M06
N110 M03 S2037 F24.4
N115 G43 H14 Z2.0 M08
N120 Z0.1
N125 G01 Z-0.6 F12.2
N130 G41 D2 X-0.375 F24.4
N135 Y4.0
N140 G02 X0.1632 Y4.7195 I0.75
N145 G01 X3.9323 Y5.8292
N150 G02 X5.375 Y4.75 I0.3177 J-1.0792
N155 G03 X5.875 Y4.3964 I0.375
N160 G02 X8.375 Y2.6287 I0.625 J-1.7678
N165 G01 Y0.5
N170 G02 X7.5 Y-0.375 I-0.875
N175 G01 X4.5528
N180 G02 X0.9472 I-1.8028 J1.125
N185 G01 X-0.375
N190 G00 Z2.0
N195 G40
N200 X3.575 Y0.75
N205 Z0.1
N210 G01 Z-0.6 F12.2
N215 G41 D2 X3.625 F24.4
N220 G03 I-0.875
N225 G00 Z2.0
N230 G40
N235 M09
N240 G00 G91 G28 Z0
N245 G49 G90 X12.0 Y8.0
N250 M30
%
```

Figure 11.84 Complete CNC milling code (SmartCAM, Point Control Company).

Another command transforms the part geometry created with AutoCAD into the CNC tool path code. The tool path can be modified by the operator and displayed on the screen. Figure 11.83 Each tool change can be assigned a different color. The tool path can be examined from different viewpoints to verify the tool path and to check for interference with fixturing. The machine to be used to fabricate the part is then specified, and the CNC program is automatically generated. Figure 11.84 The code can be printed or sent directly to the machine tool.

Other manufacturing processes can be automated with third-party software programs, using AutoCAD drawings. Special software programs have been developed that provide patterns, tablet menus, and other aids for plant layouts.

PICTORIAL DRAWINGS AND ILLUSTRATIONS

The last step in the design process is the documentation stage. The documentation of the design can take many forms depending on the design itself and the purpose that the drawings are to serve. The engineer is most familiar with drawings created for production purposes. These engineering drawings are the documentation necessary to produce the part. Working drawings are created that show orthographic detail drawings, an orthographic assembly drawing, and parts lists.

It may be necessary to create other types of documentation after the design is finalized. Although the engineer may not be concerned directly with documentation for sales, technical manuals, patent drawings, and so forth, the graphic data base created with the CADD system when the part is designed can be used for related areas of documentation other than engineering drawings. Figure 11.85 shows how the graphic data base can be used for different purposes.

Occasionally, drawings are created for design presentations that can be more easily understood by non-technical people. These drawings are usually shown in pictorial form. There are three types of pictorial drawings: axonometric, oblique, and perspective. AutoCAD can be used to create isometric drawings, which is one type of axonometric drawing, oblique drawings, and perspective drawings.

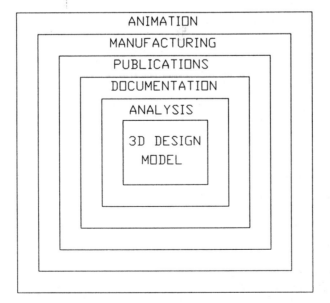

Figure 11.85 Different applications of the CADD data base.

Industrial Technical Illustration

Standard orthographic engineering drawings are used to manufacture the product. Technical illustrations are used to represent the design pictorially so that it can be understood by people who may not have engineering drawing experience. Technical illustrations can be grouped into two main areas: axonometric (parallel lines of sight), including isometric and oblique, and perspective (converging lines of sight).

Illustrations are produced, using traditional tools, from design sketches, engineering drawings, or photographs of the design. Technical illustrations can be created with CADD software programs using sketches, engineering drawings produced on the CADD system, or from the 3D models created with CADD. AutoCAD can create some types of technical illustrations and provides some commands specifically for isometric drawings. Other types of axonometric drawings can be produced by using editing commands. Rendered pictorial drawings can be created with AutoShade.

Isometric Drawings

AutoCAD simplifies the creation of isometric drawings because it provides an isometric snap grid and a command that assists in drawing isometric circles on the three isometric planes called **ISOPLANE**. Of course, isometric views can be created automatically if the model was drawn using the 3D commands explained earlier. The following steps show how to create a simple isometric cube. This process will not create a true 3D model but only a flat pictorial representation.

Creating an Isometric Drawing: Exercise 11.24

1. Open a new drawing then select the **SNAP** command.
2. Select **STYLE** from the snap prompt.
3. **Standard/Isometric {S}:**
The default setting is for a standard rectangular snap. Enter **I** and RETURN then use the default spacing of 1 to create an isometric snap grid.
4. Turn the grid on to display an isometric grid and cursor, as shown in Figure 11.86.

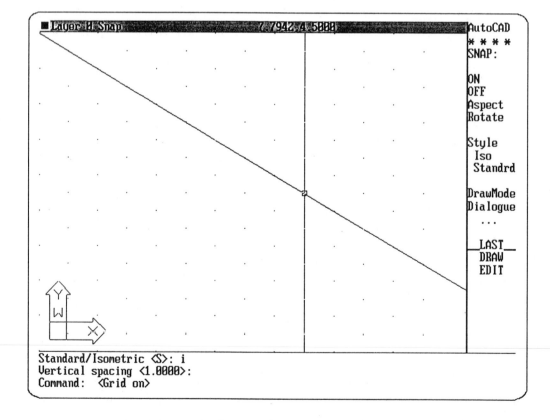

Figure 11.86 Isometric grid cursor.

5. Using the **LINE** command, draw a 2 inch isometric cube by snapping to the grid points to draw the left, right, and top surfaces, as shown in Figure 11.87.
6. The cube is used to demonstrate how to create isometric circles on the three faces of an isometric drawing. Start by picking the **ELLIPSE** command.

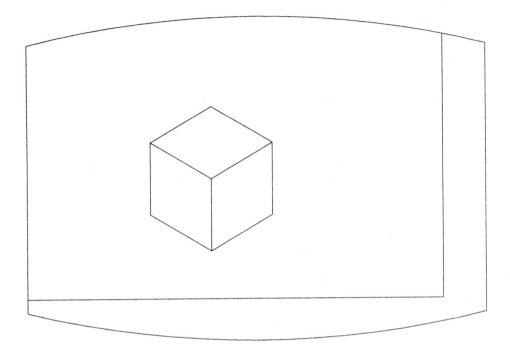

Figure 11.87 Isometric cube.

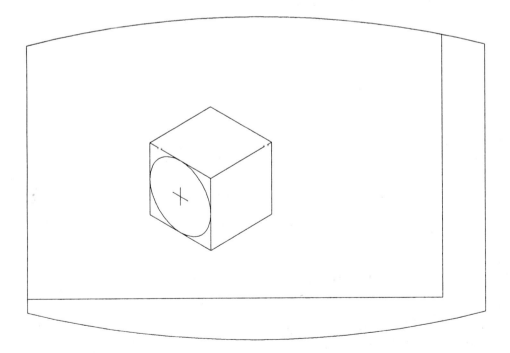

Figure 11.88 Isometric ellipse on the face of the cube.

7. **<Axis endpoint 1>/Center/Isocircle:**
Enter **I** and RETURN. The **ISOCIRCLE** option is used to draw isometric ellipses. This option is available only when the isometric snap mode is ON. The default setting draws an isometric ellipse on the left plane of the cube.

8. **Center of circle:**
Pick the grid point at the center of the left face of the cube. If the center of the isometric face is not on a grid point, diagonal lines can be drawn across the face and the **OSNAP** option **INTERSECTION** can be used.

9. **<Circle radius>/Diameter:**
Moving the cursor will drag an isometric circle on the screen. Enter the radius **1** and RETURN. An isometric ellipse is drawn, as shown in Figure 11.88.

10. To draw an isometric circle on the top or right plane of the cube, the **ISOPLANE** command must be used. At the command prompt enter **ISOPLANE**.

11. **Left/Top/Right/{Toggle}:**
Enter **T** and RETURN to draw an isometric ellipse on the top surface of the cube. Keyboard keys **Control E** can be used to toggle through the isoplanes. Notice that the cursor changes position on screen with the change in the isoplane.

12. Repeat Step 6 to add the isometric ellipse to the top surface.

13. Enter **ISOPLANE** at the command prompt and select **RIGHT** or enter **Control E**.

14. Repeat Steps 6 through 9 to add the isometric circle to the right surface of the cube (Figure 11.89).

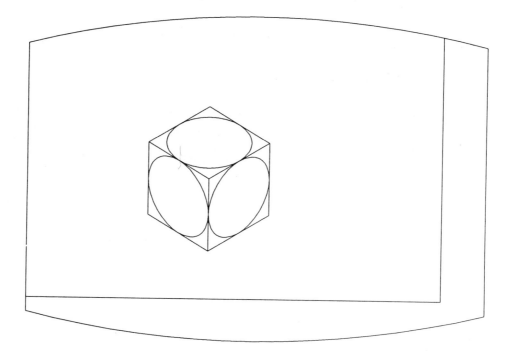

Figure 11.89 Isometric ellipses on all faces of the cube.

Isometric drawings can be created with AutoCAD using all of the **DRAW** and **EDIT** commands. To create a cylinder in isometric, draw the top and bottom of the cylinder as ellipses, **DIVIDE** the ellipses into parts, and use **LINE** to create elements on the surface of the cylinder, as shown in Figure 11.90. Hidden elements have to be erased or trimmed using the **EDIT** command. An isometric drawing produced as described is not a true 3D drawing and has limitations, but it can be used to create quickly a pictorial representation of a simple part. However, it may be easier to create a 3D model of the part and use the **VPOINT** command to create an isometric view.

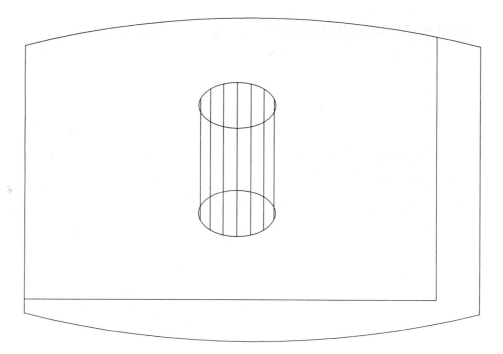

Figure 11.90 A cylinder drawn in isometric.

Oblique Drawings

Oblique drawings are another type of 2D pictorial drawing that can be created with AutoCAD. One of the most effective methods of quickly creating an oblique drawing is to draw the front face of the object and use the **COPY** command to create the back surface. The receding angle and length are determined by the position of the copy relative to the front surface. Receding **LINES** are added by picking the corners of the original and copy of the object. The following steps show how to create an oblique drawing given the front surface of the object:

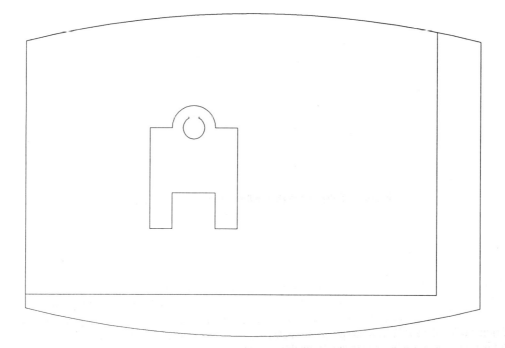

Figure 11.91 Start of the oblique drawing.

Creating an Oblique Drawing: Exercise 11.25

1. Open a new drawing then draw the front surface of the object using the **LINE, CIRCLE,** and **ARC** commands (Figure 11.91).

2. Use the **COPY** command to create the oblique drawing. Select the entities to be copied using the **WINDOW** option.

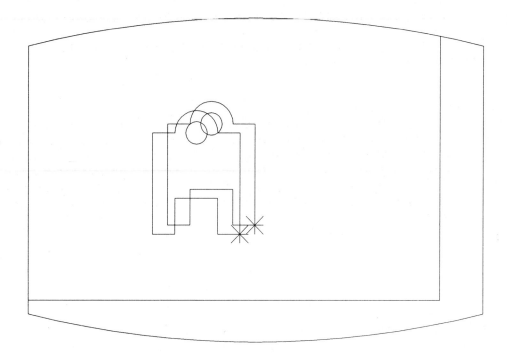

Figure 11.92 **COPY** command used to create the depth of the oblique drawing.

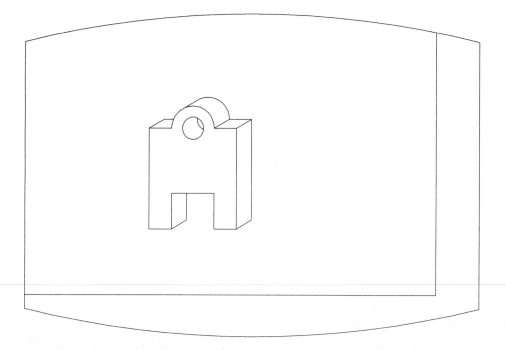

Figure 11.93 Depth lines added and hidden lines erased to complete the oblique drawing.

3. Pick a base point on the drawing, such as the bottom right corner of the object. The new base point determines the length and angle of the receding lines, in addition to the direction of the line of sight. For example, moving the copy below and to the left of the base point produces an oblique drawing that shows the bottom and left side of the object. For this example, the copy is placed above and to the right of the base point, as shown in Figure 11.92.

4. The receding lines are added to the drawing using **LINE** and the **OSNAP** option **ENDPOINT**.

5. Hidden features are deleted using **ERASE** or **TRIM**. The finished oblique drawing of the object is shown in Figure 11.93.

Perspective Drawings

Perspective drawings can be created with AutoCAD using the standard techniques with hand tools. To create a simple one-point perspective, draw the front surface using standard AutoCAD commands. A vanishing point is selected and marked with the **POINT** command, as shown in Figure 11.94. Dot lines are then drawn from the corners of the object to the vanishing point. The depth of the object is selected and drawn using the **LINE** command with the ortho toggle ON. The dot lines are erased and the object is further edited to complete the view shown in Figure 11.95. Perspective drawings can be created automatically from a 3D model with AutoShade and are explained later. Remember that perspective views of 3D drawings are automatically created by using the **VPOINT** command option **DISTANCE** as explained earlier in this chapter.

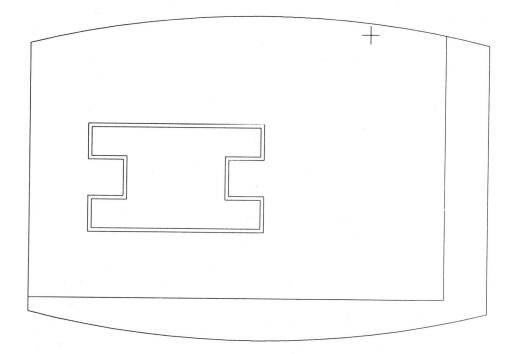

Figure 11.94 Object to be drawn in perspective.

Axonometric Drawings

Axonometric drawings can be created quickly with AutoCAD. The front or plan view of the object (Figure 11.96) is rotated, then copied to an offset position, as shown in Figure 11.97. Lines are added to connect the two surfaces. Hidden lines are deleted or trimmed to complete the axonometric view shown in Figure 11.98.

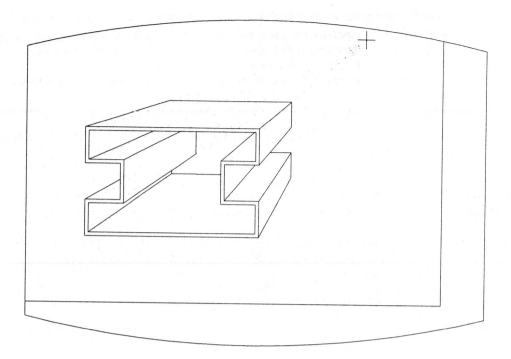

Figure 11.95 Receding lines to the vanishing point to create a one-point perspective drawing.

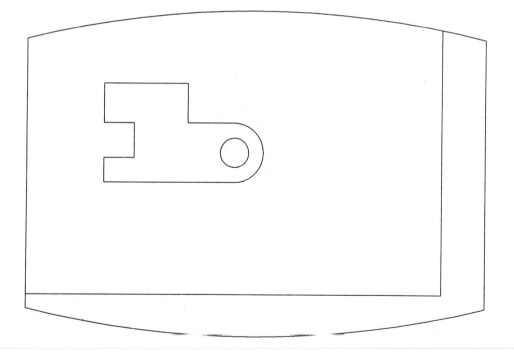

Figure 11.96 View to be used to create an axonometric drawing.

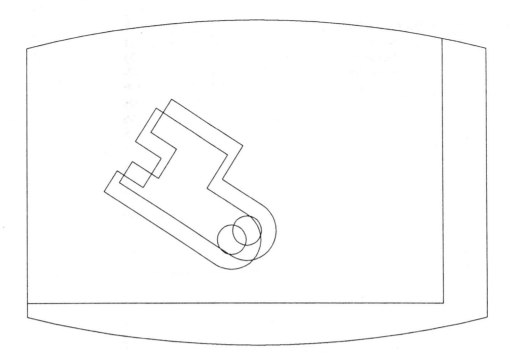

Figure 11.97 The view is rotated and copied.

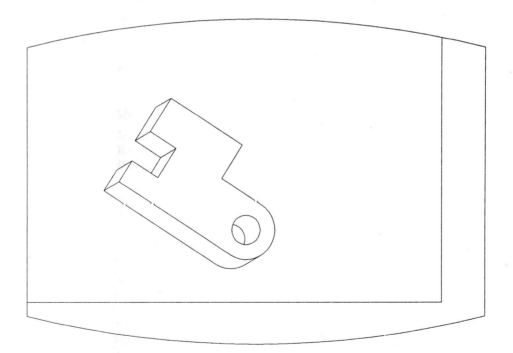

Figure 11.98 The object is edited to create the perspective view.

SHADED PICTORIAL DRAWINGS USING RENDER

Shaded illustrations can be created using the Render menu items. Figure 11.99. Render is used to create rendered images of 3D objects within AutoCAD. Render quickly renders 3D objects and gives control over colors, lighting, and cameras. Objects can appear dull or shiny by controlling reflective qualities. Lights can be placed anywhere in the scene in the form of distant sunlight coming through a window, a light bulb in a room, or a spotlight pointed at a mechanical part. Highly realistic images can be created with the Render commands. Figure 11.100.

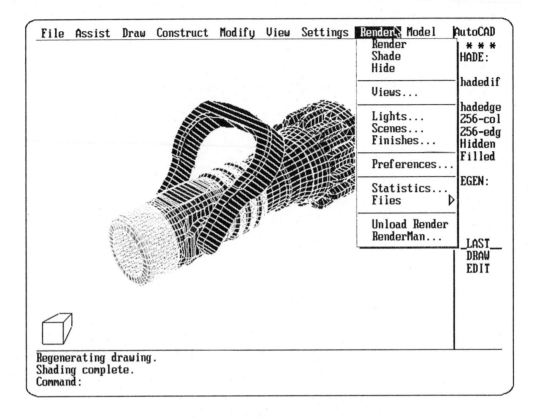

Figure 11.99 The Render Menu.

Figure 11.100 Rendered image. (Autodesk, Inc).

The Shade Command

Quick shaded renderings of 3D models in the current viewport are made with the **SHADE** command. On systems that show fewer than 256 colors, the Shade command will create an image with hidden lines removed and surface colors corresponding to the colors used to model the wireframe. Figure 11.101. Shaded images remain in the viewport until a regeneration is done. Shaded images cannot be plotted but a slide can be made by using the **MSLIDE** command. Shading in smaller viewports is much faster. Entities in a shaded image cannot be selected. You must use Regen to return to the wireframe image to select entities. To shade a 3D model, enter **SHADE** at the command prompt or pick it from the Render Pull-down Menu. The shaded image will be displayed on screen. Only 3D models made from AME solids or with faces can be shaded.

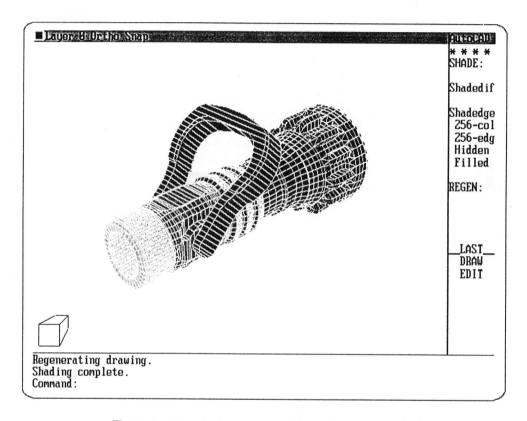

Figure 11.101 Image created with the Shade command.

Creating a Shaded Image: Exercise 11.26

1. Open **LAB11-9** from your data disk.
2. Select **Shade** from the Render Pull-down Menu or enter it at the command prompt. After a few moments the shaded image will be diaplayed on screen.

The Render Command

The Render command will create a more realistic image of the 3D model when compared to the Shade command. The Render command has many variables that can be controlled to create realistic images, such as positions and kinds of lights, surface finishes, and colors. To learn how to use most of the Render features refer to the Render tutorial found in the *AutoCAD Render Reference Manual*. To create a rendered image follow the steps shown below:

Creating a Rendered Image: Exercise 11.27

1. Open **LAB11-9** from your data disk.
2. Select Render from the Render Pull-down Menu or enter it at the command prompt. After a few moments, the rendered image will be displayed on screen. Notice that the image is more realistic than the shaded image and also took much longer to process.

DESKTOP PUBLISHING

AutoCAD and Rendered drawings can be used for desktop publishing. Desktop publishing has developed recently because of the increased capabilities of the microcomputer. Desktop publishing is used to produce newsletters, forms and other documents, magazines, books, and other types of printed media. The advantage of desktop publishing is that text files from word processors can be merged with graphics created with AutoCAD and other sources to produce a finished product. Desktop publishing software will merge graphics with text, give the text a typeset appearance, and rearrange the format to achieve the best results before printing.

This textbook was created primarily with desktop publishing software. The text was written on a word processor. Most of the drawings were created with AutoCAD or AutoShade, and then printed on a laser printer. The text files were loaded into the desktop publishing software. Different type styles and sizes were assigned to the text. The finished pages were printed on a laser printer and used as camera-ready copy. The pages then were printed and bound to produce the book.

Summary

Chapter 1 described the strengths of CADD. It was suggested that CADD drawing files are the central data base for many operations in industry. CADD can be an extremely useful tool for the engineer if used to its full capabilities. It is just as important to realize that CADD and engineering graphics can be linked to manufacturing, publishing, advertising, sales, and nearly every phase of a product's creation from the initial order to final shipment. This is referred to as Computer-integrated Manufacturing (CIM), which is a process that has engineering drawings created with CADD as its central component. Hundreds of ways exist to create a drawing with AutoCAD. This textbook has introduced some of the methods that can be used for engineering graphics. Given this introduction, it is hoped that you will use this powerful design and communications tool to increase your potential and find new and innovative uses for CADD.

THE ENGINEER OF THE FUTURE

The emergence of CADD, CAE, and powerful computer graphics programs makes engineering and design even more exciting professions. Much of the design, analysis, and documentation of a product have been automated by advanced computer programs. Engineering software provides the tools necessary to create designs in less time, test alternative designs, and actually see the behavior of a system without the use of prototypes.

The engineer of the future will be able to sit at a computer terminal and create 3D solid models of a design. Powerful input devices will make model transformations possible by a simple movement of the hand. Powerful display devices will show the model in a way similar to that of a hologram, allowing the designer to move around the part. Artificial intelligence programs will create alternative design solutions and recommend design modifications based upon the results of the design analyses. Once the part geometry is created on the CADD system, it becomes the focal point for many other activities, as shown in Figure 11.102.

The design and manufacture of the part have become more integrated. Design modifications are determined in part by the effectiveness of the design to take advantage of the tooling and plant layout. The next section of this chapter will explain the integration of design and manufacturing and how it is being accomplished with the aid of AutoCAD.

APPLICATIONS OF AUTOCAD IN MAJOR FIELDS OF ENGINEERING

AutoCAD is flexible enough to be used in many different applications. However, many third-party software programs have been developed for specific applications and for use with AutoCAD. These software programs are specialized to automate the engineer's job and take full advantage of AutoCAD.

Mechanical Engineering

Mechanical engineers are concerned with the design of power, transportation, manufacturing, and other systems. The design of mechanical devices can be performed with AutoCAD with the software, as described in the introductory chapters. Two-dimensional drawings are created using the various entities, and the design is edited and dimensioned. Three-dimensional models are produced and viewed from any position. Common mechanical devices can be made into blocks and inserted quickly into drawings. Many of the drawings described throughout this text were mechanical applications of AutoCAD. The finite element problem of the t-bracket is an application of CADD to mechanical engineering.

Electrical Engineering

Electrical engineers are of two major types: electrical power and electronics. The layout of simple circuit boards and electrical power distribution can easily be done with AutoCAD. Electronic symbols can be drawn and stored as **BLOCKS** or added to the tablet menu for quick retrieval and insertion into drawings. **ATTRIBUTES** are assigned to each inserted block for drilling information for pads. Third-party software is available that includes schematic capture, interactive part placement and route editing, and more than 5,000 available components for the design of circuit boards. Some programs have autorouter that uses artificial intelligence techniques to identify optimal routing patterns and displays it while this is taking place.

Industrial Engineering

Industrial engineers are involved with the design, integration, and improvement of the people, equipment, and materials necessary to manufacture products. AutoCAD can be used to draw plant layout diagrams and to route materials, equipment, and people. **BLOCKS** can be made of equipment for quick insertion into plant diagrams. Third-party software can be used with AutoCAD drawings to simulate a manufacturing activity for the purposes of study and analysis. The simulation software can be used to determine whether two robots will collide. It also has the capability to gather data and points in the process for statistical analysis.

Color animated graphics of several hundred objects can be shown moving about at rates many times that of the actual process. The user is able to interact with the model, trying different processes and sending the summary statistics to off line analytical programs.

Civil Engineering

Civil engineers are involved in the design and supervision of construction for buildings and transportations systems. AutoCAD can be used to draw building and transportation systems. Third-party software can be used with AutoCAD drawings and software for structural steel detailing and scheduling, concrete detailing and scheduling, mapping and site planning.

QUESTIONS FOR REVIEW

1. List and describe three types of geometric models.
2. List three ways to create wireframe models.
3. List the five commands specific to AutoCAD 3D.
4. Name the AutoCAD default view setting.
5. List three methods of using the **VPOINT** command.
6. Describe the method suggested to mark a model to prevent getting "lost in space".
7. More accurate automatic hidden line removal can be accomplished by using the _____ command.
8. List the two plotting options that are different for 3D models.
9. Define kinematics.
10. Define CAD/CAM.
11. List the two AutoCAD interchange file formats.
12. Describe how to display AutoCAD's isometric grid.
13. Describe how to change AutoCAD's isometric grid.
14. List the three AutoShade variables that are used to create perspective drawings.
15. Describe desktop publishing and how it relates to engineering graphics.
16. List other applications for AutoCAD in addition to engineering drawings.

DRAWING ASSIGNMENTS

1. Do the 3D tutorial found in the appendix.
2. From Figures 11.102 through 11.114, create 3D models with AutoCAD.
3. From Giesecke, et al., Engineering Graphics, 4th ed. Pictorial drawings from Chapters 16, 17, and 18.

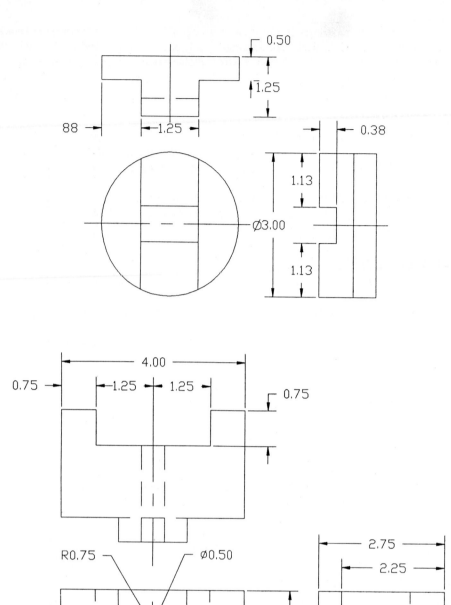

Figures 11.102 and 11.103

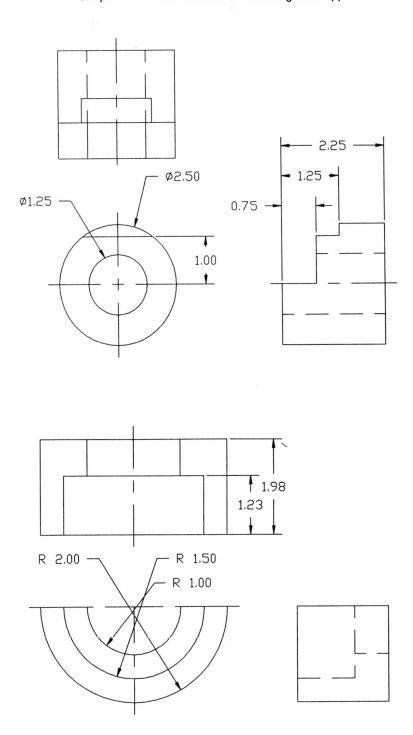

Figures 11.104 and 11.105

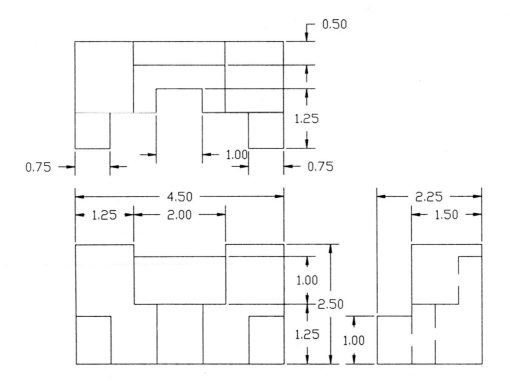

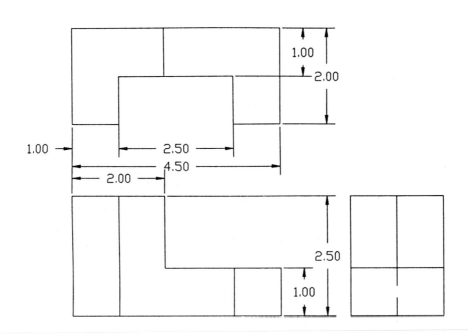

Figures 11.106 and 11.107

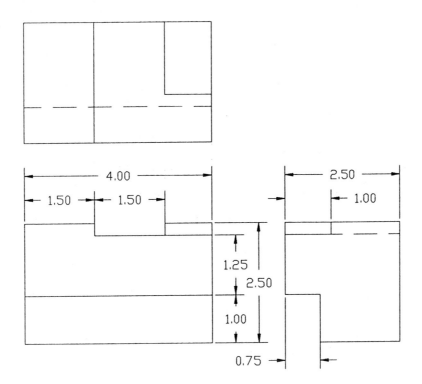

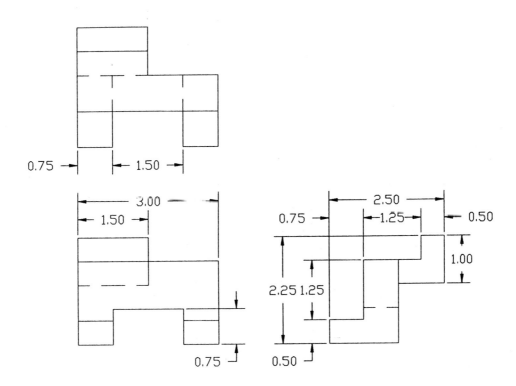

Figures 11.108 and 11.109

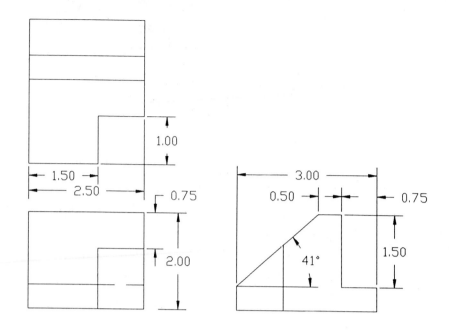

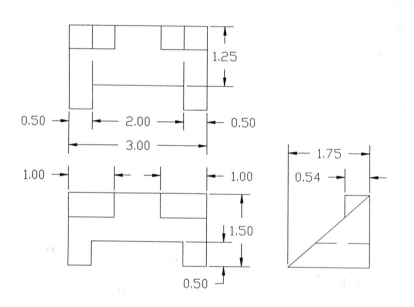

Figures 11.110 and 11.111

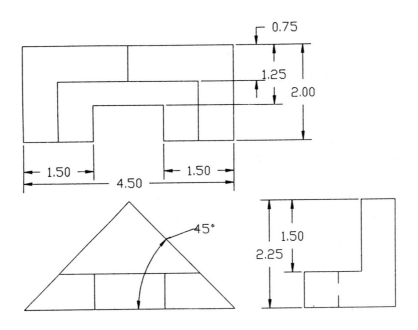

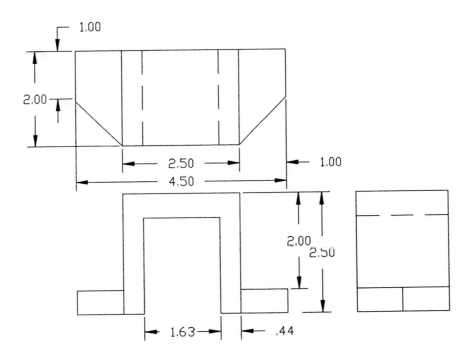

Figures 11.112 and 11.113

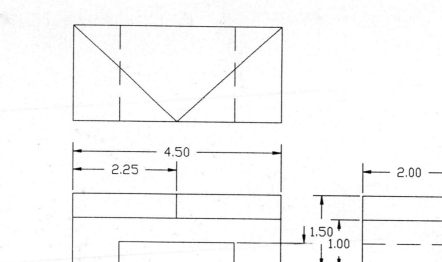

Figure 11.114

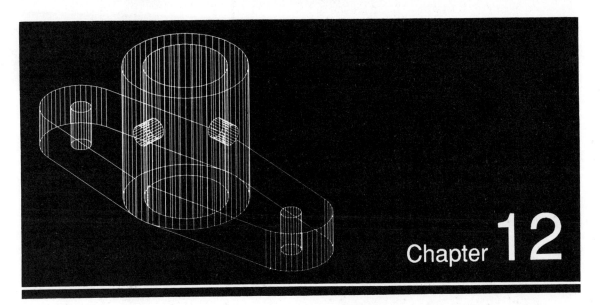

Chapter 12

SOLID MODELING

This chapter introduces AutoCAD's solid and region modeling called AME (Advanced Modeling Extensions). The region modeler creates, edits, and analyzes closed 2D areas or *regions*. The solid modeler creates composite solid 3D models using Boolean operations, primitive shape building, extrusion and revolution of 2D forms. 3D solids can also be edited and analyzed with AME. In this chapter you will learn how to create, edit, and analyze region and solid models. In addition you will experience the new design paradigm that starts with 3D modeling from which 2D drawings are extracted for documentation.

OBJECTIVES

After completing Chapter 12 you will be able to:
1. Create and analyze a region model,
2. Create, edit, and analyze solid primitive shapes,
3. Create, edit, and analyze 3D extruded solids,
4. Create, edit, and analyze 3D revolved solids,
5. Create, edit, and analyze composite solids,
6. Create 3D solid models of an assembly,
7. Extract 2D orthographic views from 3D solid models,
8. Display solid models as wireframes with and without hidden lines, shaded and rendered images.

INTRODUCTION

A solid model is a computer representation of an object, including such information as the material and mass properties of the object. The model is produced in one of two ways: boundary representation (B-rep) or constructive solid geometry (CSG). Figure 12.1. A B-rep model is produced by creating surfaces, points, and curves that define the boundary of the object. A CSG model is created by adding and subtracting solid geometric primitives. AME creates a CSG model to define the composite solid model. AME also creates B-rep models to display the solid on screen. Each solid created with AME contains CSG information for the structure and dimensions of the solid and B-rep information to describe the boundary of the solid. The B-rep information is stored in two blocks on the frozen layer AME_FRZ, which is automatically produced when a solid is created. *Never try to edit the contents of the AME_FRZ layer to prevent destroying or corrupting the solid model.*

A solid model looks similar to a surface model but is very different. Solid models contain much more information about the object, which can be an aid in determining the characteristics and behavior of the part. A solid model, unlike surface and wireframes, develops a complete description of the part. Turned parts, forgings, molding, and extrusions are common products that can be solid modeled. After the solid model is defined, it can be analyzed as in the fourth stage in the design process shown in Figure 12.1. Volume, surface area, mass, center of gravity, and moments of inertia can be calculated.

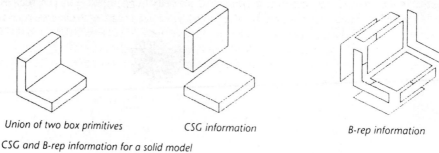

Union of two box primitives

CSG information

B-rep information

CSG and B-rep information for a solid model

Figure 12.1 CSG and B-rep information for a solid model (Courtesy of Autodesk, Inc.).

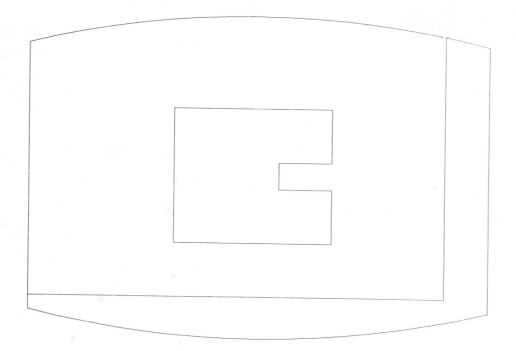

Figure 12.2 Profile created for the solid model.

A solid model is produced by creating a profile of the object, as shown in Figure 12.2. The profile is extruded to give its third dimension, as shown in Figure 12.3. The solid object is modified by creating other primitive shapes, which are added, subtracted, or intersected through Boolean operations. Complex shapes also can be created through these three Boolean operations. Figure 12.4 shows a rectangular prism that has been added to the solid. Figure 12.5 shows a circular cylinder that has been subtracted from the solid. Figure 12.6 shows the results of an intersection of a partial circular cylinder and the rectangular prism. After the solid model is created, it can be analyzed, edited, and shaded. Different views can be created to produce a multiview drawing.

ADVANCED MODELING EXTENSION (AME)

AME is loaded by entering **(xload "ame")** at the command prompt, selecting **MODEL/UTILITY/LOAD** from the screen menu or by picking **MODEL/UTILITY/LOAD MODELER** from the Pull-down Menus. Figure 12.7. After entering the load command, a prompt reads:

No modeler is loaded yet. Both AME and Region Modeler are available.
Autoload Region/<AME>:

To load AME for 3D solid modeling press Return. To load the region modeler, enter R at the prompt.

AME is unloaded to increase memory by AutoCAD by entering **(xunload"ame")** at the command prompt or by picking **UNLOAD MODELER** from the Model/Utility Pull-down Menu.

AME provides the user with the capability to build solid geometry using primitive shapes, such as boxes, cones, and wedges. Figure 12-8. Solid primitives can be added together, or subtracted, or the intersections found to create more complex geometry. These are Boolean operations called UNION, SUBTRACTION, and INTERSECTION. Solid models can have material properties assigned to describe its density, yield strength, thermal conductivity, and other characteristics. Solid models can be displayed as wireframe or mesh. The HIDE or SHADE commands can be used to display the solid model.

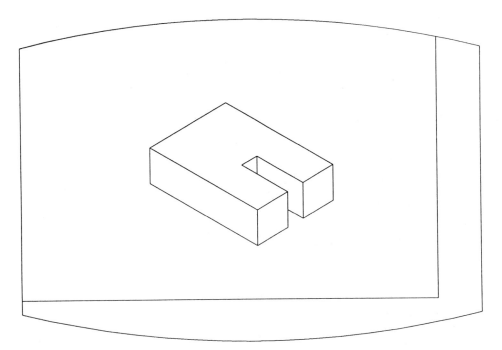

Figure 12.3 The profile is extruded to create a solid.

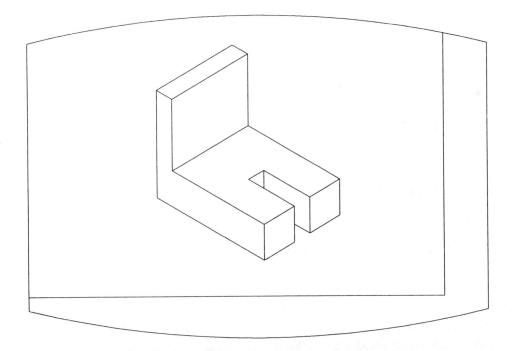

Figure 12.4 A rectangular prism is added to the solid.

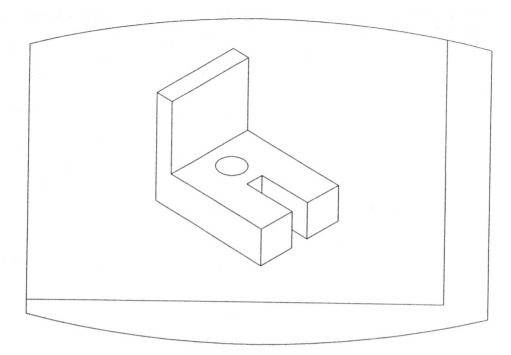

Figure 12.5 A cylinder is subtracted from the model to create a hole.

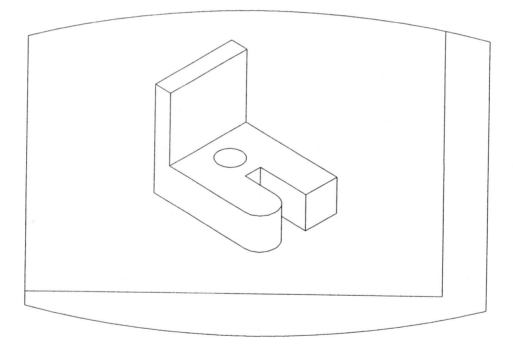

Figure 12.6 The intersection of a partial circular cylinder and the rectangular prism to create the rounded end of the model.

REGION MODELING

The region modeler creates closed 2D areas that can contain holes and be located anywhere in 3D space. The outer boundaries of the model are called outer loops and holes are called inner loops. Region models are created by solidifying polylines, circles, arcs, ellipses, polygons, traces, and donuts. 3D entities cannot be used. A composite region model is created the same as a composite solid model by using union, subtraction, and intersection commands. Figure 12.9. Region modeling is an alternative method for geometric construction as described in Chapter 5.

The use of region modeling for geometric construction can be a very effective technique. The following steps describe how to create a bicycle chain gear using region modeling:

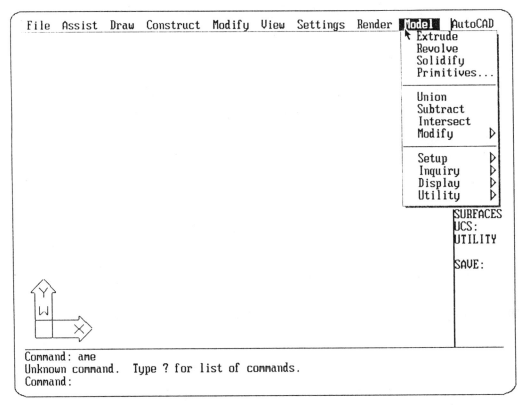

Figure 12.7 The Model menu for loading and using AME.

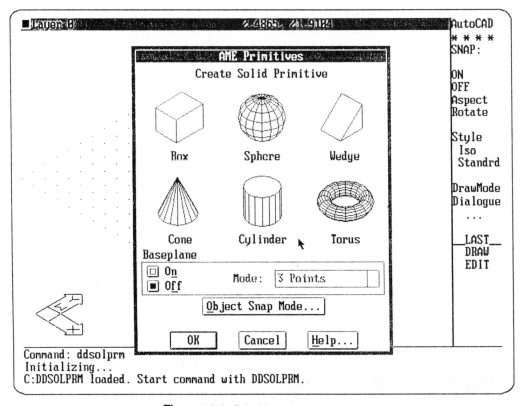

Figure 12.8 Primitive shapes for AME.

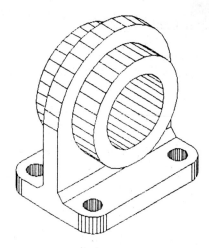
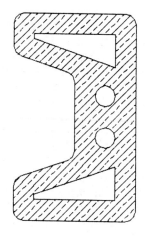

Figure 12.9 Examples of composite solid and region models.

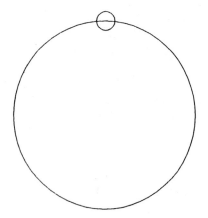

Figure 12.10 The base circles for the bicycle chain gear.

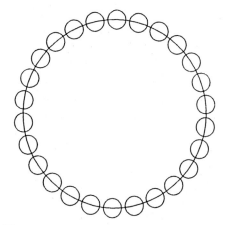

Figure 12.11 The small circles added using polar construction.

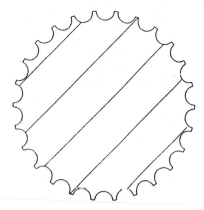

Figure 12.12 The chain gear after region subtraction.

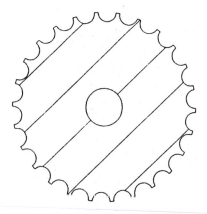

Figure 12.13 The chain gear after subtracting the center circle.

Region Modeling: Exercise 12.1

1. Open the blank drawing file **LAB12-1**.

2. Draw a 5" diameter circle by entering **C** at the command prompt.

3. **3P/2P/TTR/<CENTER POINT>:** Pick the center point location for the base circle. Enter **0,0,0** for the center point.

4. **Diameter/Radius>:** Enter **2.5** for the radius. The circle is drawn in the lower-left corner of the screen.

5. To display the whole circle enter **Z** for Zoom then **A** for all. You may want to pan the circle into the center of the screen by entering **P** at the command prompt.

6. Enter **C** at the command prompt to draw another circle.

7. **3P/2P/TTR/<CENTER POINT>:** Pick the center point location for the base circle. Enter **0,2.5,0** for the center point.

8. **Diameter/Radius>:** Enter **.25** for the radius. The circle is drawn at the 12:00 position on the circle. Figure 12.10.

9. A polar array is used to copy the small circle around the 5 diameter circle for the construction of the teeth. Pick Construct/Array from the Pull-down Menus.

10. **Select objects:** is displayed. Pick the small circle then enter Return to end the selection set.

11. **Rectangular or Polar array (r/P) <R>:** Enter **P** to select the Polar array option.

12. **Center point of array:** Enter **0,0**.

13. **Number of items:** Enter **26** to make 26 copies of the small circle.

14. **Angle to fill (+=ccw, -=cw) <360>:** Press Return to copy the circles all the way around the 5 diameter circle.

15. **Rotate objects as they are copied? <Y>:** Press Return. Figure 12.11.

16. The AME modeler must be loaded for the next step. Pick Modeler/Utility/Load Modeler from the Pull-down Menus then enter R to load the region modeler.

17. The small circles are to be subtracted from the large circle to create the teeth on the gear. From the Model Pull-down Menu pick Subtract.
Source objects...
Select objects.
Pick the large circle as the source object then enter Return.

18. **Objects to subtract from them...**
Select objects.
Use a window to select all the small circles then Return to begin the Boolean subtraction. The finished part is displayed on screen as shown in Figure 12.12.

19. Add the center hole for the bicycle pedal arms by entering C at the command prompt then adding a .5 radius circle with a center point at 0,0,0.

20. Subtract the new circle by using the Model/Subtract command. Figure 12.13.

21. The model will be analyzed to determine its surface area by picking Model/Inquiry/ Mass Property... Pull-down Menu. Pick the gear then press Return to list the mass properties of the model on screen. Figure 12.14. This listing shows the area, perimeter, centroid, and moments of the gear. The units used for calculations can be changed from British to Engineering, metric, or SI by picking Model/Setup from the Pull-down Menus.

Solid Modeling Using Primitives

Primitives can be created by extruding or revolving Polylines or by using the solid primitive commands. Figure 12.8 shows the solid primitives Pull-down Menu. These primitive shapes are defined by providing the dimensions. For example, to create a solid rectangle you must input the length, width, and depth. AutoCAD always defines the height along the positive Z-axis. There are six primitive shapes in AME:

PRIMITIVE	AUTOCAD COMMAND
BOX	SOLBOX
CONE	SOLCONE
CYLINDER	SOLCYL
SPHERE	SOLSPHERE
TORUS	SOLTORUS
WEDGE	SOLWEDGE

Creating a Solid Box

The **SOLBOX** command creates a 3D solid box of any defined size. A box is created by entering diagonally opposite corners of its base then entering its height, by defining its base rectangle then the height, or by locating the center of the box and a corner height. Another option would be to enter its length then width separately. Normally, the base of the box is located parallel to the XY plane of the current UCS. The Baseplane option is used to locate the base of the box anywhere in 3D space. The following steps describe how to create a solid box using AME:

Creating a Solid Box: Exercise 12.2

1. Begin a new drawing by selecting New from the Files Pull-down Menu. Turn the grid on with Function Key 7, snap on with Function Key 9, and coordinate display with Function Key 6.
2. To create a solid box enter **SOLBOX** at the command prompt or pick **BOX** from the Solid Primitive Pull-down Menu or **Solbox** from the Solid Menu.
2. **Baseplane/Center/<Corner of box> <0,0,0>:** The first corner is a point on the base of the box in the X-Y plane of the current UCS. Pick the corner point with the input device or enter coordinates. For this example enter **0,0,0**.
3. **Cube/Length/,Other corner.:** Enter coordinates **6,4,0** to locate the diagonal corner of the rectangular base.
4. **Height:** Enter the height measured along the Z-axis. For this example enter **4**.
5. Enter **VPOINT** at the command prompt then enter **1,-1,1**. Figure 12.15 shows the 4 x 6 x 4 rectangular solid.

Creating a Solid Cube

The cube option will make a box with equal sides. A cube is made by using the **BOX** command. The following steps describe its use:

Creating a Solid Cube: Exercise 12.3

1. Begin a new drawing by selecting New from the Files Pull-down Menu. Turn the grid on with Function Key 7, snap on with Function Key 9, and coordinate display with Function Key 6.
2. To create a solid cube enter **SOLBOX** at the command prompt or pick **BOX** from the Solid Primitive Pull-down Menu or **Solbox** from the Solid Menu.
2. **Baseplane/Center/<Corner of box> <0,0,0>:** The first corner is a point on the base of the box in the X-Y plane of the current UCS. Pick the corner point with the input device or enter coordinates. For this example enter **0,0,0**.
3. **Cube/Length/,Other corner.:** Enter **C** to pick the Cube option.
4. **Length:** Enter the length of the sides for the cube. For this example enter **4**.
5. Enter **VPOINT** at the command prompt then enter **1,-1,1**. Figure 12-16 shows the 4 x 4 x 4 cube.

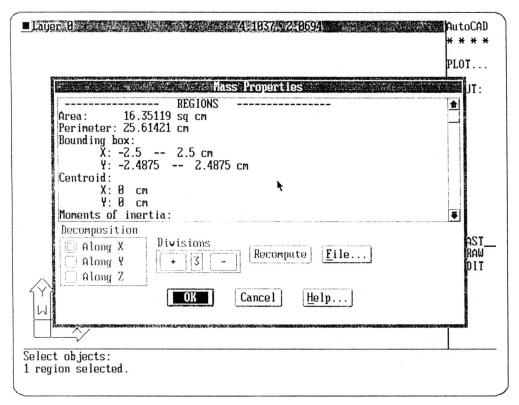

Figure 12.14 The mass properties list.

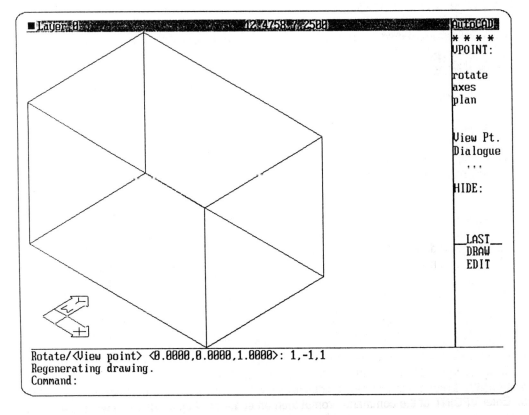

Figure 12.15 The solid box.

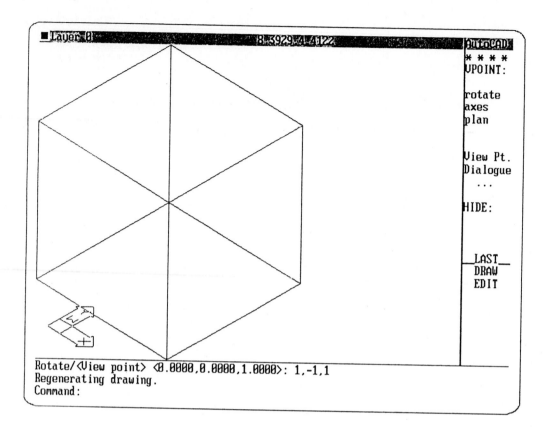

Figure 12.16 The solid cube.

Creating a Solid Circular Cone

A cone is a single curved shape with a circular or elliptical base and straight line elements that intersect at a vertex. With AME, the base of the cone lies in the X-Y plane of the current UCS and the vertex is along the Z-axis. A solid cone is created by defining the size of the circular or elliptical base and the height. The following steps show how to create a solid circular cone:

Creating a Solid Cone: Exercise 12.4

1. Begin a new drawing by selecting New from the Files Pull-down Menu. Select **CONE** from the Solid Primitives Pull-down Menu or **Solcone** from the Solid Menu.
2. **Baseplane/Elliptical/Center/<Corner point> <0,0,0>:** To create a circular cone enter the coordinate position for the center point or pick a point. For this example enter the values **0,0,0.** By locating a center point you are indicating that a circular cone is to be created.
3. **Diameter/<Radius>:** Enter a radius by picking a point or entering coordinate values. Enter a value of **1**.
4. **Height of cone:** Enter a value of **4** to create the cone.
5. Enter **VPOINT** at the command prompt then enter **1,-1,1** . Figure 12.17. A negative value would have created a cone with the vertex 4 units below the center on the negative Z-axis.

WIREFRAME AND MESH REPRESENTATION

Notice in Figure 12.17 that only 4 element lines are used to display the cone. Also notice that hidden surfaces are shown. The default setting is for solid models to be displayed as wireframes. To remove hidden lines from the displayed image, the solid model must be meshed using the **SOLMESH** command. This command displays solids as Pface entities. A mesh approximates the surface of solids by creating multi-edged faces, as shown in Figure 12.18. Exploding a solid while in the mesh mode will create Pface entities. Object snap modes such as tangent, quadrant, and center cannot be used to snap to meshed arcs and circles.

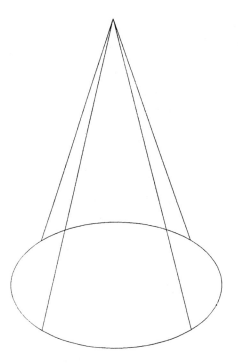

Figure 12.17 A solid cone.

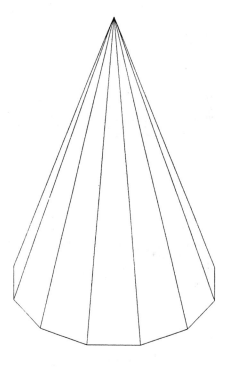

Figure 12.18 The cone after meshing and hiding showing tessellation lines used for the base circle.

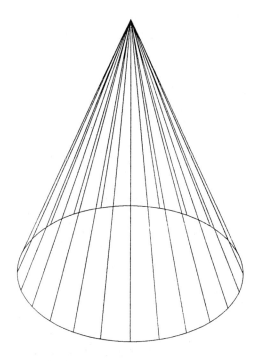

Figure 12.19 A solid cone using a solid wire density of 6.

Meshing a Solid: Exercise 12.5

1. Enter **SOLMESH** at the command prompt or pick Model/Display/Mesh from the Pull-down Menus.
2. At the **Select objects:** prompt pick the cone. Processing time varies with the hardware being used which determines how long to display the meshed cone.
3. After the cone is meshed notice how the display changes. There are more elements and the base of the cone changes from a circle to a series of straight line segments. These are referred to as *tessellation lines.* Tessellation lines are displayed for curved surfaces for better visualization.
4. Enter **HIDE** at the command prompt to display the cone with hidden lines removed. Figure 12.18.

The image used to represent the cone can be changed through use of the **SOLWDENS** variable. This variable sets the value of the wire density of a solid model at the time of creation using a setting between 1 and 12. The default setting is 1 and higher values will increase the number of wires used to display a solid. Higher settings also improve the display of shaded and hidden line renderings but causes Boolean operations to take longer to perform. Try to avoid using a wire density greater than 6. Increasing the wire density also increases the accuracy of surface calculations using the Inquiry command. Figure 12-19 shows the same cone re-created using a value of 6 for the wire density. Figure 12.20 shows the cone after meshing and hiding.

Creating a Solid Elliptical Cone

An elliptical cone is created by entering the diameter of one axis of the elliptical base and the radius of the other or by entering the center of the ellipse and the radius of each of its axes. The following steps describe how to create a solid elliptical cone:

Creating a Solid Elliptical Cone: Exercise 12.6

1. Begin a new drawing by selecting New from the Files Pull-down Menu. Select **CONE** from the Solid Primitives Pull-down Menu or **Solcone** from the Solid Menu..
2. **Baseplane/Elliptical/Center/<Corner of box> <0,0,0>:** To create an elliptical cone enter **E** at the prompt.
3. **<Axis endpoint 1>/Center:** Enter coordinate values **5,4,0** for the first axis endpoint.
4. **Axis endpoint 2:** Enter coordinate values **7,4,0** for the second axis endpoint. This will create an elliptical base with a minor axis value of 2.
5. **Other axis distance:** Enter a value of **6,2,0** to create a major axis value of 4.
6. **Apex/<Height>:** Enter a value of **4** to create the cone.
7. Enter **VPOINT** at the command prompt then enter **1,-1,1** . Figure 12.21. A negative value would have created a cone with the vertex 4 units below the center on the negative Z-axis.

Creating a Right Circular Cylinder

A circular cylinder has a circular base with straight line elements that are parallel. With AME, the base of the cylinder lies in the X-Y plane of the current UCS and the vertex is along the Z-axis. A solid cylinder is created by defining the size of the circular or elliptical base and the height. The following steps show how to create a solid circular cylinder:

Creating a Solid Circular Cylinder: Exercise 12.7

1. Open a new drawing then select **CYLINDER** from the Solid Primitives Pull-down Menu or **Solcyl** from the Solid Menu.
2. **Baseplane/Elliptical/<Center point> 0,0,0:** To create a circular cylinder enter the coordinate position for the center point or pick a point. For this example enter the values **5,4,0.** By locating a center point you are indicating that a circular cylinder is to be created.
3. **Diameter.<Radius>:** Enter a radius by picking a point or entering coordinate values. Use a radius of 1 for this example.

4. **Center of other end/<Height>:** Enter a value of **4** to create the cylinder. A negative value would have created a cylinder with the vertex 4 units below the center on the negative Z-axis.

5. Enter **VPOINT** at the command prompt then enter **1,-1,1**. Figure 12.22.

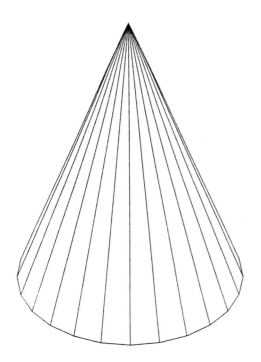

Figure 12.20 A solid cone after meshing and hiding using a solid wire density of 6.

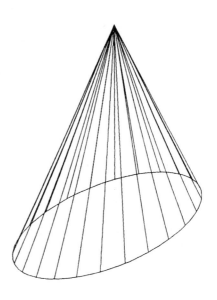

Figure 12.21 An elliptical solid cone.

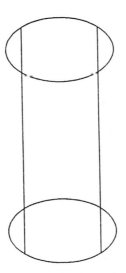

Figure 12.22 A solid cylinder.

Creating a Solid Elliptical Cylinder

An elliptical cylinder is created by entering the diameter of one axis of the elliptical base and the radius of the other or by entering the center of the ellipse and the radius of each of its axes. The following steps describe how to create a solid elliptical cylinder:

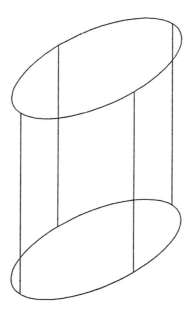

Figure 12.23 An solid elliptical cylinder.

Creating a Solid Elliptical Cylinder: Exercise 12.8

1. Open a new drawing then select **CYLINDER** from the Solid Primitives Pull-down Menu or **Solcyl** from the Solid Menu.
2. Enter **E** to select the elliptical option.
3. **<Axis endpoint 1>/Center:** Enter coordinate values **5,4,0** for the first axis endpoint.
4. **Axis endpoint 2:** Enter coordinate values **7,4,0** for the second axis endpoint. This will create an elliptical base with a minor axis value of 2.
5. **Other axis distance:** Enter a value of **6,2,0** to create a major axis value of 4.
6. **Height of cylinder:** Enter a value of **4** to create the elliptical cylinder in Figure 12.11.
5. Enter **VPOINT** at the command prompt then enter **1,-1,1**. Figure 12.23

Creating a Solid Sphere

A sphere is a solid geometric primitive with all its surface points an equal distance from the center. With AME, a sphere is created by entering the location of its center and a radius or diameter. The center point is coincident with the Z axis and latitudinal lines are parallel to the X-Y plane of the current UCS. The following steps describe how to create a solid sphere:

Creating a Solid Sphere: Exercise 12.9

1. Open a new drawing then select **SPHERE** from the Solid Primitives Pull-down Menu or **Solsphere** from the Solid Menu.
2. **Baseplane/<Center of sphere> <0,0,0>:** Enter coordinate values **5,4,0**.
3. **Diameter/<Radius> of sphere:** Enter a value of **3** to create a solid sphere with a radius of 3, as shown in Figure 12.24. Notice that half of the sphere is located in the positive Z-axis direction and half is located in a negative Z direction because the center was located at zero on the Z-axis in Step 2.
4. Enter **VPOINT** at the command prompt then enter **1,-1,1**. Figure 12.24.

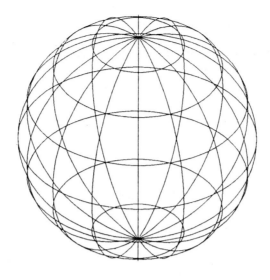

Figure 12.24 A solid sphere.

Creating a Solid Torus

A torus is a double curved geometric form created by revolving a curve about an axis that is not symmetrical with the curve. With AME, a torus is created by entering the location of the center, the diameter or radius of the torus, and the diameter or radius of the tube. The following steps describe how to create a solid torus:

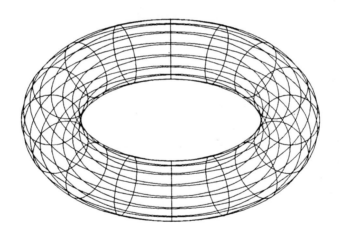

Figure 12.25 A solid torus.

Creating a Solid Torus: Exercise 12.10

1. Open a new drawing then select **TORUS** from the Solid Primitives Pull-down Menu or **Soltorus** from the Solid Menu.
2. **Baseplane/<Center of torus> <0,0,0>:** Enter the coordinate points **5,4,0** or pick it with the input device.
3. **Diameter/<Radius> of torus:** Enter a value of **4** to create a torus with a radius of 4.
4. **Diameter/<Radius> of tube:** Enter a value of **1** to create a torus with a tube radius of 1.
5. Enter **VPOINT** at the command prompt then enter **1,-1,1**. Figure 12.25.

It is possible to create other double curved geometric forms with the Soltorus command by entering a tube radius greater than the torus radius. Figure 12.26 shows a solid form created by entering a value of 2 for the torus radius in Step 3 and a value of 4 for the tube radius in Step 4. Entering a negative torus radius of -2 in Step 3 would create a football-shaped solid form, as shown in Figure 12.27.

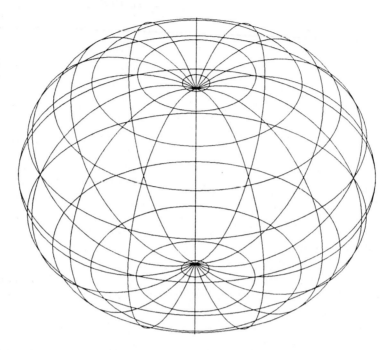

Figure 12.26 A solid torus using a tube radius greater than the torus radius.

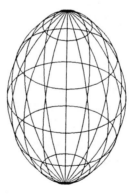

Figure 12.27 A football shaped torus created by using a negative torus radius value.

Creating a Solid Wedge

A wedge is a rectangular prism that has been cut in half diagonally along one of the faces. With AME, the base of the wedge is drawn parallel to the current UCS with the sloped face tapering along the X-axis. The following steps describe how to create a wedge:

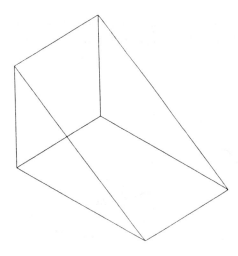

Figure 12.28 A solid wedge.

Creating a Solid Wedge: Exercise 12.11

1. To create a solid wedge enter **WEDGE** at the command prompt or pick **WEDGE** from the Solid Primitive Pull-down Menu or **Solwedge** from the Solid Menu.

2. **Baseplane/<Corner of wedge> <0,0,0>:** The first corner is a point on the base of the wedge in the X-Y plane of the current UCS. Pick the corner point with the input device or enter coordinates. For this example enter **0,0,0**.

3. **Length/<Other corner>:** Enter coordinates **6,4,0** to locate the diagonal corner of the rectangular base of the wedge.

4. **Height:** Enter the height measured along the Z-axis. For this example enter **4**.

5. Enter **VPOINT** at the command prompt then enter **1,-1,1**. Figure 12.28.

COMPOSITE SOLID MODELING

Several solids combined to form a single object is referred to as a *composite solid*. AME provides 8 commands that can be used to create composite solids:

- **SOLUNION**   UNION
- **SOLINT**   INTERSECTION
- **SOLSUB**   SUBTRACTION
- **SOLEXT**   EXTRUSION
- **SOLREV**   REVOLUTION
- **SOLCHAM**   CHAMFER
- **SOLFILL**   FILLET
- **SOLINTERF**   INTERFERENCE

Creating Solid Geometric Forms Using Extrusion

There are many examples of geometric forms used in design that are not and cannot be made of regular primitive forms. To create solids that are not made from regular primitive shapes the **Solext** (extrusion) and **Solrev** (revolution) options are used. Only polylines, polygons, circles, ellipses, and 3D poly entities can be extruded. A 2D polyline or polygon is extruded perpendicular to its 2D plane. The polyline must contain at least 3 vertices but not more than 500 to be extruded. Polylines with crossing or intersecting segments cannot be extruded. If a polyline is not closed it will be extruded as if it were closed. A taper angle can be used when creating an extrusion with AME.

The taper angle can be used to create pyramids or truncated cones. Taper angles must be greater than zero but less than 90. Tapers are only created in from the base and not out so it is impossible for the extruded end to be larger than the original polyline.

The following steps demonstrate how to create a composite 3D solid model from a polyline and circles:

Creating a Composite Solid Model Using Extrusion: Exercise 12.12

1. Open **LAB12-2** from your data disk.
2. Pick Extrude from the Model Pull-down Menu or enter **SOLEXT** from the command prompt
3. At the **Select objects:** prompt stretch a window around the geometry then press Retu m.
4. At the **Height of extrusion:** prompt enter 4.
5. At the **Extrusion taper angle <0>:** prompt enter 0.
6. To display the 3D solid model enter **VPOINT** at the command prompt then enter **1,-1,1** to display the model as shown in Figure 12.29.

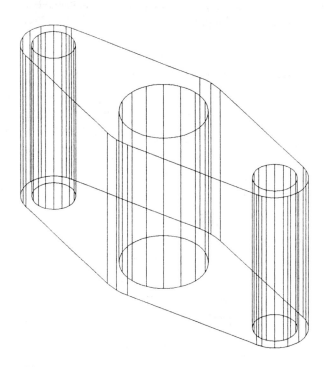

Figure 12.29 3D solid model created using extrusion.

The following steps demonstrate how to use the taper angle to create a pyramid from a polyline drawn in the shape of a rectangle:

Creating a Pyramid Using a Tapered Extrusion: Exercise 12.13

1. Open **LAB12-3** from your data disk, the select **Extrude** from the Primitives Pull-down Menu or enter **Solext** at the command prompt.
2. **Select regions, polylines and circles for extrusion...**
   Select objects: Pick the rectangular shaped polyline using the input device.
3. **Height of extrusion:** Enter a height of **6.**
4. **Extrusion taper angle <0>:** Enter a taper angle of **30.** The solid pyramid is displayed on screen, as shown in Figure 12.30.

Figure 12.31 shows a truncated cone created by extruding a circle by entering a value of 1 for the height in Step 3 and an angle of 30 in Step 4. You can try this by opening **LAB12-4**.

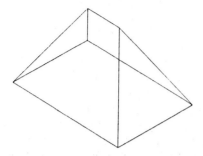

Figure 12.30 A solid pyramid created using a tapered extrusion of a rectangle.

Figure 12.31 A truncated solid cone created by using a tapered extrusion of a circle.

Creating Solid Geometric Forms Using Revolution

Unique solid shapes can be created by sweeping a polyline about an axis using the **Solrev** command. Only polylines, polygons, circles, ellipses, and 3D poly objects can be revolved. The polyline must contain at least 3 vertices but not more than 500 to be revolved. Polylines with crossing or intersecting segments cannot be revolved. If a polyline is not closed it will be revolved as if it were closed.

The following steps demonstrate how to create a revolved form from the polyline shown in Figure 12.32:

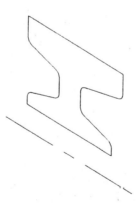

Figure 12.32 Pline to be revolved to create a solid.

Creating a Solid Using Revolution: Exercise 12.14

1. Open **LAB12-5** then select **Revolve** from the Solid Primitives Pull-down Menu or enter **Solrev** at the command prompt.

2. **Select region, polyline and circle for revolution...**
Select objects: Pick any point along the polyline. The polyline will be highlighted. Enter **Return** to terminate the selection.

3. **Axis of revolution - Entity /X/Y/<Start point of axis>:** AutoCAD provides four methods of defining the axis of revolution. The Entity option is used to select an existing line. The X option uses the positive X axis of the current UCS. The Y option uses the positive Y axis of the current UCS. The default option is to select two points on the drawing. For this example use the Entity option by entering **E** at the prompt then **Return**.

4. **Pick entity to revolve about:** Pick the line on the drawing to be used as the axis.

5. **Included angle <full circle>:** At this point it is possible to revolve the selected polyline from 1 to 360 degrees. Select the default setting by entering **Return**. After a moment the polyline profile is revolved 360 degrees creating a wheel.

6. Select **Display** from the Solid Primitives Pull-down Menu.

7. Select **Mesh** from the Display Menu and pick any point on the wheel and Return. After a moment the object is meshed and ready for hidden line removal.

8. Enter **Hide** at the command prompt to display the wheel with hidden lines removed, as shown in Figure 12.33.

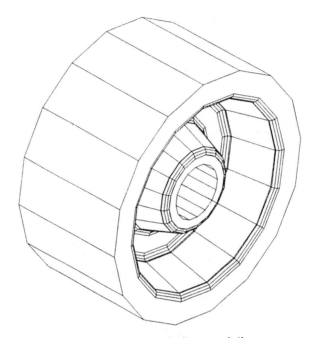

Figure 12.33 Solid formed after revolution.

Making Solids from Wireframe Geometry

The AME command **Solidify** is used to change Polylines, Polygons, Circles, Ellipses, Traces, Donuts, and 2D Solid entities with non-zero thickness to solid forms. Notice in Figure 12.34 that the polyline shape is hollow. The following steps show how to change the 3D polyline into a solid form:

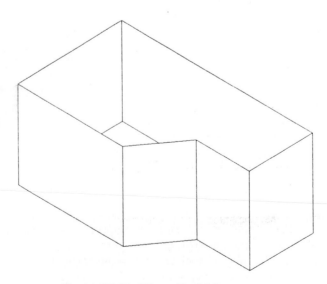

Figure 12.34 Pline with thickness.

Making a Solid From a Pline: Exercise 12.15

1. Open **LAB12-6** then select **Solidify** from the Model Pull-down Menu.
2. **Select objects:** Pick one of the entities in the polyline shape. The polylines will be highlighted. Select **Return** to begin the solidify operation.
3. After the polyline is changed into a solid form use the AME command Mesh then Hide to display the object as shown in Figure 12.35. Notice that the object no longer appears to be hollow when the hidden lines are removed.

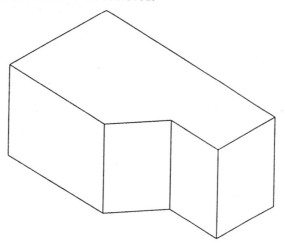

Figure 12.35 Pline solidified into a solid.

Using Boolean Operations to Create Solid Models

Boolean operators can be used to create new composite models from two or more solid objects. AME Boolean operators are:

Union- ame command **SOLUNION,** adding two or more existing solid objects to create a new composite solid.

Subtraction- ame command **SOLSUB,** subtracting two or more existing solid objects to create a new composite solid.

Intersection- AME command **SOLINT,** finding the overlapping volume of solid objects to form a new composite solid.

Figure 12.36 shows the results of various Boolean operations on two cylinders.

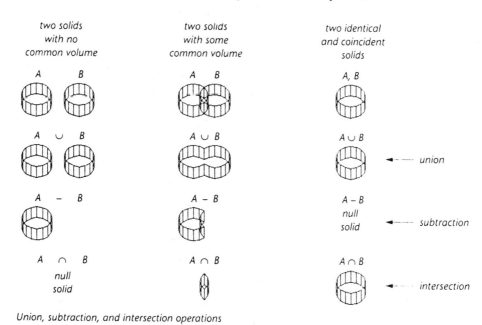

Figure 12.36 Union, subtraction, and intersection Boolean operations (Autodesk, Inc.)

Creating Solid Models using Union

The AME command used to add two or more solids is **Solunion.** Figure 12.37 shows two solid primitive shapes whose volumes share some common space. Hidden lines have been removed for visualization purposes. Notice that the corner of the box and part of the cylinder that share the same volume are shown. The following steps describe how to use the AME union operation to combine the two primitive shapes:

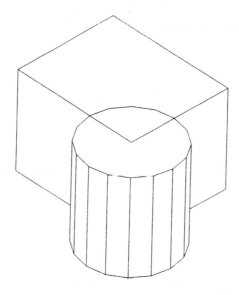

Figure 12.37 Two primitives before unioning.

Creating a Composite Solid by Union: Exercise 12.16

1. Open **LAB12-7** then select **Union** from the Solid Modify Pull-down Menu or enter **Solunion** at the command prompt.

2. **Select objects:** Pick the box and the cylinder in any order. The solids are highlighted to indicate selection. Enter **Return** to terminate the selection process and begin the union operation. Enter **Mesh** at the command prompt and pick the unioned solid then enter **Hide** to display the object shown in Figure 12.38. Notice how the area with shared volume no longer shows the corner of the box or part of the cylinder.

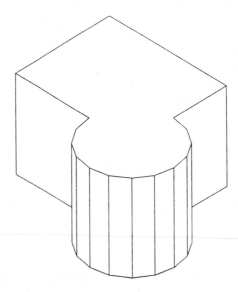

Figure 12.38 Two primitives after unioning.

Creating Solid Models using Subtraction

The AME command used to subtract two or more solids is **Solsub.** Figure 12.39 shows three solid primitive shapes whose volumes share some common space. The following steps describe how to use the AME subtraction operation to combine two or more primitive shapes:

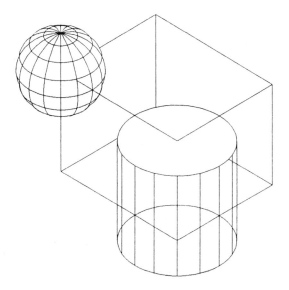 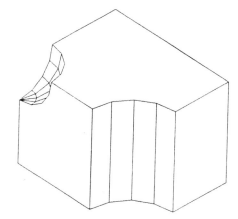

Figure 12.39 Three primitives before subtraction. Figure 12.40 Result of subtracting the cylinder and sphere from the box.

Creating a Solid by Subtraction: Exercise 12.17

1. Open **LAB12-8** then select **Subtract** from the Solid Modify Pull-down Menu or enter **Solsub** at the command prompt.
2. **Source object...**
   Select objects: Pick the box as the source object. The source object is the solid form which volume(s) will be subtracted. The box is highlighted to indicate selection. More than one object can be selected as a source. Enter **Return** to terminate the selection of source objects.
3. **Select objects:** Pick the cylinder then the sphere to indicate the solid objects to subtract from the box. Enter **Return** to terminate the selection process and begin the subtraction operation. Enter **Mesh** at the command prompt and pick the solid then enter **Hide** to display the results of the subtraction operation shown in Figure 12.40.

Creating Solid Models using Intersection

Solint is the AME command used to create a new composite solid object by determining the intersecting volume between two solids. Figure 12.41 shows two primitive shapes that share common intersecting volumes. In this example the use of the intersection operation is used to create a truncated cylinder. The following steps describe how to use AME intersection operation to create a new solid form:

Creating a Solid Using Intersection: Exercise 12.18

1. Open **LAB12-9** then select **Intersect** from the Solid Modify Pull-down Menu or enter **Solint** at the command prompt.

2. **Select objects:** Pick the cylinder and wedge then enter **Return** to terminate selection and begin the intersection operation. Figure 12.42 shows the results of the intersecting operation which creates a truncated cylinder.

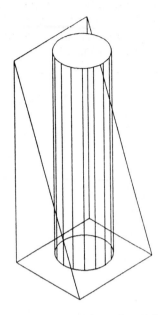

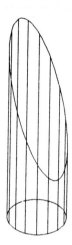

Figure 12.42 Truncated cylinder formed after intersection.

Figure 12.41 Two primitives before intersection.

Modifying Existing Solid Models

After a solid model is created it is possible to modify it using various AME commands. The modify option includes:

Fillets- add fillets to a model
Chamfers- add chamfers to a model
Separate- separates solids made from Boolean operations
Change- modifies the color, copies, moves, replaces, and changes the dimensions of solid objects.

Separating Boolean Solids

Once a solid model is created by using one of the Boolean operations it is possible to separate the resulting solid using AME command **Solsep.** To separate the result of the intersection command in Figure 12.42 select **Separate** from the Solid Modify Pull-down Menu or enter **Solsep** at the command prompt. Select the solid object to activate the separation operation. The result will be the original two solid objects shown in Figure 12.41.

Adding Fillets and Rounds to Solid Objects

The AME command **Solfill** creates a solid primitive called a fillet that automatically performs a Boolean operation of union or subtraction. The following steps describe how to create fillets and rounds with AME on the unioned objects shown in Figure 12.43:

Creating Solid Fillets: Exercise 12.19

1. Open **LAB12-10** then select **Fillet** from the Solid Modify Pull-down Menu or enter **Solfill** at the command prompt.
2. **Pick edges of solids to be filleted (Press ENTER when done):** Pick the bottom of the cylinder to create a round between the base of the cylinder and the top of the box.

Pick each corner located around the perimeter of the top of the box. Each entity is highlighted as they are selected. Enter **Return** to terminate the selection process. **Note:** The displayed geometry must be in the wireframe mode to make selections otherwise a prompt will ask if you want to change it to a wireframe to make a selection.
3. **Diameter/<Radius> of fillet <0.13>:** Enter the radius of the fillets and rounds. For this example enter the value **.25** to add fillets and rounds to the solid model. Figure 12.44 shows the results of the filleting operation on the solid model. Notice that an addition operation was performed at the base of the cylinder to add a .25 radius fillet. A subtraction operation was used along the perimeter of the top of the box to create .25 fillets.

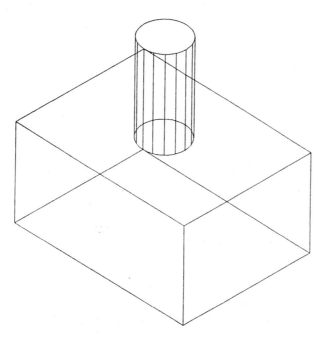

Figure 12.43 Solid model before adding fillets.

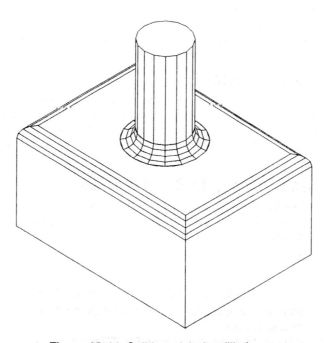

Figure 12.44 Solid model after filleting.

Adding Chamfers to Solid Objects

The AME command **Solcham** creates a solid primitive called a chamfer that will automatically perform a Boolean operation of union or subtraction. The following steps describe how to create chamfers with AME on the unioned objects shown in Figure 12.43:

Adding Chamfers to a Solid Model: Exercise 12.20

1. Open **LAB12-11** then select **Chamfer** from the Solid Modify Pull-down Menu or enter **Solcham** at the command prompt.

2. **Pick base surface:** Select the top surface of the box by picking inside of its outline.

3. **Next/<OK>:** The top surface is highlighted to give you an opportunity to change the selection by entering **N** which toggles you through the various surfaces making up the box. For this example, enter **Return** to accept the selection.

4. **Pick edges of this face to be chamfered (Press ENTER when done):** Pick each corner around the perimeter of the top surface of the box then press **Return.**

5. **Enter distance along base surface <0.00>:** Enter **.25** and **Return.**

6. **Enter distance along adjacent surface <0.25>:** Enter **Return** to accept the default setting. The solid model is updated and each corner is chamfered, as shown in Figure 12.45.

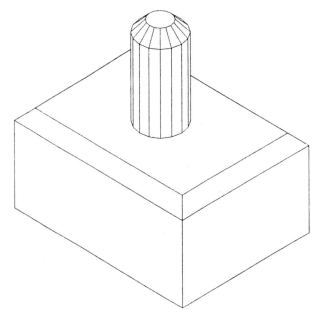

Figure 12.45 Solid model after chamfering.

Moving Solids Objects

The **Solmove** command is used to translate the solid object using a temporary coordinate system called a Motion Coordinate System (MCS) shown in Figure 12.46. The single tipped arrow is the X-axis, the double tipped arrow is the Y-axis, and the triple tipped arrow is the Z-axis on the MCS. The following is a list of motion descriptors for the MCS:

a- aligns objects with the selected coordinate system, such as **e** (edge coordinate), **f** (face coordinate), **u** (UCS), **w** (world coordinate system).

r- rotates objects about the X, Y or Z axis

t- moves or translates along the X, Y, or Z axis.

e- sets axes to align with the edge of a solid object.

f- sets axes to align with the face of a solid object.

u- sets axes to the UCS.

w- sets axes to the WCS.

o- restores object to the original orientation and position.

The following steps describe how to use the **Solmove** command to move the solid object:

Moving Solids: Exercise 12.21

1. Open **LAB12-12** then enter **Solmove** at the command prompt or select Solid Move from the Solid Modify Pull-down Menu.

2. **Select objects:** Pick the solid model and enter **Return** which will highlight the model and display the MCS, as shown in Figure 12.46.

3. **<Motion description>/?:** To rotate the solid 30 degrees about the MCS X-axis enter **RX30.** Figure 12.47 shows the results of this action. Rotation about the Y-axis is by entering **RY** and the number of degrees. Figure 12.48. Rotation about the Z-axis is by entering **RZ** and the number of degrees. Figure 12.49. The solid can be translated a distance along the MCS axes by entering **TX, TY,** or **TZ** and the distance. The MCS can also be moved relative to the model faces by entering **F** and selecting the face, moved relative to the model edge by entering **E** and selecting the edge, set to the UCS by entering **U**, set to the WCS by entering **W**, or restored to its original position by entering **O**. The new position can be cancelled by entering Ctrl-C which returns the model back to its original position.

Changing Attributes of a Solid Model

After a solid model is created it is possible to change some of the properties such as color, size, placement, and to delete or replace with another solid form. The AME command **Chprim** or Model/Modify/Change Prim... from the Pull-down Menu is used to change a solid model. To change the solid model select the model, the primitive to be changed, and the attribute to change. For example, to change the size of the chamfer on the cylinder pick the cylinder in Figure 12.45 then select **Size**. When prompted enter a new distance along the first then second surfaces, then exit. Figure 12.50 shows the results of changing the size of the chamfer on the end of the cylinder.

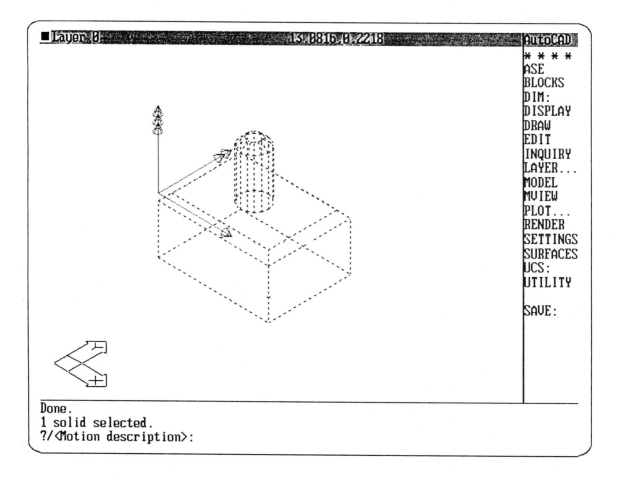

Figure 12.46 The Motion Description Coordinate System (MCS) axes.

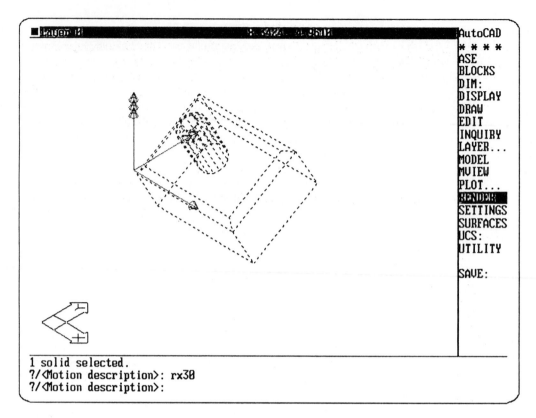

Figure 12.47 Solid rotated 30 degrees on the X-axis.

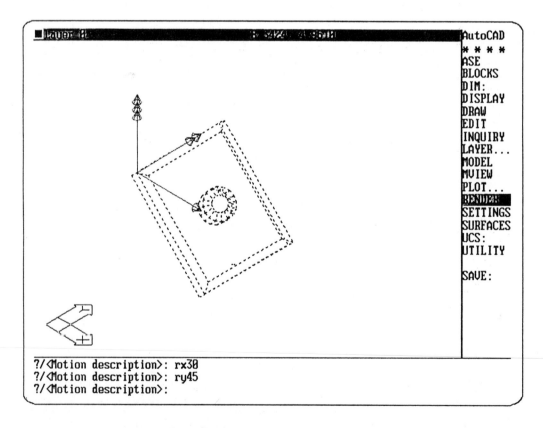

Figure 12.48 Solid rotated 45 degrees on the Y-axis.

Determining Properties of a Model

The Inquiry Pull-down Menu shown in Figure 12.51 shows the options available to determine various properties of a solid model. **List Objects** is used to display the definition information for a solid object, edge or face, as shown in Figure 12.52. **Mass Property** is used to determined the mass, center of gravity, moments of inertia, radii of gyration, moments and directions, as shown in Figure 12.53. **Solid Area** is used to determine the surface area of a solid object and displays it in the prompt line. Selecting Model/Setup from the Pull-down Menus is used to change the units used in calculations for the inquiry commands The **British Units** option is used to change displayed values into British units of feet and pounds. **CSG Units** is used to display values in centimeters and grams. **SI Units** is used to display values in meters and kilograms.

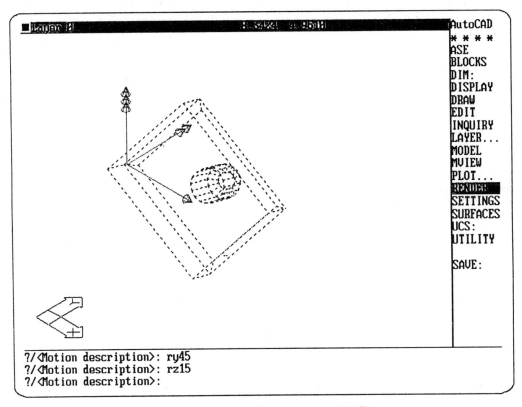

Figure 12.49 Solid rotated 15 about the Z-axes.

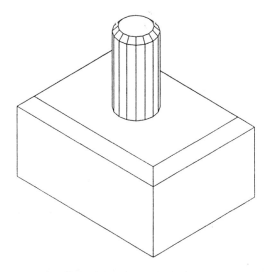

Figure 12.50 Chamfer on end of cylinder changed is size.

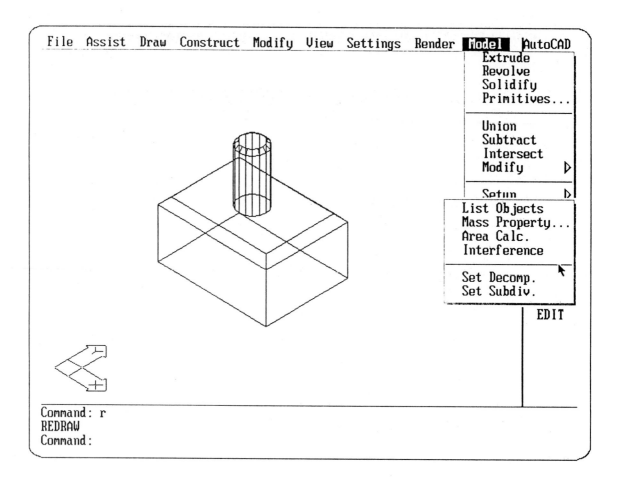

Figure 12.51 The Inquiry Menu.

```
Object type = SUBTRACTION     Handle = 1905
    Component handles:   17FD and 18CA
    Area = 55.842263    Material = MILD_STEEL
    Representation = PMESH    Render type = CSG
Rigid motion:
        +1.000000       +0.000000       +0.000000       +0.000000
        +0.000000       +1.000000       +0.000000       +0.000000
        +0.000000       +0.000000       +1.000000       +0.000000
        +0.000000       +0.000000       +0.000000       +1.000000


Command:
```

Figure 12.52 The List Object information.

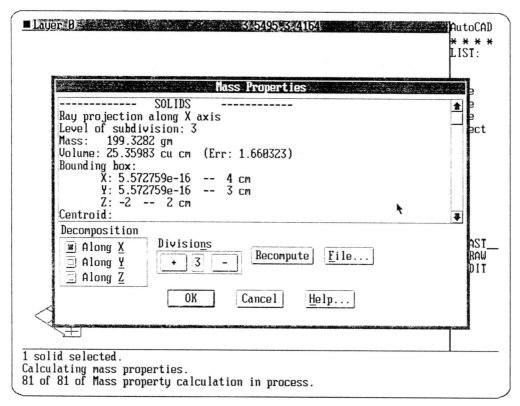

Figure 12.53 The mass property dialogue box.

CREATING 3D MODELS AND 2D DRAWINGS

This section describes how to create 3D models of a mechanical assembly. Figure 12.54. 2D profiles will be created that will be used for extrusions or revolutions to create the 3D models. Simple analysis procedures will be performed on the parts. Two-dimensional orthographic drawings will be created from the 3D models to create working drawings.

Creating the Profile and 3D Model of the Wheel

The profile of the wheel must be drawn using Polylines. The AME command **REVOLVE** is used to create the 3D model from the 2D Polylines.

Creating the Wheel Profile: Exercise 12.22

1. Open a new drawing then change the viewpoint by entering **VPOINT** at the command prompt and entering **1,-1.,1.** Set the snap spacing by entering **SNAP** at the command prompt

2. **Snap spacing or ON/OFF/Aspect/Rotate/Style <1.0000>:** Enter **.25** and **RETURN**.

3. Before drawing the profile of the Wheel a new layer is created named Wheel which is made current.

4. Change the color to **YELLOW**.

5. Change the linetype to **CENTER**.

6. A center line is drawn that will be used as the axis of revolution. Draw the center line by entering **LINE** at the command prompt.

7. **From point:** Enter coordinates **0,-2.**

8. **To point:** Enter **0,2.**

9. Pan the line onto the screen using the **PAN** command.

10. From the Settings Pull-down Menu select Layer Control... then change the color to **WHITE.**

11. Change the linetype back to **CONTINUOUS**.

12. Draw the profile of the Wheel using Polylines. Enter **PLINE** at the command prompt.

13. Enter the coordinates for the first point, **.5, -1**.

14. **Current line-width is 0.0000
Arc/Close/Halfwidth/Length/Undo/Width/<Endpoint of line>:** Enter the coordinate **.875, -1**.

15. **.875,-.25.**

16. **2.25,-.25.**

17. **2.25,-1.**

18. **2.5,-1.**

19. **2.5,1.**

20. **2.25,1.**

21. **2.25,.25.**

22. **.875,.25.**

23. **.875,1.**

24. **.5,1.**

25. **Close.** The profile of the Wheel is complete. Fillets have to be added to some of the corners before revolving it into a 3D model.

26. Enter **FILLET** at the command prompt.

27. **Polyline/Radius/<Select first object>:** Enter **R** to set the radius of the fillets.

28. **Enter fillet radius.** Enter a radius of **.125**.

29. Enter **RETURN** at the command prompt to repeat the **FILLET** command.

30. **Polyline/Radius/<Select first object>:** Pick the first line of the corner to be rounde d.

31. After picking the line the whole polyline is highlighted and the prompt reads: **Select second object:** Pick the other line that is part of the corner. The corner is changed to a fillet. Repeat Steps 30 and 31 to fillet the other 3 corners, as shown in Figure 12.55.

32. Save the drawing by entering **SAVE** at the command prompt. Use the name **WHEEL-P**.

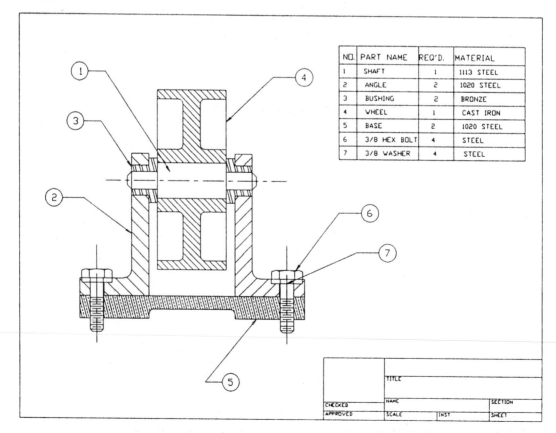

NO.	PART NAME	REQ'D.	MATERIAL
1	SHAFT	1	1113 STEEL
2	ANGLE	2	1020 STEEL
3	BUSHING	2	BRONZE
4	WHEEL	1	CAST IRON
5	BASE	2	1020 STEEL
6	3/8 HEX BOLT	4	STEEL
7	3/8 WASHER	4	STEEL

Figure 12.54 Mechanical assembly to be created as solids.

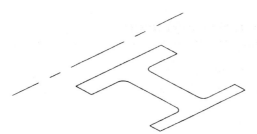

Figure 12.55 Pline profile of the wheel.

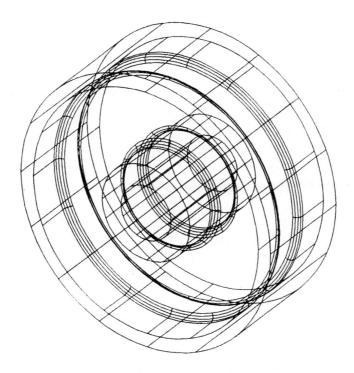

Figure 12.56 3D solid model of the wheel.

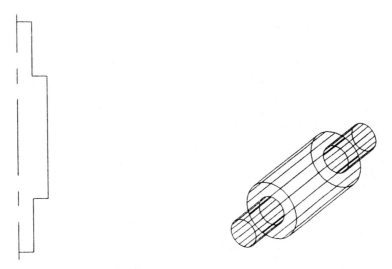

Figure 12.57 Pline profile of the shaft.   Figure 12.58 3D solid model of the shaft.

Creating a 3D Solid Model of the Wheel: Exercise 12.23

1. Set the default material that is automatically assigned to newly created solids by entering **SOLMAT** at the command prompt or by picking Model/Utility/Material... from the Pull-down Menus.
2. Enter **HSLA_STL** then load it from the ACAD.MAT directory.
3. The profile of the Wheel will be revolved into a solid model by entering **SOLREV** at the command prompt.
2. **Select region, polyline or circle for revolution...**
   Select objects: Pick the profile polyline then enter **RETURN.**
3. **Axis of revolution - Entity/X/Y/<Start point of axis>:** Enter E to select the center line as the axis of revolution.
4. **Pick entity to revolve about:** Pick the center line.
5. **Angle of revolution <full circle>:** Enter **RETURN** to select a full circle to create the wheel. Figure 12.56. Enter **SAVE** to save the file to disk using the name **WHEEL3D.**

Moving the Wheel: Exercise 12.24

The final assembly will be made by moving all the parts into position using the **SOLMOVE** command. After each 3D model is created, it will be moved away from the origin of the drawing before inserting another profile. The following steps describe how to move the wheel away from the origin before inserting the shaft profile:
1. Enter **SOLMOVE** at the command prompt or pick Model/Modify/Move Object using the Pull-down Menus.
2. Pick the wheel, then press Return.
3. The MCS is displayed on screen as green arrows. Move the model by entering **TY10.**
4. Enter **ZOOM** then **ALL** to display the 3D model of the Wheel.
5. Erase the yellow center line used for the wheel profile.

Purging Unwanted Entities

SOLPURGE is a command used to conserve memory and reduce drawing size by erasing entities associated with AME solids. This command could be used periodically when working with solids especially if you have erased solids or made changes. To execute the command enter **SOLPURGE** at the command prompt. At the **Memory/3dtree/Bfile/Pmesh/<erased>:** prompt enter the Erased option.

Creating the Profile and 3D Solid Model of the Shaft

The Shaft profile will be drawn using Polylines. Before starting the shaft profile, erase the profile of the Wheel by entering **ERASE** at the command prompt and picking the polyline. Leave the center line because it will be used as the center line for the Shaft.

Creating the Shaft Profile: Exercise 12.25

1. Make a layer called Shaft and make it current.
2. Change the color to **GREEN.**
3. Enter **PLINE** at the command prompt.
4. **From point:** Enter coordinate .25,-.375.
5. **Current line-width is 0.0000.**
   Arc/Close/Halfwidth/Length/Undo/Width/<Endpoint of line>: Enter the coordinate 0,-1.875.
6. .25,-1.875.
7. .25,-1.
8. .5,-1.
9. .5,1.
10. .25,1.
11. .25,1.875.
12. 0,1.875.
10. **Close.** The profile of the Shaft is complete, as shown in Figure 12.57.
11. Save the Shaft profile by entering **SAVE** at the command prompt. Use the name **SHAFT-P.**

Creating the 3D Solid Model of the Shaft: Exercise 12.26

1. Edit the **SHAFT-P** drawing by first zooming close to the profile drawing.
2. The profile of the Shaft will be revolved into a solid model by entering **SOLREV** at the command prompt.
3. **Select REGION, polyline or circle for revolution...**
   Select objects: Pick the profile polyline then enter **RETURN**.
4. **Axis of revolution - Entity/X/Y/<Start point of axis>:** Enter **E** to select the center line as the axis of revolution.
5. **Entity to revolve about:** Pick the center line.
6. **Included angle <full circle>:** Enter **RETURN** to select a full circle to create the shaft.
7. The ends of the Shaft must be chamfered by using the **SOLCHAM** command.
8. **Pick base surface:** Pick the end of the Shaft.
9. **Next/<OK>:** The end circle should be highlighted. If not enter **N** to select another surface. Enter **RETURN** to select the highlighted feature.
10. **Pick edges of this face to be chamfered (Press ENTER when done):** Pick the end circle with the cursor then enter **RETURN**.
11. **Enter distance along base surface <0.00>:** Enter **.125** and **RETURN**.
12, **Enter distance along second surface <.13>:** Enter **.125** and **RETURN**. The model is updated and displayed on screen.
13. Repeat the chamfer command to chamfer the other end of the Shaft. Enter **RETURN** at the command prompt.
14. **Pick base surface:** Pick the other end of the Shaft.
15. **Next/<OK>:** The end circle should be highlighted. If not enter **N** to select another surface. Enter **RETURN** to select the highlighted feature.
16. **Pick edges of this face to be chamfered (Press ENTER when done):** Pick the end circle with the cursor then enter **RETURN**.
17. **Enter distance along base surface <0.00>:** Enter **.125** and **RETURN**.
18. **Enter distance along second surface <.13>:** Enter **.125** and **RETURN**. The model is updated and displayed on screen, as shown in Figure 12.58. Enter **SAVE** to save the file to disk using the name **SHAFT3D**.

Moving the Shaft: Exercise 12.27

1. The Shaft is going to be moved into position with the Wheel by entering **SOLMOVE** at the command prompt or pick Model/Modify/Move Object using the Pull-down Menus.
2. Pick the shaft, then press Return.
3. The MCS is displayed on screen as green arrows. Move the model by entering **TY10**.
4. Enter **ZOOM** then **ALL** to display the 3D model of the Wheel and Shaft. Figure 12.59.

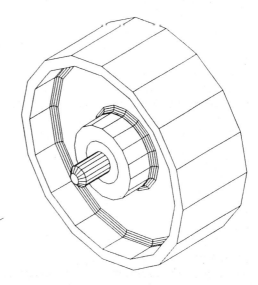

Figure 12.59 3D solid model of the assembled Shaft and Wheel.

Creating the Profile and 3D Solid Model of the Bushing

The profile of the bushing is drawn so that it can be revolved to create the solid model. The profile will be drawn using a Polyline and the existing center line from the shaft.

Creating the Bushing Profile: Exercise 12.28

1. Create a layer called Bushing and make it current.
2. Change the layer color to **BLUE.**
3. Enter **PLINE** at the command prompt.
4. **From point:** Enter coordinate .25,.375.
5. **Current line-width is 0.0000.**
   Arc/Close/Halfwidth/Length/Undo/Width/<Endpoint of line>: Enter the coordinate .25,-.375.
6. .625,-.375.
7. .625,-.125.
8. .425,-.125.
9. .425,.375.
10. **Close.** The profile of the Bushing is complete, as shown in Figure 12.60.
11. Save the Bushing profile by entering **SAVE** at the command prompt. Use the name **BUSH-P.**

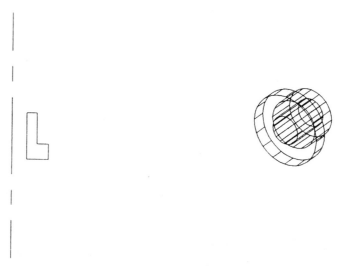

Figure 12.60 Pline profile of the bushing.   Figure 12.61 3D solid model of the bushing.

Creating a 3D Solid Model of the Bushing: Exercise 12.29

1. Zoom into the profile of the bushing.
2. Set the default material to Bronze by entering **SOLMAT** at the command prompt then **SEt** then enter **BRONZE** at the **New default material:** prompt.
3. The profile of the Bushing will be revolved into a solid model by entering **SOLREV** at the command prompt.
3. **Select region, polyline or circle for revolution...**
   Select objects: Pick the profile polyline then enter **RETURN.**
4. **Axis of revolution - Entity/X/Y/<Start point of axis>:** Enter **E** to select the center line as the axis of revolution.
5. **Entity to revolve about:** Pick the center line.
6. **Included angle <full circle>:** Enter **RETURN** to select a full circle to create the shaft.
Figure 12.61. Enter **SAVE** to save the file to disk using the name **BUSH3D.**

Moving the Bushing: Exercise 12.30

1. Enter **SOLMOVE** at the command prompt or pick Model/Modify/Move Object using the Pull-down Menus.
2. Pick the bushing, then press Return.
3. The MCS is displayed on screen as green arrows. Move the model by entering **TY11.375**. Enter Return to exit the command.
4. Enter **ZOOM** then **ALL** to display the 3D model of the Wheel.
5. Erase the center line of the bushing.

Copy/Mirroring the Second Bushing: Exercise 12.31

1. Enter **MIRROR** at the command prompt or pick it from the Construct Pull-down Menu.
2. At the **Select objects:** prompt pick the bushing then press Return.
3. At the **First point of mirror line:** prompt use Osnap Midpoint to pick a midpoint of elements on the Wheel.
4. At the **Second point:** prompt pick another midpoint of an element.
5. At the **Delete old objects? <N>:** prompt enter no. Both of the Bushings are in position as shown in Figure 12.62.

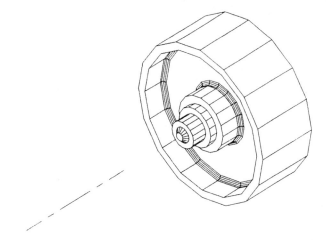

Figure 12.62 3D solid model of the assembled Shaft, Bushings, and Wheel.

Creating the Profile of the Arm

The Arm is created by drawing the profile using Lines. The lines are changed then to Polylines using the **PEDIT** command.

Creating the Arm Profile: Exercise 12.32

1. Create and make current the layer Arm.
2. Change the layer color to **CYAN**.
3. The arc will be drawn first. Enter **CIRCLE** at the command prompt.
4. **3p/2p/ttr/<Center point>:** Enter coordinate **0,0**.
5. **Diameter/<Radius>:** Enter **D** to select the diameter option.
6. **Diameter:** Enter **.75**.
7. Repeat the **CIRCLE** command to draw the circle by entering **RETURN.**
8. **3p/2p/ttr/<Center point>:** Enter coordinate **0,0**.
9. **Diameter/<Radius>:** Enter **D** to select the diameter option.
10. **Diameter:** Enter **.85**.
11. Add the lines that make up the profile of the Arm. Enter **LINE** at the command prompt.
12. **From point:** Enter coordinate value **-2,-2.75**.
13. **To point:** **-2,-3.25**.
14. **To point:** **2, -3.25**.

15. **To point: 2,-2.75.**
16. **To point:** Enter **TANGENT** in the prompt line to select the tangent OSNAP option.
17. **Tangent to:** Pick a point along the right side of the .85 diameter circle. The line will snap from the last point input tangent to the large circle.
18. Cancel the **LINE** command by entering **Ctrl-C.**
19. Repeat the **LINE** command by entering **RETURN.**
20. **From point: -2,-2.75.**
21. **To point:** Enter **TANGENT** in the prompt line to select the tangent OSNAP option.
22. **Tangent to:** Pick a point along the left side of the .85 diameter circle. The line will snap from the last point input tangent to the large circle. Cancel the **LINE** command.
23. The large circle must be trimmed to the tangent lines to complete the profile of the Arm. Enter **TRIM** at the command prompt.
24. **Select cutting edge(s)...**
    Select objects: Pick the two tangent lines then enter **RETURN.**
25. **<Select object to trim>/Undo:** Pick the bottom part of the large circle to trim it. The profile of the Arm is complete.
26. The lines used to construct the profile must be changed into Polylines to use the AME extrude command for solid modeling. Enter **PEDIT** at the command prompt.
27. **Select polyline:** Pick any one of the lines of the Arm.
28. **Entity selected is not a polyline**
    Do you want to turn it into one? <Y> Enter **RETURN** to change the lines into a polyline.
29. **Close/Join/Width/Edit vertex/Fit curve/Spline curve/Decurve/Undo/eXit <X>:** Enter **JOIN** and **RETURN.**
30. **Select objects:** Pick all the lines and the arc but not the circle in the drawing then enter **RETURN.**
31. All the selected lines are now polylines. Figure 12.63.
32. Save the profile of the Arm by entering **SAVE** at the command prompt. Enter **ARM-P** for the file name.

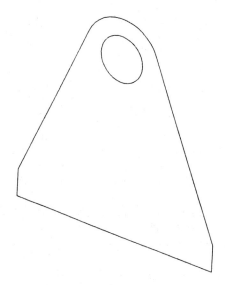

Figure 12.63 Pline profile of the arm.

Creating a Solid Model of the Arm: Exercise 12.33

1. Zoom into the profile view of the arm.
2. The profile of the Arm will be extruded into a solid model by entering **SOLEXT** at the command prompt.
3. **Select regions, polylines and circles for extrusion...**

Select objects: Pick the polyline profile after which it is highlighted. Pick the circle, then enter **RETURN.**

4. **Height of extrusion:** Enter **.5** as the height of the Arm.

5. **Extrusion taper angle from Z <0>:** No extrusion angle is necessary so enter **RETURN.** The profile is extruded into a 3D model. Figure 12.64.

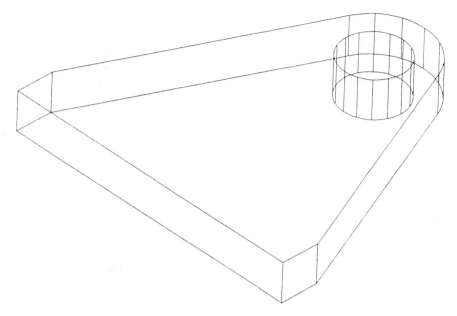

Figure 12.64 Profile after extrusion.

6. Move the UCS origin to the front lower-left corner of the Arm. Enter **UCS** at the command prompt.

7.**Origin/Zaxis/3point/Entity/View/X/Y/Z/Prev/Restore/Save/Del/?/<World>:** Enter **O** to select the Origin option.

8. **Origin point <0,0,0>:** Enter **END** to select OSNAP option Endpoint. Pick the front lower-left corner of the Arm as the new origin.

9. Move the UCS icon to its new origin by entering **UCSICON** at the command prompt.

10. **ON/OFF/All/Noorigin/ORigin <ON>:** Enter **OR** to move the UCS icon from its current position to the new origin point located at the front lower-left corner of the Arm. Figure 12.65.

11. Create a box to add to the extruded profile by entering **SOLBOX** at the command prompt

12. **Baseplane/Center/<Corner of box> <0,0,0>:** Enter **0,0,.5** and **RETURN.**

13. **Cube/Length/<Other corner>:** Enter **4,.5,.5** and **RETURN.**

14. **Height <3>:** Enter a height of **1.5** and **RETURN.** The primitive box is added to the model as shown in Figure 12.66.

15. Spot-faced holes have to be added to the Arm. Enter **SOLMOV** to move the Arm into a position that will be easier to create the box and holes.

16. **Select objects:** Pick any part of the box, then the arm profile, the hole, then enter **RETURN.**

17. **?/<Motion description>:** The solid model is highlighted and the MCS axes are displayed. Enter the descriptor **rx90** and **RETURN** twice to rotate the model 90 degrees about the X-axis. Figure 12.67.

18. Move the UCS origin to the front lower-left corner of the Arm. Enter **UCS** at the command prompt.

19. **Origin/Zaxis/3point/Entity/View/X/Y/Z/Prev/Restore/Save/Del/?/<World>:** Enter **O** to select the Origin option.

20. **Origin point <0,0,0>:** Enter **0,-2,0** and **RETURN** to move the UCS origin to the front lower-left corner of the Arm.

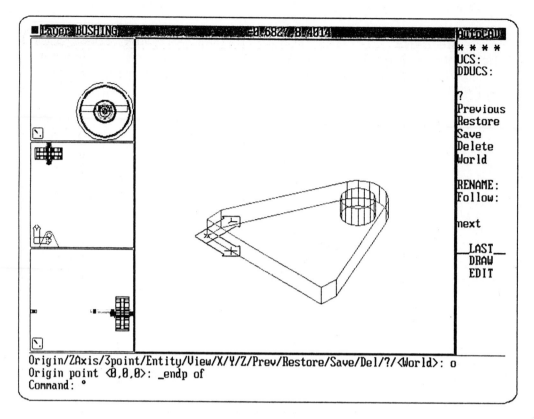

```
Origin/ZAxis/3point/Entity/View/X/Y/Z/Prev/Restore/Save/Del/?/<World>: o
Origin point <0,0,0>: _endp of
Command: °
```

Figure 12.65   Moving the UCS to a new position.

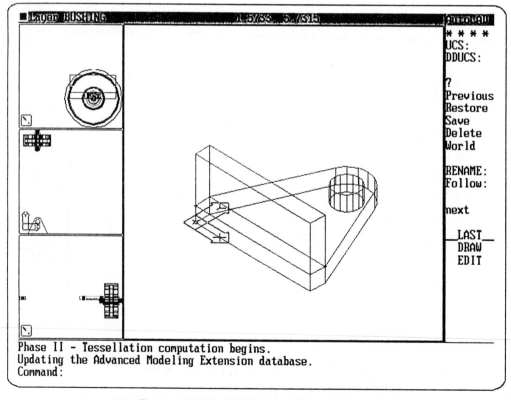

```
Phase II - Tessellation computation begins.
Updating the Advanced Modeling Extension database.
Command:
```

Figure 12.66 Adding a box to the Arm.

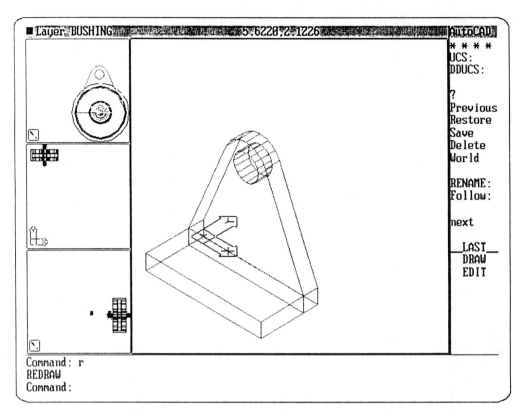

Figure 12.67 Moving the Arm.

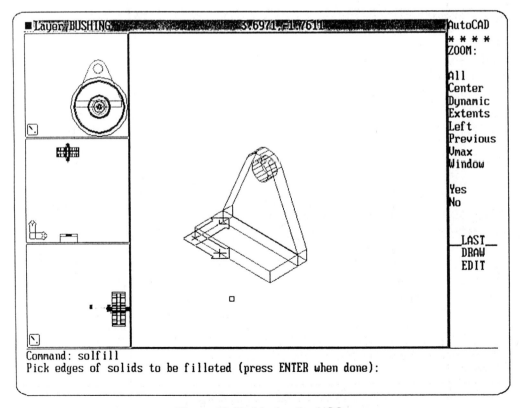

Figure 12.68 Moving the UCS.

21. **ON/OFF/All/Noorigin/ORigin <ON>:** Enter **OR** to move the UCS icon from its current position to the new origin point located at the front lower-left corner of the Arm. Figure 12.68.

22. Before making the holes add the rounds to the two corners of the box that was added to the Arm profile. Enter **SOLFILL** at the command prompt to create solid rounds.

23. **Pick edges of solid to be filleted (Press ENTER when done):** Pick the two edges then enter **RETURN**.

24. **2 edges selected.**

Diameter/<Radius> of fillet<0.25>: Enter **.25** as the fillet radius. The Boolean operations necessary to subtract the corners to create rounds are automatically performed and the results are displayed on screen. Figure 12.69.

25. To create the spot-faced holes in the Arm, cylinders must be added to the model. The small diameter cylinders will be added to the Arm first. Enter **SOLCYL** at the command prompt

26. **Baseplane/Elliptical/<Center point> <0,0,0>:** Enter the coordinate location for the cylinder as **.625,.5,0.**

27. **Diameter/<Radius>:** Use the diameter option by entering **D** and **RETURN**.

28. **Diameter:** Enter **.390** and **RETURN**.

29. **Center of other end/<Height>:** Enter a height of **.5.** The cylinder is automatically added to the Arm and displayed on screen.

30. Enter **RETURN** to repeat the **SOLCYL** command.

31. **Elliptical/<Center point>:** Enter the coordinate location for the second cylinder as **3.375,.5 ,0.**

32. **Diameter/<Radius>:** Use the diameter option by entering **D** and **RETURN**.

33. **Diameter:** Enter **.390** and **RETURN**.

34. **Center of other end/<Height>:** Enter a height of **.5.** The cylinder is automatically added to the model and displayed on screen.

35. Enter **RETURN** to repeat the **SOLCYL** command to add the spot-faces.

36. **Elliptical/<Center point>:** Enter the coordinate location for the first spot-face as **.625 ,.5, .325.**

37. **Diameter/<Radius>:** Use the diameter option by entering **D** and **RETURN**.

38. **Diameter:** Enter **.875** and **RETURN**.

39. **Center of other end/<Height>:** Enter a height of **.175.** The spot-face is automatically added to the model and displayed on screen.

40. Enter **RETURN** to repeat the **SOLCYL** command to add the spot-faces.

41. **Elliptical/<Center point>:** Enter the coordinate location for the first spot-face as **3.375,.5 ,.325.**

42. **Diameter/<Radius>:** Use the diameter option by entering **D** and **RETURN**.

43. **Diameter:** Enter **.875** and **RETURN**.

44. **Center of other end/<Height>:** Enter a height of **.175.** The spot-face is automatically added to the model and displayed on screen. Figure 12.70.

45. The base geometry is complete. Boolean operations must be performed to create a solid model of the Arm. The first step is to add the box to the extruded profile by entering **SOLUNION.**

46. **Select objects:** Pick the extruded profile and the primitive box which are highlighted on screen. Enter **RETURN** to combine the two primitives into one solid.

47. The 5 primitive cylinders that make up the spot-faced holes and the hole in the extruded portion of the Arm must be subtracted from the base geometry using Boolean operations. Enter **SOLSUB** at the command prompt to subtract the cylinders.

48. **Source objects...**

Select objects: The source object is the base geometry that was just unioned. Pick any line that highlights the unioned geometry and enter **RETURN**.

49. **Objects to subtract from them...**

Select objects: Pick all five cylinders one at a time and enter **RETURN**.

50. AME automatically subtracts the cylinders from the base geometry completing the solid model of the Arm.

51. Change the material of the Arm by entering **SOLMAT** at the command prompt or picking it from the Model menus.

52. Use the Change option then pick the arm.
53. Enter **MILD_STEEL** then exit to change the material assigned for the Arm.
51. Enter **SAVE** to save the file to disk using the name **ARM3D**.

An alternative method to create a spotface uses one of AutoCAD's bonus programs. called **CBORE**. This is a special Autolisp command specifically designed to make counterbores or spotfaces on existing holes. The following steps describe how to use this special command to spotface the holes in the arm by replacing steps 35-44:
1. At the command prompt enter **(load"hole")** or use the Files/Applications Pull-down Menu. You may have to change the directory path to open the lisp file.
2. Enter **HOLE** at the command prompt.
3. Enter **CBORE** to begin the command.
4. At the **Select planar face with hole to CBore:** prompt pick the top of one of the holes. You may need to use the Next option to get the top of the cylinder.
5. At the **Select edge of hole to CBore:** prompt pick the top of the cylinder.
6. At the **Radius or <Diameter> of CBore <0.585>:** prompt enter **.875**.
7. At the **Depth of CBore:<1.0>:** prompt enter **.175**.

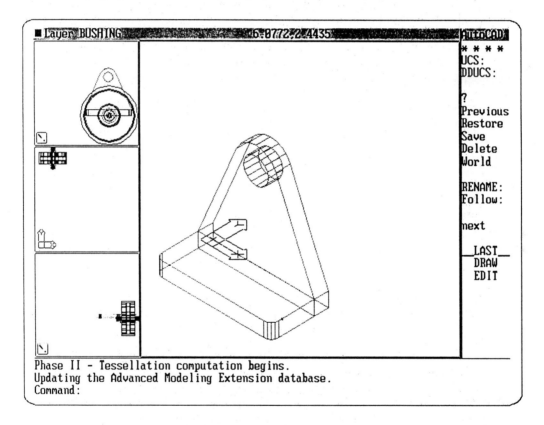

Figure 12.69 Filleting the corners.

Moving the Arm into the Assembly: Exercise 12.34

1. Use the **MOVE** command to move the Arm into the assembly by entering it at the command prompt or picking it from the Modify Pull-down Menu.
2. At the **Select objects:** prompt pick the Arm then enter Return.
3. At the **Base point or displacement:** prompt enter the Osnap command **CEN** then pick the center of the .75 diameter hole in the Arm.
4. At the **Second point of displacement:** prompt enter **'Z** to use the Zoom command.
5. Zoom into the end of the assembly close to the shaft.
6. Enter **CEN** and pick the end of the Bushing. The Arm will be moved to its new position in the assembly. Figure 12.71.

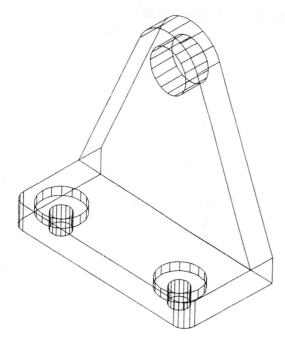

Figure 12.70 3D solid model of the Arm.

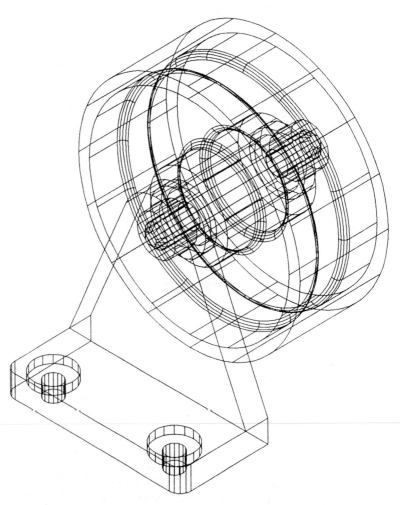

Figure 12.71 Moving the Arm into position in the assembly.

Copy/Mirroring the Second Arm: Exercise 12.35

1. In the large viewport change the viewpoint to a top view by entering **VPOINT** at the display prompt then entering **0,0,1**. Zoom if necessary to view the assembly.

2. Enter **MIRROR** at the command prompt or pick it from the Construct Pull-down Menu.

2. At the **Select objects:** prompt pick the Arm then press Return.

3. At the **First point of mirror line:** prompt use Osnap Midpoint to pick a midpoint of elements on the Wheel.

4. At the **Second point:** prompt pick another midpoint of an element.

5. At the **Delete old objects? <N>:** prompt enter no. To view the Arms in the position shown in Figure 12.72 change the Vpoint to 1,-1,1.

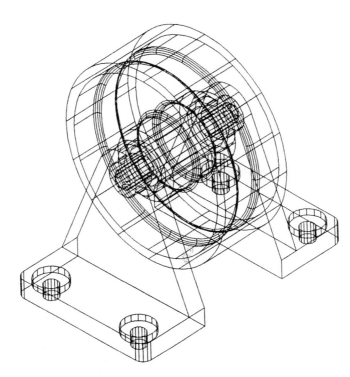

Figure 12.72 Copy/Mirroring the other Arm.

Creating the Profile of the Base Plate: Exercise 12.36

1. Create a new layer called **BASE** and make it current.

2. Set the new layer color to **RED**.

3. Enter **LINE** at the command prompt.

4. **From point:** Enter coordinate **0,0**.

5. **To point:** Enter the coordinate **2,0**.

6. **2,.25.**

7. **4.5,.25.**

8. **4.5,0.**

9. **6.5,0.**

10. **6.5,.625.**

11. **0,.625.**

12. **Close.** The profile of the Base Plate is complete except for the fillets.

13. Enter **FILLET** at the command prompt.

14. **Polyline/Radius/<Select first object>:** Enter **R** to set the radius of the fillets.

15. **Enter fillet radius.** Enter a radius of **.125**.

16. Enter **RETURN** at the command prompt to repeat the **FILLET** command.

17. **Polyline/Radius/<Select first object>:** Pick the first line of the corner to be rounde d.

18. After picking the line the whole polyline is highlighted and the prompt reads: **Select second object:** Pick the other line that is part of the corner. The corner is changed to a fillet. Repeat Steps 16 and 17 to fillet the other corner, as shown in Figure 12.73.

19. Change the lines into a Polyline by entering **PEDIT** at the command prompt.

20. Pick any of the lines in the Base Plate.

21. At the **Entity selected is not a polyline Do you want to turn it into one? <Y>:** prompt enter yes.

22. At the next prompt enter J to select the Join option.

23. At the **Select objects:** prompt use a window to pack all the lines then press Return then Return again to exit the Pedit command which joins the lines into a single polyline.

24. Save the Base Plate profile by entering **SAVE** at the command prompt. Use the name **BASE-P.**

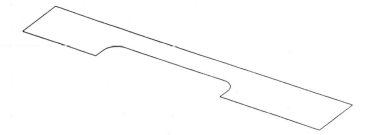

Figure 12.73 Pline profile of the base.

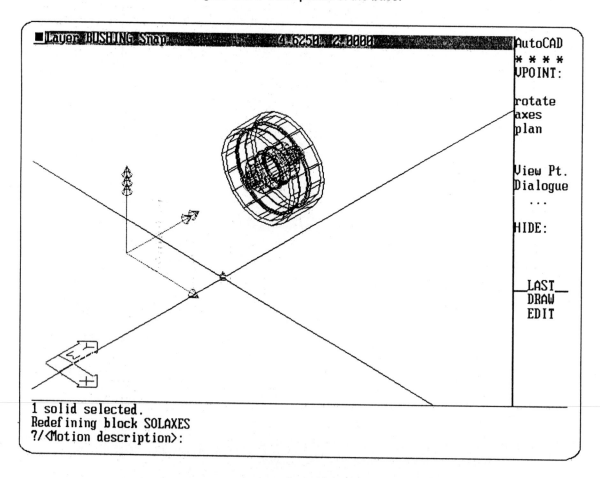

Figure 12.74 Moving the Base Plate.

Creating a 3D Solid Model of the Base Plate: Exercise 12.37

1. Zoom into the profile view of the Base.
2. The profile of the Base Plate will be extruded into a solid model by entering **SOLEXT** at the command prompt.
3. **Select polylines and circles for extrusion...**
   Select objects: Pick the polyline profile after which it is highlighted, then enter **RETURN.**
4. **Height of extrusion:** Enter **4** as the height of the Base Plate.
5. **Extrusion taper angle from Z <0>:** No extrusion angle is necessary so enter **RETURN.**
6. The profile is extruded into a 3D model. Holes have to be added to the Base Plate. Enter **SOLMOV** to move the Base Plate into a position that will be easier to create the holes.
7. **Select objects:** Pick any part of the solid model then enter **RETURN.**
8. **<Motion description>/?:** The solid model is highlighted and the MCS axes are displayed, as shown in Figure 12.74. Enter the descriptor **rx90** and **RETURN** twice to rotate the model 90 degrees about the X-axis. Figure 12.75.

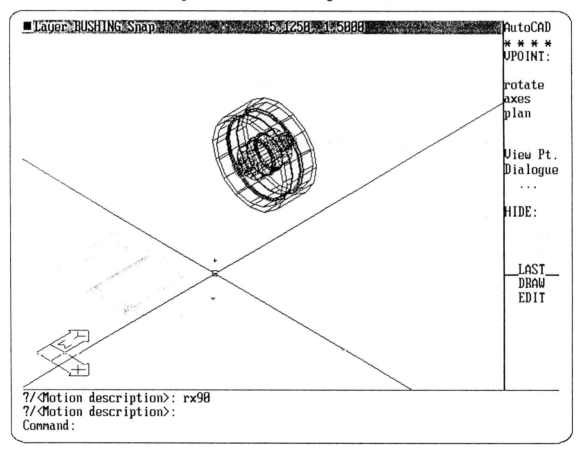

Figure 12.75 After moving the Base Plate.

9. Move the UCS origin to the front lower-left corner of the Base Plate. Enter **UCS** at the command prompt.
10. **Origin/Zaxis/3point/Entity/View/X/Y/Z/Prev/Restore/Save/Del/?/<World>:** Enter **3** to select the 3-point option.
11. **Origin point <0,0,0>:** Enter **END** to select OSNAP option Endpoint. Pick the front lower-left corner of the Base Plate as the new origin.
12. **Point on positive portion of the X-axis <1,-4,0>:** Enter **END** to select the OSNAP option Endpoint and pick the line for the X-axis, as shown in Figure 12.76.

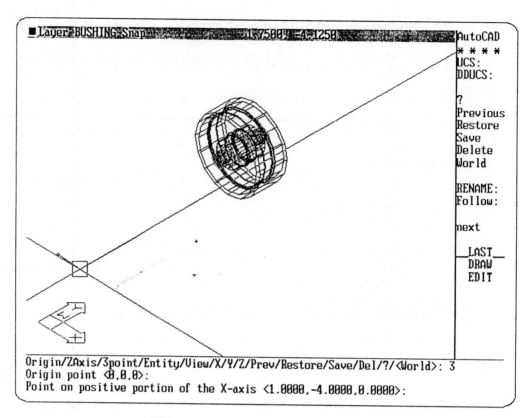

Figure 12.76 Picking the X-axis endpoint.

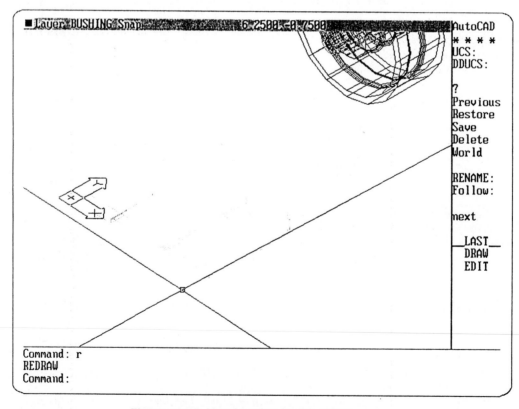

Figure 12.77 New location for the UCS icon.

13. **Point on positive-Y portion of the UCS X-Y plane <0,-3,0>:** Enter **END** to select the OSNAP option Endpoint and pick the line for the Y-axis,.

14. Move the UCS icon to its new origin by entering **UCSICON** at the command prompt.

15. **ON/OFF/All/Noorigin/ORigin <ON>:** Enter **OR** to move the UCS icon to the new origin as shown in Figure 12.77.

16. Before making the holes add the rounds to the four corners of the Base Plate. Enter **SOLFILL** at the command prompt to create solid fillets and rounds.

17. **Pick edges of solids to be filleted (Press ENTER when done):** Pick the four edges that are highlighted then enter **RETURN**.

18. **4 edges selected.**

   Diameter/<Radius> of fillet<0.13>: Enter **.25** as the fillet radius. The Boolean operations necessary to subtract the corners to create rounds are automatically performed and the results are displayed on screen.

19. To create the holes in the Base Plate, cylinders must be drawn. Enter **SOLCYL** at the command prompt.

20. **Baseplane/Elliptical/<Center point> <0,0,0>:** Enter the coordinate location for the first cylinder as **.5,3.375,0.**

21. **Diameter/<Radius>:** Use the diameter option by entering **D** and **RETURN.**

22. **Diameter:** Enter **.390** and **RETURN.**

23. **Center of other end/<Height>:** Enter a height of **.625.** The cylinder is automatically added to the Base Plate and displayed on screen.

24. The **COPY** command is used to make three copies of the cylinder. Enter **COPY** at the command prompt.

25. **Select objects:** Pick the cylinder created earlier then **RETURN** to complete the selection.

26. **<Base point or displacement>/Multiple:** More than one copy is to be made so **M** is entered.

27. **Base point:** Enter **CEN** to use the OSNAP Center option and pick the base of the cylinder.

28. **Second point of displacement:** Enter the location for the first copy of the cylinder as **6,.625,0.**

29. **Second point of displacement:** Enter the location for the second copy of the cylinder as **6,3.375,0.**

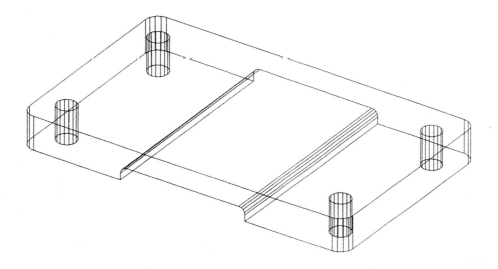

Figure 12.78 Completed 3D model of the Base Plate.

30. **Second point of displacement:** Enter the location for the third copy of the cylinder as **.5,.375,0** then **RETURN** to terminate the command. Figure 12.78.

31. The 4 primitive cylinders must be subtracted from the base geometry using Boolean operations. Enter **SOLSUB** at the command prompt to subtract the cylinders.

32. **Source objects...**

Select objects: The source object is the base geometry. Pick any line and enter **RETURN.**

33. **Objects to subtract from them...**

Select objects: Pick each cylinder and enter **RETURN.**

34. AME automatically subtracts the cylinders from the base completing the solid model of the Base Plate.

35. Change the material assigned to aluminum by entering **SOLMAT** at the command prompt

36. **Change/Edit/LIst/LOad/New/Remove/SAve/SEt/?/<eXit>:** Enter C to select the change option.

37. **Select objects:** Pick the base.

38. **New material <BRONZE>/?:** Enter **Aluminum** then Return to change the base material.

39. Enter **SAVE** to save the file to disk using the name **BASE3D.**

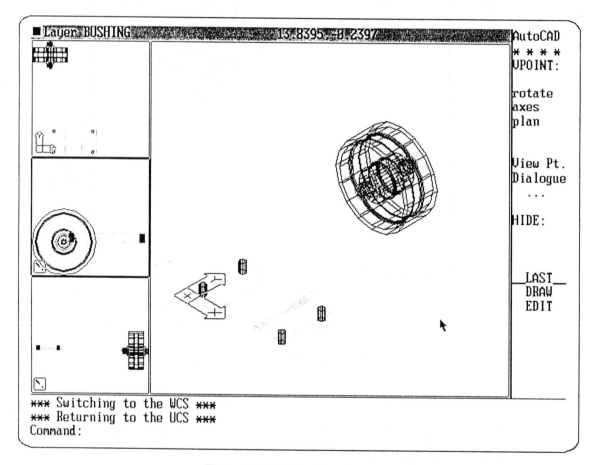

Figure 12.79 Using tiled viewports.

Moving the Base: Exercise 12.38

1. At this point you may want to change the display to four viewports, as shown in Figure 12.79.

2. Move the center of the Base to the origin by entering **MOVE** at the command prompt or picking it from the Modify Pull-down Menu.

3. Select the base then enter the base point as **3.25, 2, 0** which is the bottom center of the base.

4. Enter **0,0,0** as the second point of displacement.

5. Move the base to the center of the assembly by repeating the **MOVE** command.

6. Select the base then enter **0,0,0** as the base point.

7. Enter **0,13.875,0** to locate the base at the center of the assembly. Figure 12.80.

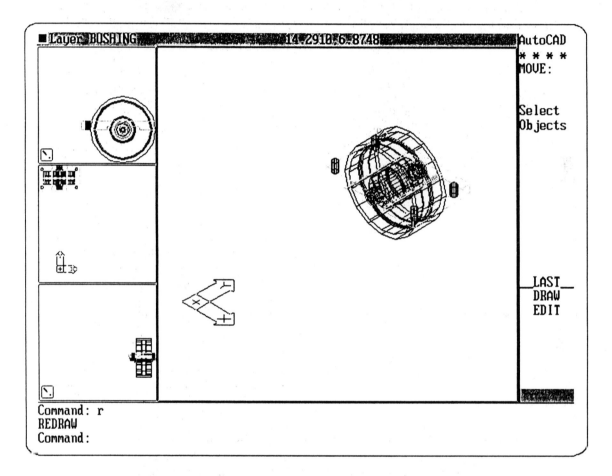

Figure 12.80 Moving the base to the center of the assembly.

8. Enter **SOLMOVE** at the command prompt or pick Model/Modify/Move Object using the Pull-down Menus.

2. Pick the base, then press Return.

3. The MCS is displayed on screen as green arrows. Move the Base to its final position by entering **rz90,tz-3.875**.

4. Enter **ZOOM** then **ALL** to display the 3D model of the assembly. Figure 12.81. Use the other viewports to verify the assembly and use **SOLMESH** then Hide and Shade to improve the visualization of the parts.

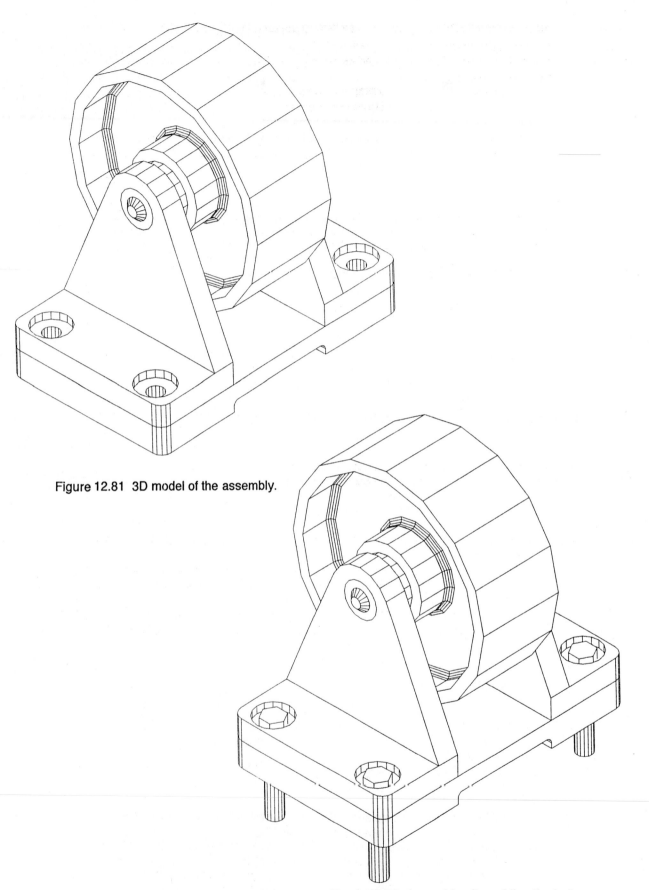

Figure 12.81 3D model of the assembly.

Figure 12.82 Assembly after adding the bolts.

Inserting Bolts into the Assembly: Exercise 12.39

The hex head bolt is used to hold the Base and arms together. The bolts could be modeled using techniques explained earlier or you could use one of the sample API programs that accompany AME. The program DESIGN.C defines 6 commands to create standard machine parts: shafts, wheels, gears, bearing brackets, hex bolts, and hex nuts. For this example a hex head bolt will be created and inserted into the assembly. Before beginning make sure the material property is set to Mild Steel.

1. From the Files Pull-down Menu pick Applications. **Design** is the name of the API program used to make machine parts. The file is located in the API/SAMPLE directory in AutoCAD.
2. After Design is loaded enter **SOLBOLT** which is the command used to create a solid model of a hex head bolt.
3. At the **Insertion base point <0,0,0>:** prompt enter **CEN** to locate the point at the center of the top large hole in one of the counterbored holes.
4. At the **Enter head diameter <2.0>:** prompt enter **.5625** found in a standards table for hexagon bolts.
5. At the **Enter head height <0.5>:** prompt enter **.25.**
6. At the **Enter screw diameter <1.0>:** prompt enter **.388.**
7. At the **Enter screw length <5.0>:** prompt enter **2.**
8. The bolt is modeled up-side-down so it must be translated into position using the **SOLMOVE** command. First the UCS origin must be moved to the insertion base point of the bolt by entering **UCS** at the command prompt then selecting the **ORIGIN** option.
9. Use Osnap Center to locate the UCS origin at the insertion base point for the bolt.
10. Enter **SOLMOVE** at the command prompt then pick the bolt.
11. Enter the motion descriptor **rx180** to turn the bolt in the right direction.
12. Use the **COPY** command to locate the other 3 bolts in the counterbored holes. Figure 12.82. Save the drawing file as **ASSEMBLY**.

SECTIONING SOLID MODELS

One way of visualizing an assembly is to create a section view to reveal interior features that are not easily visualized in wireframe mode. The section shows how to create a full section view of the assembly using the **SOLSECT** command. A section view is created by defining the location of a cutting plane in 3D space using various techniques. The variable **SOLSECTYPE** determines the type of section view produced. When Solsectype is set to 1 a block is created made of lines, arcs, and circles, if set to 2 a block is created that contains Polylines, and if set to 3 it creates a region. The default setting is 1.

An alternative method to create a section of the model is to actually cut the model in two using the **SOLCUT** command. This command separates the composite model. Both halves or one can be retained after cutting. The cut solid actually is a new composite solid model.

Creating a Full Section of the Assembly: Exercise 12.40

1. At the command prompt enter **SOLCUT** or pick Model/Modify/Cut Solids from the Pull-down Menus.
2. Use a window to pick the assembly.
3. **Cutting plane by Entity/Last/Zaxis/View/XY/YZ/ZX<3points>:** is shown in the prompt line. Use the 3-point option.
4. Use the Osnap Midpoint option to pick the midpoints of 3 lines that are on one of the Arms. The cutting plane must be positioned so that it is parallel to the axis of the Shaft and perpendicular to the top plane of the Base or Arm.
5. **Both sides/<Point on desired side of the plane>:** Pick a point on the back half of the model. After processing the cut solid model is displayed on screen. Figure 12.83 The model can be visually checked for accuracy. The two hex bolts in the front half were not deleted by the system because they were not intersected by the cutting plane.

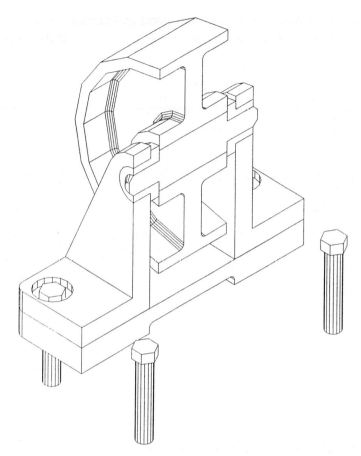

Figure 12.83 Assembly after cutting in half.

ANALYZING THE 3D MODELS

One of the great advantages of using 3D solid models for design/drawing is the analysis that can be done. In this section you will learn how to determine the accuracy of the design by using the solid interference command **SOLINTERF**. This command finds the intersection of two or more solids to determine if there is shared volume. In the case of the assembly just created, there should not be any shared volume by any of the models. One way to check for accuracy of the assembly and each model would be to use the Solinterf command.

Checking the Assembly for Interference: Exercise 12.41

1. Enter **SOLINTERF** at the command prompt or pick it from the Model/Inquiry/Interference Pull-down Menus.
2. **Select the first set of solids...**
Select objects: Use a window to pick the assembly.
3. **Select the second set of solids...**
Select objects: A second set is not needed so Return is entered to begin the interference check.
3. A prompt is displayed:
Comparing 11 solids with each other. This process may take some time to perform. After processing is complete a message could be displayed in the prompt: **Solids do not interfer e.**
4. If two or more of the solids do interfere you are given the chance to create new solids of the intersecting volumes. If you find intersecting volumes the solid models must be edited to correct the errors. For this assembly you will find that there are 4 intersections of 6 solids. All the hex head bolts interfere with the holes because the bottom of the heads are lower than the bottom of the spotface. This problem is corrected by using the **MOVE** or **SOLMOVE** command to change the hex head bolts position in 3D space. You will find that the bolts must be moved up .075 units.

Determining Mass Properties for the Assembly: Exercise 12.42

1. Enter **SOLMASSP** at the command prompt or pick Model/Inquiry/Mass Property...
from the Pull-down Menu.

2. Use a window to analyze all the models in the assembly.

3. After calculating a dialogue box is displayed giving the mass properties of the
assembly. Figure 12.84. Mass properties of each solid could by found by selective
picking. You can experiment with the mass of the assembly by assigning different
material properties to the models using the **SOLMAT** command.

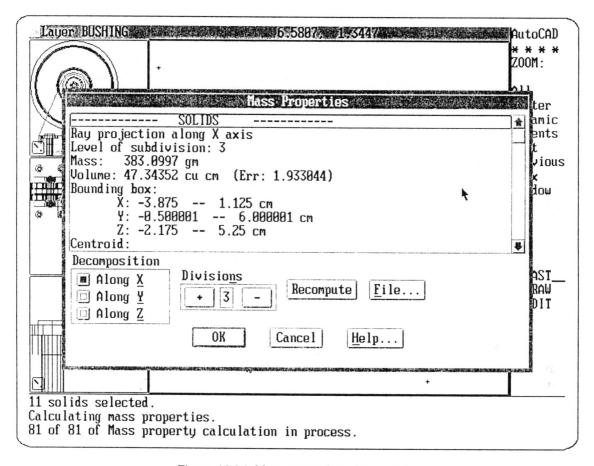

Figure 12.84 Mass properties of the solids.

CREATING ORTHOGRAPHIC VIEWS OF THE ASSEMBLY

AME provides 3 bonus features. One called **SOLVIEW**, which can be used to create paperspace viewports
and standard orthographic, sections, and auxiliary views. Solview is an ADS application that must be loaded before
using. The following steps describe how to create a front and side view of the assembly:

Creating Orthographic Views of the Assembly: Exercise 12.43

1. From the Files Pull-down Menu pick Applications. **Solview** is the name of the program
used to make orthographic views. The file is located in the SAMPLE directory in
AutoCAD.

2. Move the UCS to be parallel to the Shaft axis and perpendicular to the top plane of
the Base. This is done to automatically create an orthographic view perpendicular to the
current UCS plane. Enter **UCS** at the command prompt.

3. Rotate the UCS about the X-axis by entering X then 90 degrees.

4. Rotate the UCS about the Y-axis by entering Y then 90 degrees.

5. Enter **SOLVIEW** at the command prompt. Figure 12.85. Paper space is automatically displayed on screen along with the prompt:
Ucs/Ortho/Auxiliary/Section/<eXit>: To create an orthographic front view of the assembly enter **UCS**.

6. At the **Named/World/?/<Current>:** enter Current to make a view parallel to the current UCS XY plane.

7. At the **Enter view scale <1.00>:** enter .5 for a half scale drawing of the front view.

8. At the **View center:** prompt turn the snap on then pick a point anywhere on screen to preview the scale and location of the view.

9. **View center:** is displayed in the prompt again giving you the opportunity to reposition the view. Enter Return after the view is in the desired position. The Assembly is displayed on screen. Figure 12.86.

10. At the **Clip first corner:** prompt begin stretching a box that encloses the entire view. If the box truncates some of the entities they will not be displayed in the final view. At the **Clip other corner:** prompt pick the second corner of the box.

11. At the **View name:** prompt enter **Front**.

12 **Ucs/Ortho/Auxiliary/Section/<eXit>:** is displayed again to create more views. The side view of the assembly is created by using the Ortho option.

13. At the **Pick side of viewport to project:** pick a point along the right side of the view port box.

14. **View center:** Move the cursor to a point to the right of the current viewport. The right side view of the assembly is automatically displayed on screen. Again you are given the opportunity to reposition the view. Notice that the view is automatically created and horizontally aligned with the front view. Enter Return when you decide on the final position for the view. Figure 12.87.

15. At the **Clip first corner:** prompt begin stretching a box that encloses the entire view. At the **Clip other corner:** prompt pick the second corner of the box.

16. At the **View name:** prompt enter **Rside** then Return to exit the Solview command.

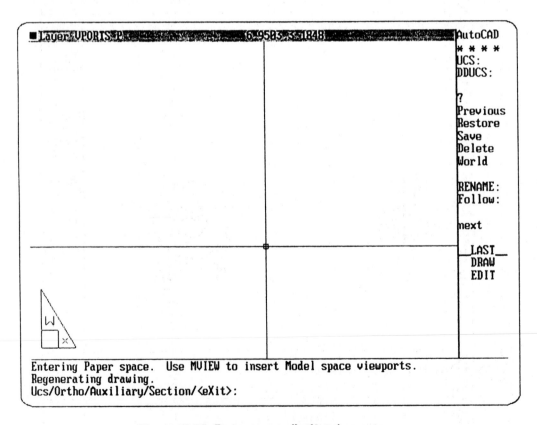

Figure 12.85 Paper space displayed on screen.

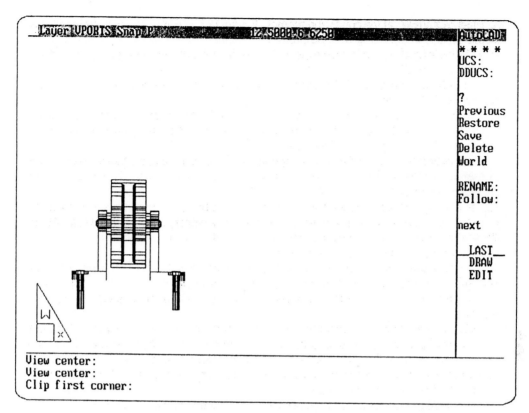

Figure 12.86 Front view created and positioned in paper space.

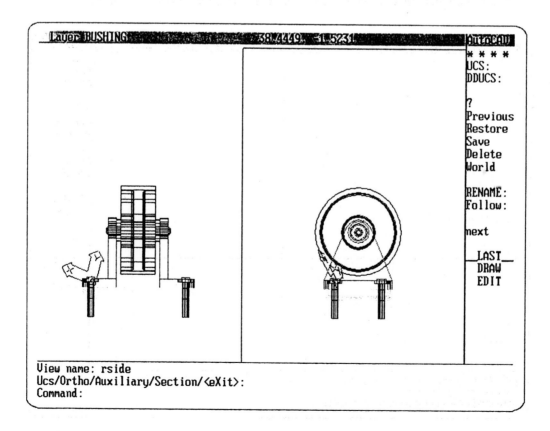

Figure 12.87 Right side view created.

The **SOLDRAW** command creates views with hidden lines removed and sections views from views created with the Solview command. To undo a viewport created using Soldraw, you must use the Back option of the Undo command. The following steps describe how to edit the views to display hidden lines:

Creating Views With Hidden Lines: Exercise 12.43

1. Load the hidden linetype by entering **LINETYPE** at the command prompt.
2. Use the load option then enter Hidden then return.
3. Enter **SOLDRAW** at the command prompt.
4. A prompt is displayed:
Viewports to draw...
Select objects: Pick the viewport border of the views to draw then press Return.
5. After some time for processing the viewports are automatically updated showing hidden lines. Figure 12.88. You may have to do some editing to erase stacked hidden lines.

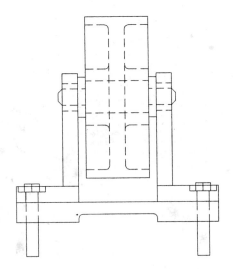 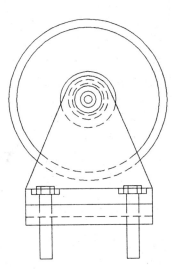

Figure 12.88 Hidden lines created for the orthographic views.

QUESTIONS FOR REVIEW

1. Define a solid model.
2. Describe how a solid model might be created using an AutoCAD drawing.
3. Define design analysis.
4. Define a finite element and describe its function.
5. List some of the AutoCAD commands that can be used to determine the property calculations of a model.
6. Describe how AutoCAD could be used to check for interference.
7. Describe a region model.
8. Name the AME_FRZ layer and state what precautions should be exercised with this layer.
9. Name the three Boolean operations used to create composite solids.
10. Name the 6 primitives that can be created with AME.
11. Identify what command must be executed before a solid model can be displayed with hidden lines removed
12. Name the command used to control the wire density of displayed solid models
13. Define tessellations.
14. Explain the technique used to create a truncated cone or a pyramid.
15. Name the 8 commands used to create composite solid models.

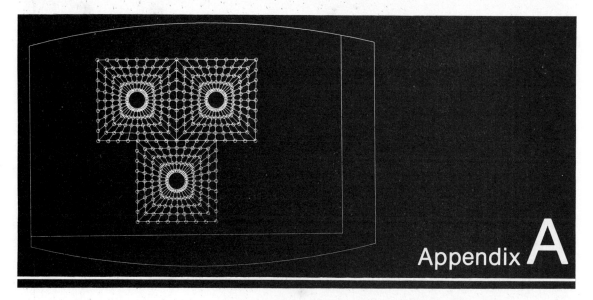

Appendix **A**

AUTOLISP PROGRAMS

This appendix contains a number of useful AutoLISP programs. Most of the programs are very short and can be used to enhance the use of AutoCAD for engineering graphics. It is suggested that you use a text editor rather than a word processor to key in the code. Save AutoLISP files with **.LSP** as the extender. These programs are printed with the permission of the authors and *CADalyst*, the journal for AutoCAD users. These files and many others are available on disk from *CADalyst* for a nominal fee, and some programs can be downloaded from within the AutoCAD User's Forum on CompuServe. All of the code appearing in the magazine is available for downloading from CompuServe's Autodesk Forum by logging onto CompuServe and GO ADESK.

Contact:
CADalyst Publications Ltd.
282-810 West Broadway
Vancouver BC Canada V5Z 4C9
Phone: 604-873-0811

```
;CADalyst  Vol.4 #7  December 1987
;Tip #201  page 89

;Easy Grid Rotation
;by Eben Kunz

;This program is used to align the grid to any line on screen.
;With S.lsp, pick any line on the drawing and the grid snaps
;to that angle.  SS.lsp is used to reset the grid to normal (0).


(DEFUN C:S (/ PT1 PT2)
   (SETVAR "ORTHOMODE" 0)
   (SETQ PT1 (OSNAP (GETPOINT "\nPick
     line to match new Grid angle: \n")
     "NEA"))
   (SETQ PT2 (OSNAP PT1 "END"))
   (COMMAND "SNAP" "R" PT1 PT2)
   (SETVAR "SNAPMODE" 0))
```

```
(DEFUN C:SS ()
   (PROMPT "\nReturn Grid to zero.")
   (COMMAND "SNAP" "R" "" 0.0)
   (SETVAR "SNAPMMODE" 0))
```

```
;CADalyst  Vol.4 #7   December 1987
;Tip #204   page 89

;Center Lines
;by Matt Slay
;This program is used to insert center marks on circles or arcs.
;This routine inserts a predefined block called "Cen1".
;The center lines are scaled to any size with cursor picks.
;The insertion point is at the intersection of the
;horizontal and vertical center lines.


(DEFUN C:CENL1 ()
 (COMMAND "INSERT" "CENL1" (GETPOINT)
   (GETPOINT) "" ""))
```

```
;CADalyst  Vol.4 #7   December 1987
;Tip #213   page93

;Outrageous Text Changes
;by Harry Geiger
;TxtChng.lsp is used globally to change text height, obliquing
;angle, width factor and style.


(DEFUN C:TXTCHG ()
(SETVAR "CMDECHO" 0)
(SETQ
  OLD (SSGET)
  TYP (STRCASE (GETSTRING "\nChange
    text A)ngle, H)eight, W)idth, or
    S)tyle: "))
  CO -1
  T2 "T"
)
(COND
  ((= "H" TYP)
    (SETQ
      X 40
      HT (GETREAL "\nNew height: ")
    )
  )
  ((= "A" TYP)
    (SETQ
      X 51
      HT (getangle "nAngle: "))
    )
  )
  ((= "W" TYP)
    (SETQ
      X 41
      HT (GETREAL "\nNew width: ")
    )
  )
  ((= "S" TYP)
    (SETQ
      X 7
      HT (GETSTRING "\nNew style: ")
    )
  )
)
```

```
  (WHILE (BOUNDP 'T2)
    (PROGN
     (SETQ
       CO (1+ CO)
       TEMP (ENTGET (SSNAME OLD CO))
       OLDHT (ASSOC X TEMP)
       NEWHT (CONS X HT)
       NEWTEXT (SUBST NEWHT OLDHT TEMP)
       T2 (SSNAME OLD (1+ CO))
     )
     (ENTMOD NEWTEXT)
     )
   )
   (SETQ TEMP "FINISHED")
)
```

```
;CADalyst   Vol.4 #7   December 1987
;Tip #206   page 90

;Layer Delete
;by Alan Henderson
;Delete.lsp will delete all or selected entities by layer.


(DEFUN C:DELETE (/ TR L TR1 L1 TR2 L2
                    TN K KK KS SS E EE)
   (SETQ TR NIL L NIL TR1 NIL L1 NIL
         TR2 NIL L2 NIL YN NIL K 0 KK 0
         KS 0)
   (SETQ TR (STRCASE
     (GETSTRING "\nEntity name to
     delete or <Enter>=all? ")))
   (SETQ L (STRCASE
     (GETSTRING "\nLayer name to
     delete or <Enter>=all ? ")))
   (SETQ YN (STRCASE
     (GETSTRING "\nSelect sets <Y> or
     <Enter>=all? ")))
   (IF (= TR "")
       (SETQ TR2 "ALL")
       (SETQ TR2 TR)
   )
   (IF (= L "")
       (SETQ L2 "ALL")
       (SETQ L2 L)
   )
   (IF (= YN "")
       (SETQ YN "ALL")
   )
   (GRTEXT -1 (STRCAT "Deleting
     entity=" TR2 " Layer=" L2 ))
   (IF (= YN "Y")
     (PROGN
     (SETQ SS (SSGET))
     (IF SS
       (PROGN
       (SETQ KS (SSLENGTH SS))
       (WHILE (< KK KS)
         (SETQ EE (ENTGET (SETQ E
           (SSNAME SS KK))))
         (SETQ TR1 (CDR (ASSOC 0 EE)))
         (SETQ L1 (CDR (ASSOC 8 EE)))
         (GRTEXT -2 (STRCAT "NO."
           (ITOA KK) " L=" L1
           " ENTITY=" TR1))
         (IF (= TR "")
           (PROGN
           (IF (= L "")
             (PROGN
```

AutoCAD Release 12 Bonus CD
AutoLISP Routines Summary   \lisp\shortdsc.txt

Here is a brief description of all the AutoLISP files in this directory located on the bonus CD which is provided with Release 12. Before you use any of these for the first time, please read the full documentation at the beginning of the file to be sure you understand its operation.

3DSPIRAL.LSP   \lisp\3dspiral.lsp
This program constructs a spiral.

ARRAY.LSP   \lisp\array.lsp
This is an example routine, illustrating how to implement multi-dimensional arrays in AutoLISP.

ASCPOINT.LSP   \lisp\ascpoint.lsp
A utility which reads coordinate data from ASCII files in CDF or SDF format, and generates AutoCAD geometry using the incoming coordinate data.

ATEXT.LSP   \lisp\atext.lsp
Draws center aligned text along an ARC.

BLK_LST.LSP   \lisp\blk_lst.lsp
For listing attributes and their values, both constant and variable.

BLOCKQ.LSP   \lisp\blockq.lsp
This lists, one-by-one, the contents of a BLOCK definition.

CASE.LSP   \lisp\case.lsp
This emulates the Common LISP (case) function.

CBLAYR.LSP   \lisp\cblayr.lsp
This program sorts entities by their color, and places all entities with the same color on a layer whose name is the color number.

CHELEV.LSP   \lisp\chelev.lsp
CHange ELEVation command replacement.

CLBHATCH.LSP   \lisp\clbhatch.lsp
A simple AutoLISP front-end for BHATCH.

CONVTEXT.LSP   \lisp\convtext.lsp
Convert all text in drawing to a new height.

COUNT.LSP   \lisp\count.lsp
Adds the COUNT command to AutoCAD, which counts, itemizes, and displays in tabular form, the number of insertions of each block in the selected objects, or the entire drawing.

CROSSREF.LSP   \lisp\crossref.lsp
Searches block definitions for references to a specified layer, linetype, style, or block, and reports the names of all blocks that contain at least one reference to the specified object(*).

CYCLE.LSP   \lisp\cycle.lsp
Creates the AutoCAD command CYCLE, which divides the display into four
viewports and reads a text file that should consist of a list of the
names of slide files, displaying each successive slide in a different viewport.

DDTRACE.LSP   \lisp\ddtrace.lsp
Turn callback tracing ON and OFF.

DENT.LSP   \lisp\dent.lsp
This changes the current LAYER, LINETYPE, THICKNESS, and COLOR settings
to those contained within the entity association list supplied as an argument.

DE_DIM.LSP   \lisp\de_dim.lsp
This file is a series of short macros to make Dimension commands available
directly from the Command prompt.

DIMSALL.LSP   \lisp\dimsall.lsp
For loading Release 10 drawings into Release 11 or 12. Control the
dimension style of exploded dimensions.

FACE.LSP   \lisp\face.lsp
This program draws parametrically controlled Chernoff faces in AutoCAD.
Two demonstration commands are defined:
  RFACE   generates a single random face at the centre of the current viewport
  DEMO   generates a series of random faces until terminated with a console
              break

FMTTIME.LSP   \lisp\fmttime.lsp
This program dissects all AutoCAD's various time & date variables.

FORMAT.LSP   \lisp\format.lsp
AutoLISP formatted string output functions.

GAME.LSP   \lisp\game.lsp
A simple 'hit the target' game.

HELIX.LSP   \lisp\helix.lsp
Draws 3D helical springs and coils of varying width.

INTFIL.LSP   \lisp\intfil.lsp
This routine will fillet two intersecting lines by allowing the user to
select which two lines he wishes to fillet.

JULIAN.LSP   \lisp\julian.lsp
AutoCAD Julian date to calendar date conversion

LOD.LSP   \lisp\lod.lsp
Basically this lets you type a shorter string without quotation marks to
reload a function - for the AutoLISP programmer who is a poor typist.

MAKE2D.LSP   \lisp\make2d.lsp
This converts a 3D polyline into a 2D polyline.

MAKE3D.LSP   \lisp\make3d.lsp
This converts a 2D polyline into a 3D polyline.

MAKELT.LSP   \lisp\makelt.lsp

MakeLT creates and edits linetypes.

MLEAD.LSP   \lisp\mlead.lsp
Command to allow multiple lines of text in a dim leader.

MODEMACRO.LSP   \lisp\modemacr\modemacr.lsp
Displays a dialogue box for creation, editing, and storing of MODEMACRO
strings.

MXPLODE.LSP   \lisp\mxplode.lsp
This routine explodes uniformly scaled blocks that have been mirrored, or
blocks inserted with both negative and positive xyz scale factors
(i.e. 1 -1 -1).

OSTACK.LSP   \lisp\ostack.lsp
This function lets you pre-stack immediate object snap modes, for faster
drawing.

PARK.LSP   \lisp\park.lsp
This program automates the layout of rows of right-angle parking spaces
(or more accurately, the striping for parking spaces).

PQCHECK.LSP   \lisp\pqcheck.lsp
This routine checks lisp programs for mismatched parentheses and closing
quotes.

PURGE.LSP   \lisp\purge.lsp
AutoCAD utility function for automatic PURGE. ** Do NOT install in your
ACAD.LSP file without reading the documentation carefully. **

SINSERT.LSP   \lisp\sinsert.lsp
Automates creation of MEASURED block insertions with additional options
not provided by the AutoCAD MEASURE command.

TCALIB.LSP   \lisp\tcalib.lsp
This routine aids in testing multi-point digitizer calibration.

TENSEL.LSP   \lisp\tensel.lsp
Allows you to selectively cycle thru, highlight and select one of several
entities that cross thru, or lie entirely within the pickbox.

TIMEIT.LSP   \lisp\timeit.lsp
This routine times the execution of one AutoCAD command (like HIDE or
REGEN) that does not require interactive user input.

VSCALE.LSP   \lisp\vscale.lsp
This displays the scale of a model space viewport.

WEBSEC.LSP   \lisp\websec.lsp
Not very practical, but a good example of parametric programming.

ZOOM9E.LSP   \lisp\zoom9e.lsp
ZOOM to Extents, then ZOOM .9X.

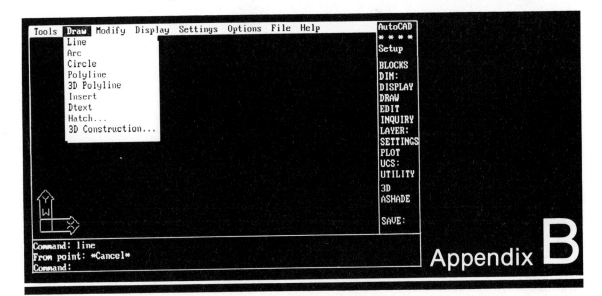

AutoCAD's SYSTEM VARIABLE SETTINGS

The following is a list of AutoCAD's system variables as set in the ACAD.DWG prototype drawing. To list this information enter Setvar at the command prompt, then ?, then Enter.

ACADPREFIX	"C:\ACAD12\SUPPORT\;C:\ACAD12\FONTS\" (read only)	
ACADVER	"12"	(read only)
AFLAGS	0	
ANGBASE	0	
ANGDIR	0	
APERTURE	10	
AREA	0.0000	(read only)
ATTDIA	0	
ATTMODE	1	
ATTREQ	1	
AUDITCTL	0	
AUNITS	0	
AUPREC	0	
BACKZ	0.0000	(read only)
BLIPMODE	1	
CDATE	19930420.07372840	(read only)
CECOLOR	"BYLAYER"	
CELTYPE	"BYLAYER"	
CHAMFERA	0.0000	
CHAMFERB	0.0000	
CIRCLERAD	0.0000	
CLAYER	"0"	
CMDACTIVE	1	(read only)
CMDDIA	1	

CMDECHO	1	
CMDNAMES	"SETVAR"	(read only)
COORDS	1	
CVPORT	2	
DATE	2449098.31778403	(read only)
DBMOD	0	(read only)
DIASTAT	1	(read only)
DIMALT	0	
DIMALTD	2	
DIMALTF	25.4000	
DIMAPOST	""	
DIMASO	1	
DIMASZ	0.1800	
DIMBLK	""	(read only)
DIMBLK1	""	(read only)
DIMBLK2	""	(read only)
DIMCEN	0.0900	
DIMCLRD	0	
DIMCLRE	0	
DIMCLRT	0	
DIMDLE	0.0000	
DIMDLI	0.3800	
DIMEXE	0.1800	
DIMEXO	0.0625	
DIMGAP	0.0900	
DIMLFAC	1.0000	
DIMLIM	0	
DIMPOST	""	
DIMRND	0.0000	
DIMSAH	0	
DIMSCALE	1.0000	
DIMSE1	0	
DIMSE2	0	
DIMSHO	1	
DIMSOXD	0	
DIMSTYLE	"*UNNAMED"	(read only)
DIMTAD	0	
DIMTFAC	1.0000	
DIMTIH	1	
DIMTIX	0	
DIMTM	0.0000	
DIMTOFL	0	
DIMTOH	1	
DIMTOL	0	
DIMTP	0.0000	
DIMTSZ	0.0000	
DIMTVP	0.0000	
DIMTXT	0.1800	
DIMZIN	0	
DISTANCE	0.0000	(read only)
DONUTID	0.5000	
DONUTOD	1.0000	
DRAGMODE	2	

```
DRAGP1        10
DRAGP2        25
DWGCODEPAGE  "ascii"
DWGNAME       "UNNAMED"              (read only)
DWGPREFIX     "C:\"                  (read only)
DWGTITLED      0                     (read only)
DWGWRITE      1
ELEVATION     0.0000
EXPERT        0
EXTMAX        -1.0000E+20,-1.0000E+20,-1.0000E+20  (read only)
EXTMIN        1.0000E+20,1.0000E+20,1.0000E+20    (read only)
FILEDIA       1
FILLETRAD     0.0000
FILLMODE      1
FRONTZ        0.0000                              (read only)
GRIDMODE      0
GRIDUNIT      0.0000,0.0000
GRIPBLOCK     0
GRIPCOLOR     5
GRIPHOT       1
GRIPS         1
GRIPSIZE      3
HANDLES       0                     (read only)
HIGHLIGHT     1
HPANG         0
HPDOUBLE      0
HPNAME        ""
HPSCALE       1.0000
HPSPACE       1.0000
INSBASE       0.0000,0.0000,0.0000
INSNAME       ""
LASTANGLE              0             (read only)
LASTPOINT     0.0000,0.0000,0.0000
LENSLENGTH    50.0000               (read only)
LIMCHECK      0
LIMMAX        12.0000,9.0000
LIMMIN        0.0000,0.0000
LOGINNAME     "Gary R. Bertoline, Purdue Univ"   (read only)
LTSCALE       1.0000
LUNITS        2
LUPREC        4
MAXACTVP      16
MAXSORT       200
MENUCTL       1
MENUECHO      0
MENUNAME      "acad"                (read only)
MIRRTEXT      1
MODEMACRO     ""
OFFSETDIST    -1.0000
ORTHOMODE     0
OSMODE        0
PDMODE        0
PDSIZE        0.0000
```

PERIMETER	0.0000	(read only)
PFACEVMAX	4	(read only)
PICKADD	1	
PICKAUTO	1	
PICKBOX	3	
PICKDRAG	0	
PICKFIRST	1	
PLATFORM	"386 DOS Extender"	(read only)
PLINEGEN	0	
PLINEWID	0.0000	
PLOTID	"HP Laserjet"	
PLOTTER	0	
POLYSIDES	4	
POPUPS	1	(read only)
PSLTSCALE	1	
PSPROLOG	""	
PSQUALITY	75	
QTEXTMODE	0	
REGENMODE	1	
SAVEFILE	"AUTO.SV$"	(read only)
SAVENAME	""	(read only)
SAVETIME	120	
SCREENBOXES	26	(read only)
SCREENMODE	0	(read only)
SCREENSIZE	574.0000,414.0000	(read only)
SHADEDGE	3	
SHADEDIF	70	
SHPNAME	""	
SKETCHINC	0.1000	
SKPOLY	0	
SNAPANG	0	
SNAPBASE	0.0000,0.0000	
SNAPISOPAIR	0	
SNAPMODE	0	
SNAPSTYL	0	
SNAPUNIT	1.0000,1.0000	
SORTENTS	96	
SPLFRAME	0	
SPLINESEGS	8	
SPLINETYPE	6	
SURFTAB1	6	
SURFTAB2	6	
SURFTYPE	6	
SURFU	6	
SURFV	6	
SYSCODEPAGE	"ascii"	(read only)
TABMODE	0	
TARGET	0.0000,0.0000,0.0000	(read only)
TDCREATE	2449098.31421250	(read only)
TDINDWG	0.00369294	(read only)
TDUPDATE	2449098.31421250	(read only)
TDUSRTIMER	0.00369352	(read only)
TEMPPREFIX	""	(read only)

```
TEXTEVAL      0
TEXTSIZE      0.2000
TEXTSTYLE     "STANDARD"
THICKNESS     0.0000
TILEMODE      1
TRACEWID      0.0500
TREEDEPTH     3020
TREEMAX       10000000
UCSFOLLOW     0
UCSICON       1
UCSNAME       ""                          (read only)
UCSORG        0.0000,0.0000,0.0000         (read only)
UCSXDIR       1.0000,0.0000,0.0000         (read only)
UCSYDIR       0.0000,1.0000,0.0000         (read only)
UNDOCTL       5                           (read only)
UNDOMARKS     0                           (read only)
UNITMODE      0
VIEWCTR       6.2433,4.5000,0.0000         (read only)
VIEWDIR       0.0000,0.0000,1.0000         (read only)
VIEWMODE      0                           (read only)
VIEWSIZE      9.0000                      (read only)
VIEWTWIST     0                           (read only)
VISRETAIN     0
VSMAX         37.4600,27.0000,0.0000       (read only)
VSMIN         -24.9734,-18.0000,0.0000     (read only)
WORLDUCS      1                           (read only)
WORLDVIEW     1
XREFCTL       0
```

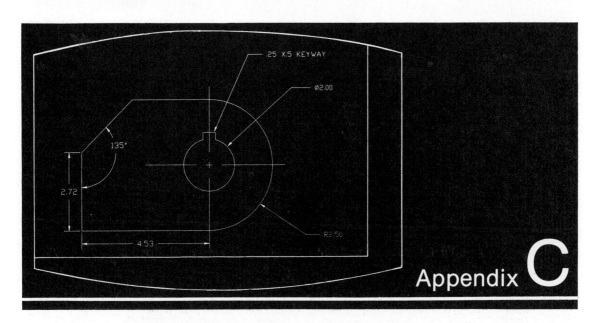

Appendix **C**

STANDARD HATCH PATTERNS

This appendix has the standard hatch pattern that come with the AutoCAD software. These patterns are located in the *acad.pat* file. The last few patterns are PostScript which are located in the *acad.psf* file.

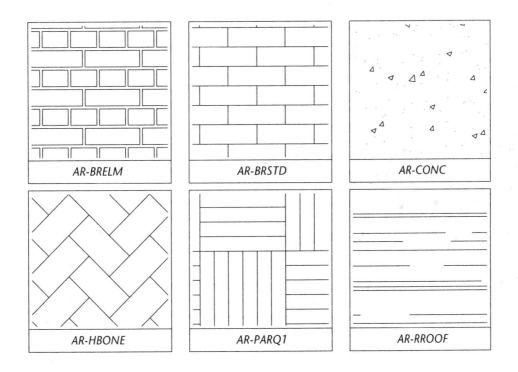

| AR-BRELM | AR-BRSTD | AR-CONC |
| AR-HBONE | AR-PARQ1 | AR-RROOF |

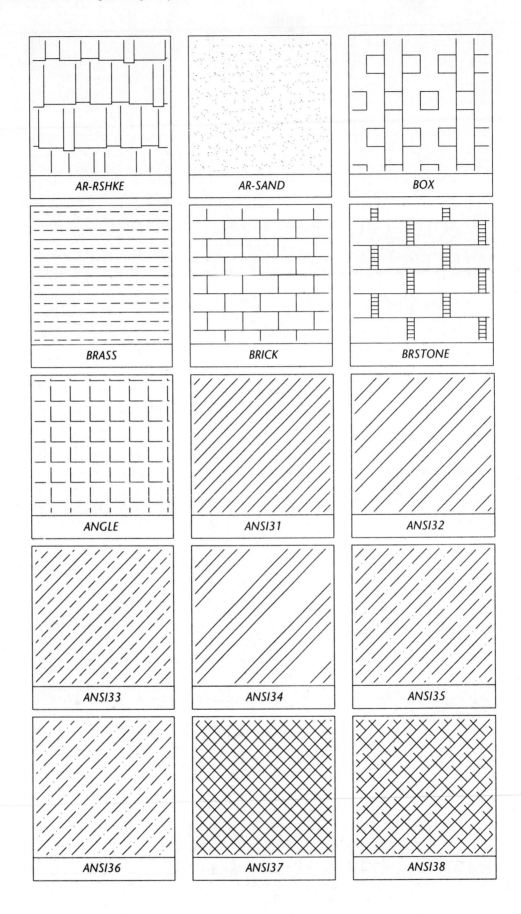

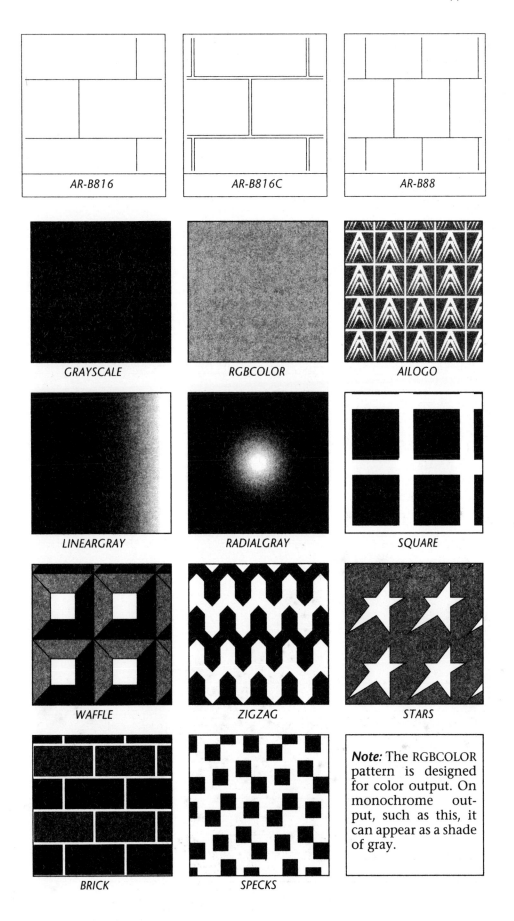

AR-B816   AR-B816C   AR-B88

GRAYSCALE   RGBCOLOR   AILOGO

LINEARGRAY   RADIALGRAY   SQUARE

WAFFLE   ZIGZAG   STARS

BRICK   SPECKS

Note: The RGBCOLOR pattern is designed for color output. On monochrome output, such as this, it can appear as a shade of gray.

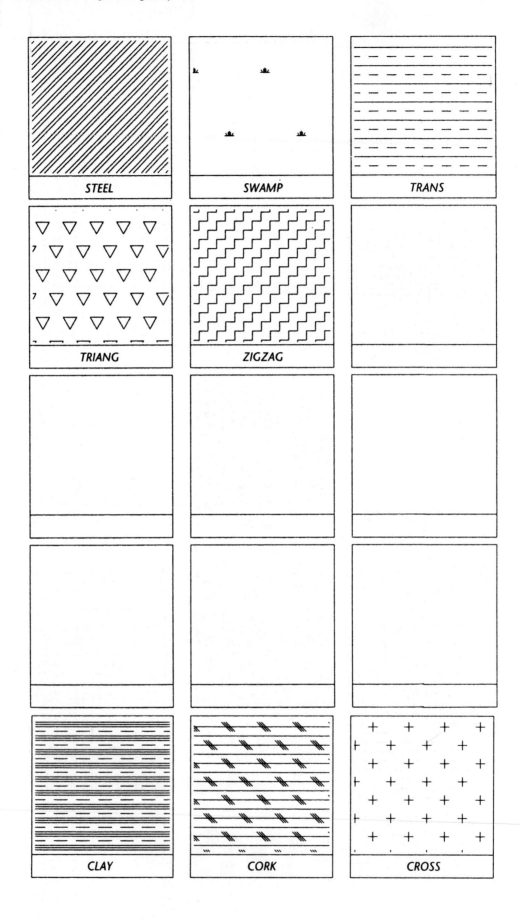

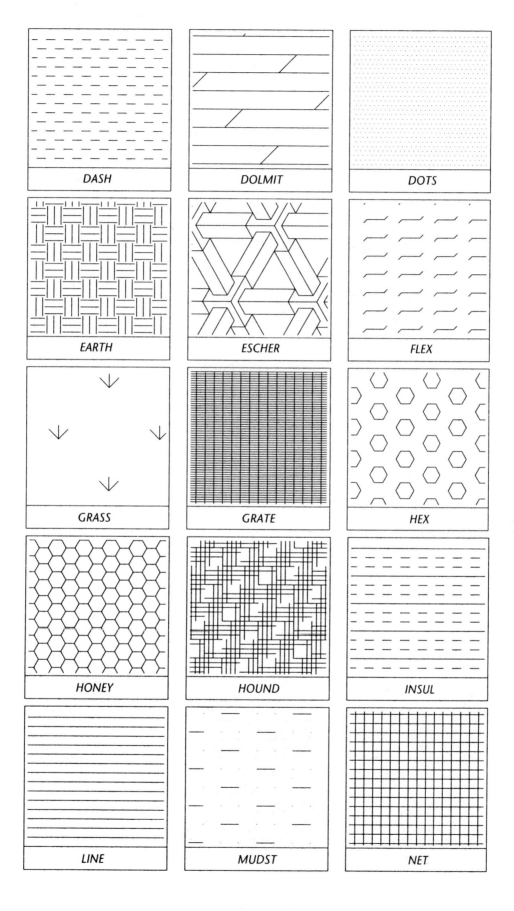

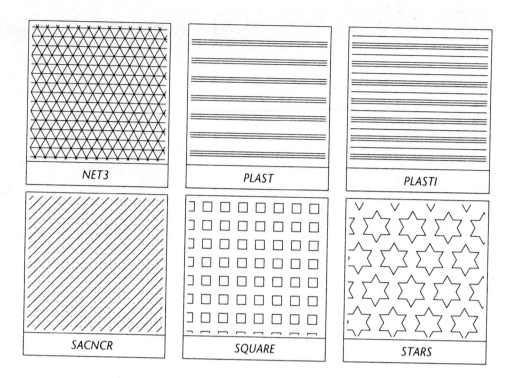

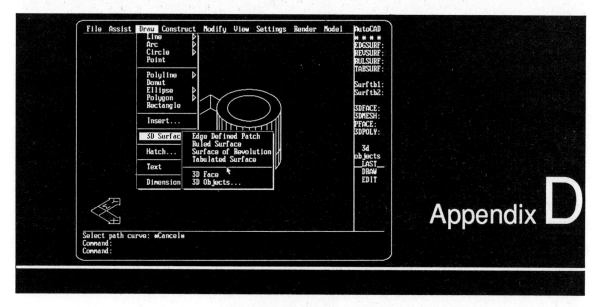

USEFUL INFORMATION

This appendix lists various important information useful when using AutoCAD. Refer to this list or the end pages for reference information. Use this appendix as a reference for:

Text scaling factors
Special characters
Control and function keys
Layer conventions for engineering drawings
Coordinate input summary
Viewport settings for principal and pictorial views
Command aliases

TEXT SCALING FACTORS FOR PLOTTING

Plotting scale	Text height
1/8"=1'	12
1/4"=1'	6
1/2"=1'	3
1/4 size	.5
1/2 size	.25
full size	.125
2/1	.0625
3/1	.0416
4/1	.0312
5/1	.0250
10/1	.0125

SPECIAL CHARACTERS
%%d degree symbol.
%%p plus/minus symbol.
%%c ANSI standard diameter symbol.
%%o overscore.
%%u underscore.

CONTROL & FUNCTION KEY COMMANDS
Coordinate toggle= **Ctrl D** or **F6.**
Grid toggle= **Ctrl G** or **F7.**
Ortho mode= **Ctrl O** or **F8.**
Snap toggle= **Ctrl B** or **F9.**
Tablet mode= **Ctrl T** or **F10.**
Print echo= **Ctrl Q.**
Isometric cursor= **Ctrl E.**

THE VIEWPOINT COMMAND

Principal View	View Coordinates
Top (plan)	0,0,1
Front	0,-1,0
Right side	1,0,0
Left side	-1,0,0
Rear	0,1,0
Bottom	0,0,-1

Pictorial View	View Coordinates
Front Above/Right	1,-1,1
Front Above/Left	-1,-1,1
Rear Above/Right	-1,1,1
Rear Above/Left	1,1,1
Front Below/Right	-1,1,-1
Front Below/Left	1,1,-1
Rear Below/Right	1,-1,-1
Rear Below/Left	-1,-1,-1

VIEW PRESETS

Principal View	Angle from X-axis	Angle from XY plane
Top (plan)	270	90
Front	270	0
Right side	0	0
Left side	180	0
Rear	90	0
Bottom	270	-90

Pictorial View	Angle from X-axis	Angle from XY plane
Front Above/Right	315	10 to 75
Front Above/Left	225	10 to 75
Rear Above/Right	135	10 to 75
Rear Above/Left	45	10 to 75
Front Below/Right	315	-10 to -75
Front Below/Left	225	-10 to -75
Rear Below/Righr	135	-10 to -75
Rear Below/Left	45	-10 to -75

LAYERING CONVENTIONS FOR ENGINEERING DRAWINGS

Layer Name	Color	Linetype
0	White 7	Continuous
Hidden	Green 3	Hidden
Center	Magenta 6	Center
Object	White 7	Continuous
Text	White 7	Continuous
Dimension	Yellow 2	Continuous
Border	Blue 5	Continuous
Section	Red 1	Continuous

COORDINATE INPUT SUMMARY

Coordinate		Example
Cartesian Absolute	X,Y,Z	3,9,0
Cartesian Relative	@X,Y,Z	@2,5,1
Polar Absolute	Distance<Angle	5.25<45
Polar Relative	@Distance<Angle	@4<30
Cylindrical Absolute	Distance<Angle in XY Plane,Z Distance	4<45,4.5
Cylindrical Relative	@Distance<Angle in XY Plane,Z Distance	@6.5<30,4.5
Spherical Absolute	Distance<Angle in XY Plane<Angle	10<35<63
Spherical Relative	@Distance<Angle in XY Plane<Angle	@10<35<63
Last Point	@Specifies a zero offset from the last point	@
World	*Specifies world coordinates	*4,2,7.5

ACAD.PGP - EXTERNAL COMMAND AND COMMAND ALIAS DEFINITIONS
SAMPLE ALIASES FOR AUTOCAD COMMANDS

A,	*ARC
AR,	*ARRAY
B,	*BREAK
BOX,	*SOLBOX
C,	*CIRCLE
CON,	*SOLCONE
CP,	*COPY
CYL,	*SOLCYL
DT,	*DTEXT
DV,	*DVIEW
E,	*ERASE
ET,	*EXTEND
EP,	*EXPLODE
F,	*FILLET
H,	*HIDE
HA,	*HATCH
L,	*LINE
LA,	*LAYER
M,	*MOVE
ME,	*SOLMESH
MI,	*MIRROR
N,	*NEW
O,	*OFFSET
OP,	*OPEN
P,	*PAN
PE,	*PEDIT
PL,	*PLINE
Q,	*QUIT
QS,	*QSAVE
R,	*REDRAW
RE,	*REGEN
RO,	*ROTATE
S,	*SAVE
SC,	*SCALE
SH,	*SHADE
SM,	*SOLMOVE
SPH,	*SOLSPHERE
ST,	*STRETCH
SW,	*SOLWIRE
T,	*TRIM
TOR,	*SOLTORUS
U,	*UCS
V,	*VPOINT
WED,	*SOLWEDGE
Z,	*ZOOM

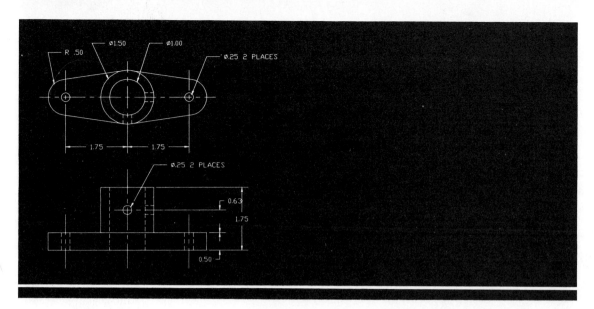

AutoCAD 2D TUTORIAL

This tutorial is an introduction to AutoCAD's 2D drawing capabilities. It starts with the creation of a drawing border and a title strip. Lines, arcs, and circles are added to create a part called Spacer. Colors, linetypes, and layers are changed during the tutorial to provide an overview of some of the more common 2D drawing features of AutoCAD.

SECTION 1
CREATING THE BORDER LINE AND TITLE BLOCK

An A-size border line is created for the Spacer. The layers, linetypes, and colors are created before the border line is drawn. This saves time because all the layers have been created for every new drawing that uses an A-size sheet. The border line and title strip are then added to the drawing. This title block is saved as a drawing file and can be used for any other drawings in the future that require an A-size sheet. It is recommended that drawing sheets for B-, C- and D-size formats be created for larger drawing formats. The C-size sheet is created by doubling the scale of the A-size. After drawing the B-size sheet, the D-size can be created by doubling the scale.

After loading the AutoCAD program, begin by creating the layer information for all drawings using an A-size border. Enter **LAYER** at the command prompt in the Drawing Editor. Create new layers by entering **NEW** at the layer prompt, and enter the names of the layers necessary to create most engineering drawings. It is good practice to separate different drawing entities or parts of a drawing by placing them on different layers. If a color display is being used, it is good practice to separate entities by color. Some of the important elements that should be located on separate layers include, the border line, object, center, and hidden linetypes, dimensions, section lines, and text.

After entering **NEW** at the layer prompt, enter the names of the layers, separated by a comma, with no spaces.

Command: layer
?/Make/Set/New/ON/OFF/Color/Ltype/Freeze/Thaw/LOck/Unlock: NEW

New layer name(s): BORDER,HIDDEN,DIMENSIONS,SECTIONS,CENTER,OBJECT,TEXT

Some layers have to be assigned different linetypes by entering LTYPE at the layer prompt. Assign the center linetype to the CENTER layer and the hidden linetype to the HIDDEN layer.

?/Make/Set/New/ON/OFF/Color/Ltype/Freeze/Thaw/LOck/Unlock: LTYPE

Linetype (or ?) <CONTINUOUS>: HIDDEN

Layer name(s) for linetype HIDDEN <0>: HIDDEN
?/Make/Set/New/ON/OFF/Color/Ltype/Freeze/Thaw/LOck/Unlock: LTYPE

Linetype (or ?) <CONTINUOUS>: CENTER

Layer name(s) for linetype CENTER <0>: CENTER

Assign colors to some of the layers by entering COLOR at the layer prompt. Enter the color desired for each layer, and then enter the name of the layer to assign the color.

?/Make/Set/New/ON/OFF/Color/Ltype/Freeze/Thaw/LOck/Unlock: COLOR

Color: BLUE

Layer name(s) for color 5 (blue) <0>: OBJECT
?/Make/Set/New/ON/OFF/Color/Ltype/Freeze/Thaw/LOck/Unlock: COLOR

Color: RED

Layer name(s) for color 1 (red) <0>: CENTER,DIMENSIONS
?/Make/Set/New/ON/OFF/Color/Ltype/Freeze/Thaw/LOck/Unlock: COLOR

Color: YELLOW

Layer name(s) for color 2 (yellow) <0>: SECTIONS

After all the layer information has been created, get a listing by entering ? at the layer prompt.

?/Make/Set/New/ON/OFF/Color/Ltype/Freeze/Thaw/LOck/Unlock: ?

Layer name(s) to list <*>:

Layer name	State	Color	Linetype
0	On	7 (white)	CONTINUOUS
BORDER	On	7 (white)	CONTINUOUS
CENTER	On	1 (red)	CENTER
DIMENSIONS	On	1 (red)	CONTINUOUS
HIDDEN	On	7 (white)	HIDDEN
OBJECT	On	5 (blue)	CONTINUOUS
SECTIONS	On	2 (yellow)	CONTINUOUS
TEXT	On	7 (white)	CONTINUOUS

Current layer: 0

Finally, set the current layer to **BORDER** by entering **SET** at the layer prompt. Enter the layer name **BORDER** to set the current layer. To end the layer changes press enter again to return to the command prompt.

?/Make/Set/New/ON/OFF/Color/Ltype/Freeze/Thaw/LOck/Unlock: SET

New current layer <0>: BORDER
?/Make/Set/New/ON/OFF/Color/Ltype/Freeze/Thaw/LOck/Unlock:

Turn the grid on (F7), and the snap on (F9). At the command prompt, enter **SNAP** to change the snap setting. Enter **.25** to change the snap. Check the limits of the current drawing by entering **LIMITS** at the command prompt. Set the lower left corner at **0,0** and the upper right corner at **12,9** if they are not already set.

Command: <Grid on> <Snap on> SNAP

Snap spacing or ON/OFF/Aspect/Rotate/Style <1.0000>: .25

Command: LIMITS

Reset Model space limits:
ON/OFF/<Lower left corner> <0.0000,0.0000>:

Upper right corner <12.0000,9.0000>:

Begin drawing the border line by entering **LINE** at the command prompt. Lines are drawn by entering coordinate points or picking the points with the input device, using the grid and snap setting selected earlier (Figure T1).

Command: LINE
From point: 0,0

To point: 10.5,0

To point: 10.5,8

To point: 0,8

To point: CLOSE

The title strip is created by repeating the **LINE** command. Enter coordinate points for the title strip because the snap setting is not set to the correct increments. Or enter **SNAP** at the command prompt and change the setting to **.125**, then use the input device to pick points (Figure T2).

Command: LINE
From point: 0,.375

To point: 10.5,.375

To point:

Command:
LINE From point: 3.5,0

To point: 3.5,.375

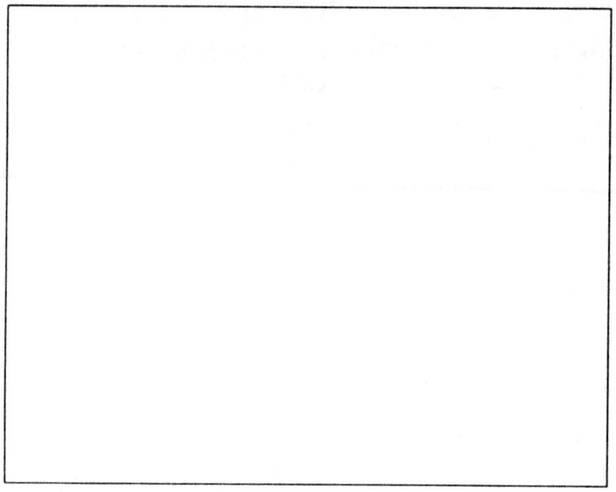

Figure T1

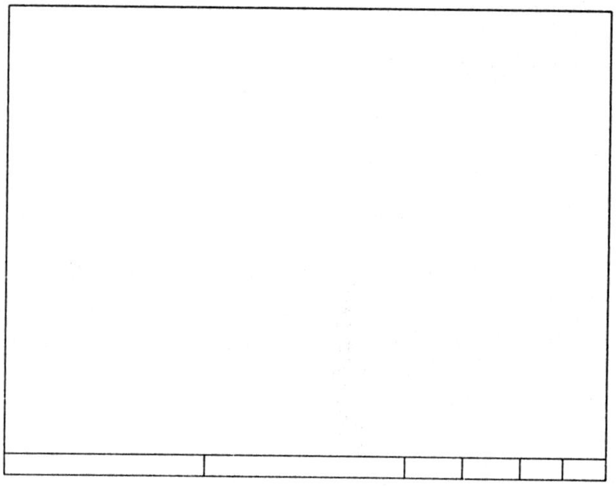

Figure T2

To point:

Command:
LINE From point: 7,0

To point: 7,.375

To point:

Command:
LINE From point: 8,0

To point: 8,.375

To point:

Use the **ZOOM-SCALE** option to move the border lines away from the edge of the drawing area. Save the drawing by entering **SAVE** at the command prompt and enter the name **BORDER-A**..

Command: ZOOM

All/Center/Dynamic/Extents/Left/Previous/Vmax/Window/<Scale(X/XP)>: ALL
Regenerating drawing.

Command: ZOOM

All/Center/Dynamic/Extents/Left/Previous/Vmax/Window/<Scale(X/XP)>: .9X

Command: SAVE
Save current changes as: BORDER-A
Current drawing name set to BORDER-A.

SECTION 2
CREATING A TWO-VIEW DRAWING OF THE SPACER

Before starting on the drawing of the Spacer, set a new layer by entering **LAYER** at the command prompt. Enter **SET**; then the name of the new layer, **OBJECT**.

LAYER
?/Make/Set/New/ON/OFF/Color/Ltype/Freeze/Thaw/LOck/Unlock: SET

New current layer <BORDER>: OBJECT
?/Make/Set/New/ON/OFF/Color/Ltype/Freeze/Thaw/LOck/Unlock:

The top view is drawn first by drawing the circles. Enter **CIRCLE** at the command prompt and pick the center point of the circle or enter coordinate points **5,5**. Enter the radius **.5** to draw the first circle. Repeat the **CIRCLE** command, use the same center point and enter a radius of **.75** to draw the second circle. Repeat the **CIRCLE** command to draw the remaining four circles, as shown in Figure T3.

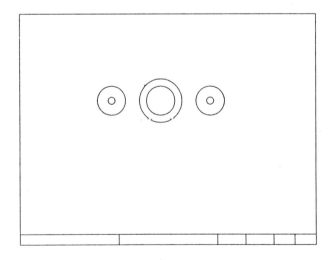

Figure T3

Command: CIRCLE
3P/2P/TTR/<Center point>: 5,5
Diameter/<Radius>: .5

Command:
CIRCLE 3P/2P/TTR/<Center point>: 5,5
Diameter/<Radius> <0.5000>: .75

Command:
CIRCLE 3P/2P/TTR/<Center point>: 6.75,5
Diameter/<Radius> <0.7500>: D
Diameter <1.5000>: .25

Command:
CIRCLE 3P/2P/TTR/<Center point>: 6.75,5
Diameter/<Radius> <0.1250>: .5

Command:
CIRCLE 3P/2P/TTR/<Center point>: 3.25,5
Diameter/<Radius> <0.5000>: D
Diameter <1.0000>: .25

Command:
CIRCLE 3P/2P/TTR/<Center point>: 3.25,5
Diameter/<Radius> <0.1250>: .5

To draw lines tangent to the large circle in the center and the large circles on the ends, set the object snap to tangent by entering **OSNAP** at the command prompt, then enter **TANGENT**.

Command: OSNAP
Object snap modes: TANGENT

Enter **LINE** at the command prompt. Pick the circles that the lines are to be drawn tangent to by repeating the **LINE** command (Figure T4).

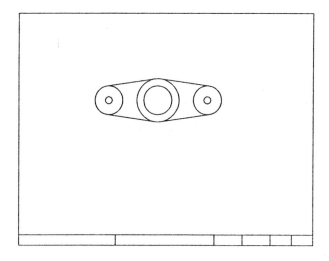

Figure T4

Command: LINE
From point:
To point:
To point:

Command:
LINE From point:
To point:
To point:

Command:
LINE From point:
To point:
To point:

Command:
LINE From point:
To point:
To point:

Turn the **OSNAP** mode to **NONE**. Use the **TRIM** command to erase part of the large circles on the ends of the Spacer. Enter **TRIM** at the command prompt. Select the two tangent lines as the two cutting edges, then enter **RETURN**. Pick the part of the circle to be erased then **RETURN** to end the command. Repeat the **TRIM** command to erase part of the other circle. (Figure T5). Save the drawing by entering **SAVE** at the command and entering the file name **SPACER**.

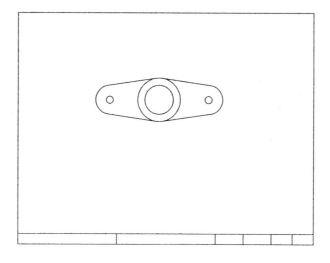

Figure T5

Command: OSNAP
Object snap modes: NONE

Command: TRIM

Select cutting edge(s)...
Select objects: 1 found

Select objects: 1 found

Select objects:

<Select object to trim>/Undo:
<Select object to trim>/Undo:

```
Command:
TRIM
Select cutting edge(s)...
Select objects: 1 found

Select objects: 1 found

Select objects:

<Select object to trim>/Undo:
<Select object to trim>/Undo:

Command: SAVE
Save current changes as <C:\BORDER-A>: SPACER
```

Draw the outline of the front view by entering **LINE** at the command prompt and picking points with the cursor or entering coordinate points.

```
Command: LINE
From point: 2.75,1.25

To point: 7.25,1.25

To point: 7.25,1.75

To point: 2.75,1.75

To point: CLOSE

Command: LINE
From point: 4.25,1.75

To point: 4.25,3

To point: 5.75,3

To point: 5.75,1.75

To point:
```

Add the circle in the front view by entering **CIRCLE** at the command prompt. Locate the center point at **5,2.375** and enter the diameter by entering **D** and **.25** (Figure T6).

```
Command: CIRCLE
3P/2P/TTR/<Center point>: 5,2.375
Diameter/<Radius> <0.5000>: D
Diameter <1.0000>: .25
```

Change the layer before adding center lines. Center lines are added to the drawing by first changing the layer. Enter **LAYER** at the command prompt. Enter **SET** at the layer prompt and enter **CENTER** to change the layer.

```
Command: LAYER
?/Make/Set/New/ON/OFF/Color/Ltype/Freeze/Thaw/LOck/Unlock: SET

New current layer <OBJECT>: CENTER
?/Make/Set/New/ON/OFF/Color/Ltype/Freeze/Thaw/LOck/Unlock:
```

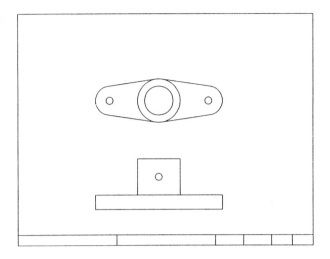

Figure T6

Change the linetype scale by entering **LTSCALE** at the command prompt. Enter a new scale factor of **.5** before drawing the center lines.

Command: LTSCALE
New scale factor <1.0000>: .5
Regenerating drawing.

Draw the center lines by entering **LINE** at the command prompt. Enter the points with the cursor or enter coordinate points, as shown (Figure T7).

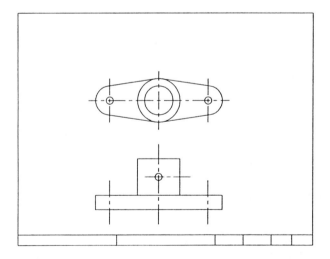

Figure T7

Command: LINE
From point: 3.25,.75

To point: 3.25,2.25

To point:

Command: LINE
From point: 6.75,2.25

To point: 6.75,.75

To point:

Command: LINE
From point: 5,3.5

To point: 5,.75

To point:

Command: LINE
From point: 2.5,5

To point: 7.5,5

To point:

Command: LINE
From point: 3.25,4.25

To point: 3.25,5.75

To point:

Command: LINE
From point: 5,4

To point: 5,6

To point:

Command: LINE
From point: 6.75,5.75

To point: 6.75,4.25

To point:

Command: LINE
From point: 4.5,2.375

To point: 6,2.375

To point:

Set the layer to **HIDDEN** before adding hidden lines to the front view.
Use the **ZOOM** command to window-in on the two views. Set the object snap to
.125. Draw the hidden lines in the front view by entering coordinate points or
snapping to the positions (Figure T8).

Command: LAYER
?/Make/Set/New/ON/OFF/Color/Ltype/Freeze/Thaw/LOck/Unlock: SET

New current layer <CENTER>: HIDDEN
?/Make/Set/New/ON/OFF/Color/Ltype/Freeze/Thaw/LOck/Unlock:

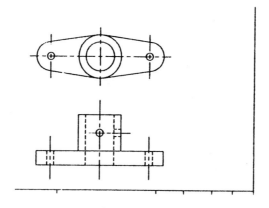

Figure T8

Command: ZOOM

All/Center/Dynamic/Extents/Left/Previous/Vmax/Window/<Scale(X/XP)>:WINDOW
Other corner:
Command: SAVE
Save current changes as <C:\BORDER-A>: SPACER
A drawing with this name already exists.
Do you want to replace it? <N> Y

Command: SNAP

Snap spacing or ON/OFF/Aspect/Rotate/Style <0.2500>: .125

Command: LINE
From point: 3.125,1.25

To point: 3.125,1.75

To point:

Command: LINE

From point: 3.375,1.75

To point: 3.375,1.25

To point:

Command: LINE
From point: 4.5,1.25

To point: 4.5,3

To point:

Command: LINE
From point: 5.5,3

To point: 5.5,1.25

To point:

Command: LINE
From point: 6.625,1.25

To point: 6.625,1.75

To point:

Command: LINE
From point: 6.875,1.75

To point: 6.875,1.25

To point:

Command: LINE
From point: 5.5,2.25

To point: 5.75,2.25

To point:

Command: LINE
From point: 5.75,2.5

To point: 5.5,2.5

To point:

Use the **ZOOM** command to create a new window for the top view (Figure T9). Use the **LINE** command to draw hidden lines in the top view for the holes drilled in the cylinder. The lines are drawn too long (Figure T10) and then trimmed to the circles to create hidden lines of the proper length. After the lines are drawn, enter **ZOOM-ALL** to display the completed two-view drawing of the Spacer (Figure T11). Save the drawing by entering **SAVE** at the command prompt.

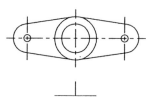

Figure T9

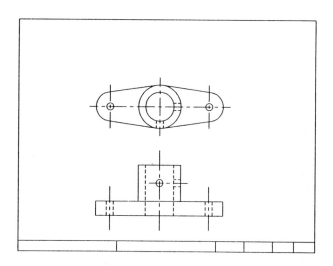

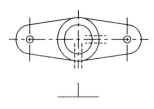

Figure T10

Figure T11

Command: ZOOM

All/Center/Dynamic/Extents/Left/Previous/Vmax/Window/<Scale(X/XP)>:
Other corner:

Command: LINE
From point: 4.875,4

To point: 4.875,4.875

To point:

Command: LINE
From point: 5.125,4.875

To point: 5.125,4

To point:

Command: LINE
From point: 5.25,4.875

To point: 6,4.875

To point:

Command: LINE
From point: 6,5.125

To point: 5.25,5.125

To point:

Trim the hidden lines by picking the circles as the cutting edges then picking the four parts of the lines to be erased.

Command: TRIM

Select cutting edge(s)...
Select objects: 1 found

Select objects: 1 found

Select objects:

<Select object to trim>/Undo:
<Select object to trim>/Undo:
<Select object to trim>/Undo:
<Select object to trim>/Undo:
<Select object to trim>/Undo:
<Select object to trim>/Undo:
<Select object to trim>/Undo:
<Select object to trim>/Undo:
<Select object to trim>/Undo:

Command: ZOOM

All/Center/Dynamic/Extents/Left/Previous/Vmax/Window/<Scale(X/XP)>: ALL
Regenerating drawing.

Command: SAVE
Save current changes as <C:\BORDER-A>: SPACER
A drawing with this name already exists.
Do you want to replace it? <N> Y

SECTION 3
ADDING DIMENSIONS TO THE SPACER DRAWING
The distance between the front and top views is too small if dimensions are to be added. Use the **EDIT** option **MOVE** to locate the top view farther from the front. Stretch a window around the top view to define all of the entities to be moved. Use the center of the cylinder in the top view as the base point. Move the top view vertically .5 inch by entering **5, 5.5** for the second point (Figure T12).

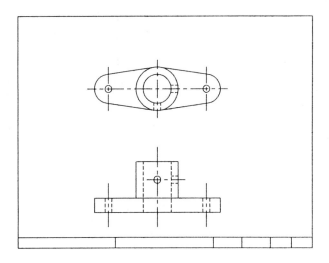

Figure T12

Command: MOVE

Select objects: WINDOW

First corner: Other corner: 18 found

Select objects:
Base point or displacement: 5,5
Second point of displacement: 5,5.5

Before adding dimensions, set the layer to **DIMENSIONS**.

Command: LAYER
?/Make/Set/New/ON/OFF/Color/Ltype/Freeze/Thaw/LOck/Unlock: SET

New current layer <HIDDEN>: DIMENSIONS
?/Make/Set/New/ON/OFF/Color/Ltype/Freeze/Thaw/LOck/Unlock:

Determine the current settings of the dimension variables by entering **DIM** at the command prompt; then enter **STATUS** to list the current settings.

Command: DIM

Dim: STATUS

DIMALT Off	Alternate units selected
DIMALTD 2	Alternate unit decimal places
DIMALTF 25.4000	Alternate unit scale factor
DIMAPOST	Suffix for alternate text

DIMASO   On   Create associative dimensions
DIMASZ   0.1800   Arrow size
DIMBLK   Arrow block name
DIMBLK1   First arrow block name
DIMBLK2   Second arrow block name
DIMCEN   0.0900   Center mark size
DIMCLRD BYBLOCK   Dimension line color
DIMCLRE BYBLOCK   Extension line & leader color
DIMCLRT BYBLOCK   Dimension text color
DIMDLE   0.0000   Dimension line extension
DIMDLI   0.3800   Dimension line increment for continuation
DIMEXE   0.1800   Extension above dimension line
DIMEXO   0.0625   Extension line origin offset
DIMGAP   0.0900   Gap from dimension line to text
DIMLFAC 1.0000   Linear unit scale factor
-- Press RETURN for more --
DIMLIM   Off   Generate dimension limits
DIMPOST   Default suffix for dimension text
DIMRND   0.0000   Rounding value
DIMSAH   Off   Separate arrow blocks
DIMSCALE 1.0000   Overall scale factor
DIMSE1   Off   Suppress the first extension line
DIMSE2   Off   Suppress the second extension line
DIMSHO   On   Update dimensions while dragging
DIMSOXD Off   Suppress outside extension dimension
DIMSTYLE *UNNAMED   Current dimension style (read-only)
DIMTAD   Off   Place text above the dimension line
DIMTFAC 1.0000   Tolerance text height scaling factor
DIMTIH   On   Text inside extensions is horizontal
DIMTIX   Off   Place text inside extensions
DIMTM   0.0000   Minus tolerance
DIMTOFL Off   Force line inside extension lines
DIMTOH   On   Text outside extensions is horizontal
DIMTOL   Off   Generate dimension tolerances
DIMTP   0.0000   Plus tolerance
DIMTSZ   0.0000   Tick size
-- Press RETURN for more --
DIMTVP   0.0000   Text vertical position
DIMTXT   0.1800   Text height
DIMZIN   0   Zero suppression

Dim: EXIT

Use the **F1** key to return to the drawing screen. Change the dimension text and arrow size by entering **EXIT** at the dimension prompt. Enter **SETVAR** at the command prompt; then enter **DIMTXT** to change the size of the dimension text to **.125** inch. Repeat the **SETVAR** command and enter **DIMASZ** to change the arrow size to **.125** inch.

Command: SETVAR
Variable name or ?: DIMTXT

New value for DIMTXT <0.1800>: .125

Command: SETVAR
Variable name or ? <DIMTXT>: DIMASZ

New value for DIMASZ <0.1800>: .125

The number of decimal places for the dimension text is set to two places by entering **UNITS** at the command prompt. Enter the number **2** for decimal modes, **2** for the number of decimal places, **1** for decimal degrees, and **0** for the fractional places for angles.

Command: UNITS
Report formats: (Examples)

  1. Scientific   1.55E+01
  2. Decimal   15.50
  3. Engineering   1'-3.50"
  4. Architectural   1'-3 1/2"
  5. Fractional   15 1/2

With the exception of Engineering and Architectural formats, these formats can be used with any basic unit of measurement. For example, Decimal mode is perfect for metric units as well as decimal English units.

Enter choice, 1 to 5 <2>: 2
Number of digits to right of decimal point (0 to 8) <4>: 2

Systems of angle measure: (Examples)

  1. Decimal degrees   45.0000
  2. Degrees/minutes/seconds   45d0'0"
  3. Grads   50.0000g
  4. Radians   0.7854r
  5. Surveyor's units   N 45d0'0" E

Enter choice, 1 to 5 <1>: 1
Number of fractional places for display of angles (0 to 8) <0>: 0

Direction for angle 0:
  East   3 o'clock = 0
  North   12 o'clock = 90
  West   9 o'clock = 180
  South   6 o'clock = 270
Enter direction for angle 0 <0>: 0

Do you want angles measured clockwise? <N> N

Use the **F1** key to return to the drawing screen. Enter **DIM** at the command prompt to begin placing dimensions on the drawing. The two horizontal dimensions in the top view are placed first by entering **HORIZ** at the dimension prompt. Figure T13 shows the location of all the points picked (X) with the input device to dimension the Spacer. Pick the first and second dimension line origins, and then the location for the text for each horizontal dimension.

Command: DIM

Dim: HORIZ

First extension line origin or RETURN to select: <Snap on>
Second extension line origin:
Dimension line location (Text/Angle):
Dimension text <1.75>:

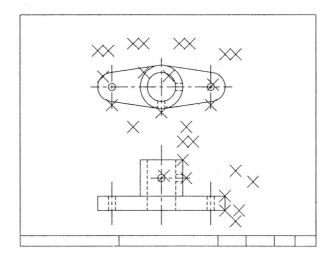

Figure T13

Dim:
HORIZ
First extension line origin or RETURN to select:
Second extension line origin:
Dimension line location (Text/Angle):

Dimension text <1.75>:

To place vertical dimensions in the front view, enter **VERTICAL** at the dimension prompt. Pick each point for the extension lines and the location for text. For the smaller dimension values, pick a point outside the extension lines to place the text .50, for example.

Dim: VERTICAL

First extension line origin or RETURN to select:
Second extension line origin:
Dimension line location (Text/Angle):
Dimension text <0.50>:

Dim:
VERTICAL
First extension line origin or RETURN to select:
Second extension line origin:
Dimension line location (Text/Angle):
Dimension text <0.63>:

Dim:
VERTICAL
First extension line origin or RETURN to select:
Second extension line origin:
Dimension line location (Text/Angle):
Dimension text <1.75>:

Enter **LEADER** to create leader lines and text for each hole. Enter **%%c** to create the phi symbol necessary for diameter dimensions. Begin by turning the snap off and picking a point on the circumference of the circle. Turn the snap on and pick the endpoints of the leader line. Enter the text from the keyboard. Repeat this sequence for each hole. (Figure T14). Save the drawing by entering **SAVE** at the command prompt.

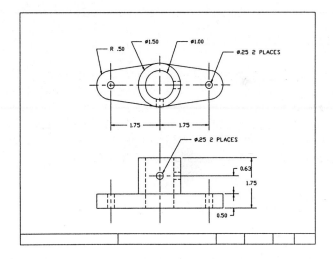

Figure T14

Dim: LEADER
Leader start: <Snap off>
To point: <Snap on>
To point:
To point:
To point:

Dimension text <1.75>: %%C.25 2 PLACES

Dim: DIAMETER

Select arc or circle: <Snap off>
Dimension text <0.25>:

Enter leader length for text:
Dim:
DIAMETER
Select arc or circle:
Dimension text <1.00>:

Enter leader length for text:

Dim:
DIAMETER
Select arc or circle:
Dimension text <1.50>:

Enter leader length for text:
Dim: RADIUS

Select arc or circle:
Dimension text <0.50>:

Enter leader length for text:
Dim: *Cancel*

SECTION 4
SECTION VIEW TUTORIAL

The section view tutorial demonstrates how to use AutoCAD to create crosshatching for sectional views. The front view of the Spacer is edited, then crosshatching lines are added to create a full-section view. The text is added to the title block to complete the section view drawing of the Spacer.

Some of the lines must be removed to create a section view. Use the **TRIM** command to erase parts of the lines in the front view.

Command: TRIM

Select cutting edge(s)...
Select objects: 1 found

Select objects: 1 found

Select objects:

<Select object to trim>/Undo:
<Select object to trim>/Undo:

The hidden lines in the front view must be changed to object lines using the **CHANGE** command to change the hidden lines to the object layer.

Command: CHANGE

Select objects: 1 found

Select objects: 1 found

Select objects: 1 found

Select objects: 1 found

Select objects: 1 found

Select objects: 1 found

Select objects: 1 found

Select objects: 1 found

Select objects:
Properties/<Change point>: P

Change what property (Color/Elev/LAyer/LType/Thickness) ? LAYER

New layer <HIDDEN>: OBJECT

Change what property (Color/Elev/LAyer/LType/Thickness) ?

The current layer is set to **SECTIONS** by entering **LAYER** and **SET**.

Command: LAYER
?/Make/Set/New/ON/OFF/Color/Ltype/Freeze/Thaw/LOck/Unlock: SET

New current layer <DIMENSIONS>: SECTIONS
?/Make/Set/New/ON/OFF/Color/Ltype/Freeze/Thaw/LOck/Unlock:

The crosshatching is added to the front view using the BHATCH command. The hatching style is set ANSI31 using the Bhatch dialogue box.

Command: BHATCH
Select internal point Selecting everything...
Selecting everything visible...
Analyzing the selected data...
Select internal point Select internal point Select internal point Select internal point Select internal point

The small hole is erased by entering **ERASE** at the command prompt (Figure T15).

Command: ERASE

Select objects: 1 found

Select objects:

Text is added to the title block by using the **ZOOM** command and a **WINDOW** to enlarge the left half of the title block. The **DTEXT** command is used to enter the first two strings of text. The **CENTER** option is used for the drawing name and the name of the designer. The **PAN** option is used to display the right half of the title block. Repeat the **DTEXT** command but use a height of **.125** inch for the text. Enter **ZOOM** at the command prompt and **EXTENTS** to display the completed drawing (Figure T15).

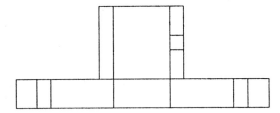

Figure T15

Command: ZOOM

All/Center/Dynamic/Extents/Left/Previous/Vmax/Window/<Scale(X/XP)>: W

First corner: Other corner:
Command: DTEXT
Justify/Style/<Start point>: J
Align/Fit/Center/Middle/Right/TL/TC/TR/ML/MC/MR/BL/BC/BR: C

Center point:
Height <0.20>: .2

Rotation angle <0>:

Text: SPACER
Text: JIM LACHEY
Text:
Command: PAN
Displacement: Second point:
Command: DTEXT
Justify/Style/<Start point>:
Height <0.20>: .125

Rotation angle <0>:

Text: 4-12-93
Text:
Command:
DTEXT Justify/Style/<Start point>:
Height <0.13>:

Rotation angle <0>:

Text: 1 OF 1
Text:
Command:
DTEXT Justify/Style/<Start point>:
Height <0.13>:

Rotation angle <0>:

Text: FULL
Text:

Command: Z
ZOOM
All/Center/Dynamic/Extents/Left/Previous/Vmax/Window/<Scale(X/XP)>: E
Regenerating drawing.

Command: SAVE
Save current changes as <C:\SPACER>:

Command: QUIT

End AutoCAD.

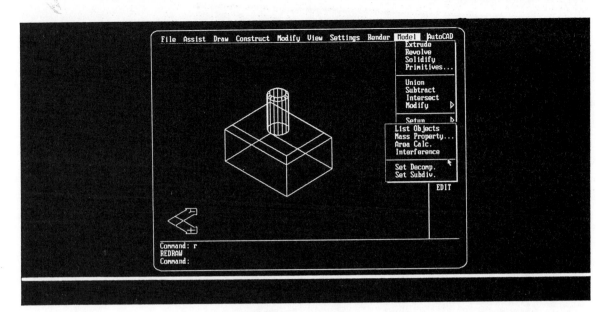

AutoCAD 3D TUTORIAL

This 3D tutorial is an introduction to creating a 3D drawing of a part. Three-dimensional cylinders, arcs, lines, and holes will be created. The model will be edited, and the UCS icon will be moved to draw 3D entities on various surfaces. The tutorial is meant to provide a quick introduction to the AutoCAD 3D drawing capabilities. The part to be drawn is the Spacer that was created in the 2D tutorial.

The first step in this drawing is to create the viewports necessary to visualize the object as it is being drawn. Move the cursor to the **VIEW** option in the menu bar at the top of the screen or enter **VPORTS** at the command prompt. Select the option shown in Figure T16. The screen is divided as shown in Figure T17. Each viewport will have a different view of the spacer. The upper left viewport will be the top view or plan view. The lower left viewport will be the front view. The viewport to the right will be an isometric view. This arrangement provides the user with the maximum visualization capabilities without having the views displayed too small.

Command: VPORTS

Save/Restore/Delete/Join/SIngle/?/2/<3>/4: 3

Horizontal/Vertical/Above/Below/Left/<Right>: RIGHT
Regenerating drawing.

The plan view is the default setting for all of the viewports. The **VPOINT** command is used to change the view in a viewport. Before entering the **VPOINT** command, use the mouse to click in the right viewport on screen. Enter **VPOINT** at the command prompt or select it from the View/Set View Pull-down Menu.

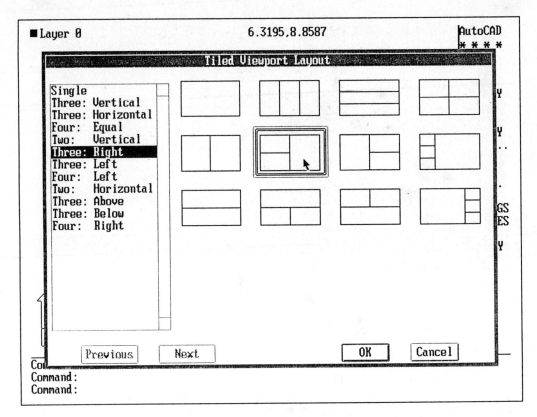

Figure T16

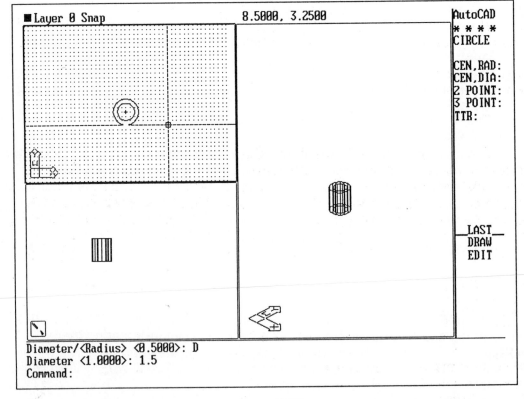

Figure T17

Move the cursor to the lower-left viewport and activate it by clicking in it with the cursor. Use the View/Set Pull-down Menu **Vpoint** and select the **FRONT** option from the Icon Menu.

```
Command: VPOINT
Rotate/<View point> <0.0000,0.0000,1.0000>: ROTATE
Enter angle in XY plane from X axis <270>: 315
Enter angle from XY plane <90>: 30
Regenerating drawing.
```

Pick the top viewport with the cursor to activate it. Turn the coordinate display readout on by selecting function key **F6** or **CTRL-D**. Turn the grid on by selecting function key **F7** or **CTRL-G**. Turn the snap on by selecting function key **F9** or **CTRL-B**. Change the snap increment by entering **SNAP** at the command prompt and entering **.25.**

```
Command:
VPOINT Rotate/<View point> <0.0000,0.0000,1.0000>: ROTATE
Enter angle in XY plane from X axis <270>: 270


Enter angle from XY plane <90>: 0
Regenerating drawing.

Command: <Coords off> <Coords on> <Grid on> <Snap on> SNAP

Snap spacing or ON/OFF/Aspect/Rotate/Style <1.0000>: .25
```

To extrude entities for 3D drawings, the thickness must be set. Enter **ELEV** at the command prompt to set the thickness. The elevation is not changed, so press RETURN at the new elevation prompt. Enter a value of **1.75** at the new thickness prompt. This is the height of the cylinders for the Spacer.

```
Command: ELEV
New current elevation <0.0000>:

New current thickness <0.0000>: 1.75
```

The first items to be drawn for the Spacer are the cylinder and hole. This is drawn in the top or plan view. Enter **CIRCLE** at the command prompt and enter coordinate values of **6,4** for the location of the center. Enter the letter **D** for a diameter input. Enter a value of 1 for the size of the hole. Each viewport is updated as the hole is being drawn. Repeat the **CIRCLE** command by entering Return. Select the center point by entering values of **6,4**. Enter **D** to input a diameter. The diameter of the cylinder is 1.5, which is entered (Figure T17).

```
Command: CIRCLE
3P/2P/TTR/<Center point>: 6,4
Diameter/<Radius>: D
Diameter: 1

Command:
CIRCLE 3P/2P/TTR/<Center point>: 6,4
Diameter/<Radius> <0.5000>: D
Diameter <1.0000>: 1.5
```

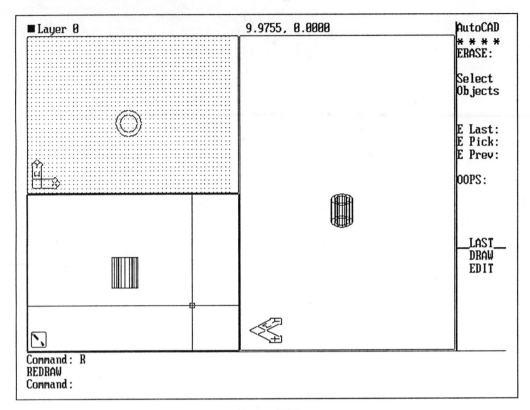

Figure T18

Activate the front view viewport with the cursor. The view is centered by entering **ZOOM** at the command prompt then **ALL**. The **ZOOM** command is repeated then a scale of **1** is used to center the view. (Figure T18).

Command: ZOOM

All/Center/Dynamic/Extents/Left/Previous/Vmax/Window/<Scale(X/XP)>: A
Regenerating drawing.

The base of the Spacer is drawn next, but first the thickness must be changed from 1.75 to .5. Enter **ELEV** at the command prompt, and leave the elevation the same by entering Return. Enter **.5** for the thickness of the base.

Command: ELEV
New current elevation <0.0000>:

New current thickness <1.7500>: .5

The ends of the base are constructed by drawing circles, which will be trimmed later. Enter **CIRCLE** at the command prompt, and locate the center point with coordinate values of **7.75,4**. Enter **D** for the diameter option and enter **.25** for the size of the drilled hole. Repeat the **CIRCLE** command and enter coordinate values of **7.75,4**. Enter **D** for the diameter option and a value of **1** to draw the circle.

The circles at the other end of the base are drawn by repeating the **CIRCLE** command and entering coordinate values of **4.25,4** and the same diameters (Figure T19).

Command: CIRCLE
3P/2P/TTR/<Center point>: 7.75,4
Diameter/<Radius> <0.7500>: D
Diameter <1.5000>: .25

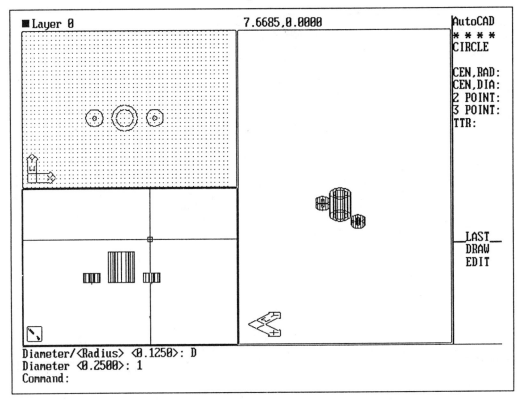

Figure T19

Command:
CIRCLE 3P/2P/TTR/<Center point>: 7.75,4
Diameter/<Radius> <0.1250>: D
Diameter <0.2500>: 1

Command:
CIRCLE 3P/2P/TTR/<Center point>: 4.24,4
Diameter/<Radius> <0.5000>: D
Diameter <1.0000>: .25

Command:
CIRCLE 3P/2P/TTR/<Center point>: 4.25,4
Diameter/<Radius> <0.1250>: D
Diameter <0.2500>: 1

To complete the base of the Spacer, lines are drawn tangent to the 1-inch-diameter circles on each end and the large cylinder in the center of the part. Set the **OSNAP** mode to **TANGENT** by entering **OSNAP** at the command prompt. Set the snap mode by entering **TANGENT** at the prompt.

Pick the top viewport with the cursor to activate it. The **LINE** command is entered at the command prompt. Select one of the large circles at the end of the Spacer. Then select the large cylinder at the center of the Spacer. A .5-inch-thick tangent line is drawn between each circle. Cancel the Line Command then repeat the sequence for the other three tangent lines to complete the base of the spacer (Figure T20).

Command: OSNAP
Object snap modes: TANGENT

Command: LINE
From point: OSNAP
Object snap modes: TANGENT

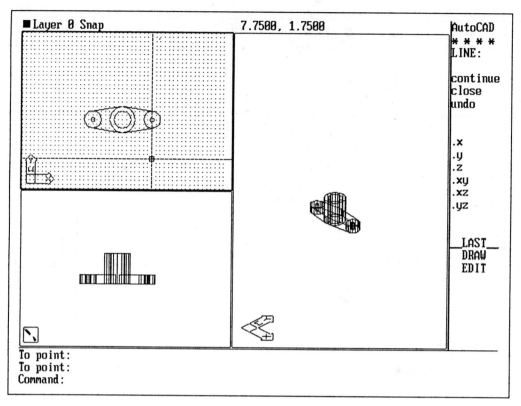

Figure T20

Command: LINE
From point:
To point:
To point:

Command:

LINE From point:
To point:
To point:

Command:
LINE From point:
To point:
To point:

Command:
LINE From point:
To point:
To point:

Two small drilled holes are added to the cylinders near the center of the spacer. This operation requires UCS elevation and position changes. The first step is to turn the tangent snap mode off by entering **OSNAP** at the command prompt, and then entering **NONE**.

The UCS must be changed to draw the small holes in the cylinder. To display the new orientation and position of the UCS in each viewport, enter the **UCSICON** option at the command prompt. Enter **OR** at the UCSICON prompt. This step must be repeated for each viewport after it is activated with the cursor.

Command: OSNAP
Object snap modes: NONE

Command: UCSICON

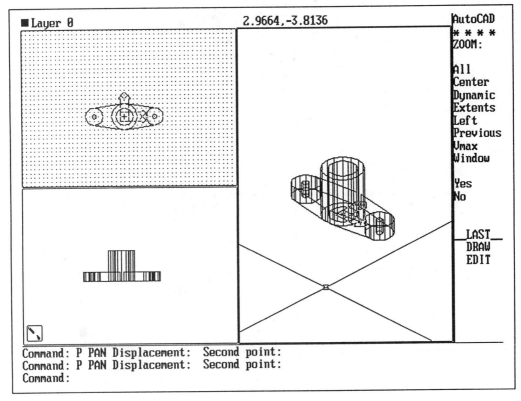

Figure T21

ON/OFF/All/Noorigin/ORigin <ON>: OR

Command:
UCSICON
ON/OFF/All/Noorigin/ORigin <ON>: OR

Command:
UCSICON
ON/OFF/All/Noorigin/ORigin <ON>: OR

The origin point of the current UCS is changed by entering **UCS** at the command prompt. Select **ORIGIN** by entering **O** at the UCS prompt. Move the origin to the center of the Spacer by entering coordinate points **6,4**. The UCS icon is moved to that position in each viewport, as shown in Figure T21.

Command: UCS

Origin/ZAxis/3point/Entity/View/X/Y/Z/Prev/Restore/Save/Del/?/<World>: O

Origin point <0,0,0>: 6,4

The UCS must be rotated into position to draw the small hole in the front of the Spacer. Repeat the UCS command and enter **X** to rotate the UCS about the X axis. Enter a rotation angle of **90** at the prompt. Each viewport displays the new position of the UCS, as shown in Figure T22.

Command: UCS

Origin/ZAxis/3point/Entity/View/X/Y/Z/Prev/Restore/Save/Del/?/<World>: X

Rotation angle about X axis <0>: 90

Grid too dense to display

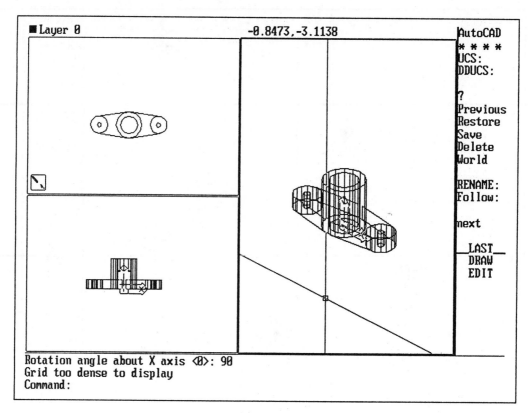

Figure T22

To draw the small holes, a new thickness is set by entering **ELEV** at the command prompt. The elevation is changed to **.25** and the thickness to **1.00**

The hole is created by entering **CIRCLE** at the command prompt. The center of the hole is located 1.125 inches above the base of the Spacer, which is the current origin point of the UCS. This distance is entered as a Y value. Enter **0,1.125** to locate the center of the hole. Enter **D** for diameter, and then enter **.25** for the diameter of the hole. The hole is drawn on screen, as shown in Figure T23. The hole is much longer than necessary but Boolean operations will be performed on the 3D model to create the holes.

```
Command: ELEV
New current elevation <0.0000>: .25

New current thickness <0.2500>: 1

Command: CIRCLE
3P/2P/TTR/<Center point>: 0,1.125
Diameter/<Radius> <0.1250>: D
Diameter <0.2500>: .25
```

The second hole is drawn by again changing the UCS. Enter **UCS** at the command prompt and enter **Y**. By rotating the Y axis 90 degrees, the second small hole in the cylinder can be created. Enter a value of **90** to change the UCS, as shown in Figure T23.

```
Command: UCS

Origin/ZAxis/3point/Entity/View/X/Y/Z/Prev/Restore/Save/Del/?/<World>: Y
```

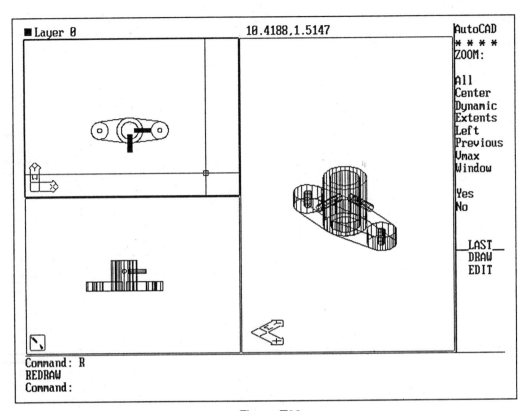

Figure T23

Rotation angle about Y axis <0>: 90

Enter **CIRCLE** at the command prompt and enter the center point as **0,1.125**. Enter **D** for diameter and the diameter of **.25** (Figure T23).

Command: CIRCLE
3P/2P/TTR/<Center point>: 0,1.125
Diameter/<Radius> <0.1250>: D
Diameter <0.2500>: .25

The circles at the ends of the base of the Spacer have to be trimmed to complete the part. The UCS axis is returned to its default position by entering **UCS** at the command prompt. Enter **W** for the **WORLD** option to change the UCS back to its original position (Figure T24).

Command: UCS

Origin/ZAxis/3point/Entity/View/X/Y/Z/Prev/Restore/Save/Del/?/<World>: W

Activate the top viewport by picking it with the cursor then turn off the snap with **F9**. Enter **TRIM** at the command prompt, and select the cutting edges by picking the two tangent lines for one of the large circles at the end of the Spacer; then press Return. Pick the part of the circle to be trimmed with the cursor. Repeat the **TRIM** command to trim the other circle, and complete the 3D model of the Spacer (Figure T24).

Command: <Snap off> TRIM

Select cutting edge(s)...
Select objects: 1 found

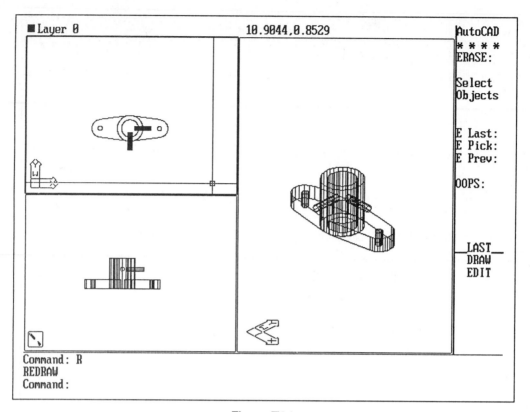

Figure T24

Select objects: 1 found

Select objects:

<Select object to trim>/Undo:
<Select object to trim>/Undo:

Command: TRIM

Select cutting edge(s)...
Select objects: 1 found

Select objects: 1 found

Select objects:

<Select object to trim>/Undo:
<Select object to trim>/Undo:

The two ends of the part must be made into a Pline so the part can be made into a solid model. This is done by adding an arc between the lines and points of tangency on the outside of the large cylinder. First activate the top viewport then use the **ZOOM** option to zoom-in on the top view. Figure T25. Enter **ELEV** and set the elevation to **0** and the thickness to **.50**. Enter **ARC** at the command prompt then pick the **C,S,E** (center, start, end) option from the menu. Enter **CEN** to activate the Osnap center option then pick one of the large circles in the top view. Enter **INT** to activate the Osnap intersection option then pick the first tangent point between the line and the outside of the cylinder.

Remember that AutoCAD draws arcs in a counterclockwise direction so the first point selected determines the direction of the drawn arc. Enter **INT** to activate the Osnap intersection option again then pick the second tangent point between the line and the outside of the cylinder.   Repeat these steps to make the other arc.

Command: ZOOM

All/Center/Dynamic/Extents/Left/Previous/Vmax/Window/<Scale(X/XP)>:
Other corner:

Command: ELEV
New current elevation <0.2500>: 0

New current thickness <1.0000>: .50

Command:
Command: _ARC Center/<Start point>: _C Center: CEN
of
Start point: INT
of
Angle/Length of chord/<End point>: DRAG INT
of

Command:
Command: _ARC Center/<Start point>: _C Center: CEN
of
Start point: INT
of
Angle/Length of chord/<End point>: DRAG INT
of

Activate the isometric viewport by picking it with the cursor, then enter **ZOOM**. Tightly window into the part as shown in Figure T25. Use the **PEDIT** command to create a polyline of the two arcs and two lines. Use the **PAN** command to pan to other side of the object. Figure T26. Repeat the **PEDIT** command to create a pline of the other side. Use **ZOOM** to view all of the part in the isometric view after editing the lines to plines.

Command: ZOOM

All/Center/Dynamic/Extents/Left/Previous/Vmax/Window/<Scale(X/XP)>: W
Other corner:
Command: PEDIT
Select polyline:
Entity selected is not a polyline
Do you want to turn it into one? <Y>
Close/Join/Width/Edit vertex/Fit/Spline/Decurve/Ltype gen/Undo/eXit <X>: J

Select objects: 1 found

Select objects: 1 found

Select objects: 1 found

Select objects: 1 found

Select objects:

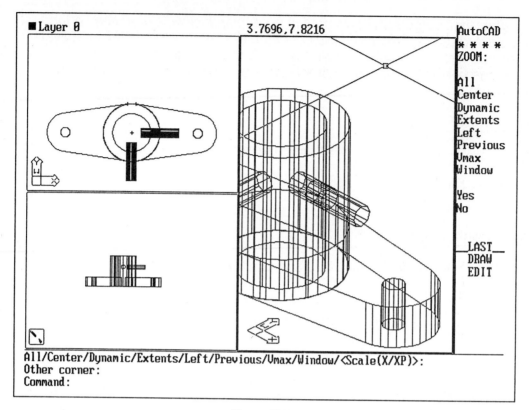

Figure T25

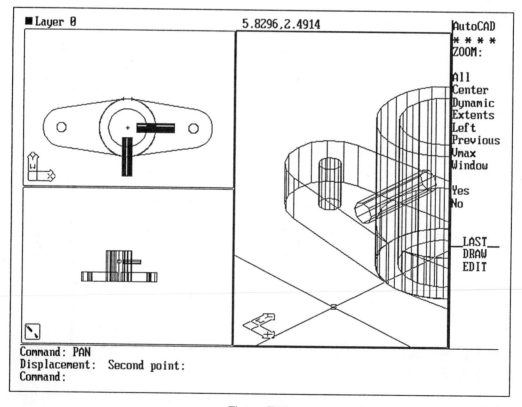

Figure T26

Entity selected is not a polyline
Do you want to turn it into one? <Y>

Close/Join/Width/Edit vertex/Fit/Spline/Decurve/Ltype gen/Undo/eXit <X>: J

Select objects: 1 found

Select objects: 1 found

Select objects: 1 found

Select objects: 1 found

Select objects:

3 segments added to polyline

Open/Join/Width/Edit vertex/Fit/Spline/Decurve/Ltype gen/Undo/eXit <X>: X

Command: ZOOM

All/Center/Dynamic/Extents/Left/Previous/Vmax/Window/<Scale(X/XP)>: A
Regenerating drawing.

**Redisplay required by change in drawing extents.

Change the wireframe model into a solid model by entering **SOLIDIFY** at
the command prompt. Load the AME modeler as prompted. Use a window to
select all of the Spacer. After processing the model is displayed as shown in
Figure T27.

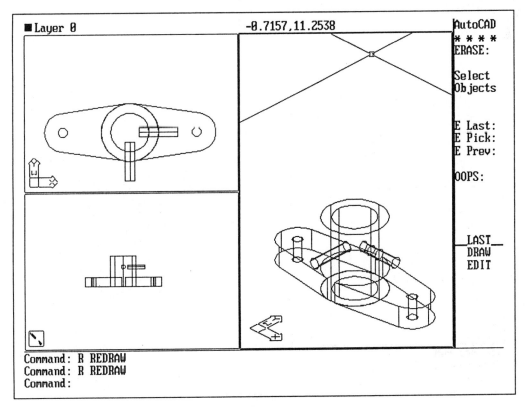

Figure T27

3 segments added to polyline

Open/Join/Width/Edit vertex/Fit/Spline/Decurve/Ltype gen/Undo/eXit <X>: X

Command: PAN
Displacement: Second point:
Command: PEDIT
Select polyline:

Command: SOLIDIFY

Initializing...
No modeler is loaded yet. Both AME and Region Modeler are available.
Autoload Region/<AME>: AME

Initializing Advanced Modeling Extension.

Select objects: Other corner: 12 found

Select objects:
Phase I - Boundary evaluation begins.
Tessellation computation begins.
Updating the Advanced Modeling Extension database.

After solidifying the Spacer the cylinders must be subtracted to create the holes. Enter **SOLSUB** at the command prompt then pick the large cylinder and the two plines on the ends of the Spacer. Pick the 4 small holes and the large hole in the center of the large cylinder which will be subtracted to make holes. Figure T28.

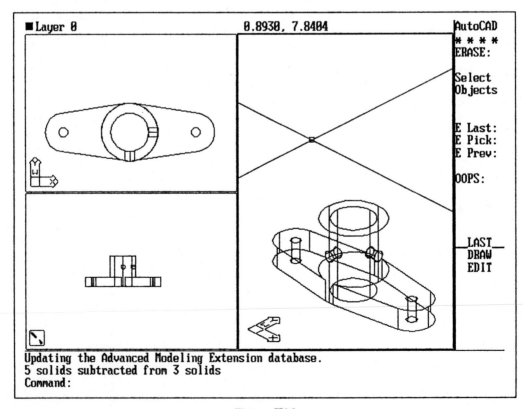

Figure T28

Command: SOLSUB

Source objects...

Select objects: 1 found

Select objects: 1 found

Select objects: 1 found

Select objects:
3 solids selected.

Objects to subtract from them...

Select objects: 1 found

Select objects: 1 found

Select objects: 1 found

Select objects: 1 found

Select objects: 1 found

Select objects:
5 solids selected.
Phase I - Boundary evaluation begins.
Updating the Advanced Modeling Extension database.
5 solids subtracted from 3 solids

Use the **SOLMESH** command to create a surface model of the Spacer
(Figure T29) then use **HIDE** to remove hidden lines. Figure T30.

Command: SOLMESH

Select objects: 1 found

Select objects:
1 solid selected.
Surface meshing of current solid is completed.
Creating block for mesh representation...
Done.

Command: HIDE
Regenerating drawing.
Hiding lines: done 0%Hiding lines: done 76%Hiding lines: done 100%

Command:

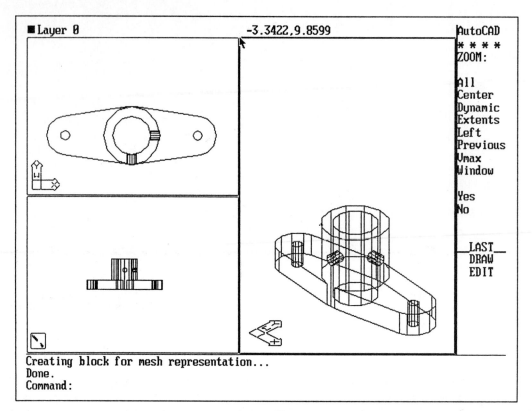

Figure T29

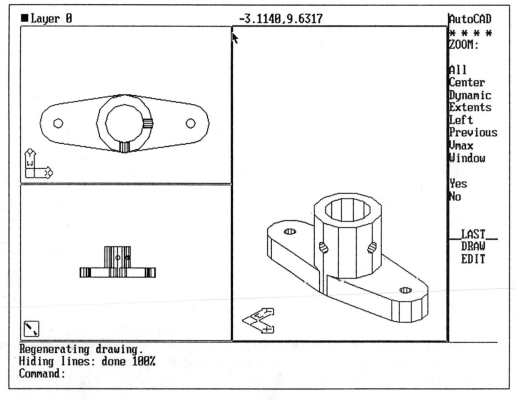

Figure T30

CAD LITERACY

As with most technologies, there are many words that have specific meanings. This is especially true of CAD, which has borrowed many terms from other disciplines and applied them to computer graphics. This glossary defines many of the terms that have special meaning and is illustrated to increase your understanding of CAD.

ILLUSTRATED GLOSSARY

Aliasing Related to the resolution of the screen and the stair-stepping or jaggies of screen images.

Array When more than one copy is created in a series of rows and columns.

Associative dimensions Process that automatically updates dimensions to edited entities. For example, if a dimensioned object is scaled to half-size, all dimensions will automatically be changed to reflect the different size.

Block A group of entities that are stored and can be retrieved and placed into any drawing. Sometimes called a *symbol*.

BOM Bill of materials. Some CAD systems have automated the creation of bills of materials by associating text information with geometric entities. The text data are extracted and automatically placed in a bill of materials.

Boolean operations A theory of operation used when creating solid models with primitive shapes. To drill a hole in a cube, boolean operations are used to define the hole as a cylinder that is subtracted from the cube.

Break An editing command that is used to make gaps in entities, such as making a circle into an arc by breaking the circle and removing part of it.

CAD Computer-aided design/drafting.

CAM Computer-aided manufacturing, which includes robots, automated measuring machines, NC (numerical machine) tools, and factory automation.

Chamfer Command used to turn a square corner into a chamfered corner.

CIM Computer-integrated manufacturing, which combines the whole design process, manufacturing, assembly, sales, and other components of a factory into one integrated process.

Configure The process used to match the software to the hardware devices used on a particular CAD workstation.

Crosshatch   Section lines that are added to a drawing by defining the area.

Cursor   A large plus (+) that is moved around the screen by movement of the cursor control device which typically is the mouse, stylus, or puck.

Digitizer   An input device used to enter existing drawings into a CAD system.

Drag   A function that shows the new position of entities as the cursor changes position on the screen, such as a block that is being positioned on a drawing.

Default   The original settings of the CAD software.

Edit   Commands used to change existing drawing entities, such as linetype, color, layer, text parameters, and others.

Entities   The basic geometric elements used to create drawings.

Extend   Used to lengthen an entity such as a line from the current endpoint to a new point, such as the endpoint of another line.

Extrude   Technique used when creating a 3D wireframe model where a 2D profile is copied and extended to a depth resulting in a 3D wireframe of the profile.

FEA   Finite element analysis. A method of analyzing a wireframe mesh model.

Fillet   Automatically adds fillets or rounds to corners at any specified radius by selecting the corner.

Graphic card   An electronic circuit board that determines the type of display monitor, resolution, and number of colors that are used with a CADD workstation.

Geometric model   A mathematical representation of a design created with CADD.

Grid   Is a series of small marks displayed on screen similar to grid paper.

Group   A method of linking entities to assist in copying, moving, erasing, and other editing functions.

Handle   A defined point that is used to copy, move, or place entities or blocks on a drawing.

Hatching   A term used to describe the section lines or shading patterns used for sectional drawings.

Hide   Command used to remove hidden lines automatically from a 3D wireframe model.

ICON   A graphic representation of menu items used on some CAD systems.

IGES   Initial graphics exchange specification. A standard file format that is used to move CAD drawing files from one system to another.

Input device   Used to enter data and/or control some features of the CAD software.

Layers   A display option used to separate entities. Similar in nature to using overlays or separate drawings sheets when using hand tools.

Macro   A number of chained commands to execute a function. Sometimes called a *symbol* or *parametric program*.

Mask   A method of selecting entities that are excluded from a task.

Menu   A method of displaying commands on screen or a tablet.

Mirror   An operation that makes a mirror image of the defined entities around an axis.

Model   A 3D drawing of an object that is represented as a wireframe, surface, or solid.

Mouse   An input device used to control cursor movement and select or cancel program commands.

Move   An operation that is used to move selected entities to a new position.

NC   Numerical control. The control of machine tools with computers.

Origin   Defined as the intersection of the X, Y, and Z axes and assigned coordinate values of 0, 0, 0.

Output device   Used to present, in a form common to engineers and designers, the graphics created with a CADD system.

Palette   The range of colors available to the user of a CAD system.

Pan   A display option that allows the user to change the window or view of the drawing by moving to the left or right and up or down.

Parametric program A chained sequence of commands that perform a function. Sometimes called a *macro* or *symbol*.

Pattern A defined set of entities that are stored and can be retrieved and placed on other drawings. Sometimes called a *symbol*.

Peripheral Computer hardware device controlled by the CPU.

Pick The act of selecting or choosing entities and menu commands.

Pixel The individual picture element that determines the resolution of a display screen.

Plotter An output device used to make hard copies of CAD drawings.

Polar coordinates A method of entering the location of entities by entering a distance and an angle.

Primitive Basic geometric shapes that are defined to produce a 3D model.

Prompt A message that appears on the screen to assist the user of the CAD software.

Recall A function that undeletes entities at a new angle and can be combined with the copy and move commands.

Redraw Command used to refresh the screen image to remove temporary markers.

Resolution The number of pixels on a display screen.

Rotate Used to position entities at a new angle and can be combined with the copy and move commands.

Scanner A device that automatically converts a paper drawing to data that are used by a CAD system.

Snap Command used to make the screen cursor snap or jump in specified increments.

Solid model A graphic representation of an object that is the most realistic and least abstract of the three types of models.

Splines A series of smooth curves drawn through a string of points.

Stretch A method of moving selected points of an object and leaving unselected points behind by stretching or lengthening selected entities.

Surface model One of three models that is a graphic representation of an object created by defining surfaces

Symbol Any defined group of entities that can be stored, retrieved, and placed on an existing drawing.

Tablet An input device used to control cursor movement and to select menu options.

Trim An editing command that is used to erase parts of lines, arcs, circles, and other entities by picking the entity and the start point and endpoint to be erased.

View coordinates Term used with 3D modeling to describe the relative location of the X, Y, and Z axes on the screen. In the view coordinate system, the X, Y, and Z axes changes as a new view is defined. Sometimes referred to as a *user coordinate system*.

Window The current view displayed on screen.

Wireframe One of three types of 3D models, where only the edges of the object are defined. The most abstract and least realistic type of model.

Workstation A group of hardware devices used to run CAD software programs.

World Coordinate System Term used in 3D modeling to describe the relative location of the X, Y, and Z axes to the model. In the world coordinate system, the X, Y, and Z axes do not change when the view is changed because they move with the model.

Zoom A display option used to magnify or reduce the displayed size of the drawing on the screen.

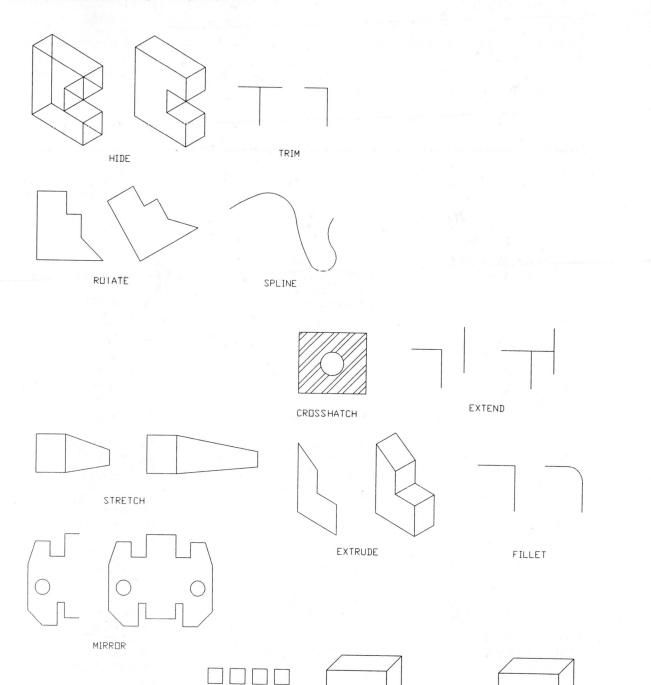

HIDE

TRIM

ROTATE

SPLINE

CROSSHATCH

EXTEND

STRETCH

EXTRUDE

FILLET

MIRROR

4 × 4 ARRAY

BOOLEAN OPERATION

BREAK

CHAMFER

INDEX